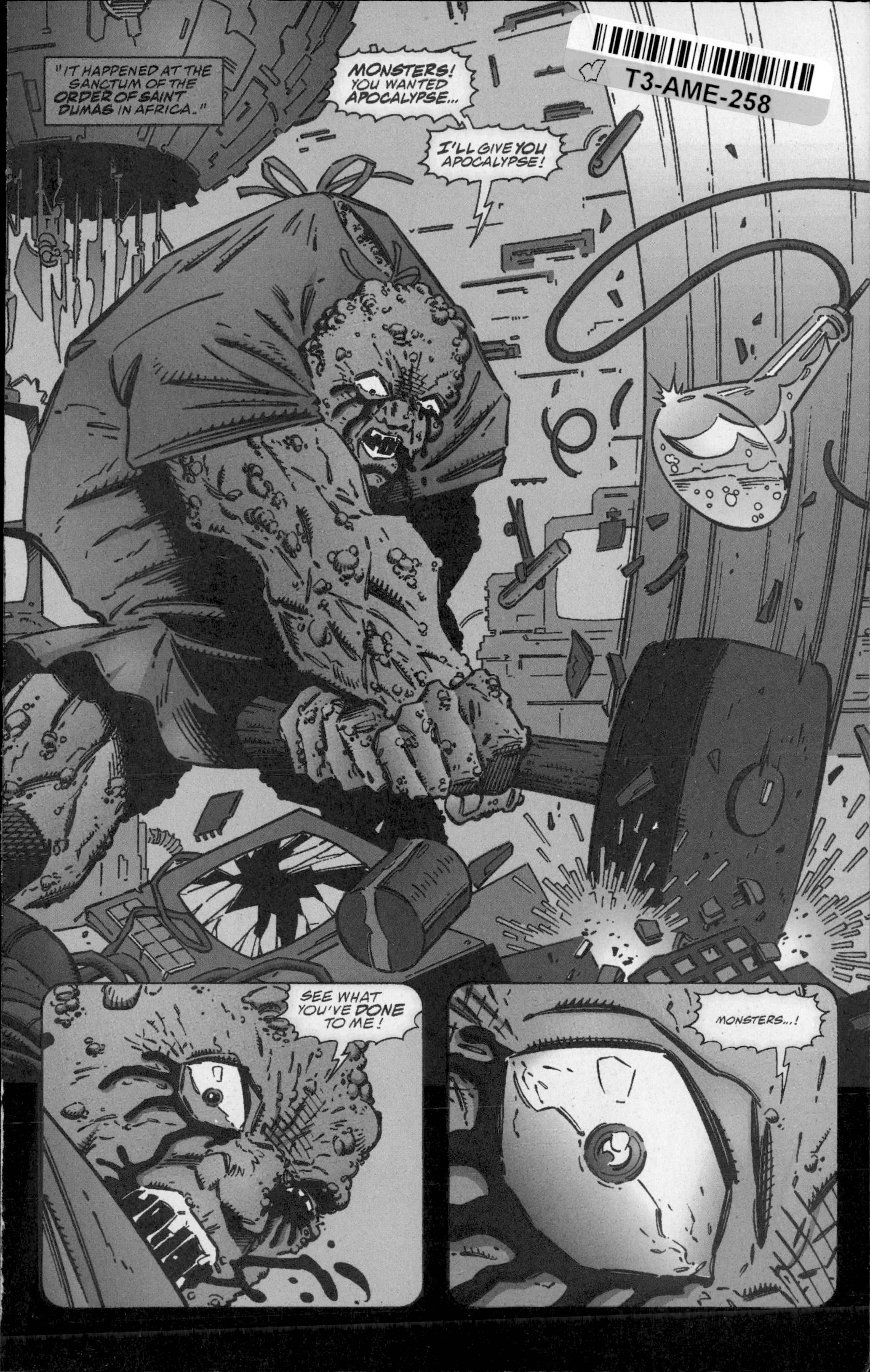

"IT HAPPENED AT THE SANCTUM OF THE ORDER OF SAINT DUMAS IN AFRICA."
MONSTERS! YOU WANTED APOCALYPSE...
I'LL GIVE YOU APOCALYPSE!
SEE WHAT YOU'VE DONE TO ME!
MONSTERS...!

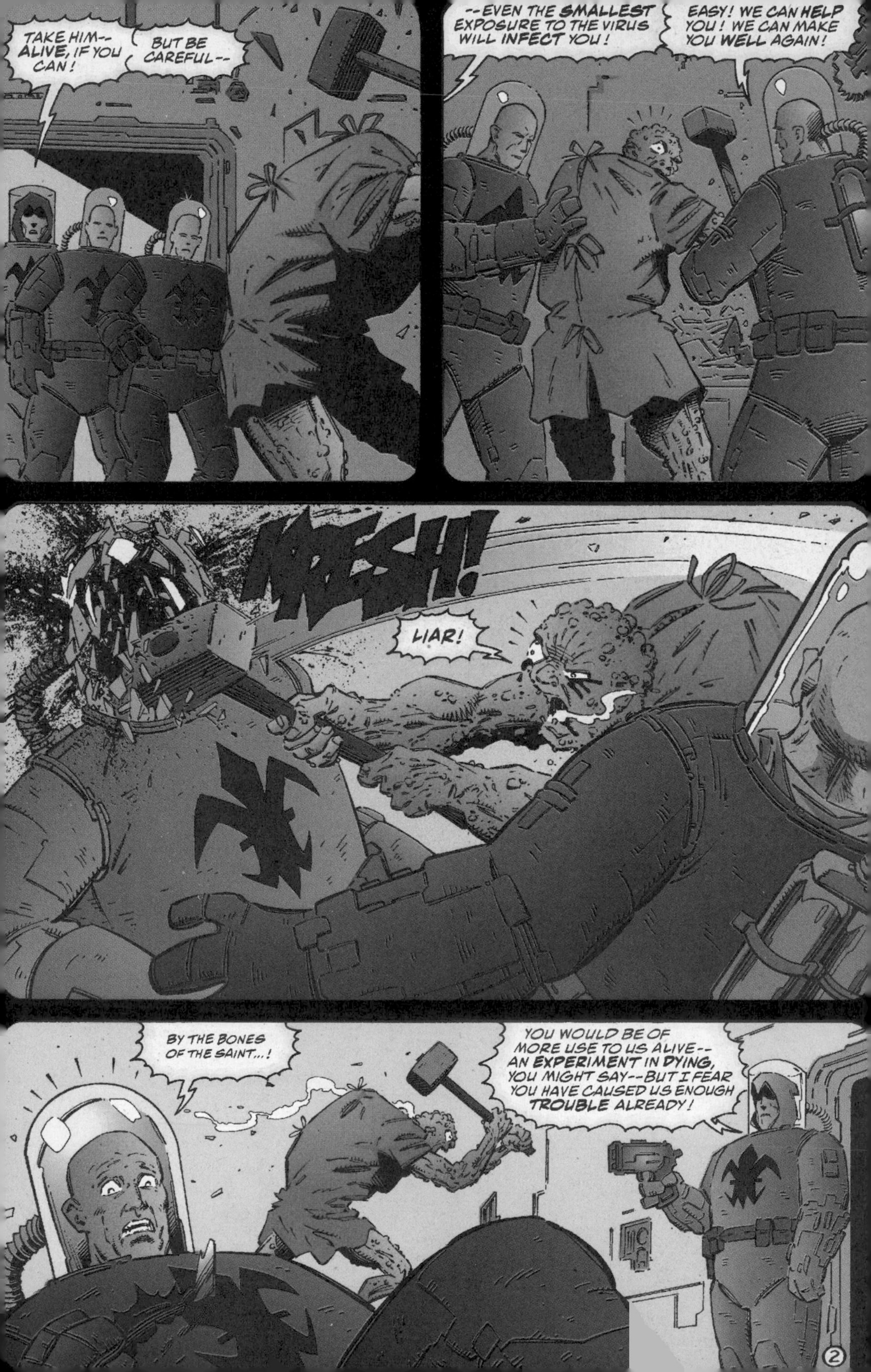
TAKE HIM-- ALIVE, IF YOU CAN!
BUT BE CAREFUL--
--EVEN THE SMALLEST EXPOSURE TO THE VIRUS WILL INFECT YOU!
EASY! WE CAN HELP YOU! WE CAN MAKE YOU WELL AGAIN!
KRESH!
LIAR!
BY THE BONES OF THE SAINT...!
YOU WOULD BE OF MORE USE TO US ALIVE-- AN EXPERIMENT IN DYING, YOU MIGHT SAY--BUT I FEAR YOU HAVE CAUSED US ENOUGH TROUBLE ALREADY!

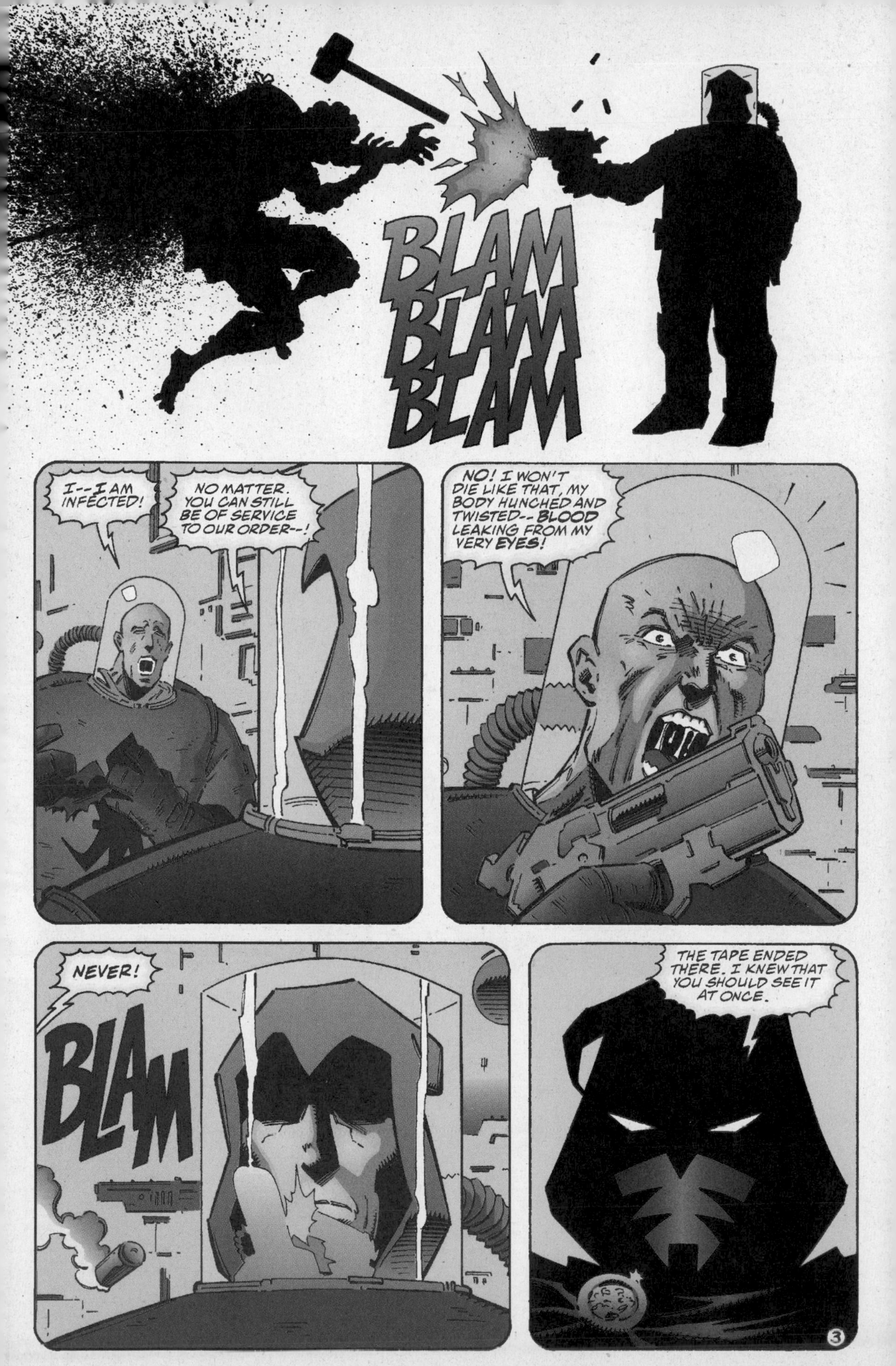
BLAM
BLAM
BLAM
I--I AM INFECTED!
NO MATTER. YOU CAN STILL BE OF SERVICE TO OUR ORDER--!
NO! I WON'T DIE LIKE THAT, MY BODY HUNCHED AND TWISTED-- BLOOD LEAKING FROM MY VERY EYES!
NEVER!
BLAM
THE TAPE ENDED THERE. I KNEW THAT YOU SHOULD SEE IT AT ONCE.
3

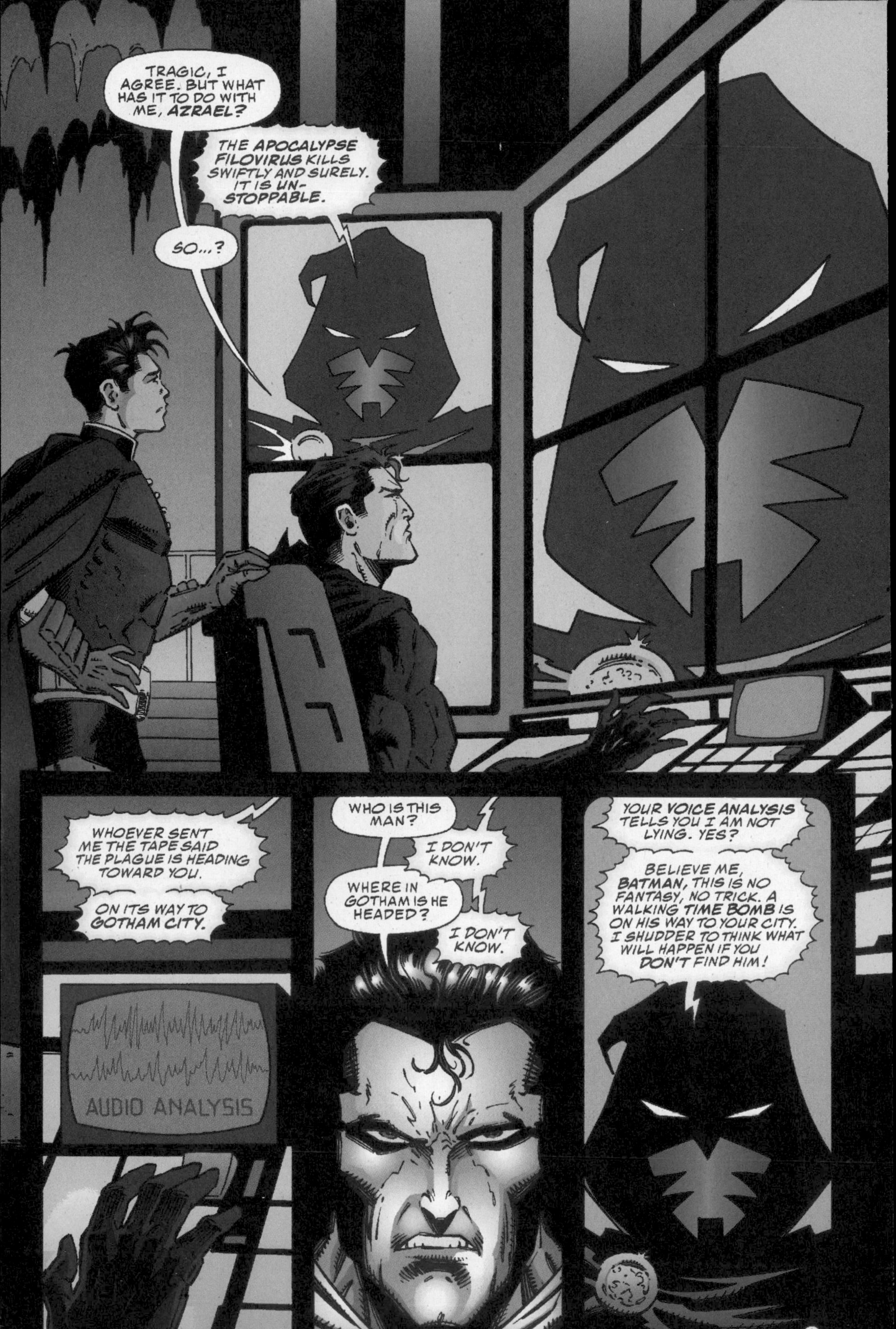
TRAGIC, I AGREE. BUT WHAT HAS IT TO DO WITH ME, AZRAEL?
THE APOCALYPSE FILOVIRUS KILLS SWIFTLY AND SURELY. IT IS UN-STOPPABLE.
SO...?
WHOEVER SENT ME THE TAPE SAID THE PLAGUE IS HEADING TOWARD YOU.
ON ITS WAY TO GOTHAM CITY.
WHO IS THIS MAN?
I DON'T KNOW.
WHERE IN GOTHAM IS HE HEADED?
I DON'T KNOW.
YOUR VOICE ANALYSIS TELLS YOU I AM NOT LYING. YES?
BELIEVE ME, BATMAN, THIS IS NO FANTASY, NO TRICK. A WALKING TIME BOMB IS ON HIS WAY TO YOUR CITY. I SHUDDER TO THINK WHAT WILL HAPPEN IF YOU DON'T FIND HIM!
AUDIO ANALYSIS

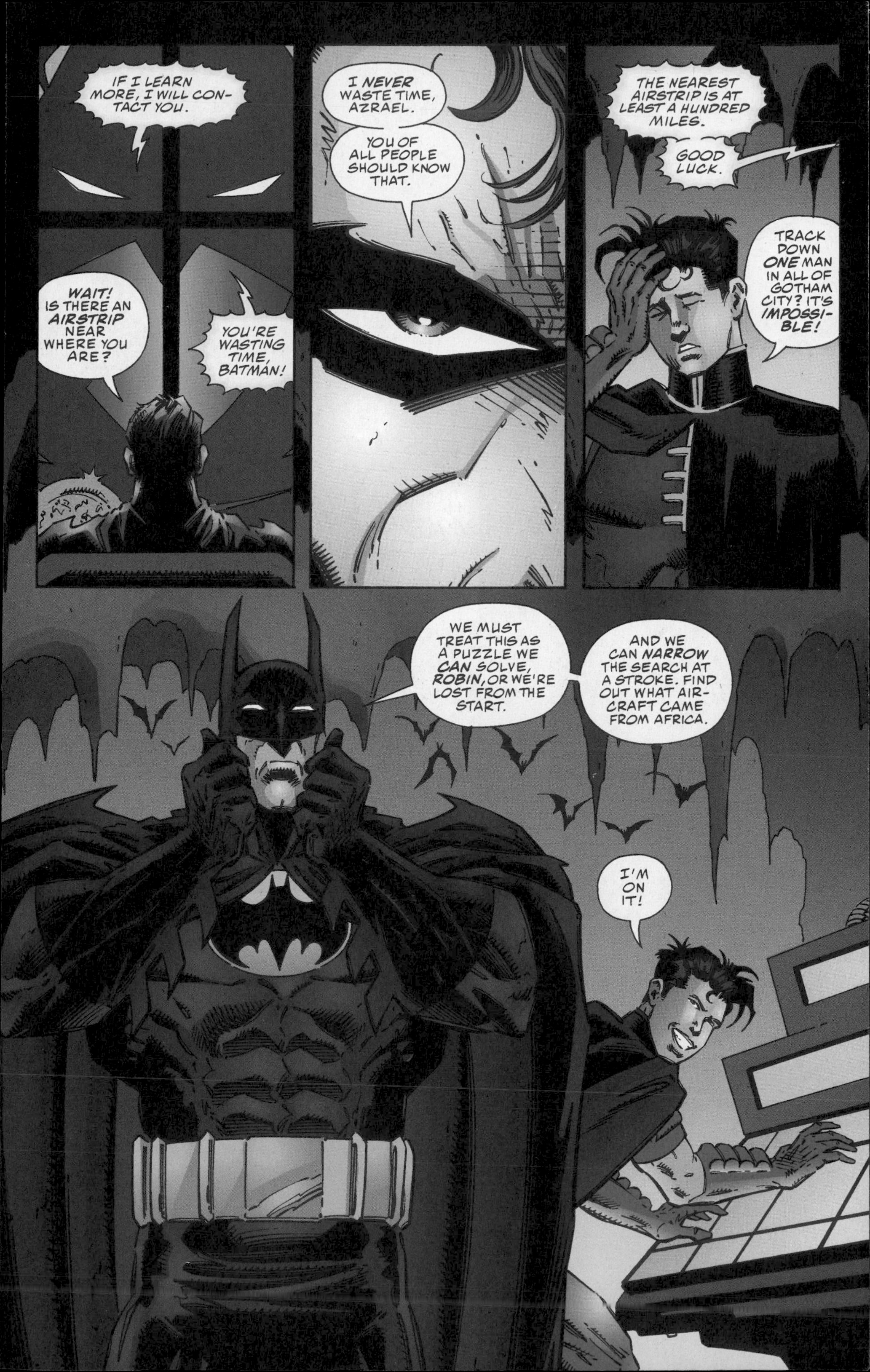
IF I LEARN MORE, I WILL CONTACT YOU.
WAIT! IS THERE AN AIRSTRIP NEAR WHERE YOU ARE?
YOU'RE WASTING TIME, BATMAN!
I NEVER WASTE TIME, AZRAEL.
YOU OF ALL PEOPLE SHOULD KNOW THAT.
THE NEAREST AIRSTRIP IS AT LEAST A HUNDRED MILES.
GOOD LUCK.
TRACK DOWN ONE MAN IN ALL OF GOTHAM CITY? IT'S IMPOSSIBLE!
WE MUST TREAT THIS AS A PUZZLE WE CAN SOLVE, ROBIN, OR WE'RE LOST FROM THE START.
AND WE CAN NARROW THE SEARCH AT A STROKE. FIND OUT WHAT AIRCRAFT CAME FROM AFRICA.
I'M ON IT!

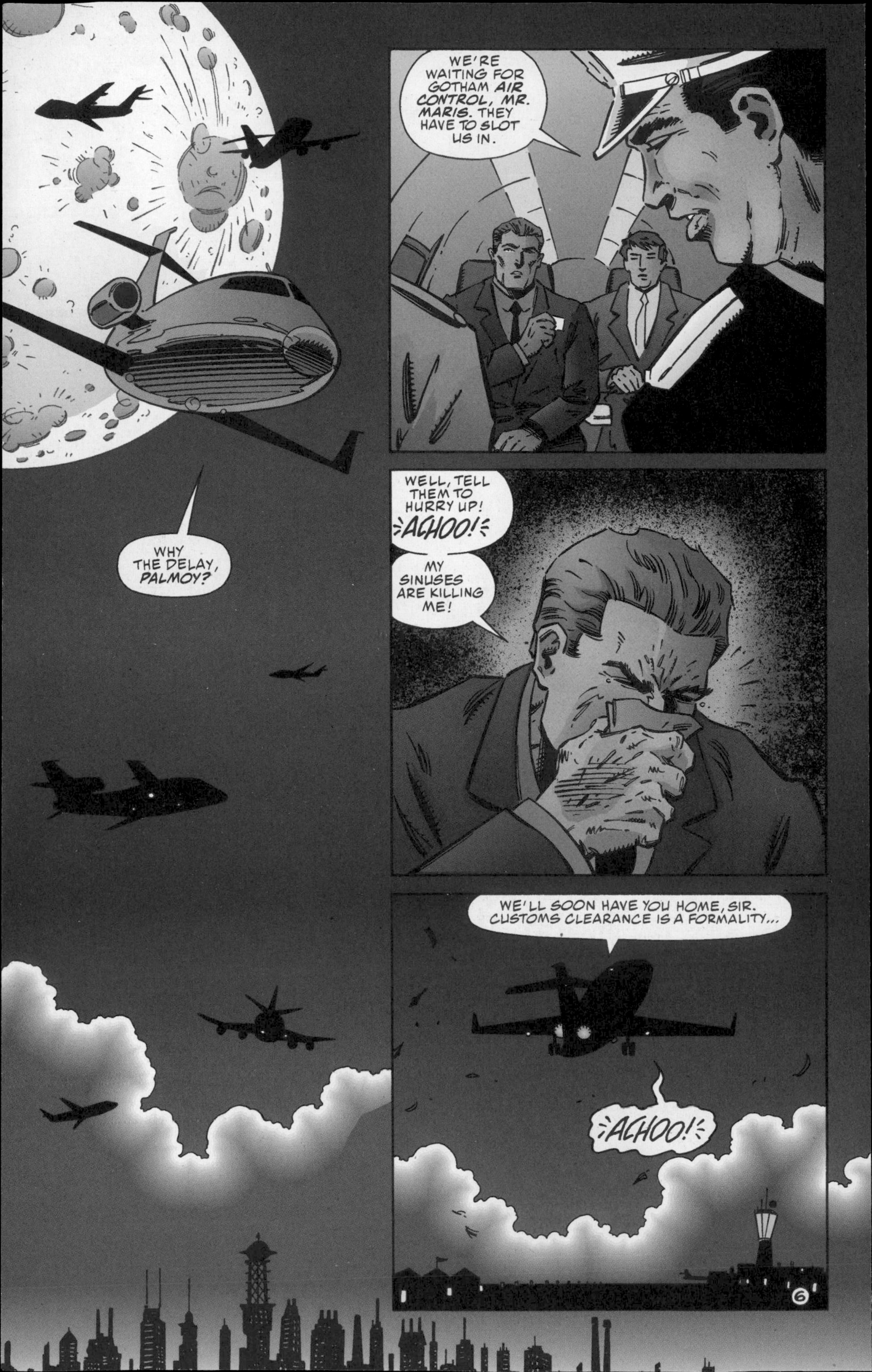
WE'RE WAITING FOR GOTHAM AIR CONTROL, MR. MARIS. THEY HAVE TO SLOT US IN.
WHY THE DELAY, PALMOY?
WELL, TELL THEM TO HURRY UP!
ACHOO!
MY SINUSES ARE KILLING ME!
WE'LL SOON HAVE YOU HOME, SIR. CUSTOMS CLEARANCE IS A FORMALITY...
ACHOO!
6

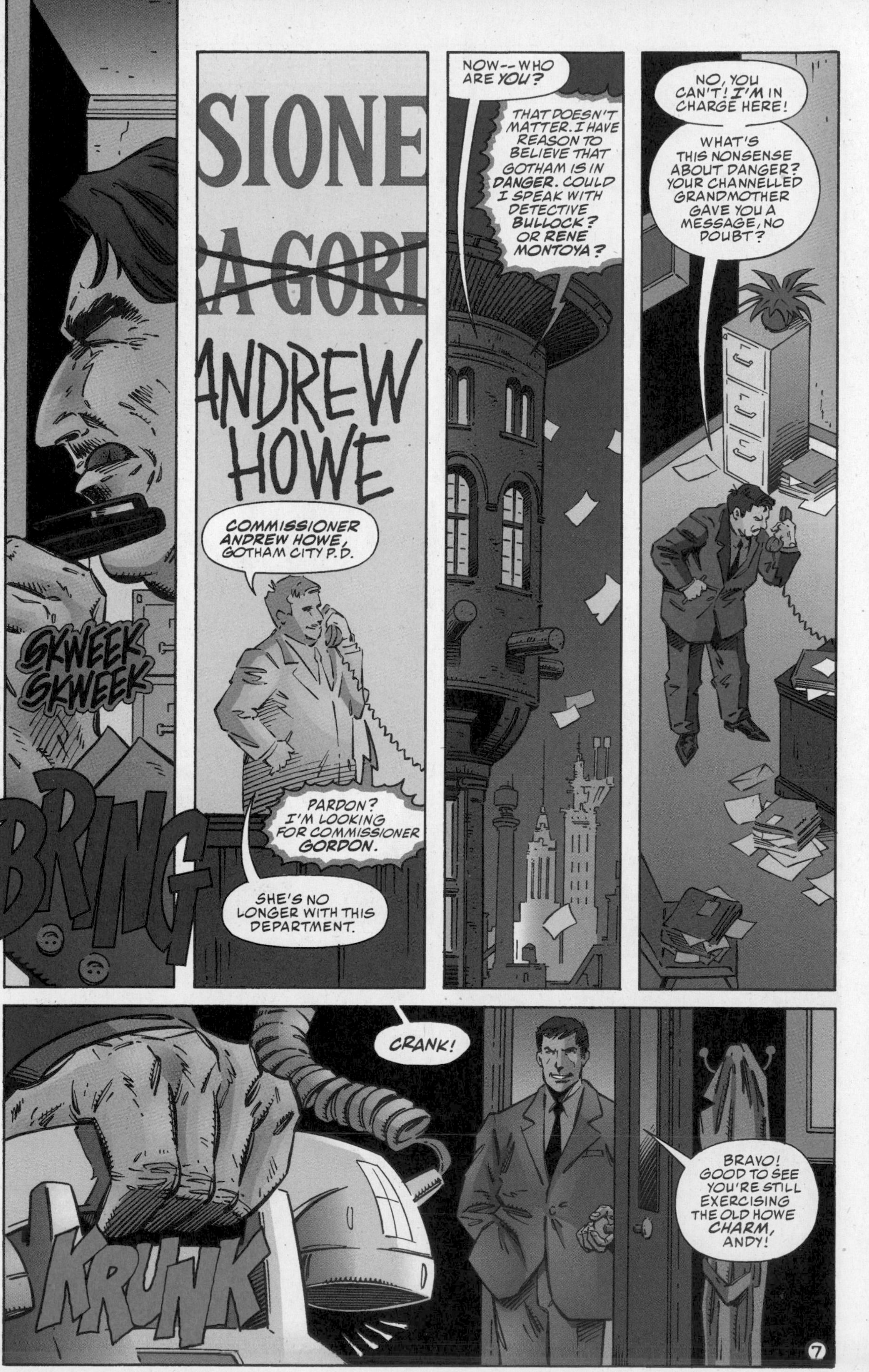
SKWEEK SKWEEK
BRING
SIONE
RA GORD
ANDREW HOWE
COMMISSIONER ANDREW HOWE, GOTHAM CITY P.D.
PARDON? I'M LOOKING FOR COMMISSIONER GORDON.
SHE'S NO LONGER WITH THIS DEPARTMENT.
NOW--WHO ARE YOU?
THAT DOESN'T MATTER. I HAVE REASON TO BELIEVE THAT GOTHAM IS IN DANGER. COULD I SPEAK WITH DETECTIVE BULLOCK? OR RENE MONTOYA?
NO, YOU CAN'T! I'M IN CHARGE HERE!
WHAT'S THIS NONSENSE ABOUT DANGER? YOUR CHANNELLED GRANDMOTHER GAVE YOU A MESSAGE, NO DOUBT?
CRANK!
KRUNK
BRAVO! GOOD TO SEE YOU'RE STILL EXERCISING THE OLD HOWE CHARM, ANDY!
7

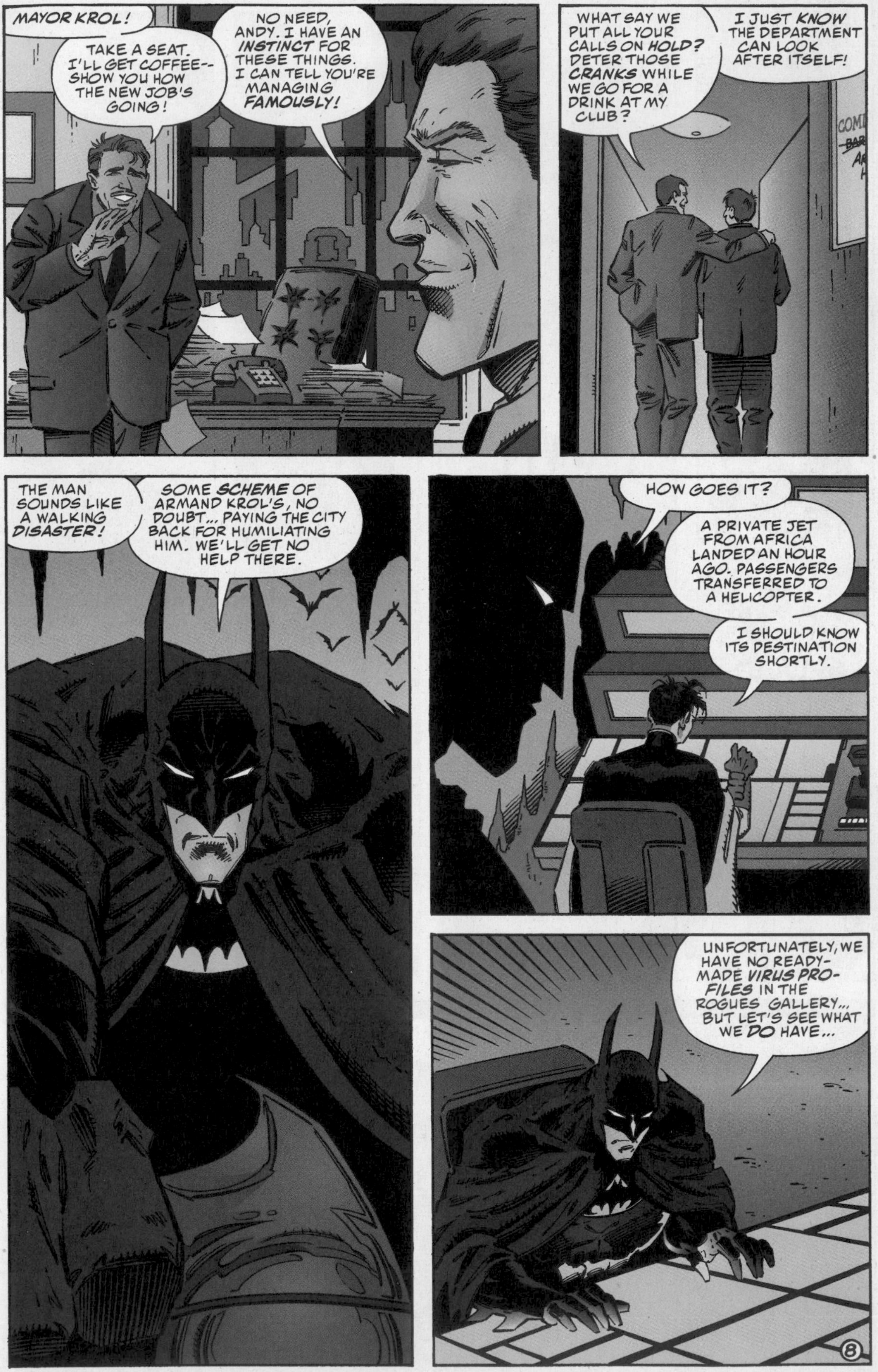
MAYOR KROL!
TAKE A SEAT. I'LL GET COFFEE-- SHOW YOU HOW THE NEW JOB'S GOING!
NO NEED, ANDY. I HAVE AN INSTINCT FOR THESE THINGS. I CAN TELL YOU'RE MANAGING FAMOUSLY!
WHAT SAY WE PUT ALL YOUR CALLS ON HOLD? DETER THOSE CRANKS WHILE WE GO FOR A DRINK AT MY CLUB?
I JUST KNOW THE DEPARTMENT CAN LOOK AFTER ITSELF!
THE MAN SOUNDS LIKE A WALKING DISASTER!
SOME SCHEME OF ARMAND KROL'S, NO DOUBT... PAYING THE CITY BACK FOR HUMILIATING HIM. WE'LL GET NO HELP THERE.
HOW GOES IT?
A PRIVATE JET FROM AFRICA LANDED AN HOUR AGO. PASSENGERS TRANSFERRED TO A HELICOPTER.
I SHOULD KNOW ITS DESTINATION SHORTLY.
UNFORTUNATELY, WE HAVE NO READY-MADE VIRUS PROFILES IN THE ROGUES GALLERY... BUT LET'S SEE WHAT WE DO HAVE...
8

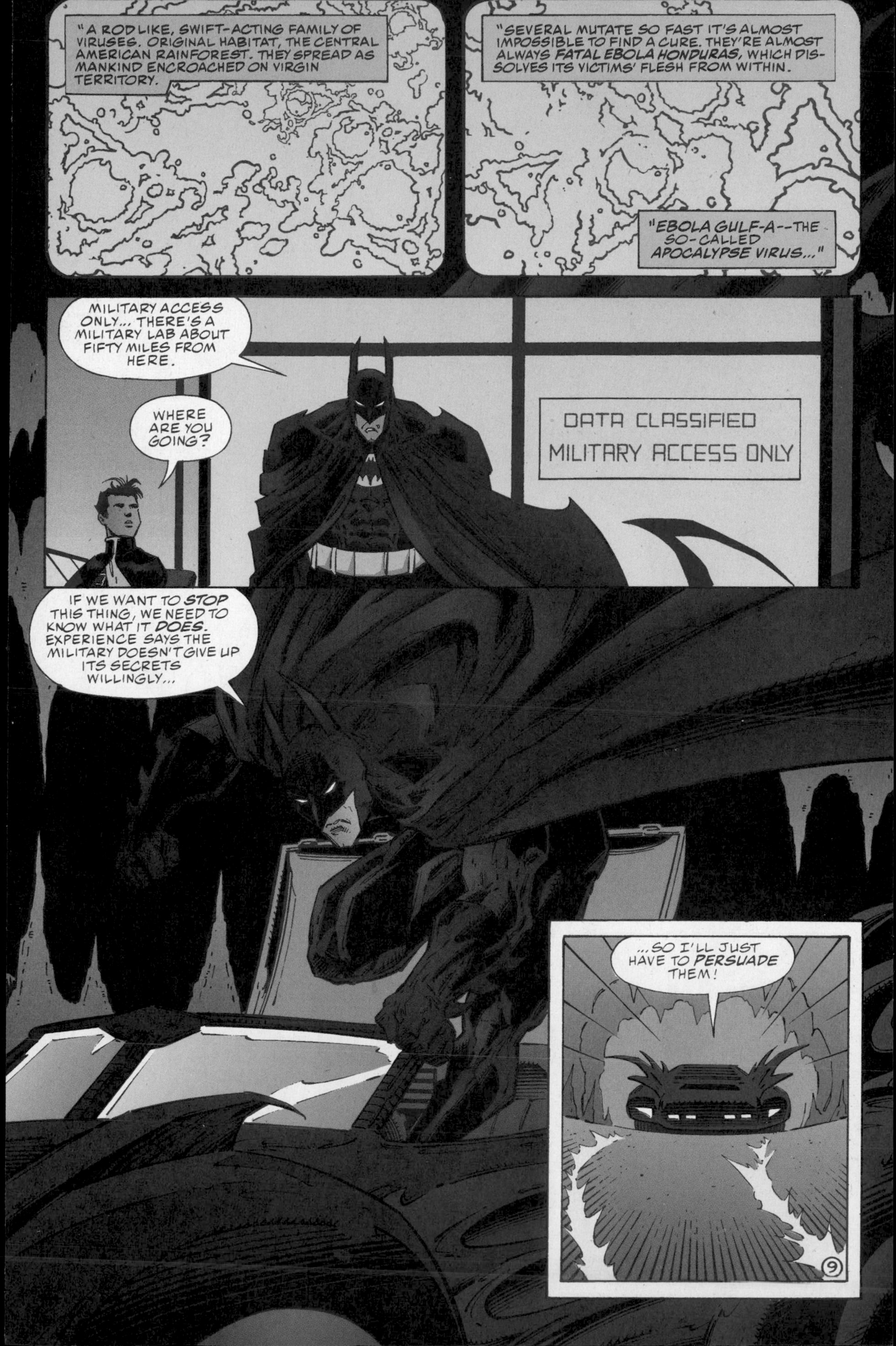
"A ROD LIKE, SWIFT-ACTING FAMILY OF VIRUSES. ORIGINAL HABITAT, THE CENTRAL AMERICAN RAINFOREST. THEY SPREAD AS MANKIND ENCROACHED ON VIRGIN TERRITORY.
"SEVERAL MUTATE SO FAST IT'S ALMOST IMPOSSIBLE TO FIND A CURE. THEY'RE ALMOST ALWAYS FATAL EBOLA HONDURAS, WHICH DISSOLVES ITS VICTIMS' FLESH FROM WITHIN.
"EBOLA GULF-A--THE SO-CALLED APOCALYPSE VIRUS..."
MILITARY ACCESS ONLY... THERE'S A MILITARY LAB ABOUT FIFTY MILES FROM HERE.
WHERE ARE YOU GOING?
DATA CLASSIFIED
MILITARY ACCESS ONLY
IF WE WANT TO STOP THIS THING, WE NEED TO KNOW WHAT IT DOES. EXPERIENCE SAYS THE MILITARY DOESN'T GIVE UP ITS SECRETS WILLINGLY...
...SO I'LL JUST HAVE TO PERSUADE THEM!

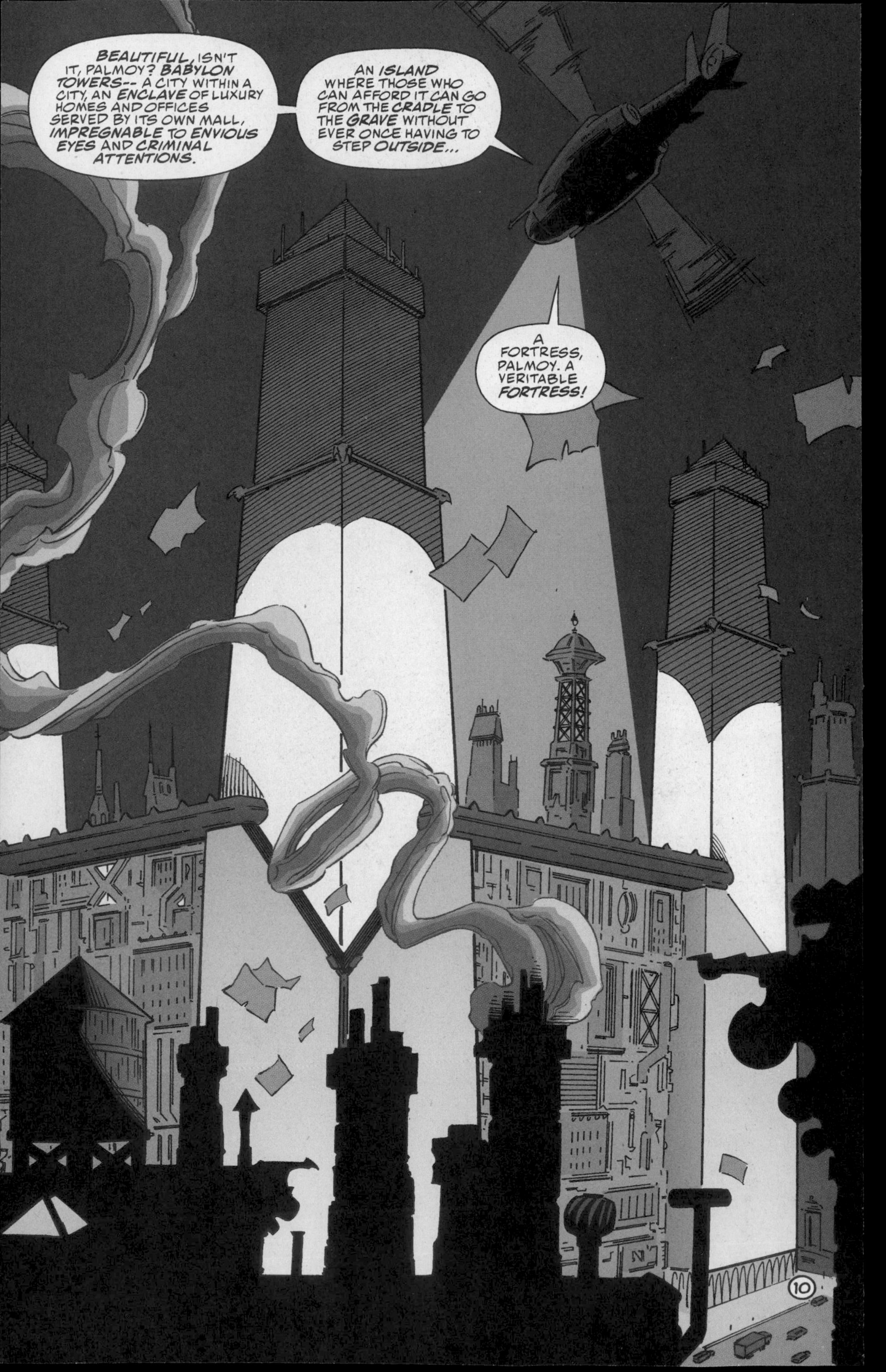
BEAUTIFUL, ISN'T IT, PALMOY? BABYLON TOWERS-- A CITY WITHIN A CITY, AN ENCLAVE OF LUXURY HOMES AND OFFICES SERVED BY ITS OWN MALL, IMPREGNABLE TO ENVIOUS EYES AND CRIMINAL ATTENTIONS.
AN ISLAND WHERE THOSE WHO CAN AFFORD IT CAN GO FROM THE CRADLE TO THE GRAVE WITHOUT EVER ONCE HAVING TO STEP OUTSIDE...
A FORTRESS, PALMOY. A VERITABLE FORTRESS!
10

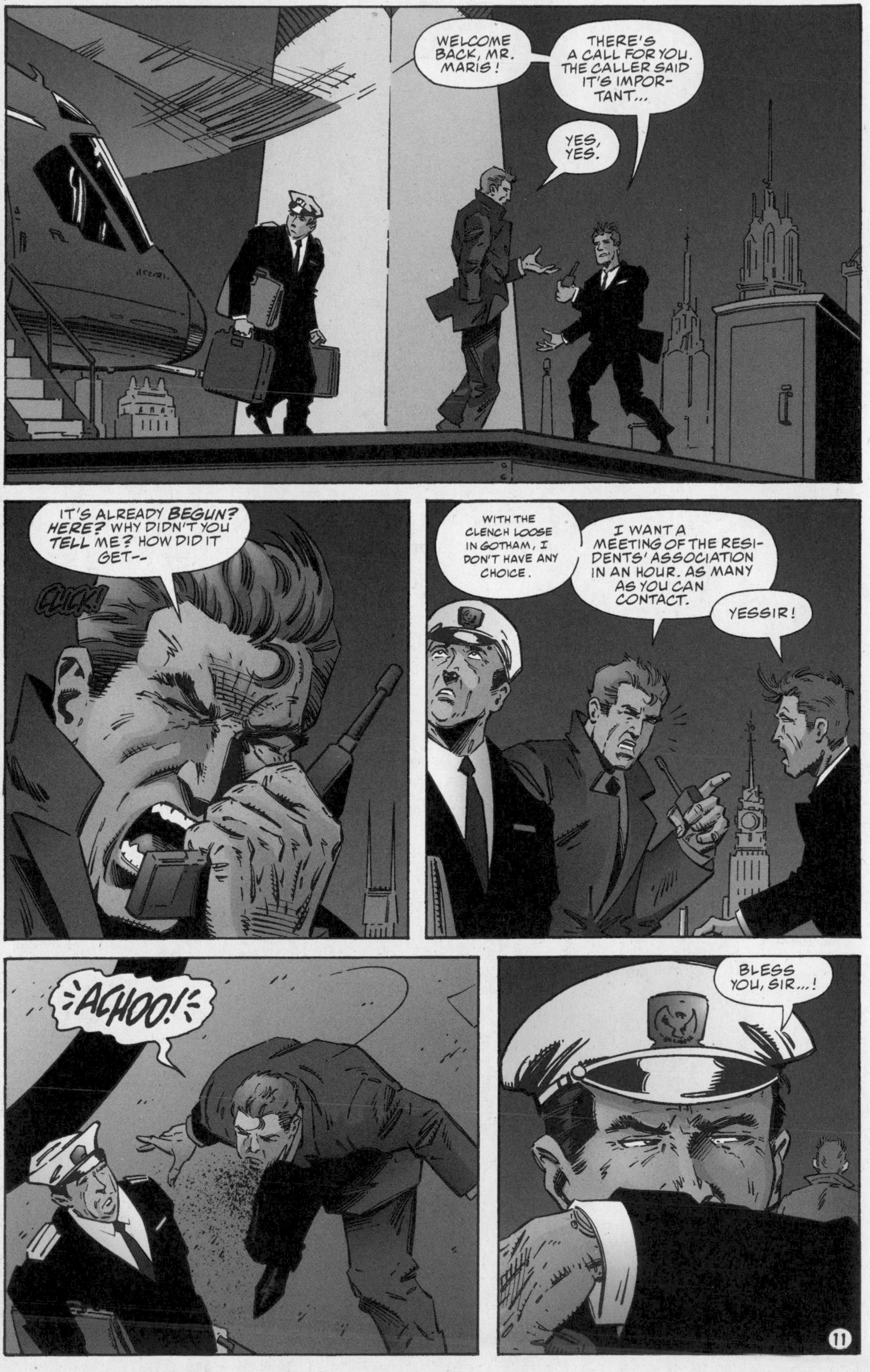

WELCOME BACK, MR. MARIS!
THERE'S A CALL FOR YOU. THE CALLER SAID IT'S IMPORTANT...
YES, YES.
IT'S ALREADY BEGUN? HERE? WHY DIDN'T YOU TELL ME? HOW DID IT GET--
CLICK!
WITH THE CLENCH LOOSE IN GOTHAM, I DON'T HAVE ANY CHOICE.
I WANT A MEETING OF THE RESIDENTS' ASSOCIATION IN AN HOUR. AS MANY AS YOU CAN CONTACT.
YESSIR!
ACHOO!
BLESS YOU, SIR...!
11

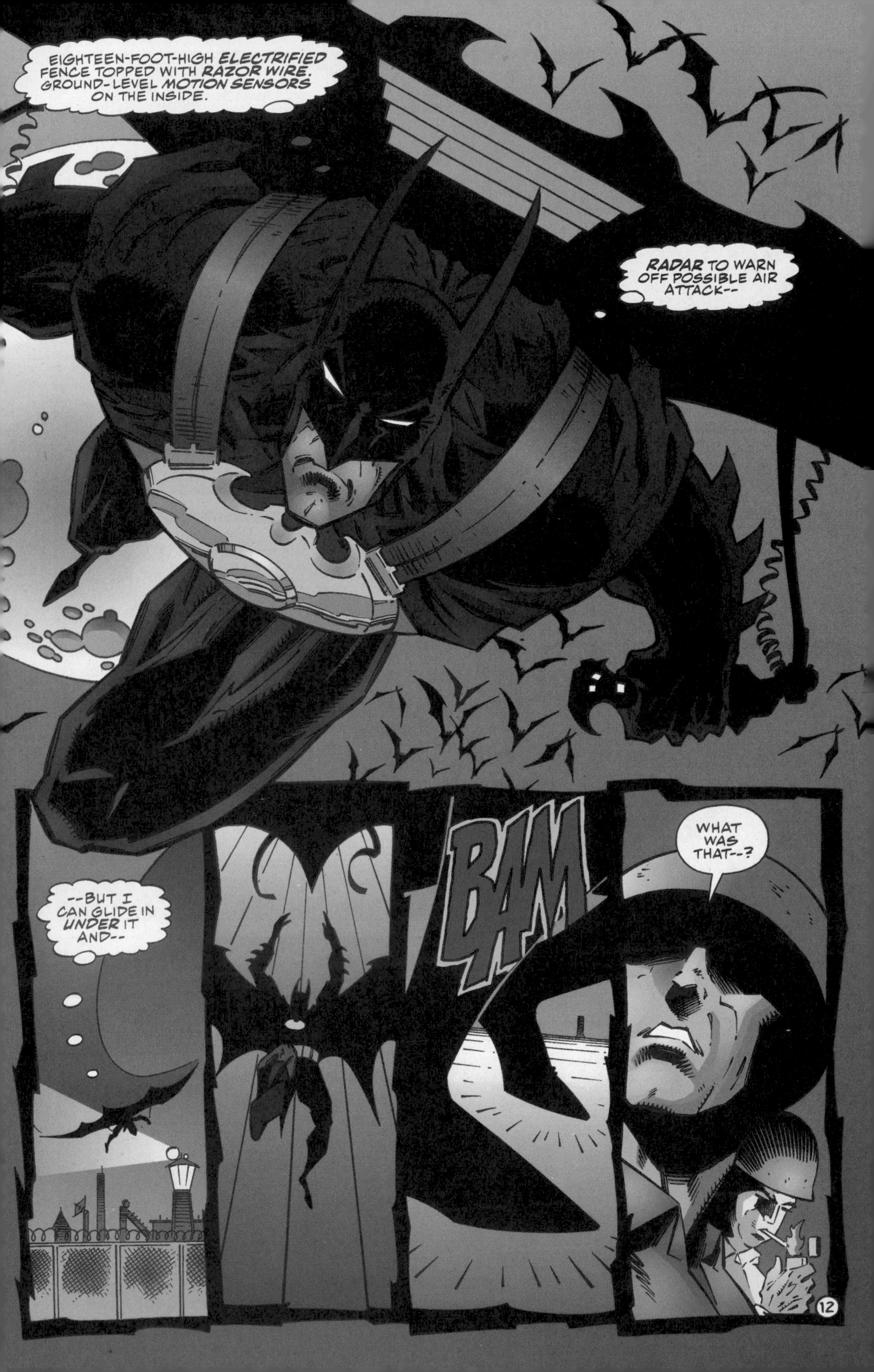
EIGHTEEN-FOOT-HIGH ELECTRIFIED FENCE TOPPED WITH RAZOR WIRE. GROUND-LEVEL MOTION SENSORS ON THE INSIDE.
RADAR TO WARN OFF POSSIBLE AIR ATTACK--
--BUT I CAN GLIDE IN UNDER IT AND--
BAM
WHAT WAS THAT--?
12

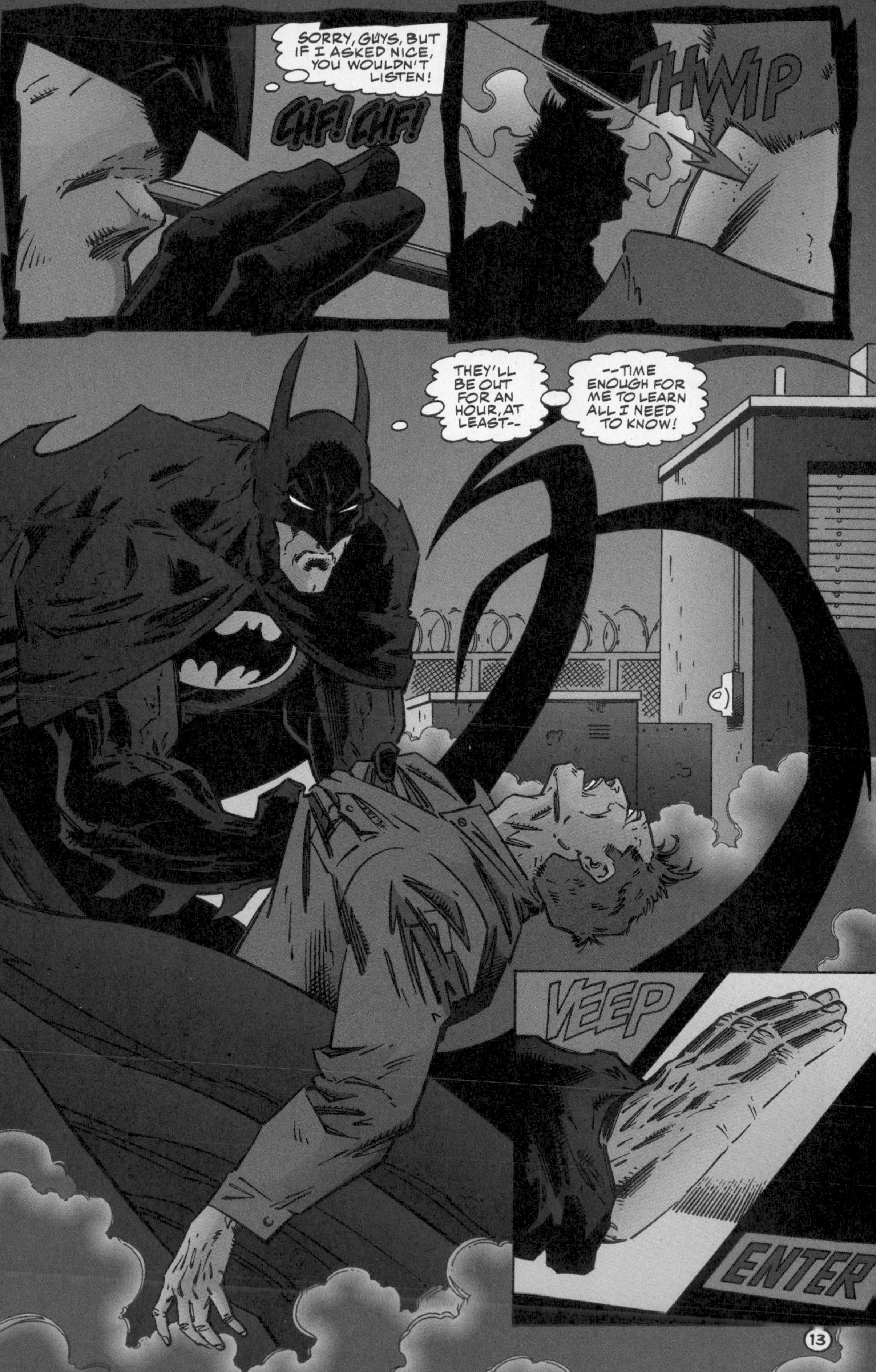

SORRY, GUYS, BUT IF I ASKED NICE, YOU WOULDN'T LISTEN!
CHF! CHF!
THWIP
THEY'LL BE OUT FOR AN HOUR, AT LEAST--
--TIME ENOUGH FOR ME TO LEARN ALL I NEED TO KNOW!
VEEP
ENTER

mmff!

I NEED TO SPEAK WITH *GENERAL MONDIAL DERWENT*, YOUR SENIOR *RESEARCH* CHEMIST.

HE-- HE ISN'T *HERE!*

I'VE CHECKED. HE HASN'T BEEN HOME FOR *DAYS.* WHERE *IS* HE?

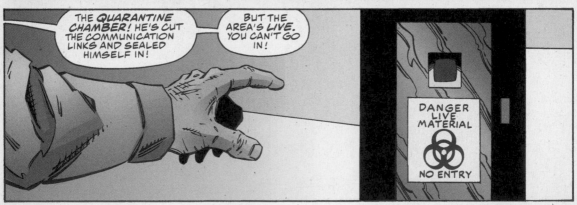

THE *QUARANTINE CHAMBER!* HE'S CUT THE COMMUNICATION LINKS AND SEALED HIMSELF IN!

BUT THE AREA'S *LIVE.* YOU CAN'T GO IN!

DANGER
LIVE
MATERIAL

NO ENTRY

I HAVE NO OPTION.

FORGIVE ME. YOU'LL RECOVER SOON.

�14

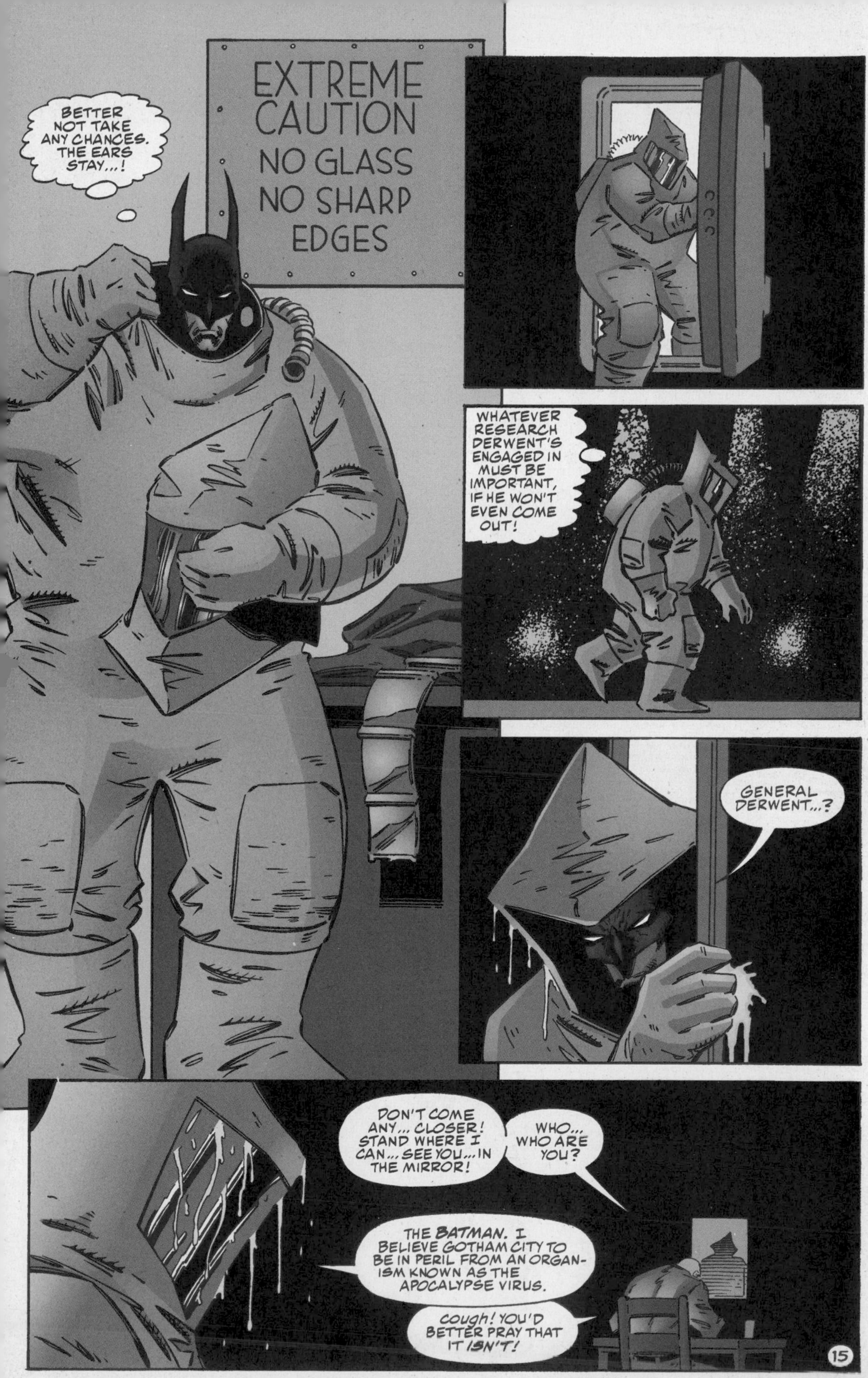
EXTREME CAUTION NO GLASS NO SHARP EDGES
BETTER NOT TAKE ANY CHANCES. THE EARS STAY...!
WHATEVER RESEARCH DERWENT'S ENGAGED IN MUST BE IMPORTANT, IF HE WON'T EVEN COME OUT!
GENERAL DERWENT...?
DON'T COME ANY... CLOSER! STAND WHERE I CAN... SEE YOU... IN THE MIRROR!
WHO... WHO ARE YOU?
THE BATMAN. I BELIEVE GOTHAM CITY TO BE IN PERIL FROM AN ORGANISM KNOWN AS THE APOCALYPSE VIRUS.
Cough! YOU'D BETTER PRAY THAT IT ISN'T!
15

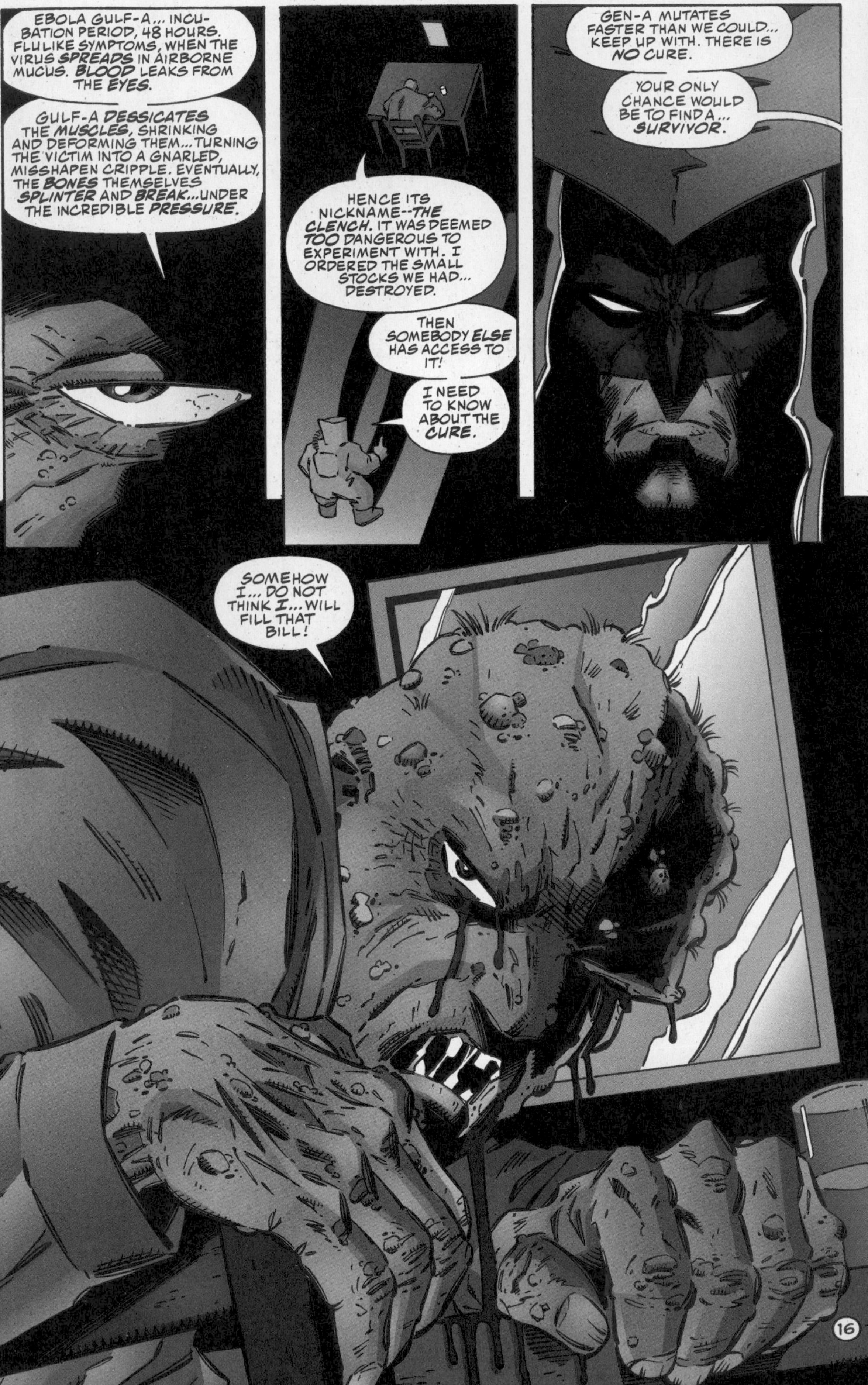

EBOLA GULF-A... INCUBATION PERIOD, 48 HOURS. FLULIKE SYMPTOMS, WHEN THE VIRUS SPREADS IN AIRBORNE MUCUS. BLOOD LEAKS FROM THE EYES.
GULF-A DESSICATES THE MUSCLES, SHRINKING AND DEFORMING THEM... TURNING THE VICTIM INTO A GNARLED, MISSHAPEN CRIPPLE. EVENTUALLY, THE BONES THEMSELVES SPLINTER AND BREAK... UNDER THE INCREDIBLE PRESSURE.
HENCE ITS NICKNAME--THE CLENCH. IT WAS DEEMED TOO DANGEROUS TO EXPERIMENT WITH. I ORDERED THE SMALL STOCKS WE HAD... DESTROYED.
THEN SOMEBODY ELSE HAS ACCESS TO IT!
I NEED TO KNOW ABOUT THE CURE.
GEN-A MUTATES FASTER THAN WE COULD... KEEP UP WITH. THERE IS NO CURE.
YOUR ONLY CHANCE WOULD BE TO FIND A... SURVIVOR.
SOMEHOW I... DO NOT THINK I... WILL FILL THAT BILL!

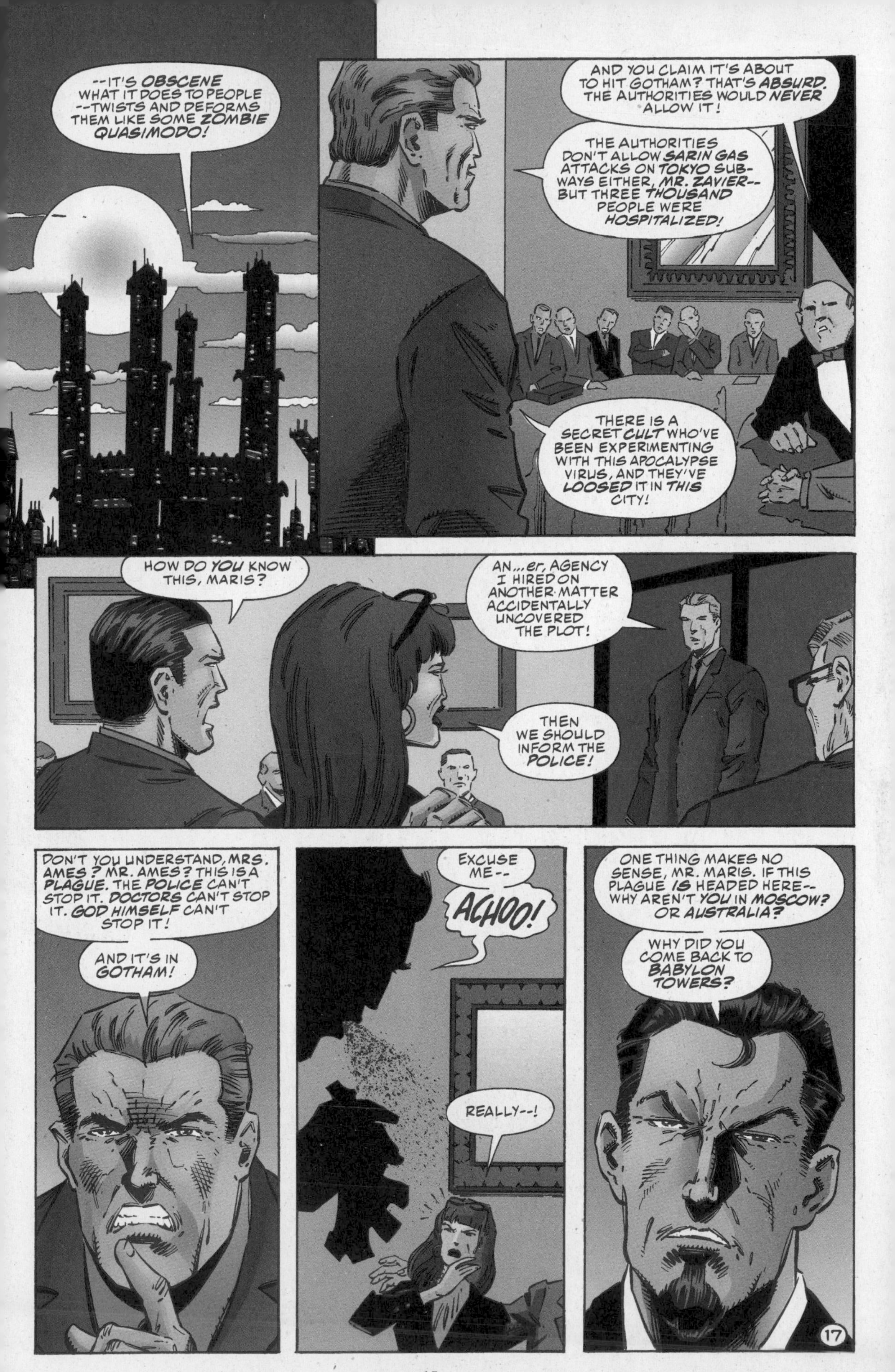
--IT'S OBSCENE WHAT IT DOES TO PEOPLE --TWISTS AND DEFORMS THEM LIKE SOME ZOMBIE QUASIMODO!
AND YOU CLAIM IT'S ABOUT TO HIT GOTHAM? THAT'S ABSURD. THE AUTHORITIES WOULD NEVER ALLOW IT!
THE AUTHORITIES DON'T ALLOW SARIN GAS ATTACKS ON TOKYO SUBWAYS EITHER, MR. ZAVIER-- BUT THREE THOUSAND PEOPLE WERE HOSPITALIZED!
THERE IS A SECRET CULT WHO'VE BEEN EXPERIMENTING WITH THIS APOCALYPSE VIRUS, AND THEY'VE LOOSED IT IN THIS CITY!
HOW DO YOU KNOW THIS, MARIS?
AN...er, AGENCY I HIRED ON ANOTHER MATTER ACCIDENTALLY UNCOVERED THE PLOT!
THEN WE SHOULD INFORM THE POLICE!
DON'T YOU UNDERSTAND, MRS. AMES? MR. AMES? THIS IS A PLAGUE. THE POLICE CAN'T STOP IT. DOCTORS CAN'T STOP IT. GOD HIMSELF CAN'T STOP IT!
AND IT'S IN GOTHAM!
EXCUSE ME--
ACHOO!
REALLY--!
ONE THING MAKES NO SENSE, MR. MARIS. IF THIS PLAGUE IS HEADED HERE-- WHY AREN'T YOU IN MOSCOW? OR AUSTRALIA?
WHY DID YOU COME BACK TO BABYLON TOWERS?
17

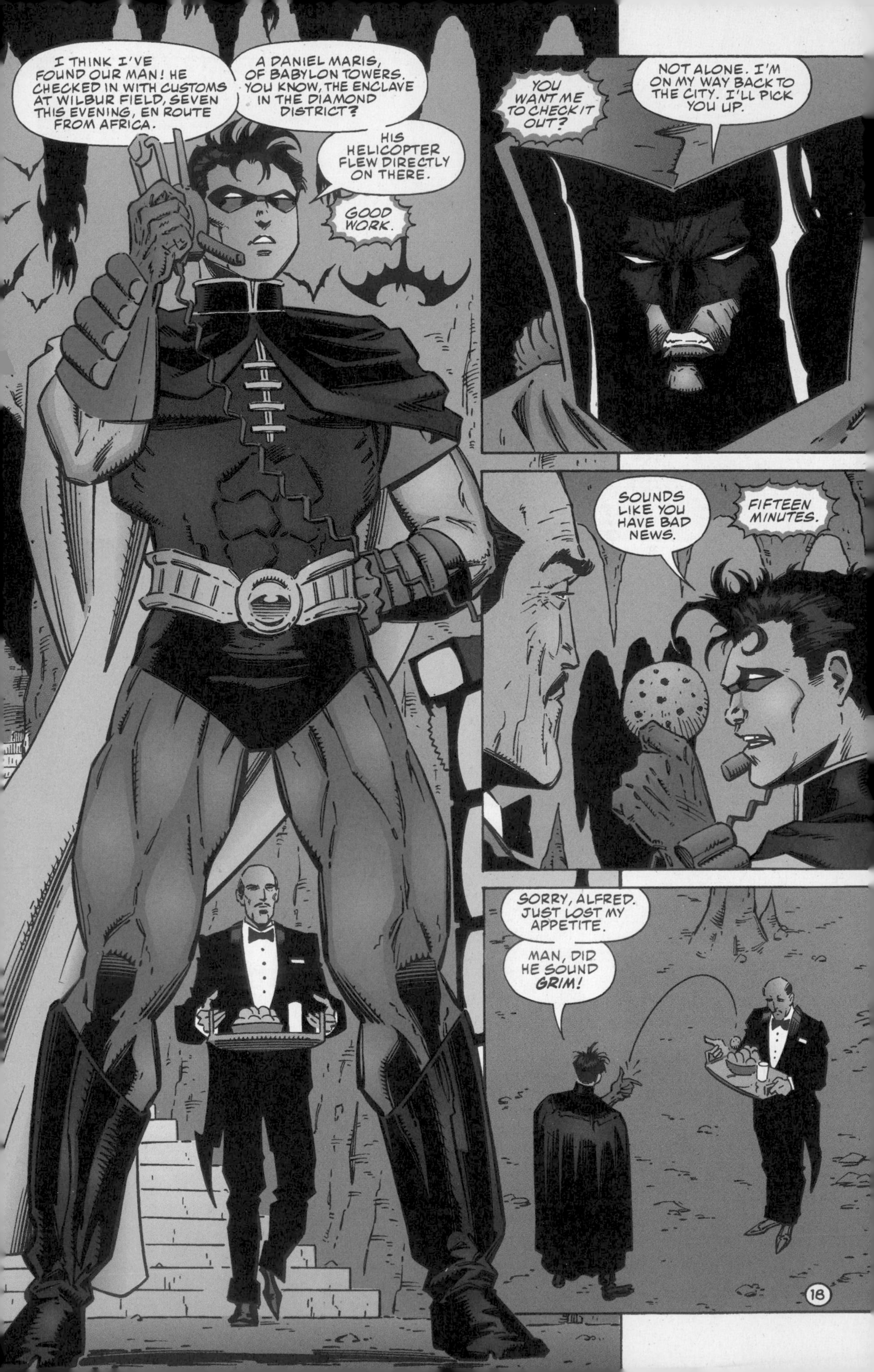

I THINK I'VE FOUND OUR MAN! HE CHECKED IN WITH CUSTOMS AT WILBUR FIELD, SEVEN THIS EVENING, EN ROUTE FROM AFRICA.
A DANIEL MARIS, OF BABYLON TOWERS. YOU KNOW, THE ENCLAVE IN THE DIAMOND DISTRICT?
HIS HELICOPTER FLEW DIRECTLY ON THERE.
GOOD WORK.
YOU WANT ME TO CHECK IT OUT?
NOT ALONE. I'M ON MY WAY BACK TO THE CITY. I'LL PICK YOU UP.
SOUNDS LIKE YOU HAVE BAD NEWS.
FIFTEEN MINUTES.
SORRY, ALFRED. JUST LOST MY APPETITE.
MAN, DID HE SOUND GRIM!

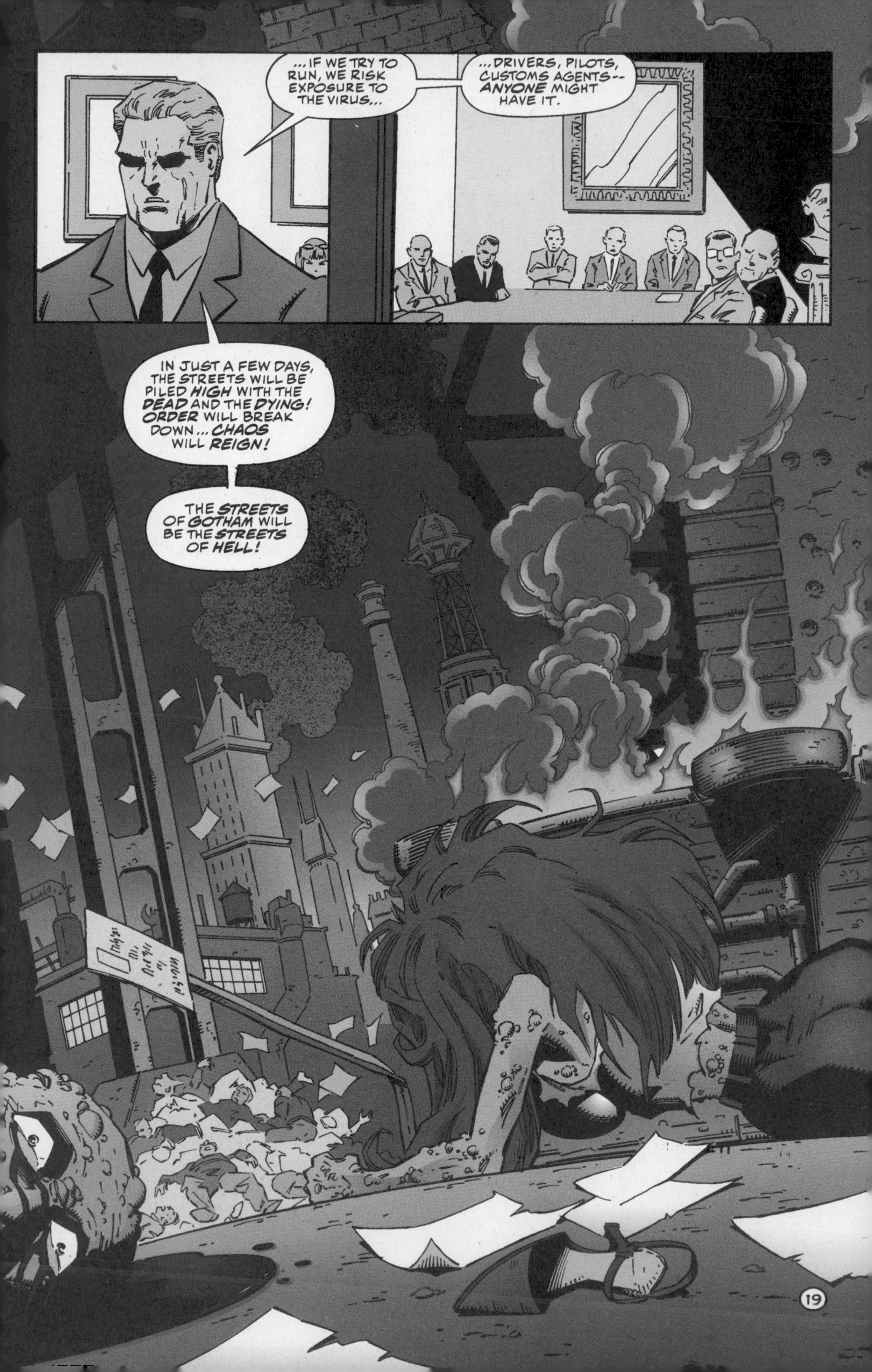
...IF WE TRY TO RUN, WE RISK EXPOSURE TO THE VIRUS...
...DRIVERS, PILOTS, CUSTOMS AGENTS-- ANYONE MIGHT HAVE IT.
IN JUST A FEW DAYS, THE STREETS WILL BE PILED HIGH WITH THE DEAD AND THE DYING! ORDER WILL BREAK DOWN... CHAOS WILL REIGN!
THE STREETS OF GOTHAM WILL BE THE STREETS OF HELL!

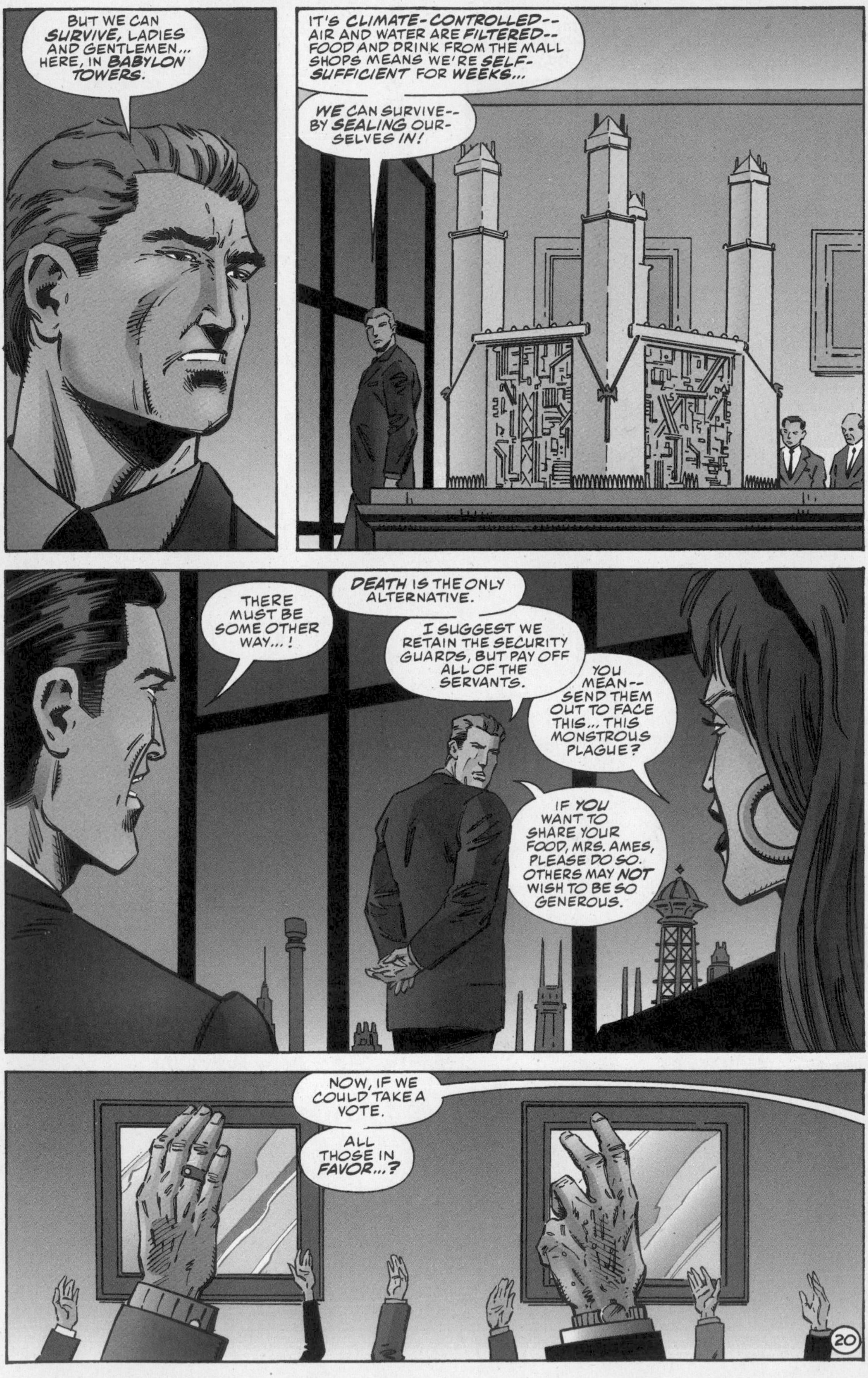
BUT WE CAN SURVIVE, LADIES AND GENTLEMEN... HERE, IN BABYLON TOWERS.
IT'S CLIMATE-CONTROLLED-- AIR AND WATER ARE FILTERED-- FOOD AND DRINK FROM THE MALL SHOPS MEANS WE'RE SELF-SUFFICIENT FOR WEEKS...
WE CAN SURVIVE-- BY SEALING OURSELVES IN!
THERE MUST BE SOME OTHER WAY...!
DEATH IS THE ONLY ALTERNATIVE.
I SUGGEST WE RETAIN THE SECURITY GUARDS, BUT PAY OFF ALL OF THE SERVANTS.
YOU MEAN-- SEND THEM OUT TO FACE THIS... THIS MONSTROUS PLAGUE?
IF YOU WANT TO SHARE YOUR FOOD, MRS. AMES, PLEASE DO SO. OTHERS MAY NOT WISH TO BE SO GENEROUS.
NOW, IF WE COULD TAKE A VOTE.
ALL THOSE IN FAVOR...?
20

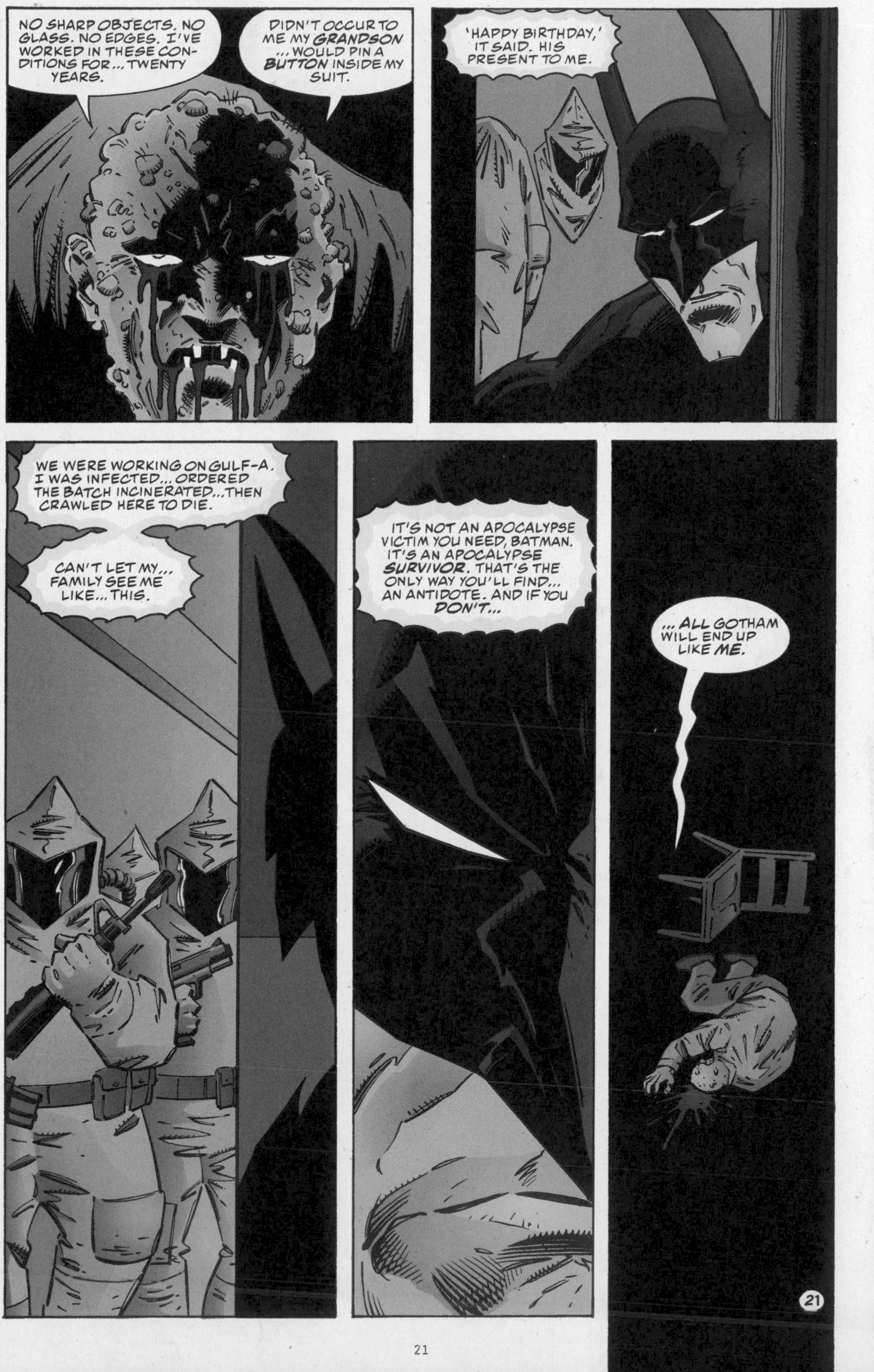
NO SHARP OBJECTS. NO GLASS. NO EDGES. I'VE WORKED IN THESE CONDITIONS FOR... TWENTY YEARS.
DIDN'T OCCUR TO ME MY GRANDSON ...WOULD PIN A BUTTON INSIDE MY SUIT.
'HAPPY BIRTHDAY,' IT SAID. HIS PRESENT TO ME.
WE WERE WORKING ON GULF-A. I WAS INFECTED... ORDERED THE BATCH INCINERATED... THEN CRAWLED HERE TO DIE.
CAN'T LET MY... FAMILY SEE ME LIKE... THIS.
IT'S NOT AN APOCALYPSE VICTIM YOU NEED, BATMAN. IT'S AN APOCALYPSE SURVIVOR. THAT'S THE ONLY WAY YOU'LL FIND... AN ANTIDOTE. AND IF YOU DON'T...
...ALL GOTHAM WILL END UP LIKE ME.
21

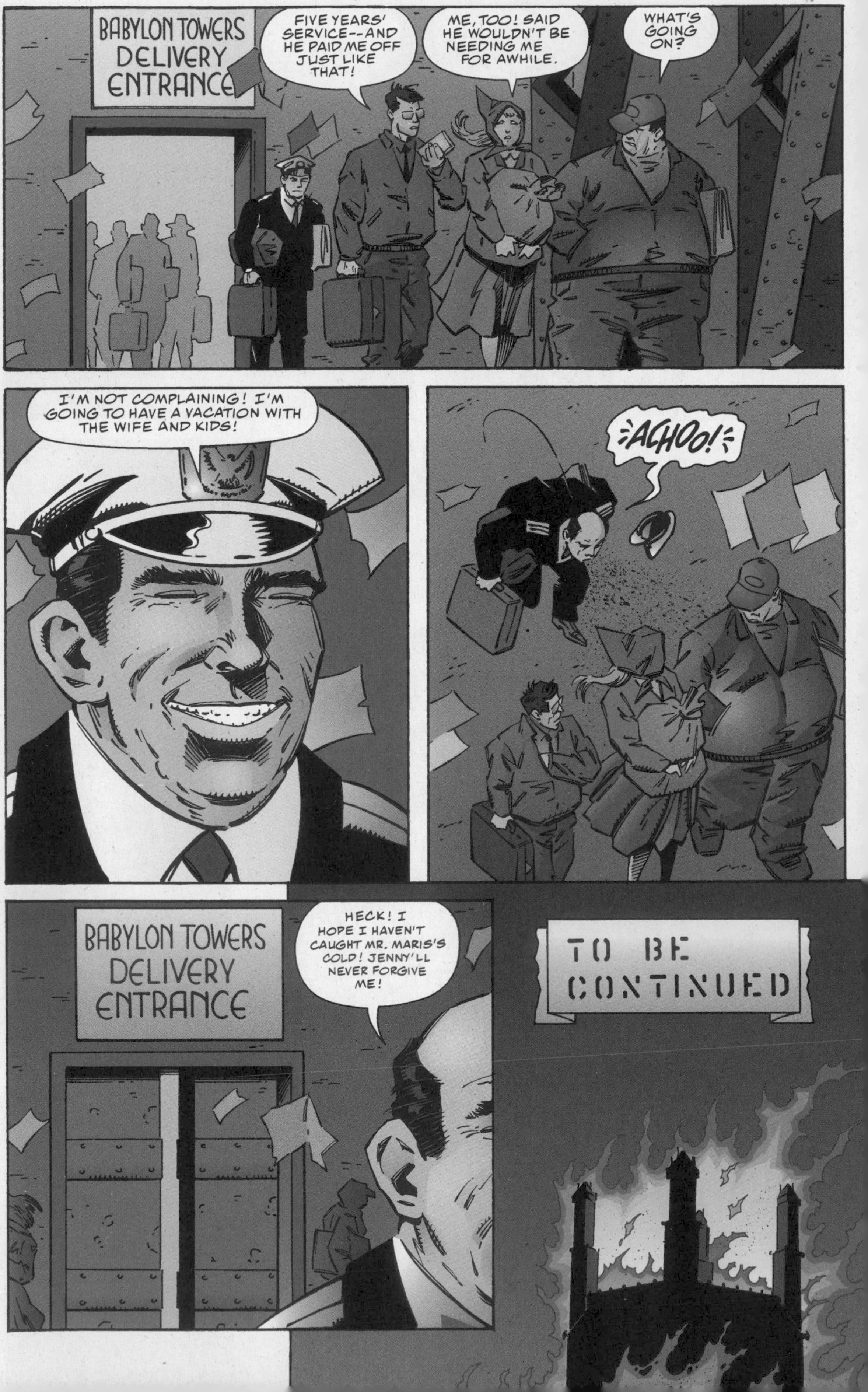
BABYLON TOWERS DELIVERY ENTRANCE
FIVE YEARS' SERVICE--AND HE PAID ME OFF JUST LIKE THAT!
ME, TOO! SAID HE WOULDN'T BE NEEDING ME FOR AWHILE.
WHAT'S GOING ON?
I'M NOT COMPLAINING! I'M GOING TO HAVE A VACATION WITH THE WIFE AND KIDS!
ACHOO!
BABYLON TOWERS DELIVERY ENTRANCE
HECK! I HOPE I HAVEN'T CAUGHT MR. MARIS'S COLD! JENNY'LL NEVER FORGIVE ME!
TO BE CONTINUED

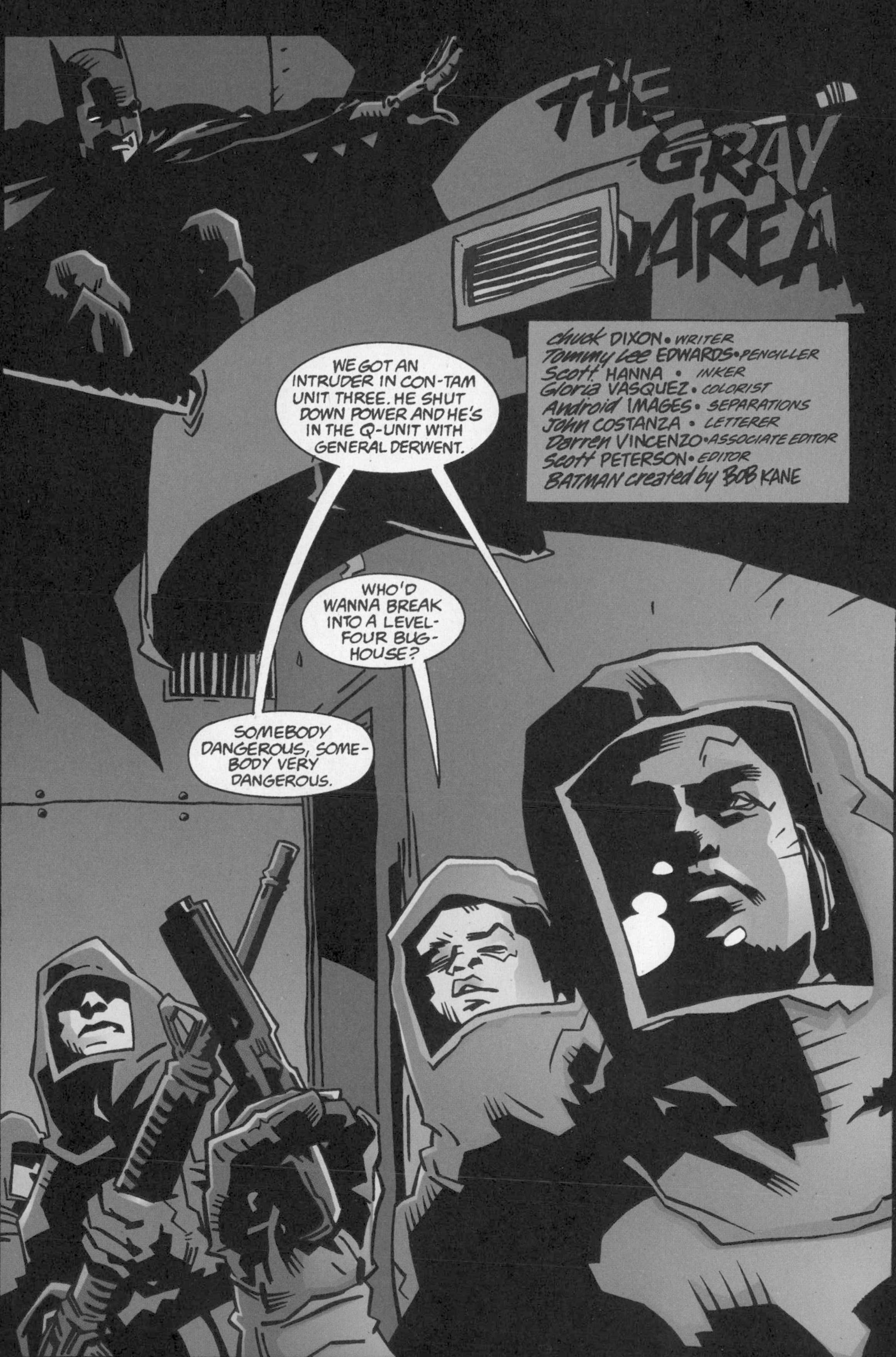

THE GRAY AREA
Chuck DIXON • WRITER
Tommy Lee EDWARDS • PENCILLER
Scott HANNA • INKER
Gloria VASQUEZ • COLORIST
Android IMAGES • SEPARATIONS
John COSTANZA • LETTERER
Darren VINCENZO • ASSOCIATE EDITOR
Scott PETERSON • EDITOR
BATMAN created by BOB KANE
WE GOT AN INTRUDER IN CON-TAM UNIT THREE. HE SHUT DOWN POWER AND HE'S IN THE Q-UNIT WITH GENERAL DERWENT.
WHO'D WANNA BREAK INTO A LEVEL-FOUR BUG-HOUSE?
SOMEBODY DANGEROUS, SOMEBODY VERY DANGEROUS.

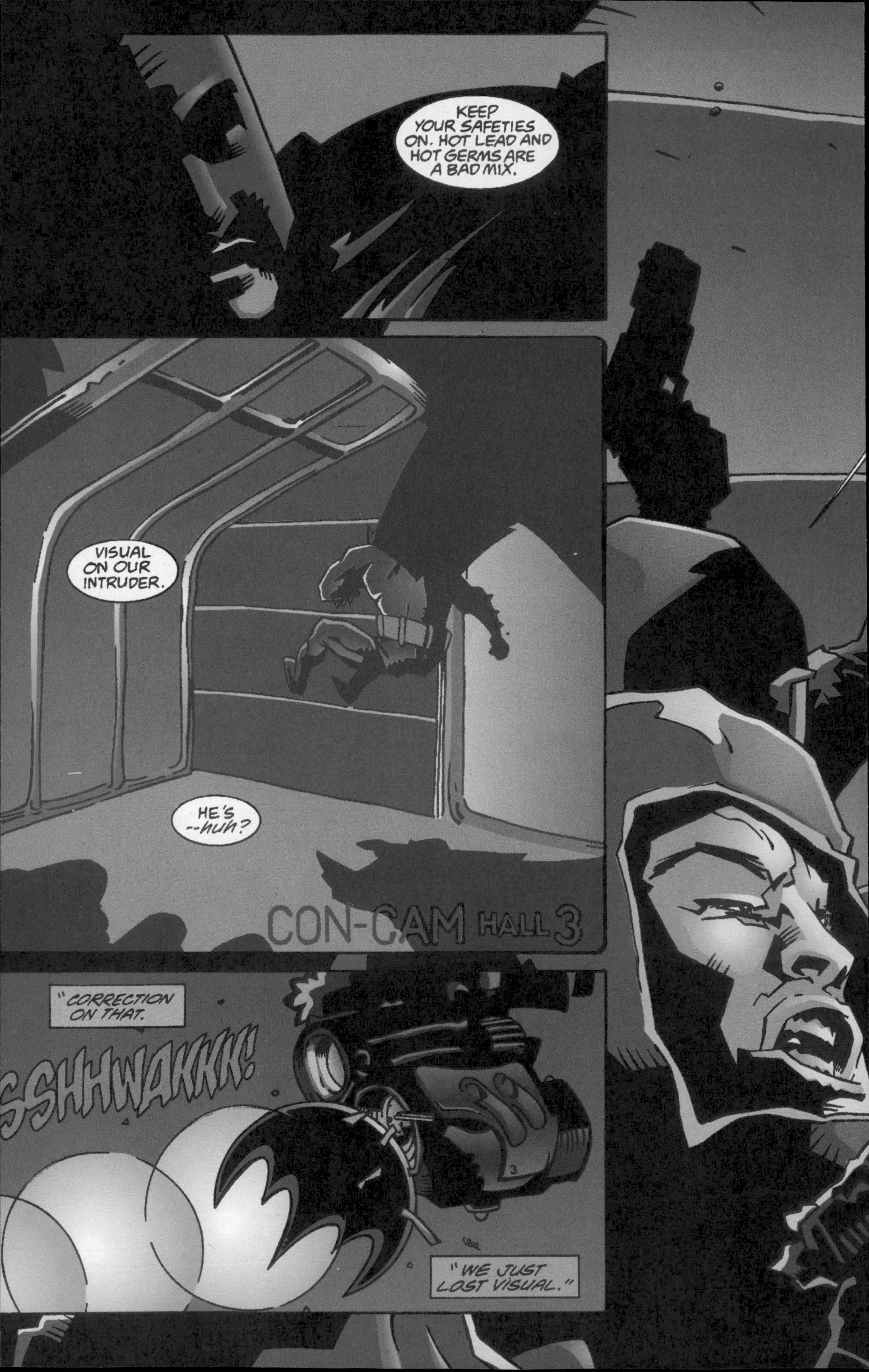
KEEP YOUR SAFETIES ON. HOT LEAD AND HOT GERMS ARE A BAD MIX.
VISUAL ON OUR INTRUDER.
HE'S --huh?
CON-CAM HALL 3
"CORRECTION ON THAT.
SSHHWAKKK!
"WE JUST LOST VISUAL."

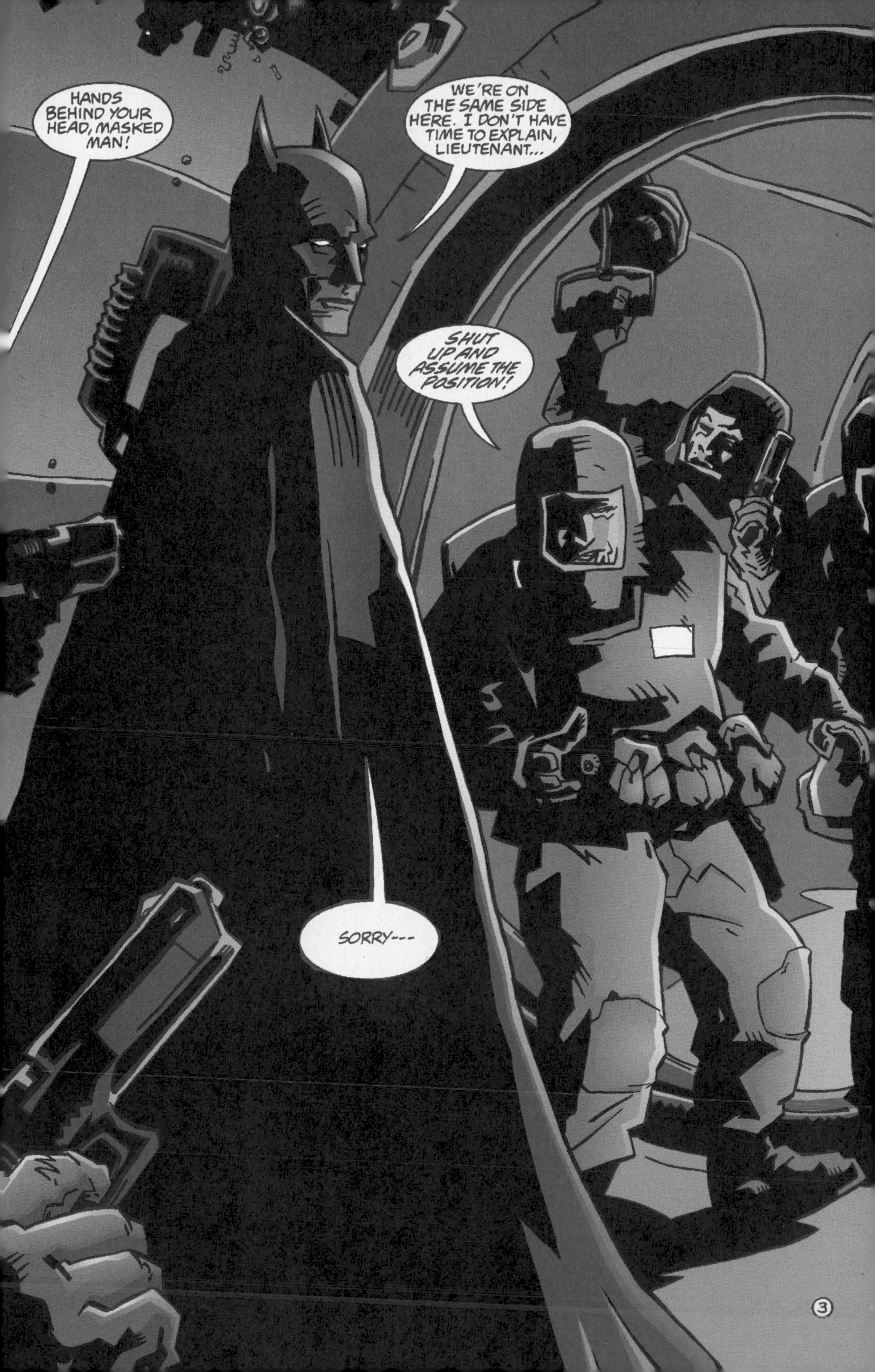
HANDS BEHIND YOUR HEAD, MASKED MAN!
WE'RE ON THE SAME SIDE HERE. I DON'T HAVE TIME TO EXPLAIN, LIEUTENANT...
SHUT UP AND ASSUME THE POSITION!
SORRY---

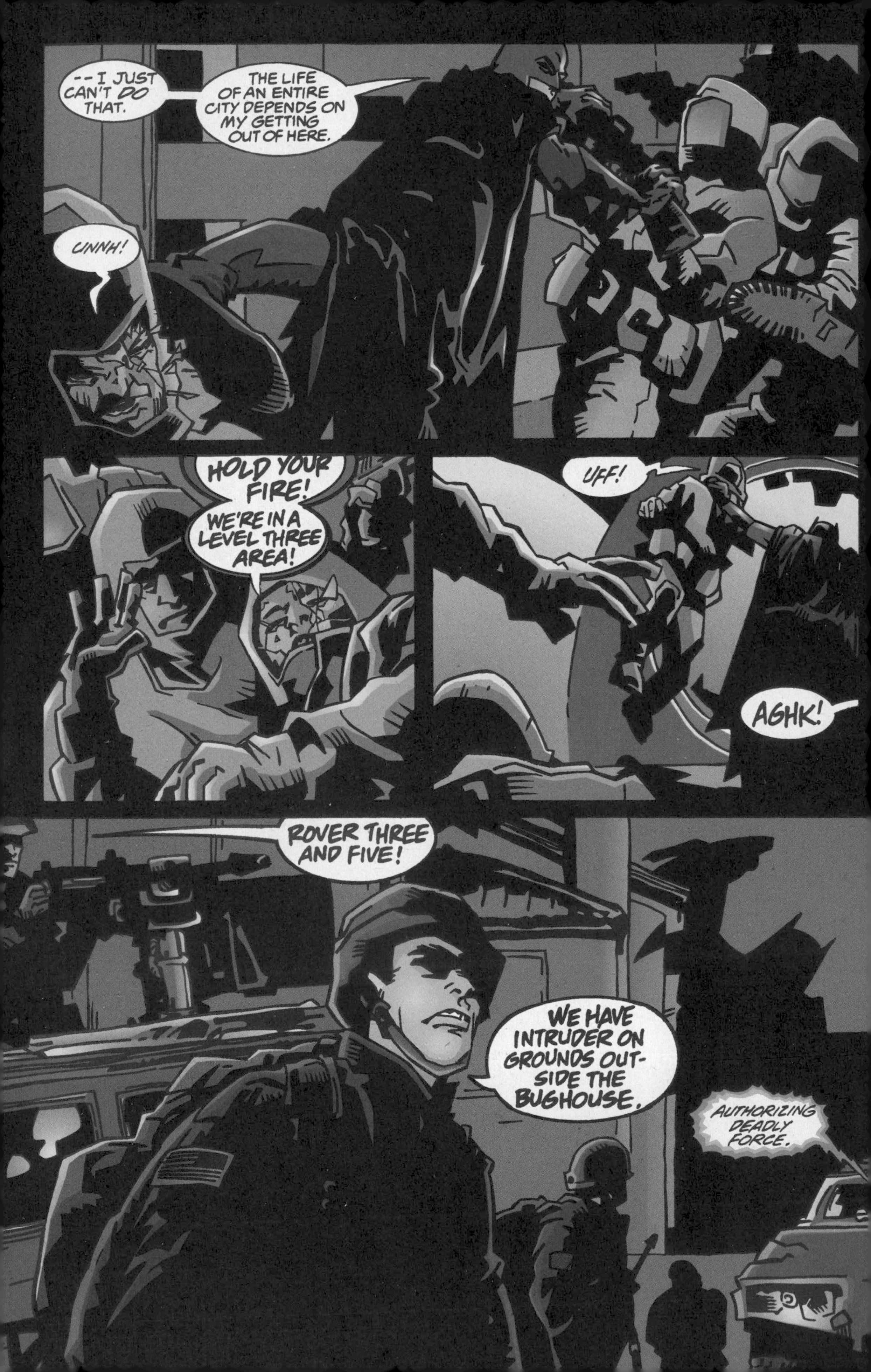
--I JUST CAN'T DO THAT.
THE LIFE OF AN ENTIRE CITY DEPENDS ON MY GETTING OUT OF HERE.
UNNH!
HOLD YOUR FIRE!
WE'RE IN A LEVEL THREE AREA!
UFF!
AGHK!
ROVER THREE AND FIVE!
WE HAVE INTRUDER ON GROUNDS OUT-SIDE THE BUGHOUSE.
AUTHORIZING DEADLY FORCE.

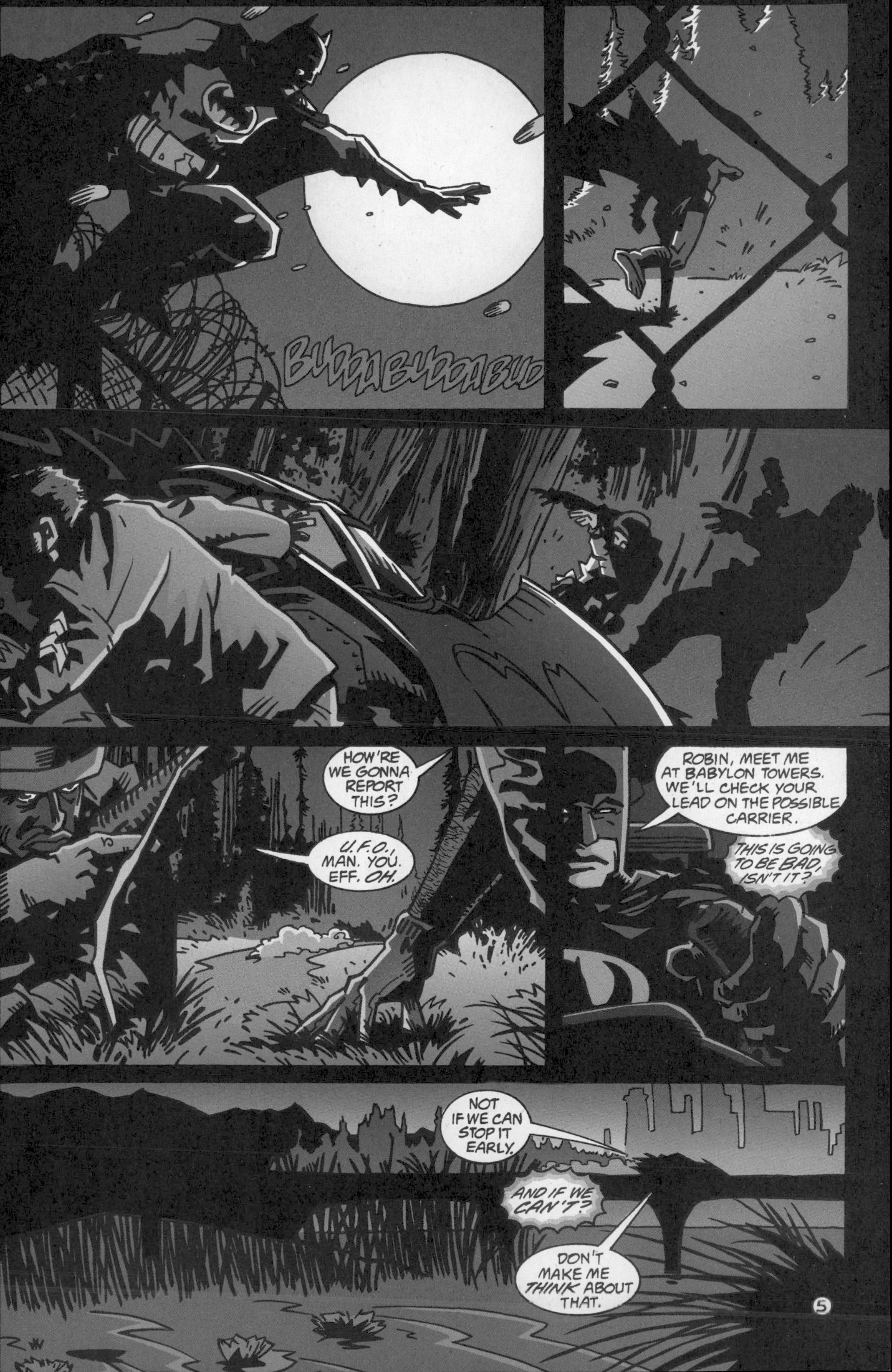
BUDDABUDDABUD
HOW'RE WE GONNA REPORT THIS?
U.F.O., MAN. YOU. EFF. *OH.*
ROBIN, MEET ME AT BABYLON TOWERS. WE'LL CHECK YOUR LEAD ON THE POSSIBLE CARRIER.
THIS IS GOING TO BE BAD, ISN'T IT?
NOT IF WE CAN STOP IT EARLY.
AND IF WE CAN'T?
DON'T MAKE ME *THINK* ABOUT THAT.

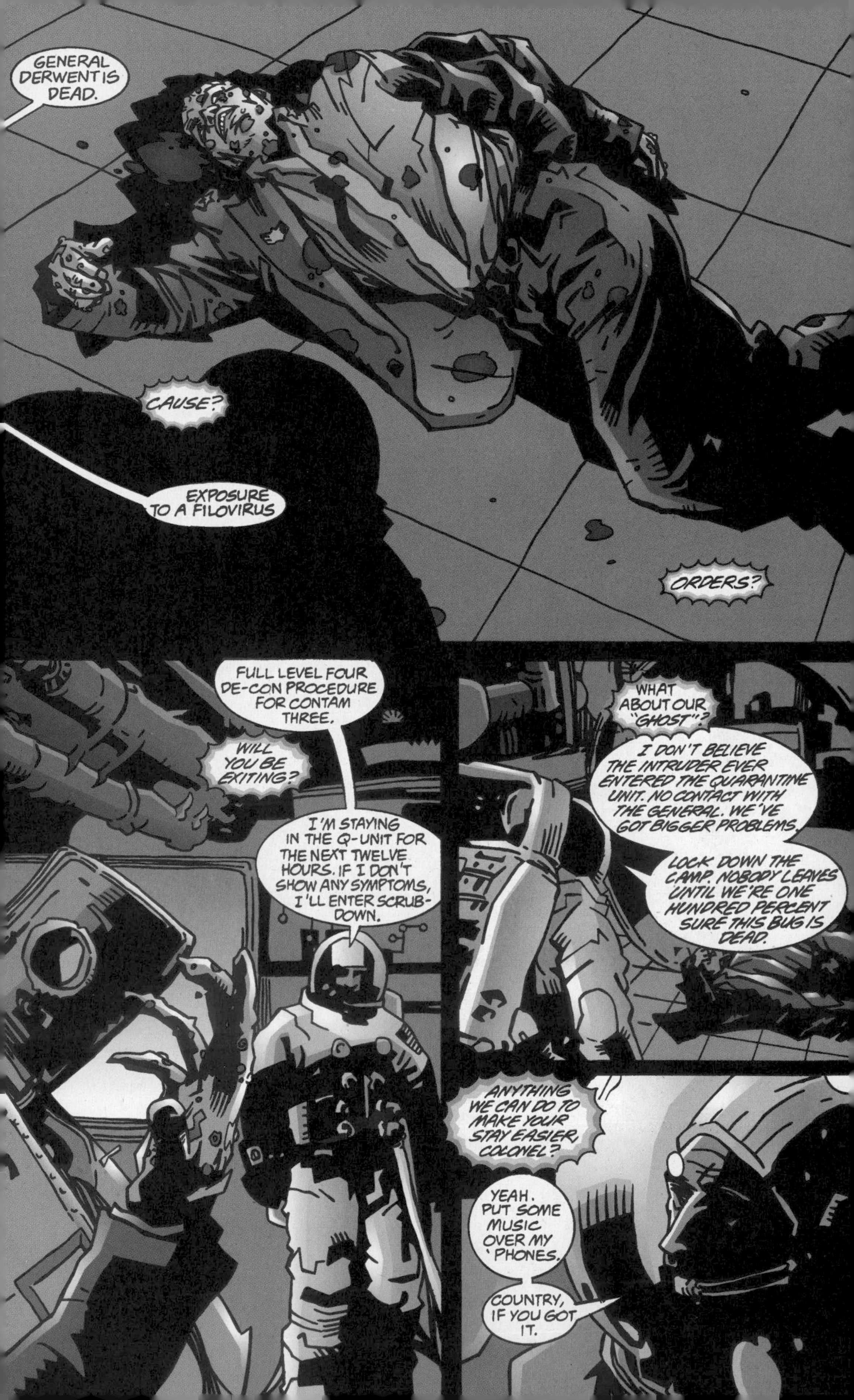
GENERAL DERWENT IS DEAD.
CAUSE?
EXPOSURE TO A FILOVIRUS
ORDERS?
FULL LEVEL FOUR DE-CON PROCEDURE FOR CONTAM THREE.
WILL YOU BE EXITING?
I'M STAYING IN THE Q-UNIT FOR THE NEXT TWELVE HOURS. IF I DON'T SHOW ANY SYMPTOMS, I'LL ENTER SCRUB-DOWN.
WHAT ABOUT OUR "GHOST"?
I DON'T BELIEVE THE INTRUDER EVER ENTERED THE QUARANTINE UNIT. NO CONTACT WITH THE GENERAL. WE'VE GOT BIGGER PROBLEMS.
LOCK DOWN THE CAMP. NOBODY LEAVES UNTIL WE'RE ONE HUNDRED PERCENT SURE THIS BUG IS DEAD.
ANYTHING WE CAN DO TO MAKE YOUR STAY EASIER, COLONEL?
YEAH. PUT SOME MUSIC OVER MY 'PHONES.
COUNTRY, IF YOU GOT IT.

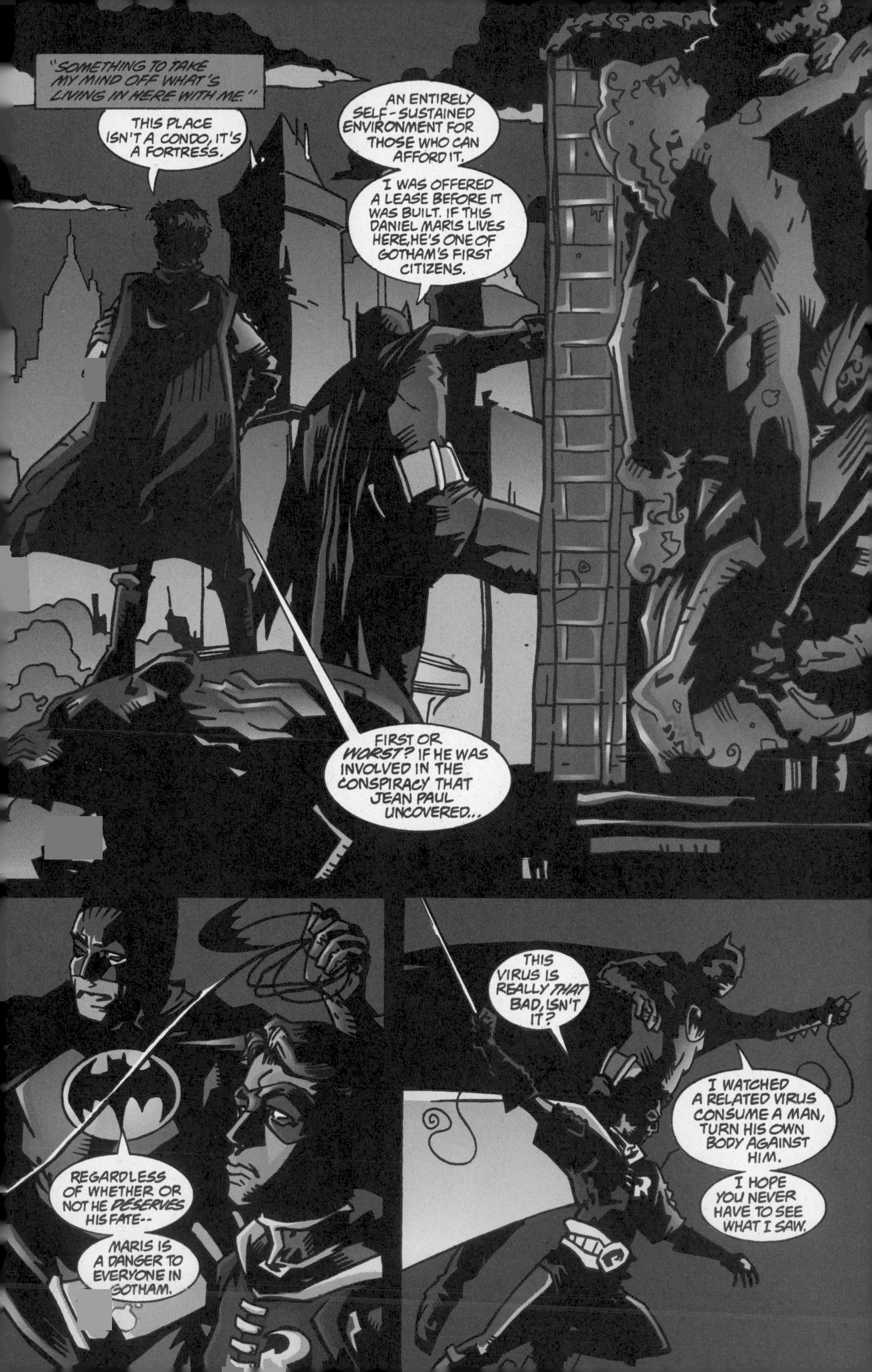
"SOMETHING TO TAKE MY MIND OFF WHAT'S LIVING IN HERE WITH ME."
THIS PLACE ISN'T A CONDO, IT'S A FORTRESS.
AN ENTIRELY SELF-SUSTAINED ENVIRONMENT FOR THOSE WHO CAN AFFORD IT.
I WAS OFFERED A LEASE BEFORE IT WAS BUILT. IF THIS DANIEL MARIS LIVES HERE, HE'S ONE OF GOTHAM'S FIRST CITIZENS.
FIRST OR WORST? IF HE WAS INVOLVED IN THE CONSPIRACY THAT JEAN PAUL UNCOVERED...
REGARDLESS OF WHETHER OR NOT HE DESERVES HIS FATE--
MARIS IS A DANGER TO EVERYONE IN GOTHAM.
THIS VIRUS IS REALLY THAT BAD, ISN'T IT?
I WATCHED A RELATED VIRUS CONSUME A MAN, TURN HIS OWN BODY AGAINST HIM.
I HOPE YOU NEVER HAVE TO SEE WHAT I SAW.

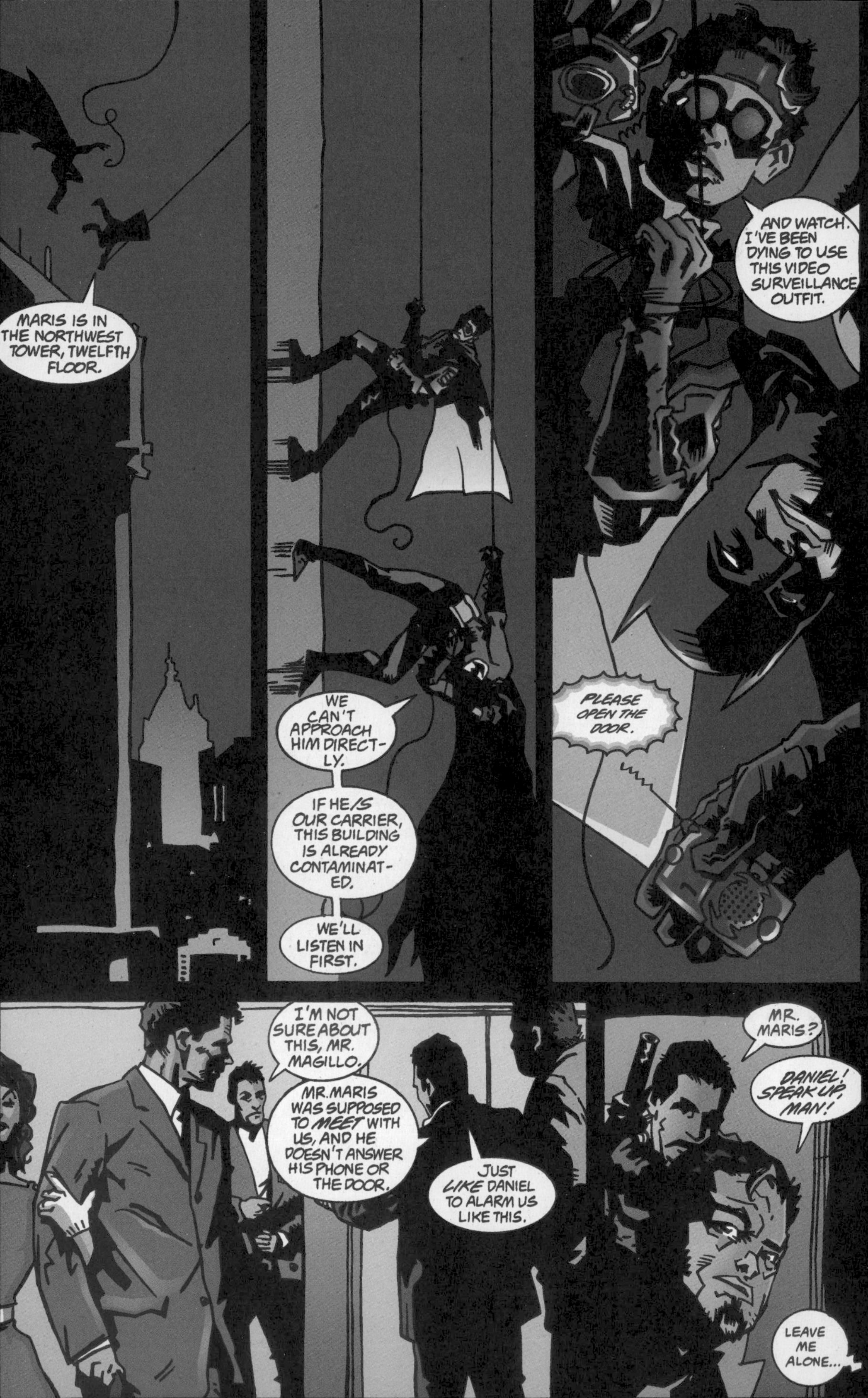
MARIS IS IN THE NORTHWEST TOWER, TWELFTH FLOOR.
WE CAN'T APPROACH HIM DIRECTLY.
IF HE *IS* OUR CARRIER, THIS BUILDING IS ALREADY CONTAMINATED.
WE'LL LISTEN IN FIRST.
AND WATCH. I'VE BEEN DYING TO USE THIS VIDEO SURVEILLANCE OUTFIT.
PLEASE OPEN THE DOOR.
I'M NOT SURE ABOUT THIS, MR. MAGILLO.
MR. MARIS WAS SUPPOSED TO *MEET* WITH US, AND HE DOESN'T ANSWER HIS PHONE OR THE DOOR.
JUST *LIKE* DANIEL TO ALARM US LIKE THIS.
MR. MARIS?
DANIEL! SPEAK UP, MAN!
LEAVE ME ALONE...

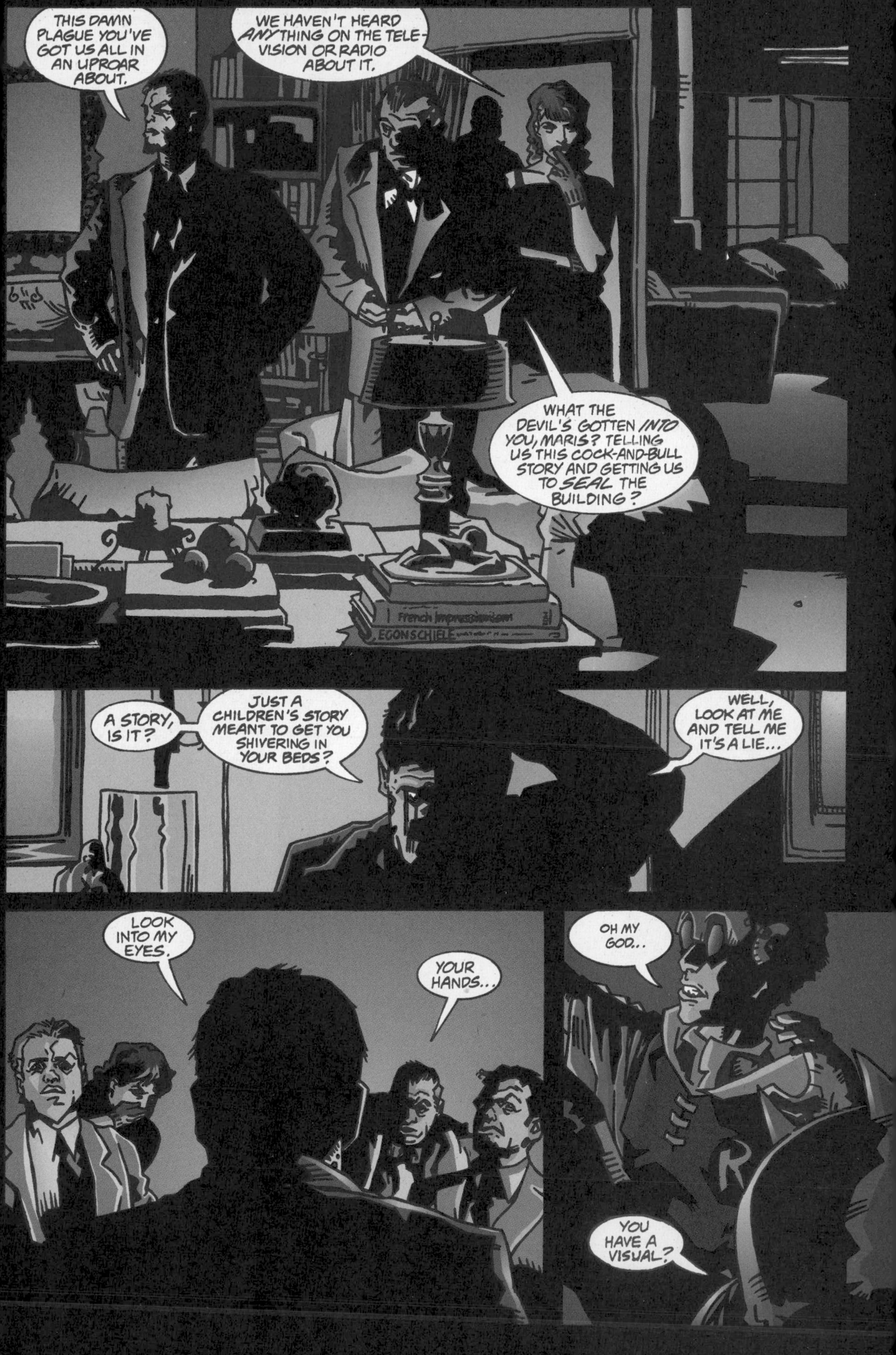
THIS DAMN PLAGUE YOU'VE GOT US ALL IN AN UPROAR ABOUT.
WE HAVEN'T HEARD ANYTHING ON THE TELEVISION OR RADIO ABOUT IT.
WHAT THE DEVIL'S GOTTEN INTO YOU, MARIS? TELLING US THIS COCK-AND-BULL STORY AND GETTING US TO SEAL THE BUILDING?
French Impressionism
EGON SCHIELE
A STORY, IS IT?
JUST A CHILDREN'S STORY MEANT TO GET YOU SHIVERING IN YOUR BEDS?
WELL, LOOK AT ME AND TELL ME IT'S A LIE...
LOOK INTO MY EYES.
YOUR HANDS...
OH MY GOD...
YOU HAVE A VISUAL?

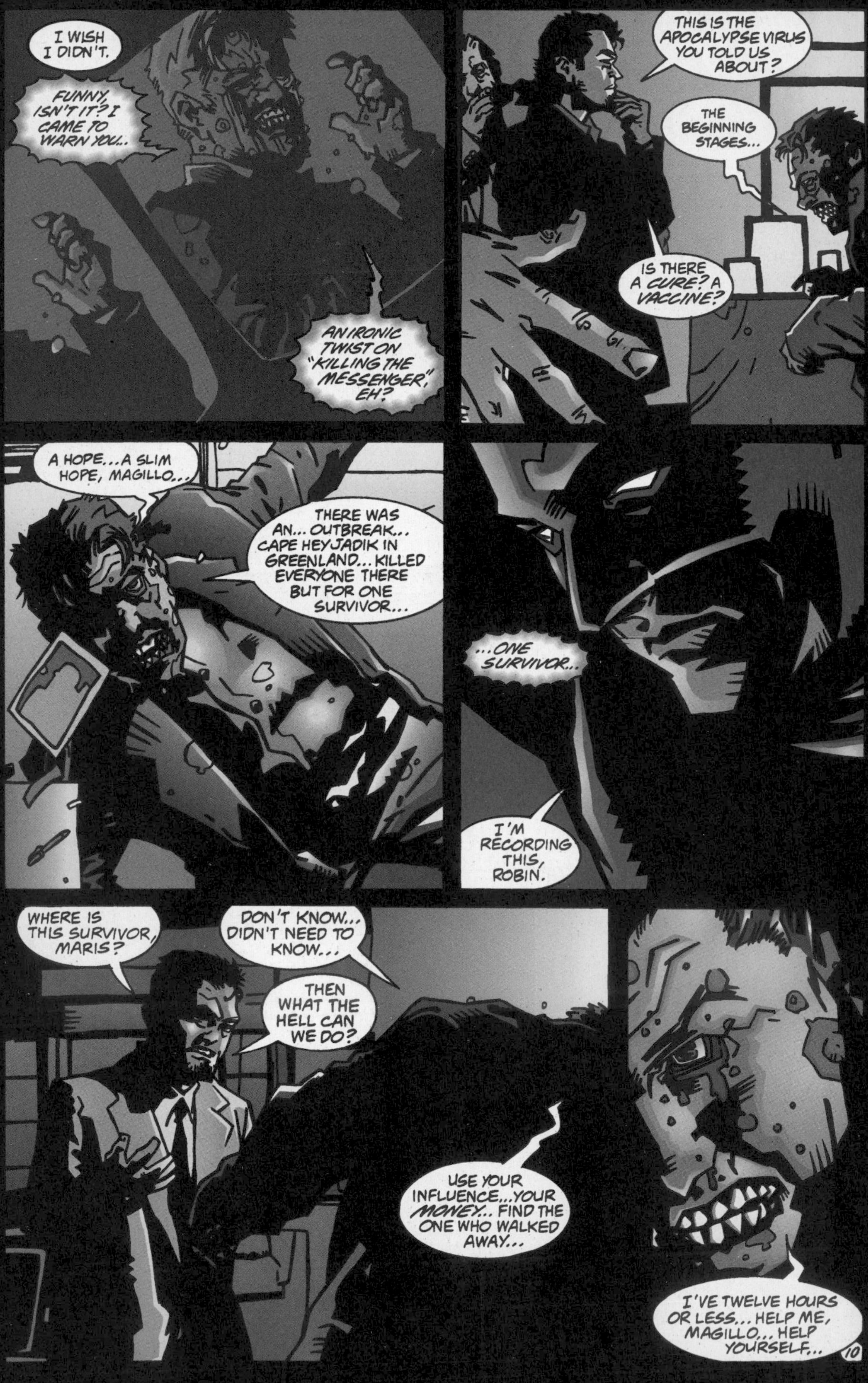
I WISH I DIDN'T.
FUNNY, ISN'T IT? I CAME TO WARN YOU..
AN IRONIC TWIST ON "KILLING THE MESSENGER," EH?
THIS IS THE APOCALYPSE VIRUS YOU TOLD US ABOUT?
THE BEGINNING STAGES...
IS THERE A CURE? A VACCINE?
A HOPE...A SLIM HOPE, MAGILLO...
THERE WAS AN... OUTBREAK... CAPE HEYJADIK IN GREENLAND... KILLED EVERYONE THERE BUT FOR ONE SURVIVOR...
...ONE SURVIVOR...
I'M RECORDING THIS, ROBIN.
WHERE IS THIS SURVIVOR, MARIS?
DON'T KNOW... DIDN'T NEED TO KNOW...
THEN WHAT THE HELL CAN WE DO?
USE YOUR INFLUENCE...YOUR MONEY... FIND THE ONE WHO WALKED AWAY...
I'VE TWELVE HOURS OR LESS... HELP ME, MAGILLO... HELP YOURSELF...
10

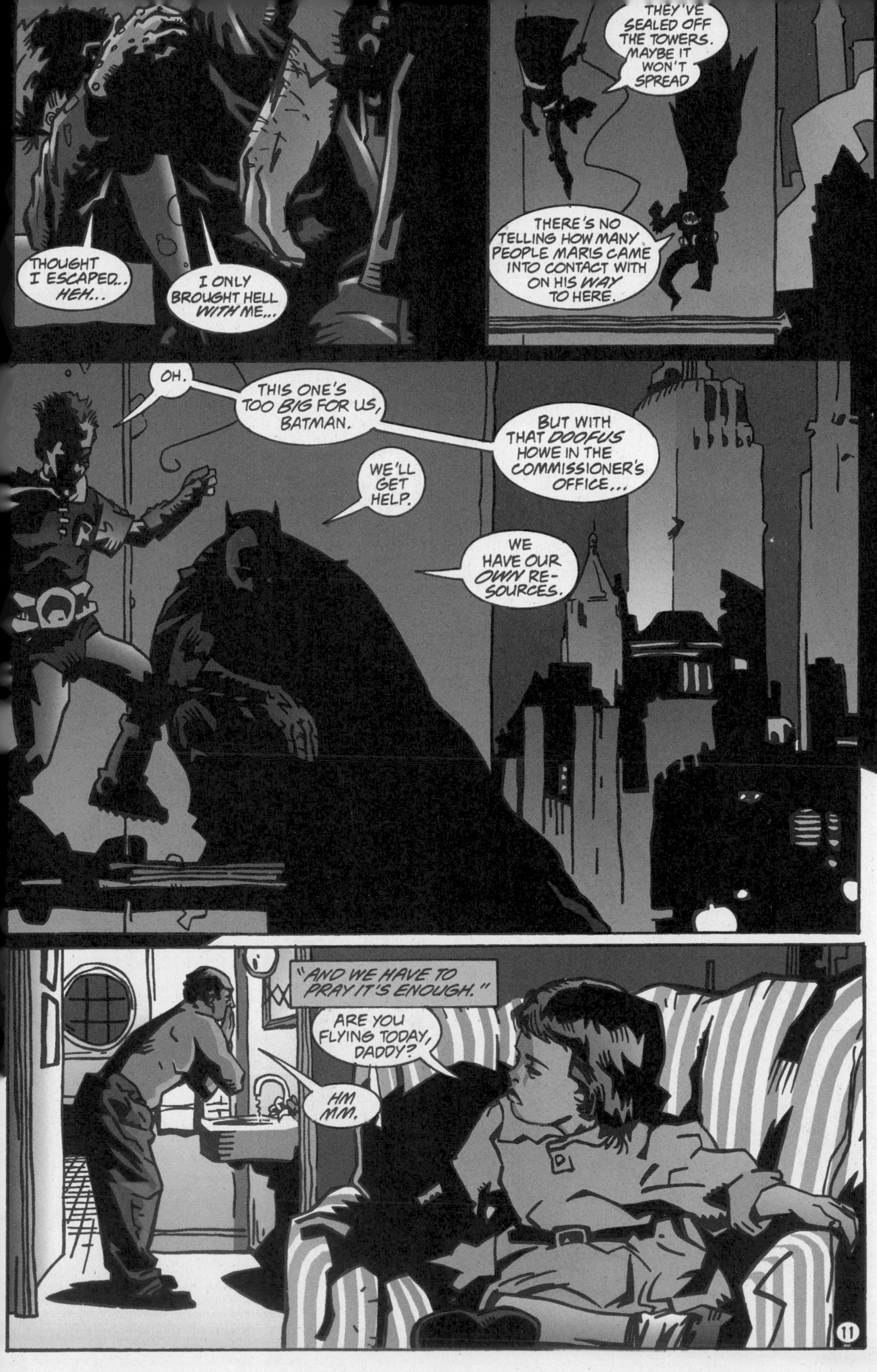
THOUGHT I ESCAPED... HEH...
I ONLY BROUGHT HELL WITH ME...
THEY'VE SEALED OFF THE TOWERS. MAYBE IT WON'T SPREAD
THERE'S NO TELLING HOW MANY PEOPLE MARIS CAME INTO CONTACT WITH ON HIS WAY TO HERE.
OH.
THIS ONE'S TOO BIG FOR US, BATMAN.
BUT WITH THAT DOOFUS HOWE IN THE COMMISSIONER'S OFFICE...
WE'LL GET HELP.
WE HAVE OUR OWN RE-SOURCES.
"AND WE HAVE TO PRAY IT'S ENOUGH."
ARE YOU FLYING TODAY, DADDY?
HM MM.
11

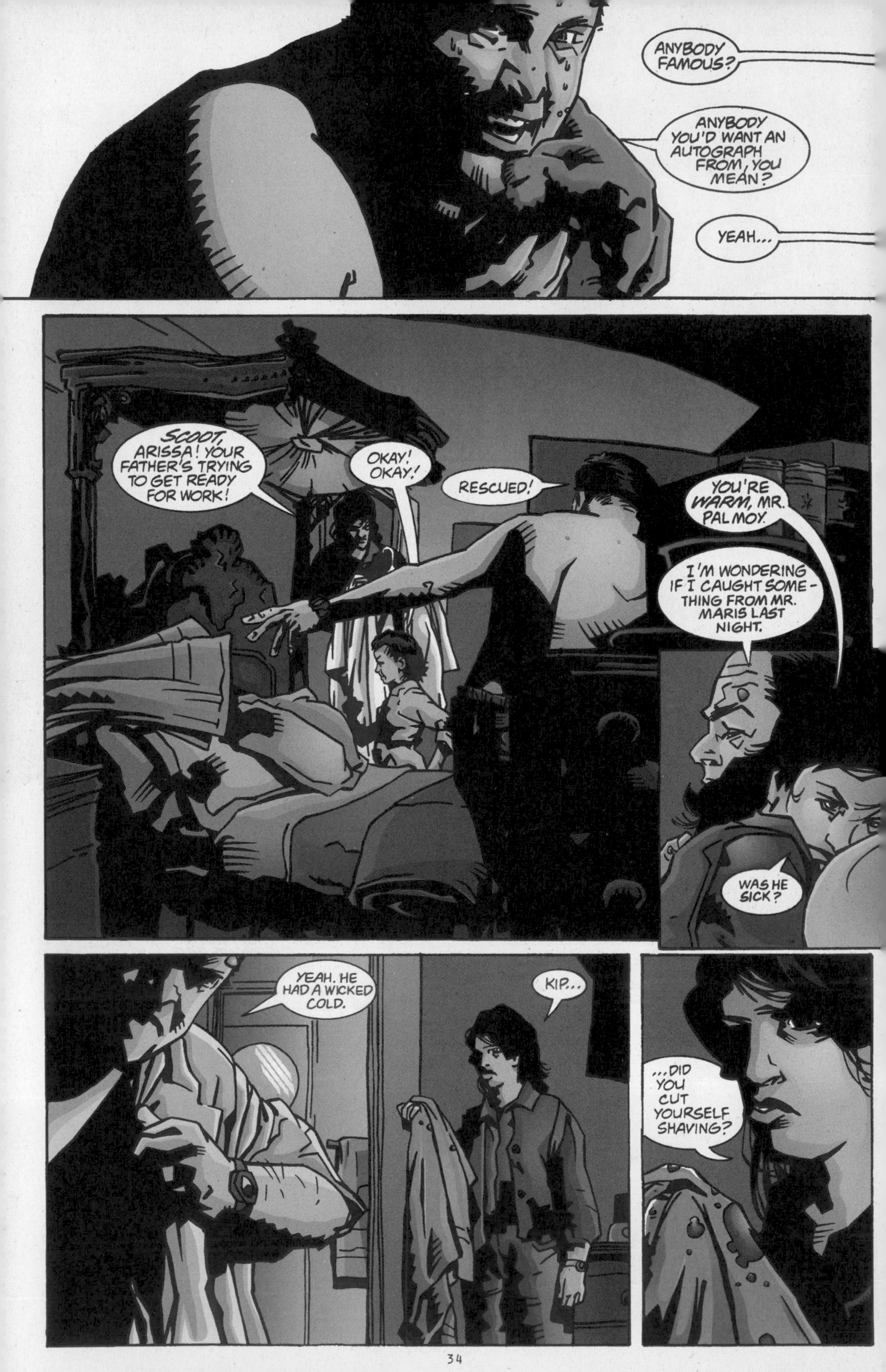
ANYBODY FAMOUS?
ANYBODY YOU'D WANT AN AUTOGRAPH FROM, YOU MEAN?
YEAH...
SCOOT, ARISSA! YOUR FATHER'S TRYING TO GET READY FOR WORK!
OKAY! OKAY!
RESCUED!
YOU'RE WARM, MR. PALMOY.
I'M WONDERING IF I CAUGHT SOME-THING FROM MR. MARIS LAST NIGHT.
WAS HE SICK?
YEAH. HE HAD A WICKED COLD.
KIP...
...DID YOU CUT YOURSELF SHAVING?

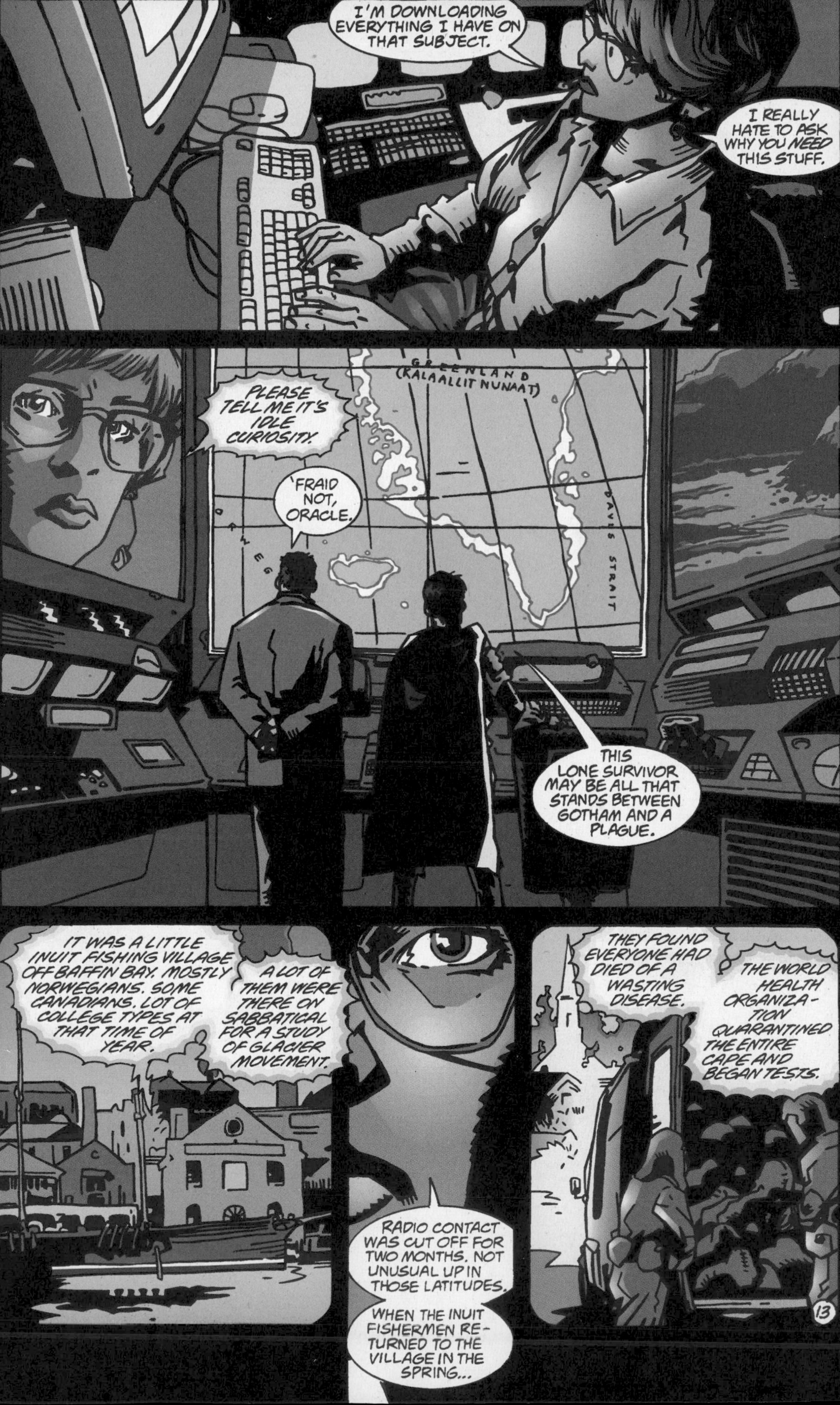
I'M DOWNLOADING EVERYTHING I HAVE ON THAT SUBJECT.
I REALLY HATE TO ASK WHY YOU NEED THIS STUFF.
GREENLAND (KALAALLIT NUNAAT)
PLEASE TELL ME IT'S IDLE CURIOSITY.
'FRAID NOT, ORACLE.
DAVIS STRAIT
THIS LONE SURVIVOR MAY BE ALL THAT STANDS BETWEEN GOTHAM AND A PLAGUE.
IT WAS A LITTLE INUIT FISHING VILLAGE OFF BAFFIN BAY. MOSTLY NORWEGIANS. SOME CANADIANS. LOT OF COLLEGE TYPES AT THAT TIME OF YEAR.
A LOT OF THEM WERE THERE ON SABBATICAL FOR A STUDY OF GLACIER MOVEMENT.
RADIO CONTACT WAS CUT OFF FOR TWO MONTHS. NOT UNUSUAL UP IN THOSE LATITUDES.
WHEN THE INUIT FISHERMEN RE-TURNED TO THE VILLAGE IN THE SPRING...
THEY FOUND EVERYONE HAD DIED OF A WASTING DISEASE.
THE WORLD HEALTH ORGANIZA-TION QUARANTINED THE ENTIRE CAPE AND BEGAN TESTS.

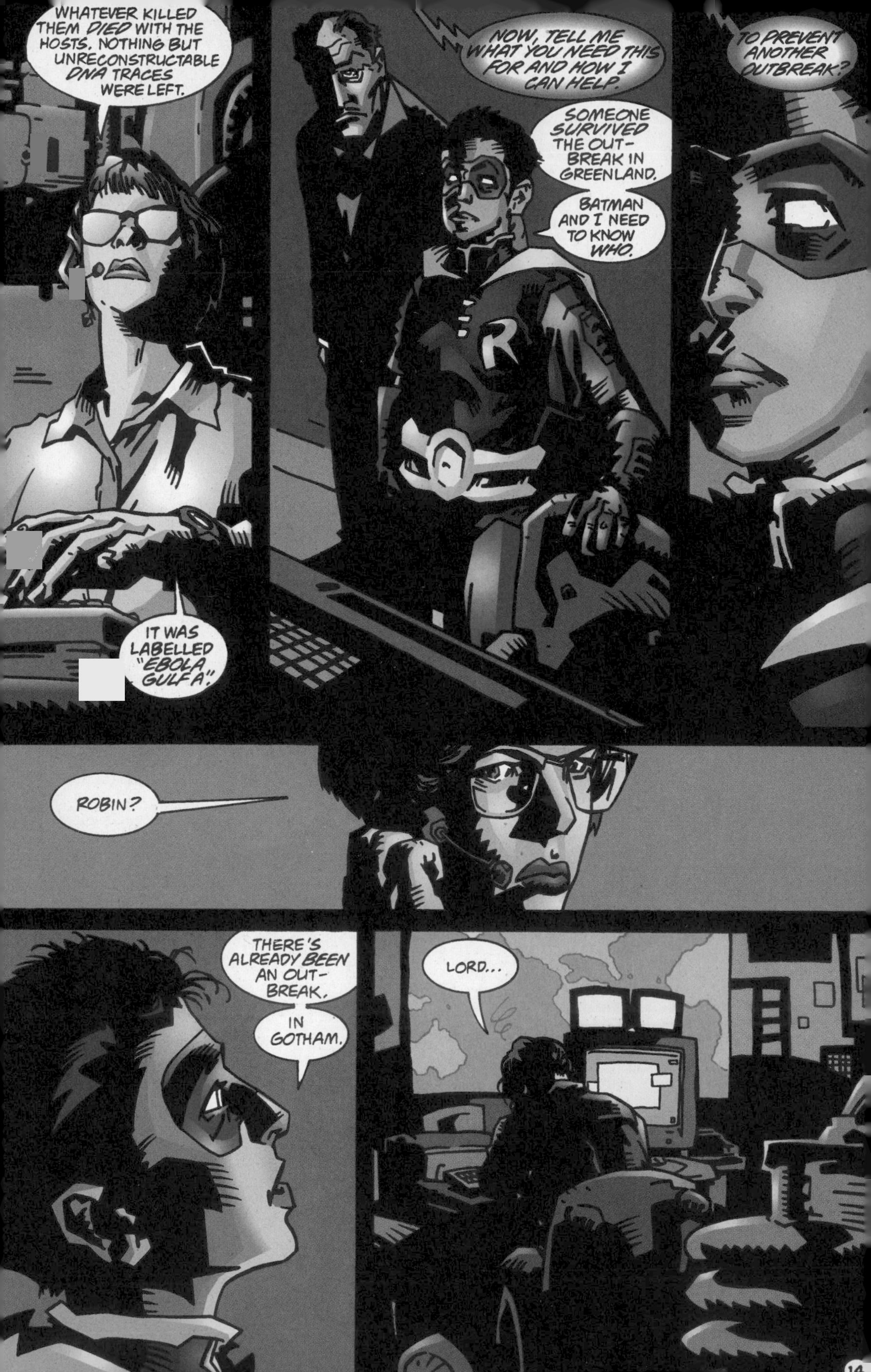
WHATEVER KILLED THEM DIED WITH THE HOSTS. NOTHING BUT UNRECONSTRUCTABLE DNA TRACES WERE LEFT.
IT WAS LABELLED "EBOLA GULF A".
NOW, TELL ME WHAT YOU NEED THIS FOR AND HOW I CAN HELP.
SOMEONE SURVIVED THE OUT-BREAK IN GREENLAND.
BATMAN AND I NEED TO KNOW WHO.
TO PREVENT ANOTHER OUTBREAK?
ROBIN?
THERE'S ALREADY BEEN AN OUT-BREAK.
IN GOTHAM.
LORD...

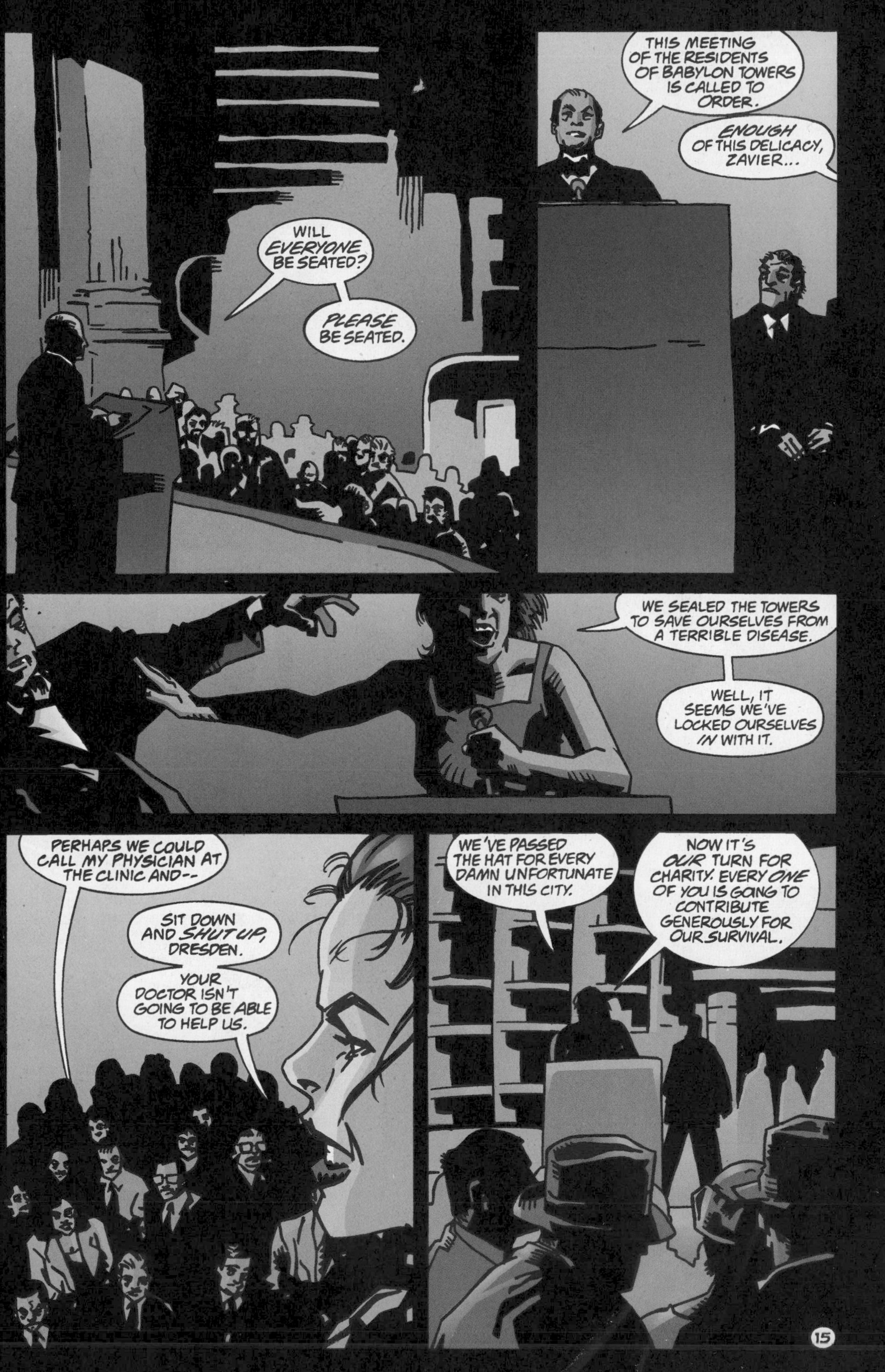
WILL EVERYONE BE SEATED?
PLEASE BE SEATED.
THIS MEETING OF THE RESIDENTS OF BABYLON TOWERS IS CALLED TO ORDER.
ENOUGH OF THIS DELICACY, ZAVIER...
WE SEALED THE TOWERS TO SAVE OURSELVES FROM A TERRIBLE DISEASE.
WELL, IT SEEMS WE'VE LOCKED OURSELVES IN WITH IT.
PERHAPS WE COULD CALL MY PHYSICIAN AT THE CLINIC AND--
SIT DOWN AND SHUT UP, DRESDEN.
YOUR DOCTOR ISN'T GOING TO BE ABLE TO HELP US.
WE'VE PASSED THE HAT FOR EVERY DAMN UNFORTUNATE IN THIS CITY.
NOW IT'S OUR TURN FOR CHARITY. EVERY ONE OF YOU IS GOING TO CONTRIBUTE GENEROUSLY FOR OUR SURVIVAL.

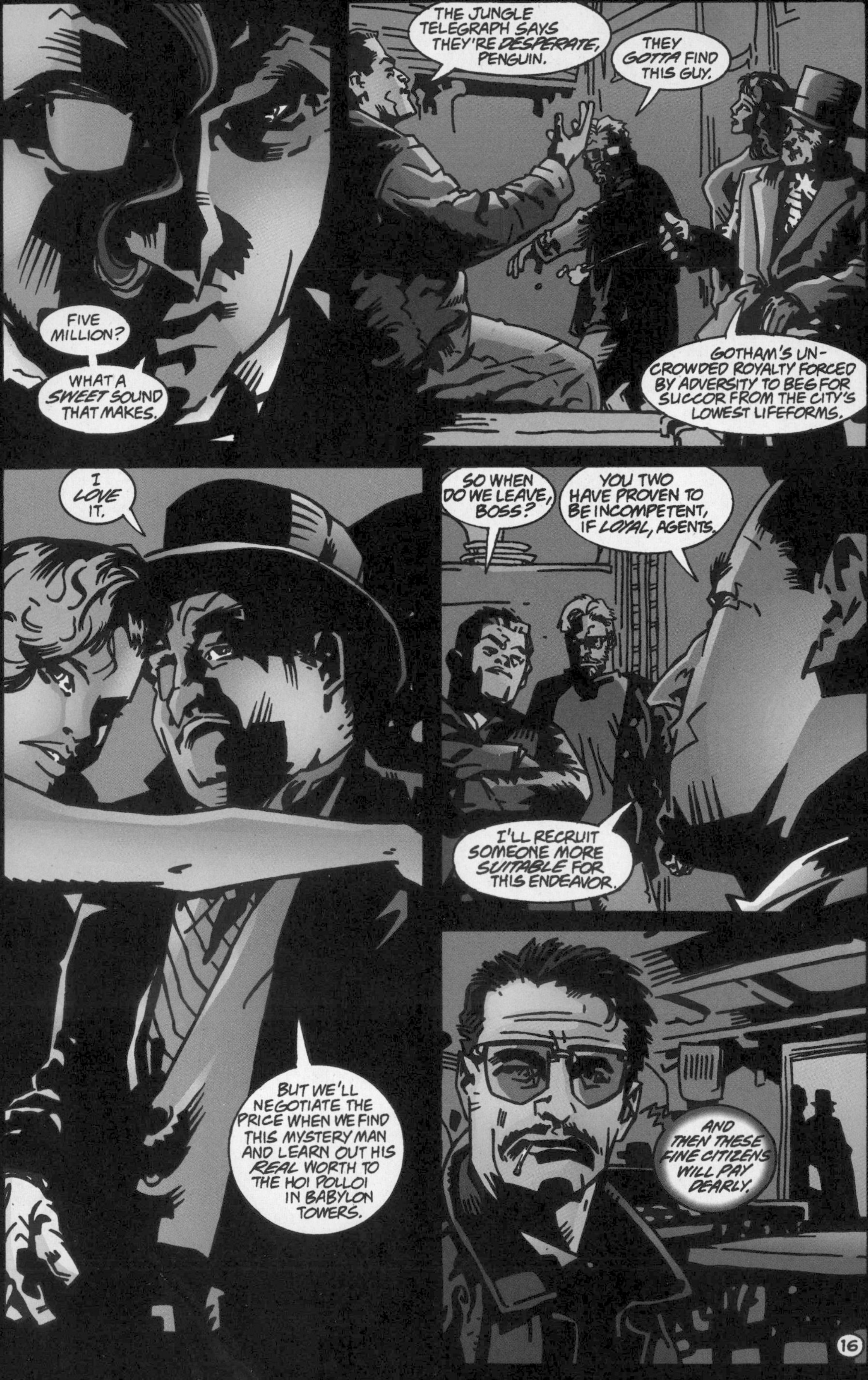
THE JUNGLE TELEGRAPH SAYS THEY'RE DESPERATE, PENGUIN.
THEY GOTTA FIND THIS GUY.
FIVE MILLION?
WHAT A SWEET SOUND THAT MAKES.
GOTHAM'S UN-CROWDED ROYALTY FORCED BY ADVERSITY TO BEG FOR SUCCOR FROM THE CITY'S LOWEST LIFEFORMS.
I LOVE IT.
SO WHEN DO WE LEAVE, BOSS?
YOU TWO HAVE PROVEN TO BE INCOMPETENT, IF LOYAL, AGENTS.
I'LL RECRUIT SOMEONE MORE SUITABLE FOR THIS ENDEAVOR.
BUT WE'LL NEGOTIATE THE PRICE WHEN WE FIND THIS MYSTERY MAN AND LEARN OUT HIS REAL WORTH TO THE HOI POLLOI IN BABYLON TOWERS.
AND THEN THESE FINE CITIZENS WILL PAY DEARLY.

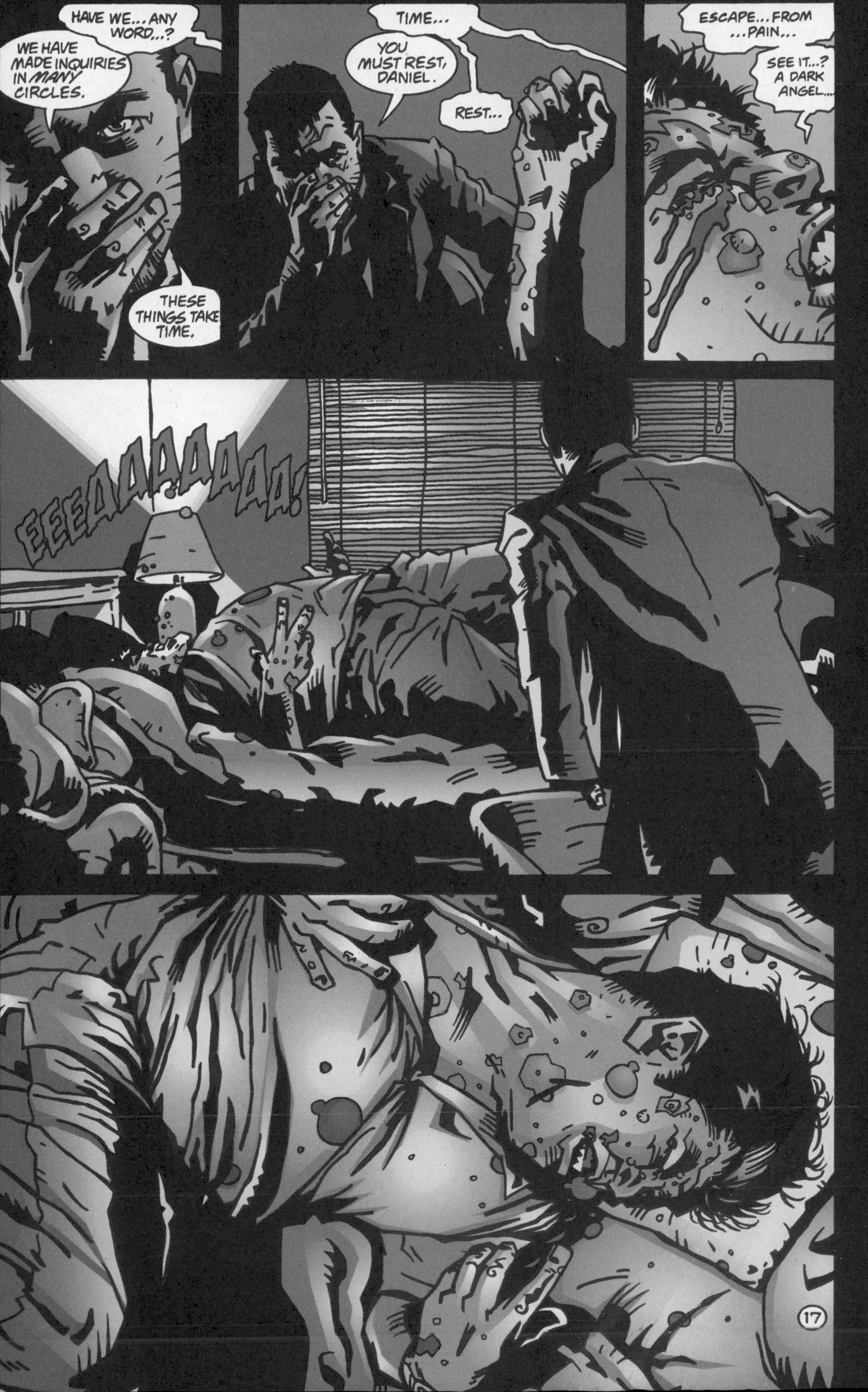
HAVE WE... ANY WORD...?
WE HAVE MADE INQUIRIES IN MANY CIRCLES.
THESE THINGS TAKE TIME.
TIME...
YOU MUST REST, DANIEL.
REST...
ESCAPE... FROM ...PAIN...
SEE IT...? A DARK ANGEL...
EEEAAAAAAAA!

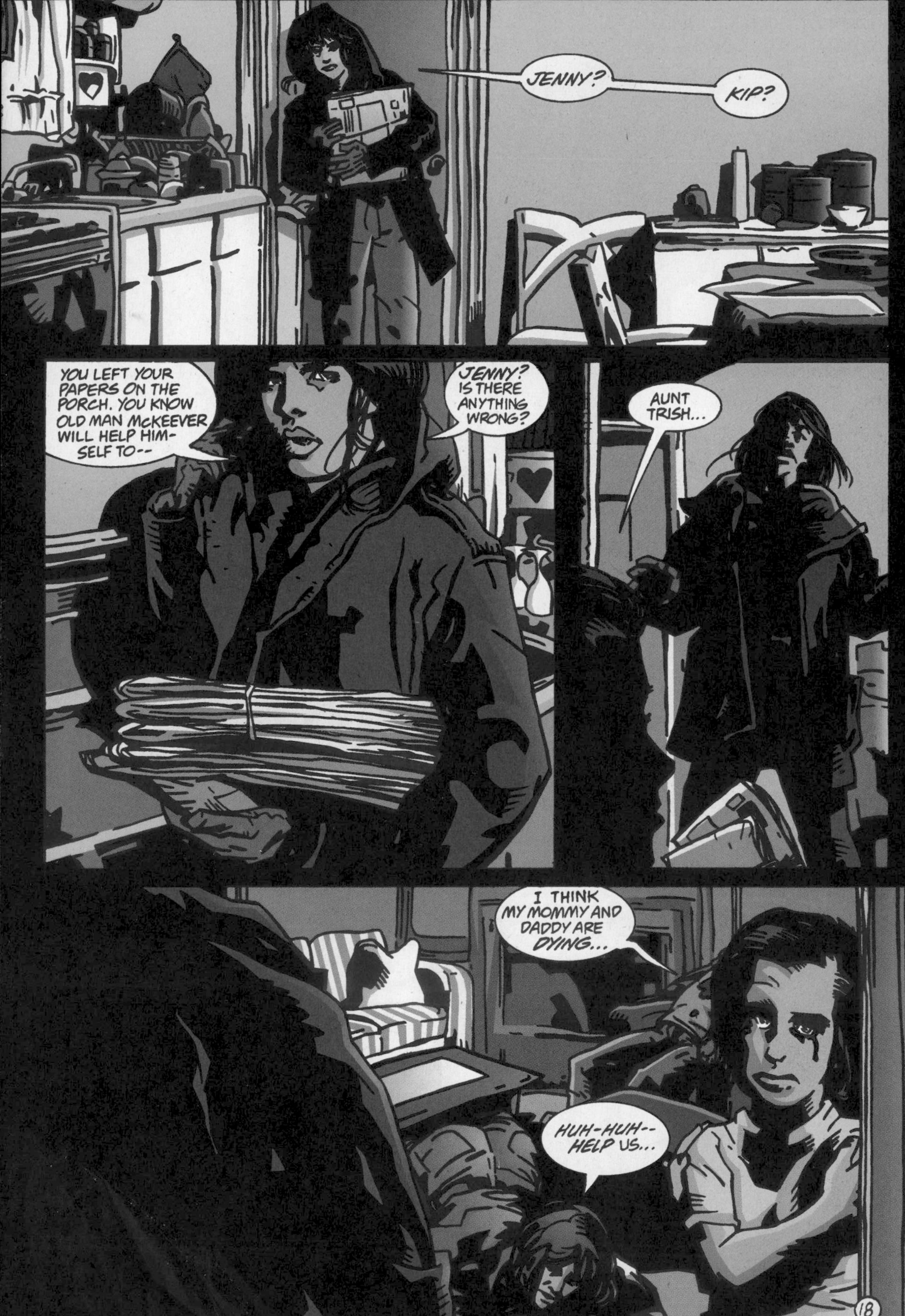
JENNY?
KIP?
YOU LEFT YOUR PAPERS ON THE PORCH. YOU KNOW OLD MAN McKEEVER WILL HELP HIM-SELF TO--
JENNY? IS THERE ANYTHING WRONG?
AUNT TRISH...
I THINK MY MOMMY AND DADDY ARE DYING...
HUH-HUH-- HELP US...

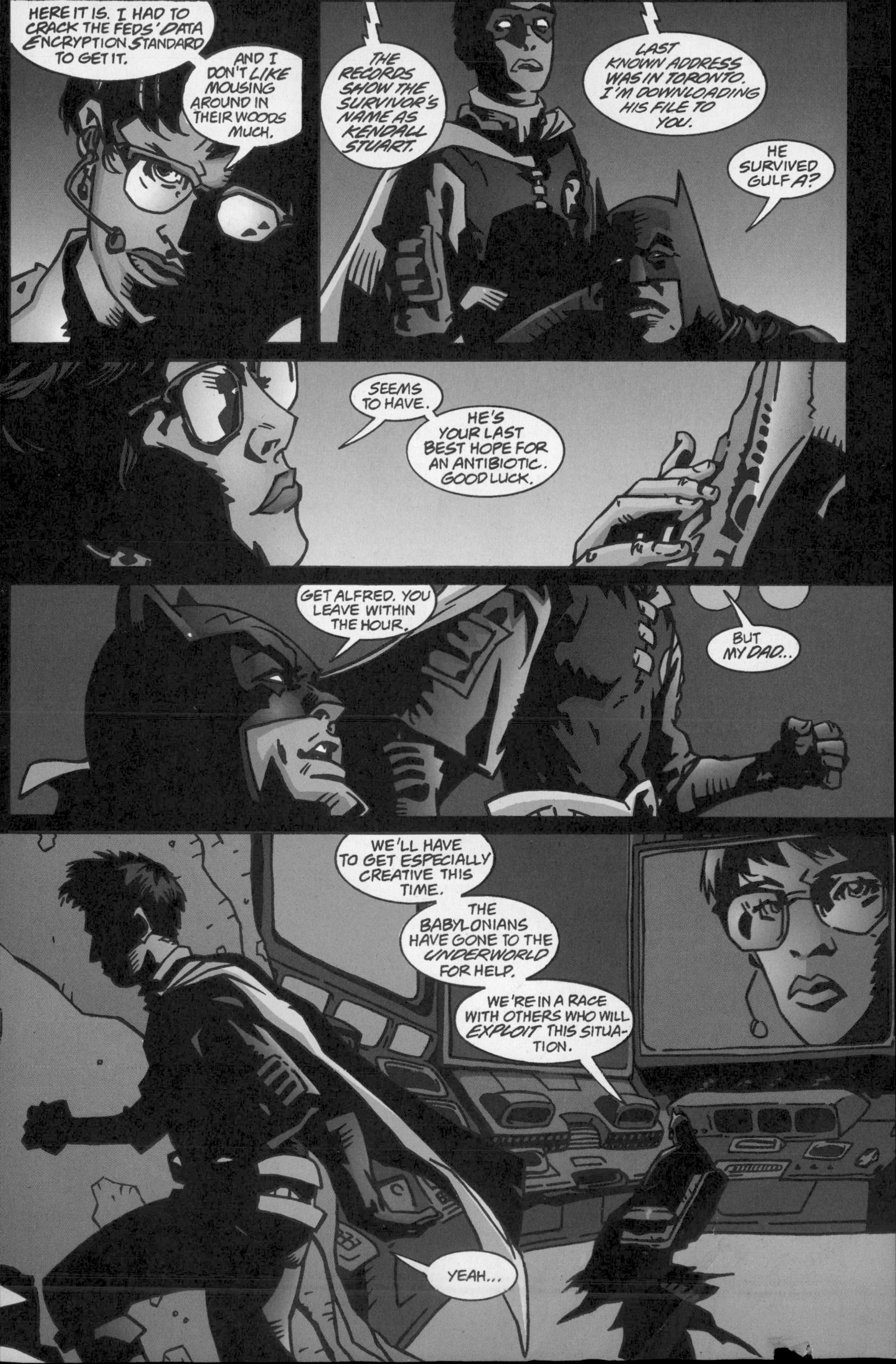
HERE IT IS. I HAD TO CRACK THE FEDS' DATA ENCRYPTION STANDARD TO GET IT.
AND I DON'T LIKE MOUSING AROUND IN THEIR WOODS MUCH.
THE RECORDS SHOW THE SURVIVOR'S NAME AS KENDALL STUART.
LAST KNOWN ADDRESS WAS IN TORONTO. I'M DOWNLOADING HIS FILE TO YOU.
HE SURVIVED GULF A?
SEEMS TO HAVE.
HE'S YOUR LAST BEST HOPE FOR AN ANTIBIOTIC. GOOD LUCK.
GET ALFRED. YOU LEAVE WITHIN THE HOUR.
BUT MY DAD...
WE'LL HAVE TO GET ESPECIALLY CREATIVE THIS TIME.
THE BABYLONIANS HAVE GONE TO THE UNDERWORLD FOR HELP.
WE'RE IN A RACE WITH OTHERS WHO WILL EXPLOIT THIS SITUATION.
YEAH...

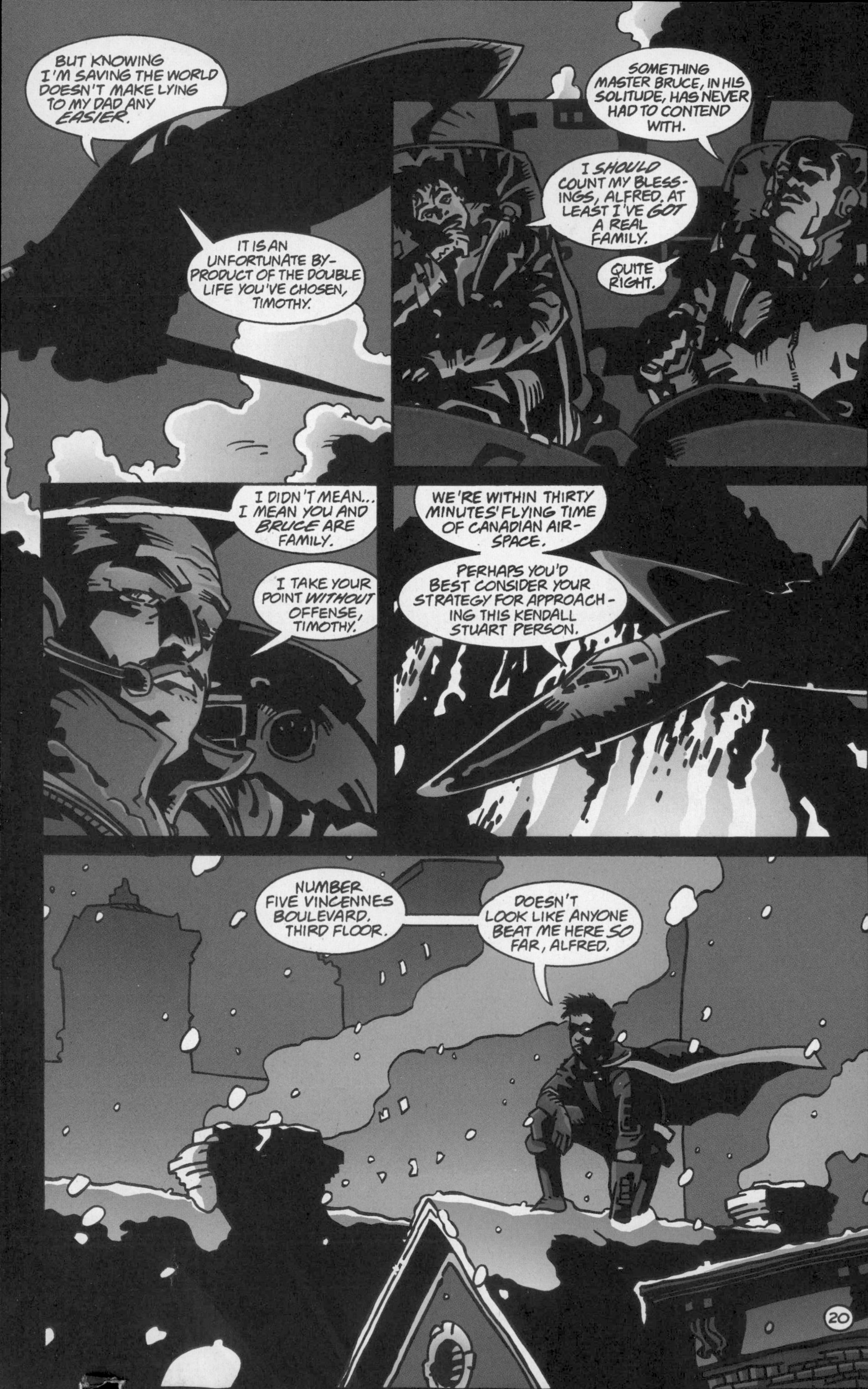
BUT KNOWING I'M SAVING THE WORLD DOESN'T MAKE LYING TO MY DAD ANY EASIER.
IT IS AN UNFORTUNATE BY-PRODUCT OF THE DOUBLE LIFE YOU'VE CHOSEN, TIMOTHY.
SOMETHING MASTER BRUCE, IN HIS SOLITUDE, HAS NEVER HAD TO CONTEND WITH.
I SHOULD COUNT MY BLESS-INGS, ALFRED. AT LEAST I'VE GOT A REAL FAMILY.
QUITE RIGHT.
I DIDN'T MEAN... I MEAN YOU AND BRUCE ARE FAMILY.
I TAKE YOUR POINT WITHOUT OFFENSE, TIMOTHY.
WE'RE WITHIN THIRTY MINUTES' FLYING TIME OF CANADIAN AIR-SPACE.
PERHAPS YOU'D BEST CONSIDER YOUR STRATEGY FOR APPROACH-ING THIS KENDALL STUART PERSON.
NUMBER FIVE VINCENNES BOULEVARD, THIRD FLOOR.
DOESN'T LOOK LIKE ANYONE BEAT ME HERE SO FAR, ALFRED.

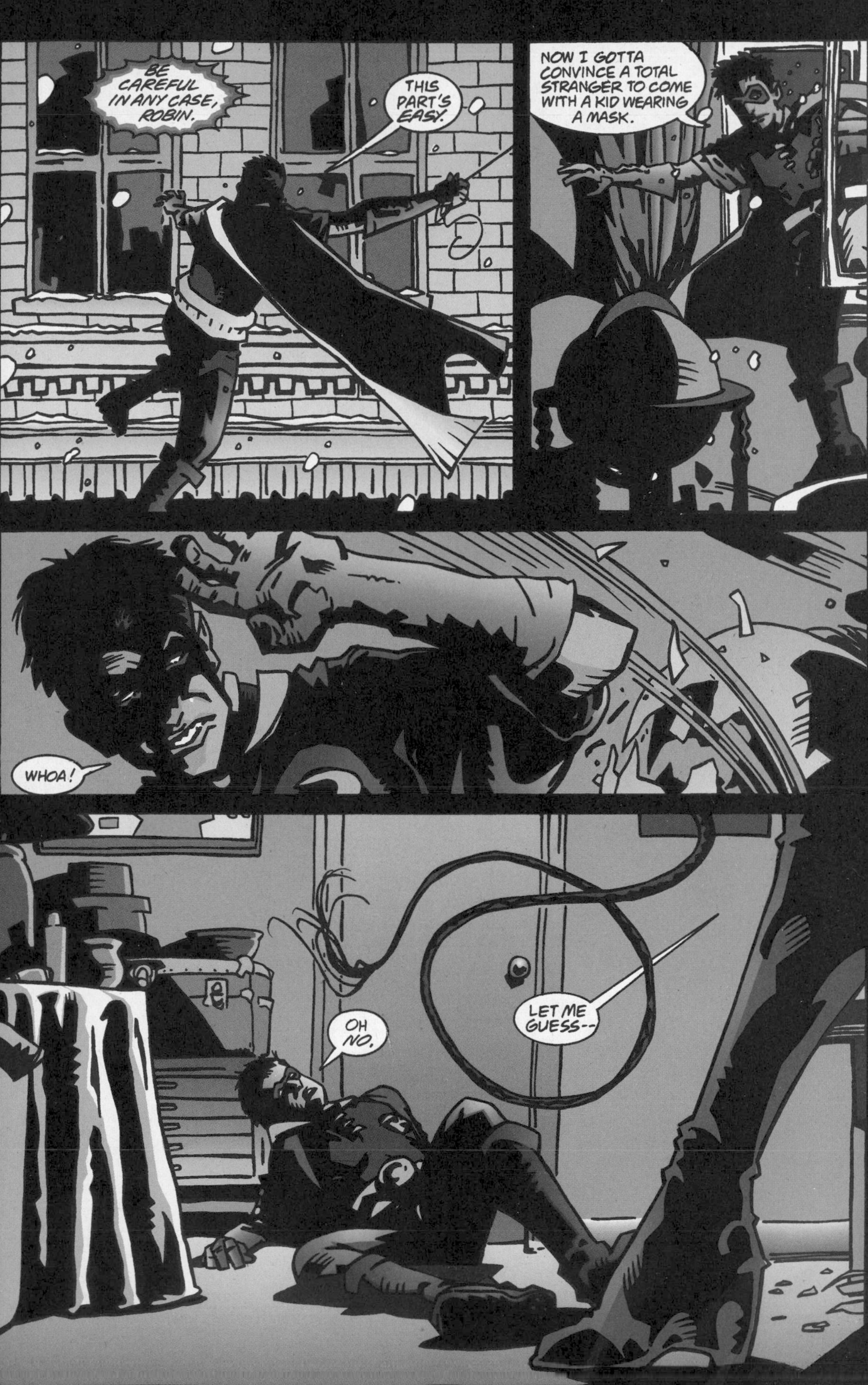
BE CAREFUL IN ANY CASE, ROBIN.
THIS PART'S EASY.
NOW I GOTTA CONVINCE A TOTAL STRANGER TO COME WITH A KID WEARING A MASK.
WHOA!
OH NO.
LET ME GUESS--

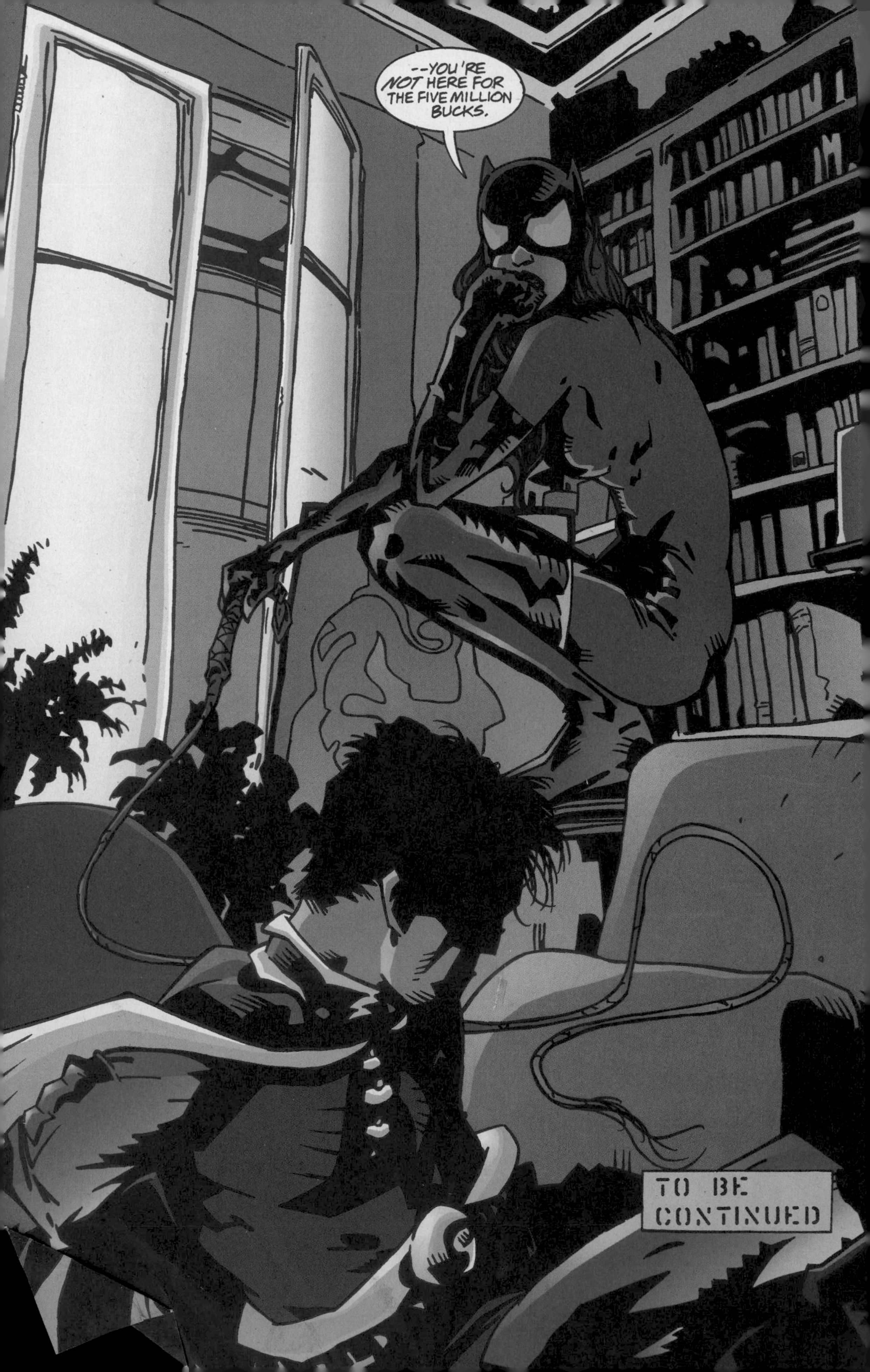
--YOU'RE NOT HERE FOR THE FIVE MILLION BUCKS.
TO BE CONTINUED

NATURAL BORN HEALER
I'LL GIVE YOU THIS, BOY WONDER...
...YOU'VE GOT THE SPEED TO KEEP UP WITH YOUR ROLE MODEL.
I DON'T HAVE TIME FOR THIS, CATWOMAN!
MOBY DICK
HERMAN MELVILLE
JOHN GRISHAM
CHUCK DIXON WRITER
MIKE WIERINGO PENCILLER
STAN WOCH INKER
ADRIENNE ROY COLORIST
HARKINS LETTERER
JORDAN B. GORFINKEL ASSOCIATE EDITOR
DENNY O'NEIL EDITOR

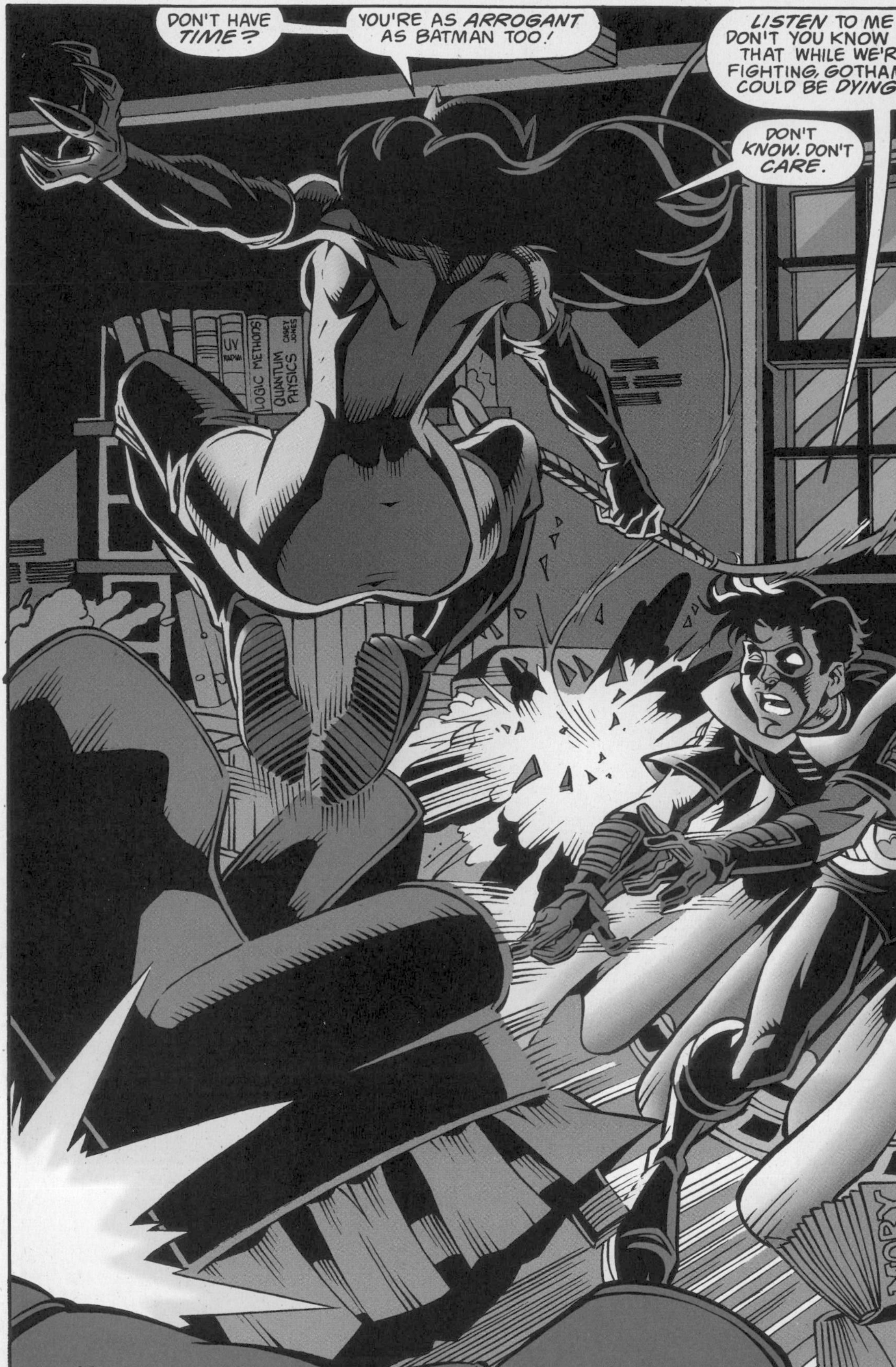
DON'T HAVE TIME?
YOU'RE AS ARROGANT AS BATMAN TOO!
LISTEN TO ME! DON'T YOU KNOW THAT WHILE WE'RE FIGHTING, GOTHAM COULD BE DYING!
DON'T KNOW. DON'T CARE.
LOGIC METHODS
QUANTUM PHYSICS
CASEY JONES
MOBY

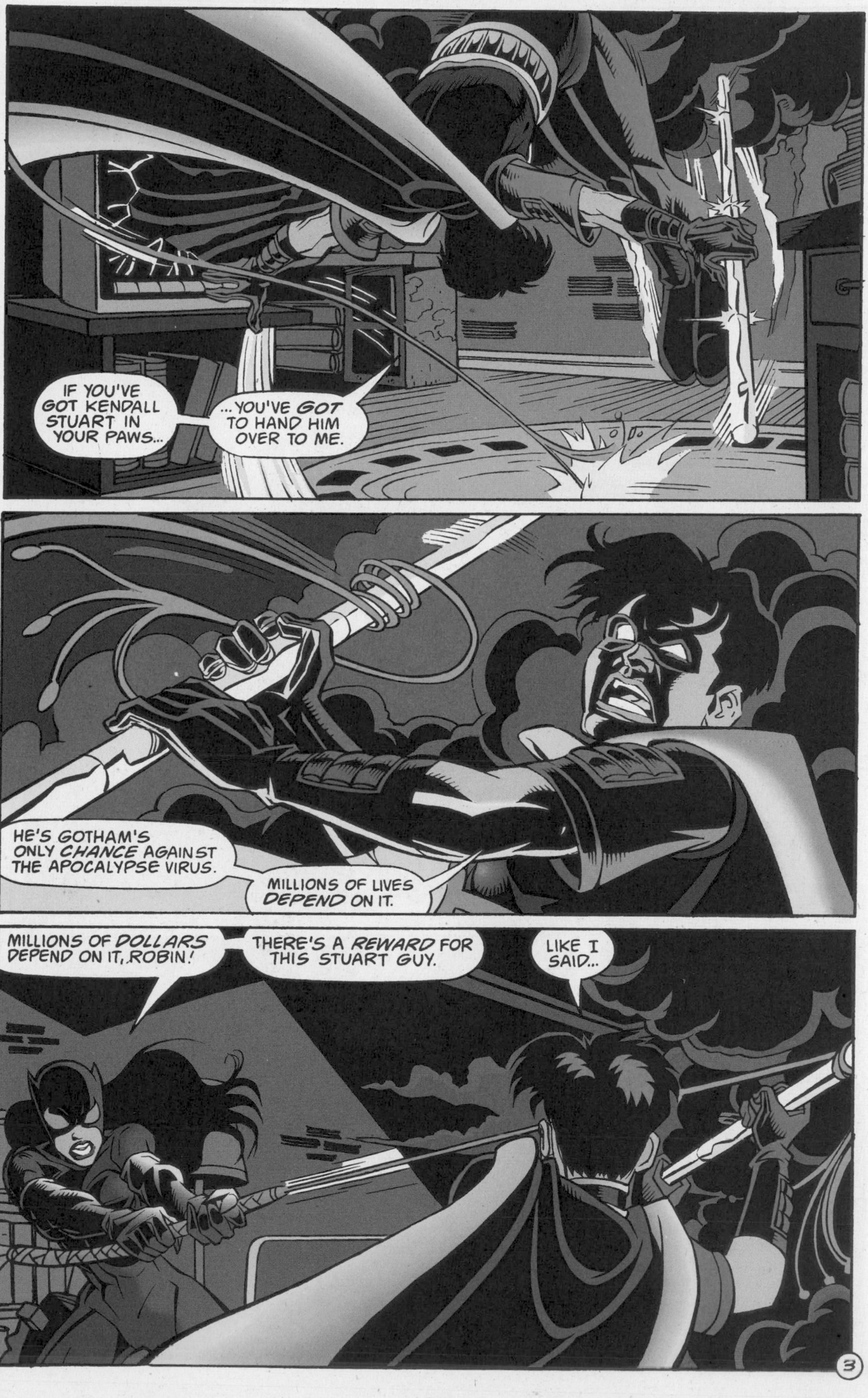
IF YOU'VE GOT KENDALL STUART IN YOUR PAWS...
...YOU'VE *GOT* TO HAND HIM OVER TO ME.
HE'S GOTHAM'S ONLY *CHANCE* AGAINST THE APOCALYPSE VIRUS.
MILLIONS OF LIVES *DEPEND* ON IT.
MILLIONS OF *DOLLARS* DEPEND ON IT, ROBIN!
THERE'S A *REWARD* FOR THIS STUART GUY.
LIKE I SAID...
3

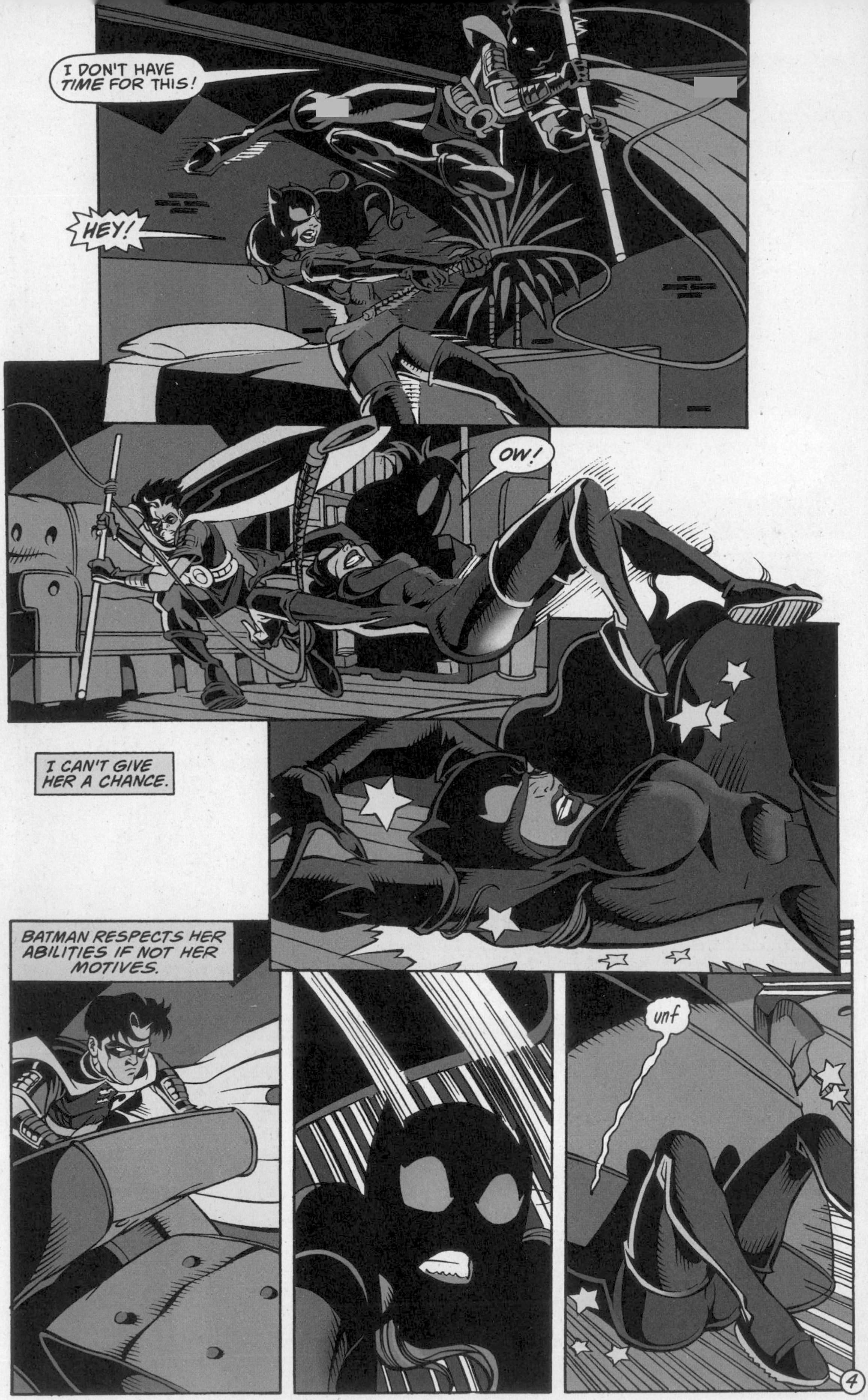
I DON'T HAVE TIME FOR THIS!
HEY!
OW!
I CAN'T GIVE HER A CHANCE.
BATMAN RESPECTS HER ABILITIES IF NOT HER MOTIVES.
unf
4

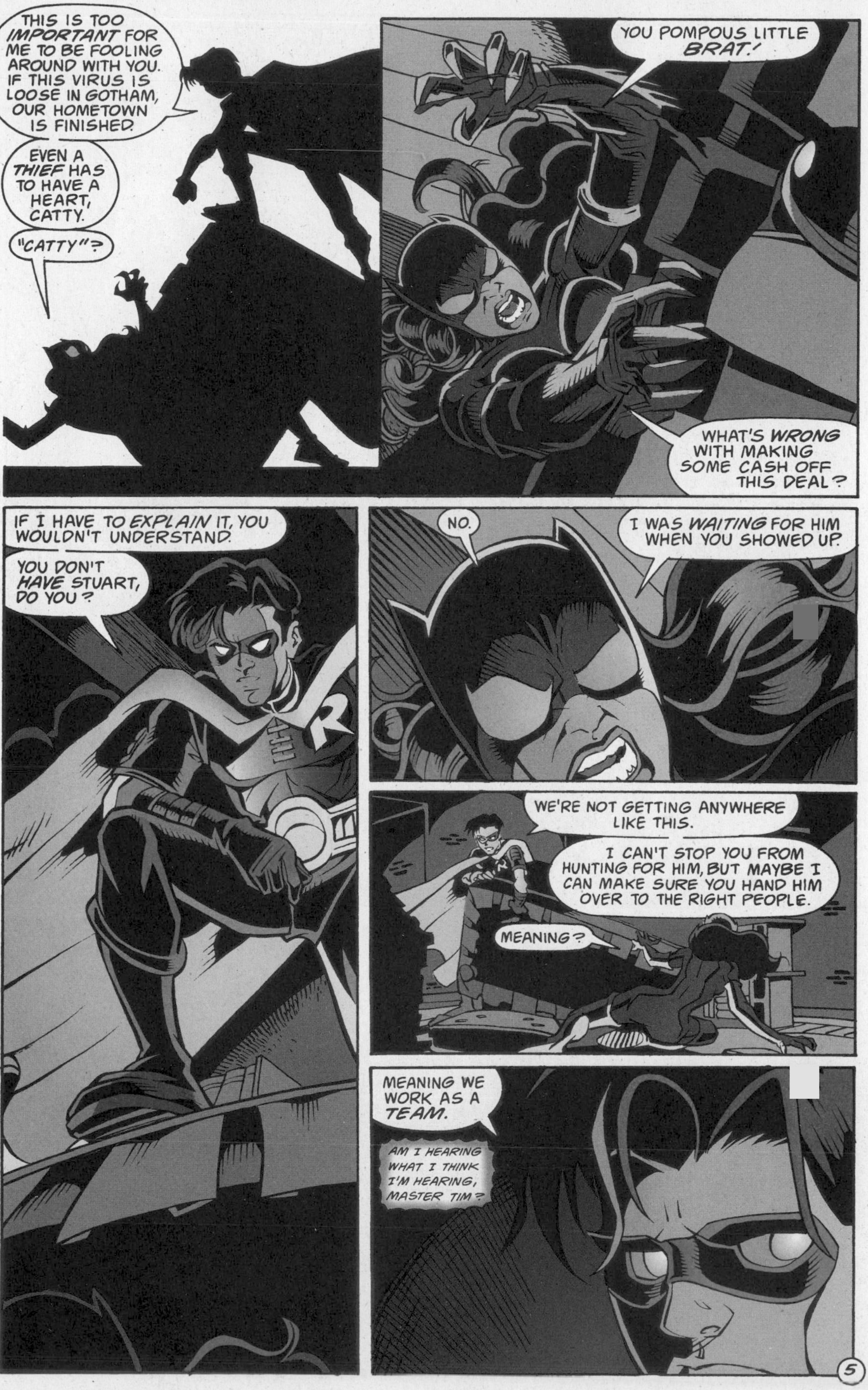
THIS IS TOO IMPORTANT FOR ME TO BE FOOLING AROUND WITH YOU. IF THIS VIRUS IS LOOSE IN GOTHAM, OUR HOMETOWN IS FINISHED.
EVEN A THIEF HAS TO HAVE A HEART, CATTY.
"CATTY"?
YOU POMPOUS LITTLE BRAT!
WHAT'S WRONG WITH MAKING SOME CASH OFF THIS DEAL?
IF I HAVE TO EXPLAIN IT, YOU WOULDN'T UNDERSTAND.
YOU DON'T HAVE STUART, DO YOU?
NO.
I WAS WAITING FOR HIM WHEN YOU SHOWED UP.
WE'RE NOT GETTING ANYWHERE LIKE THIS.
I CAN'T STOP YOU FROM HUNTING FOR HIM, BUT MAYBE I CAN MAKE SURE YOU HAND HIM OVER TO THE RIGHT PEOPLE.
MEANING?
MEANING WE WORK AS A TEAM.
AM I HEARING WHAT I THINK I'M HEARING, MASTER TIM?
5

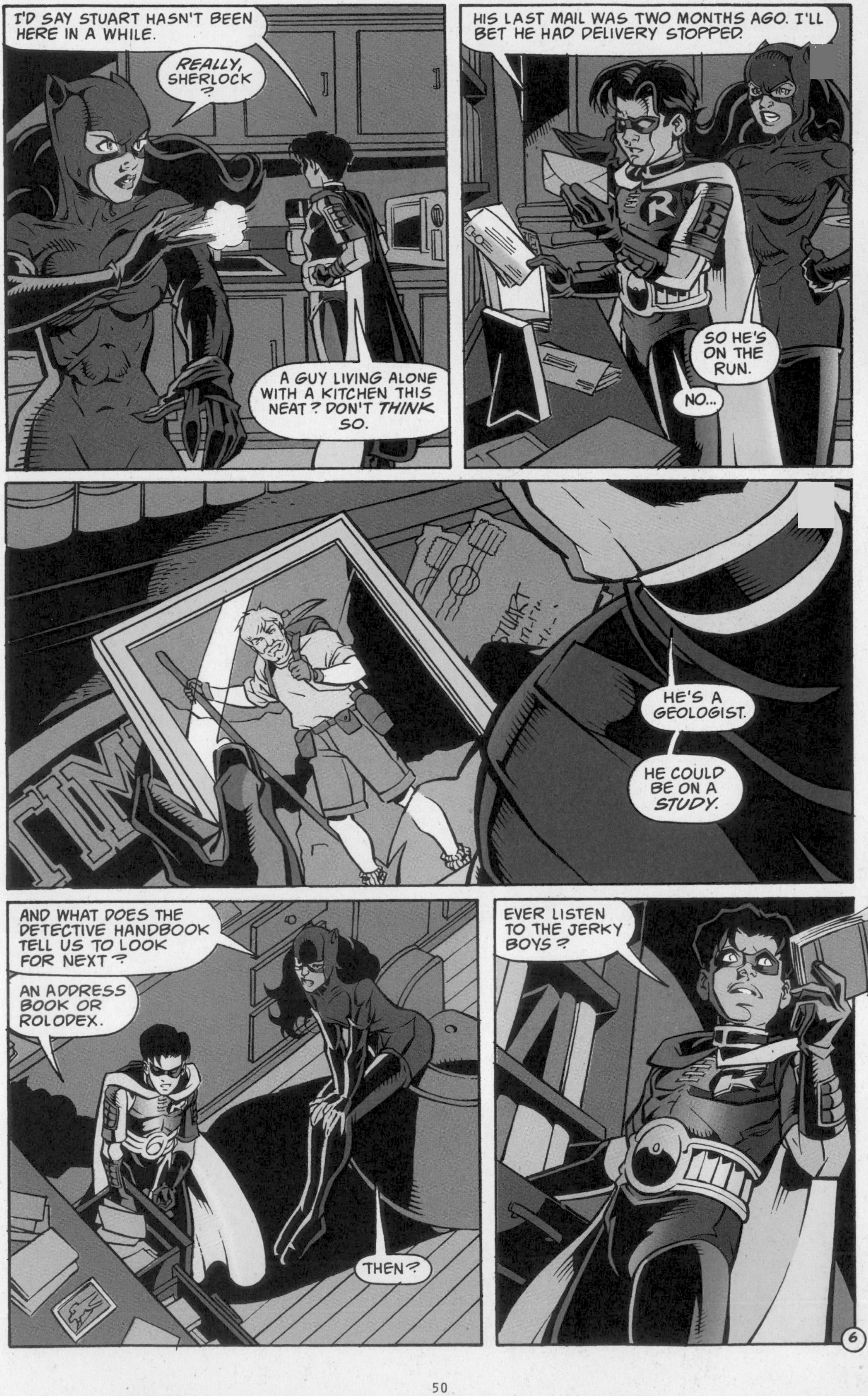

I'D SAY STUART HASN'T BEEN HERE IN A WHILE.
REALLY, SHERLOCK?
A GUY LIVING ALONE WITH A KITCHEN THIS NEAT? DON'T THINK SO.
HIS LAST MAIL WAS TWO MONTHS AGO. I'LL BET HE HAD DELIVERY STOPPED.
SO HE'S ON THE RUN.
NO...
HE'S A GEOLOGIST.
HE COULD BE ON A STUDY.
AND WHAT DOES THE DETECTIVE HANDBOOK TELL US TO LOOK FOR NEXT?
AN ADDRESS BOOK OR ROLODEX.
THEN?
EVER LISTEN TO THE JERKY BOYS?
6

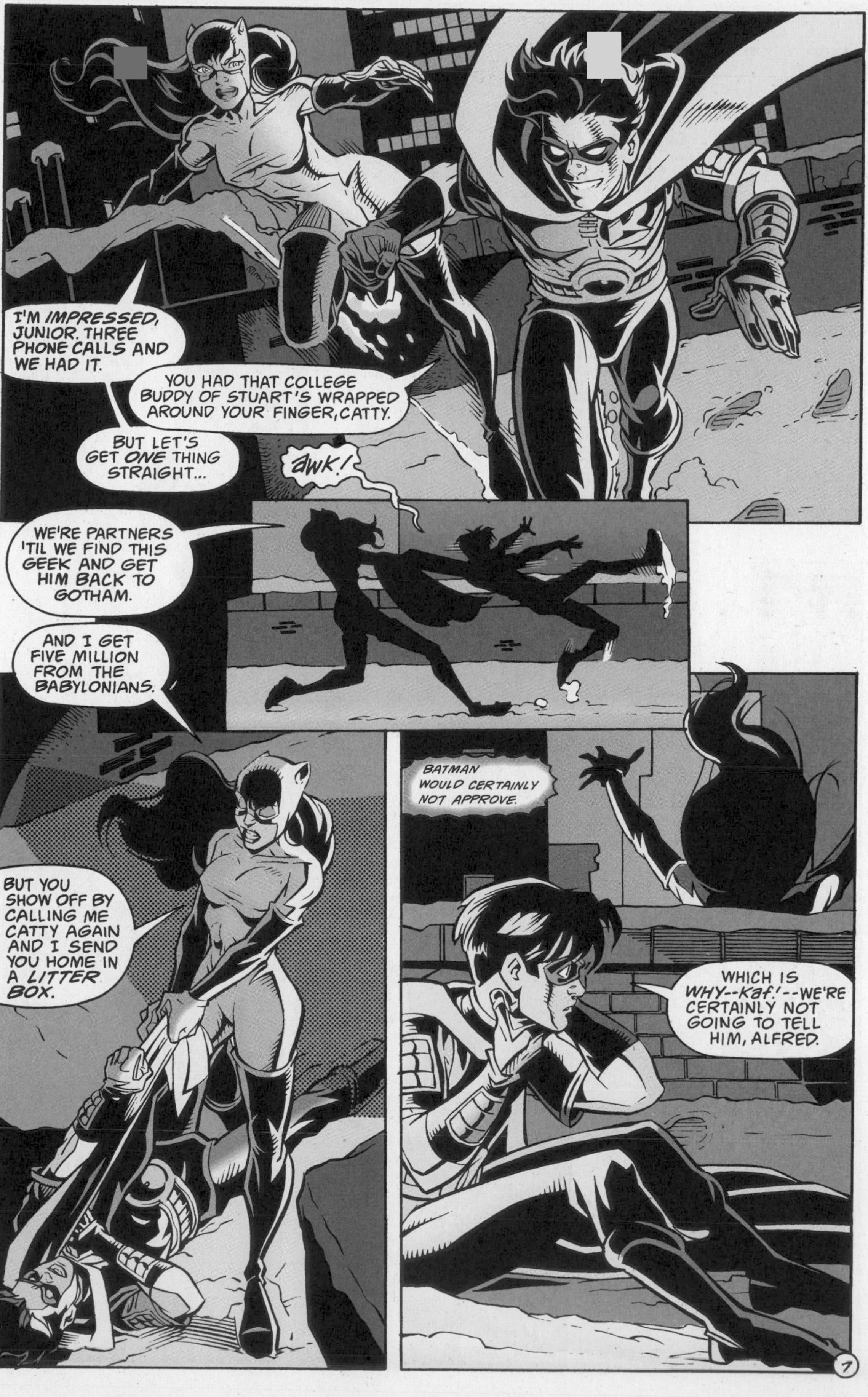

I'M IMPRESSED, JUNIOR. THREE PHONE CALLS AND WE HAD IT.
YOU HAD THAT COLLEGE BUDDY OF STUART'S WRAPPED AROUND YOUR FINGER, CATTY.
BUT LET'S GET ONE THING STRAIGHT...
AWK!
WE'RE PARTNERS 'TIL WE FIND THIS GEEK AND GET HIM BACK TO GOTHAM.
AND I GET FIVE MILLION FROM THE BABYLONIANS.
BUT YOU SHOW OFF BY CALLING ME CATTY AGAIN AND I SEND YOU HOME IN A LITTER BOX.
BATMAN WOULD CERTAINLY NOT APPROVE.
WHICH IS WHY--Kaf!--WE'RE CERTAINLY NOT GOING TO TELL HIM, ALFRED.
7

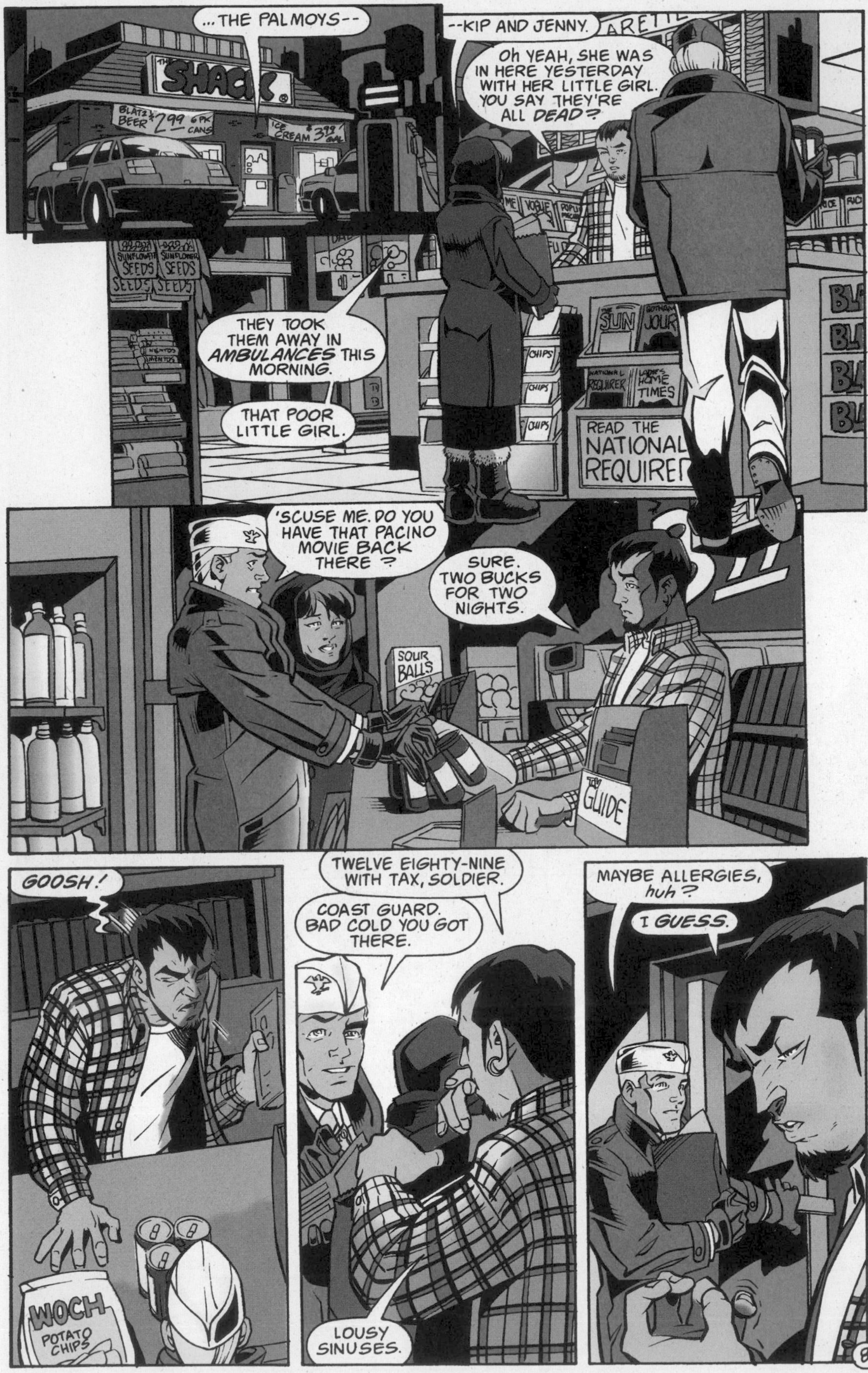
... THE PALMOYS--
--KIP AND JENNY.
Oh YEAH, SHE WAS IN HERE YESTERDAY WITH HER LITTLE GIRL. YOU SAY THEY'RE ALL DEAD?
THEY TOOK THEM AWAY IN AMBULANCES THIS MORNING.
THAT POOR LITTLE GIRL.
READ THE NATIONAL REQUIRER
'SCUSE ME. DO YOU HAVE THAT PACINO MOVIE BACK THERE?
SURE. TWO BUCKS FOR TWO NIGHTS.
SOUR BALLS
TV GUIDE
GOOSH!
WOCH POTATO CHIPS
TWELVE EIGHTY-NINE WITH TAX, SOLDIER.
COAST GUARD. BAD COLD YOU GOT THERE.
LOUSY SINUSES.
MAYBE ALLERGIES, huh?
I GUESS.
8

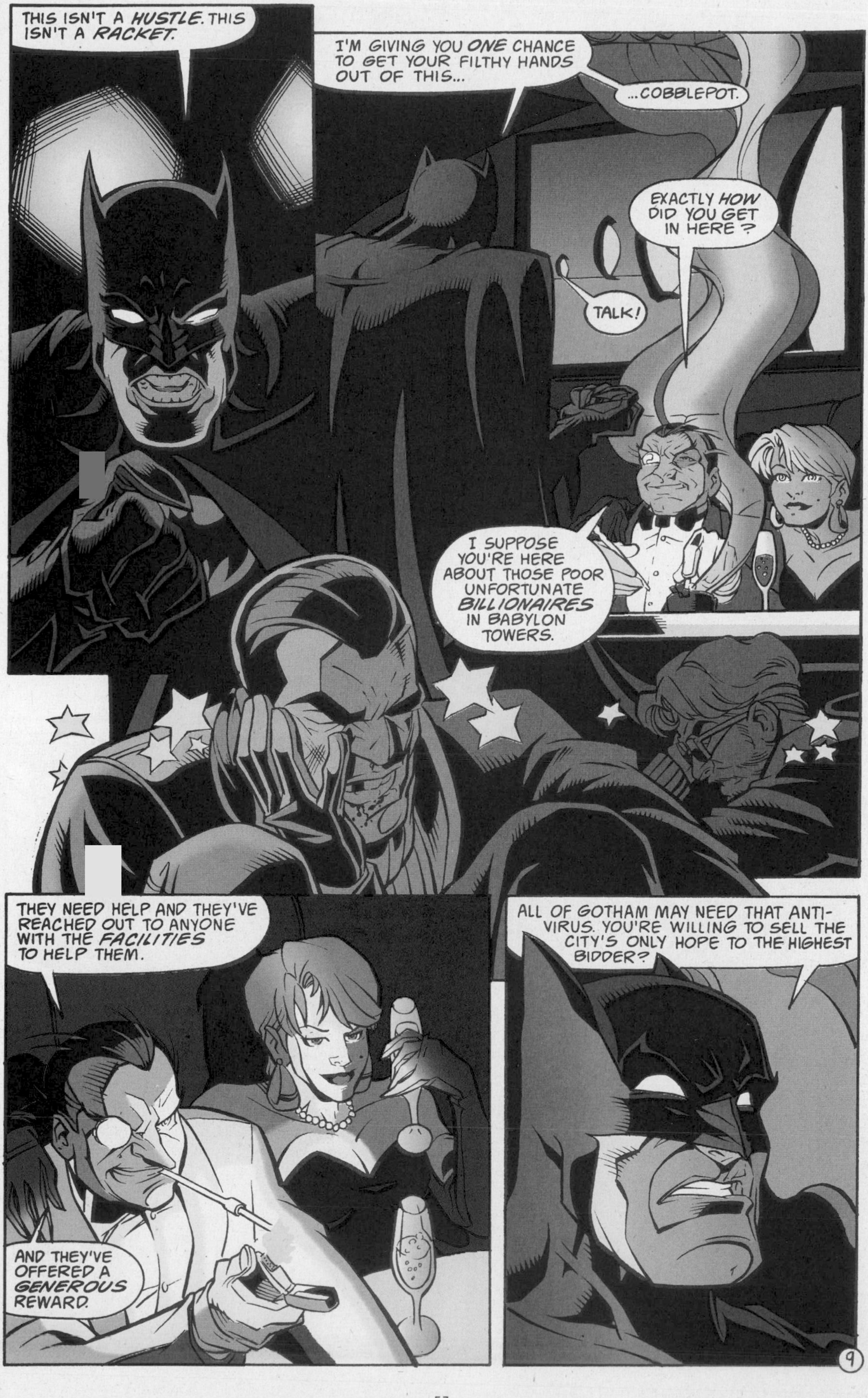
THIS ISN'T A HUSTLE. THIS ISN'T A RACKET.
I'M GIVING YOU ONE CHANCE TO GET YOUR FILTHY HANDS OUT OF THIS...
...COBBLEPOT.
EXACTLY HOW DID YOU GET IN HERE?
TALK!
I SUPPOSE YOU'RE HERE ABOUT THOSE POOR UNFORTUNATE BILLIONAIRES IN BABYLON TOWERS.
THEY NEED HELP AND THEY'VE REACHED OUT TO ANYONE WITH THE FACILITIES TO HELP THEM.
AND THEY'VE OFFERED A GENEROUS REWARD.
ALL OF GOTHAM MAY NEED THAT ANTI-VIRUS. YOU'RE WILLING TO SELL THE CITY'S ONLY HOPE TO THE HIGHEST BIDDER?
9

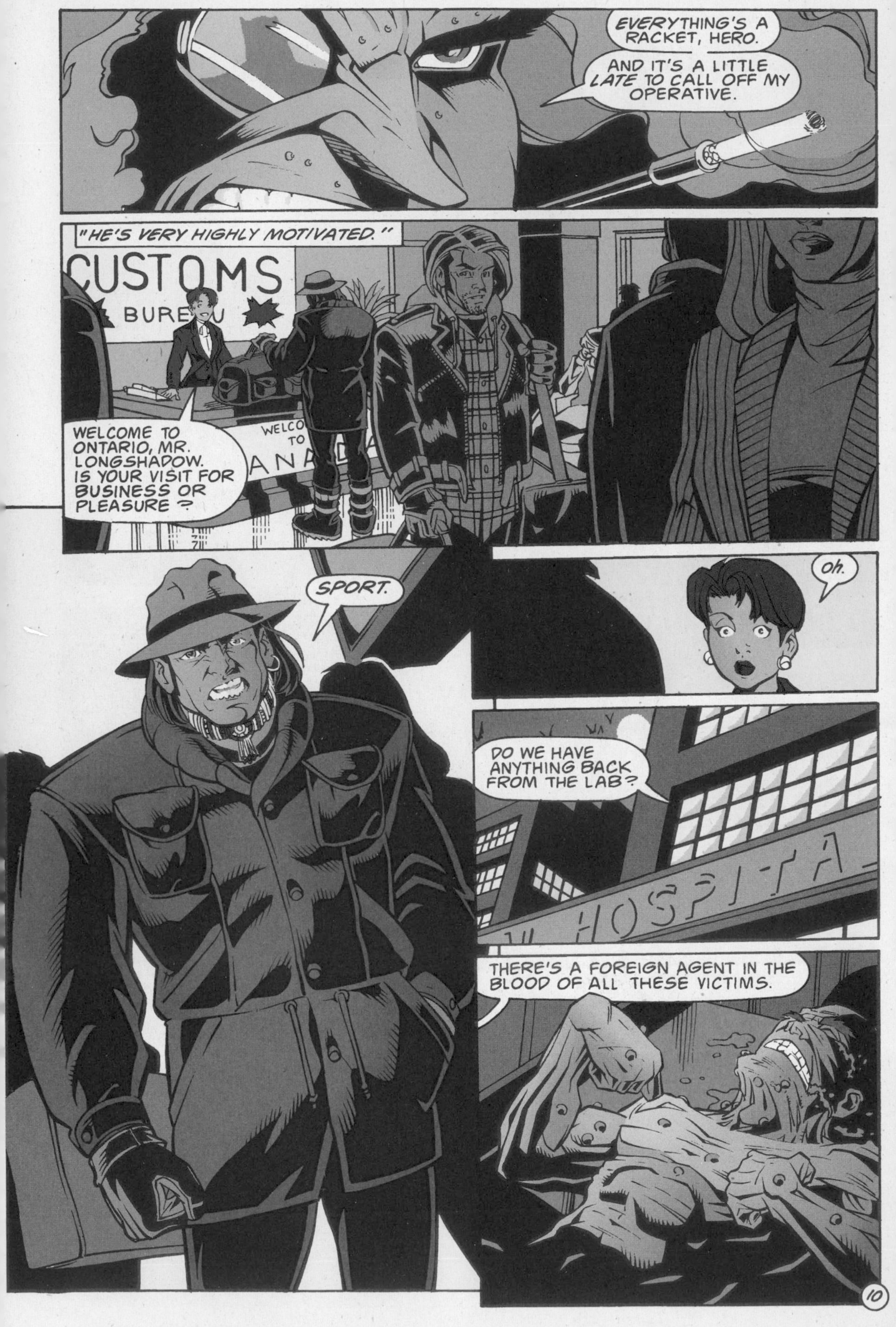
EVERYTHING'S A RACKET, HERO.
AND IT'S A LITTLE LATE TO CALL OFF MY OPERATIVE.
"HE'S VERY HIGHLY MOTIVATED."
CUSTOMS
BUREAU
WELCOME TO ONTARIO, MR. LONGSHADOW. IS YOUR VISIT FOR BUSINESS OR PLEASURE?
SPORT.
oh.
DO WE HAVE ANYTHING BACK FROM THE LAB?
HOSPITA
THERE'S A FOREIGN AGENT IN THE BLOOD OF ALL THESE VICTIMS.
10

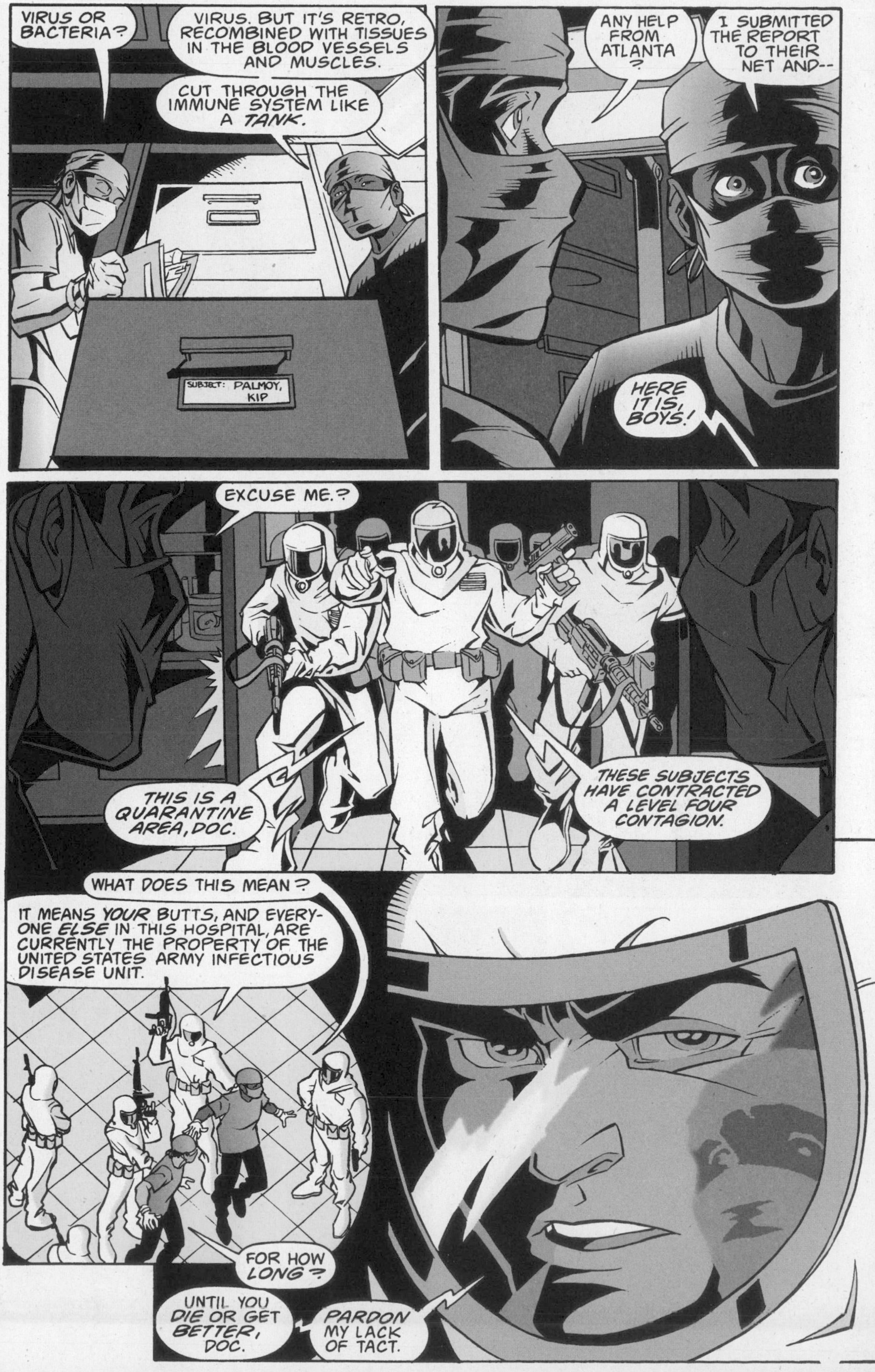
VIRUS OR BACTERIA?
VIRUS. BUT IT'S RETRO, RECOMBINED WITH TISSUES IN THE BLOOD VESSELS AND MUSCLES.
CUT THROUGH THE IMMUNE SYSTEM LIKE A TANK.
SUBJECT: PALMOY, KIP
ANY HELP FROM ATLANTA?
I SUBMITTED THE REPORT TO THEIR NET AND--
HERE IT IS, BOYS!
EXCUSE ME.?
THIS IS A QUARANTINE AREA, DOC.
THESE SUBJECTS HAVE CONTRACTED A LEVEL FOUR CONTAGION.
WHAT DOES THIS MEAN?
IT MEANS YOUR BUTTS, AND EVERYONE ELSE IN THIS HOSPITAL, ARE CURRENTLY THE PROPERTY OF THE UNITED STATES ARMY INFECTIOUS DISEASE UNIT.
FOR HOW LONG?
UNTIL YOU DIE OR GET BETTER, DOC.
PARDON MY LACK OF TACT.

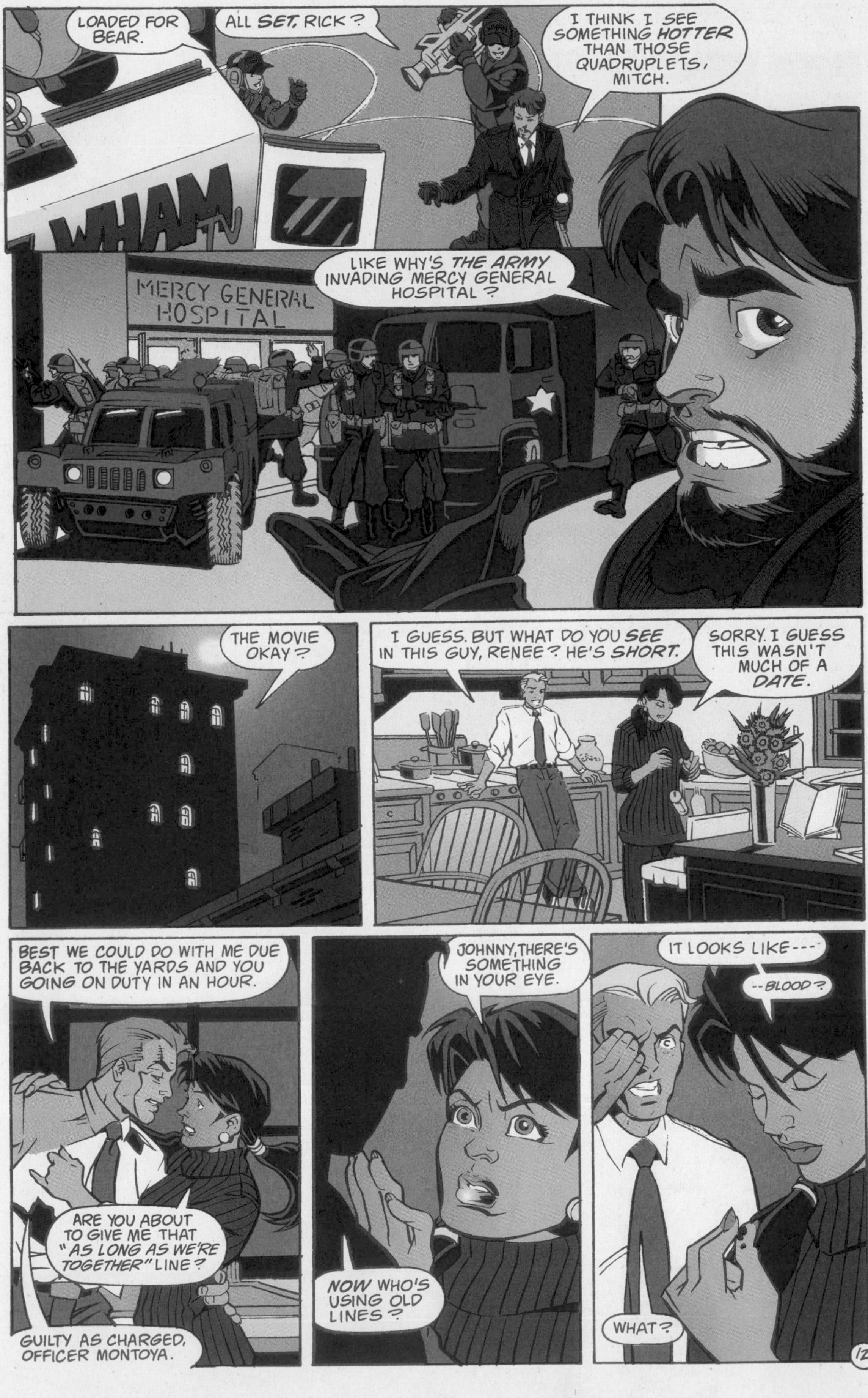
LOADED FOR BEAR.
ALL SET, RICK?
I THINK I SEE SOMETHING HOTTER THAN THOSE QUADRUPLETS, MITCH.
WHAM TV
MERCY GENERAL HOSPITAL
LIKE WHY'S THE ARMY INVADING MERCY GENERAL HOSPITAL?
THE MOVIE OKAY?
I GUESS. BUT WHAT DO YOU SEE IN THIS GUY, RENEE? HE'S SHORT.
SORRY. I GUESS THIS WASN'T MUCH OF A DATE.
BEST WE COULD DO WITH ME DUE BACK TO THE YARDS AND YOU GOING ON DUTY IN AN HOUR.
ARE YOU ABOUT TO GIVE ME THAT "AS LONG AS WE'RE TOGETHER" LINE?
GUILTY AS CHARGED, OFFICER MONTOYA.
JOHNNY, THERE'S SOMETHING IN YOUR EYE.
NOW WHO'S USING OLD LINES?
IT LOOKS LIKE---
--BLOOD?
WHAT?
12

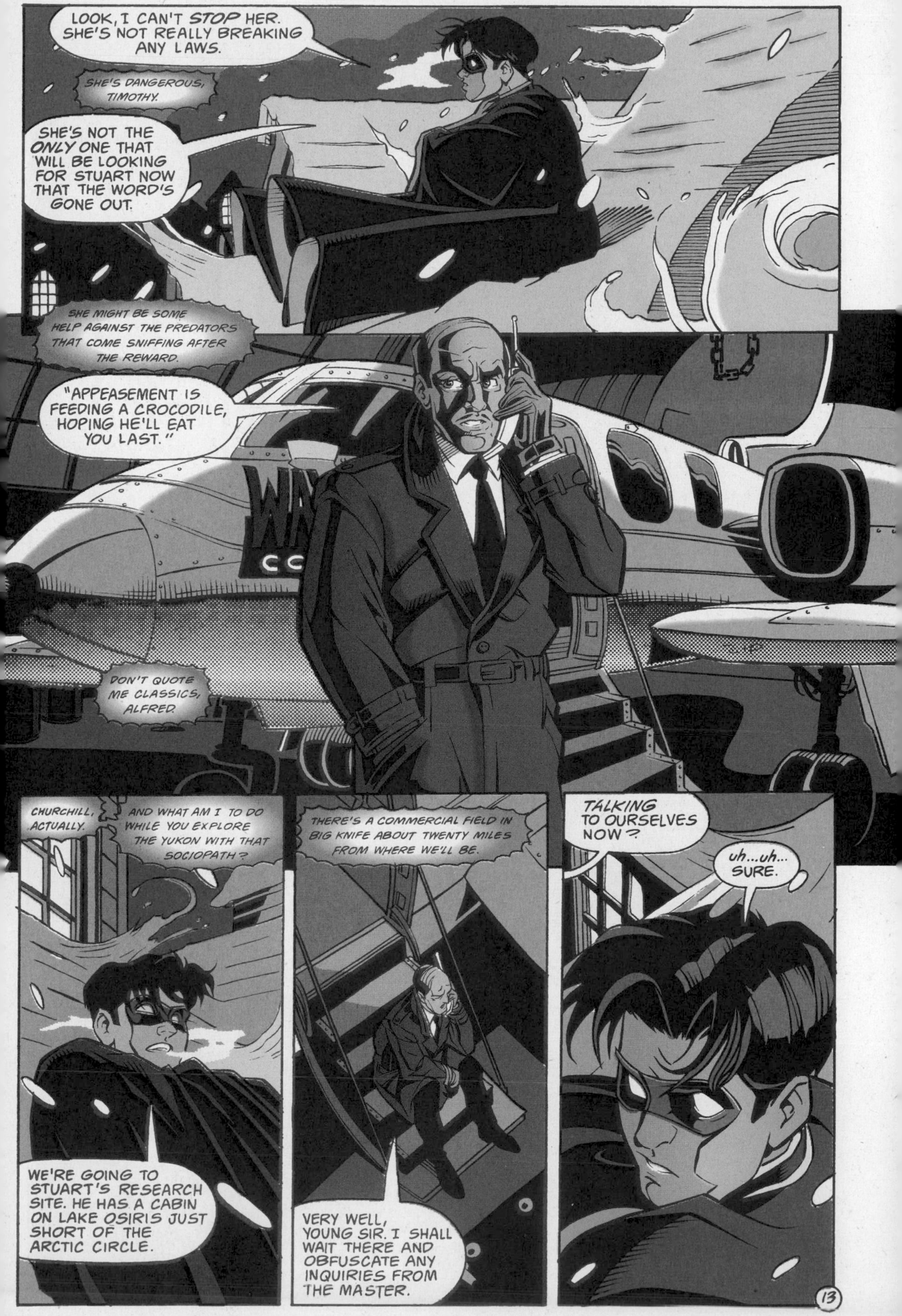

LOOK, I CAN'T STOP HER. SHE'S NOT REALLY BREAKING ANY LAWS.
SHE'S DANGEROUS, TIMOTHY.
SHE'S NOT THE ONLY ONE THAT WILL BE LOOKING FOR STUART NOW THAT THE WORD'S GONE OUT.
SHE MIGHT BE SOME HELP AGAINST THE PREDATORS THAT COME SNIFFING AFTER THE REWARD.
"APPEASEMENT IS FEEDING A CROCODILE, HOPING HE'LL EAT YOU LAST."
DON'T QUOTE ME CLASSICS, ALFRED.
CHURCHILL, ACTUALLY.
AND WHAT AM I TO DO WHILE YOU EXPLORE THE YUKON WITH THAT SOCIOPATH?
WE'RE GOING TO STUART'S RESEARCH SITE. HE HAS A CABIN ON LAKE OSIRIS JUST SHORT OF THE ARCTIC CIRCLE.
THERE'S A COMMERCIAL FIELD IN BIG KNIFE ABOUT TWENTY MILES FROM WHERE WE'LL BE.
VERY WELL, YOUNG SIR. I SHALL WAIT THERE AND OBFUSCATE ANY INQUIRIES FROM THE MASTER.
TALKING TO OURSELVES NOW?
uh...uh... SURE.
13

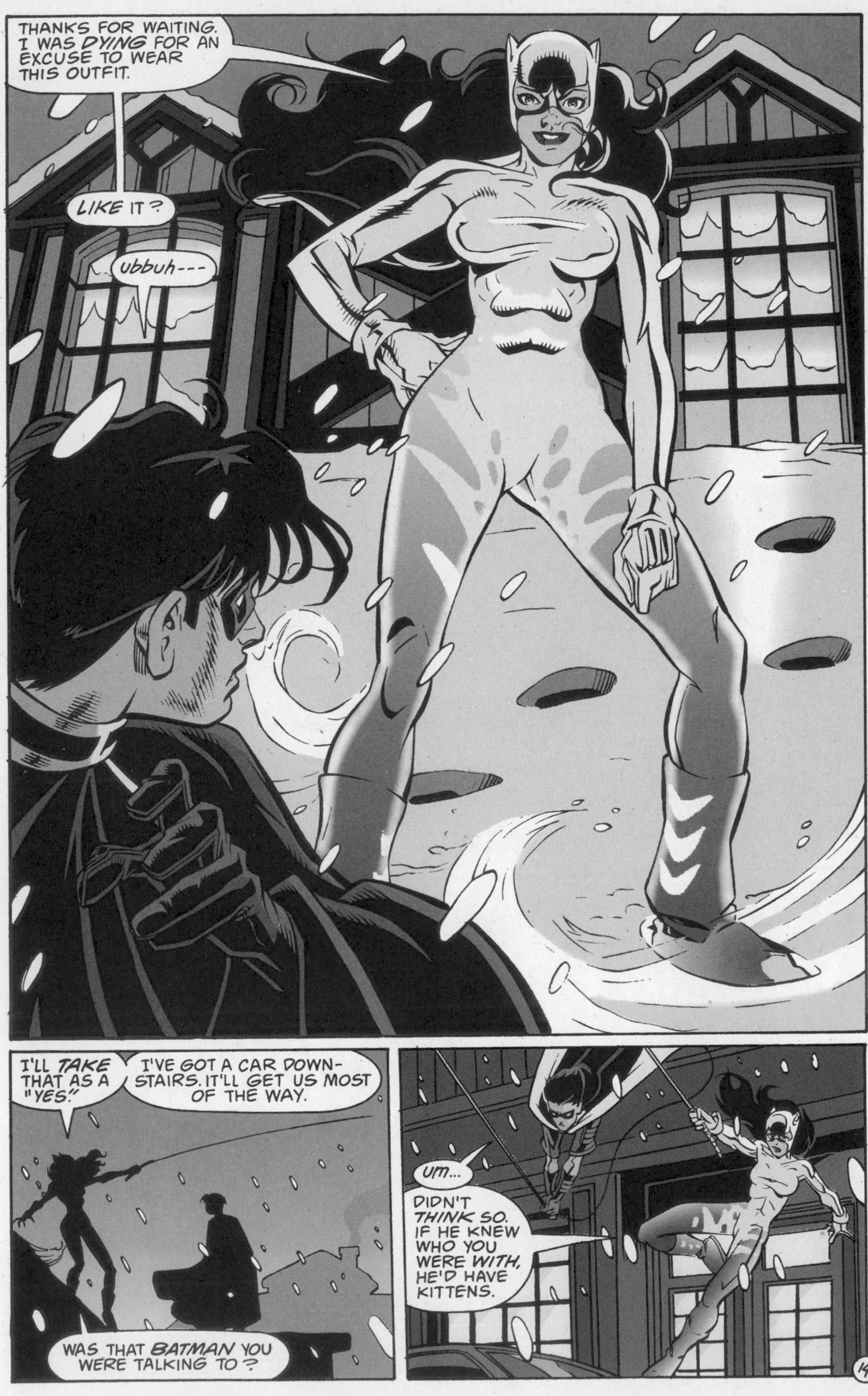
THANKS FOR WAITING. I WAS DYING FOR AN EXCUSE TO WEAR THIS OUTFIT.
LIKE IT?
ubbuh---
I'LL TAKE THAT AS A "YES."
I'VE GOT A CAR DOWN-STAIRS. IT'LL GET US MOST OF THE WAY.
WAS THAT BATMAN YOU WERE TALKING TO?
um...
DIDN'T THINK SO. IF HE KNEW WHO YOU WERE WITH, HE'D HAVE KITTENS.
14

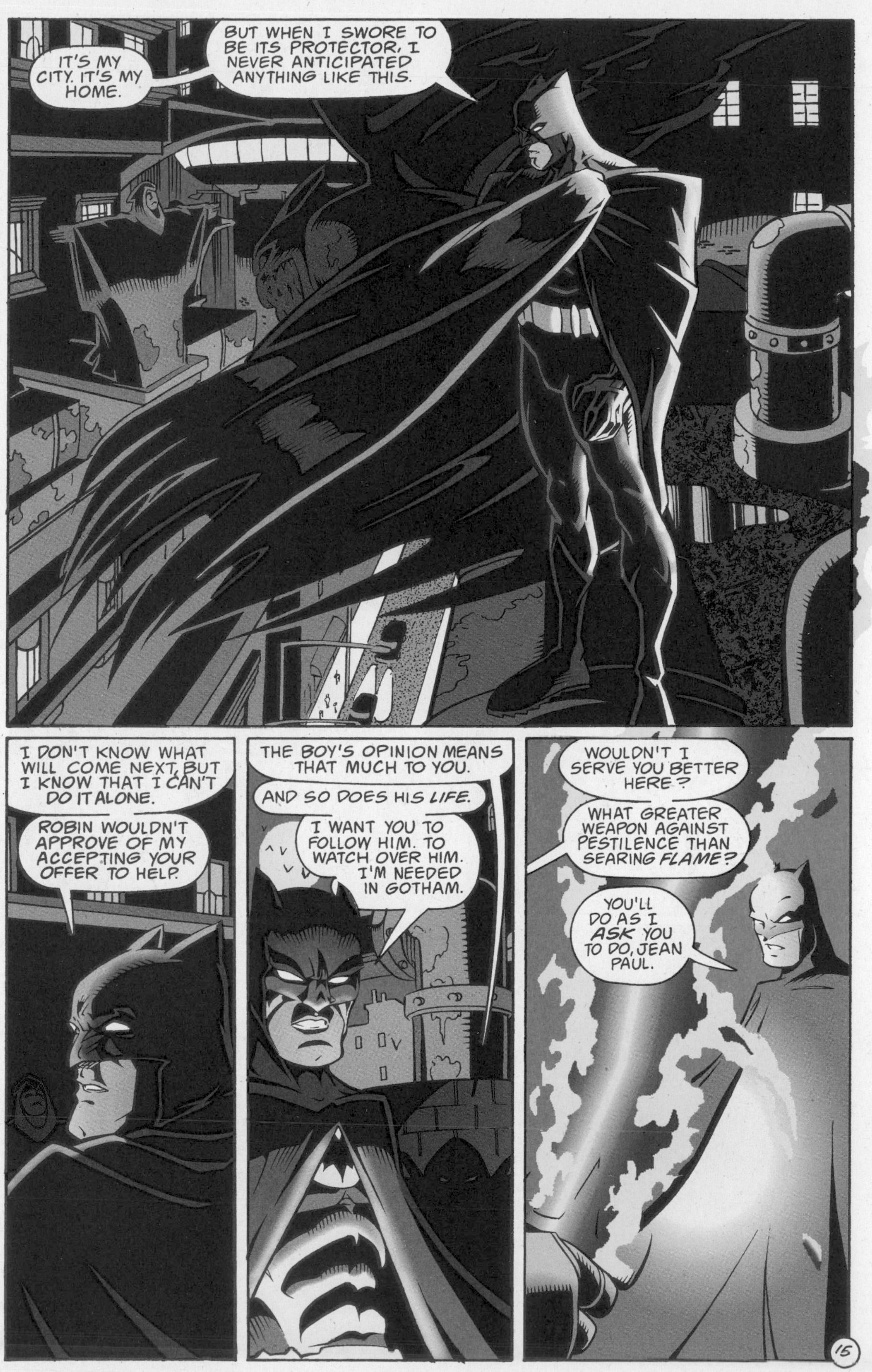
IT'S MY CITY. IT'S MY HOME.
BUT WHEN I SWORE TO BE ITS PROTECTOR, I NEVER ANTICIPATED ANYTHING LIKE THIS.
I DON'T KNOW WHAT WILL COME NEXT, BUT I KNOW THAT I CAN'T DO IT ALONE.
ROBIN WOULDN'T APPROVE OF MY ACCEPTING YOUR OFFER TO HELP.
THE BOY'S OPINION MEANS THAT MUCH TO YOU.
AND SO DOES HIS LIFE.
I WANT YOU TO FOLLOW HIM. TO WATCH OVER HIM. I'M NEEDED IN GOTHAM.
WOULDN'T I SERVE YOU BETTER HERE?
WHAT GREATER WEAPON AGAINST PESTILENCE THAN SEARING FLAME?
YOU'LL DO AS I ASK YOU TO DO, JEAN PAUL.
15

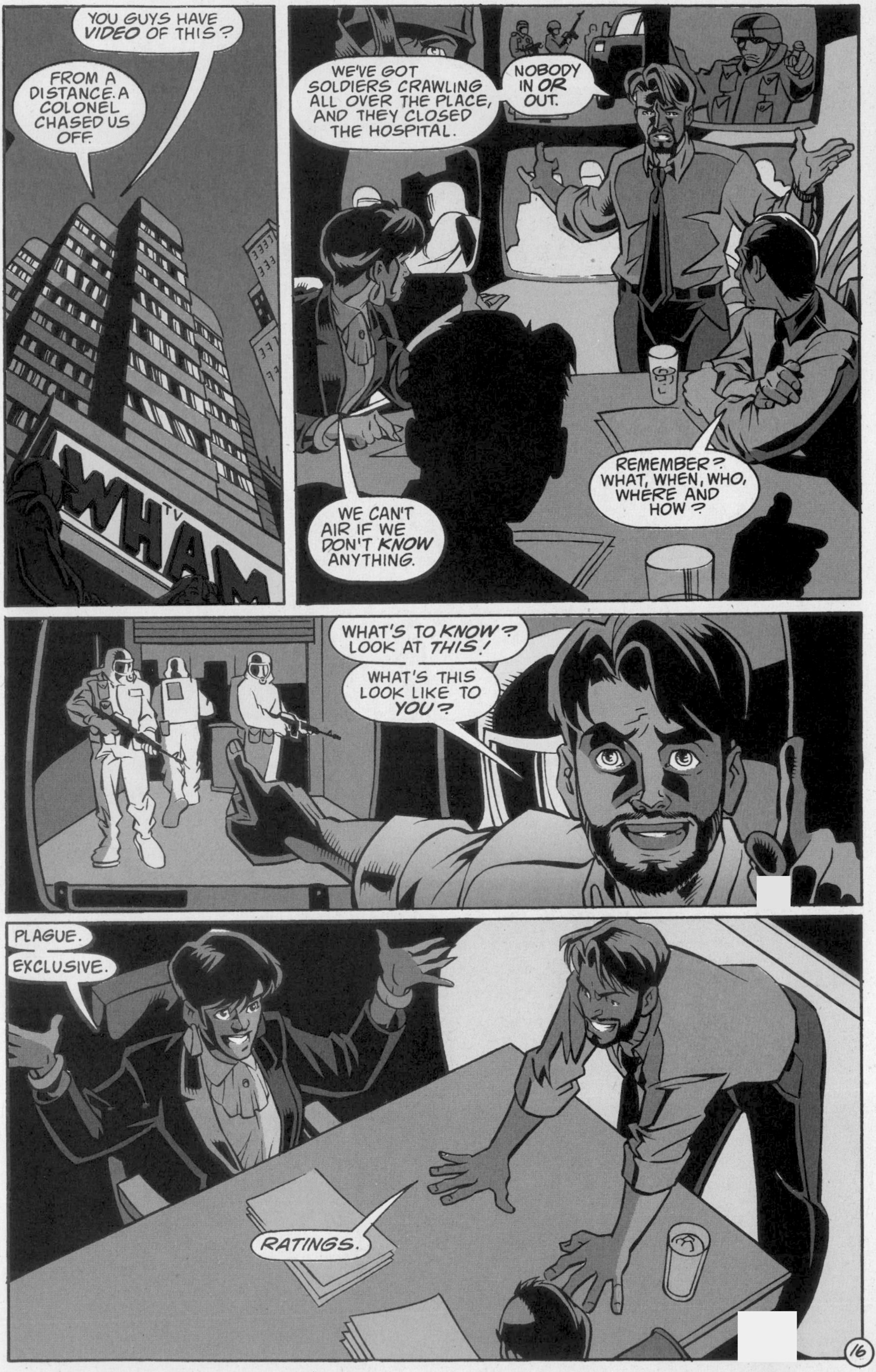

YOU GUYS HAVE VIDEO OF THIS?
FROM A DISTANCE. A COLONEL CHASED US OFF.
WHAM TV
WE'VE GOT SOLDIERS CRAWLING ALL OVER THE PLACE, AND THEY CLOSED THE HOSPITAL.
NOBODY IN OR OUT.
WE CAN'T AIR IF WE DON'T KNOW ANYTHING.
REMEMBER? WHAT, WHEN, WHO, WHERE AND HOW?
WHAT'S TO KNOW? LOOK AT THIS!
WHAT'S THIS LOOK LIKE TO YOU?
PLAGUE.
EXCLUSIVE.
RATINGS.
16

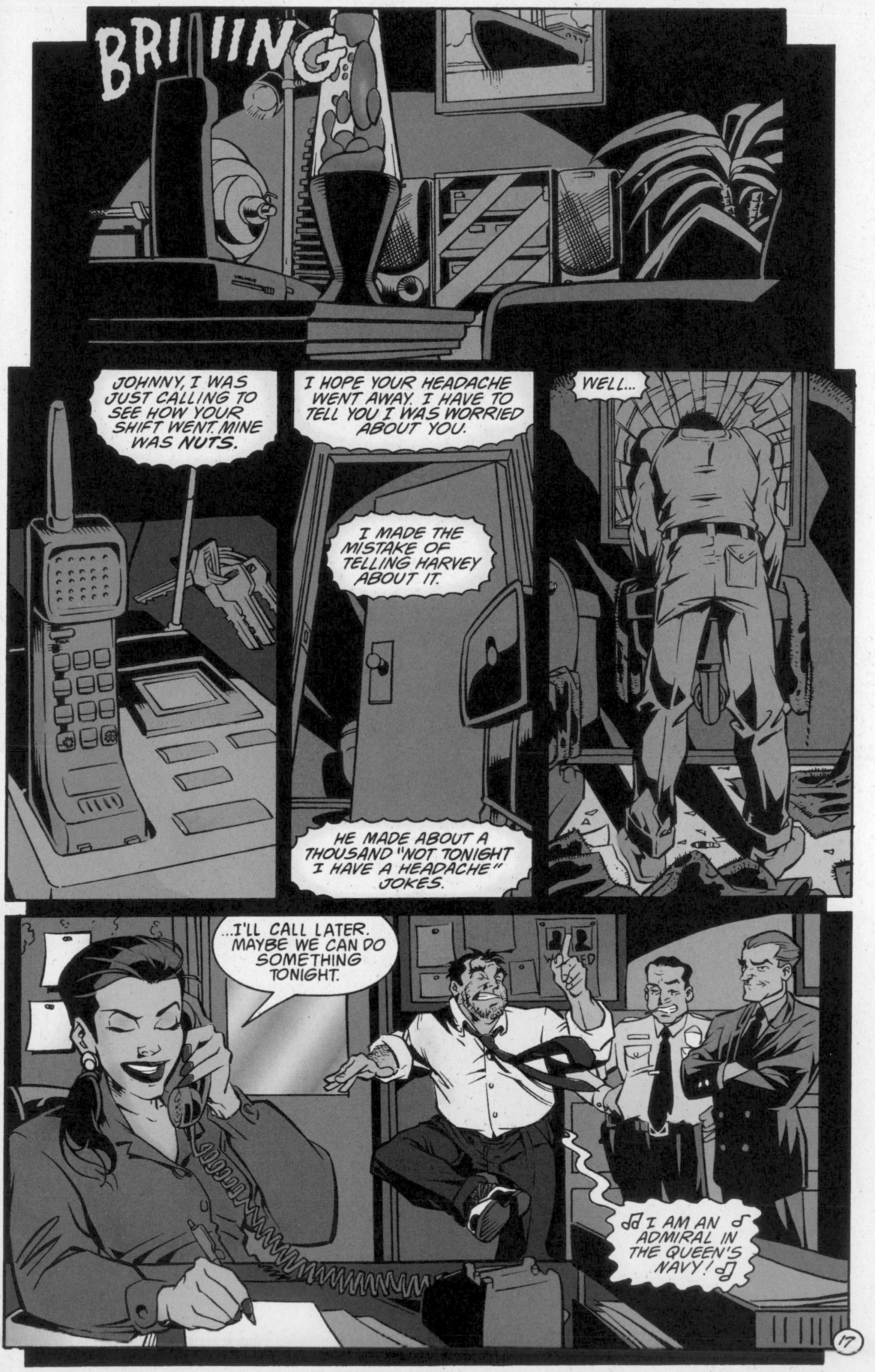
BRIIIING
JOHNNY, I WAS JUST CALLING TO SEE HOW YOUR SHIFT WENT. MINE WAS NUTS.
I HOPE YOUR HEADACHE WENT AWAY. I HAVE TO TELL YOU I WAS WORRIED ABOUT YOU.
I MADE THE MISTAKE OF TELLING HARVEY ABOUT IT.
HE MADE ABOUT A THOUSAND "NOT TONIGHT I HAVE A HEADACHE" JOKES.
WELL...
...I'LL CALL LATER. MAYBE WE CAN DO SOMETHING TONIGHT.
♫ I AM AN ADMIRAL IN THE QUEEN'S NAVY! ♫
17

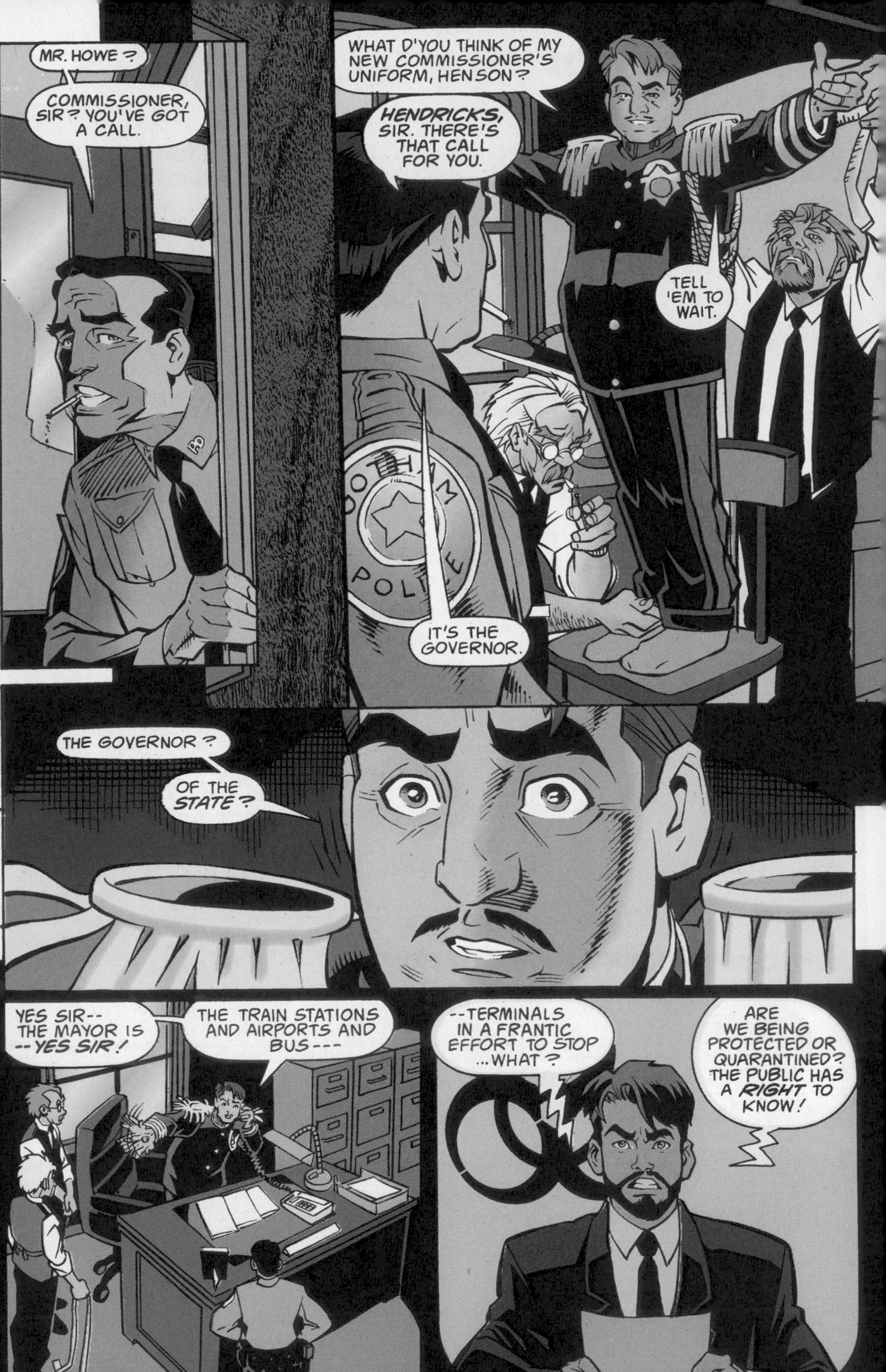

MR. HOWE?
COMMISSIONER, SIR? YOU'VE GOT A CALL.
WHAT D'YOU THINK OF MY NEW COMMISSIONER'S UNIFORM, HENSON?
HENDRICKS, SIR. THERE'S THAT CALL FOR YOU.
TELL 'EM TO WAIT.
IT'S THE GOVERNOR.
THE GOVERNOR?
OF THE STATE?
YES SIR-- THE MAYOR IS --YES SIR!
THE TRAIN STATIONS AND AIRPORTS AND BUS---
--TERMINALS IN A FRANTIC EFFORT TO STOP ...WHAT?
ARE WE BEING PROTECTED OR QUARANTINED? THE PUBLIC HAS A RIGHT TO KNOW!

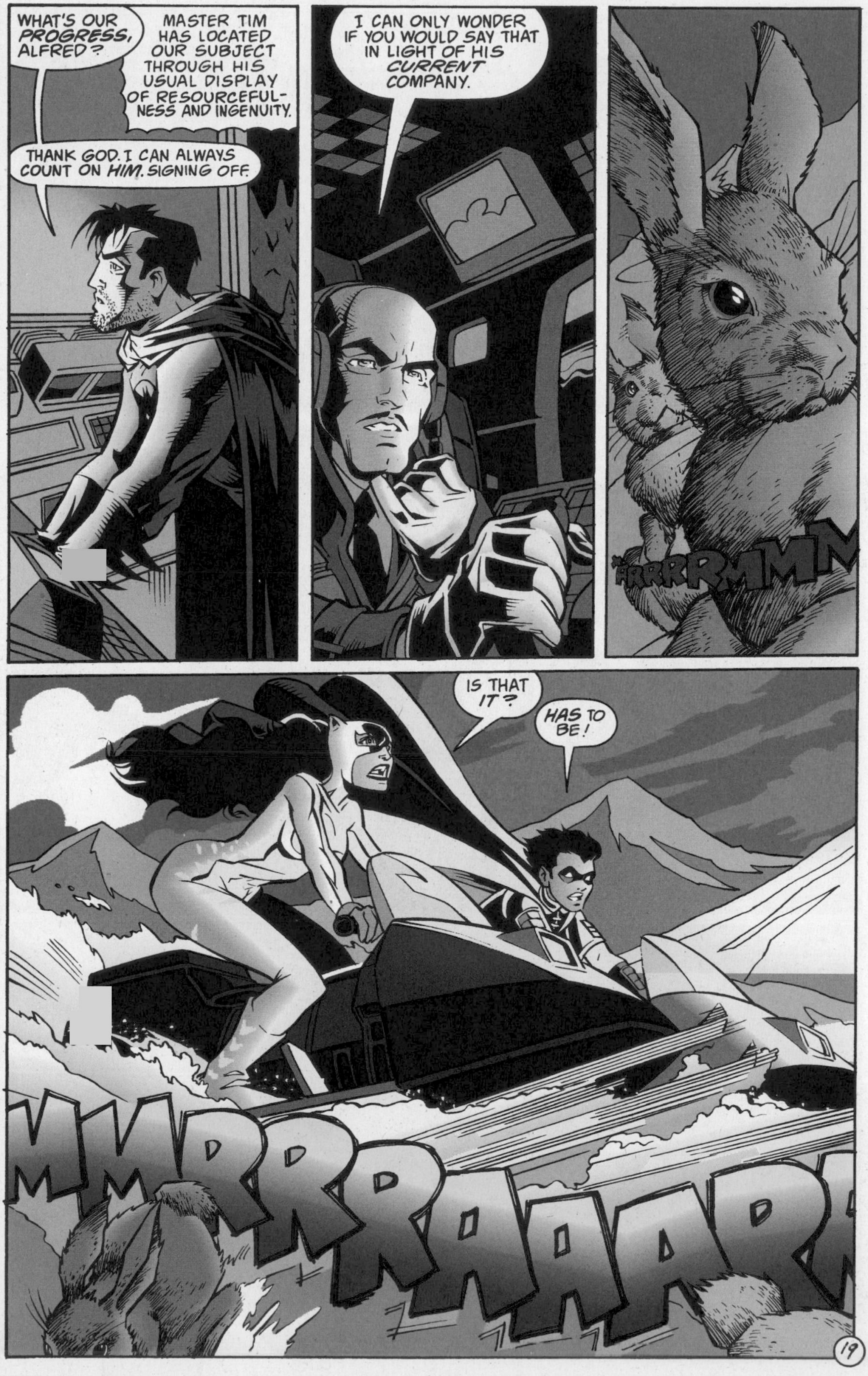
WHAT'S OUR PROGRESS, ALFRED?
MASTER TIM HAS LOCATED OUR SUBJECT THROUGH HIS USUAL DISPLAY OF RESOURCEFULNESS AND INGENUITY.
THANK GOD. I CAN ALWAYS COUNT ON HIM. SIGNING OFF.
I CAN ONLY WONDER IF YOU WOULD SAY THAT IN LIGHT OF HIS CURRENT COMPANY.
FRRRRRMMMM
IS THAT IT?
HAS TO BE!
MMRRAAAR
19

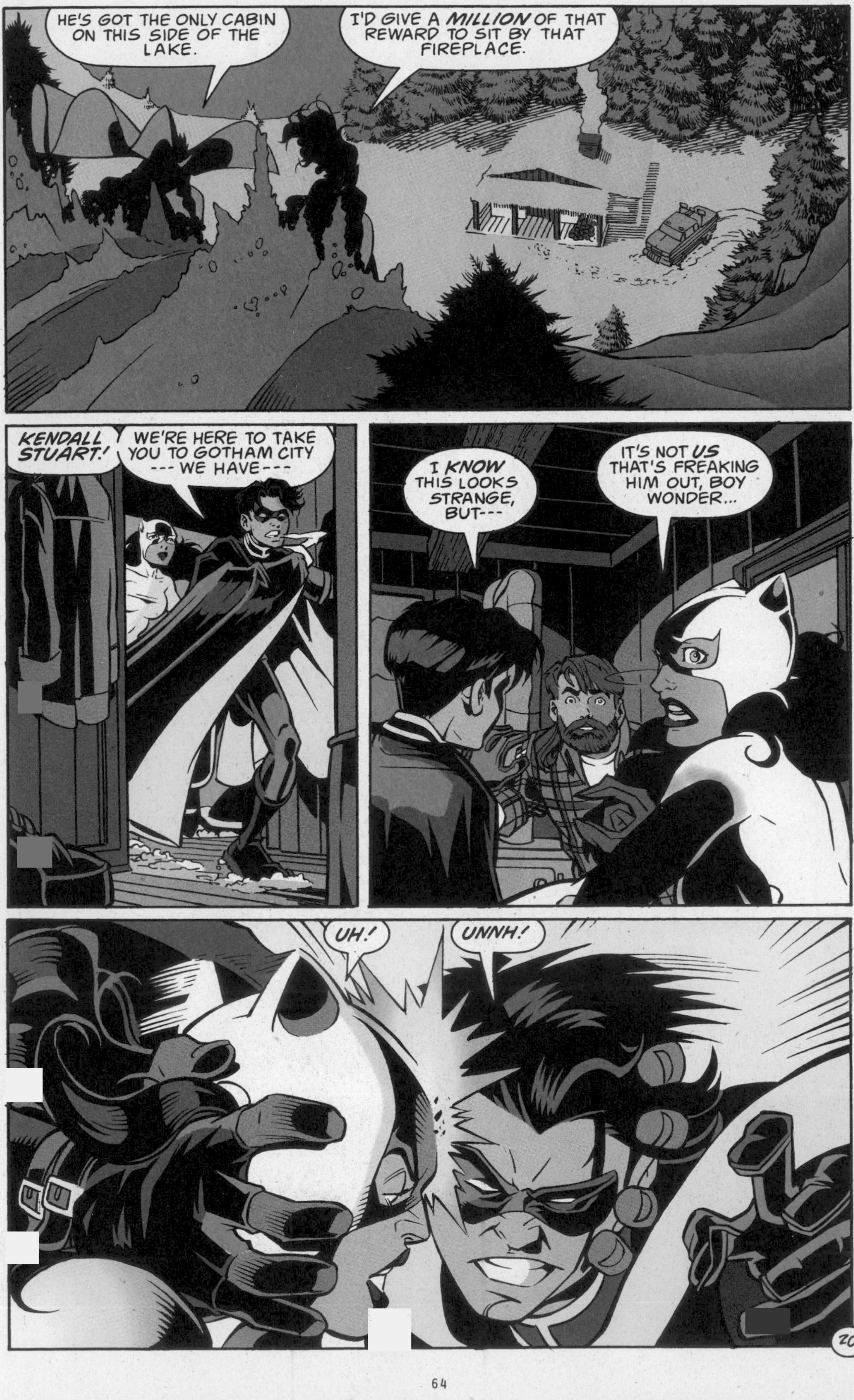
HE'S GOT THE ONLY CABIN ON THIS SIDE OF THE LAKE.
I'D GIVE A MILLION OF THAT REWARD TO SIT BY THAT FIREPLACE.
KENDALL STUART!
WE'RE HERE TO TAKE YOU TO GOTHAM CITY --- WE HAVE---
I KNOW THIS LOOKS STRANGE, BUT---
IT'S NOT US THAT'S FREAKING HIM OUT, BOY WONDER...
UH!
UNNH!
20

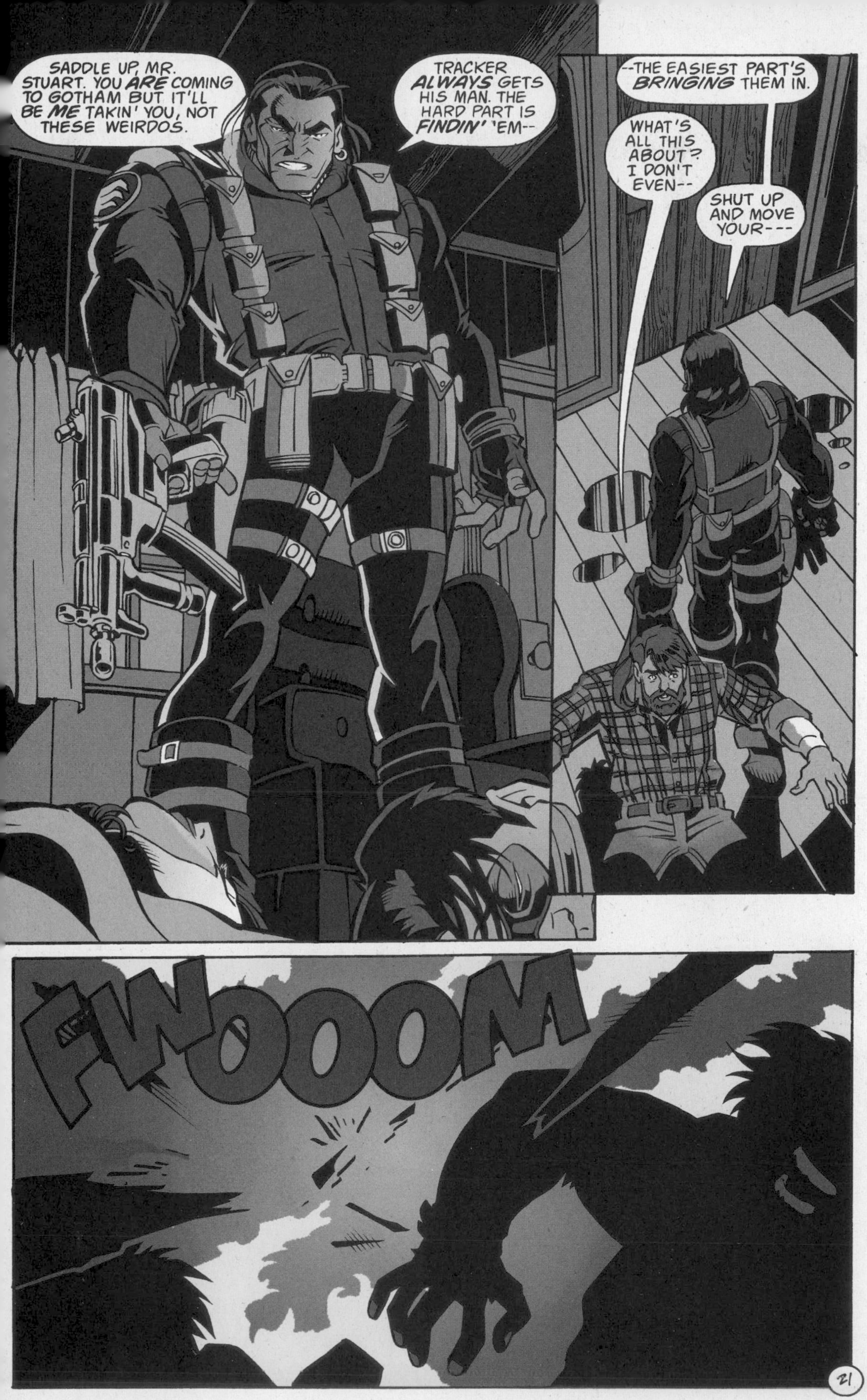
SADDLE UP, MR. STUART. YOU ARE COMING TO GOTHAM BUT IT'LL BE ME TAKIN' YOU, NOT THESE WEIRDOS.
TRACKER ALWAYS GETS HIS MAN. THE HARD PART IS FINDIN' 'EM--
--THE EASIEST PART'S BRINGING THEM IN.
WHAT'S ALL THIS ABOUT? I DON'T EVEN--
SHUT UP AND MOVE YOUR---
FWOOOM

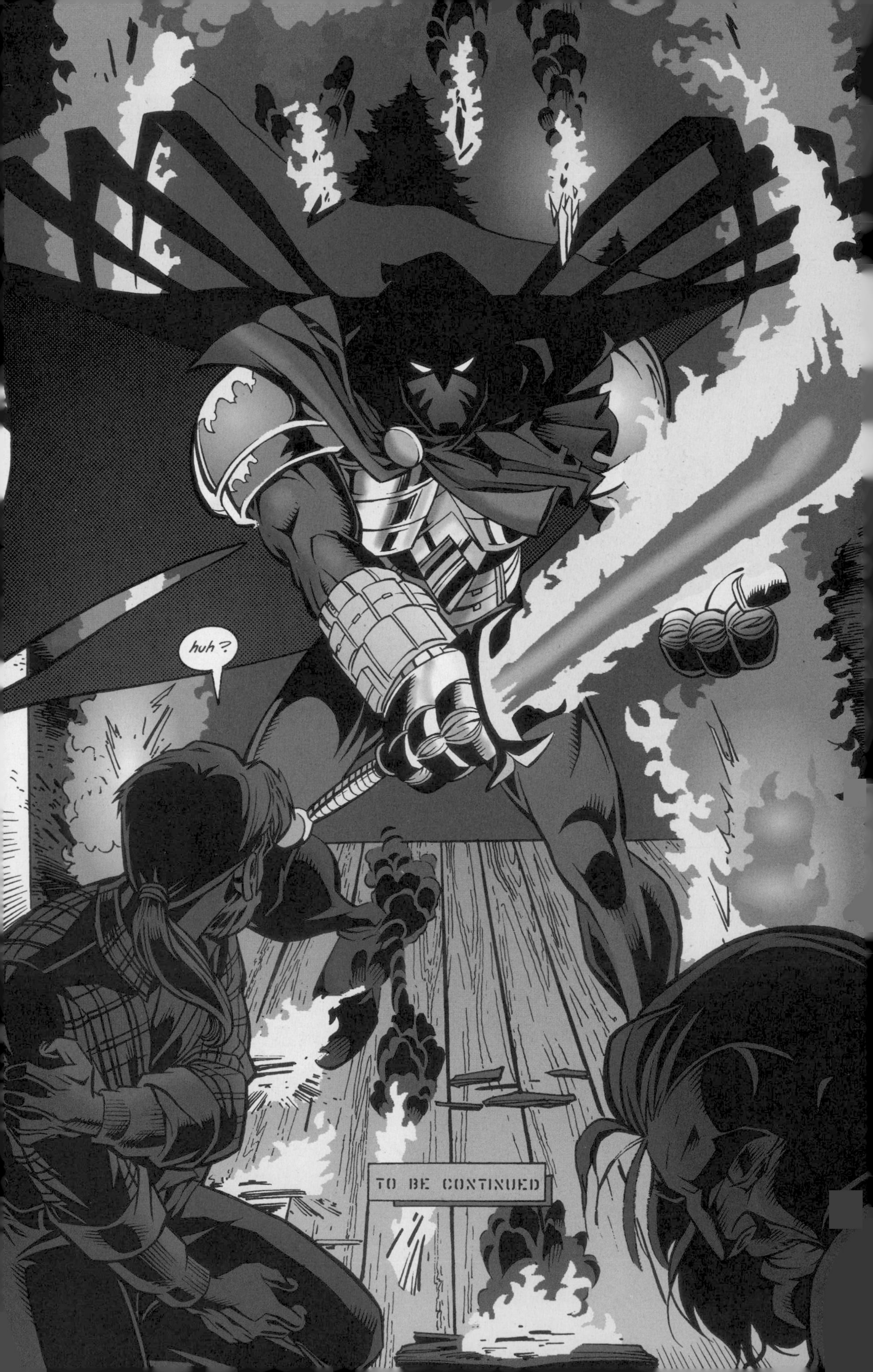
huh?
TO BE CONTINUED

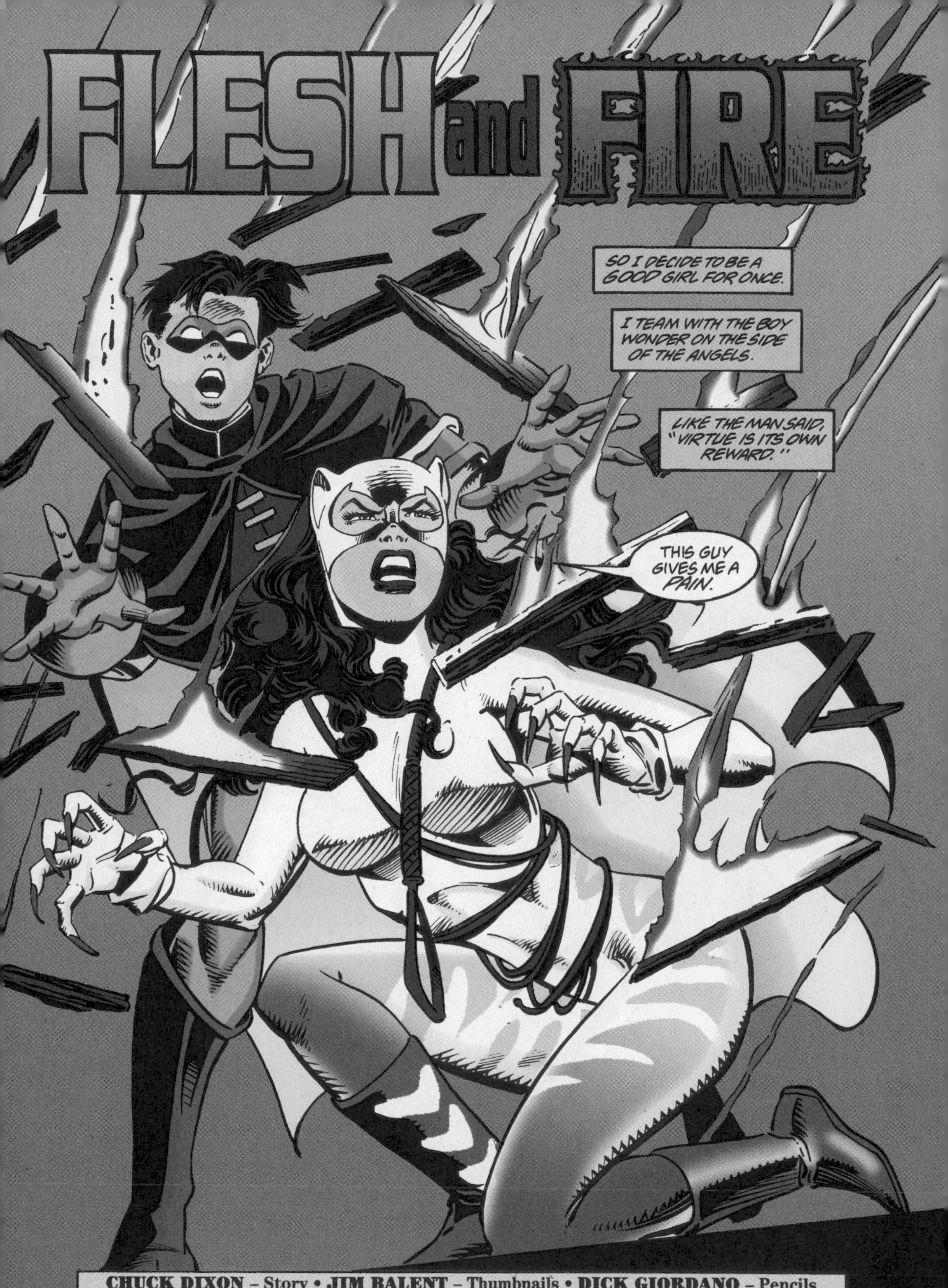
FLESH and FIRE
SO I DECIDE TO BE A GOOD GIRL FOR ONCE.
I TEAM WITH THE BOY WONDER ON THE SIDE OF THE ANGELS.
LIKE THE MAN SAID, "VIRTUE IS ITS OWN REWARD."
THIS GUY GIVES ME A PAIN.

CHUCK DIXON – Story • **JIM BALENT** – Thumbnails • **DICK GIORDANO** – Pencils
BOB SMITH – Inks • **BUZZ SETZER** – Colors • **ALBERT DE GUZMAN** – Letters
JORDAN B. GORFINKEL – Associate Editor • **DENNIS O'NEIL** – Editor

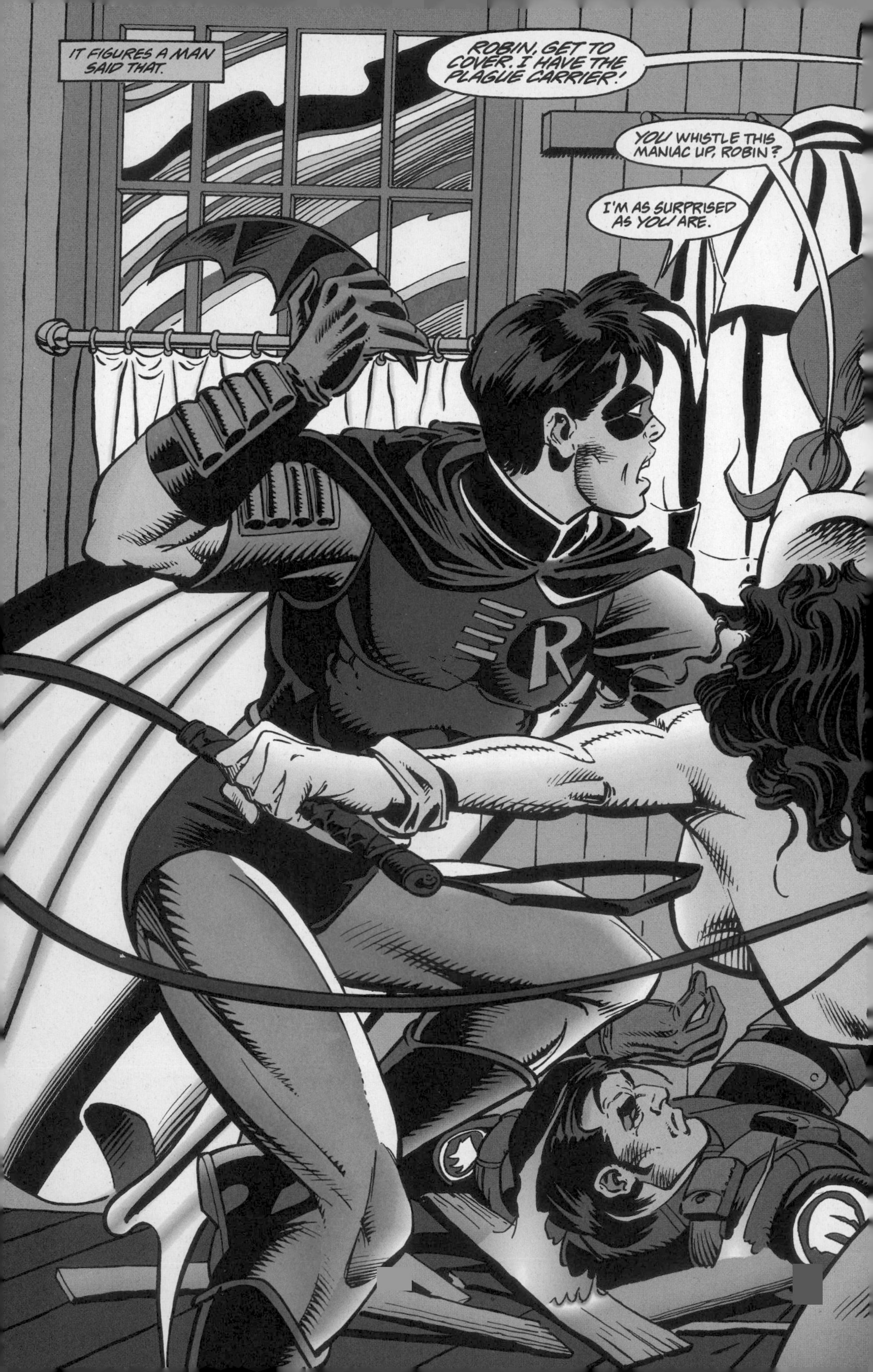
IT FIGURES A MAN SAID THAT.
ROBIN, GET TO COVER. I HAVE THE PLAGUE CARRIER!
YOU WHISTLE THIS MANIAC UP, ROBIN?
I'M AS SURPRISED AS YOU ARE.

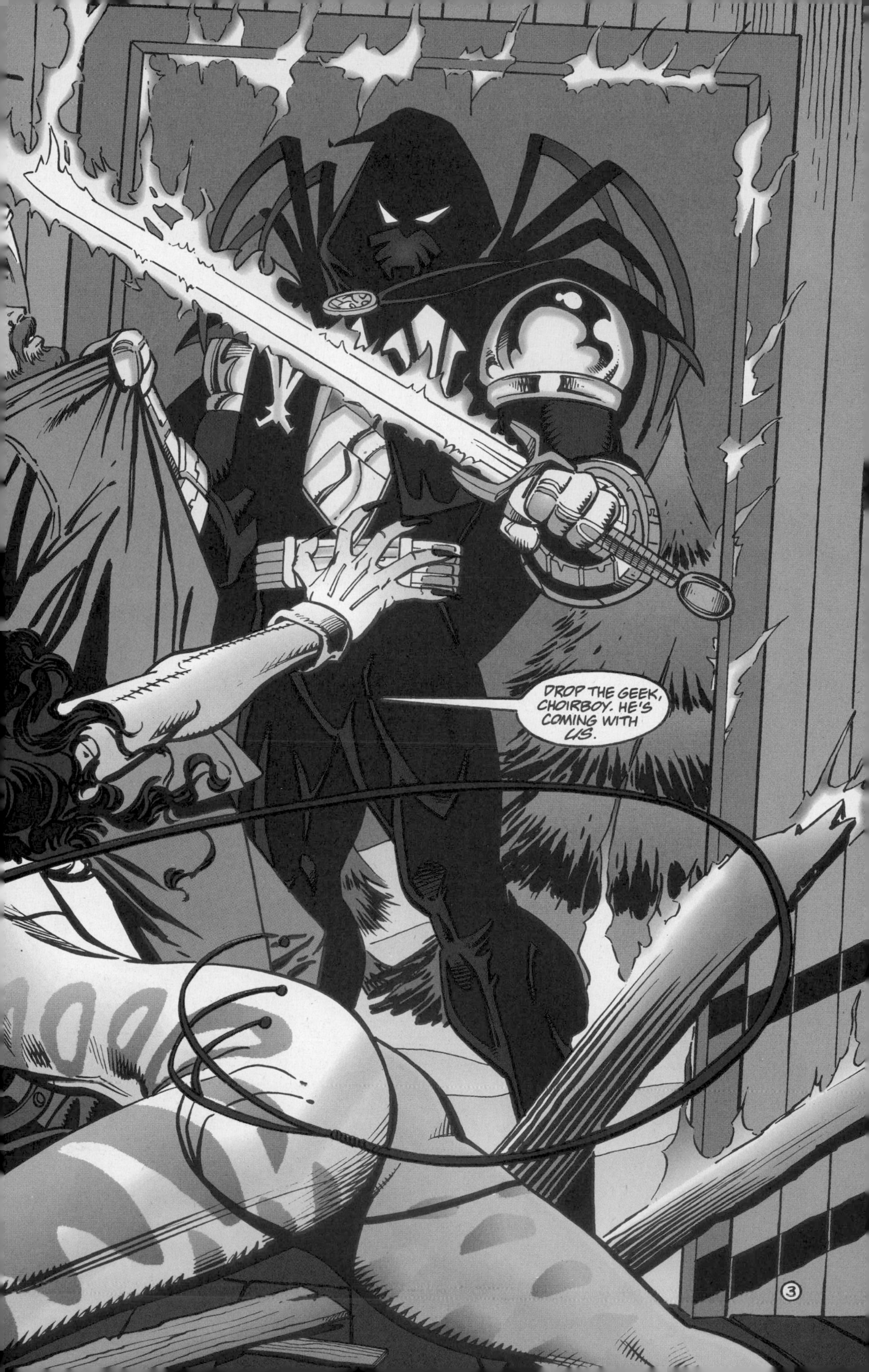
DROP THE GEEK, CHOIRBOY. HE'S COMING WITH US.

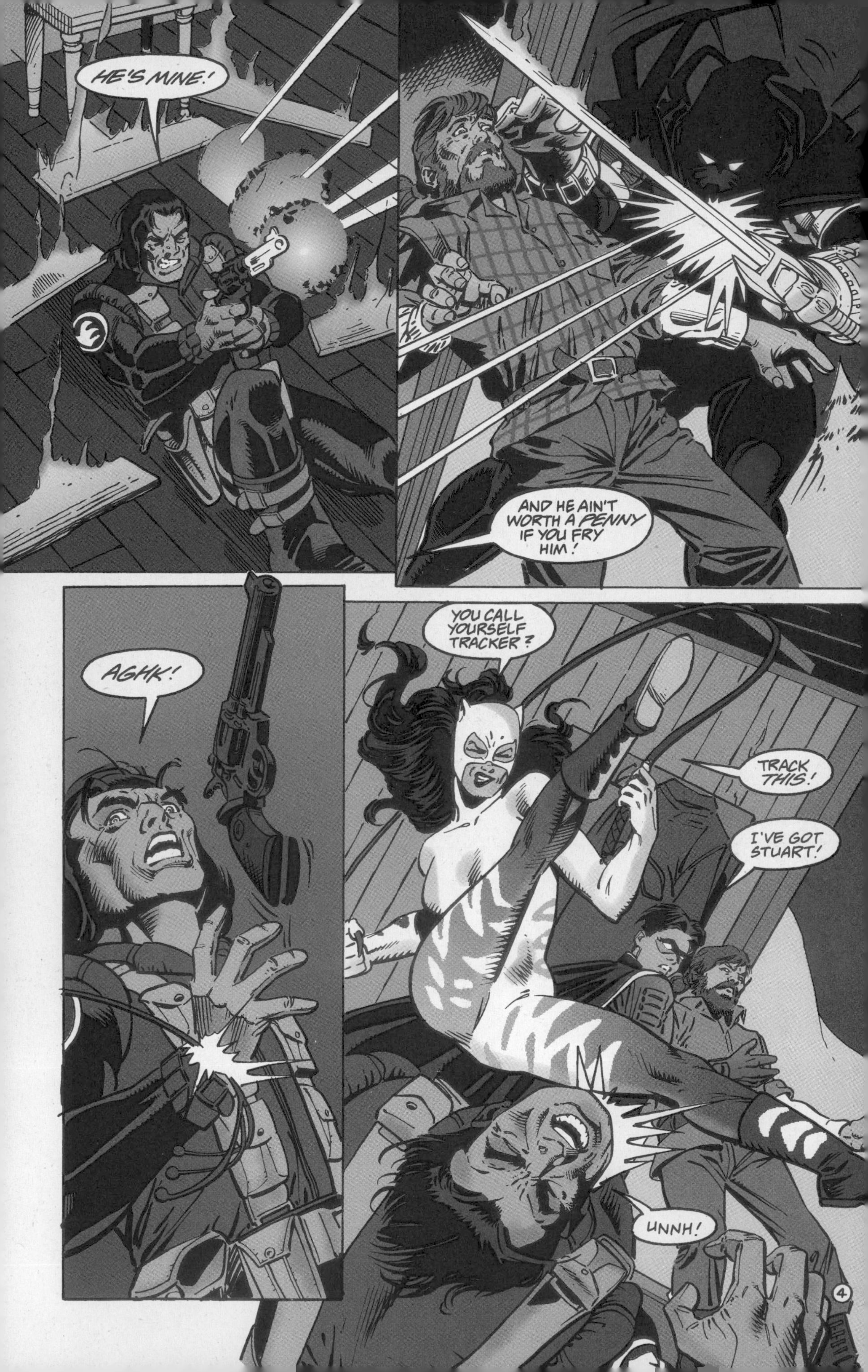
HE'S MINE!
AND HE AIN'T WORTH A PENNY IF YOU FRY HIM!
AGHK!
YOU CALL YOURSELF TRACKER?
TRACK THIS!
I'VE GOT STUART!
UNNH!
4

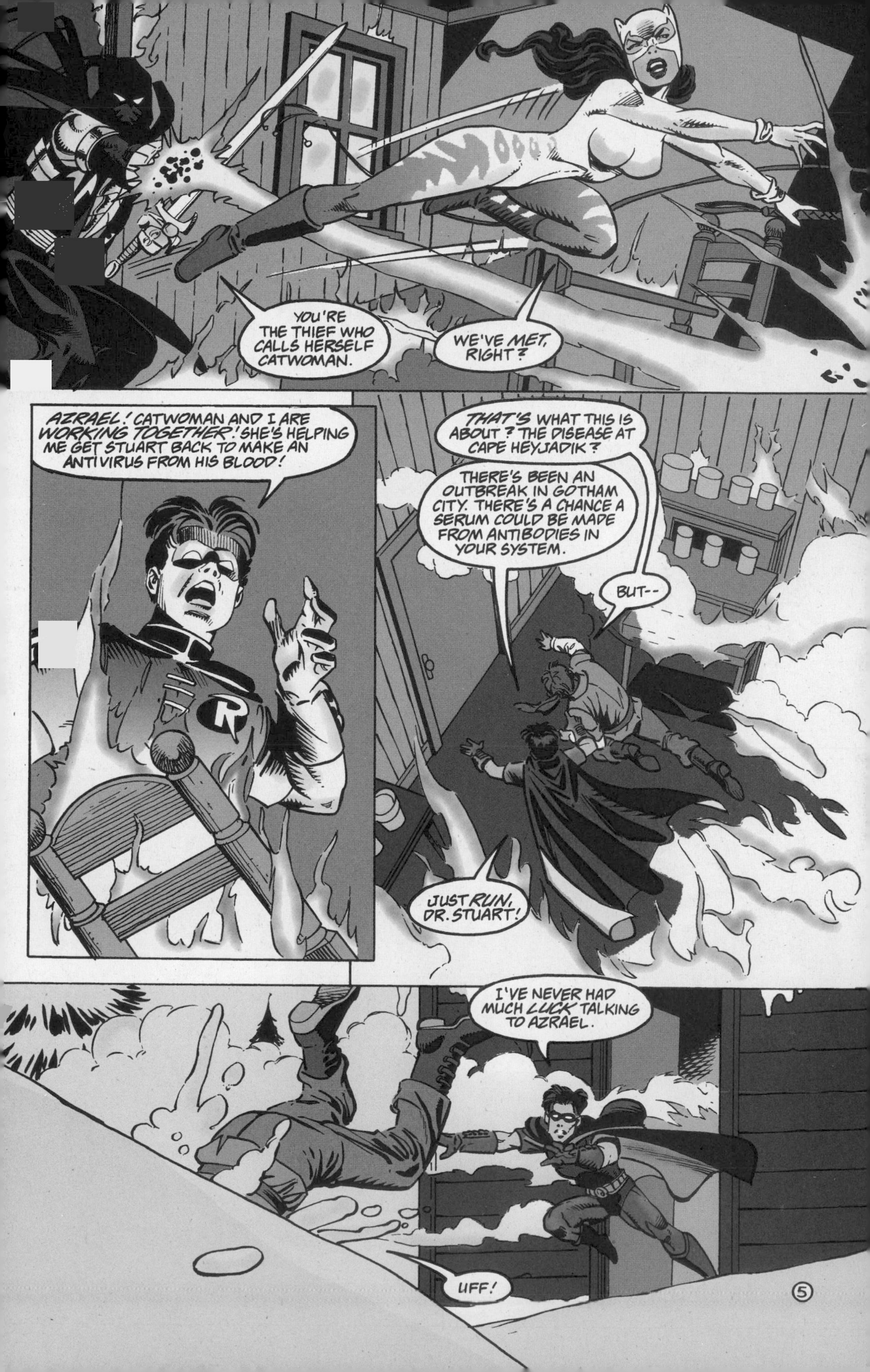
YOU'RE THE THIEF WHO CALLS HERSELF CATWOMAN.
WE'VE MET, RIGHT?
AZRAEL! CATWOMAN AND I ARE WORKING TOGETHER! SHE'S HELPING ME GET STUART BACK TO MAKE AN ANTIVIRUS FROM HIS BLOOD!
THAT'S WHAT THIS IS ABOUT? THE DISEASE AT CAPE HEYJADIK?
THERE'S BEEN AN OUTBREAK IN GOTHAM CITY. THERE'S A CHANCE A SERUM COULD BE MADE FROM ANTIBODIES IN YOUR SYSTEM.
BUT--
JUST RUN, DR. STUART!
I'VE NEVER HAD MUCH LUCK TALKING TO AZRAEL.
UFF!

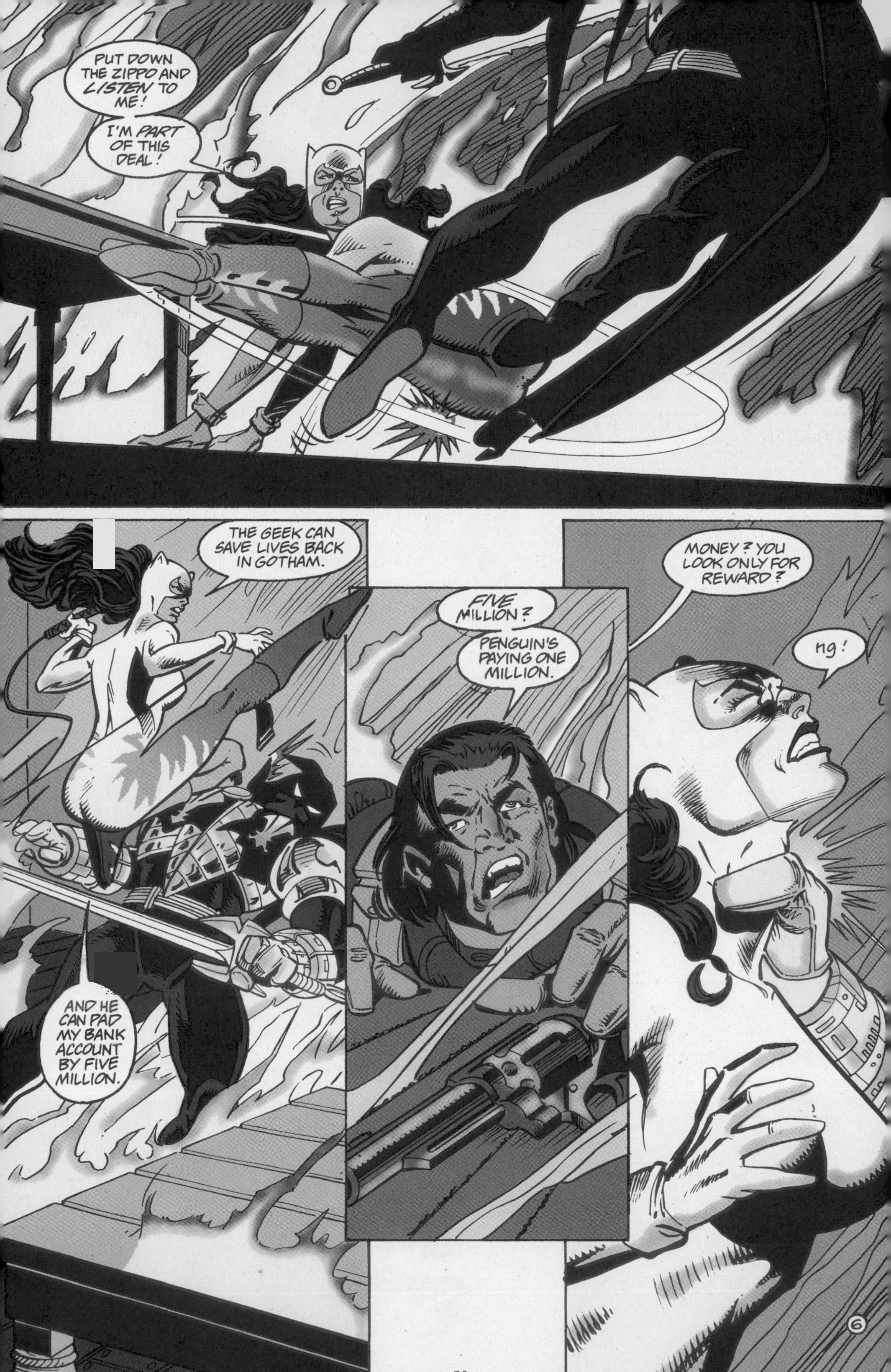
PUT DOWN THE ZIPPO AND LISTEN TO ME!
I'M PART OF THIS DEAL!
THE GEEK CAN SAVE LIVES BACK IN GOTHAM.
AND HE CAN PAD MY BANK ACCOUNT BY FIVE MILLION.
FIVE MILLION?
PENGUIN'S PAYING ONE MILLION.
MONEY? YOU LOOK ONLY FOR REWARD?
ng!
6

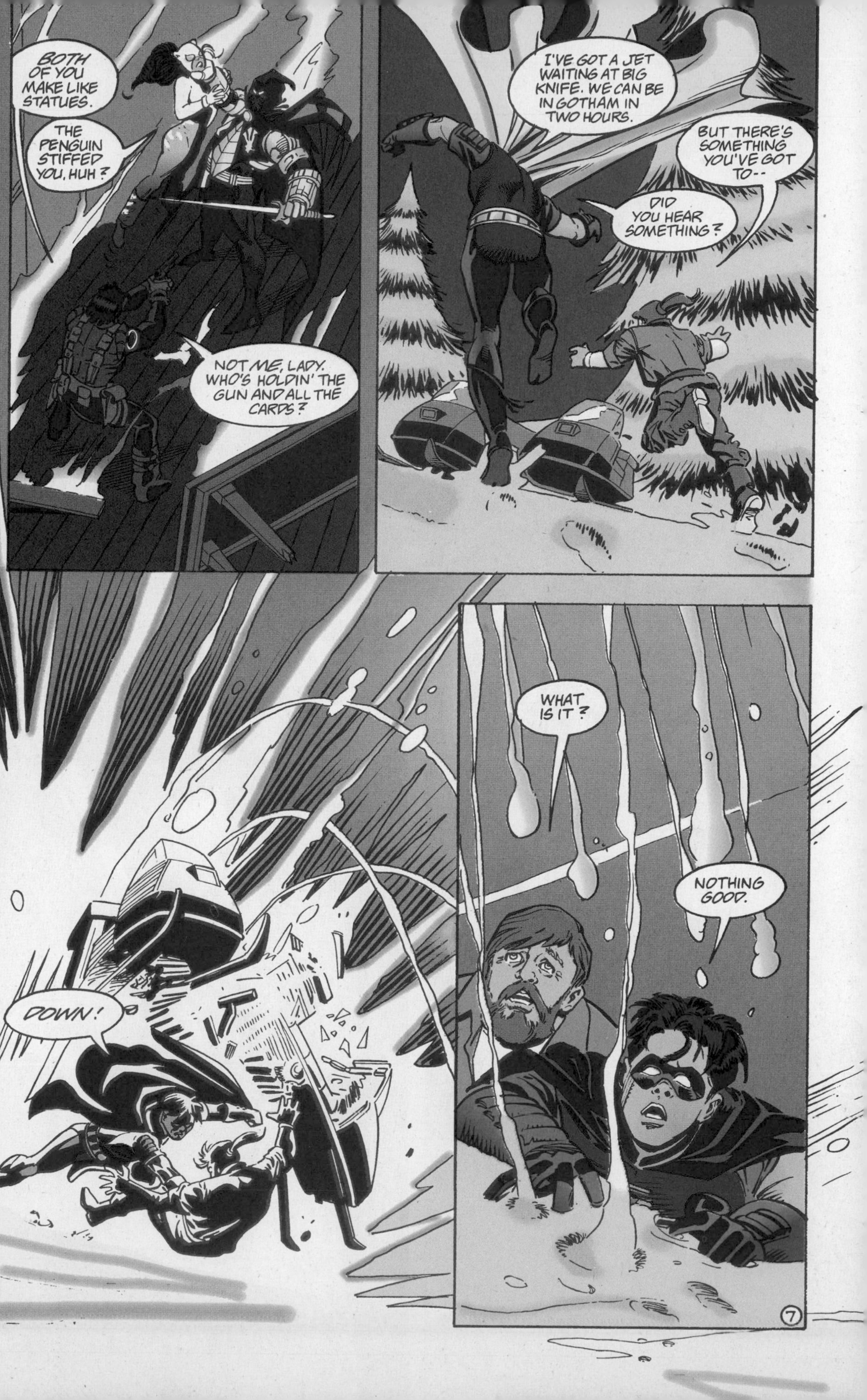
BOTH OF YOU MAKE LIKE STATUES.
THE PENGUIN STIFFED YOU, HUH?
NOT ME, LADY. WHO'S HOLDIN' THE GUN AND ALL THE CARDS?
I'VE GOT A JET WAITING AT BIG KNIFE. WE CAN BE IN GOTHAM IN TWO HOURS.
BUT THERE'S SOMETHING YOU'VE GOT TO--
DID YOU HEAR SOMETHING?
WHAT IS IT?
NOTHING GOOD.
DOWN!
7

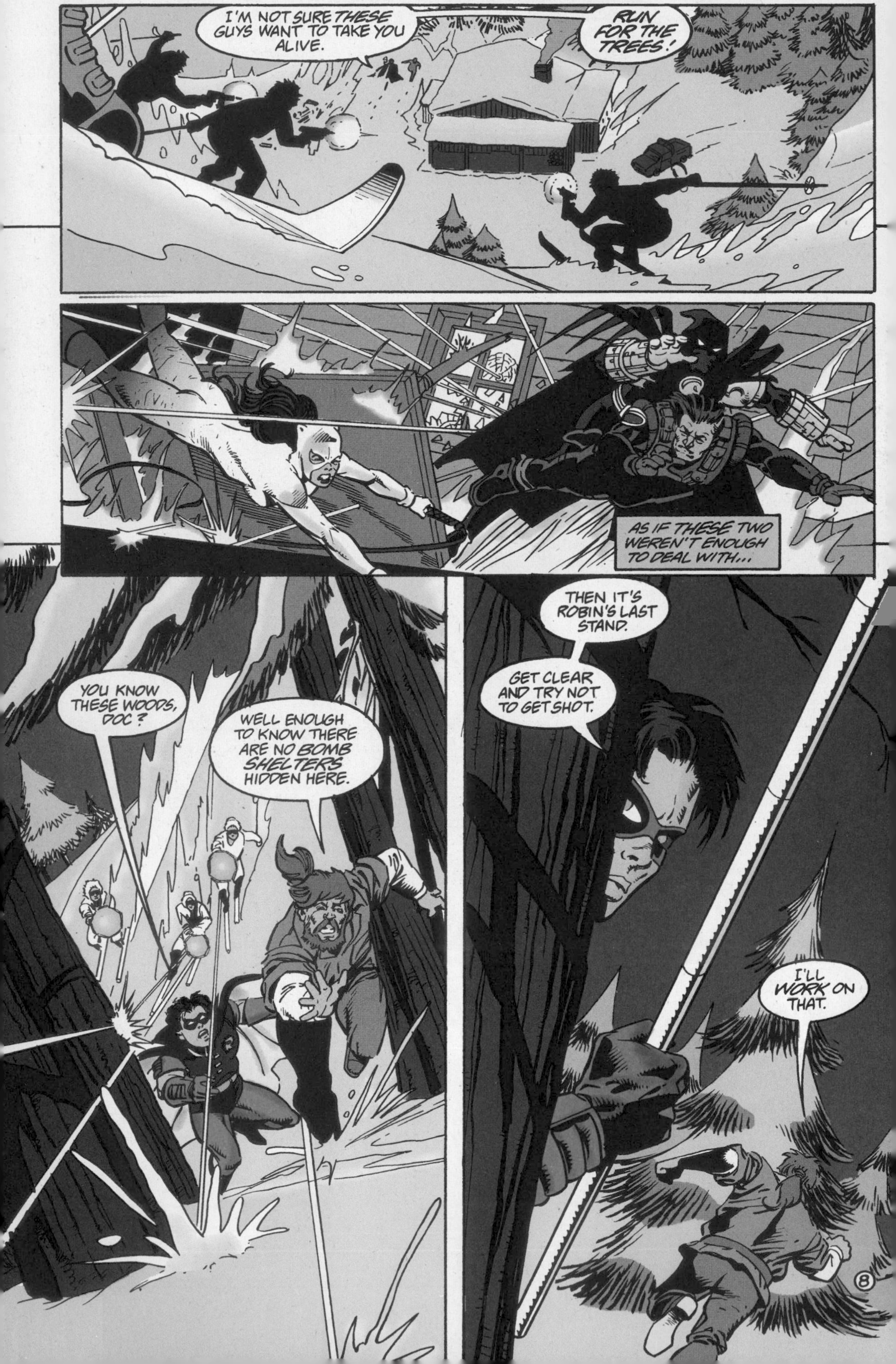
I'M NOT SURE THESE GUYS WANT TO TAKE YOU ALIVE.
RUN FOR THE TREES!
AS IF THESE TWO WEREN'T ENOUGH TO DEAL WITH...
YOU KNOW THESE WOODS, DOC?
WELL ENOUGH TO KNOW THERE ARE NO BOMB SHELTERS HIDDEN HERE.
THEN IT'S ROBIN'S LAST STAND.
GET CLEAR AND TRY NOT TO GET SHOT.
I'LL WORK ON THAT.
8

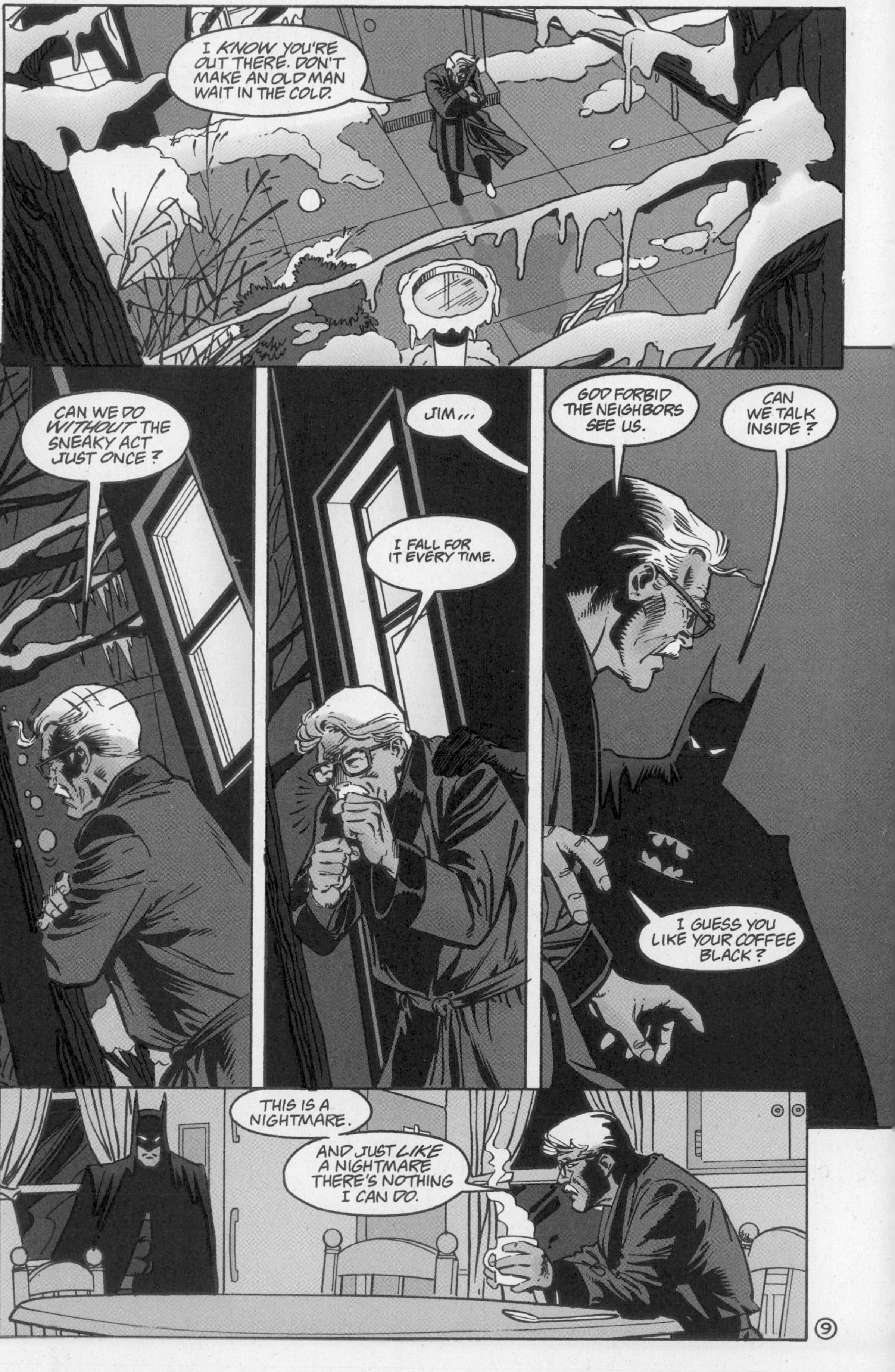
I KNOW YOU'RE OUT THERE. DON'T MAKE AN OLD MAN WAIT IN THE COLD.
CAN WE DO WITHOUT THE SNEAKY ACT JUST ONCE ?
JIM,,,
I FALL FOR IT EVERY TIME.
GOD FORBID THE NEIGHBORS SEE US.
CAN WE TALK INSIDE ?
I GUESS YOU LIKE YOUR COFFEE BLACK ?
THIS IS A NIGHTMARE.
AND JUST LIKE A NIGHTMARE THERE'S NOTHING I CAN DO.
9

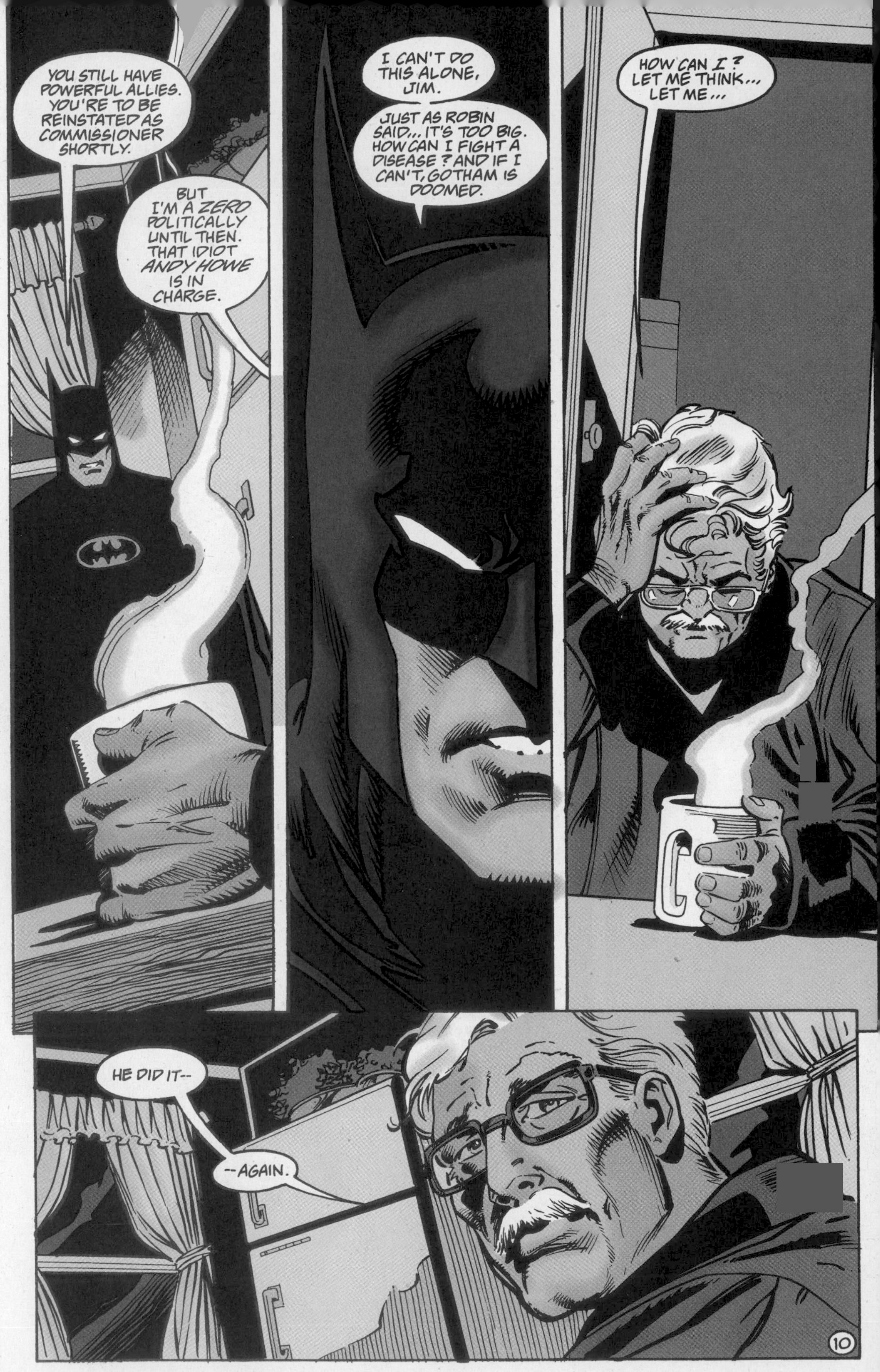
YOU STILL HAVE POWERFUL ALLIES. YOU'RE TO BE REINSTATED AS COMMISSIONER SHORTLY.
BUT I'M A ZERO POLITICALLY UNTIL THEN. THAT IDIOT ANDY HOWE IS IN CHARGE.
I CAN'T DO THIS ALONE, JIM.
JUST AS ROBIN SAID,.. IT'S TOO BIG. HOW CAN I FIGHT A DISEASE ? AND IF I CAN'T, GOTHAM IS DOOMED.
HOW CAN I ? LET ME THINK... LET ME...
HE DID IT--
--AGAIN.
10

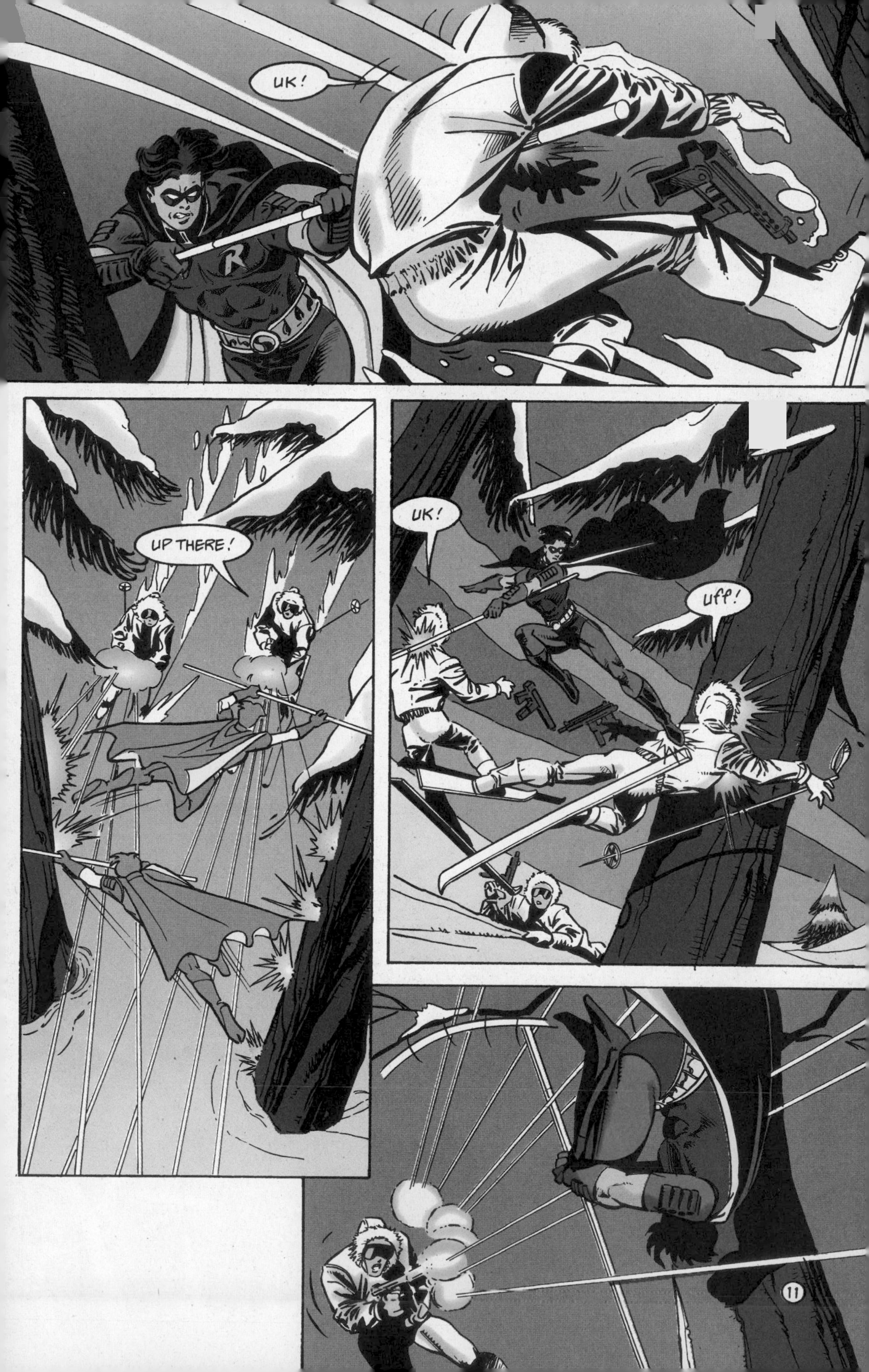
UK!
UP THERE!
UK!
UFF!
11

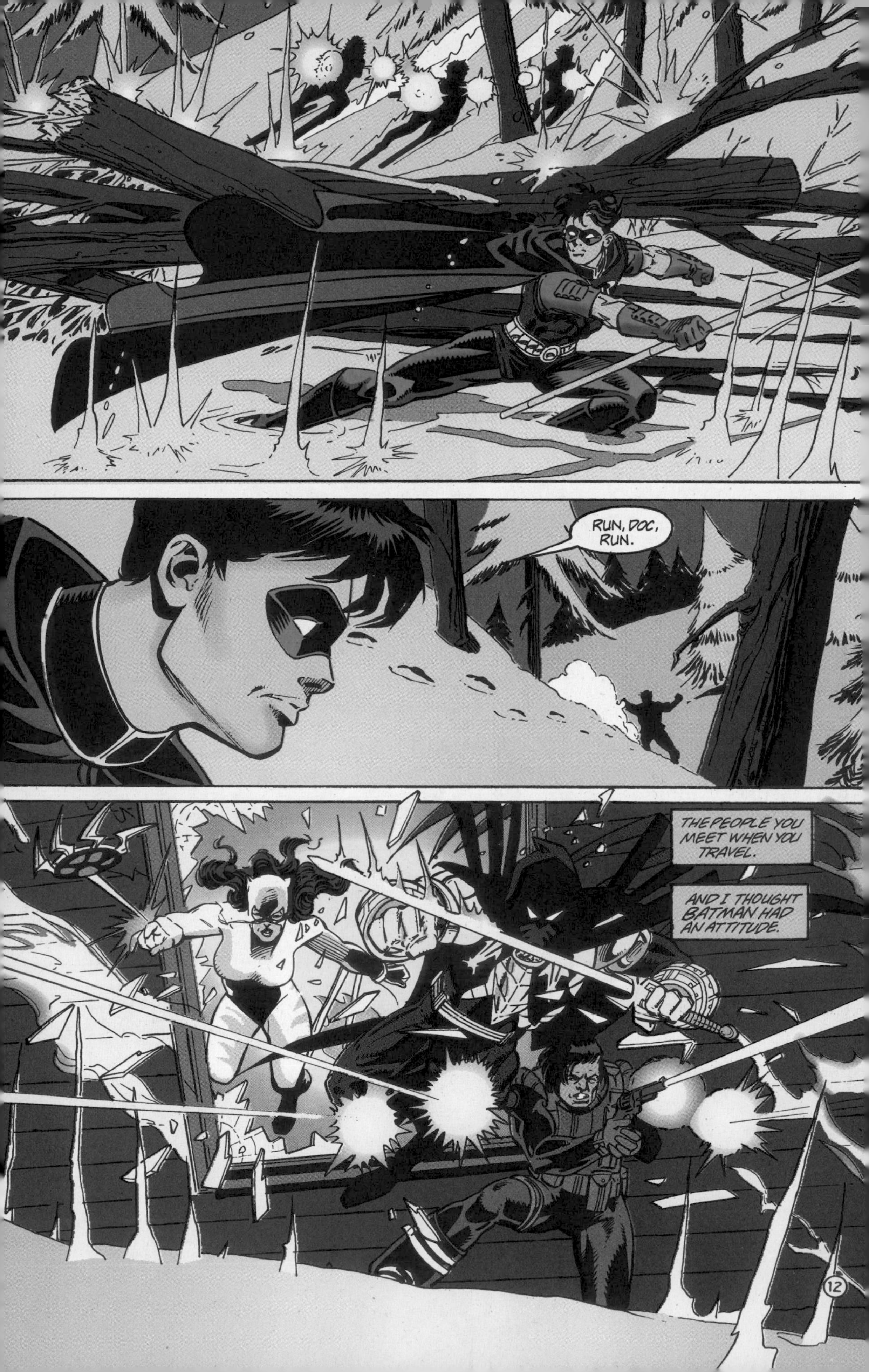
RUN, DOC, RUN.
THE PEOPLE YOU MEET WHEN YOU TRAVEL.
AND I THOUGHT BATMAN HAD AN ATTITUDE.

THE PIOUS ALTAR BOY WITH THE GINSU KNIFE ONLY A PYROMANIAC COULD LOVE.

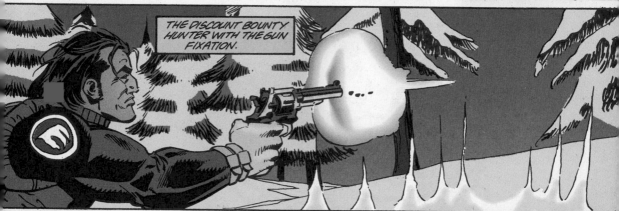

THE DISCOUNT BOUNTY HUNTER WITH THE GUN FIXATION.

AND ME.

JUST A HARD-WORKING GIRL TRYING TO MAKE IT IN A MAN'S WORLD.

WHO ARE THESE GUYS?

I INTEND TO FIND OUT.

WHO SENT YOU?

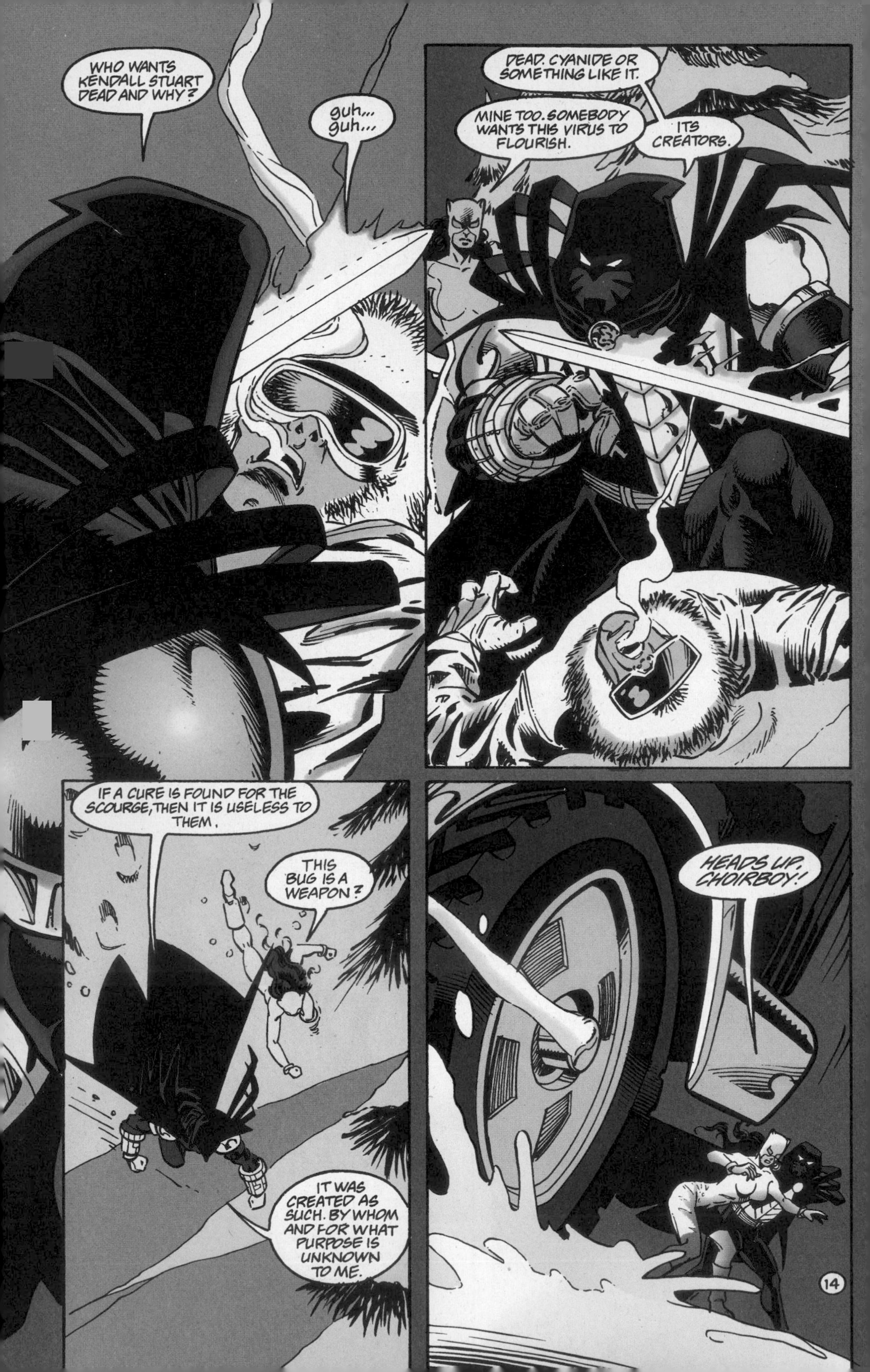
WHO WANTS KENDALL STUART DEAD AND WHY?
guh... guh...
DEAD. CYANIDE OR SOMETHING LIKE IT.
MINE TOO. SOMEBODY WANTS THIS VIRUS TO FLOURISH.
ITS CREATORS.
IF A CURE IS FOUND FOR THE SCOURGE, THEN IT IS USELESS TO THEM.
THIS BUG IS A WEAPON?
IT WAS CREATED AS SUCH. BY WHOM AND FOR WHAT PURPOSE IS UNKNOWN TO ME.
HEADS UP, CHOIRBOY!
14

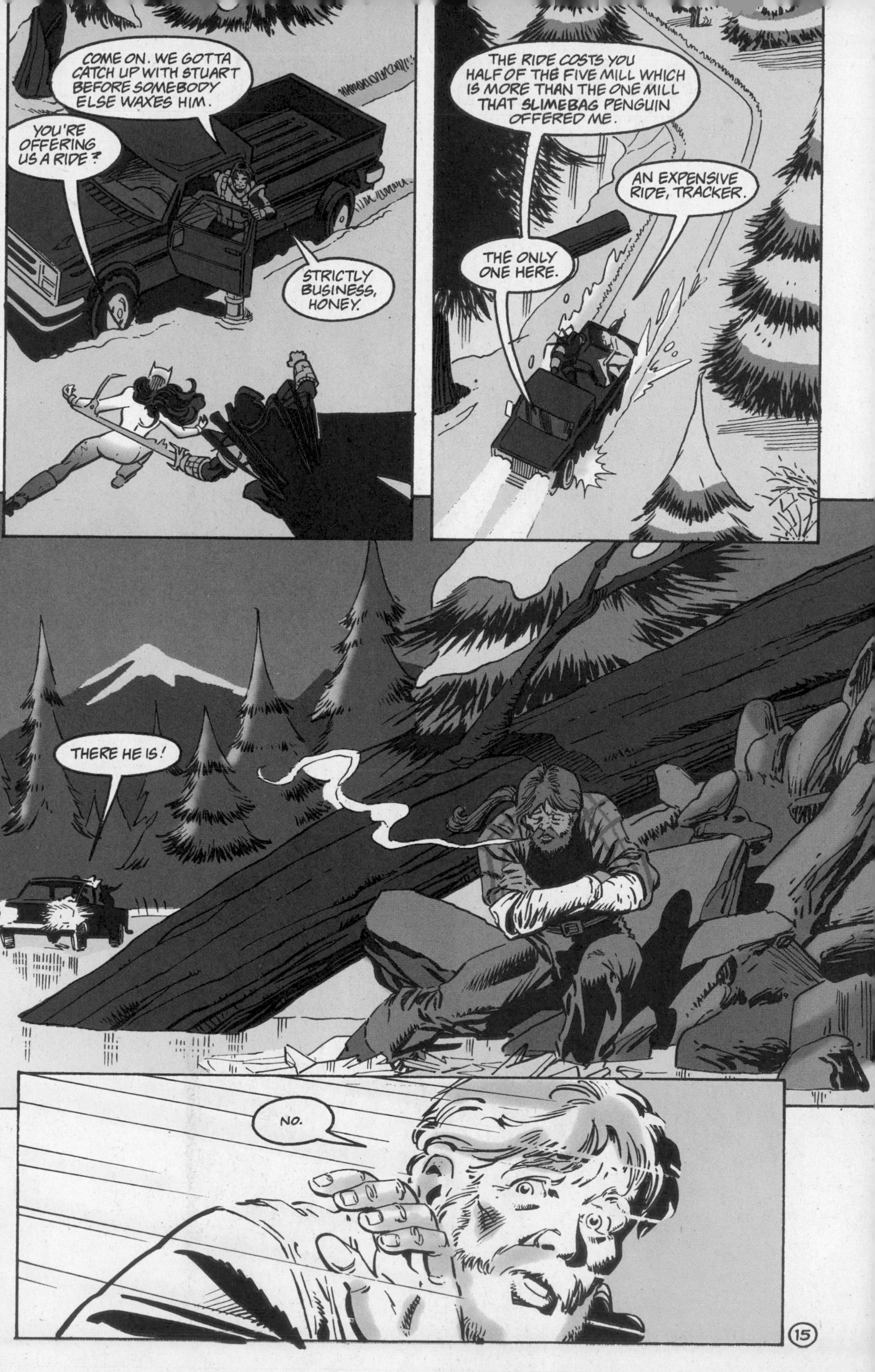
COME ON. WE GOTTA CATCH UP WITH STUART BEFORE SOMEBODY ELSE WAXES HIM.
YOU'RE OFFERING US A RIDE?
STRICTLY BUSINESS, HONEY.
THE RIDE COSTS YOU HALF OF THE FIVE MILL WHICH IS MORE THAN THE ONE MILL THAT SLIMEBAG PENGUIN OFFERED ME.
AN EXPENSIVE RIDE, TRACKER.
THE ONLY ONE HERE.
THERE HE IS!
NO.
15

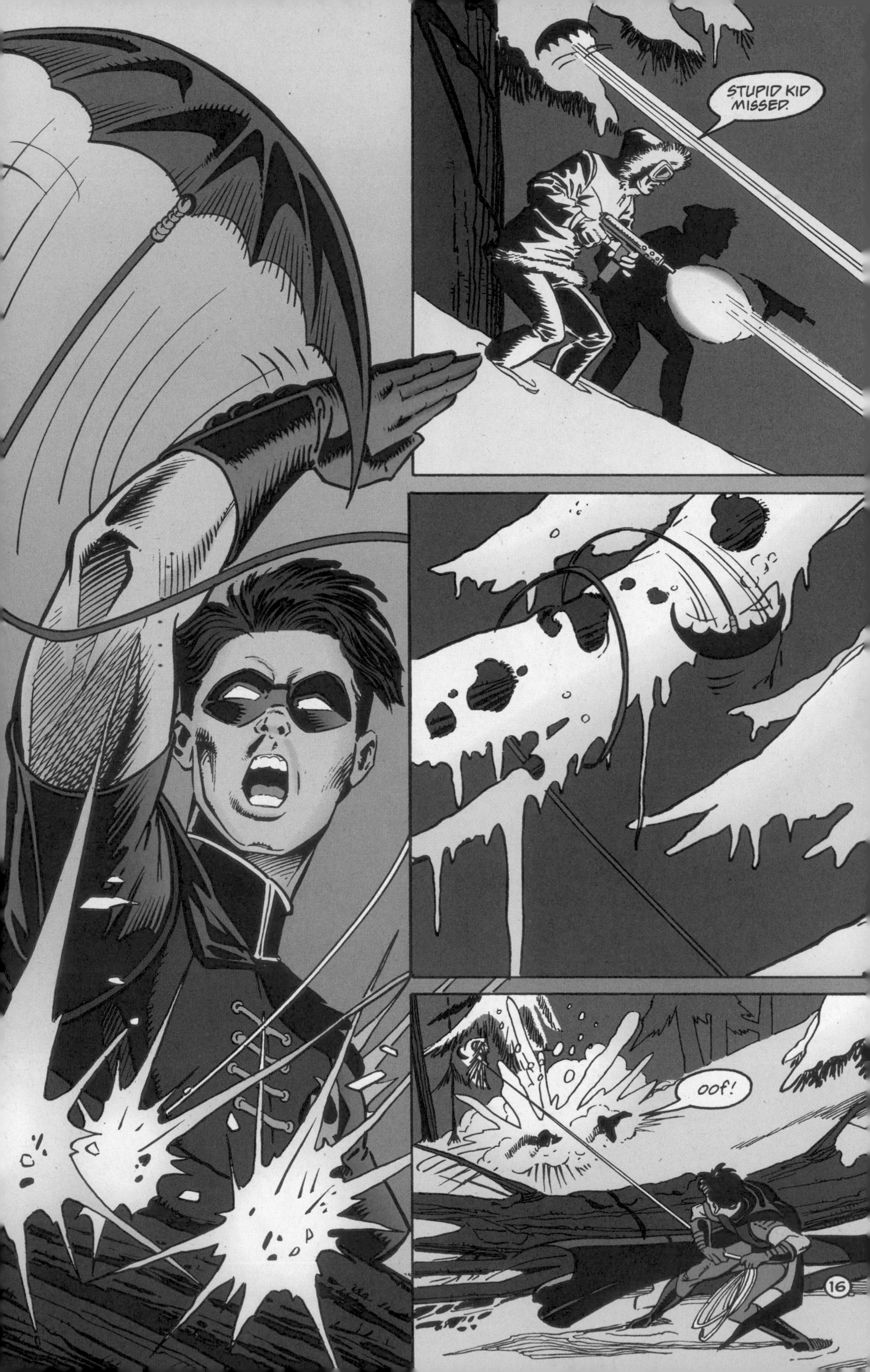
STUPID KID MISSED.
oof!
16

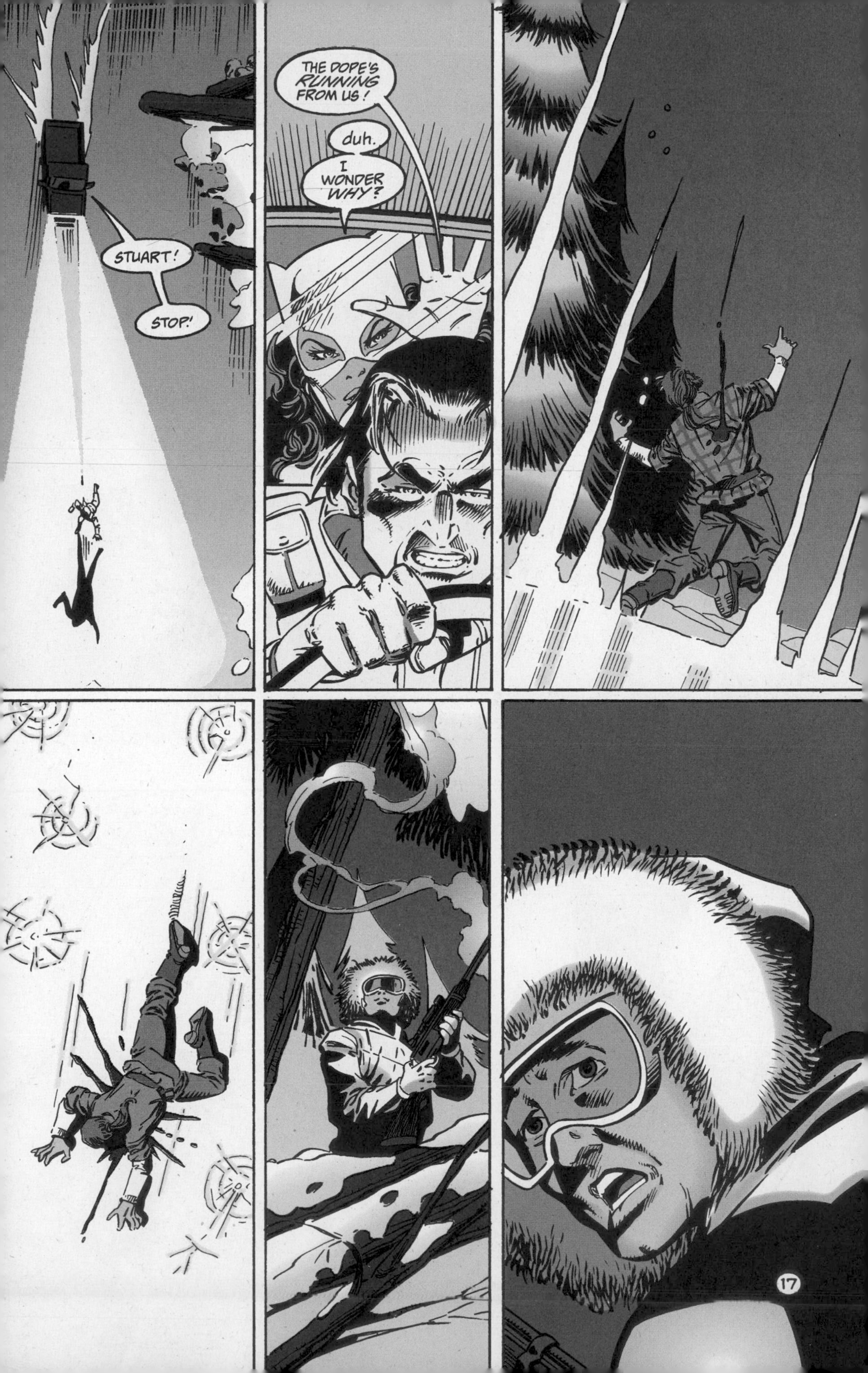
STUART!
STOP!
THE DOPE'S RUNNING FROM US!
duh.
I WONDER WHY?

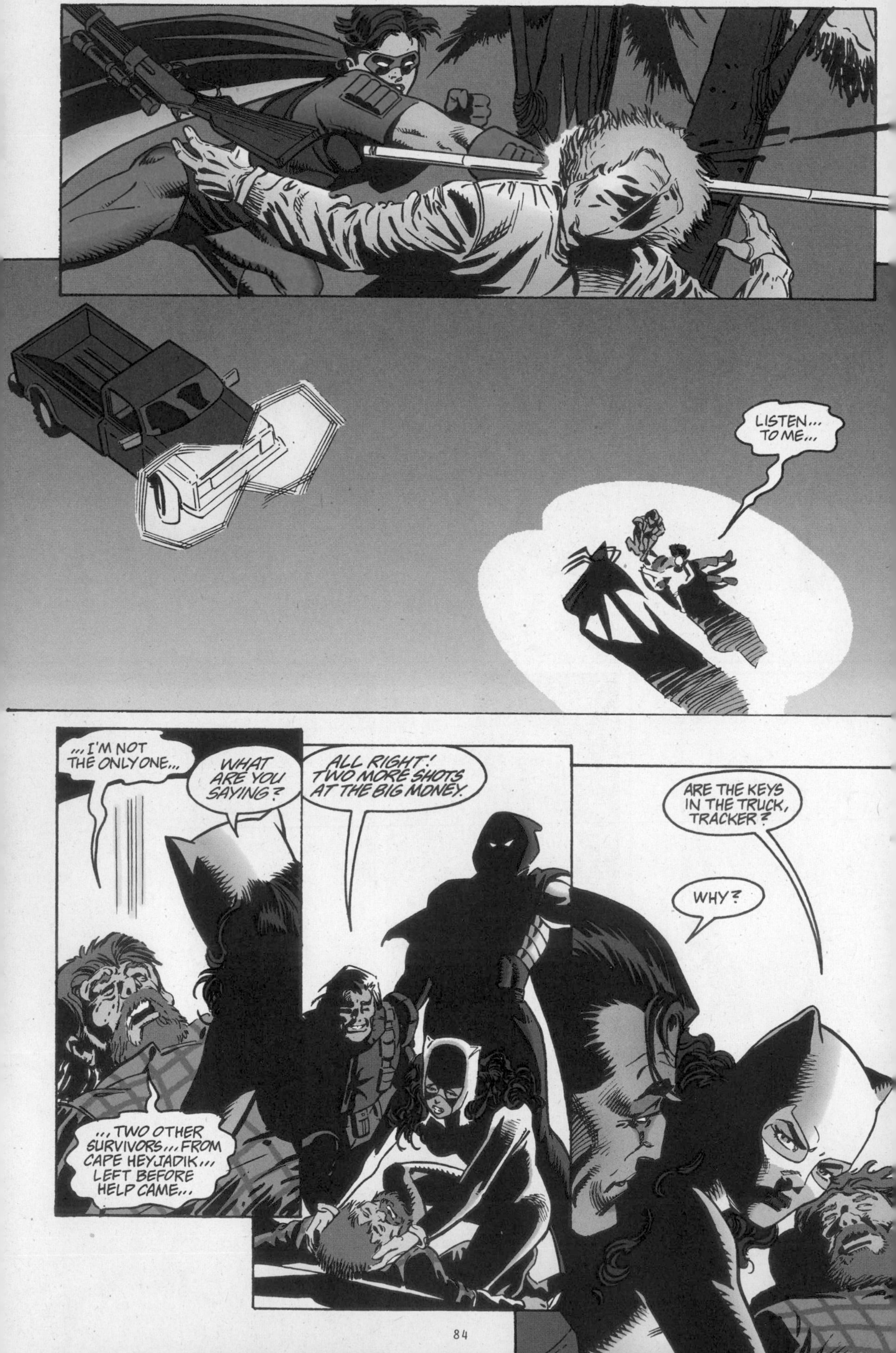
LISTEN... TO ME...
...I'M NOT THE ONLY ONE...
WHAT ARE YOU SAYING?
...TWO OTHER SURVIVORS... FROM CAPE HEYJADIK... LEFT BEFORE HELP CAME...
ALL RIGHT! TWO MORE SHOTS AT THE BIG MONEY.
ARE THE KEYS IN THE TRUCK, TRACKER?
WHY?

OKAY IF **I** DRIVE, CHOIRBOY?

STUART IS--

DEAD, ROBIN.

THERE'S STILL TIME.

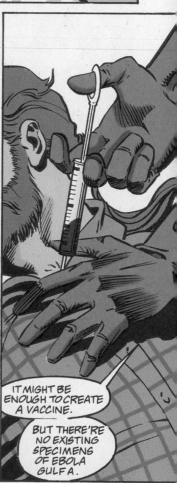

IT MIGHT BE ENOUGH TO CREATE A VACCINE.

BUT THERE'RE NO EXISTING SPECIMENS OF EBOLA GULF A.

DID HE SAY ANYTHING?

NOTHING.

19

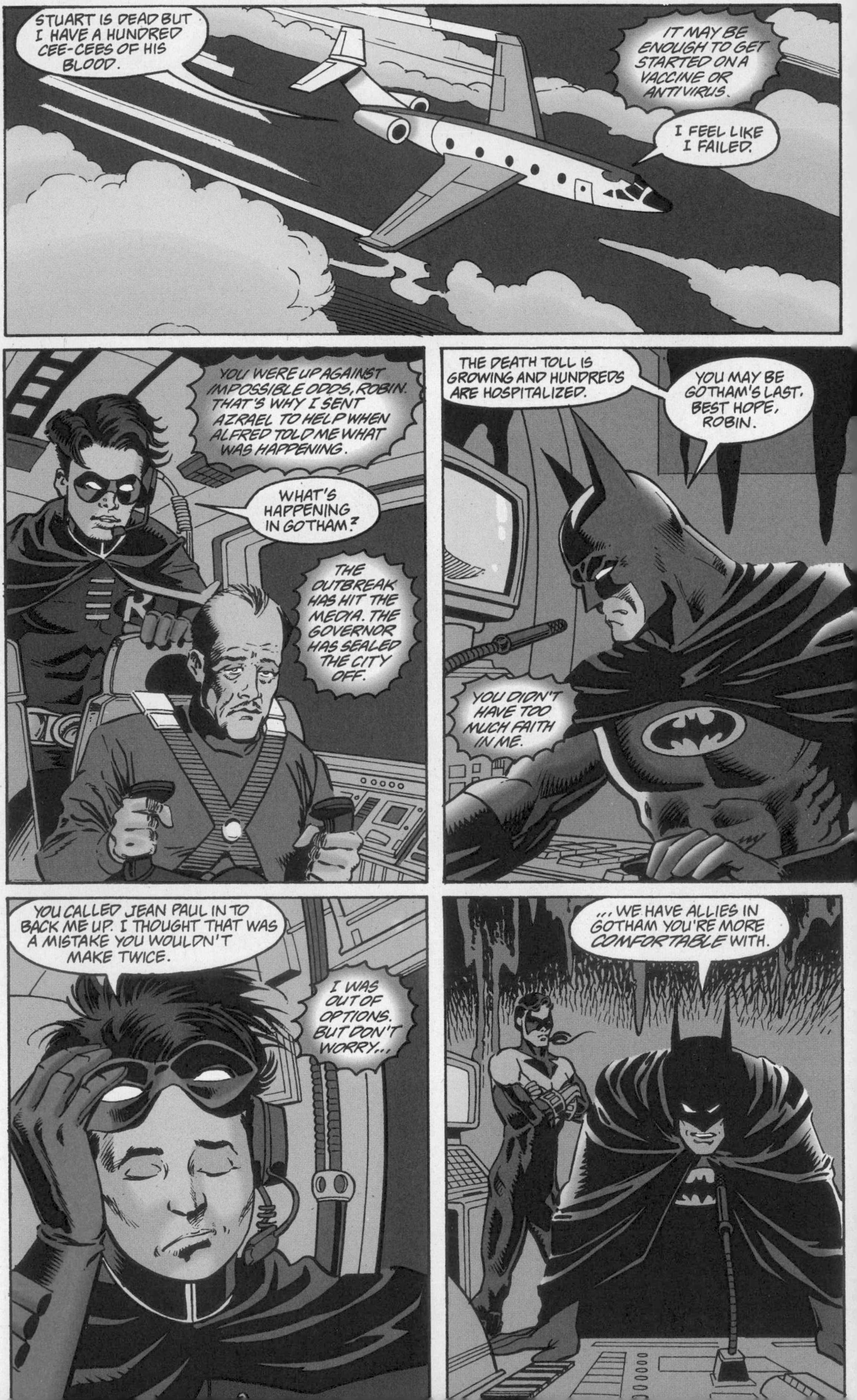
STUART IS DEAD BUT I HAVE A HUNDRED CEE-CEES OF HIS BLOOD.
IT MAY BE ENOUGH TO GET STARTED ON A VACCINE OR ANTIVIRUS.
I FEEL LIKE I FAILED.
YOU WERE UP AGAINST IMPOSSIBLE ODDS, ROBIN. THAT'S WHY I SENT AZRAEL TO HELP WHEN ALFRED TOLD ME WHAT WAS HAPPENING.
WHAT'S HAPPENING IN GOTHAM?
THE OUTBREAK HAS HIT THE MEDIA. THE GOVERNOR HAS SEALED THE CITY OFF.
THE DEATH TOLL IS GROWING AND HUNDREDS ARE HOSPITALIZED.
YOU MAY BE GOTHAM'S LAST, BEST HOPE, ROBIN.
YOU DIDN'T HAVE TOO MUCH FAITH IN ME.
YOU CALLED JEAN PAUL IN TO BACK ME UP. I THOUGHT THAT WAS A MISTAKE YOU WOULDN'T MAKE TWICE.
I WAS OUT OF OPTIONS. BUT DON'T WORRY...
...WE HAVE ALLIES IN GOTHAM YOU'RE MORE COMFORTABLE WITH.

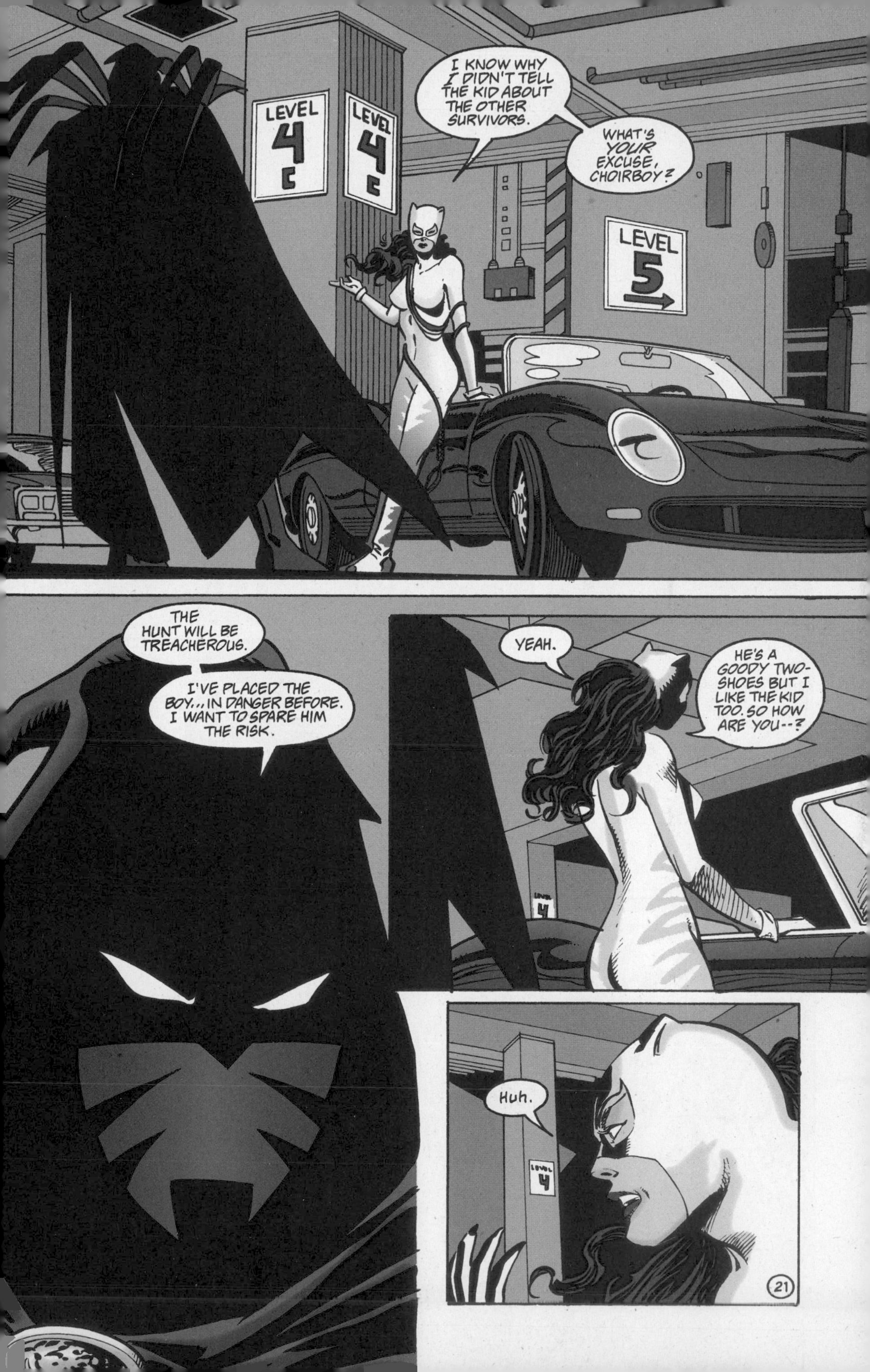

I KNOW WHY I DIDN'T TELL THE KID ABOUT THE OTHER SURVIVORS.
WHAT'S YOUR EXCUSE, CHOIRBOY?
LEVEL 4 C
LEVEL 4 C
LEVEL 5
THE HUNT WILL BE TREACHEROUS.
I'VE PLACED THE BOY... IN DANGER BEFORE. I WANT TO SPARE HIM THE RISK.
YEAH.
HE'S A GOODY TWO-SHOES BUT I LIKE THE KID TOO. SO HOW ARE YOU--?
Huh.
21

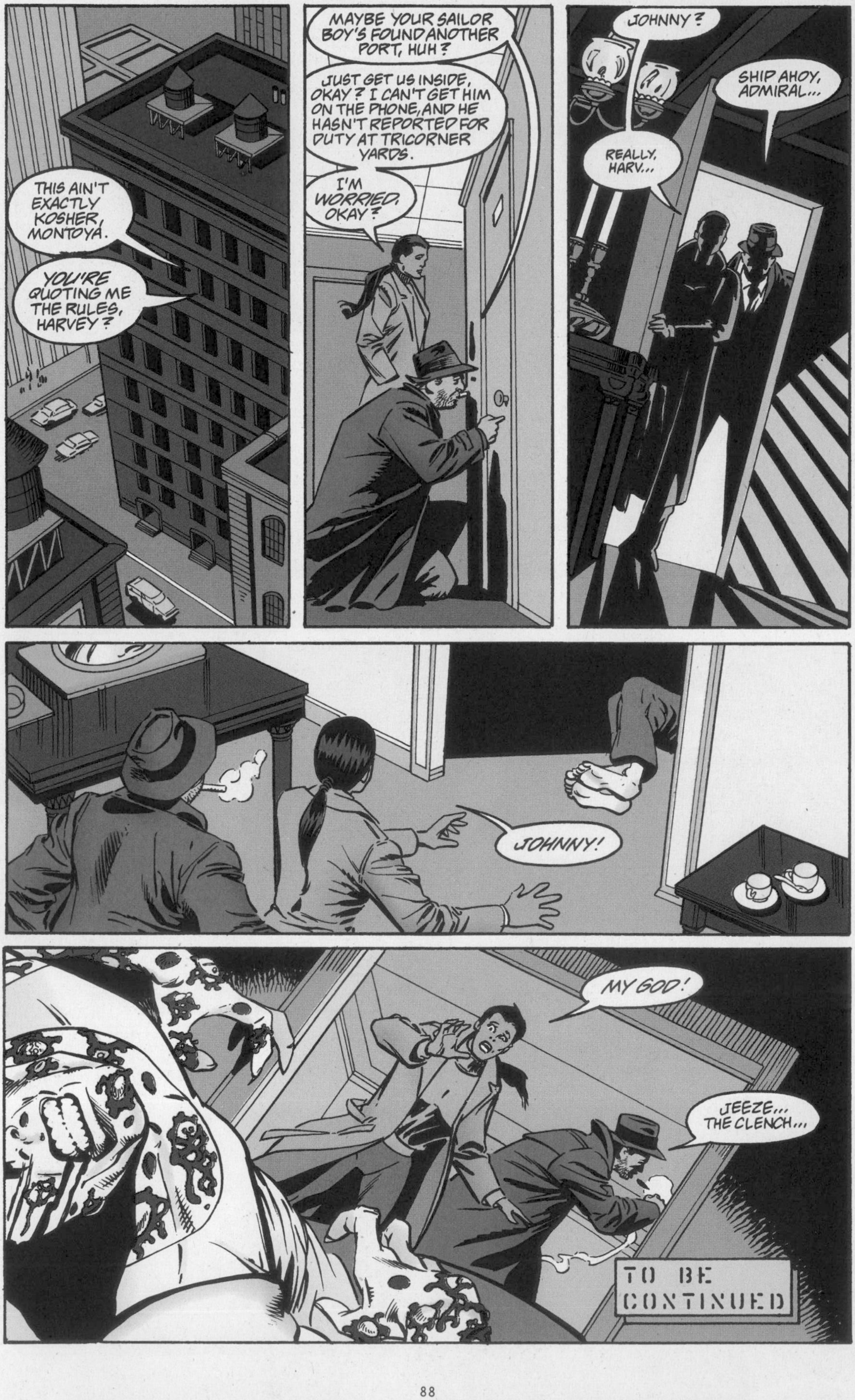
THIS AIN'T EXACTLY KOSHER, MONTOYA.
YOU'RE QUOTING ME THE RULES, HARVEY?
MAYBE YOUR SAILOR BOY'S FOUND ANOTHER PORT, HUH?
JUST GET US INSIDE, OKAY? I CAN'T GET HIM ON THE PHONE, AND HE HASN'T REPORTED FOR DUTY AT TRICORNER YARDS.
I'M WORRIED, OKAY?
JOHNNY?
SHIP AHOY, ADMIRAL...
REALLY, HARV...
JOHNNY!
MY GOD!
JEEZE... THE CLENCH...
TO BE CONTINUED

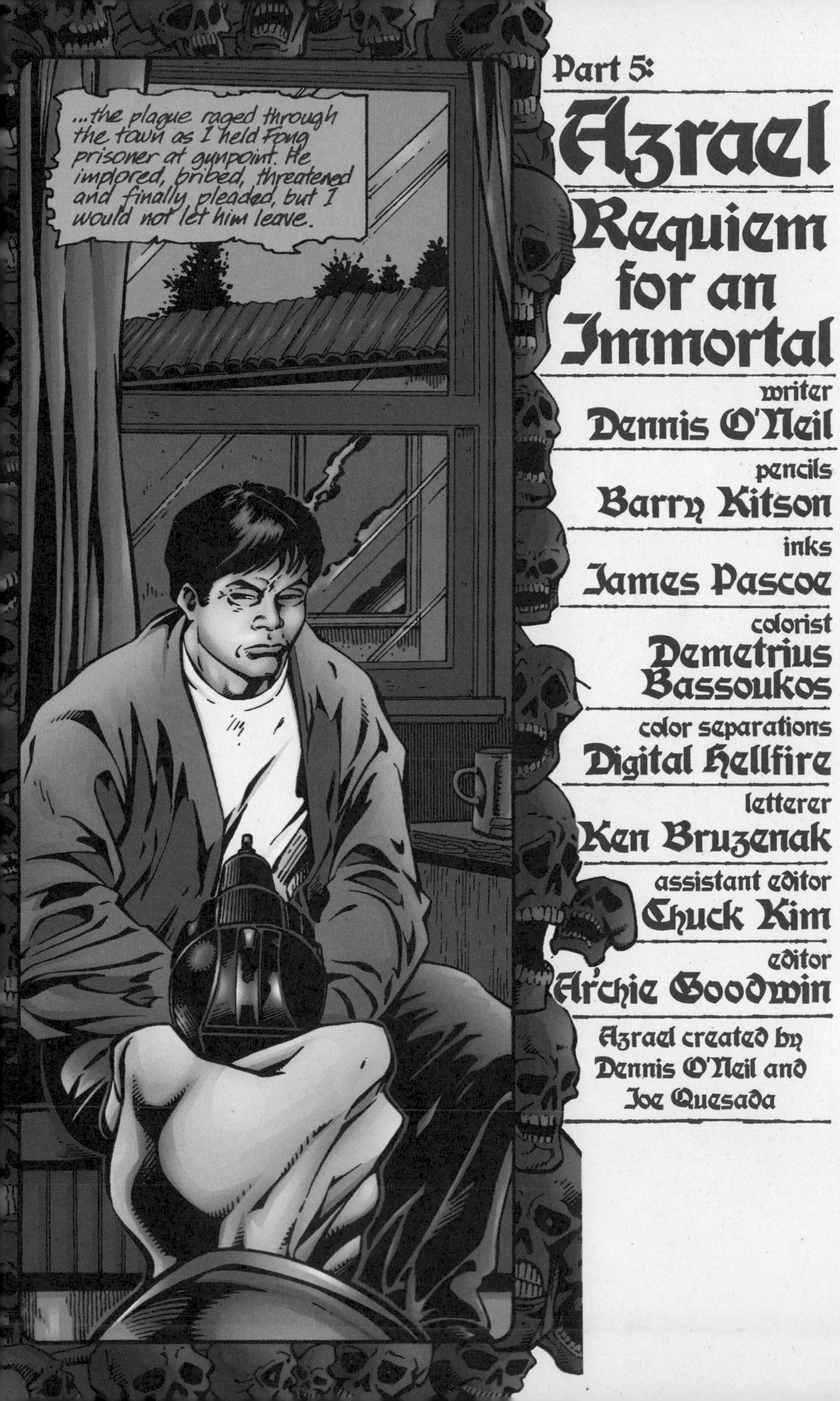
...the plague raged through the town as I held Fong prisoner at gunpoint. He implored, bribed, threatened and finally pleaded, but I would not let him leave.

Part 5:

Azrael

Requiem for an Immortal

writer
Dennis O'Neil

pencils
Barry Kitson

inks
James Pascoe

colorist
Demetrius Bassoukos

color separations
Digital Hellfire

letterer
Ken Bruzenak

assistant editor
Chuck Kim

editor
Archie Goodwin

Azrael created by Dennis O'Neil and Joe Quesada

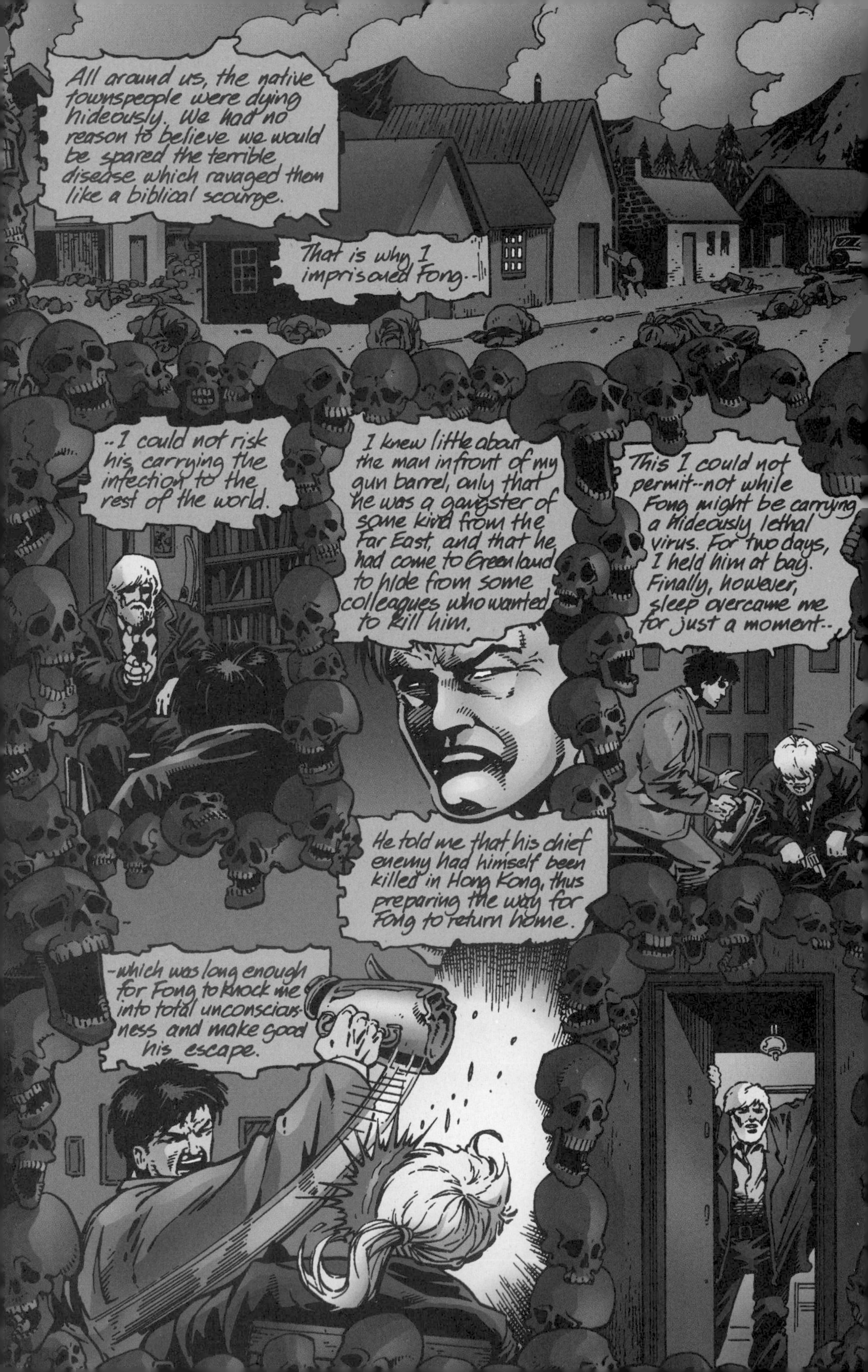
All around us, the native townspeople were dying hideously. We had no reason to believe we would be spared the terrible disease which ravaged them like a biblical scourge.
That is why I imprisoned Fong.--
..I could not risk his carrying the infection to the rest of the world.
I knew little about the man in front of my gun barrel, only that he was a gangster of some kind from the Far East, and that he had come to Greenland to hide from some colleagues who wanted to kill him.
He told me that his chief enemy had himself been killed in Hong Kong, thus preparing the way for Fong to return home.
This I could not permit--not while Fong might be carrying a hideously lethal virus. For two days, I held him at bay. Finally, however, sleep overcame me for just a moment..
-which was long enough for Fong to knock me into total unconsciousness and make good his escape.

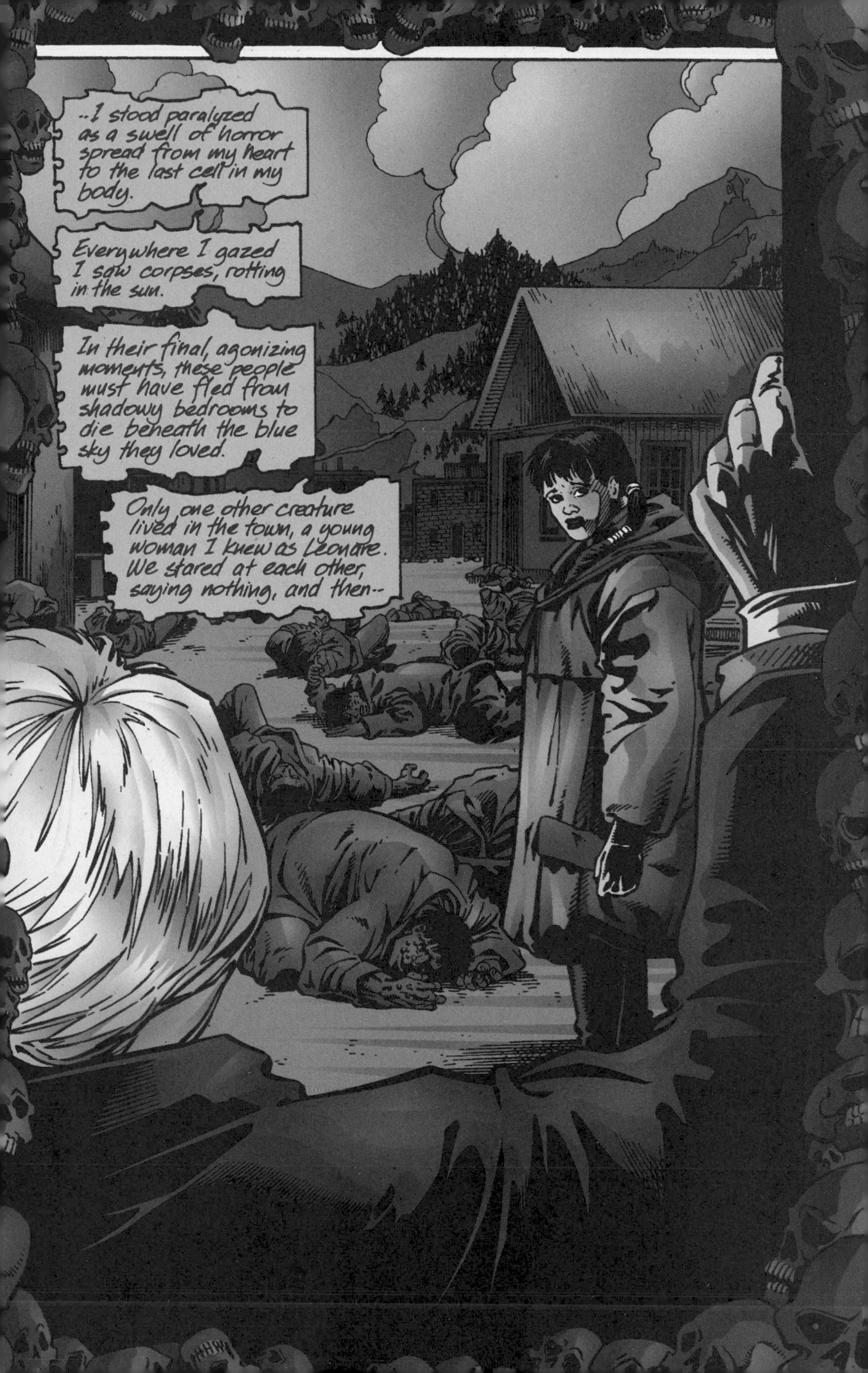
..I stood paralyzed as a swell of horror spread from my heart to the last cell in my body.
Everywhere I gazed I saw corpses, rotting in the sun.
In their final, agonizing moments, these people must have fled from shadowy bedrooms to die beneath the blue sky they loved.
Only one other creature lived in the town, a young woman I knew as Leonare. We stared at each other, saying nothing, and then--

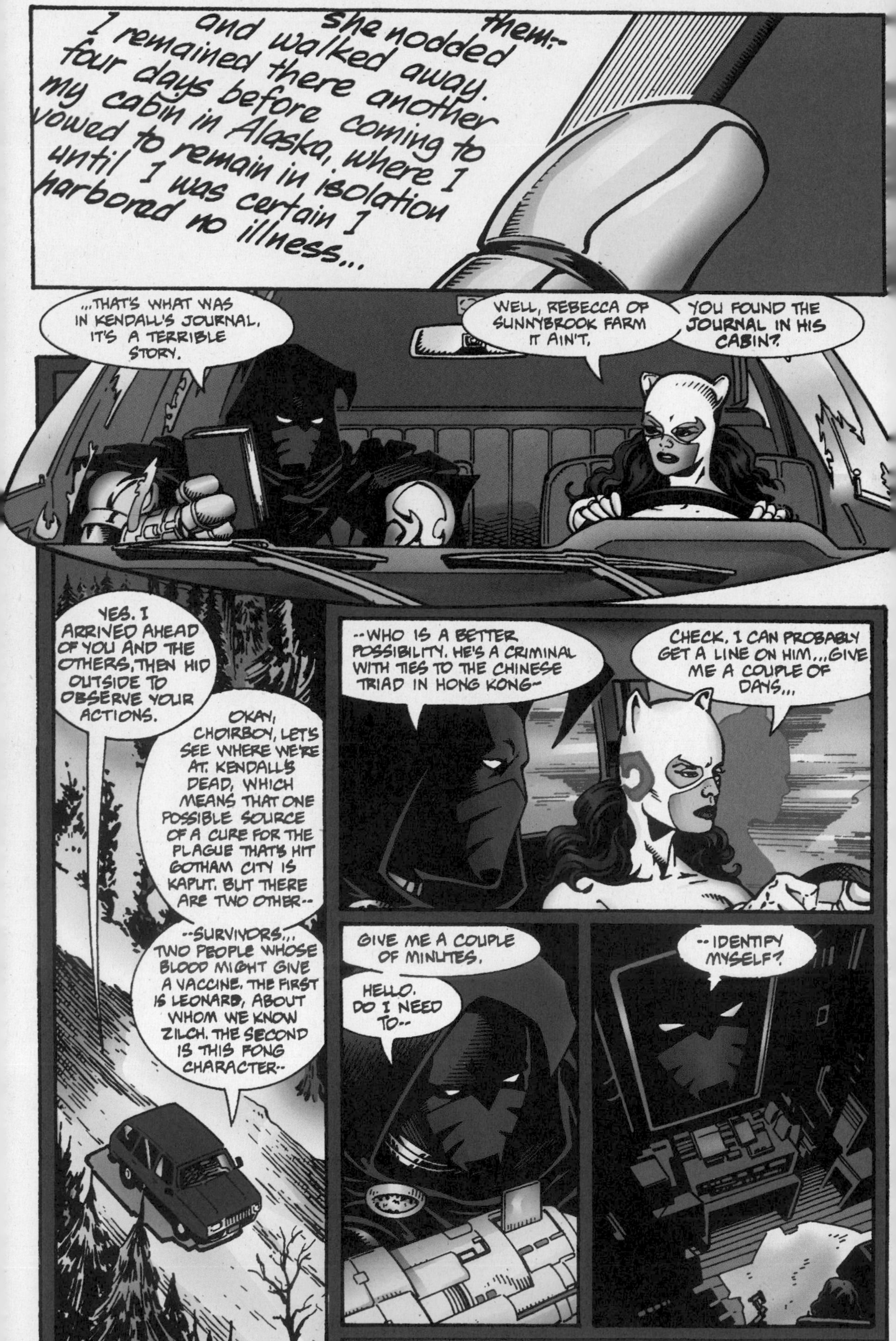
and she nodded them:- walked away.
I remained there another four days before coming to my cabin in Alaska, where I vowed to remain in isolation until I was certain I harbored no illness...
...THAT'S WHAT WAS IN KENDALL'S JOURNAL. IT'S A TERRIBLE STORY.
WELL, REBECCA OF SUNNYBROOK FARM IT AIN'T.
YOU FOUND THE JOURNAL IN HIS CABIN?
YES. I ARRIVED AHEAD OF YOU AND THE OTHERS, THEN HID OUTSIDE TO OBSERVE YOUR ACTIONS.
OKAY, CHOIRBOY, LET'S SEE WHERE WE'RE AT. KENDALL'S DEAD, WHICH MEANS THAT ONE POSSIBLE SOURCE OF A CURE FOR THE PLAGUE THAT'S HIT GOTHAM CITY IS KAPUT. BUT THERE ARE TWO OTHER--
--SURVIVORS... TWO PEOPLE WHOSE BLOOD MIGHT GIVE A VACCINE. THE FIRST IS LEONARD, ABOUT WHOM WE KNOW ZILCH. THE SECOND IS THIS FONG CHARACTER--
--WHO IS A BETTER POSSIBILITY. HE'S A CRIMINAL WITH TIES TO THE CHINESE TRIAD IN HONG KONG--
CHECK. I CAN PROBABLY GET A LINE ON HIM...GIVE ME A COUPLE OF DAYS...
GIVE ME A COUPLE OF MINUTES.
HELLO. DO I NEED TO--
--IDENTIFY MYSELF?

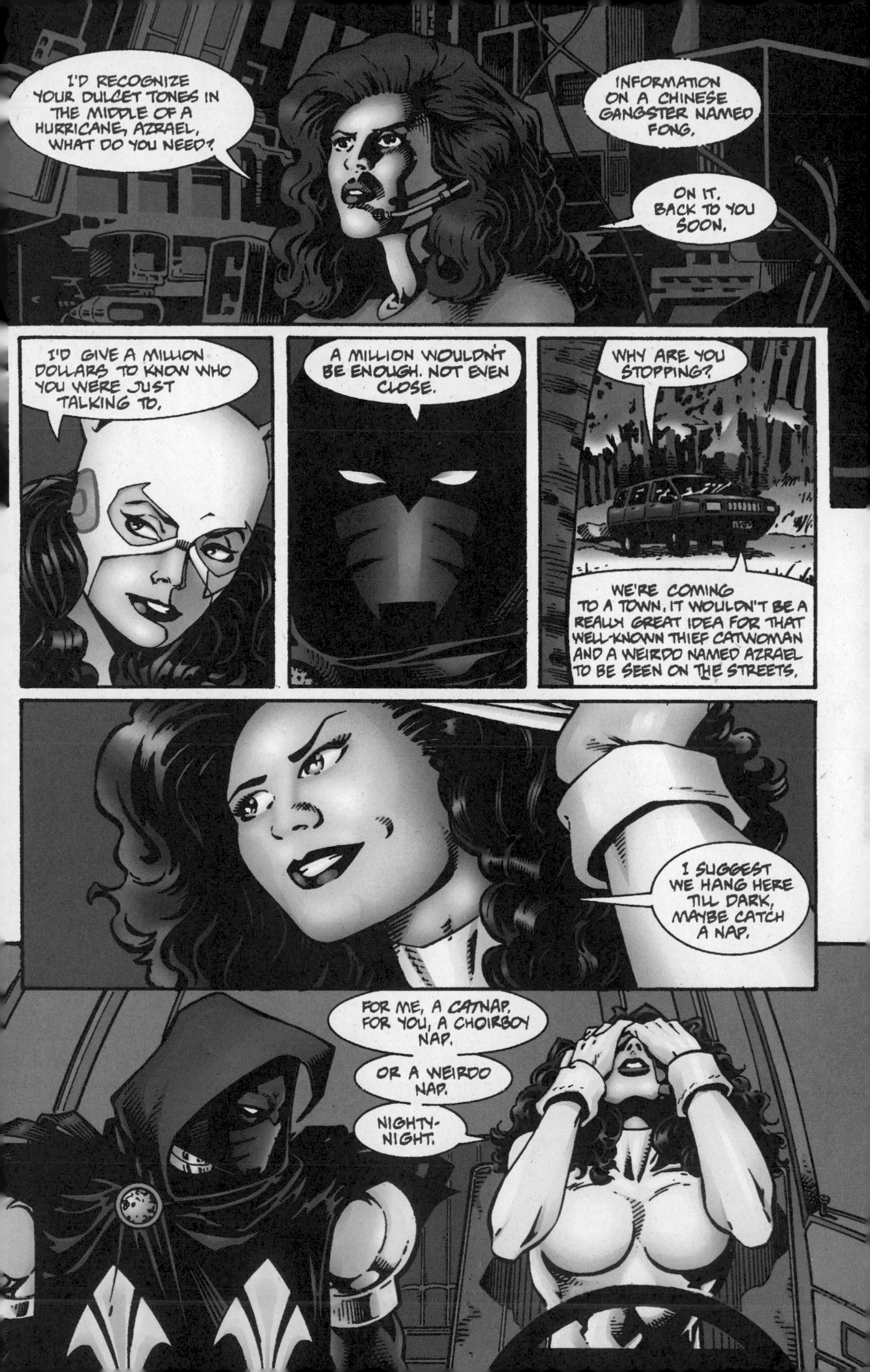
I'D RECOGNIZE YOUR DULCET TONES IN THE MIDDLE OF A HURRICANE, AZRAEL. WHAT DO YOU NEED?
INFORMATION ON A CHINESE GANGSTER NAMED FONG.
ON IT. BACK TO YOU SOON.
I'D GIVE A MILLION DOLLARS TO KNOW WHO YOU WERE JUST TALKING TO.
A MILLION WOULDN'T BE ENOUGH. NOT EVEN CLOSE.
WHY ARE YOU STOPPING?
WE'RE COMING TO A TOWN. IT WOULDN'T BE A REALLY GREAT IDEA FOR THAT WELL-KNOWN THIEF CATWOMAN AND A WEIRDO NAMED AZRAEL TO BE SEEN ON THE STREETS.
I SUGGEST WE HANG HERE TILL DARK, MAYBE CATCH A NAP.
FOR ME, A CATNAP. FOR YOU, A CHOIRBOY NAP.
OR A WEIRDO NAP.
NIGHTY-NIGHT.

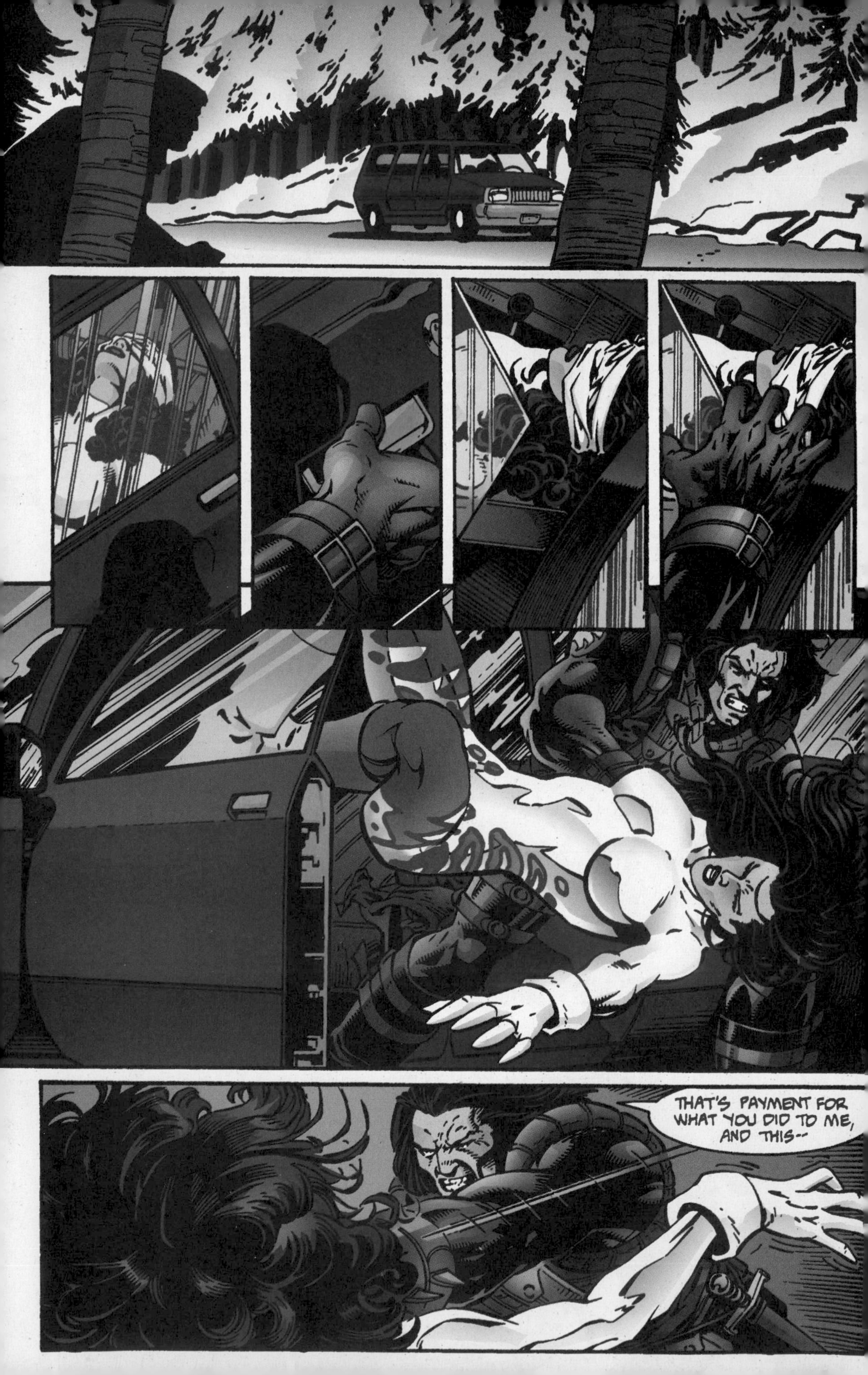
THAT'S PAYMENT FOR WHAT YOU DID TO ME, AND THIS--

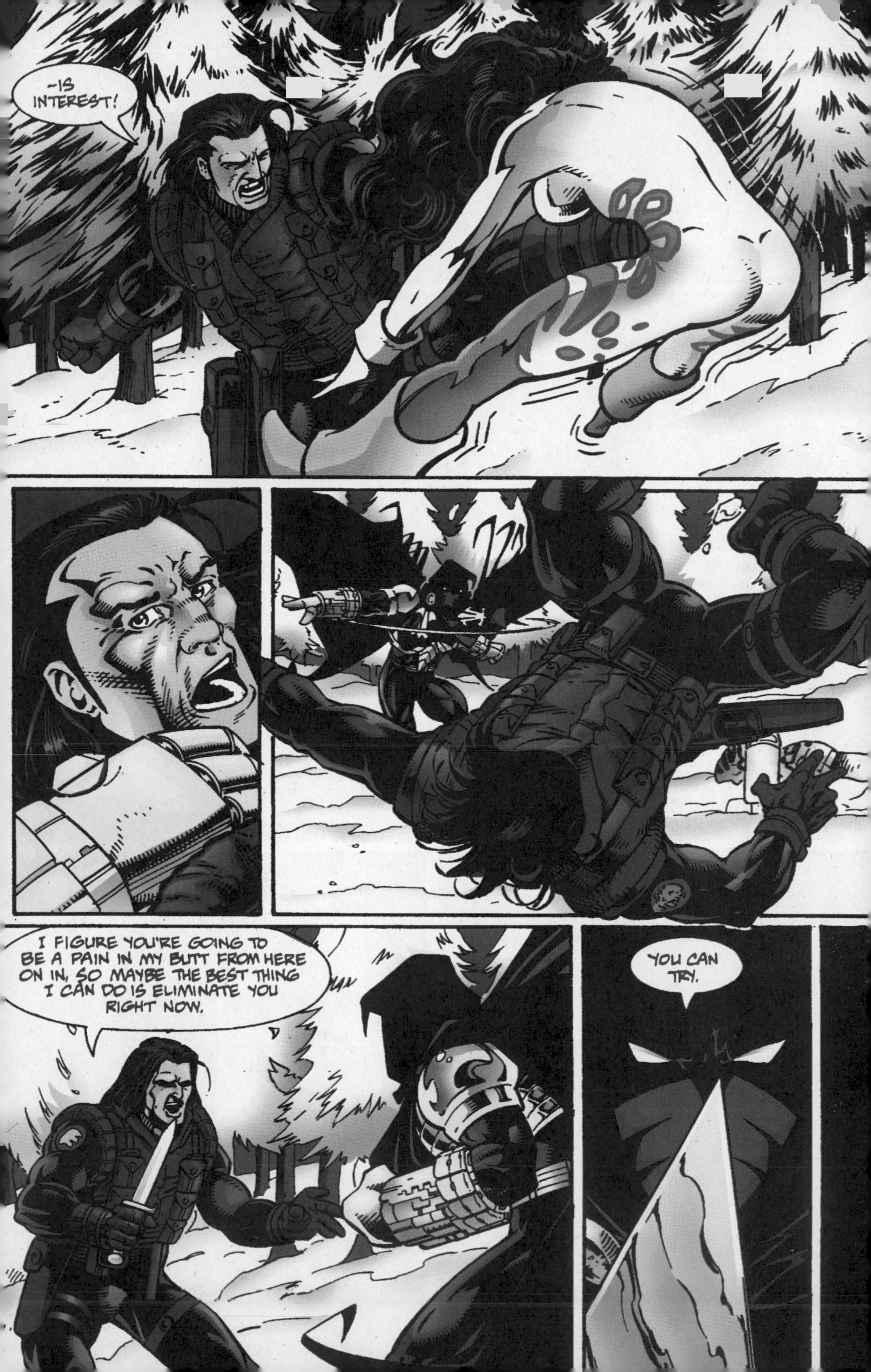
-IS INTEREST!
I FIGURE YOU'RE GOING TO BE A PAIN IN MY BUTT FROM HERE ON IN, SO MAYBE THE BEST THING I CAN DO IS ELIMINATE YOU RIGHT NOW.
YOU CAN TRY.

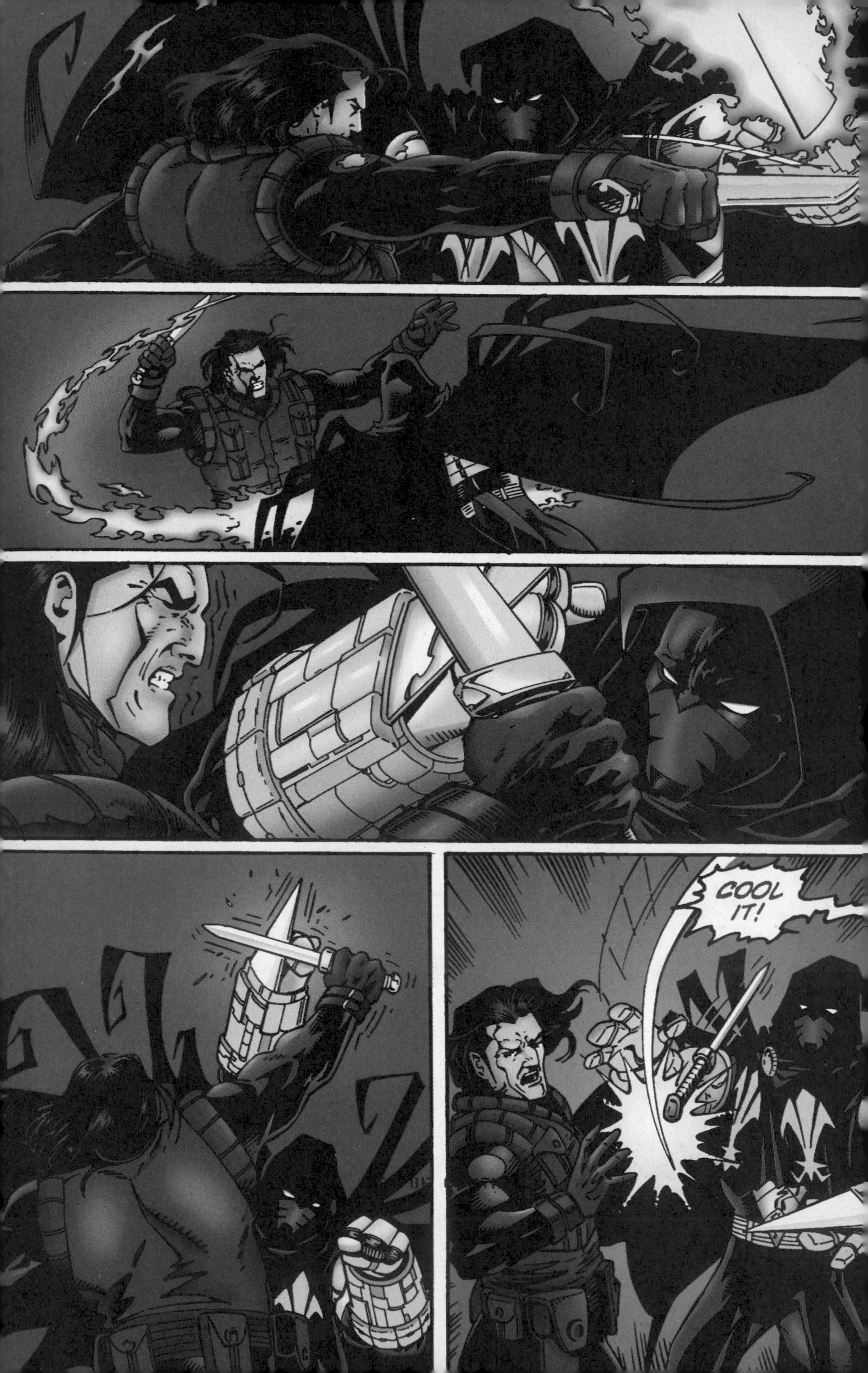
COOL IT!

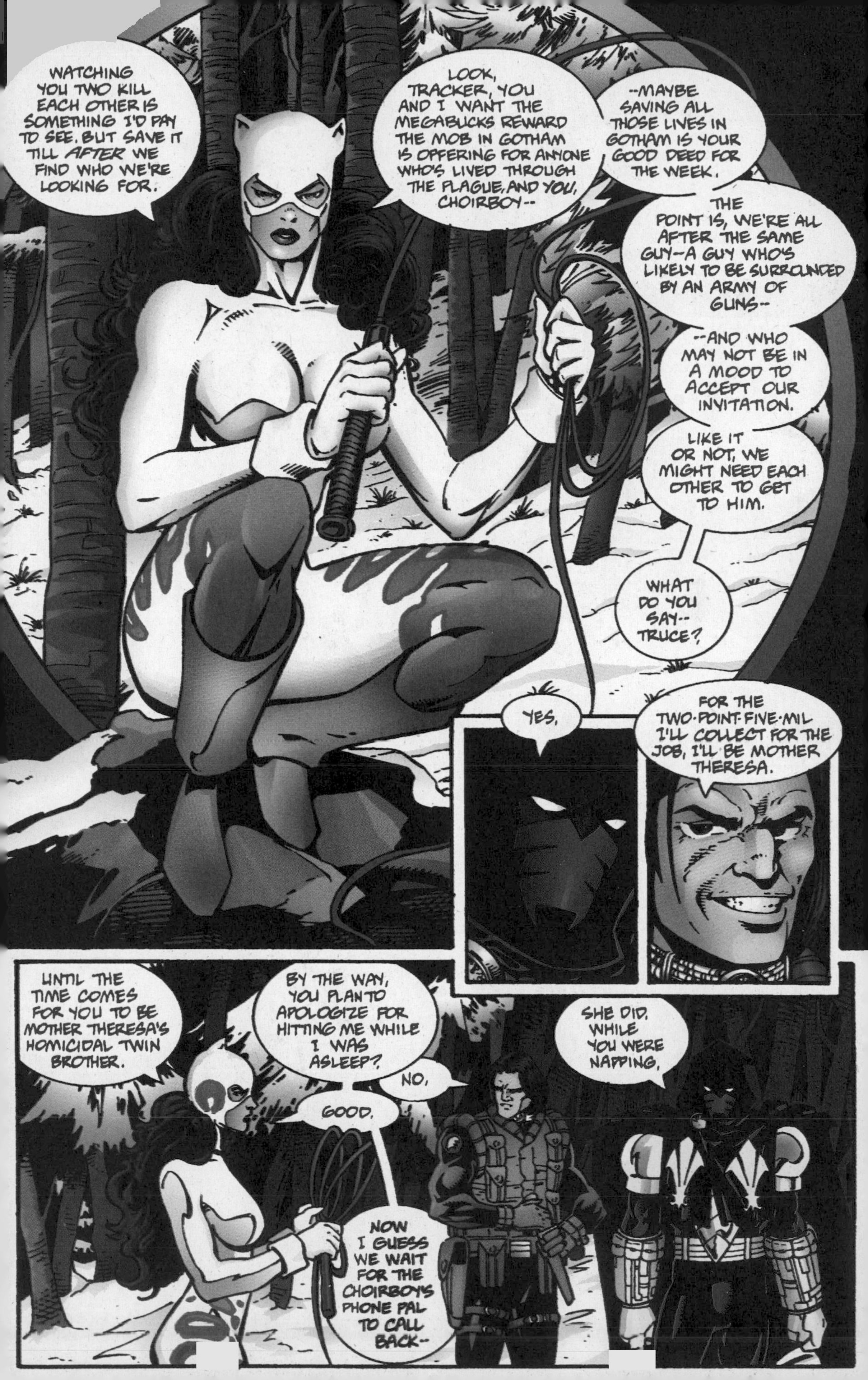
WATCHING YOU TWO KILL EACH OTHER IS SOMETHING I'D PAY TO SEE. BUT SAVE IT TILL *AFTER* WE FIND WHO WE'RE LOOKING FOR.
LOOK, TRACKER, YOU AND I WANT THE MEGABUCKS REWARD THE MOB IN GOTHAM IS OFFERING FOR ANYONE WHO'S LIVED THROUGH THE PLAGUE. AND YOU, CHOIRBOY--
--MAYBE SAVING ALL THOSE LIVES IN GOTHAM IS YOUR GOOD DEED FOR THE WEEK.
THE POINT IS, WE'RE ALL AFTER THE SAME GUY--A GUY WHO'S LIKELY TO BE SURROUNDED BY AN ARMY OF GUNS--
--AND WHO MAY NOT BE IN A MOOD TO ACCEPT OUR INVITATION.
LIKE IT OR NOT, WE MIGHT NEED EACH OTHER TO GET TO HIM.
WHAT DO YOU SAY-- TRUCE?
YES.
FOR THE TWO-POINT-FIVE-MIL I'LL COLLECT FOR THE JOB, I'LL BE MOTHER THERESA.
UNTIL THE TIME COMES FOR YOU TO BE MOTHER THERESA'S HOMICIDAL TWIN BROTHER.
BY THE WAY, YOU PLAN TO APOLOGIZE FOR HITTING ME WHILE I WAS ASLEEP?
NO.
GOOD.
SHE DID. WHILE YOU WERE NAPPING.
NOW I GUESS WE WAIT FOR THE CHOIRBOY'S PHONE PAL TO CALL BACK--

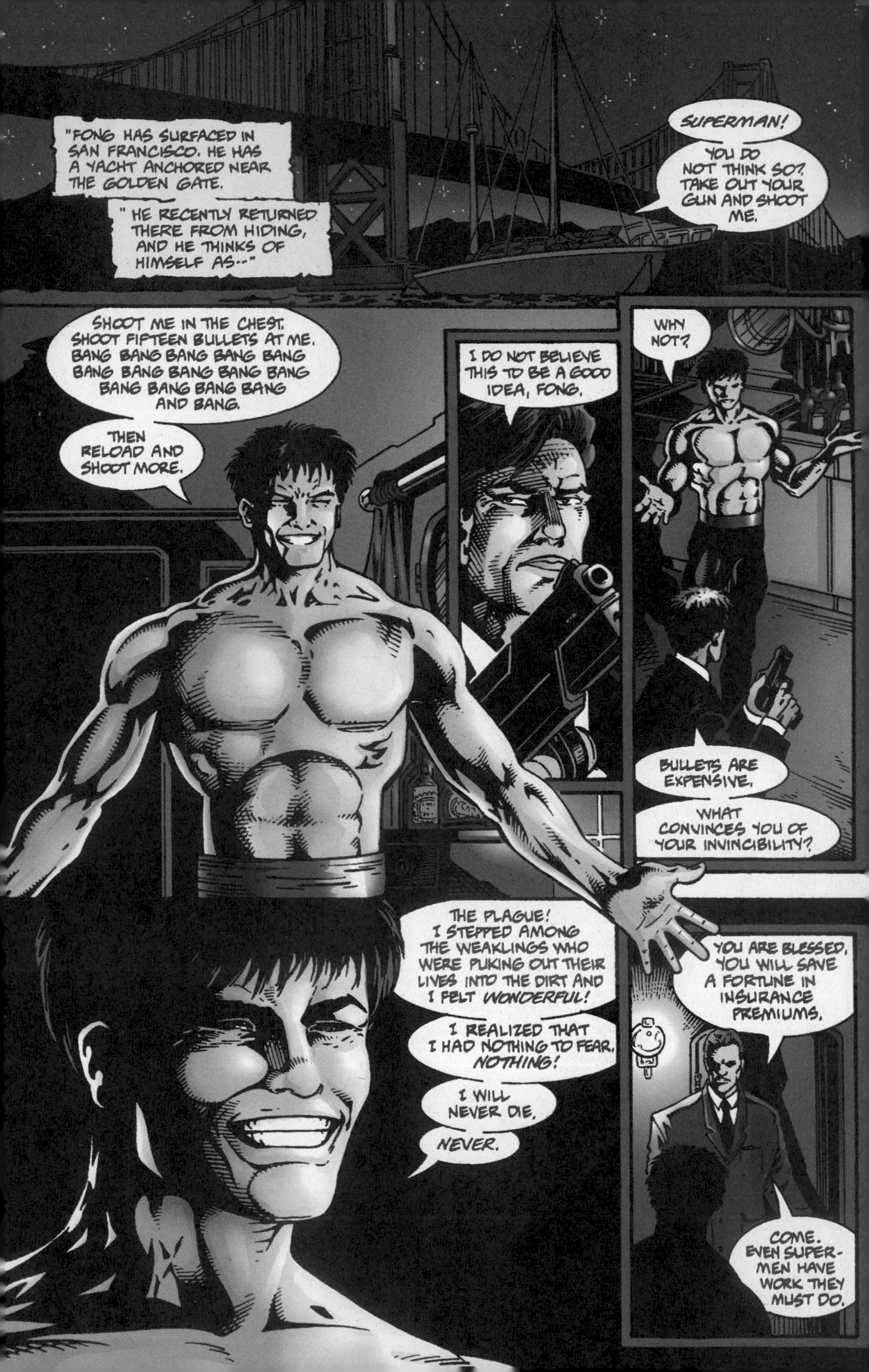
"FONG HAS SURFACED IN SAN FRANCISCO. HE HAS A YACHT ANCHORED NEAR THE GOLDEN GATE.
" HE RECENTLY RETURNED THERE FROM HIDING, AND HE THINKS OF HIMSELF AS--"
SUPERMAN!
YOU DO NOT THINK SO? TAKE OUT YOUR GUN AND SHOOT ME.
SHOOT ME IN THE CHEST. SHOOT FIFTEEN BULLETS AT ME. BANG BANG BANG BANG BANG BANG BANG BANG BANG BANG BANG BANG BANG BANG AND BANG.
THEN RELOAD AND SHOOT MORE.
I DO NOT BELIEVE THIS TO BE A GOOD IDEA, FONG.
WHY NOT?
BULLETS ARE EXPENSIVE.
WHAT CONVINCES YOU OF YOUR INVINCIBILITY?
THE PLAGUE! I STEPPED AMONG THE WEAKLINGS WHO WERE PUKING OUT THEIR LIVES INTO THE DIRT AND I FELT WONDERFUL!
I REALIZED THAT I HAD NOTHING TO FEAR. NOTHING!
I WILL NEVER DIE.
NEVER.
YOU ARE BLESSED. YOU WILL SAVE A FORTUNE IN INSURANCE PREMIUMS.
COME. EVEN SUPER-MEN HAVE WORK THEY MUST DO.

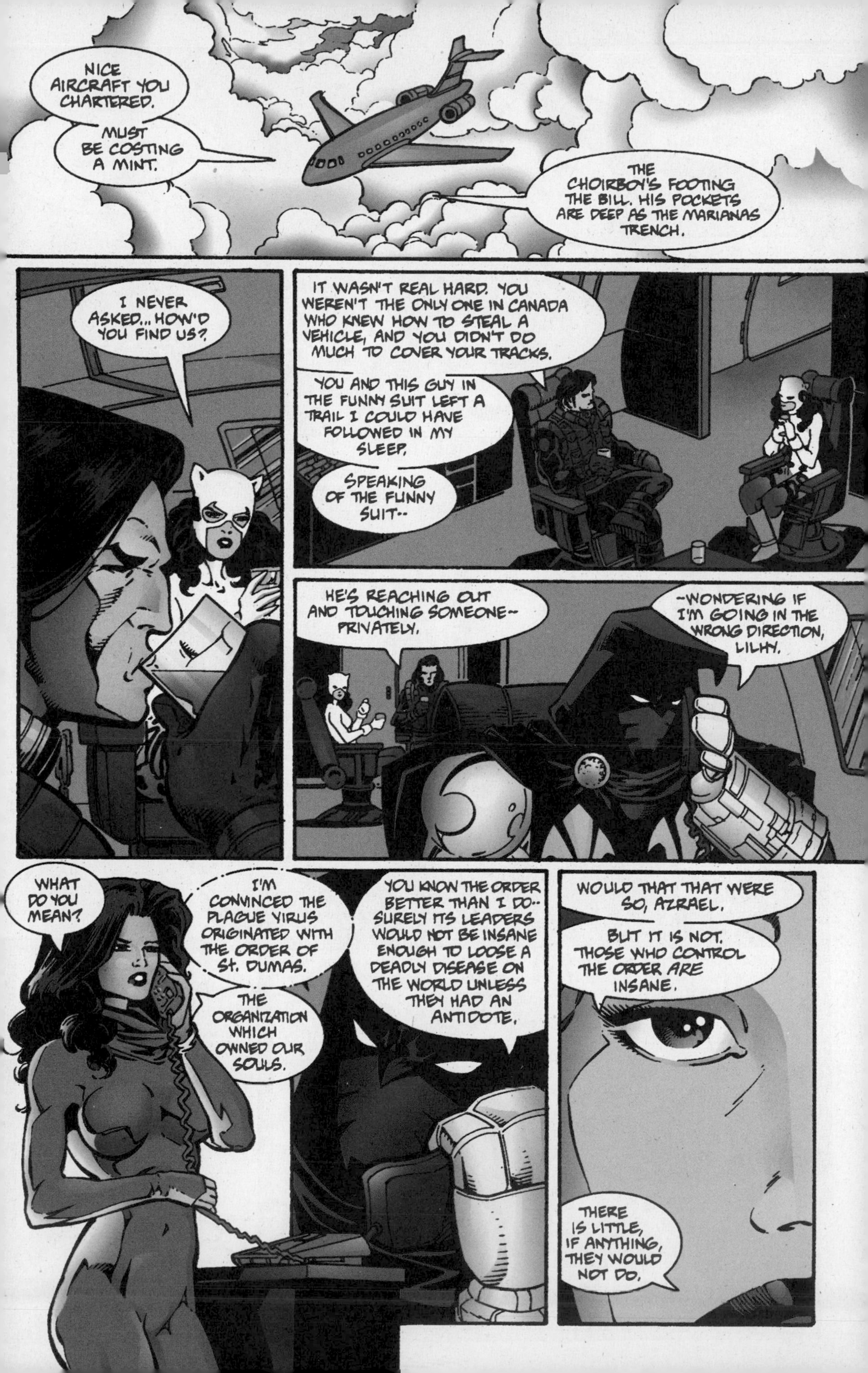
NICE AIRCRAFT YOU CHARTERED.
MUST BE COSTING A MINT.
THE CHOIRBOY'S FOOTING THE BILL. HIS POCKETS ARE DEEP AS THE MARIANAS TRENCH.
I NEVER ASKED... HOW'D YOU FIND US?
IT WASN'T REAL HARD. YOU WEREN'T THE ONLY ONE IN CANADA WHO KNEW HOW TO STEAL A VEHICLE, AND YOU DIDN'T DO MUCH TO COVER YOUR TRACKS.
YOU AND THIS GUY IN THE FUNNY SUIT LEFT A TRAIL I COULD HAVE FOLLOWED IN MY SLEEP.
SPEAKING OF THE FUNNY SUIT--
HE'S REACHING OUT AND TOUCHING SOMEONE-- PRIVATELY.
--WONDERING IF I'M GOING IN THE WRONG DIRECTION, LILHY.
WHAT DO YOU MEAN?
I'M CONVINCED THE PLAGUE VIRUS ORIGINATED WITH THE ORDER OF St. DUMAS.
THE ORGANIZATION WHICH OWNED OUR SOULS.
YOU KNOW THE ORDER BETTER THAN I DO-- SURELY ITS LEADERS WOULD NOT BE INSANE ENOUGH TO LOOSE A DEADLY DISEASE ON THE WORLD UNLESS THEY HAD AN ANTIDOTE.
WOULD THAT THAT WERE SO, AZRAEL.
BUT IT IS NOT. THOSE WHO CONTROL THE ORDER ARE INSANE.
THERE IS LITTLE, IF ANYTHING, THEY WOULD NOT DO.

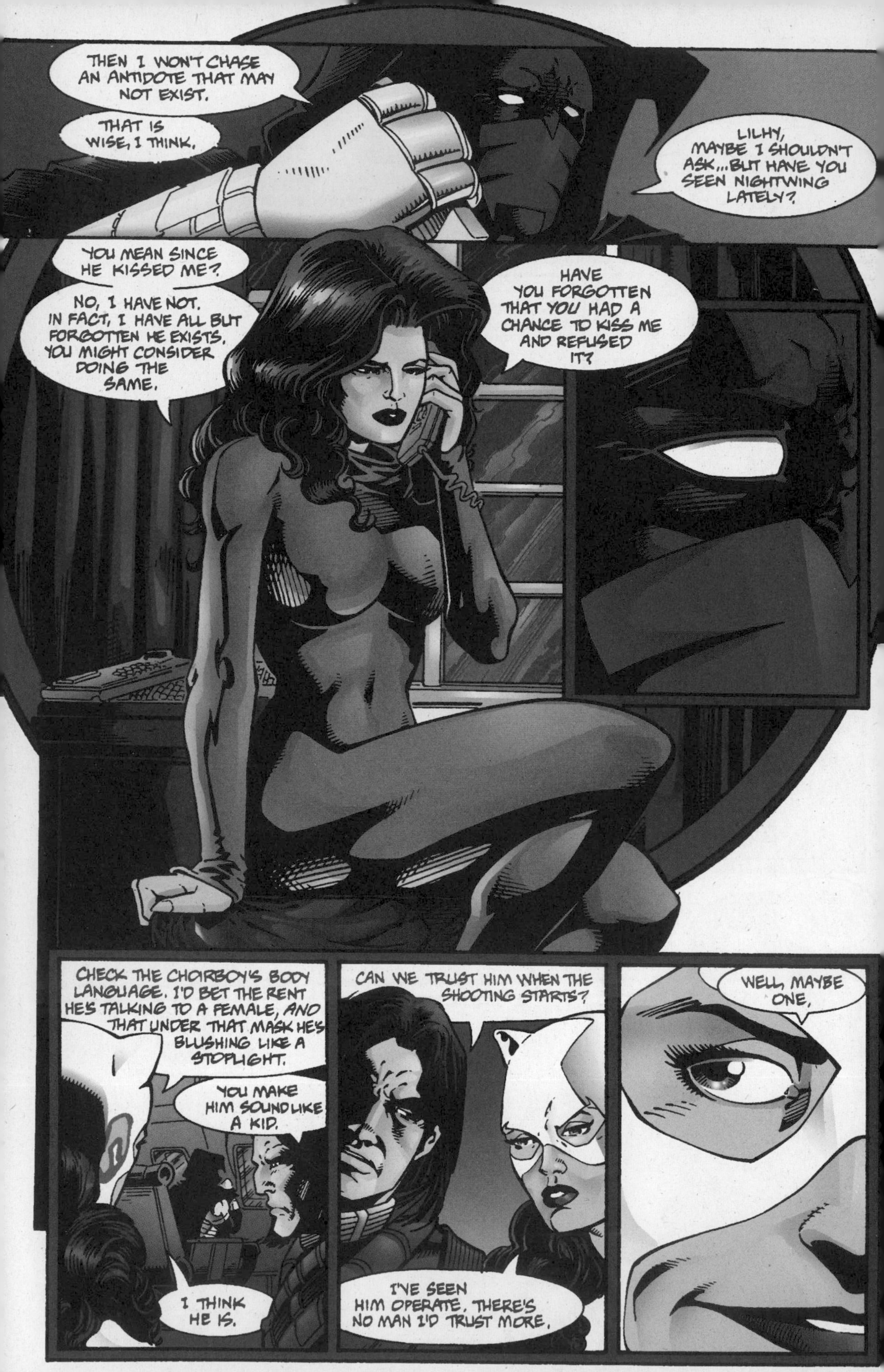
THEN I WON'T CHASE AN ANTIDOTE THAT MAY NOT EXIST.
THAT IS WISE, I THINK.
LILHY, MAYBE I SHOULDN'T ASK...BUT HAVE YOU SEEN NIGHTWING LATELY?
YOU MEAN SINCE HE KISSED ME?
NO, I HAVE NOT. IN FACT, I HAVE ALL BUT FORGOTTEN HE EXISTS. YOU MIGHT CONSIDER DOING THE SAME.
HAVE YOU FORGOTTEN THAT YOU HAD A CHANCE TO KISS ME AND REFUSED IT?
CHECK THE CHOIRBOY'S BODY LANGUAGE. I'D BET THE RENT HE'S TALKING TO A FEMALE, AND THAT UNDER THAT MASK HE'S BLUSHING LIKE A STOPLIGHT.
YOU MAKE HIM SOUND LIKE A KID.
I THINK HE IS.
CAN WE TRUST HIM WHEN THE SHOOTING STARTS?
I'VE SEEN HIM OPERATE. THERE'S NO MAN I'D TRUST MORE.
WELL, MAYBE ONE.

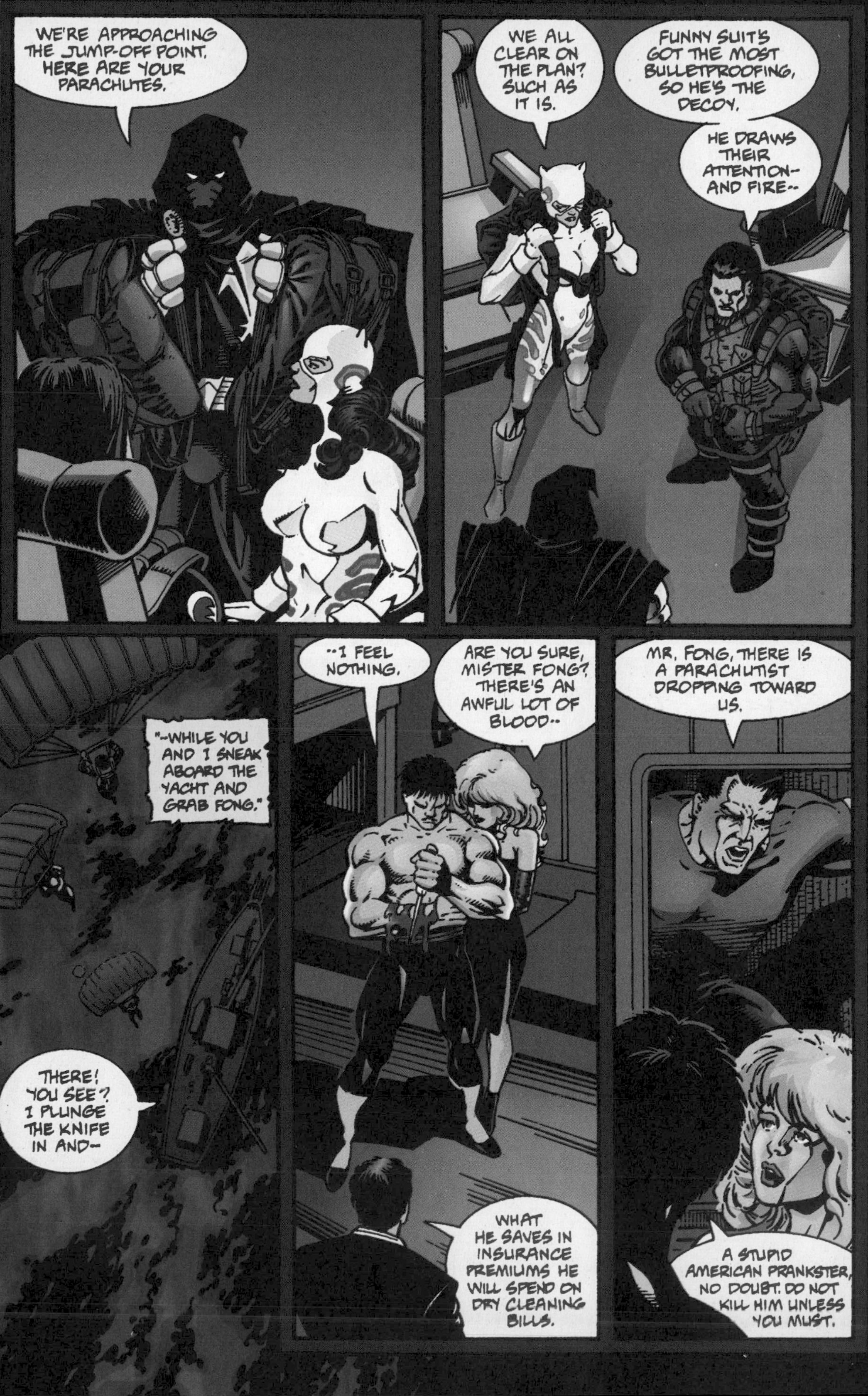
WE'RE APPROACHING THE JUMP-OFF POINT. HERE ARE YOUR PARACHUTES.
WE ALL CLEAR ON THE PLAN? SUCH AS IT IS.
FUNNY SUIT'S GOT THE MOST BULLETPROOFING, SO HE'S THE DECOY.
HE DRAWS THEIR ATTENTION-- AND FIRE--
"--WHILE YOU AND I SNEAK ABOARD THE YACHT AND GRAB FONG."
THERE! YOU SEE? I PLUNGE THE KNIFE IN AND--
--I FEEL NOTHING.
ARE YOU SURE, MISTER FONG? THERE'S AN AWFUL LOT OF BLOOD--
WHAT HE SAVES IN INSURANCE PREMIUMS HE WILL SPEND ON DRY CLEANING BILLS.
MR. FONG, THERE IS A PARACHUTIST DROPPING TOWARD US.
A STUPID AMERICAN PRANKSTER, NO DOUBT. DO NOT KILL HIM UNLESS YOU MUST.

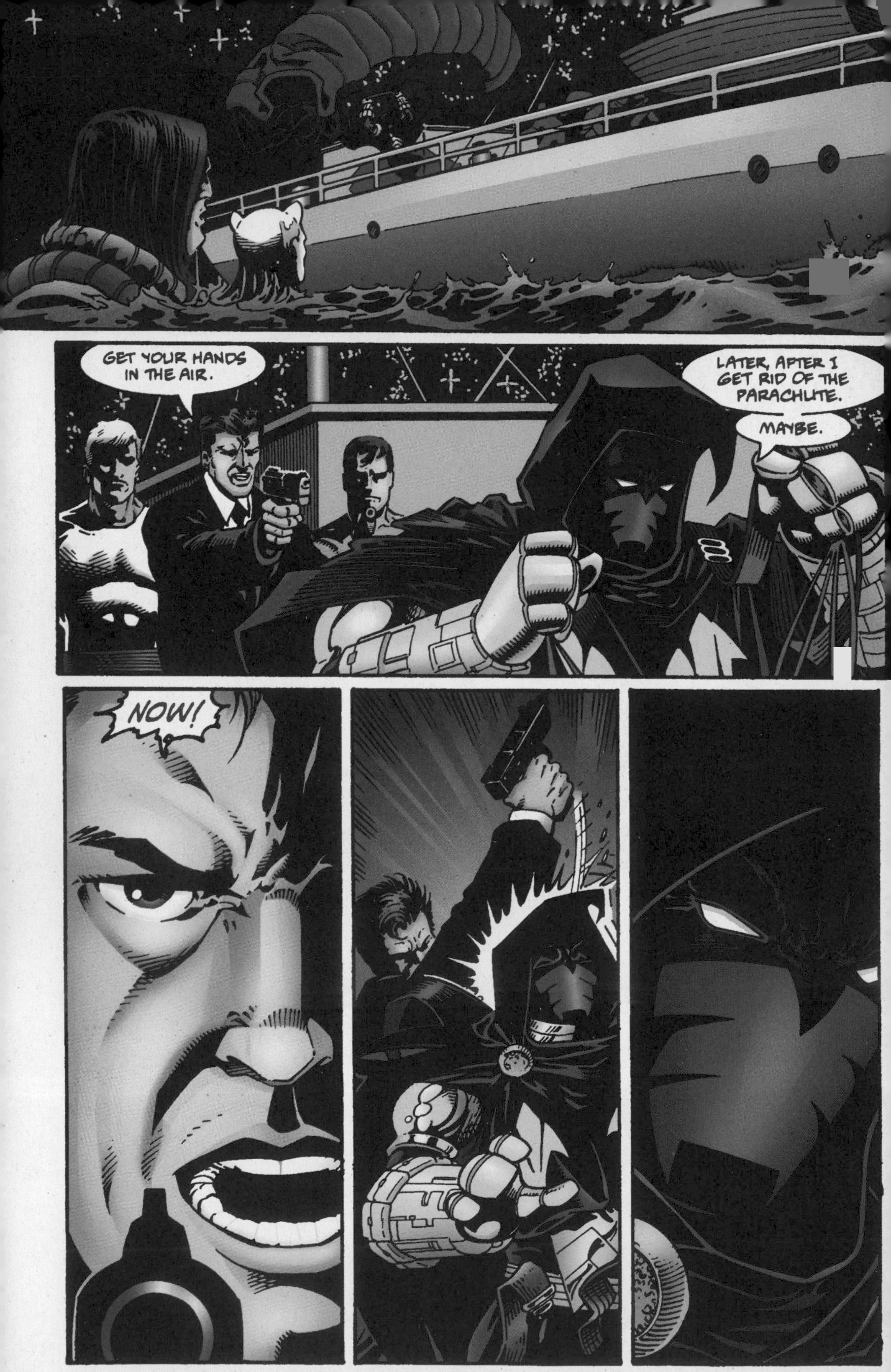
GET YOUR HANDS IN THE AIR.
LATER, AFTER I GET RID OF THE PARACHUTE.
MAYBE.
NOW!

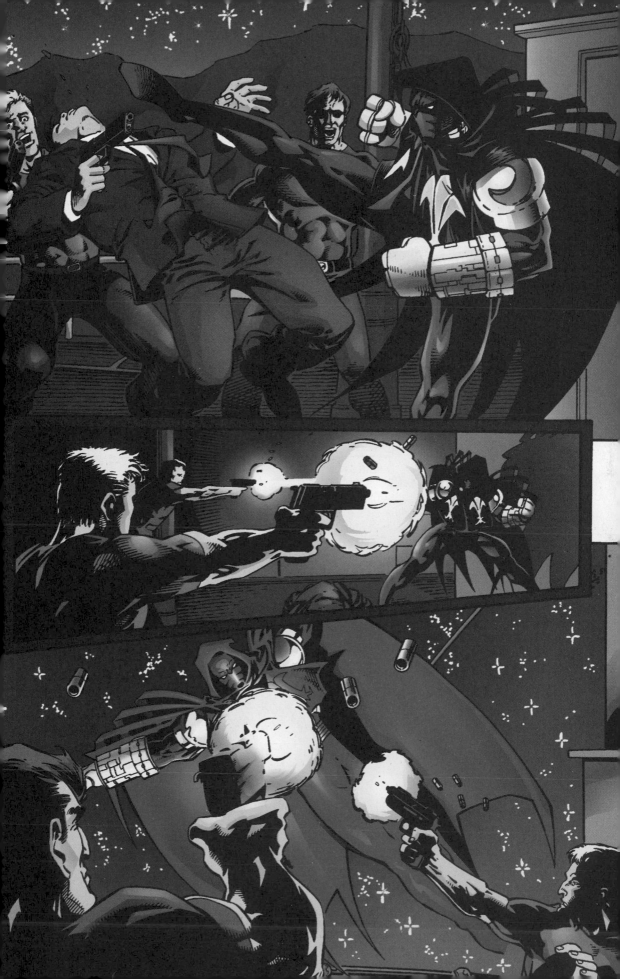

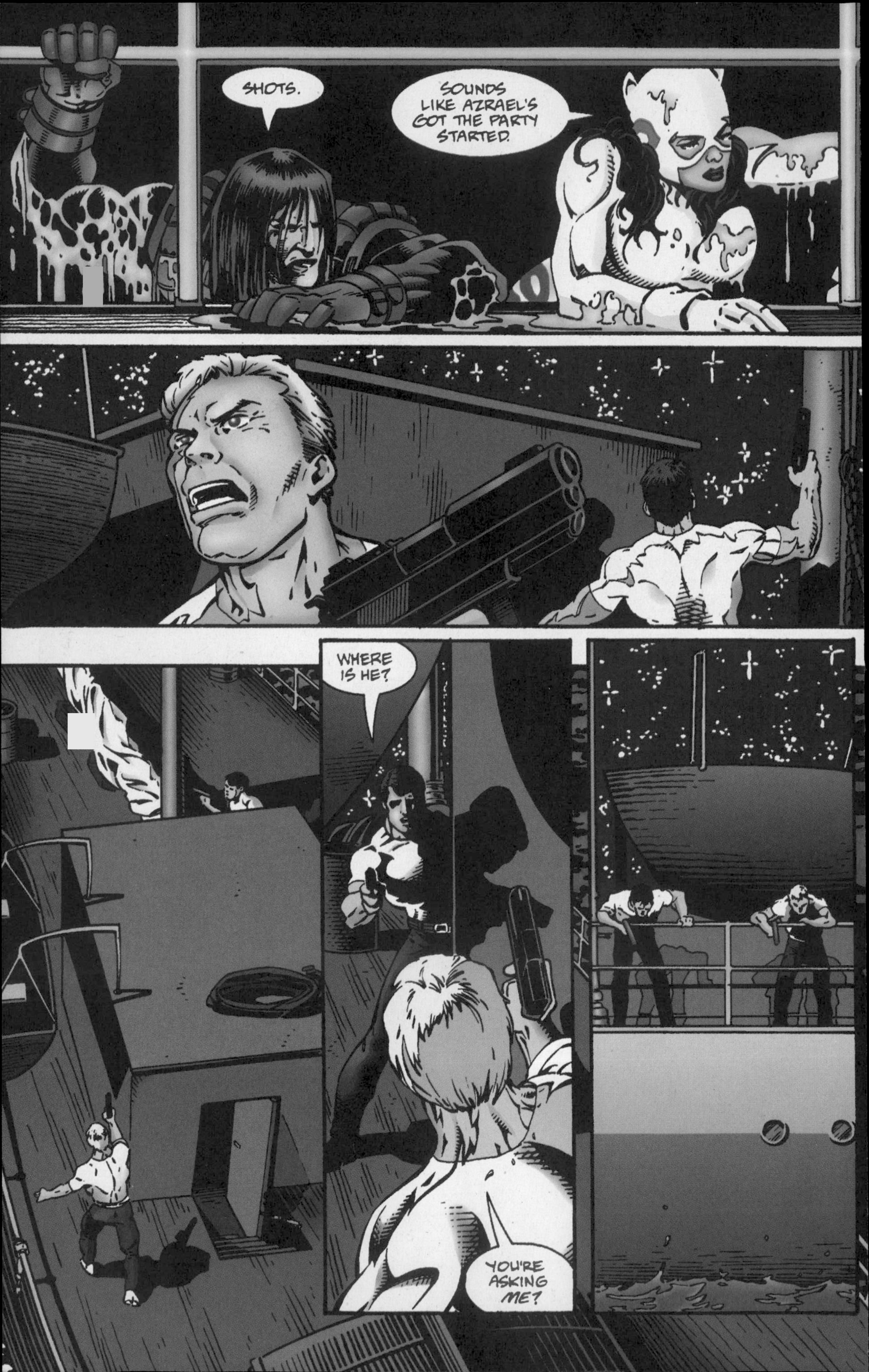
SHOTS.
SOUNDS LIKE AZRAEL'S GOT THE PARTY STARTED.
WHERE IS HE?
YOU'RE ASKING ME?

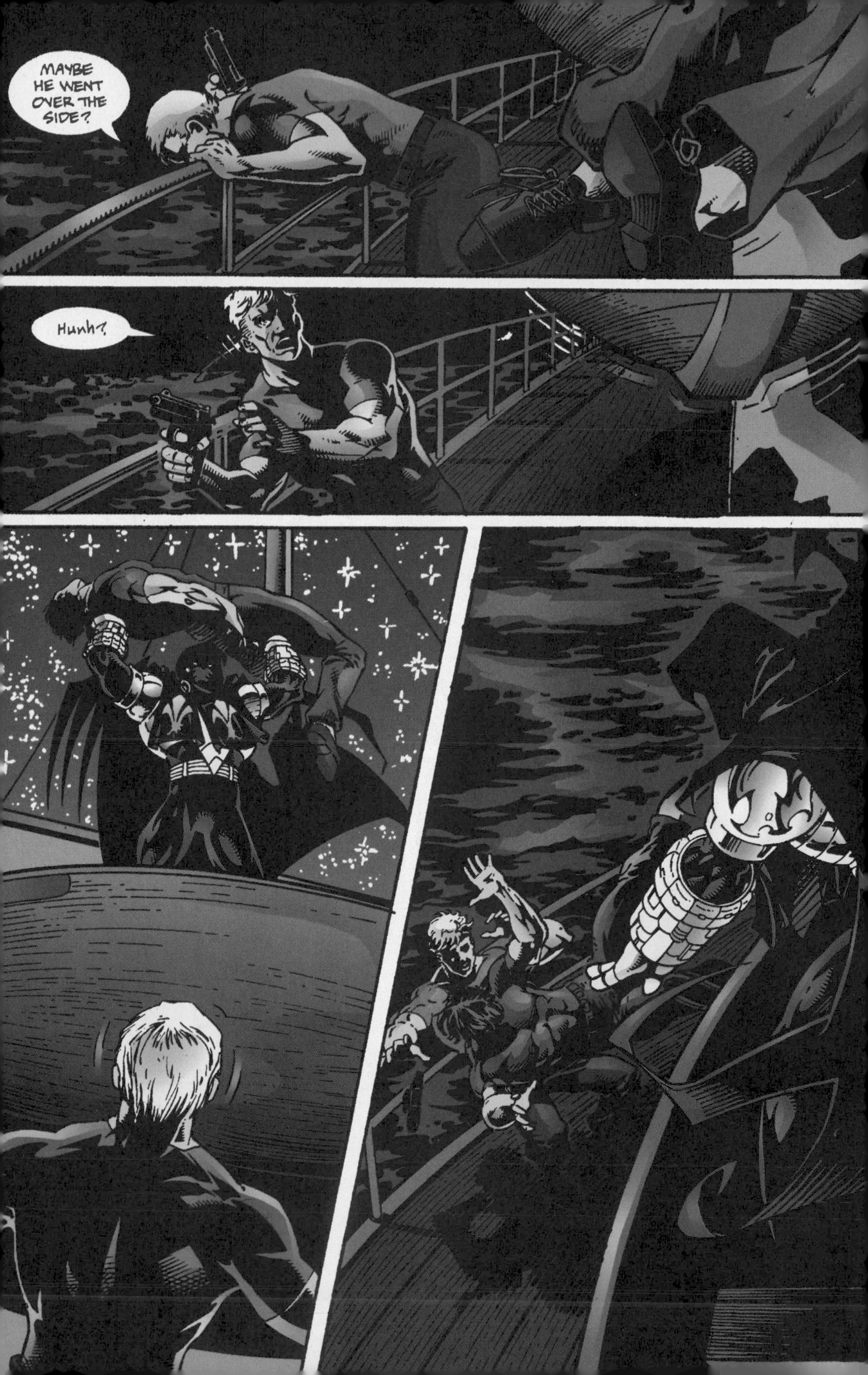
MAYBE HE WENT OVER THE SIDE?
Hunh?

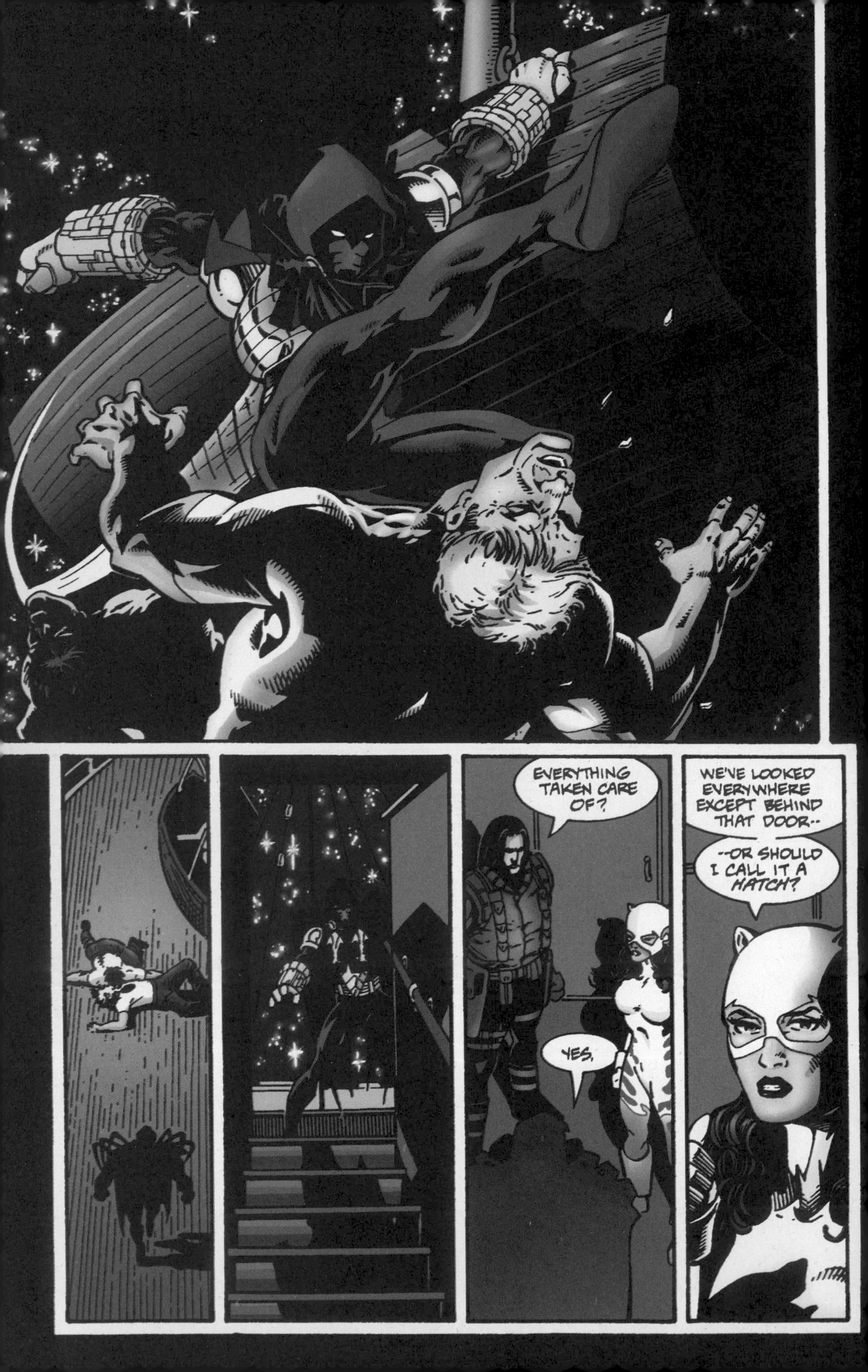
EVERYTHING TAKEN CARE OF?
YES.
WE'VE LOOKED EVERYWHERE EXCEPT BEHIND THAT DOOR--
--OR SHOULD I CALL IT A HATCH?

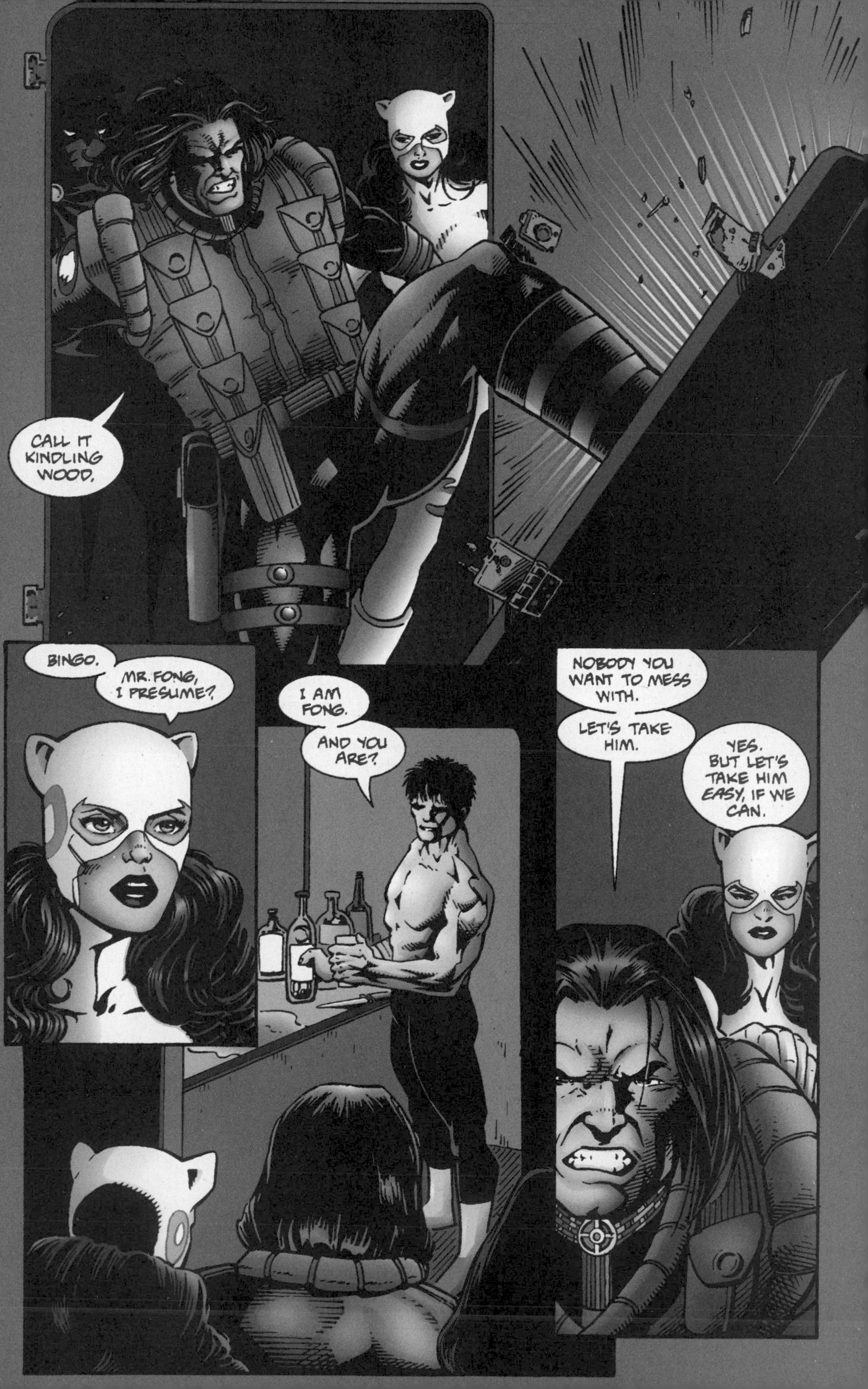
CALL IT KINDLING WOOD.
BINGO.
MR. FONG, I PRESUME?
I AM FONG.
AND YOU ARE?
NOBODY YOU WANT TO MESS WITH.
LET'S TAKE HIM.
YES. BUT LET'S TAKE HIM EASY, IF WE CAN.

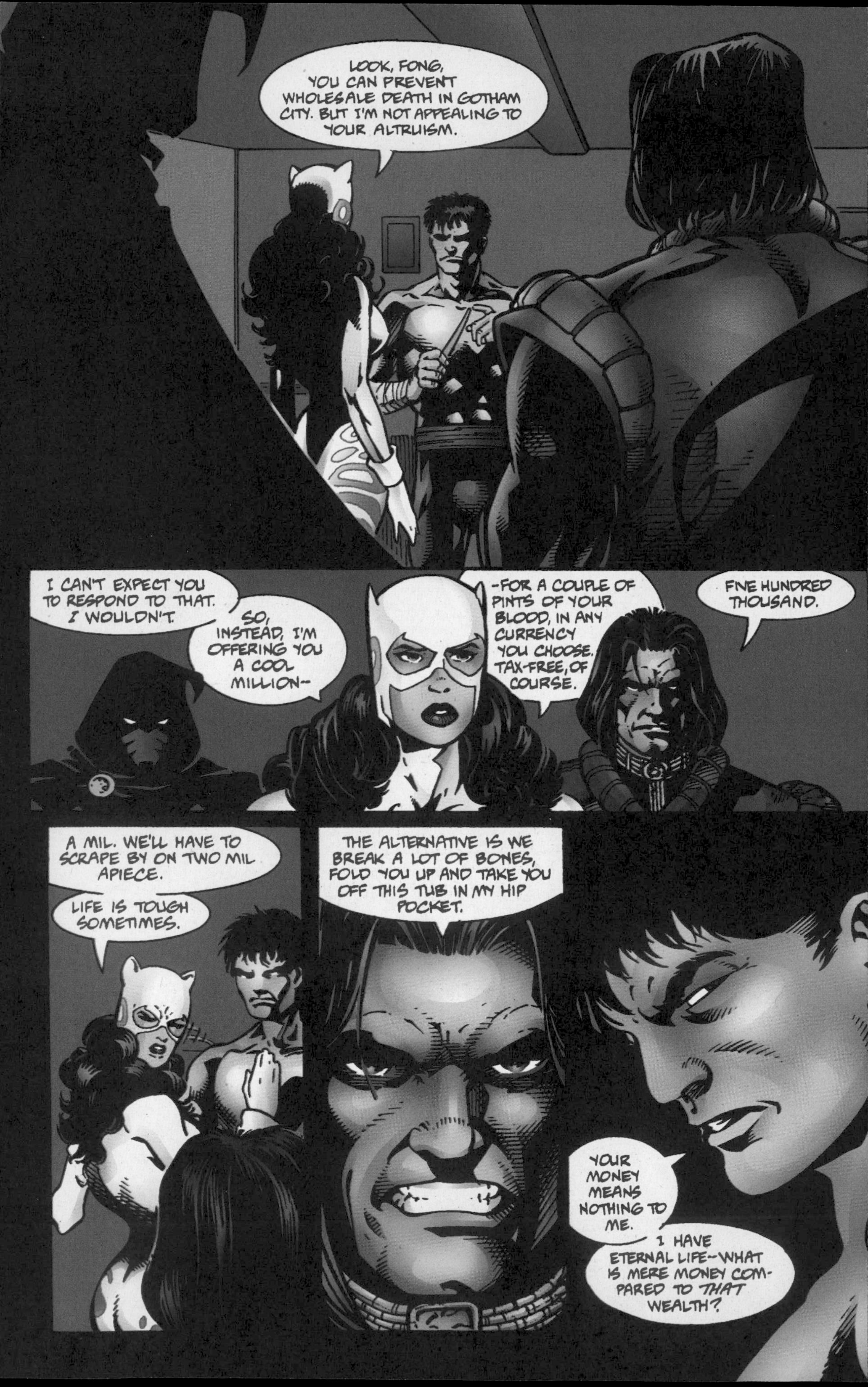
LOOK, FONG, YOU CAN PREVENT WHOLESALE DEATH IN GOTHAM CITY. BUT I'M NOT APPEALING TO YOUR ALTRUISM.
I CAN'T EXPECT YOU TO RESPOND TO THAT. I WOULDN'T.
SO, INSTEAD, I'M OFFERING YOU A COOL MILLION--
-FOR A COUPLE OF PINTS OF YOUR BLOOD, IN ANY CURRENCY YOU CHOOSE. TAX-FREE, OF COURSE.
FIVE HUNDRED THOUSAND.
A MIL. WE'LL HAVE TO SCRAPE BY ON TWO MIL APIECE.
LIFE IS TOUGH SOMETIMES.
THE ALTERNATIVE IS WE BREAK A LOT OF BONES, FOLD YOU UP AND TAKE YOU OFF THIS TUB IN MY HIP POCKET.
YOUR MONEY MEANS NOTHING TO ME.
I HAVE ETERNAL LIFE--WHAT IS MERE MONEY COMPARED TO THAT WEALTH?

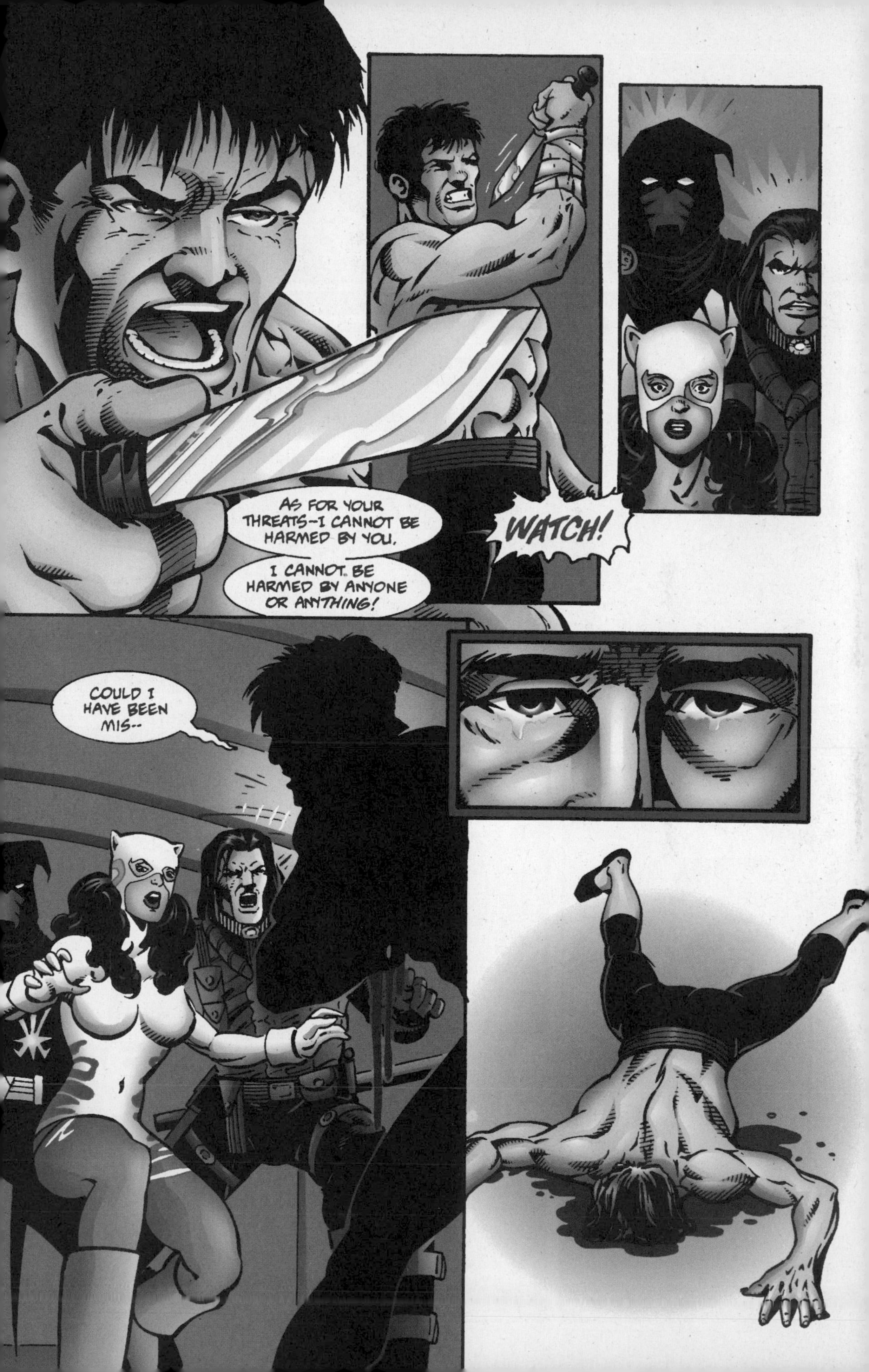
AS FOR YOUR THREATS--I CANNOT BE HARMED BY YOU.
I CANNOT BE HARMED BY ANYONE OR ANYTHING!
WATCH!
COULD I HAVE BEEN MIS--

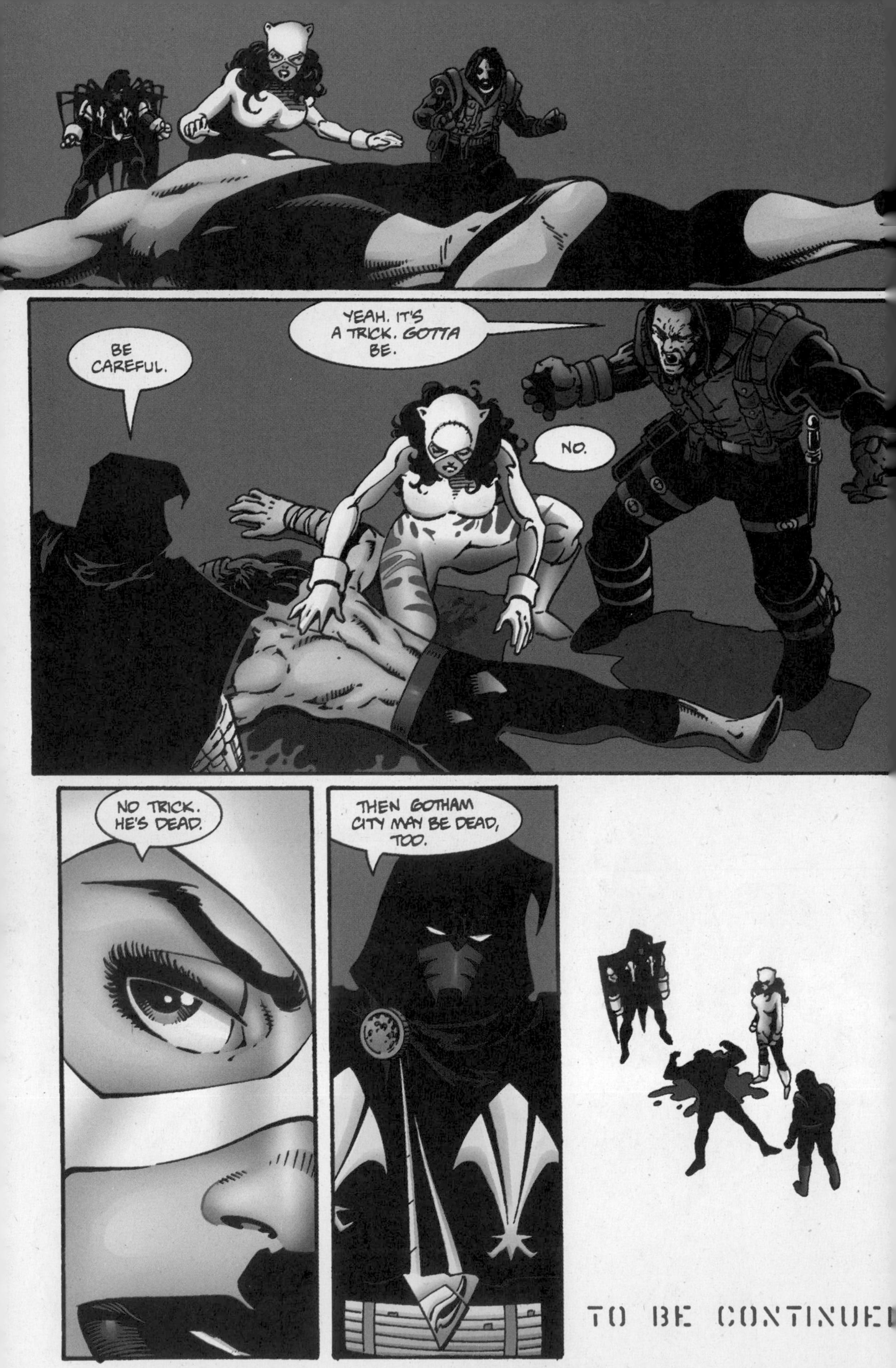
BE CAREFUL.
YEAH. IT'S A TRICK. GOTTA BE.
NO.
NO TRICK. HE'S DEAD.
THEN GOTHAM CITY MAY BE DEAD, TOO.

TO BE CONTINUED

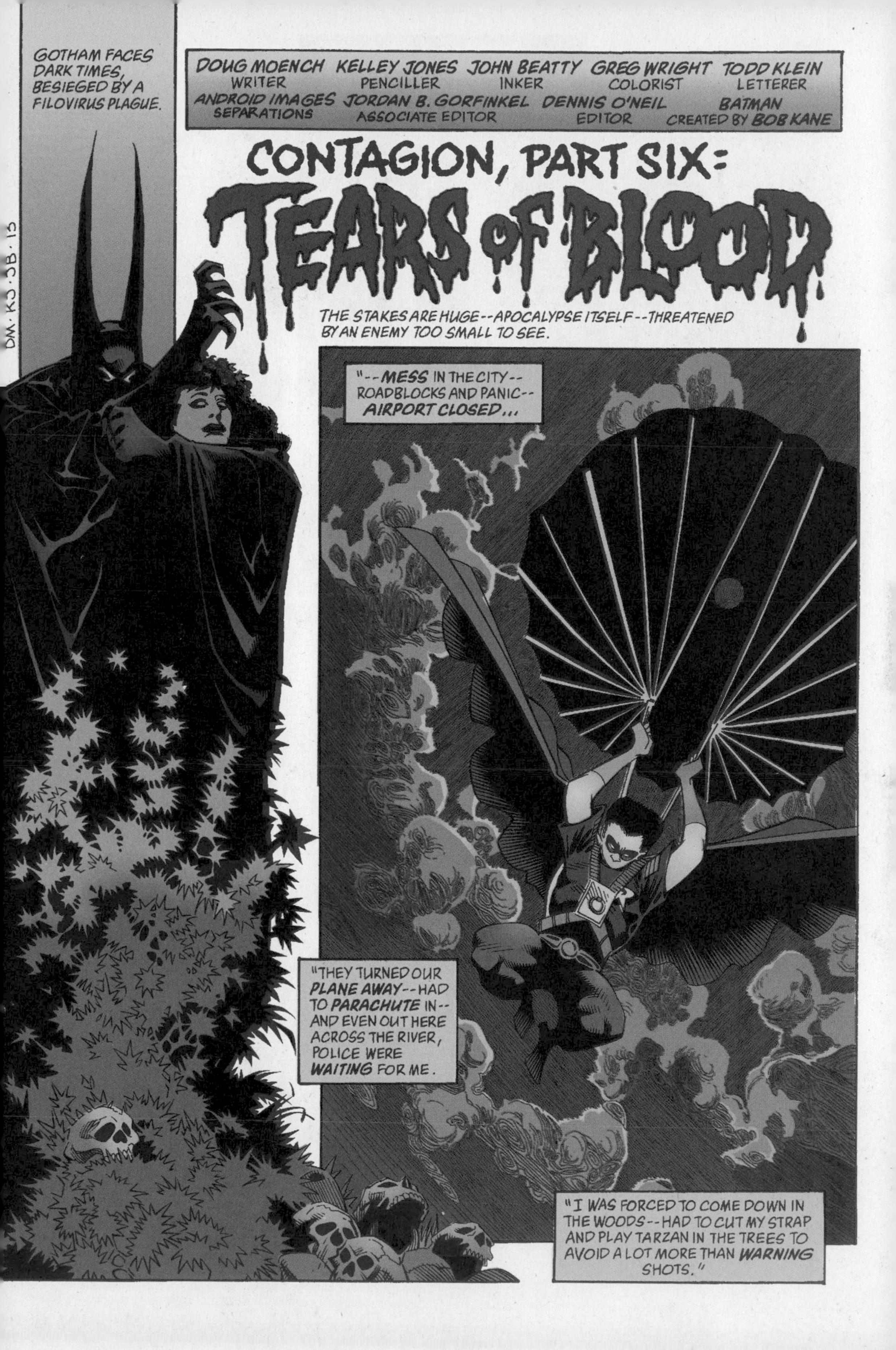

GOTHAM FACES DARK TIMES, BESIEGED BY A FILOVIRUS PLAGUE.
DOUG MOENCH WRITER KELLEY JONES PENCILLER JOHN BEATTY INKER GREG WRIGHT COLORIST TODD KLEIN LETTERER
ANDROID IMAGES SEPARATIONS JORDAN B. GORFINKEL ASSOCIATE EDITOR DENNIS O'NEIL EDITOR BATMAN CREATED BY BOB KANE
CONTAGION, PART SIX:
TEARS OF BLOOD
THE STAKES ARE HUGE--APOCALYPSE ITSELF--THREATENED BY AN ENEMY TOO SMALL TO SEE.
"--MESS IN THE CITY--ROADBLOCKS AND PANIC--AIRPORT CLOSED...
"THEY TURNED OUR PLANE AWAY--HAD TO PARACHUTE IN--AND EVEN OUT HERE ACROSS THE RIVER, POLICE WERE WAITING FOR ME.
"I WAS FORCED TO COME DOWN IN THE WOODS--HAD TO CUT MY STRAP AND PLAY TARZAN IN THE TREES TO AVOID A LOT MORE THAN WARNING SHOTS."
DM·KJ·JB·15

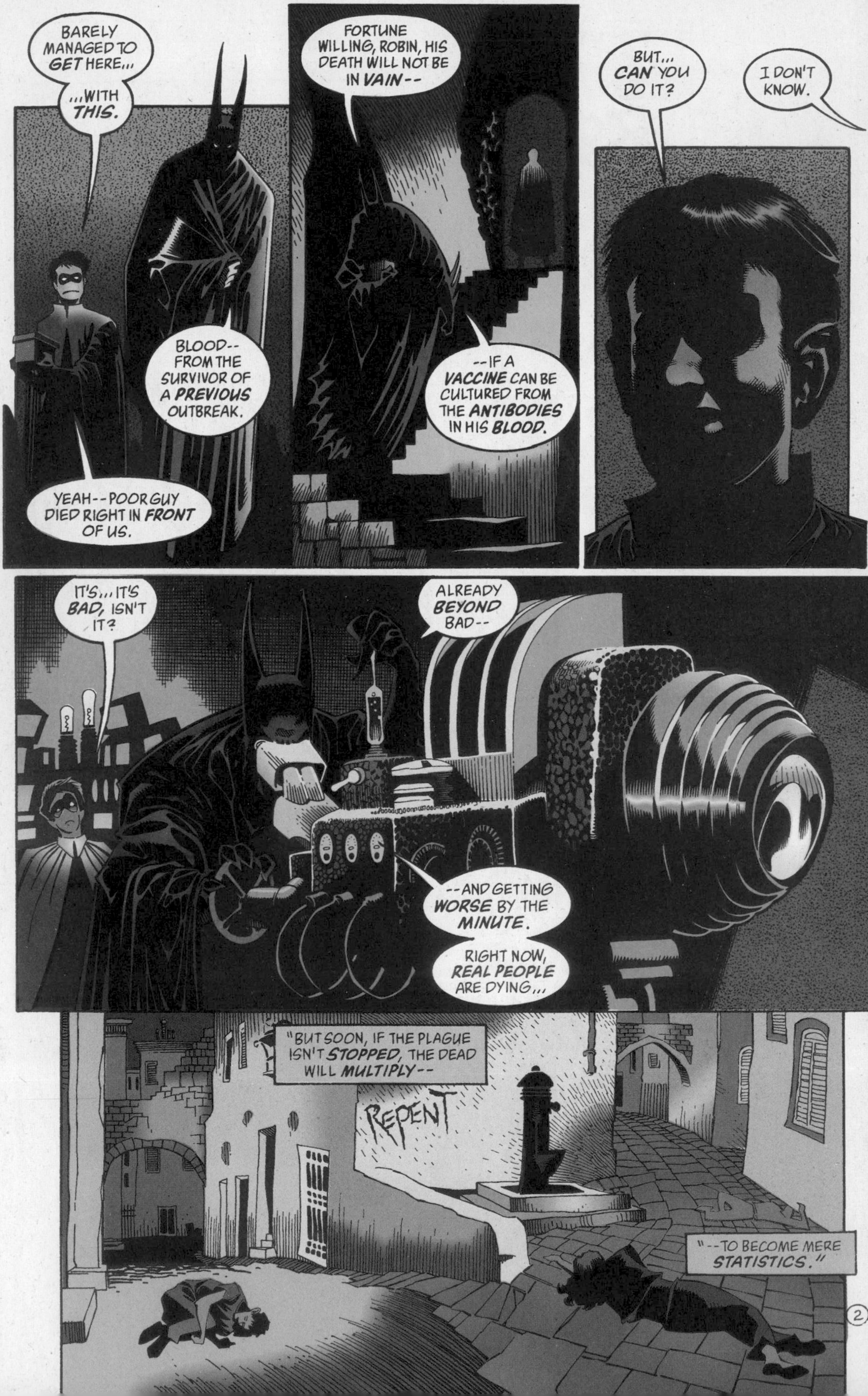
BARELY MANAGED TO GET HERE...
...WITH THIS.
BLOOD-- FROM THE SURVIVOR OF A PREVIOUS OUTBREAK.
YEAH--POOR GUY DIED RIGHT IN FRONT OF US.
FORTUNE WILLING, ROBIN, HIS DEATH WILL NOT BE IN VAIN--
--IF A VACCINE CAN BE CULTURED FROM THE ANTIBODIES IN HIS BLOOD.
BUT... CAN YOU DO IT?
I DON'T KNOW.
IT'S... IT'S BAD, ISN'T IT?
ALREADY BEYOND BAD--
--AND GETTING WORSE BY THE MINUTE.
RIGHT NOW, REAL PEOPLE ARE DYING...
"BUT SOON, IF THE PLAGUE ISN'T STOPPED, THE DEAD WILL MULTIPLY--
REPENT
"--TO BECOME MERE STATISTICS."
2

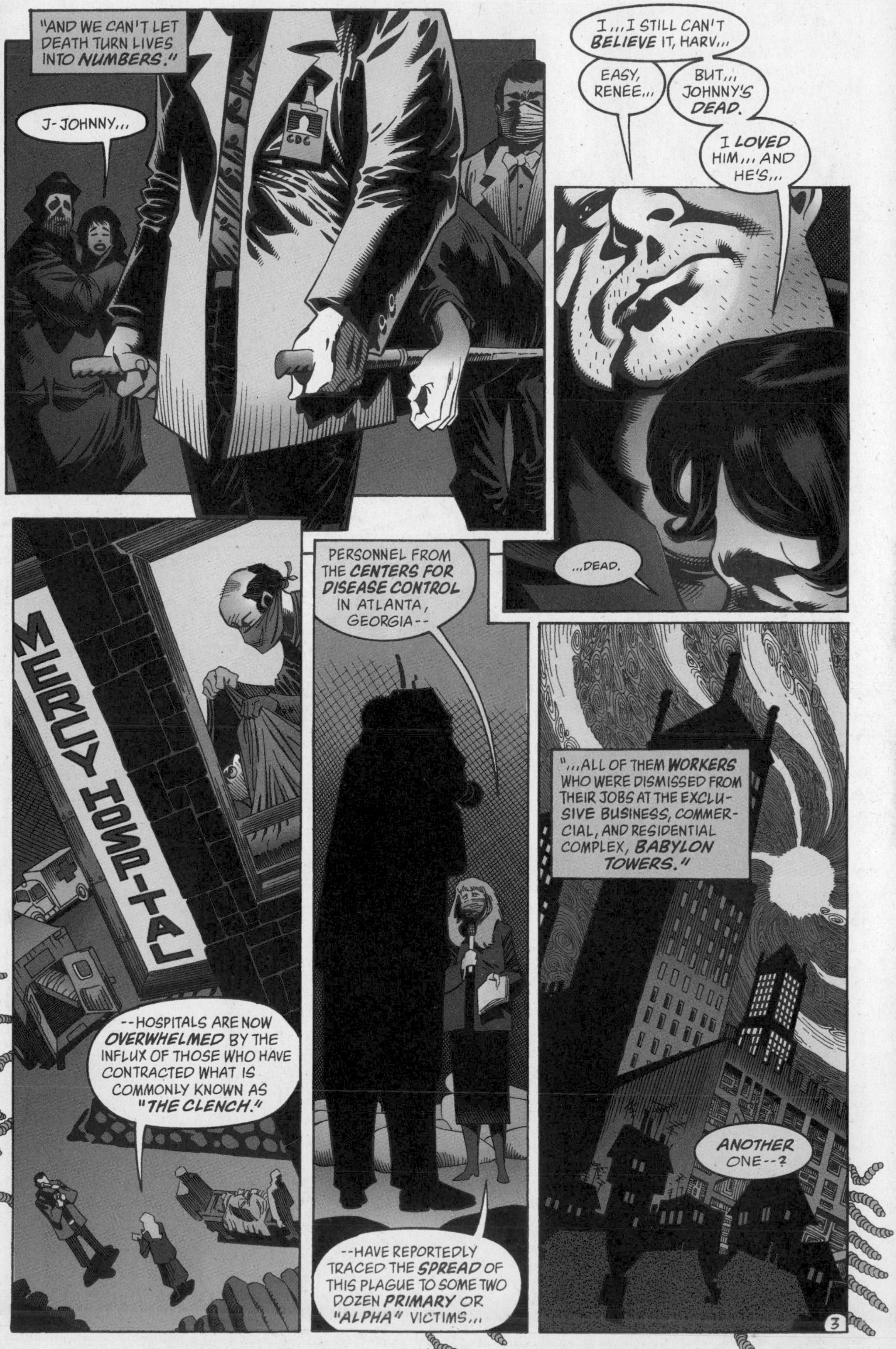
"AND WE CAN'T LET DEATH TURN LIVES INTO NUMBERS."
J-JOHNNY...
CDC
I... I STILL CAN'T BELIEVE IT, HARV...
EASY, RENEE...
BUT... JOHNNY'S DEAD.
I LOVED HIM... AND HE'S...
...DEAD.
MERCY HOSPITAL
--HOSPITALS ARE NOW OVERWHELMED BY THE INFLUX OF THOSE WHO HAVE CONTRACTED WHAT IS COMMONLY KNOWN AS "THE CLENCH."
PERSONNEL FROM THE CENTERS FOR DISEASE CONTROL IN ATLANTA, GEORGIA--
--HAVE REPORTEDLY TRACED THE SPREAD OF THIS PLAGUE TO SOME TWO DOZEN PRIMARY OR "ALPHA" VICTIMS...
"...ALL OF THEM WORKERS WHO WERE DISMISSED FROM THEIR JOBS AT THE EXCLUSIVE BUSINESS, COMMERCIAL, AND RESIDENTIAL COMPLEX, BABYLON TOWERS."
ANOTHER ONE--?
3

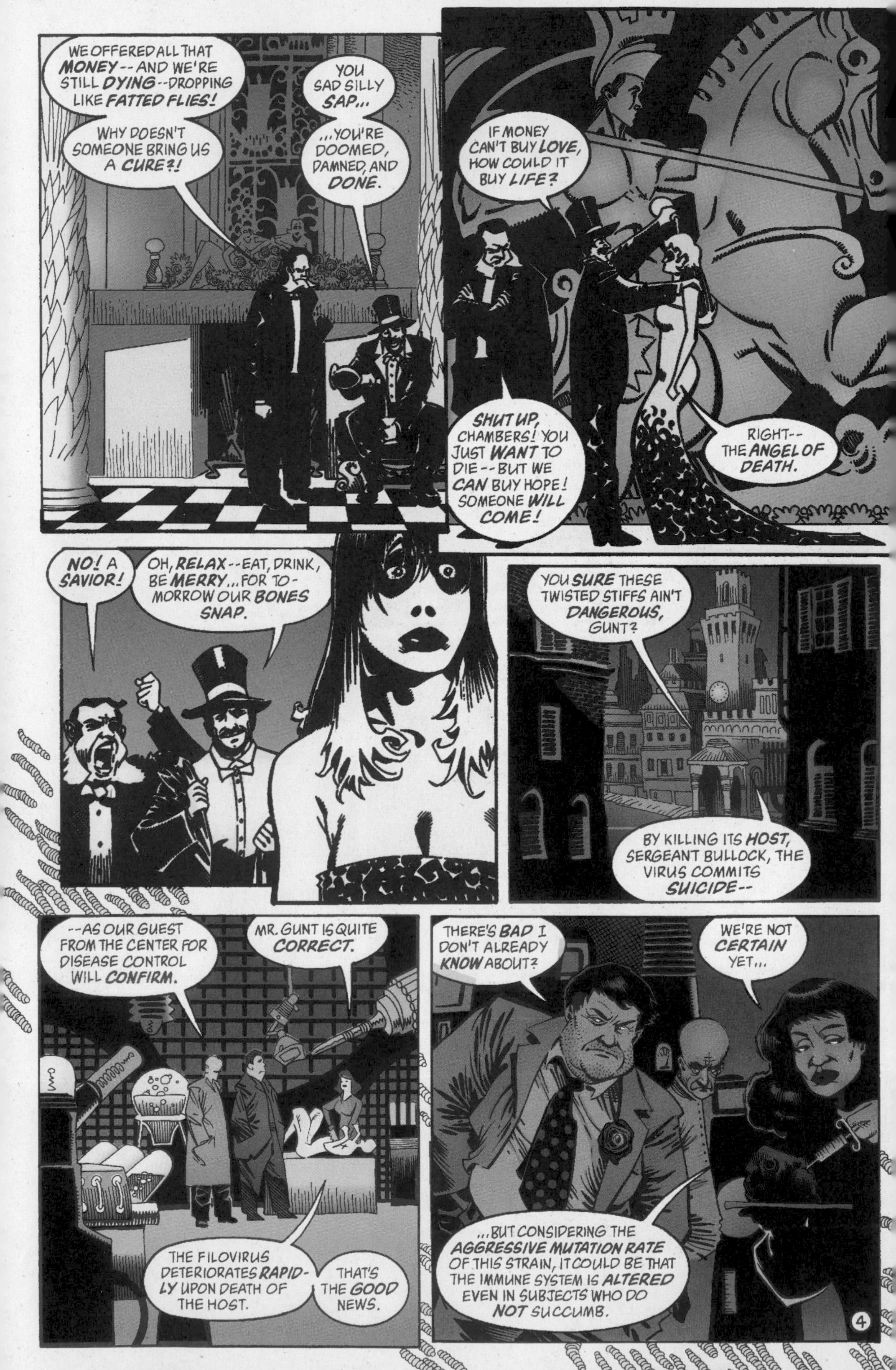
WE OFFERED ALL THAT MONEY--AND WE'RE STILL DYING--DROPPING LIKE FATTED FLIES!
WHY DOESN'T SOMEONE BRING US A CURE?!
YOU SAD SILLY SAP...
...YOU'RE DOOMED, DAMNED, AND DONE.
IF MONEY CAN'T BUY LOVE, HOW COULD IT BUY LIFE?
SHUT UP, CHAMBERS! YOU JUST WANT TO DIE--BUT WE CAN BUY HOPE! SOMEONE WILL COME!
RIGHT-- THE ANGEL OF DEATH.
NO! A SAVIOR!
OH, RELAX--EAT, DRINK, BE MERRY...FOR TO-MORROW OUR BONES SNAP.
YOU SURE THESE TWISTED STIFFS AIN'T DANGEROUS, GUNT?
BY KILLING ITS HOST, SERGEANT BULLOCK, THE VIRUS COMMITS SUICIDE--
--AS OUR GUEST FROM THE CENTER FOR DISEASE CONTROL WILL CONFIRM.
MR. GUNT IS QUITE CORRECT.
THE FILOVIRUS DETERIORATES RAPID-LY UPON DEATH OF THE HOST.
THAT'S THE GOOD NEWS.
THERE'S BAD I DON'T ALREADY KNOW ABOUT?
WE'RE NOT CERTAIN YET...
...BUT CONSIDERING THE AGGRESSIVE MUTATION RATE OF THIS STRAIN, IT COULD BE THAT THE IMMUNE SYSTEM IS ALTERED EVEN IN SUBJECTS WHO DO NOT SUCCUMB.
4

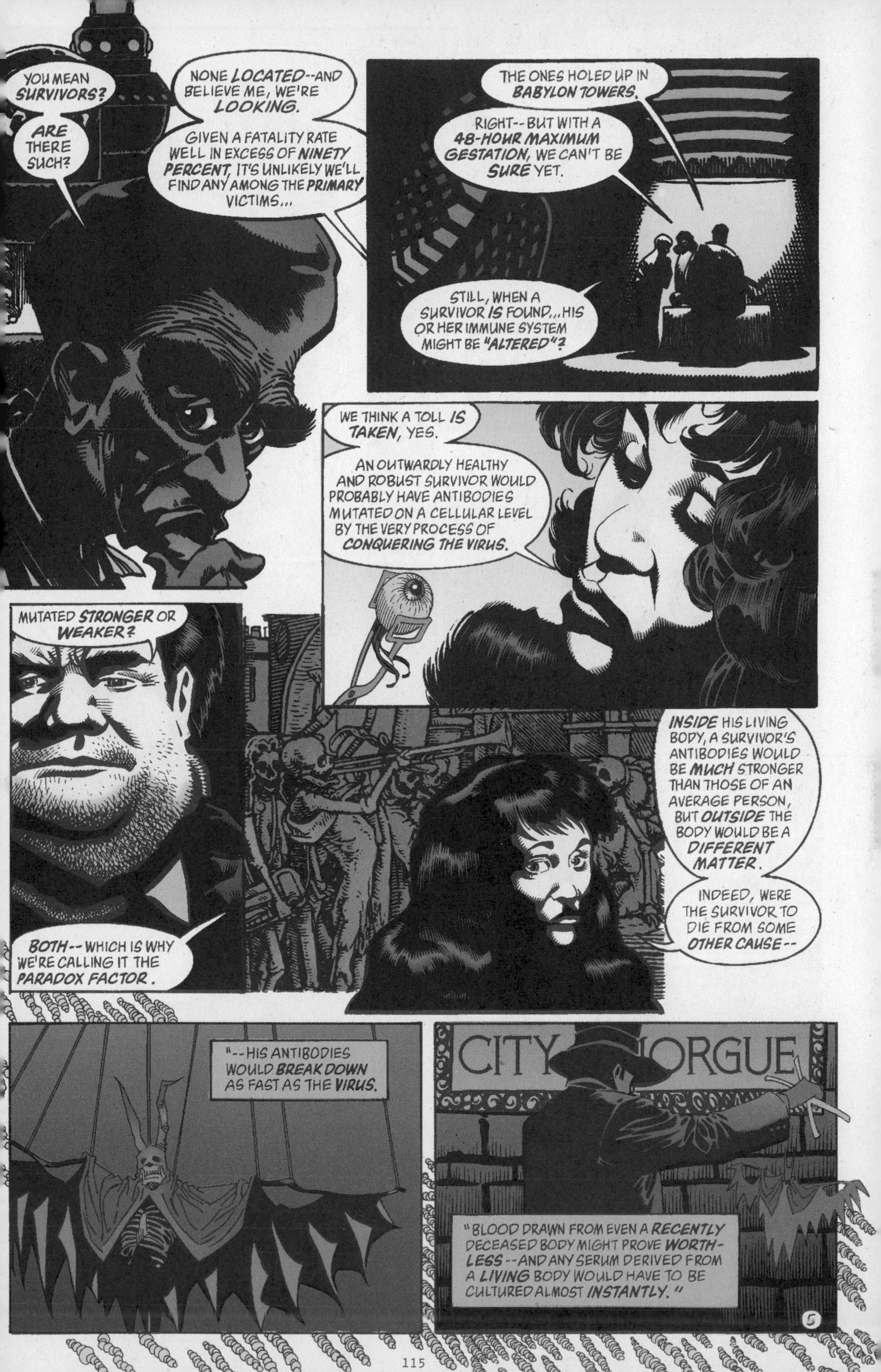
YOU MEAN SURVIVORS?
ARE THERE SUCH?
NONE LOCATED--AND BELIEVE ME, WE'RE LOOKING.
GIVEN A FATALITY RATE WELL IN EXCESS OF NINETY PERCENT, IT'S UNLIKELY WE'LL FIND ANY AMONG THE PRIMARY VICTIMS...
THE ONES HOLED UP IN BABYLON TOWERS.
RIGHT--BUT WITH A 48-HOUR MAXIMUM GESTATION, WE CAN'T BE SURE YET.
STILL, WHEN A SURVIVOR IS FOUND... HIS OR HER IMMUNE SYSTEM MIGHT BE "ALTERED"?
WE THINK A TOLL IS TAKEN, YES.
AN OUTWARDLY HEALTHY AND ROBUST SURVIVOR WOULD PROBABLY HAVE ANTIBODIES MUTATED ON A CELLULAR LEVEL BY THE VERY PROCESS OF CONQUERING THE VIRUS.
MUTATED STRONGER OR WEAKER?
INSIDE HIS LIVING BODY, A SURVIVOR'S ANTIBODIES WOULD BE MUCH STRONGER THAN THOSE OF AN AVERAGE PERSON, BUT OUTSIDE THE BODY WOULD BE A DIFFERENT MATTER.
INDEED, WERE THE SURVIVOR TO DIE FROM SOME OTHER CAUSE--
BOTH--WHICH IS WHY WE'RE CALLING IT THE PARADOX FACTOR.
"--HIS ANTIBODIES WOULD BREAK DOWN AS FAST AS THE VIRUS.
CITY ORGUE
"BLOOD DRAWN FROM EVEN A RECENTLY DECEASED BODY MIGHT PROVE WORTHLESS--AND ANY SERUM DERIVED FROM A LIVING BODY WOULD HAVE TO BE CULTURED ALMOST INSTANTLY."
5

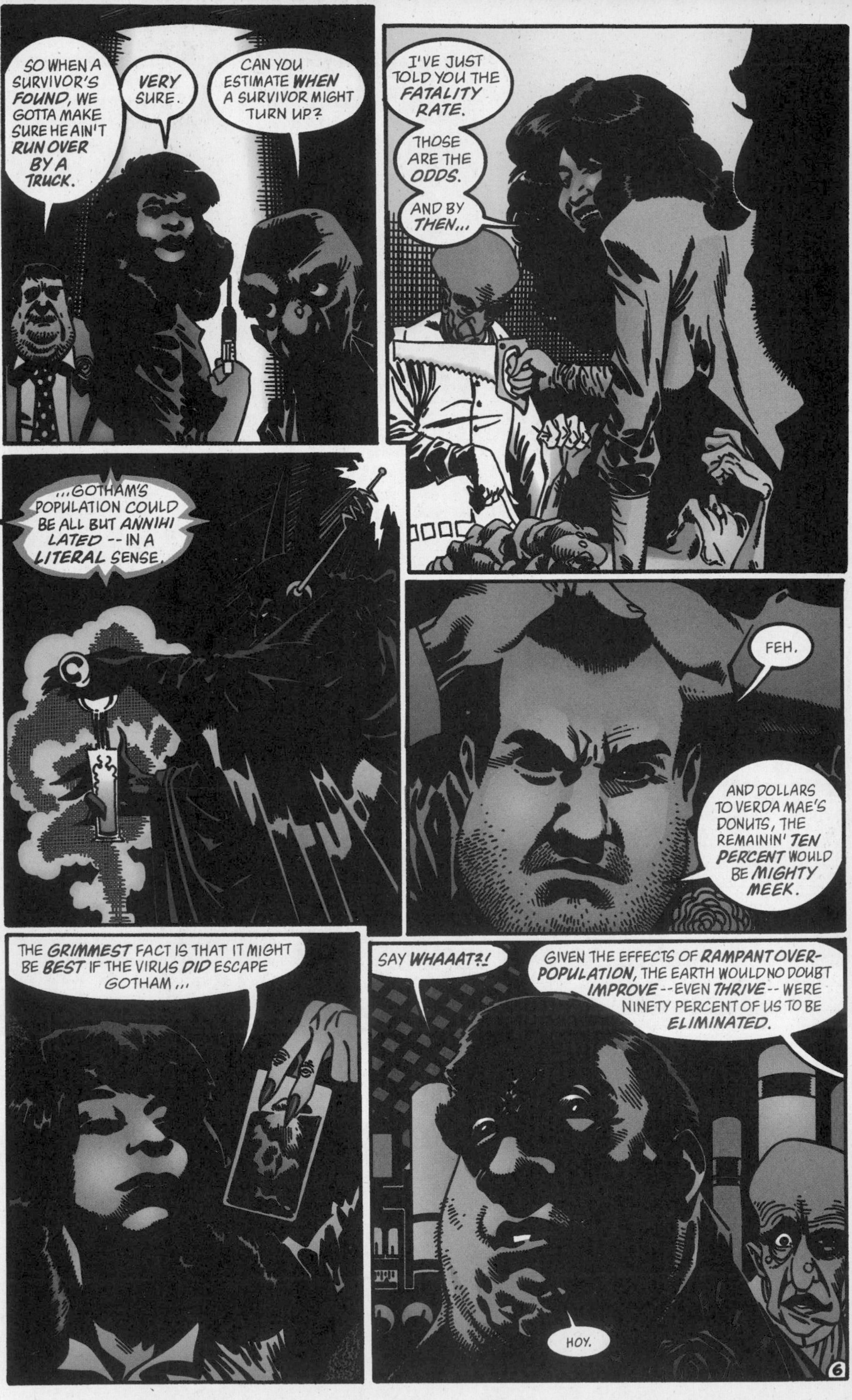
SO WHEN A SURVIVOR'S FOUND, WE GOTTA MAKE SURE HE AIN'T RUN OVER BY A TRUCK.
VERY SURE.
CAN YOU ESTIMATE WHEN A SURVIVOR MIGHT TURN UP?
I'VE JUST TOLD YOU THE FATALITY RATE.
THOSE ARE THE ODDS.
AND BY THEN...
...GOTHAM'S POPULATION COULD BE ALL BUT ANNIHI LATED -- IN A LITERAL SENSE.
FEH.
AND DOLLARS TO VERDA MAE'S DONUTS, THE REMAININ' TEN PERCENT WOULD BE MIGHTY MEEK.
THE GRIMMEST FACT IS THAT IT MIGHT BE BEST IF THE VIRUS DID ESCAPE GOTHAM...
SAY WHAAAT?!
GIVEN THE EFFECTS OF RAMPANT OVER-POPULATION, THE EARTH WOULD NO DOUBT IMPROVE -- EVEN THRIVE -- WERE NINETY PERCENT OF US TO BE ELIMINATED.
HOY.
6

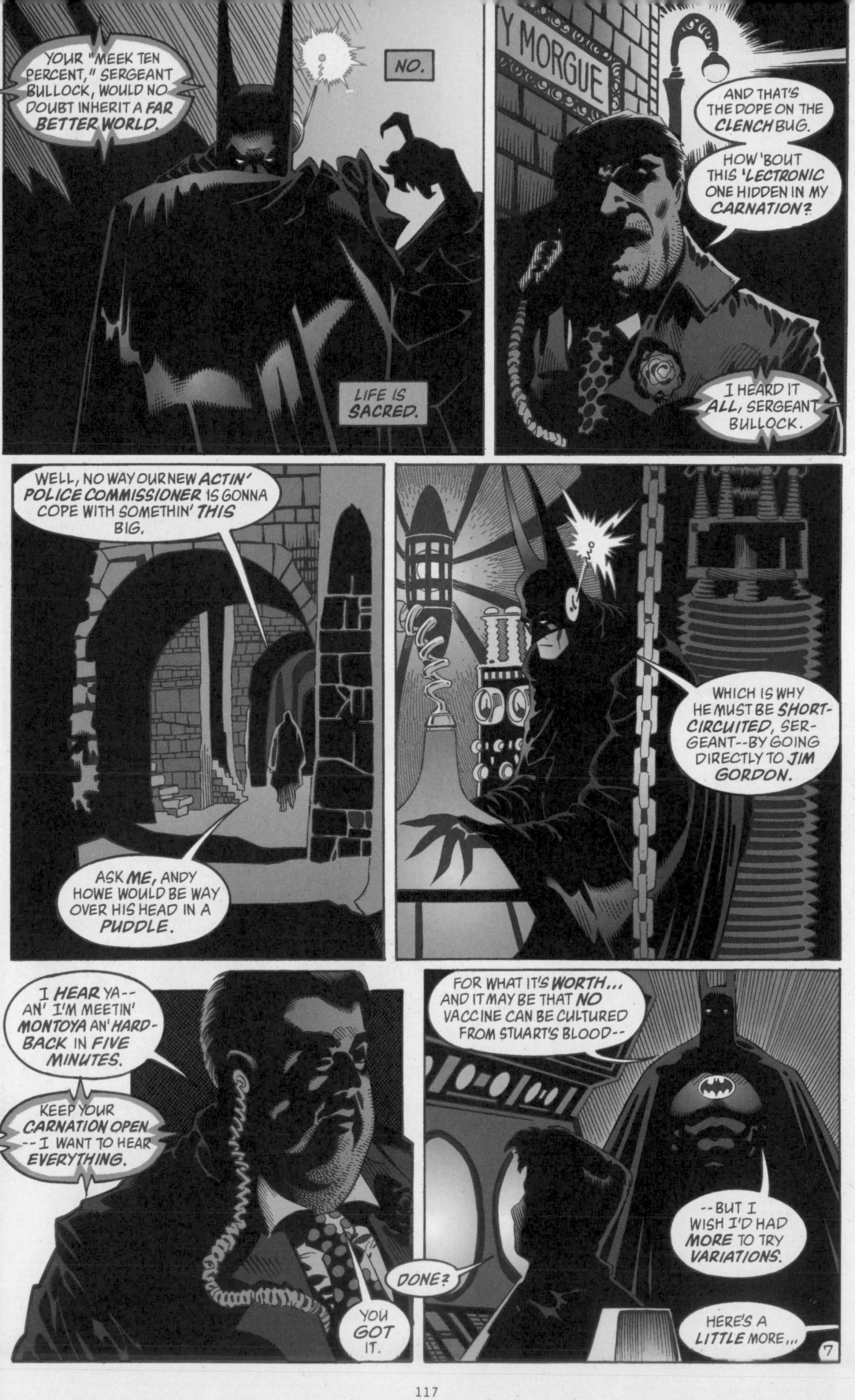
YOUR "MEEK TEN PERCENT," SERGEANT BULLOCK, WOULD NO DOUBT INHERIT A FAR BETTER WORLD.
NO.
LIFE IS SACRED.
Y MORGUE
AND THAT'S THE DOPE ON THE CLENCH BUG.
HOW 'BOUT THIS 'LECTRONIC ONE HIDDEN IN MY CARNATION?
I HEARD IT ALL, SERGEANT BULLOCK.
WELL, NO WAY OUR NEW ACTIN' POLICE COMMISSIONER IS GONNA COPE WITH SOMETHIN' THIS BIG.
ASK ME, ANDY HOWE WOULD BE WAY OVER HIS HEAD IN A PUDDLE.
WHICH IS WHY HE MUST BE SHORT-CIRCUITED, SERGEANT--BY GOING DIRECTLY TO JIM GORDON.
I HEAR YA-- AN' I'M MEETIN' MONTOYA AN' HARDBACK IN FIVE MINUTES.
KEEP YOUR CARNATION OPEN --I WANT TO HEAR EVERYTHING.
YOU GOT IT.
FOR WHAT IT'S WORTH... AND IT MAY BE THAT NO VACCINE CAN BE CULTURED FROM STUART'S BLOOD--
--BUT I WISH I'D HAD MORE TO TRY VARIATIONS.
DONE?
HERE'S A LITTLE MORE...
7

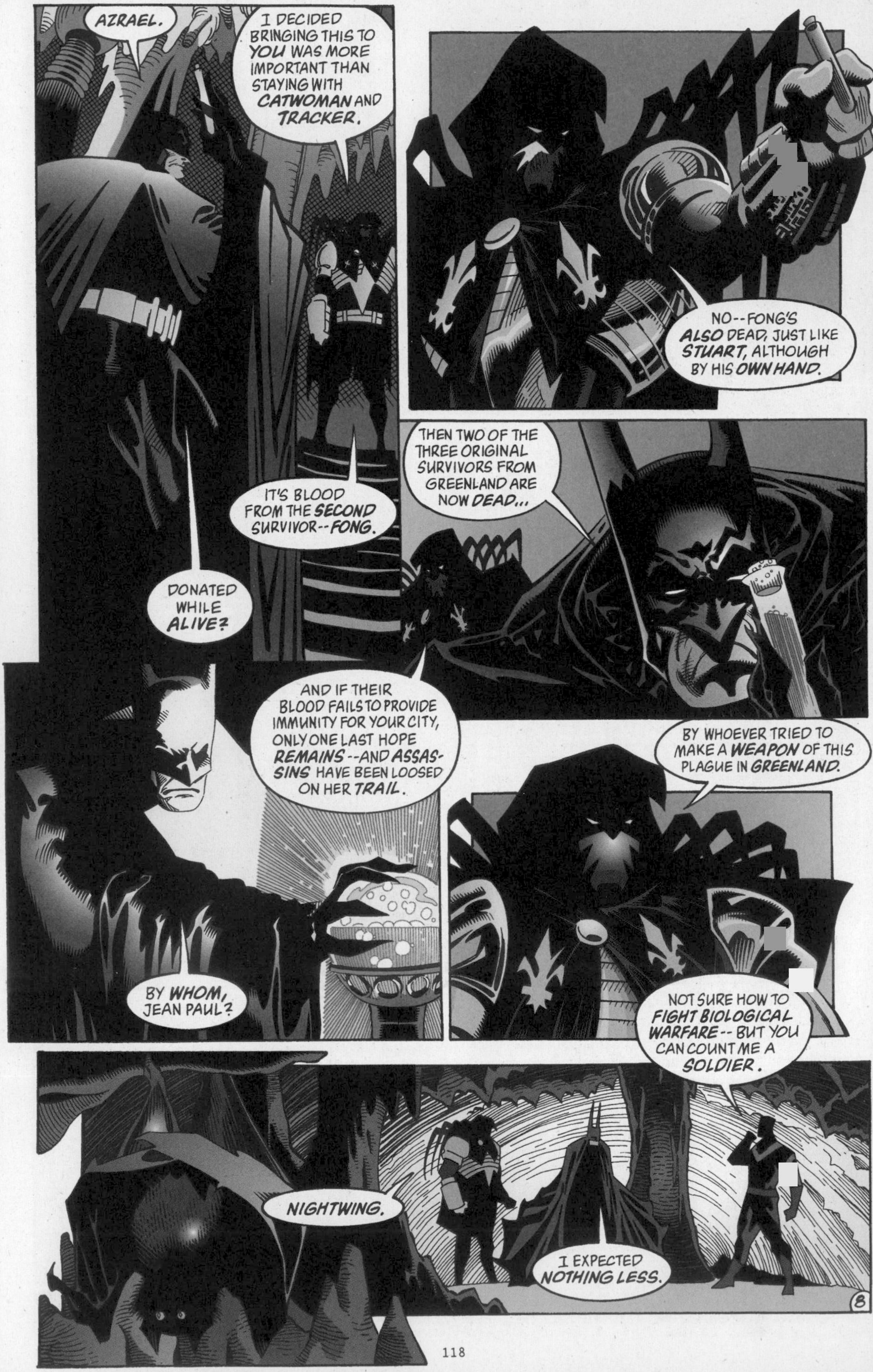
AZRAEL.
I DECIDED BRINGING THIS TO YOU WAS MORE IMPORTANT THAN STAYING WITH CATWOMAN AND TRACKER.
NO--FONG'S ALSO DEAD, JUST LIKE STUART, ALTHOUGH BY HIS OWN HAND.
IT'S BLOOD FROM THE SECOND SURVIVOR--FONG.
THEN TWO OF THE THREE ORIGINAL SURVIVORS FROM GREENLAND ARE NOW DEAD...
DONATED WHILE ALIVE?
AND IF THEIR BLOOD FAILS TO PROVIDE IMMUNITY FOR YOUR CITY, ONLY ONE LAST HOPE REMAINS--AND ASSASSINS HAVE BEEN LOOSED ON HER TRAIL.
BY WHOEVER TRIED TO MAKE A WEAPON OF THIS PLAGUE IN GREENLAND.
BY WHOM, JEAN PAUL?
NOT SURE HOW TO FIGHT BIOLOGICAL WARFARE--BUT YOU CAN COUNT ME A SOLDIER.
NIGHTWING.
I EXPECTED NOTHING LESS.
8

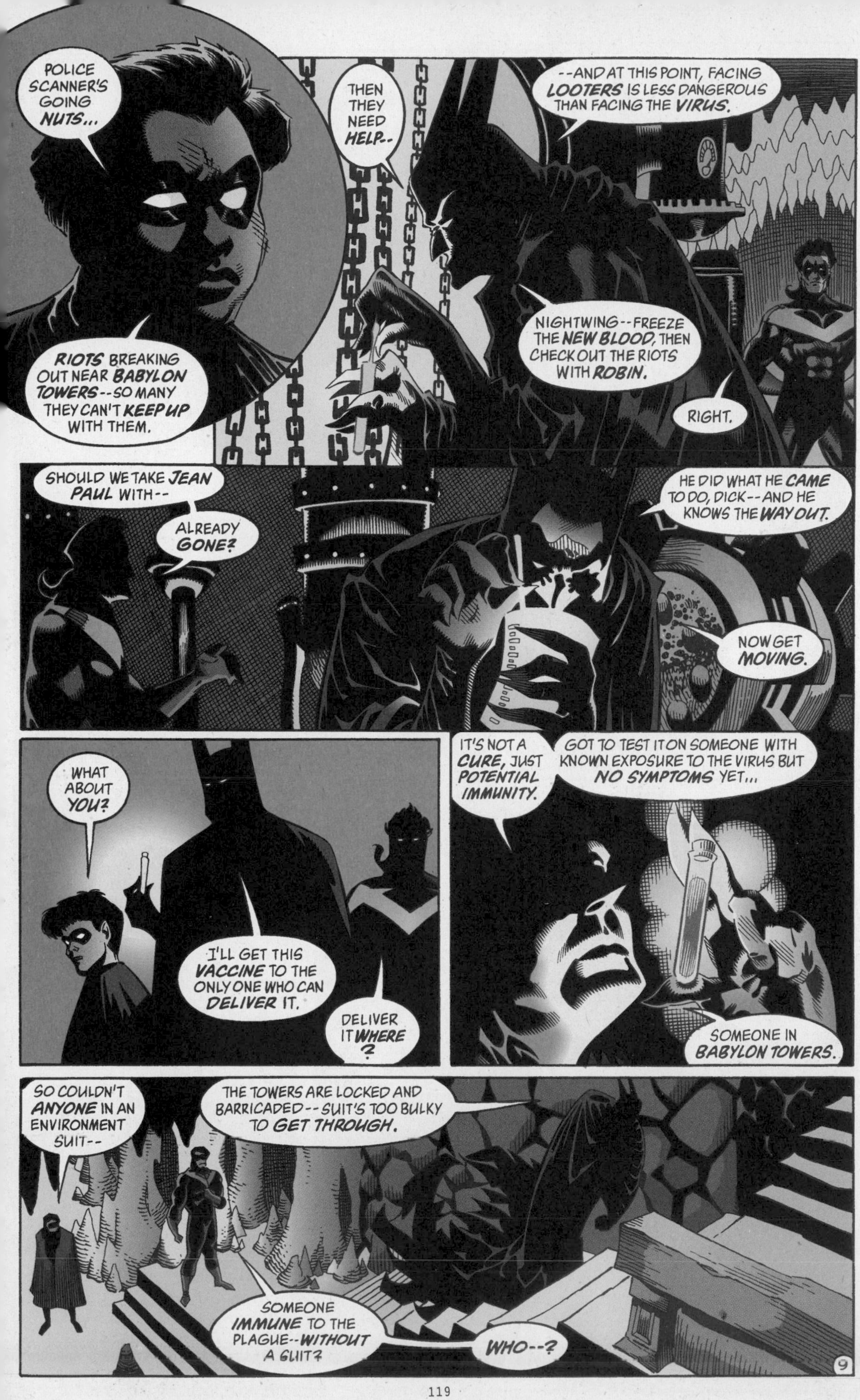
POLICE SCANNER'S GOING NUTS...
RIOTS BREAKING OUT NEAR BABYLON TOWERS--SO MANY THEY CAN'T KEEP UP WITH THEM.
THEN THEY NEED HELP--
--AND AT THIS POINT, FACING LOOTERS IS LESS DANGEROUS THAN FACING THE VIRUS.
NIGHTWING--FREEZE THE NEW BLOOD, THEN CHECK OUT THE RIOTS WITH ROBIN.
RIGHT.
SHOULD WE TAKE JEAN PAUL WITH--
ALREADY GONE?
HE DID WHAT HE CAME TO DO, DICK--AND HE KNOWS THE WAY OUT.
NOW GET MOVING.
WHAT ABOUT YOU?
I'LL GET THIS VACCINE TO THE ONLY ONE WHO CAN DELIVER IT.
DELIVER IT WHERE?
IT'S NOT A CURE, JUST POTENTIAL IMMUNITY.
GOT TO TEST IT ON SOMEONE WITH KNOWN EXPOSURE TO THE VIRUS BUT NO SYMPTOMS YET...
SOMEONE IN BABYLON TOWERS.
SO COULDN'T ANYONE IN AN ENVIRONMENT SUIT--
THE TOWERS ARE LOCKED AND BARRICADED--SUIT'S TOO BULKY TO GET THROUGH.
SOMEONE IMMUNE TO THE PLAGUE--WITHOUT A SUIT?
WHO--?
9

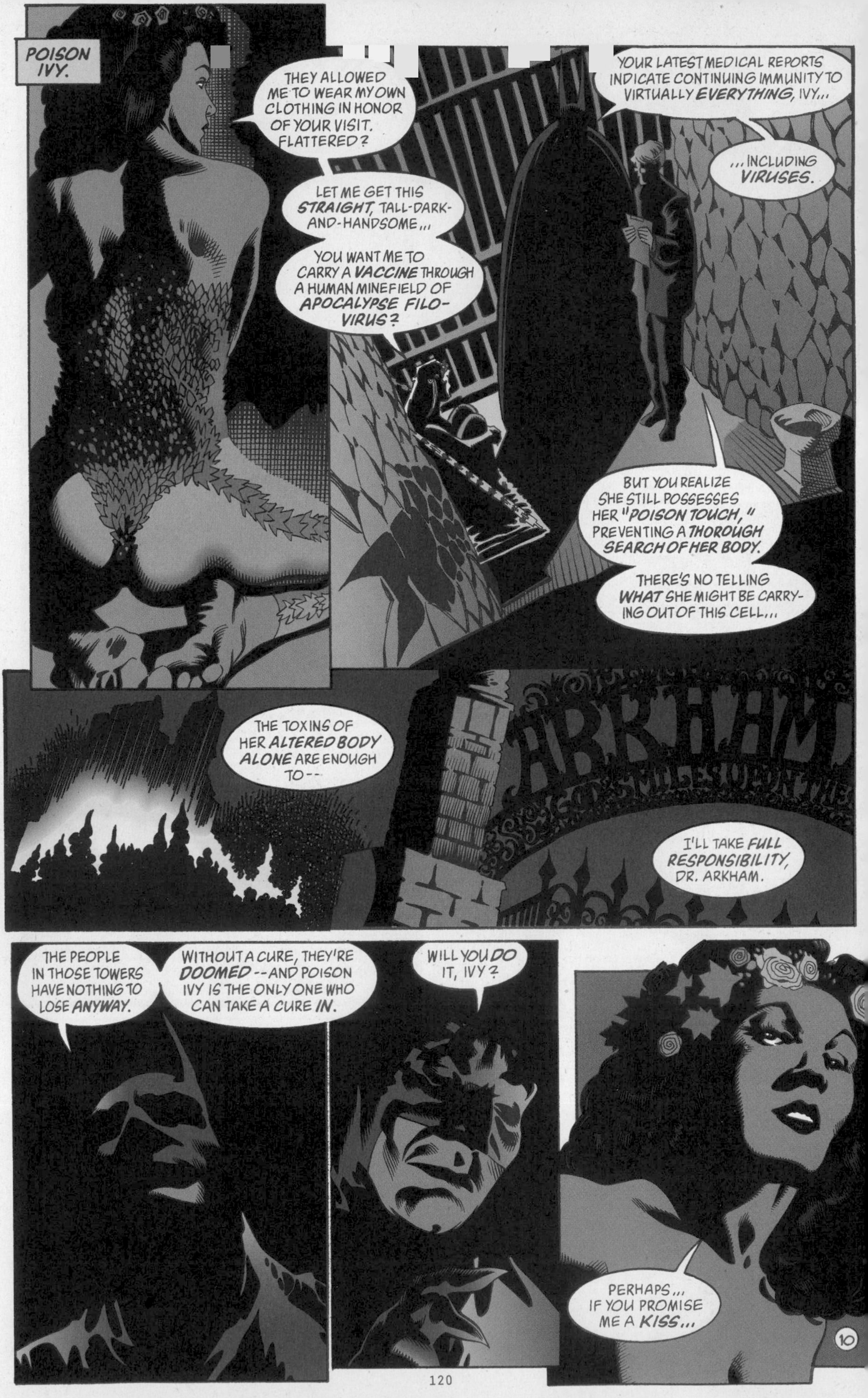
POISON IVY.
THEY ALLOWED ME TO WEAR MY OWN CLOTHING IN HONOR OF YOUR VISIT. FLATTERED?
LET ME GET THIS STRAIGHT, TALL-DARK-AND-HANDSOME...
YOU WANT ME TO CARRY A VACCINE THROUGH A HUMAN MINEFIELD OF APOCALYPSE FILO-VIRUS?
YOUR LATEST MEDICAL REPORTS INDICATE CONTINUING IMMUNITY TO VIRTUALLY EVERYTHING, IVY...
...INCLUDING VIRUSES.
BUT YOU REALIZE SHE STILL POSSESSES HER "POISON TOUCH," PREVENTING A THOROUGH SEARCH OF HER BODY.
THERE'S NO TELLING WHAT SHE MIGHT BE CARRYING OUT OF THIS CELL...
THE TOXINS OF HER ALTERED BODY ALONE ARE ENOUGH TO--
I'LL TAKE FULL RESPONSIBILITY, DR. ARKHAM.
THE PEOPLE IN THOSE TOWERS HAVE NOTHING TO LOSE ANYWAY.
WITHOUT A CURE, THEY'RE DOOMED--AND POISON IVY IS THE ONLY ONE WHO CAN TAKE A CURE IN.
WILL YOU DO IT, IVY?
PERHAPS... IF YOU PROMISE ME A KISS...
10

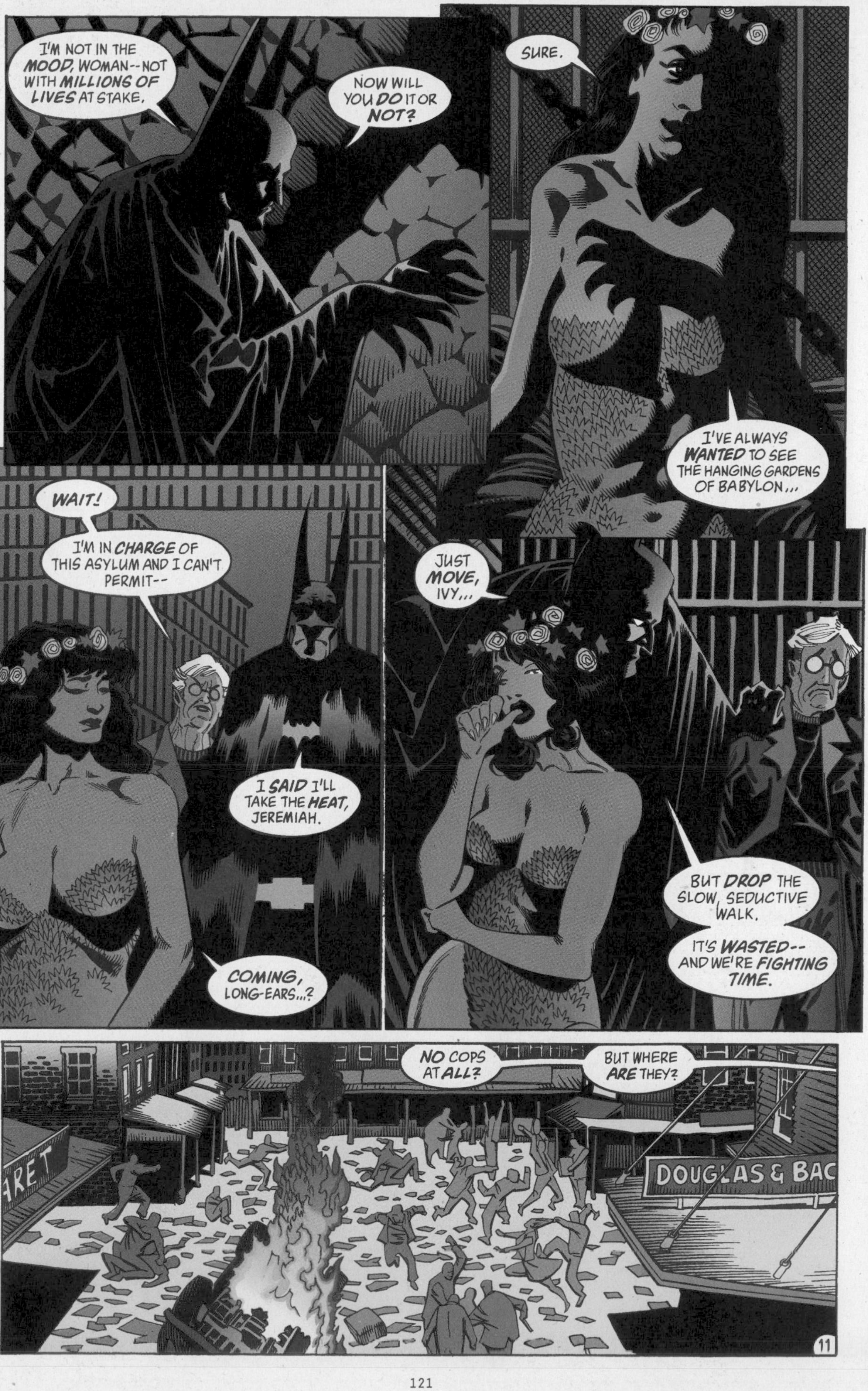

I'M NOT IN THE MOOD, WOMAN--NOT WITH MILLIONS OF LIVES AT STAKE.
NOW WILL YOU DO IT OR NOT?
SURE.
I'VE ALWAYS WANTED TO SEE THE HANGING GARDENS OF BABYLON...
WAIT!
I'M IN CHARGE OF THIS ASYLUM AND I CAN'T PERMIT--
I SAID I'LL TAKE THE HEAT, JEREMIAH.
COMING, LONG-EARS...?
JUST MOVE, IVY...
BUT DROP THE SLOW, SEDUCTIVE WALK.
IT'S WASTED--AND WE'RE FIGHTING TIME.
NO COPS AT ALL?
BUT WHERE ARE THEY?
ARET
DOUGLAS & BAC
11

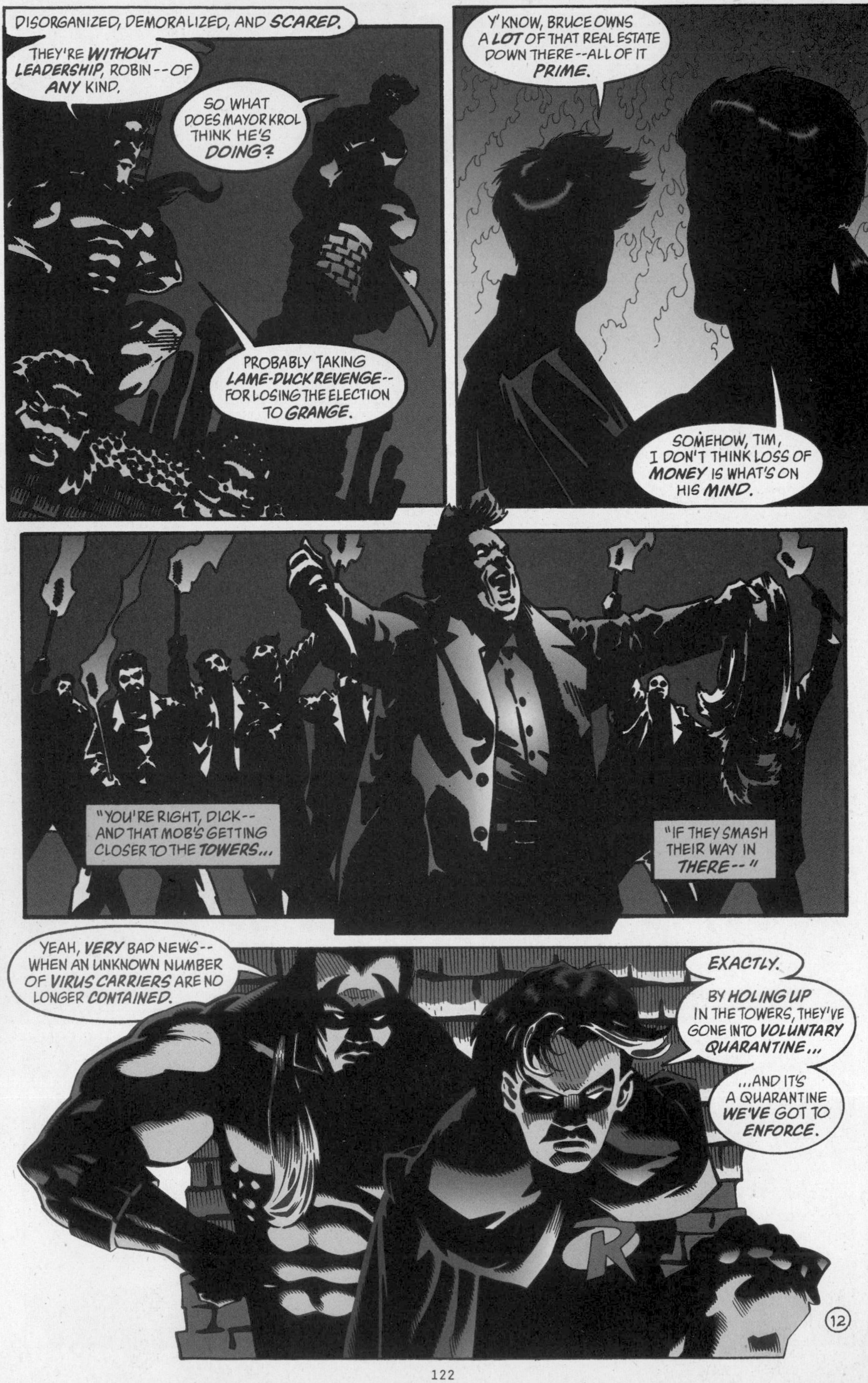
DISORGANIZED, DEMORALIZED, AND SCARED.
THEY'RE WITHOUT LEADERSHIP, ROBIN--OF ANY KIND.
SO WHAT DOES MAYOR KROL THINK HE'S DOING?
PROBABLY TAKING LAME-DUCK REVENGE--FOR LOSING THE ELECTION TO GRANGE.
Y'KNOW, BRUCE OWNS A LOT OF THAT REAL ESTATE DOWN THERE--ALL OF IT PRIME.
SOMEHOW, TIM, I DON'T THINK LOSS OF MONEY IS WHAT'S ON HIS MIND.
"YOU'RE RIGHT, DICK--AND THAT MOB'S GETTING CLOSER TO THE TOWERS...
"IF THEY SMASH THEIR WAY IN THERE--"
YEAH, VERY BAD NEWS--WHEN AN UNKNOWN NUMBER OF VIRUS CARRIERS ARE NO LONGER CONTAINED.
EXACTLY.
BY HOLING UP IN THE TOWERS, THEY'VE GONE INTO VOLUNTARY QUARANTINE...
...AND IT'S A QUARANTINE WE'VE GOT TO ENFORCE.
12

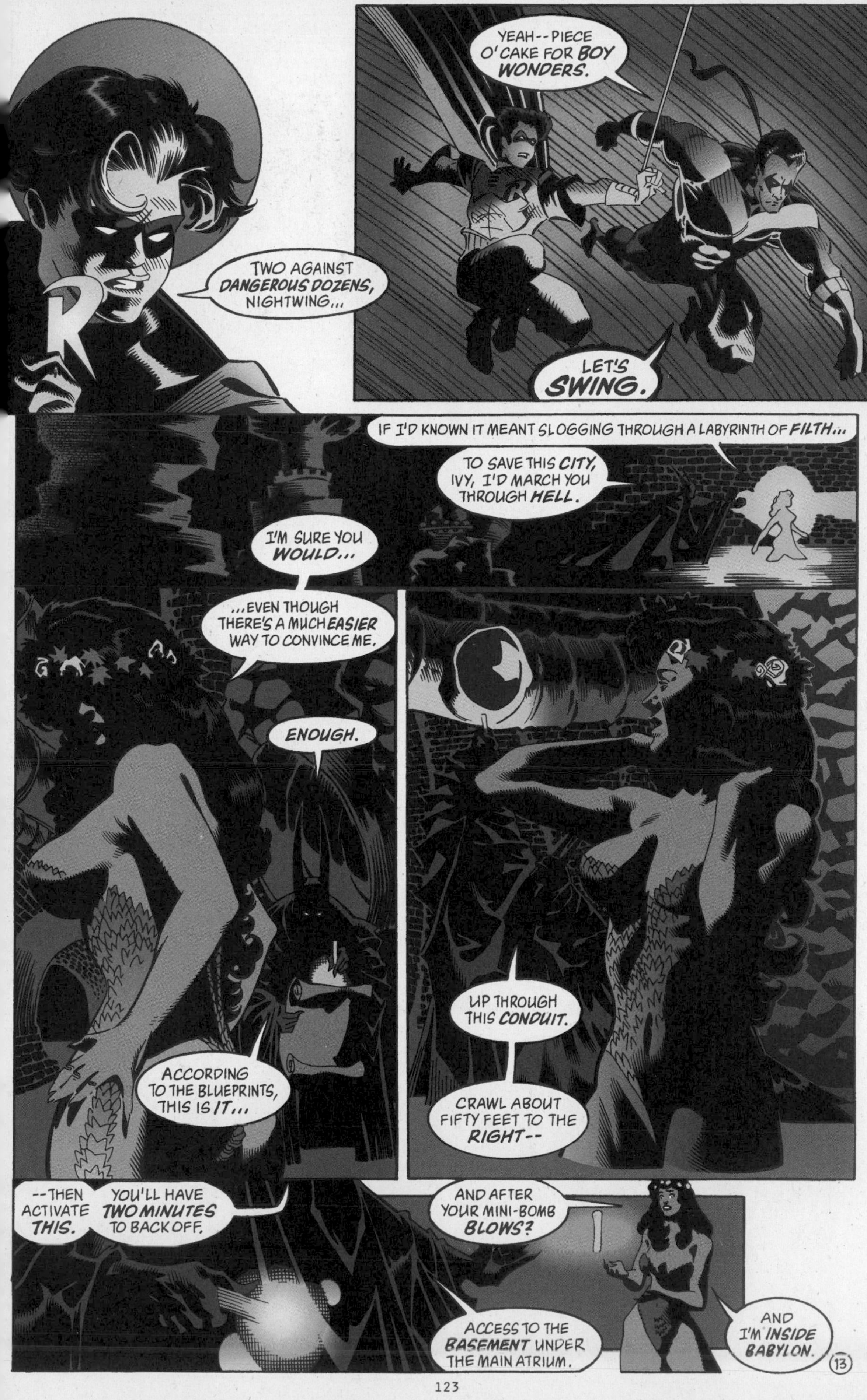
TWO AGAINST DANGEROUS DOZENS, NIGHTWING...
YEAH--PIECE O'CAKE FOR BOY WONDERS.
LET'S SWING.
IF I'D KNOWN IT MEANT SLOGGING THROUGH A LABYRINTH OF FILTH...
TO SAVE THIS CITY, IVY, I'D MARCH YOU THROUGH HELL.
I'M SURE YOU WOULD...
...EVEN THOUGH THERE'S A MUCH EASIER WAY TO CONVINCE ME.
ENOUGH.
ACCORDING TO THE BLUEPRINTS, THIS IS IT...
UP THROUGH THIS CONDUIT.
CRAWL ABOUT FIFTY FEET TO THE RIGHT--
--THEN ACTIVATE THIS.
YOU'LL HAVE TWO MINUTES TO BACK OFF.
AND AFTER YOUR MINI-BOMB BLOWS?
ACCESS TO THE BASEMENT UNDER THE MAIN ATRIUM.
AND I'M INSIDE BABYLON.
13

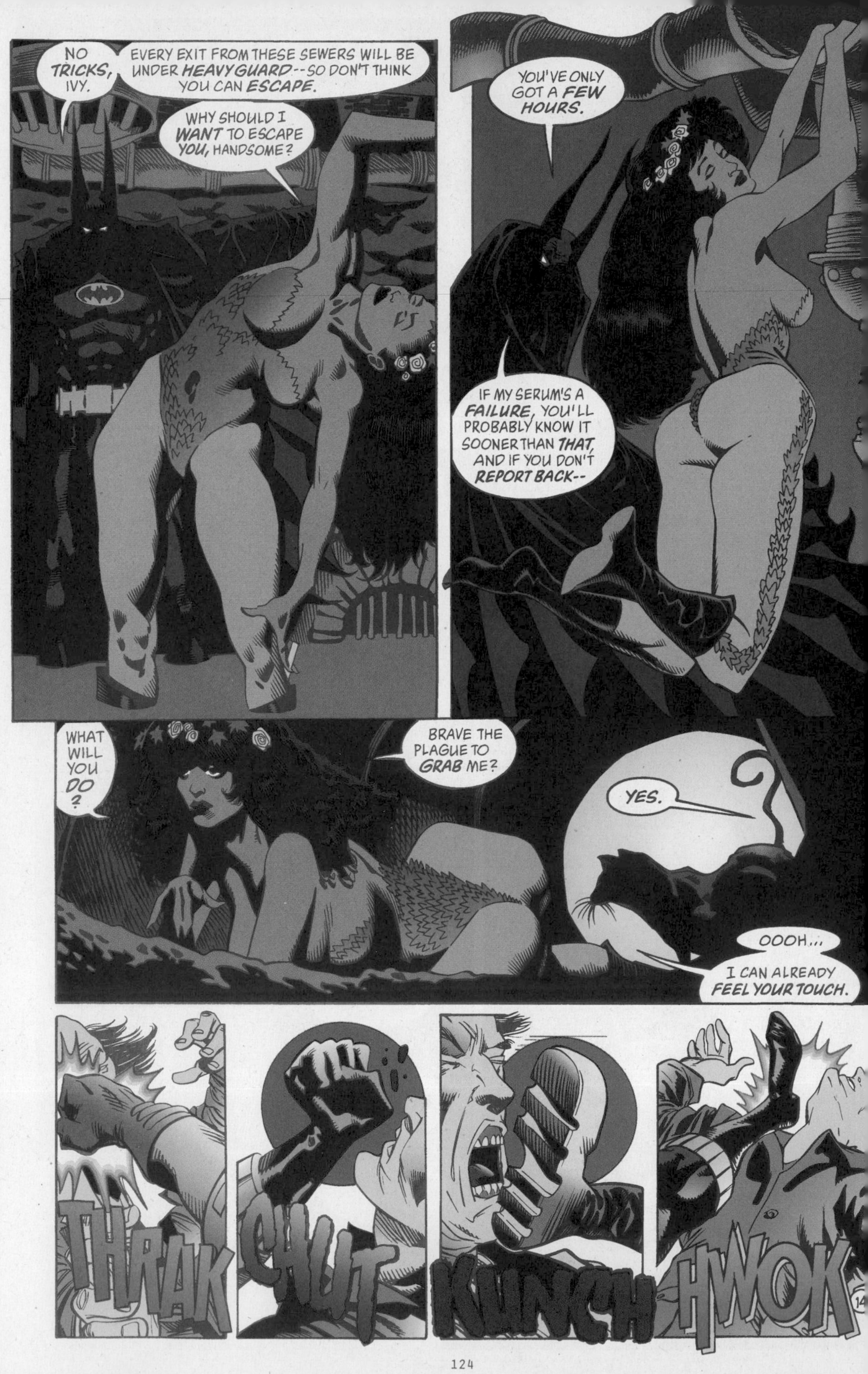
NO TRICKS, IVY.
EVERY EXIT FROM THESE SEWERS WILL BE UNDER HEAVY GUARD--SO DON'T THINK YOU CAN ESCAPE.
WHY SHOULD I WANT TO ESCAPE YOU, HANDSOME?
YOU'VE ONLY GOT A FEW HOURS.
IF MY SERUM'S A FAILURE, YOU'LL PROBABLY KNOW IT SOONER THAN THAT, AND IF YOU DON'T REPORT BACK--
WHAT WILL YOU DO?
BRAVE THE PLAGUE TO GRAB ME?
YES.
OOOH...
I CAN ALREADY FEEL YOUR TOUCH.
THRAK
CHUT
KUNCH
HWOK
14

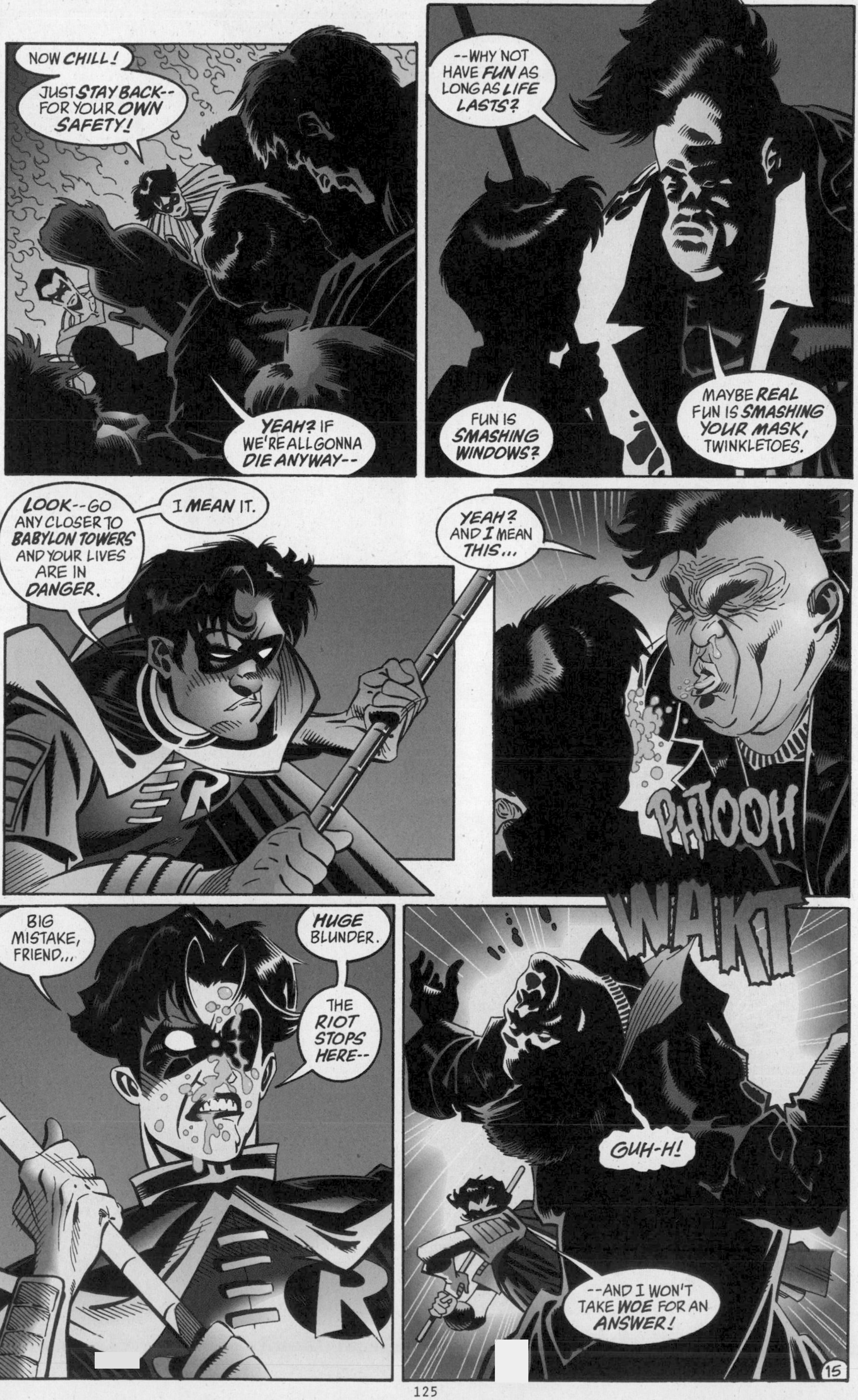

NOW CHILL!
JUST STAY BACK-- FOR YOUR OWN SAFETY!
YEAH? IF WE'RE ALL GONNA DIE ANYWAY--
--WHY NOT HAVE FUN AS LONG AS LIFE LASTS?
FUN IS SMASHING WINDOWS?
MAYBE REAL FUN IS SMASHING YOUR MASK, TWINKLETOES.
LOOK--GO ANY CLOSER TO BABYLON TOWERS AND YOUR LIVES ARE IN DANGER.
I MEAN IT.
YEAH? AND I MEAN THIS...
PHTOOH
BIG MISTAKE, FRIEND...
HUGE BLUNDER.
THE RIOT STOPS HERE--
WAKT
GUH-H!
--AND I WON'T TAKE WOE FOR AN ANSWER!
15

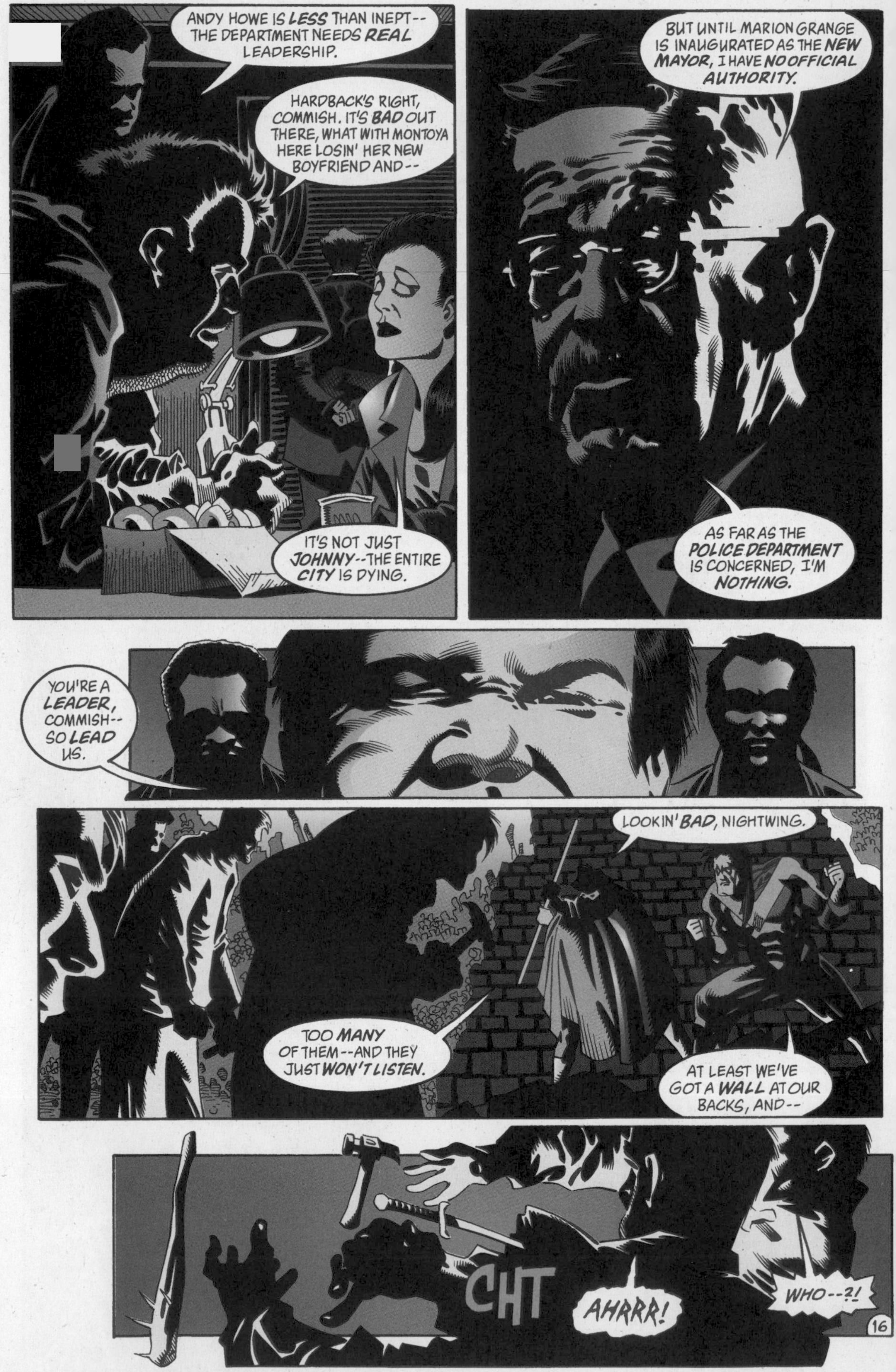
ANDY HOWE IS LESS THAN INEPT-- THE DEPARTMENT NEEDS REAL LEADERSHIP.
HARDBACK'S RIGHT, COMMISH. IT'S BAD OUT THERE, WHAT WITH MONTOYA HERE LOSIN' HER NEW BOYFRIEND AND--
IT'S NOT JUST JOHNNY--THE ENTIRE CITY IS DYING.
BUT UNTIL MARION GRANGE IS INAUGURATED AS THE NEW MAYOR, I HAVE NO OFFICIAL AUTHORITY.
AS FAR AS THE POLICE DEPARTMENT IS CONCERNED, I'M NOTHING.
YOU'RE A LEADER, COMMISH-- SO LEAD US.
LOOKIN' BAD, NIGHTWING.
TOO MANY OF THEM--AND THEY JUST WON'T LISTEN.
AT LEAST WE'VE GOT A WALL AT OUR BACKS, AND--
CHT
AHRRR!
WHO--?!
16

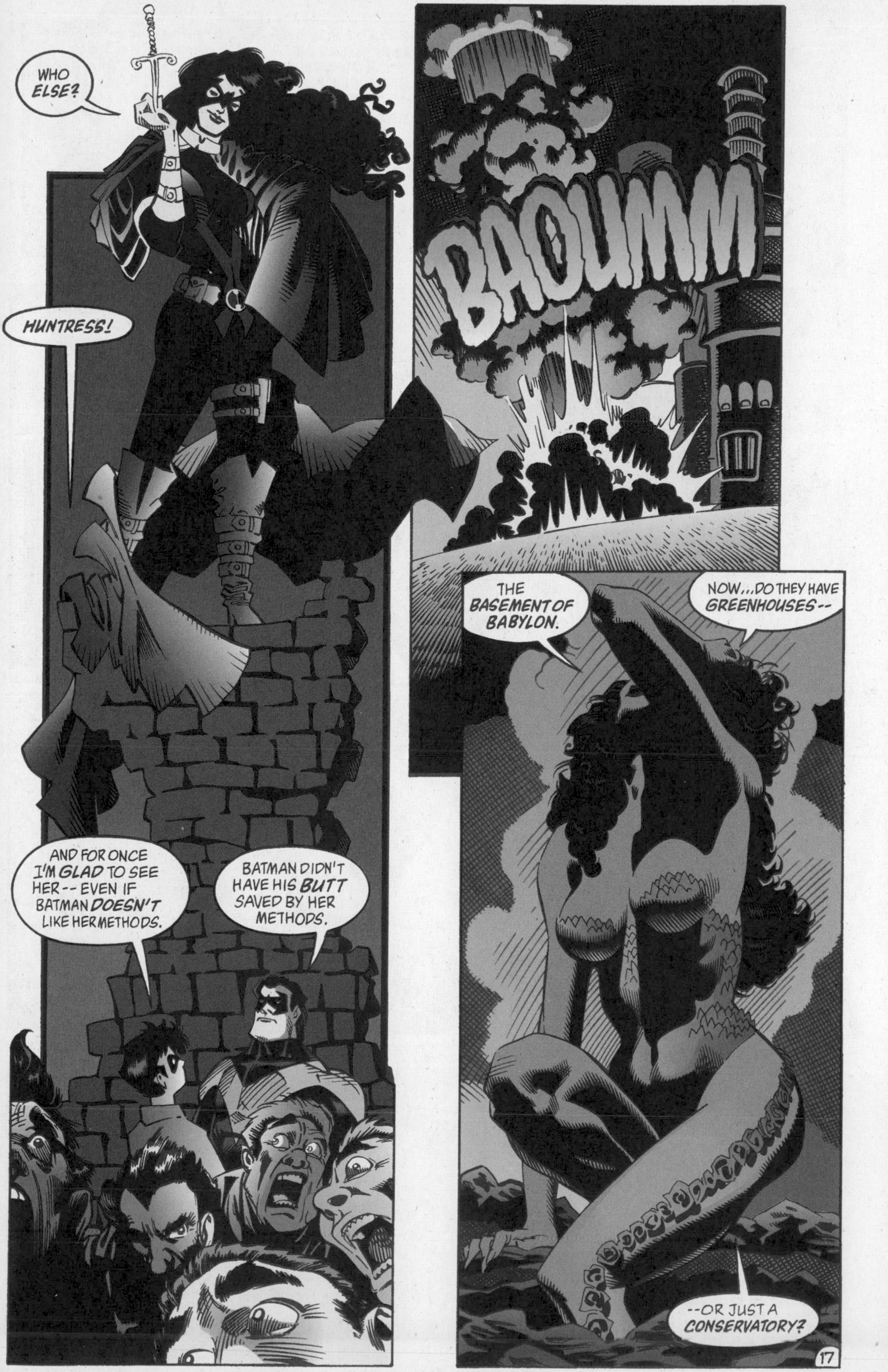
WHO ELSE?
HUNTRESS!
AND FOR ONCE I'M GLAD TO SEE HER -- EVEN IF BATMAN DOESN'T LIKE HER METHODS.
BATMAN DIDN'T HAVE HIS BUTT SAVED BY HER METHODS.
BAOUMM
THE BASEMENT OF BABYLON.
NOW... DO THEY HAVE GREENHOUSES --
-- OR JUST A CONSERVATORY?
17

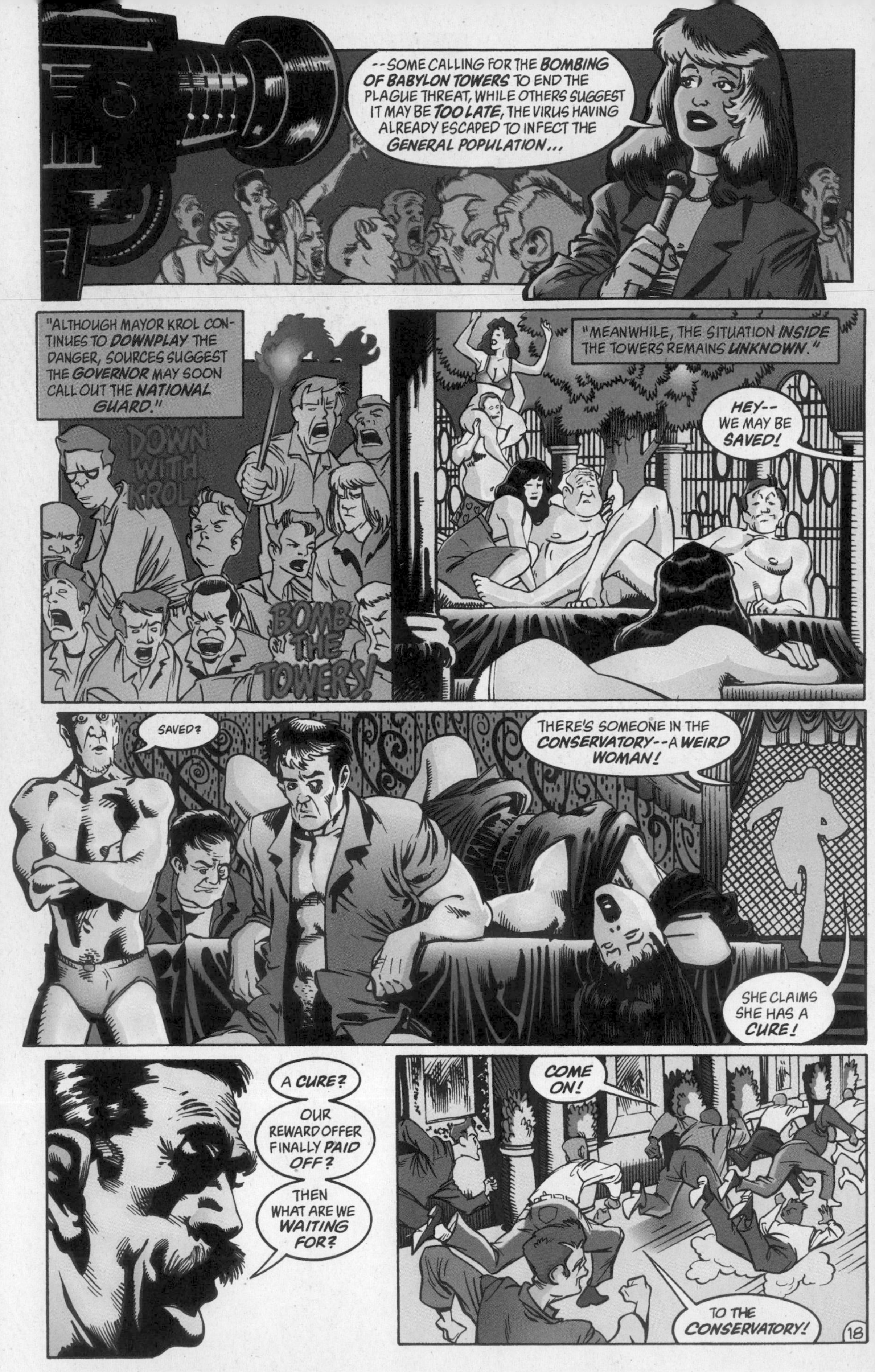
--SOME CALLING FOR THE BOMBING OF BABYLON TOWERS TO END THE PLAGUE THREAT, WHILE OTHERS SUGGEST IT MAY BE TOO LATE, THE VIRUS HAVING ALREADY ESCAPED TO INFECT THE GENERAL POPULATION...
"ALTHOUGH MAYOR KROL CONTINUES TO DOWNPLAY THE DANGER, SOURCES SUGGEST THE GOVERNOR MAY SOON CALL OUT THE NATIONAL GUARD."
DOWN WITH KROL!
BOMB THE TOWERS!
"MEANWHILE, THE SITUATION INSIDE THE TOWERS REMAINS UNKNOWN."
HEY-- WE MAY BE SAVED!
SAVED?
THERE'S SOMEONE IN THE CONSERVATORY--A WEIRD WOMAN!
SHE CLAIMS SHE HAS A CURE!
A CURE?
OUR REWARD OFFER FINALLY PAID OFF?
THEN WHAT ARE WE WAITING FOR?
COME ON!
TO THE CONSERVATORY!
18

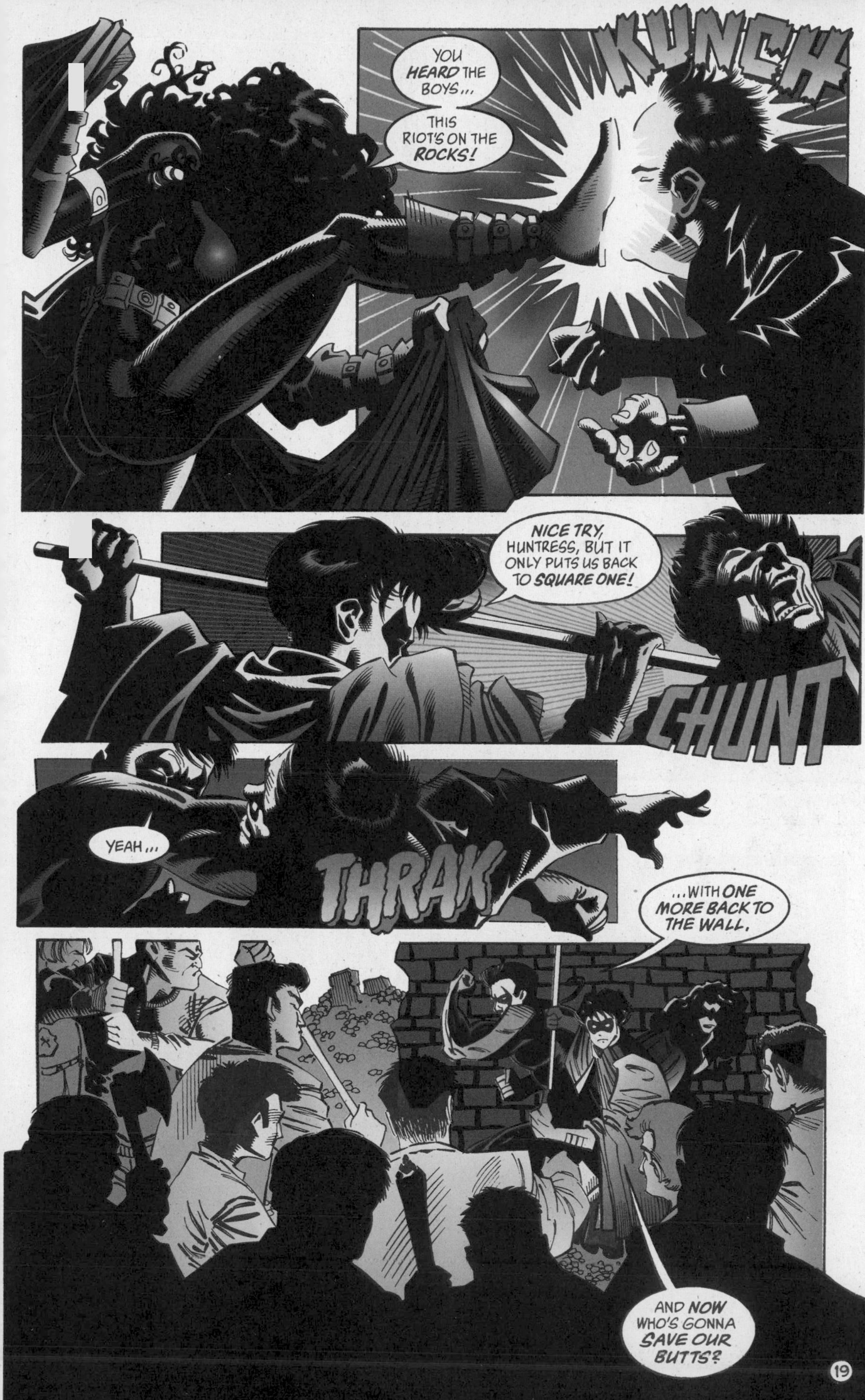
YOU HEARD THE BOYS...
THIS RIOT'S ON THE ROCKS!
KUNCH
NICE TRY, HUNTRESS, BUT IT ONLY PUTS US BACK TO SQUARE ONE!
CHUNT
YEAH...
THRAK
...WITH ONE MORE BACK TO THE WALL.
AND NOW WHO'S GONNA SAVE OUR BUTTS?

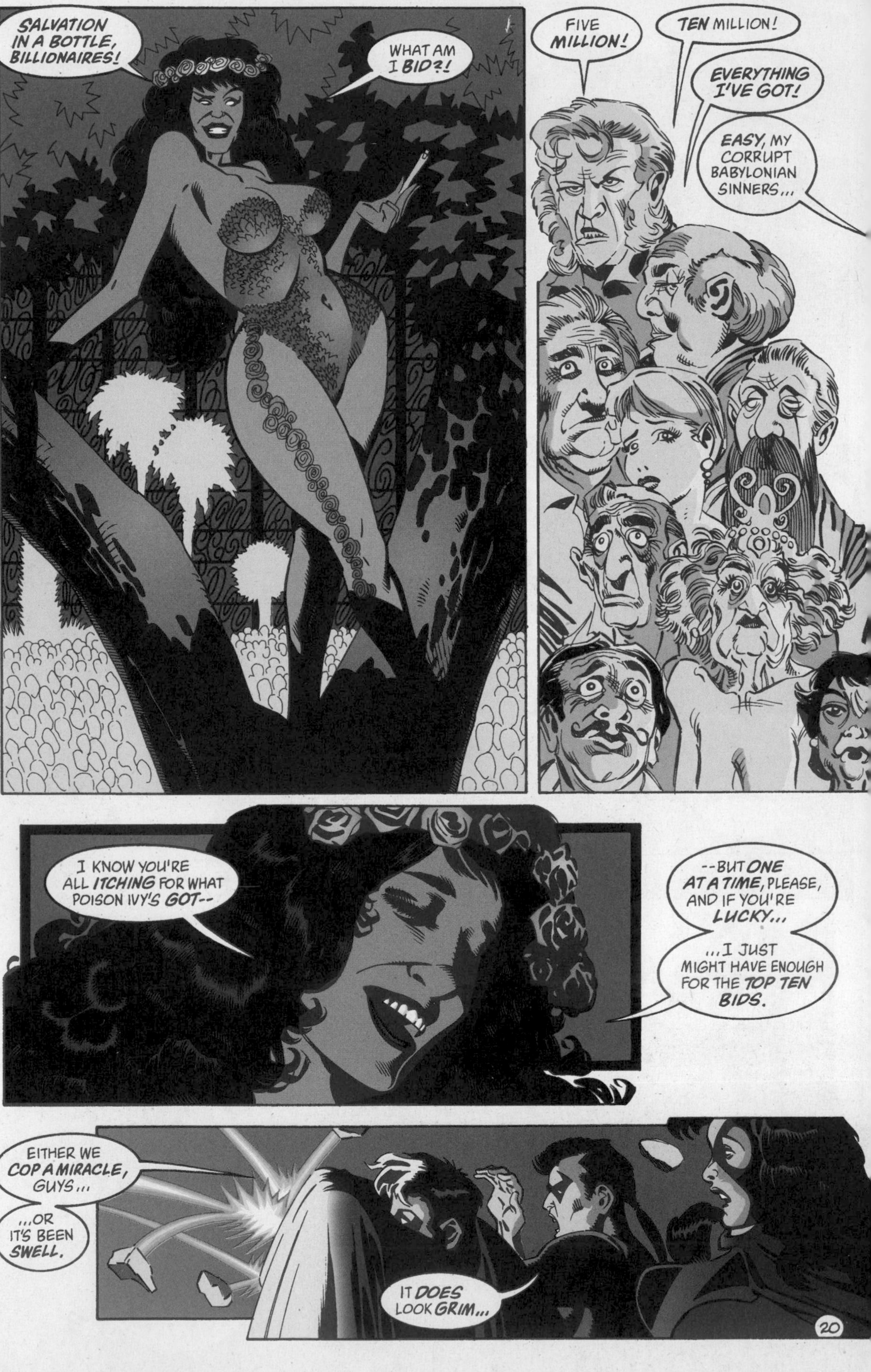
SALVATION IN A BOTTLE, BILLIONAIRES!
WHAT AM I BID?!
FIVE MILLION!
TEN MILLION!
EVERYTHING I'VE GOT!
EASY, MY CORRUPT BABYLONIAN SINNERS...
I KNOW YOU'RE ALL ITCHING FOR WHAT POISON IVY'S GOT--
--BUT ONE AT A TIME, PLEASE, AND IF YOU'RE LUCKY...
...I JUST MIGHT HAVE ENOUGH FOR THE TOP TEN BIDS.
EITHER WE COP A MIRACLE, GUYS...
...OR IT'S BEEN SWELL.
IT DOES LOOK GRIM...
20

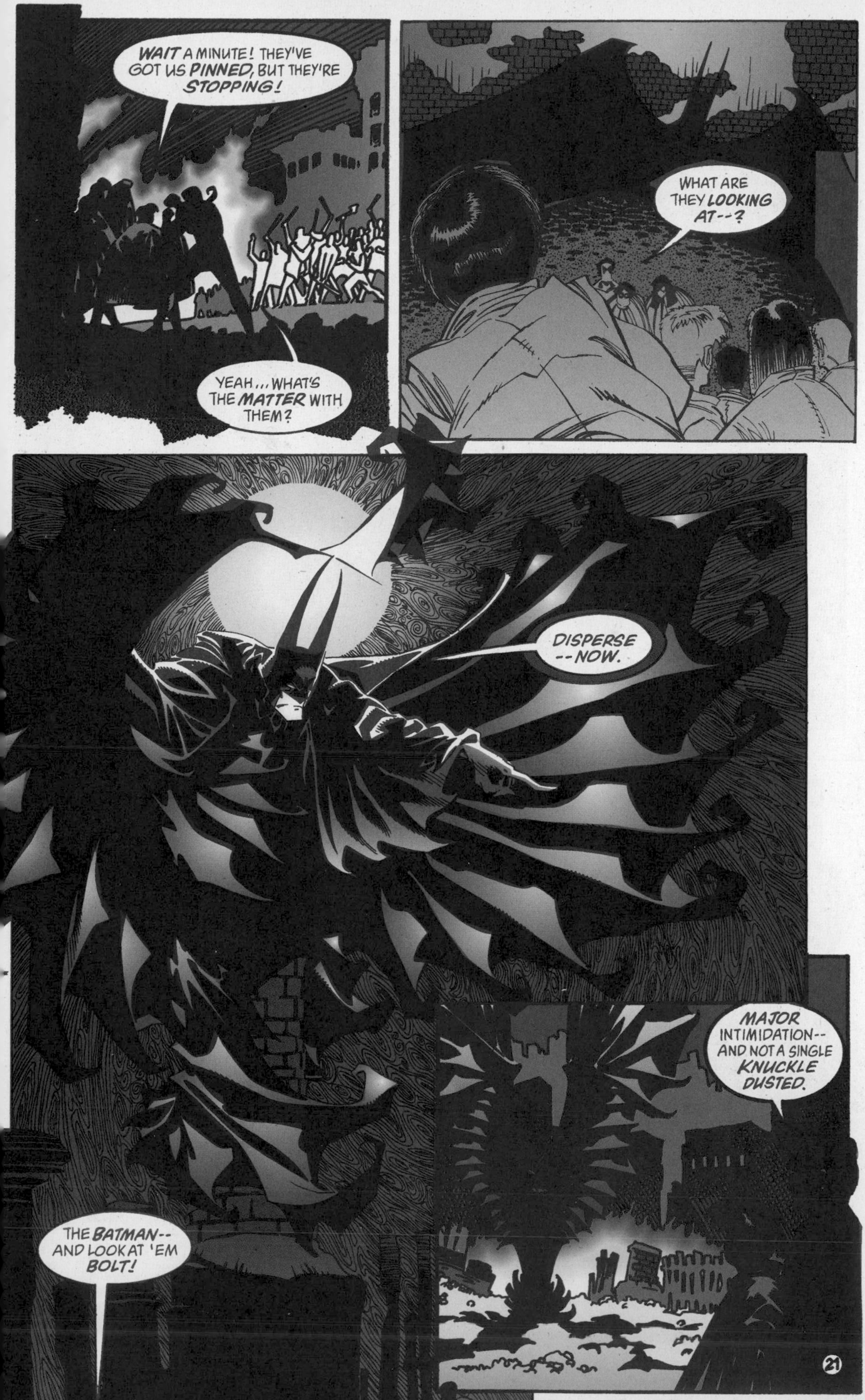
WAIT A MINUTE! THEY'VE GOT US PINNED, BUT THEY'RE STOPPING!
YEAH... WHAT'S THE MATTER WITH THEM?
WHAT ARE THEY LOOKING AT--?
DISPERSE --NOW.
MAJOR INTIMIDATION-- AND NOT A SINGLE KNUCKLE DUSTED.
THE BATMAN-- AND LOOK AT 'EM BOLT!

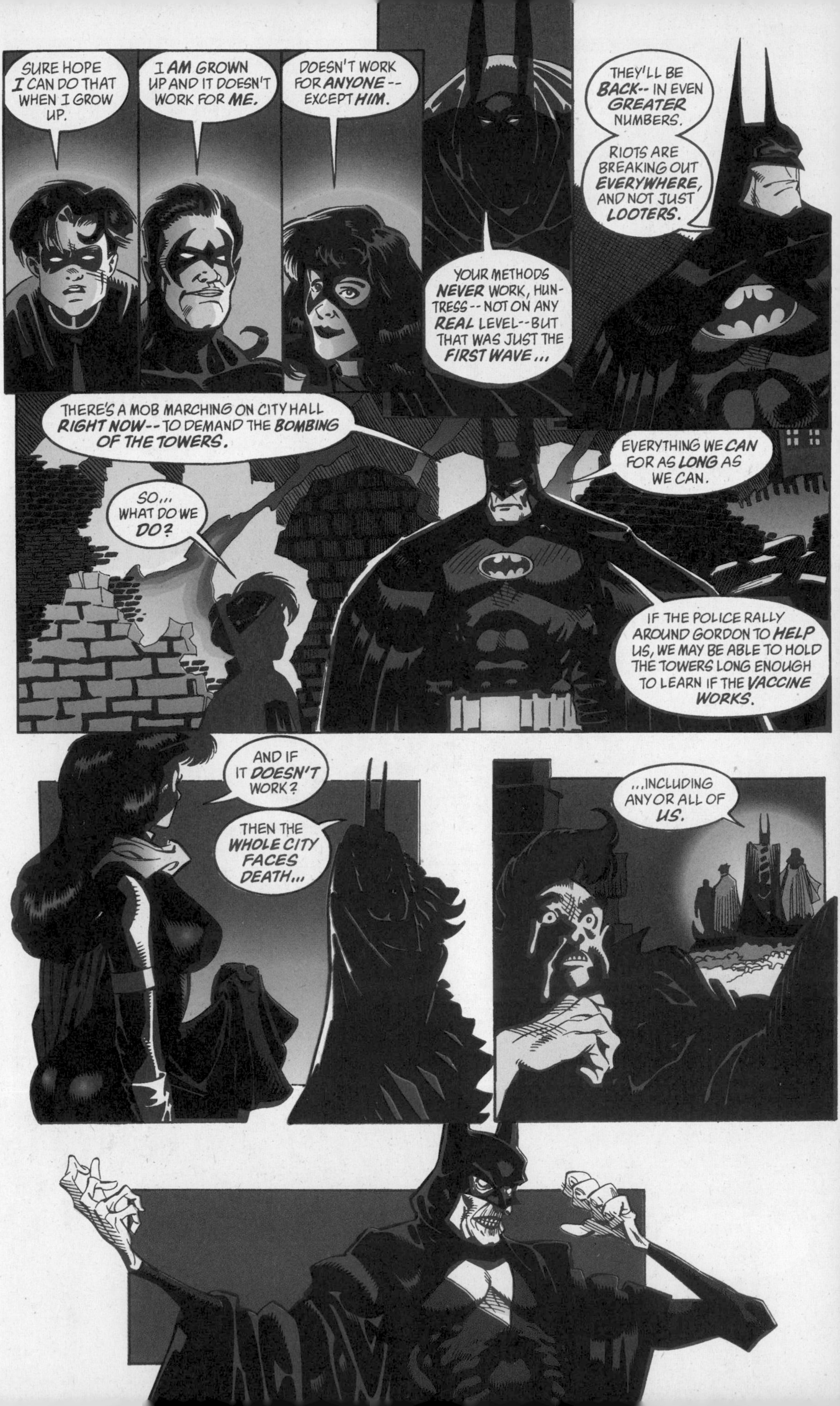
SURE HOPE I CAN DO THAT WHEN I GROW UP.
I AM GROWN UP AND IT DOESN'T WORK FOR ME.
DOESN'T WORK FOR ANYONE -- EXCEPT HIM.
YOUR METHODS NEVER WORK, HUNTRESS -- NOT ON ANY REAL LEVEL -- BUT THAT WAS JUST THE FIRST WAVE...
THEY'LL BE BACK -- IN EVEN GREATER NUMBERS.
RIOTS ARE BREAKING OUT EVERYWHERE, AND NOT JUST LOOTERS.
THERE'S A MOB MARCHING ON CITY HALL RIGHT NOW -- TO DEMAND THE BOMBING OF THE TOWERS.
SO... WHAT DO WE DO?
EVERYTHING WE CAN FOR AS LONG AS WE CAN.
IF THE POLICE RALLY AROUND GORDON TO HELP US, WE MAY BE ABLE TO HOLD THE TOWERS LONG ENOUGH TO LEARN IF THE VACCINE WORKS.
AND IF IT DOESN'T WORK?
THEN THE WHOLE CITY FACES DEATH...
...INCLUDING ANY OR ALL OF US.

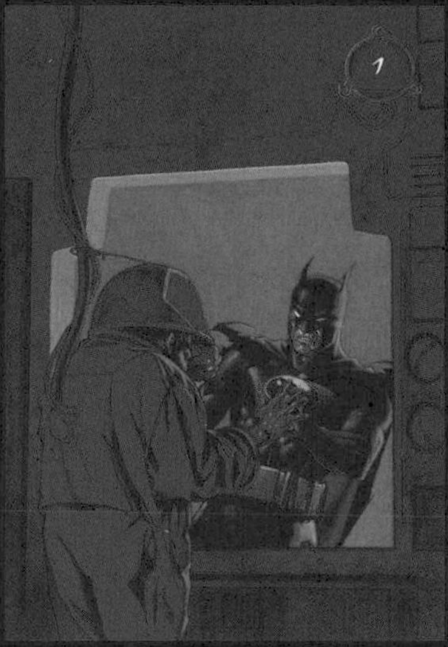
1
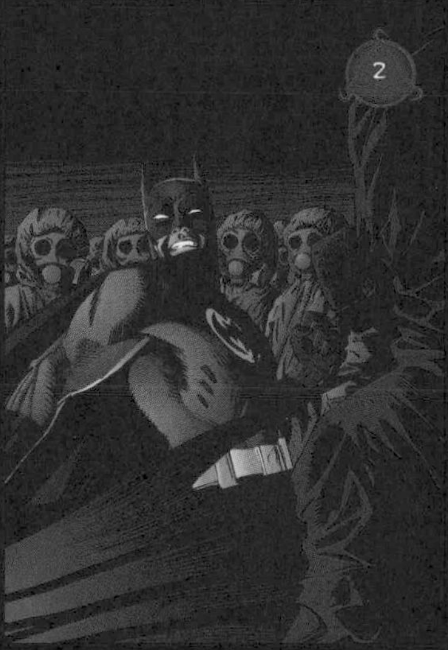
2
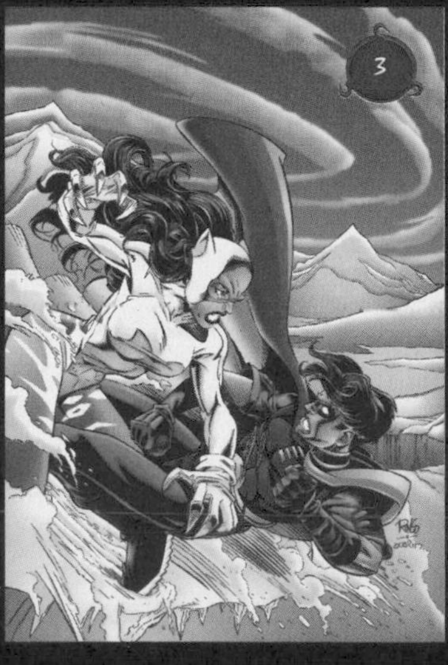
3
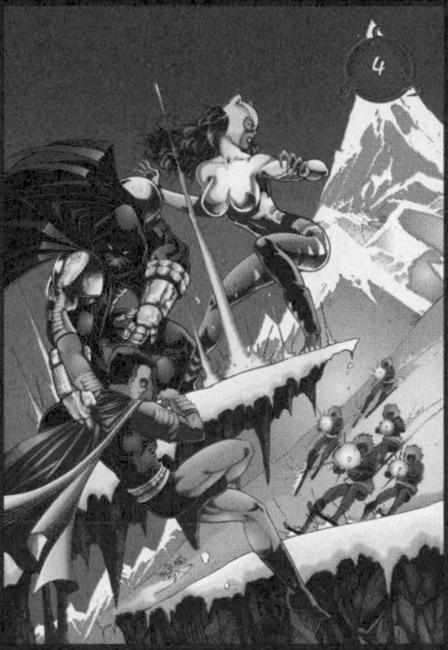
4
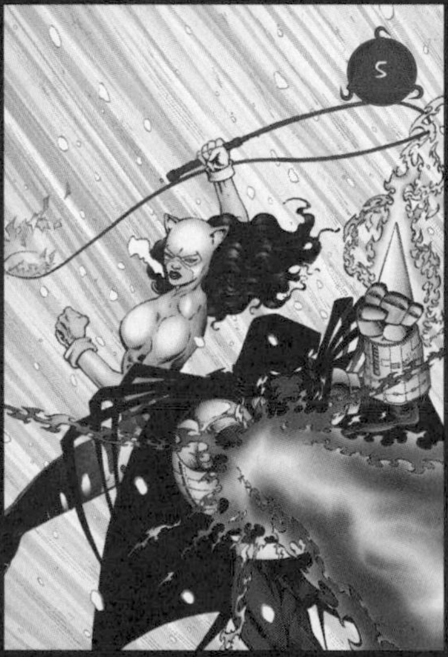
5
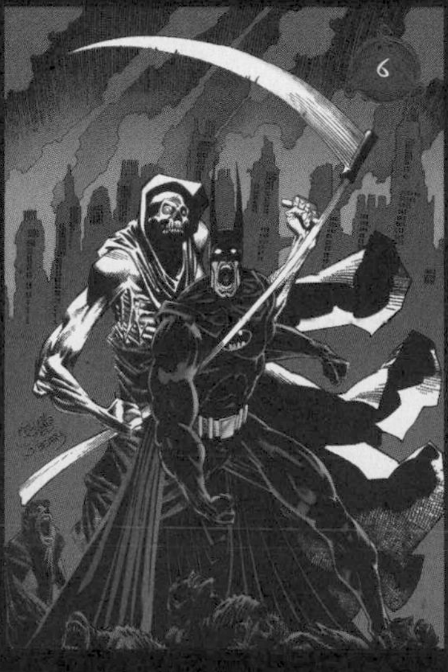
6

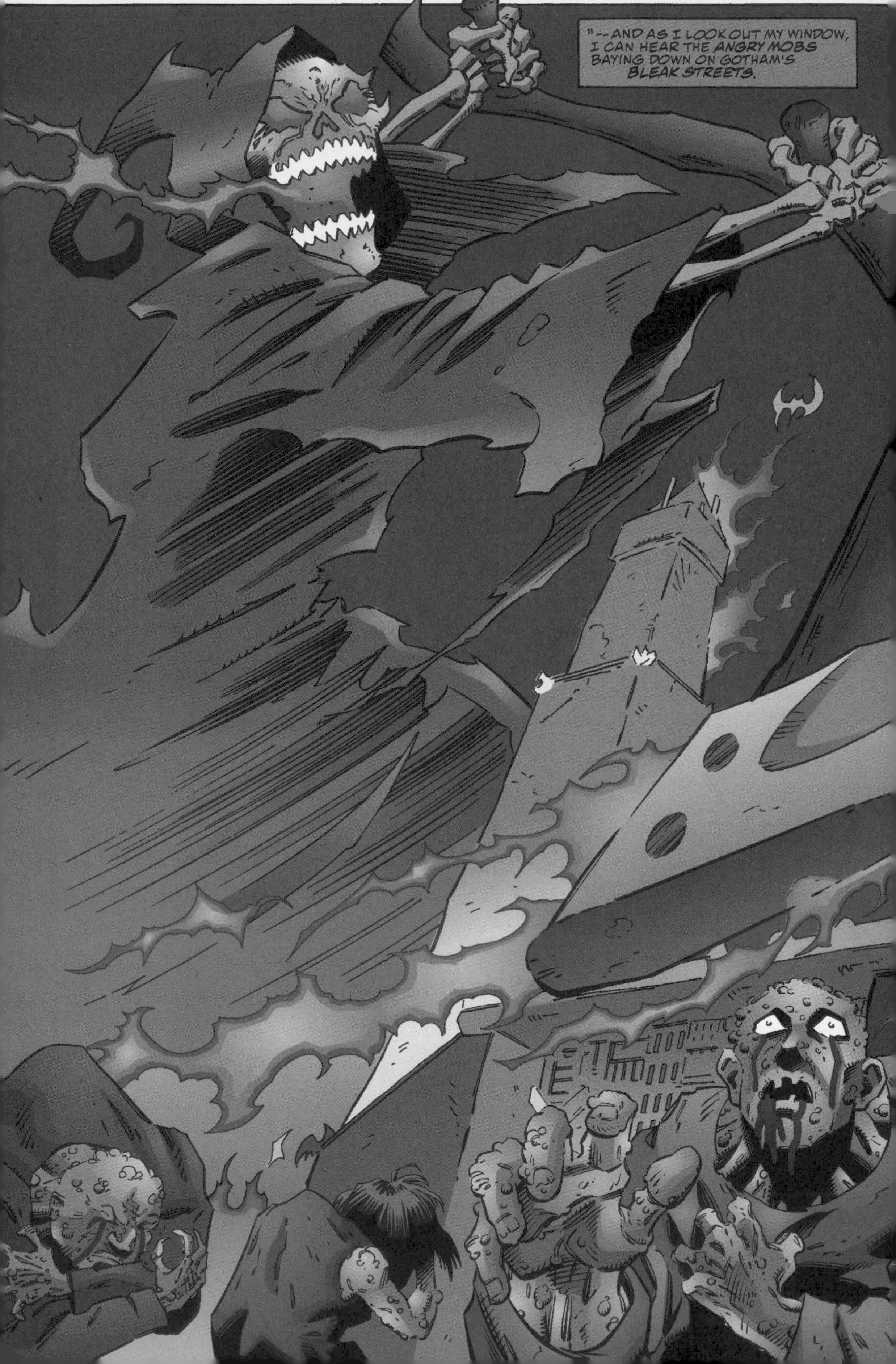
"--AND AS I LOOK OUT MY WINDOW, I CAN HEAR THE ANGRY MOBS BAYING DOWN ON GOTHAM'S BLEAK STREETS.

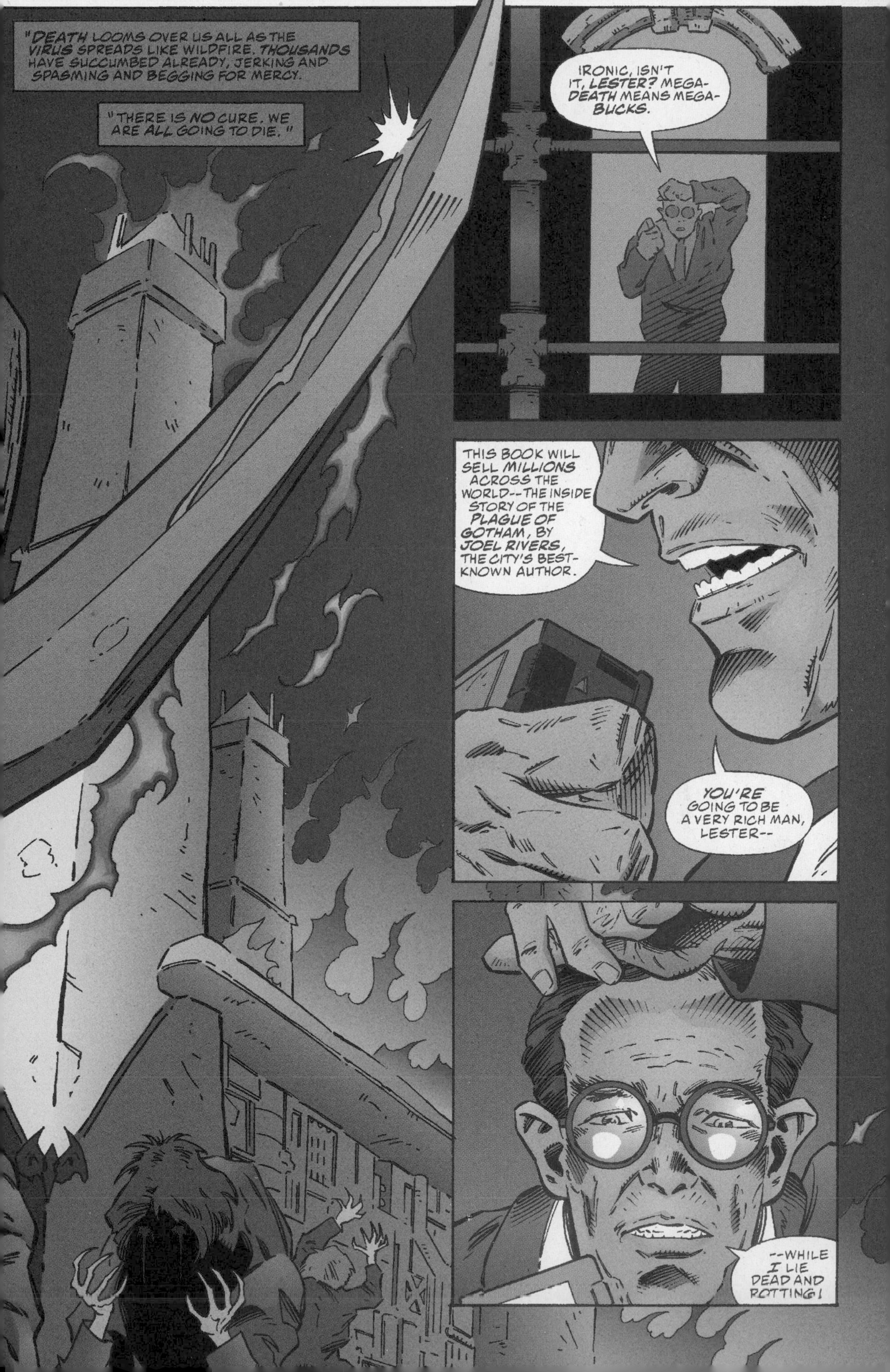
"DEATH LOOMS OVER US ALL AS THE VIRUS SPREADS LIKE WILDFIRE. THOUSANDS HAVE SUCCUMBED ALREADY, JERKING AND SPASMING AND BEGGING FOR MERCY.
"THERE IS NO CURE. WE ARE ALL GOING TO DIE."
IRONIC, ISN'T IT, LESTER? MEGA-DEATH MEANS MEGA-BUCKS.
THIS BOOK WILL SELL MILLIONS ACROSS THE WORLD--THE INSIDE STORY OF THE PLAGUE OF GOTHAM, BY JOEL RIVERS, THE CITY'S BEST-KNOWN AUTHOR.
YOU'RE GOING TO BE A VERY RICH MAN, LESTER--
--WHILE I LIE DEAD AND ROTTING!

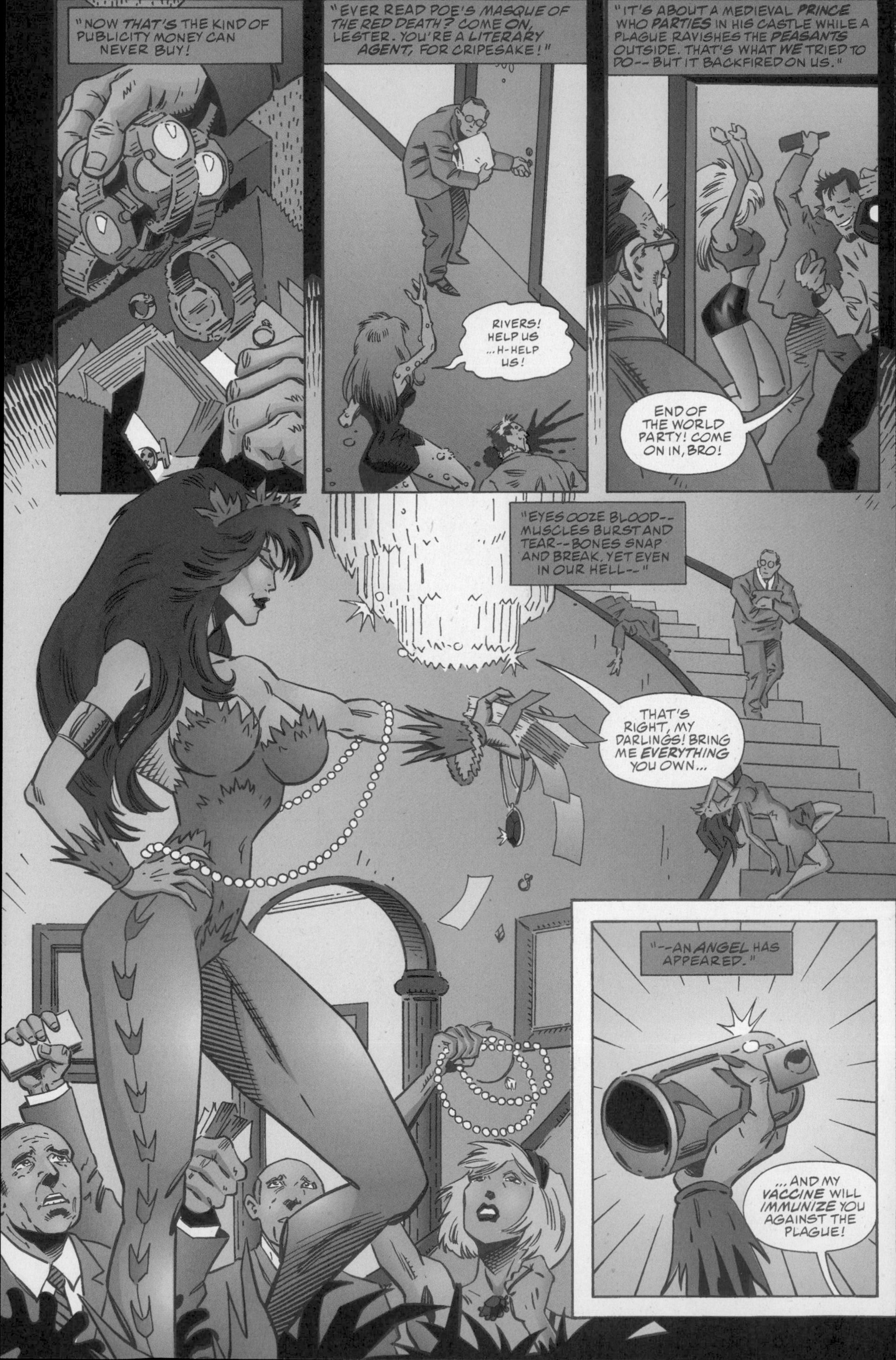
"NOW THAT'S THE KIND OF PUBLICITY MONEY CAN NEVER BUY!
"EVER READ POE'S MASQUE OF THE RED DEATH? COME ON, LESTER. YOU'RE A LITERARY AGENT, FOR CRIPESAKE!"
RIVERS! HELP US ...H-HELP US!
"IT'S ABOUT A MEDIEVAL PRINCE WHO PARTIES IN HIS CASTLE WHILE A PLAGUE RAVISHES THE PEASANTS OUTSIDE. THAT'S WHAT WE TRIED TO DO-- BUT IT BACKFIRED ON US."
END OF THE WORLD PARTY! COME ON IN, BRO!
"EYES OOZE BLOOD-- MUSCLES BURST AND TEAR--BONES SNAP AND BREAK, YET EVEN IN OUR HELL--"
THAT'S RIGHT, MY DARLINGS! BRING ME EVERYTHING YOU OWN...
"--AN ANGEL HAS APPEARED."
...AND MY VACCINE WILL IMMUNIZE YOU AGAINST THE PLAGUE!

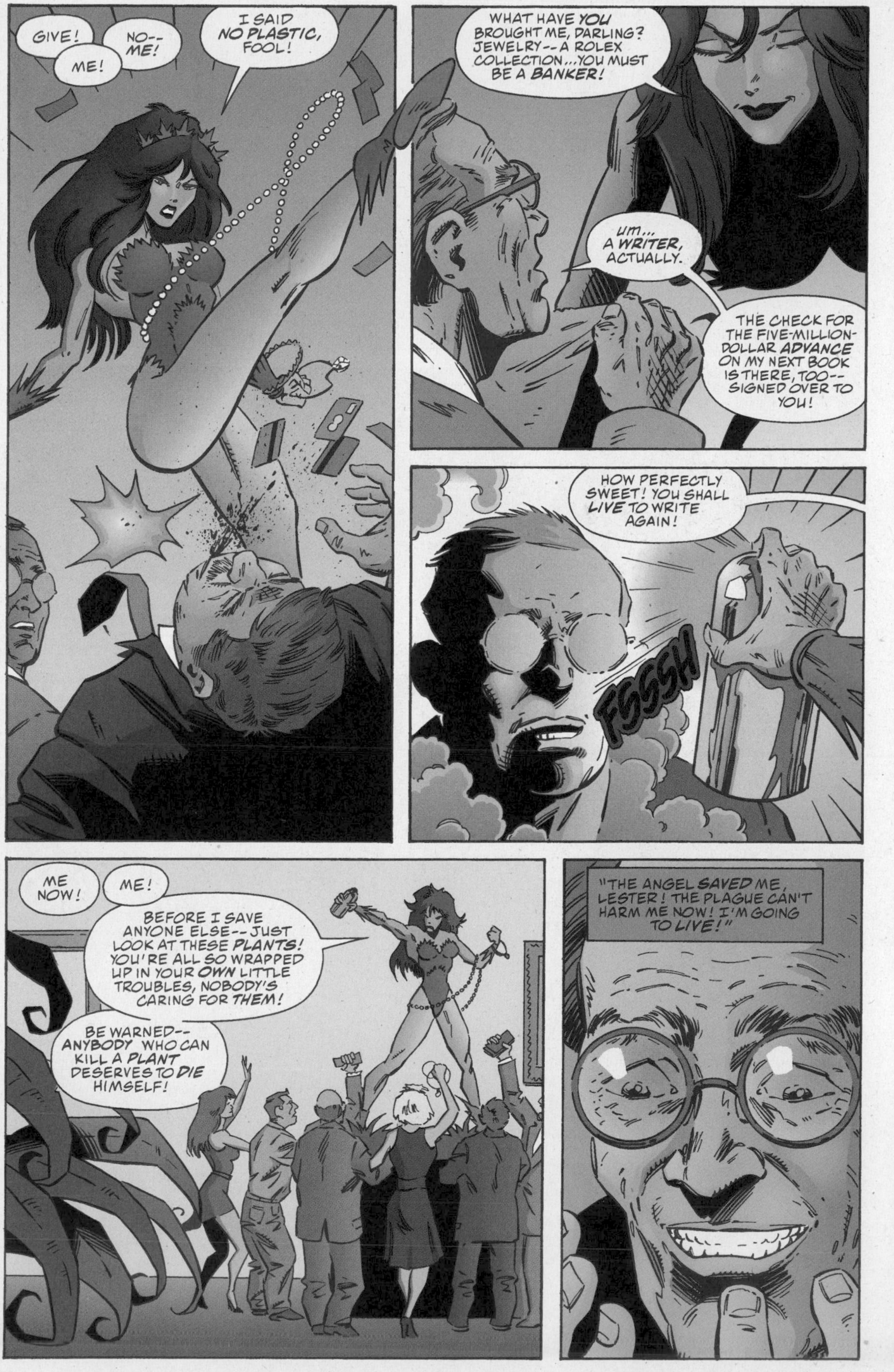
GIVE!
ME!
NO-- ME!
I SAID NO PLASTIC, FOOL!
WHAT HAVE YOU BROUGHT ME, DARLING? JEWELRY-- A ROLEX COLLECTION... YOU MUST BE A BANKER!
UM... A WRITER, ACTUALLY.
THE CHECK FOR THE FIVE-MILLION-DOLLAR ADVANCE ON MY NEXT BOOK IS THERE, TOO-- SIGNED OVER TO YOU!
HOW PERFECTLY SWEET! YOU SHALL LIVE TO WRITE AGAIN!
FSSSH
ME NOW!
ME!
BEFORE I SAVE ANYONE ELSE-- JUST LOOK AT THESE PLANTS! YOU'RE ALL SO WRAPPED UP IN YOUR OWN LITTLE TROUBLES, NOBODY'S CARING FOR THEM!
BE WARNED-- ANYBODY WHO CAN KILL A PLANT DESERVES TO DIE HIMSELF!
"THE ANGEL SAVED ME, LESTER! THE PLAGUE CAN'T HARM ME NOW! I'M GOING TO LIVE!"

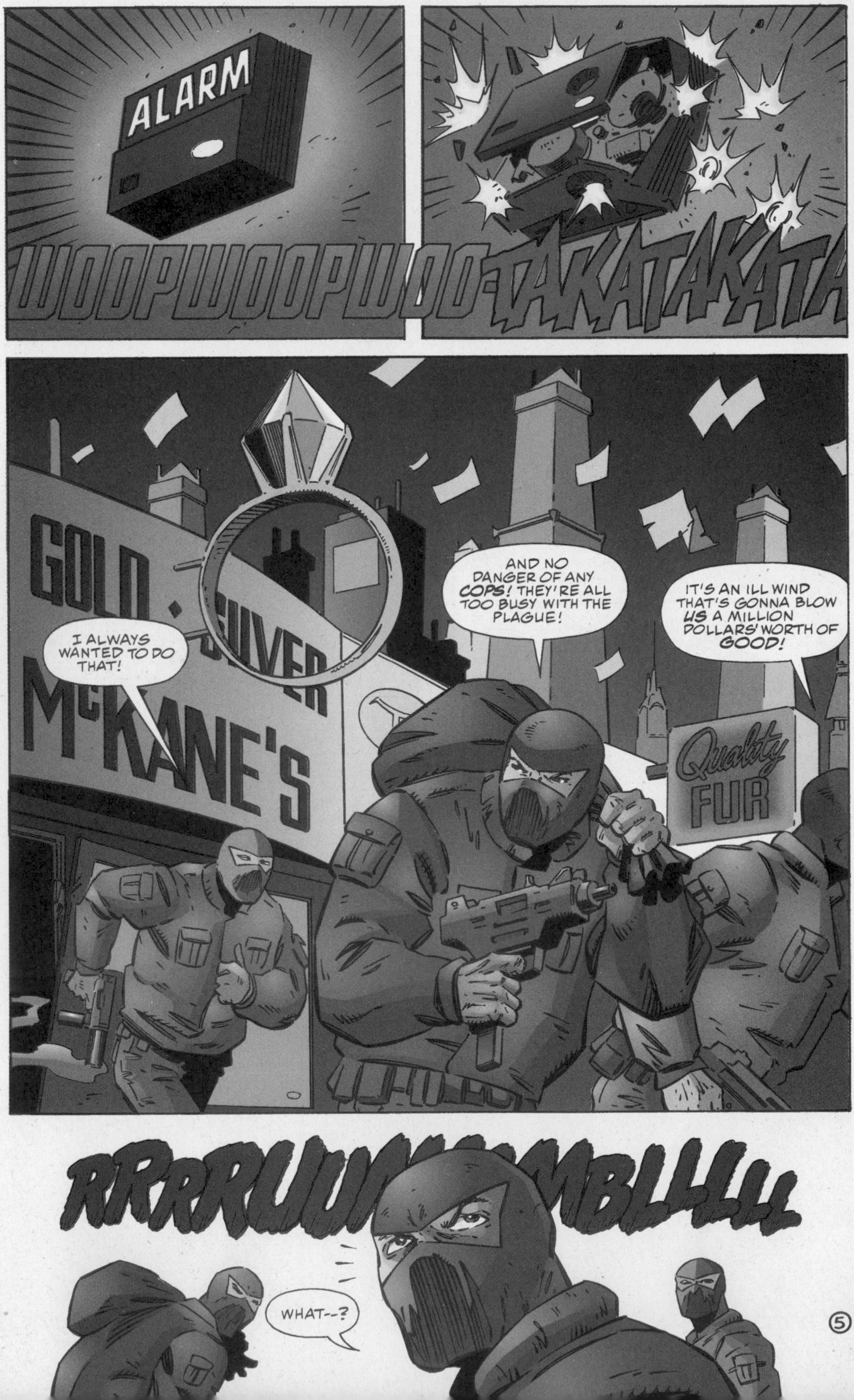
ALARM
WOOPWOOPWOO-TAKATAKATA
GOLD · SILVER
McKANE'S
Quality FUR
I ALWAYS WANTED TO DO THAT!
AND NO DANGER OF ANY COPS! THEY'RE ALL TOO BUSY WITH THE PLAGUE!
IT'S AN ILL WIND THAT'S GONNA BLOW US A MILLION DOLLARS' WORTH OF GOOD!
WHAT--?

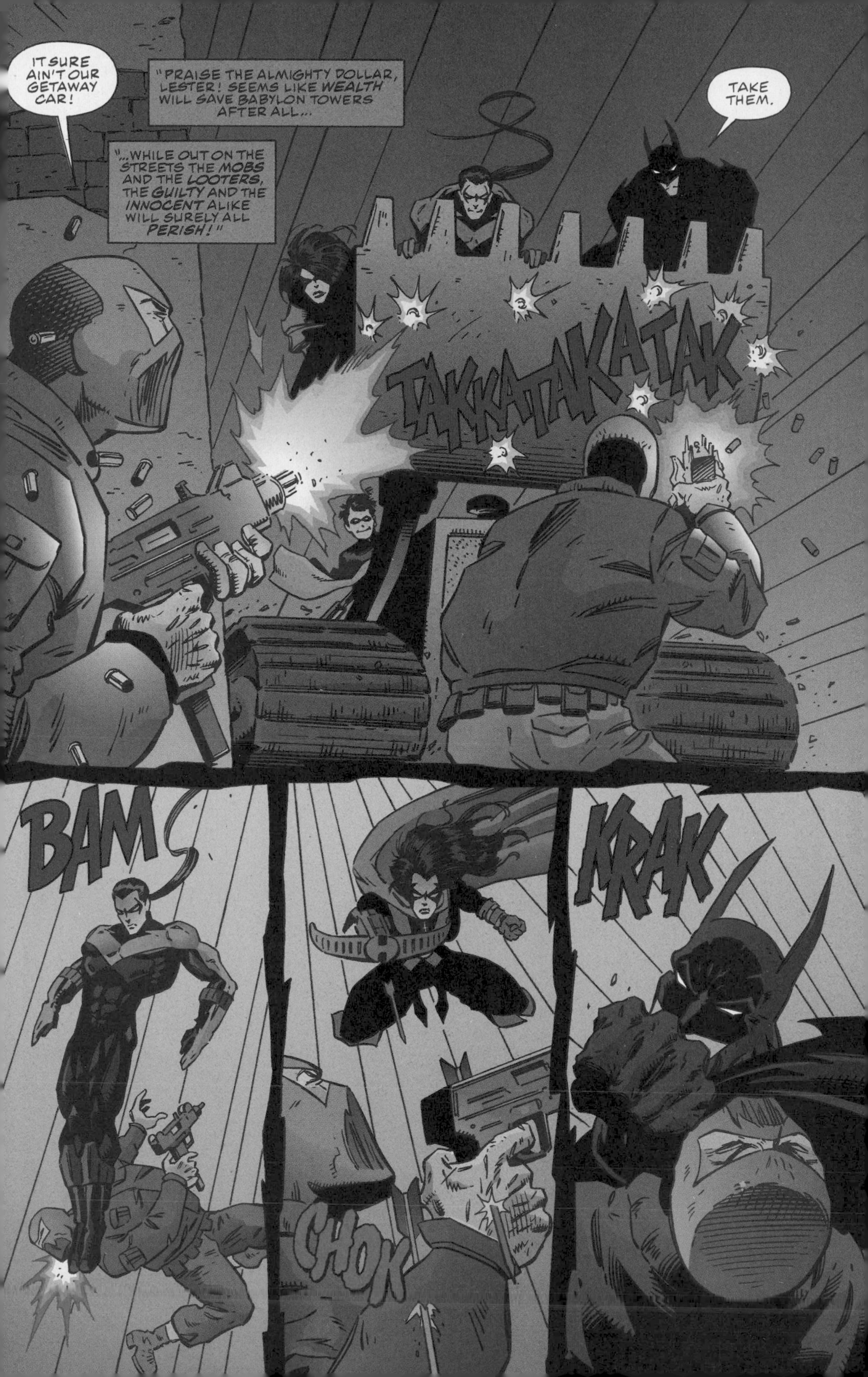
IT SURE AIN'T OUR GETAWAY CAR!
"PRAISE THE ALMIGHTY DOLLAR, LESTER! SEEMS LIKE WEALTH WILL SAVE BABYLON TOWERS AFTER ALL...
"...WHILE OUT ON THE STREETS THE MOBS AND THE LOOTERS, THE GUILTY AND THE INNOCENT ALIKE WILL SURELY ALL PERISH!"
TAKE THEM.
TAKKATAKKATAK
BAM
CHOK
KRAK

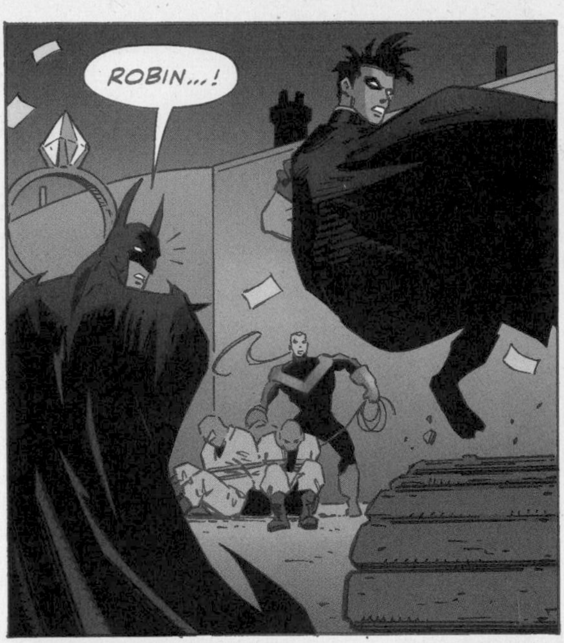
ROBIN...!

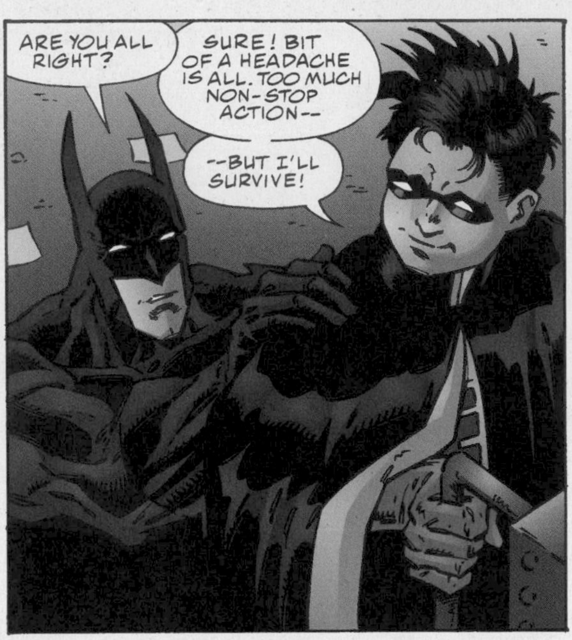
ARE YOU ALL RIGHT?
SURE! BIT OF A HEADACHE IS ALL. TOO MUCH NON-STOP ACTION--
--BUT I'LL SURVIVE!

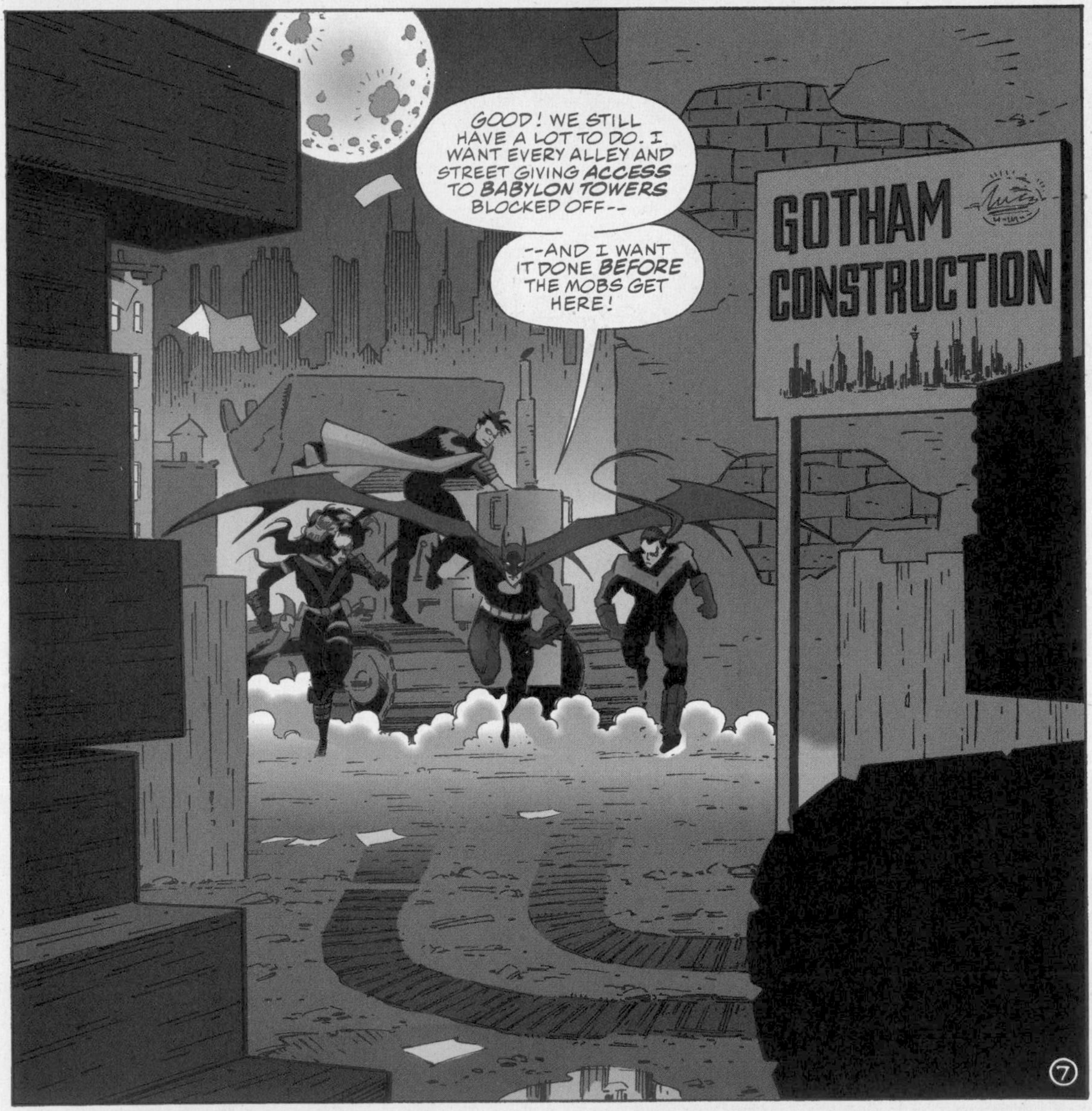
GOOD! WE STILL HAVE A LOT TO DO. I WANT EVERY ALLEY AND STREET GIVING ACCESS TO BABYLON TOWERS BLOCKED OFF--
--AND I WANT IT DONE BEFORE THE MOBS GET HERE!
GOTHAM CONSTRUCTION
7

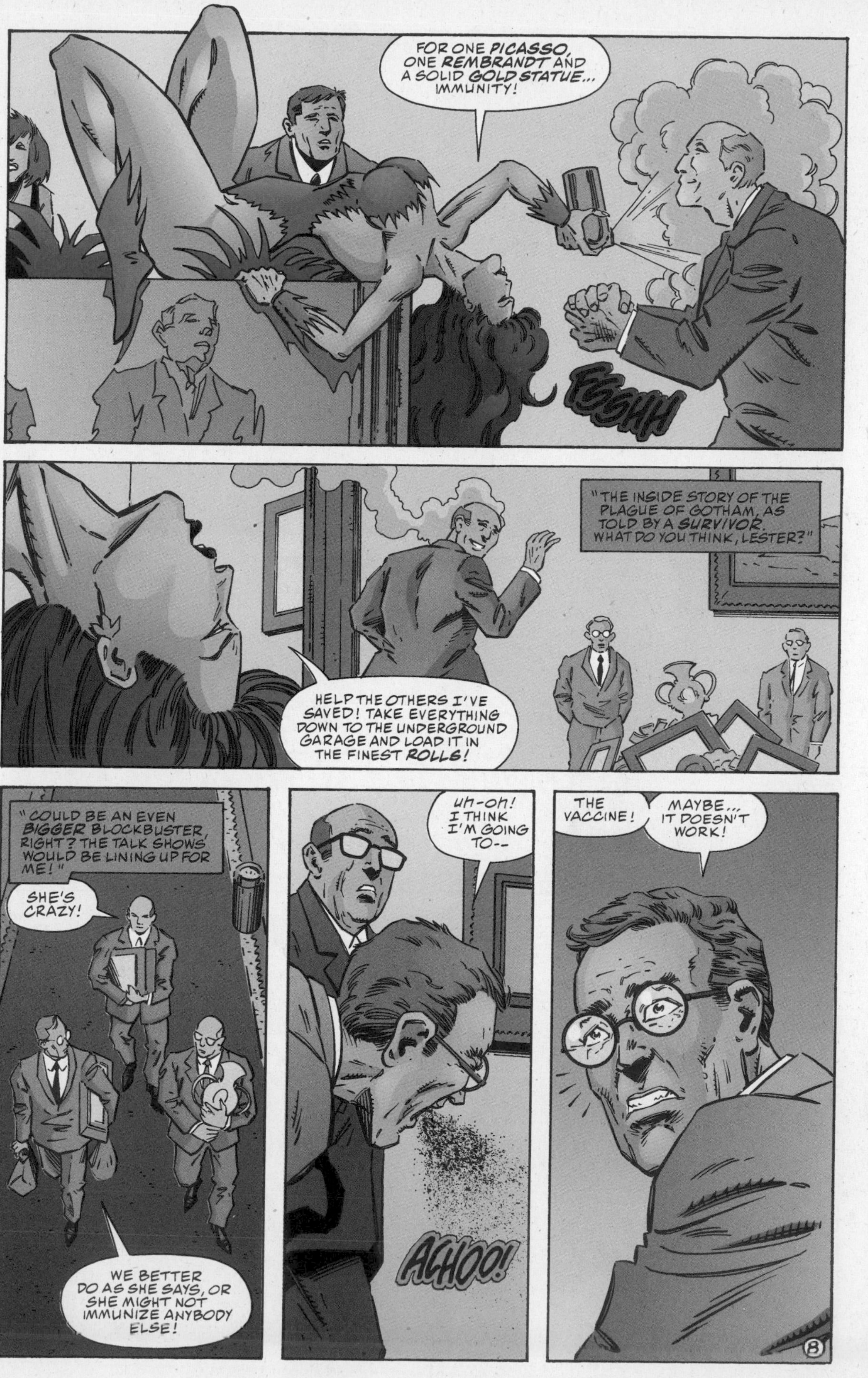
FOR ONE PICASSO, ONE REMBRANDT AND A SOLID GOLD STATUE... IMMUNITY!
FSSHH
"THE INSIDE STORY OF THE PLAGUE OF GOTHAM, AS TOLD BY A SURVIVOR. WHAT DO YOU THINK, LESTER?"
HELP THE OTHERS I'VE SAVED! TAKE EVERYTHING DOWN TO THE UNDERGROUND GARAGE AND LOAD IT IN THE FINEST ROLLS!
"COULD BE AN EVEN BIGGER BLOCKBUSTER, RIGHT? THE TALK SHOWS WOULD BE LINING UP FOR ME!"
SHE'S CRAZY!
WE BETTER DO AS SHE SAYS, OR SHE MIGHT NOT IMMUNIZE ANYBODY ELSE!
UH-OH! I THINK I'M GOING TO--
ACHOO!
THE VACCINE!
MAYBE... IT DOESN'T WORK!
8

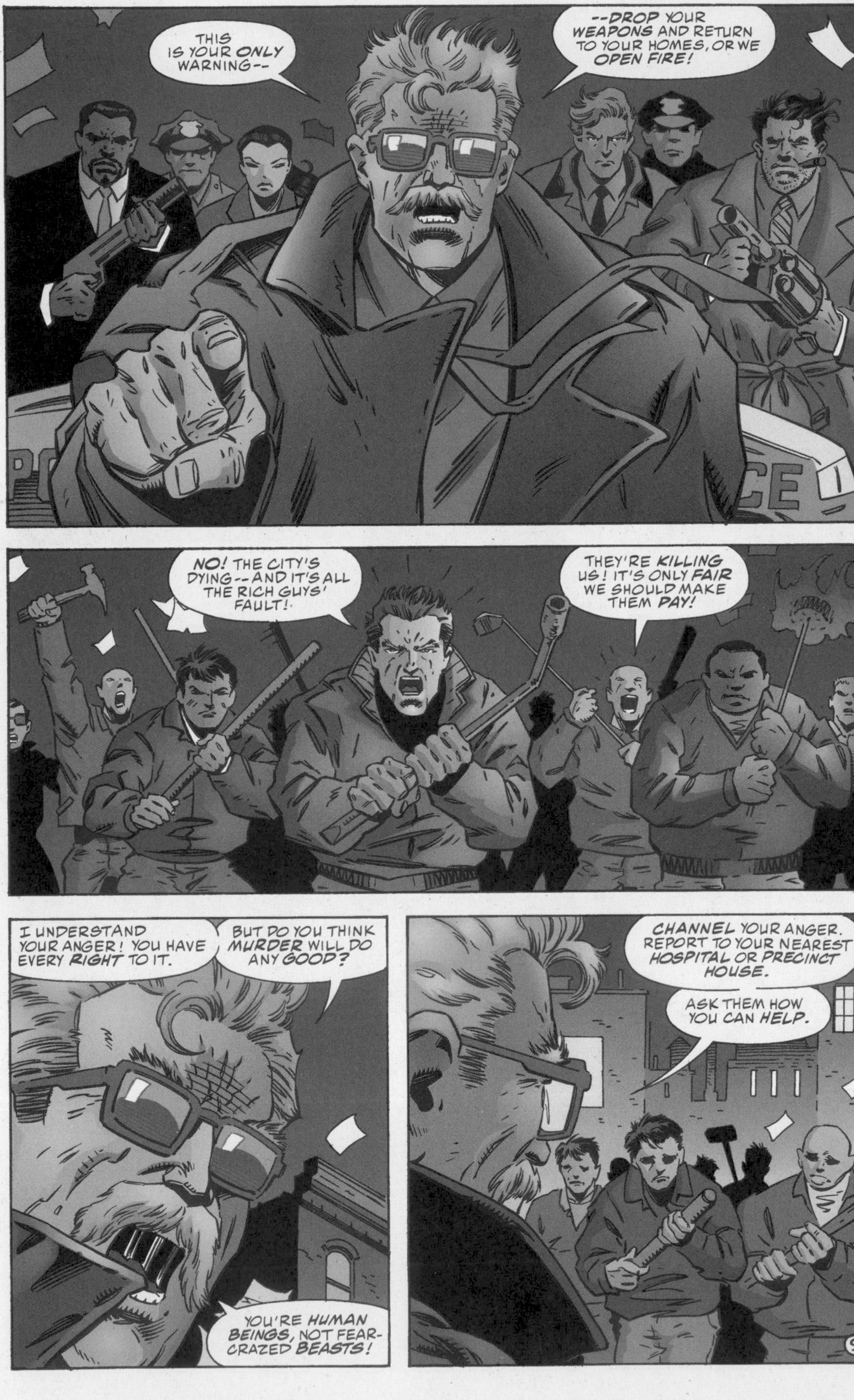
THIS IS YOUR ONLY WARNING--
--DROP YOUR WEAPONS AND RETURN TO YOUR HOMES, OR WE OPEN FIRE!
NO! THE CITY'S DYING--AND IT'S ALL THE RICH GUYS' FAULT!
THEY'RE KILLING US! IT'S ONLY FAIR WE SHOULD MAKE THEM PAY!
I UNDERSTAND YOUR ANGER! YOU HAVE EVERY RIGHT TO IT.
BUT DO YOU THINK MURDER WILL DO ANY GOOD?
YOU'RE HUMAN BEINGS, NOT FEAR-CRAZED BEASTS!
CHANNEL YOUR ANGER. REPORT TO YOUR NEAREST HOSPITAL OR PRECINCT HOUSE.
ASK THEM HOW YOU CAN HELP.
9

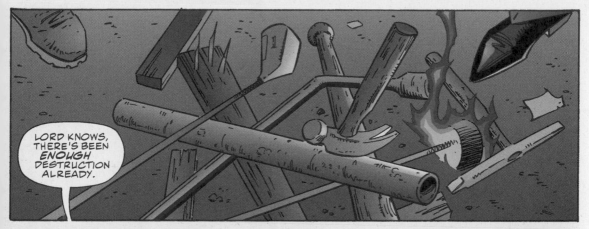

LORD KNOWS, THERE'S BEEN *ENOUGH* DESTRUCTION ALREADY.

NICE WORK, SIR!

THEY'LL BE BACK, LIEUTENANT. THEM, OR OTHERS LIKE THEM.

KITCH-- THERE ARE REPORTS OF *LOOTERS* IN THE CENTRAL MALLS. TAKE WHAT BACKUP YOU CAN SCROUNGE!

MONTOYA--HARDBACK-- I WANT AS MANY STREETS *BLOCKED OFF* AS POSSIBLE!

JUST LIKE THE OLD DAYS, COMMISH!

THAT'S STILL *EX-COMMISH, HARVEY.* AND THERE'LL BE *HELL* TO PAY WHEN *ANDY HOWE* DISCOVERS THAT SERVING OFFICERS HAVE *DESERTED* HIM TO TAKE ORDERS FROM *ME!*

THERE'S HELL TO PAY *NOW...*

...COMMISH!

⑩

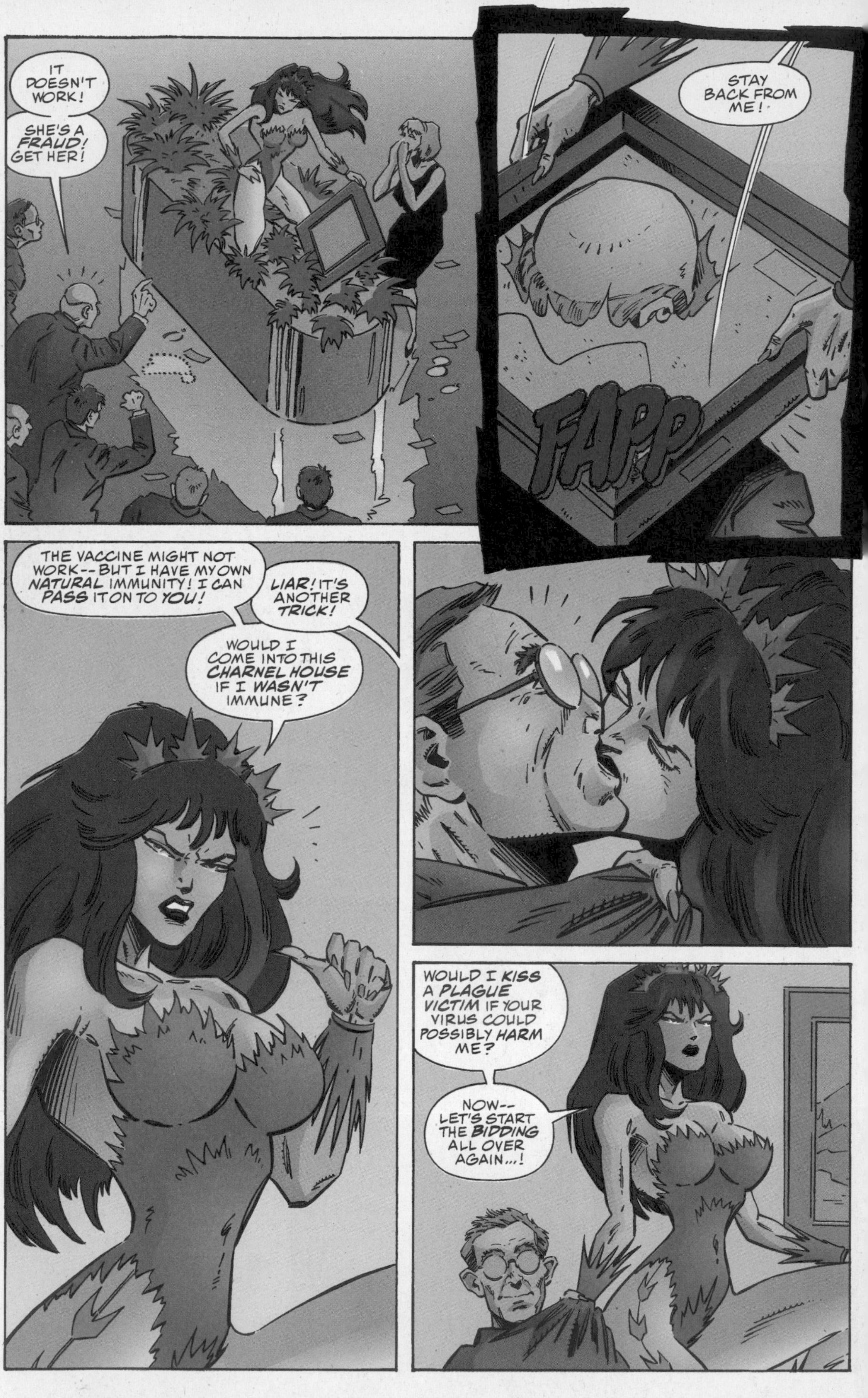
IT DOESN'T WORK!
SHE'S A FRAUD! GET HER!
STAY BACK FROM ME!
FAPP
THE VACCINE MIGHT NOT WORK--BUT I HAVE MY OWN NATURAL IMMUNITY! I CAN PASS IT ON TO YOU!
LIAR! IT'S ANOTHER TRICK!
WOULD I COME INTO THIS CHARNEL HOUSE IF I WASN'T IMMUNE?
WOULD I KISS A PLAGUE VICTIM IF YOUR VIRUS COULD POSSIBLY HARM ME?
NOW-- LET'S START THE BIDDING ALL OVER AGAIN...!

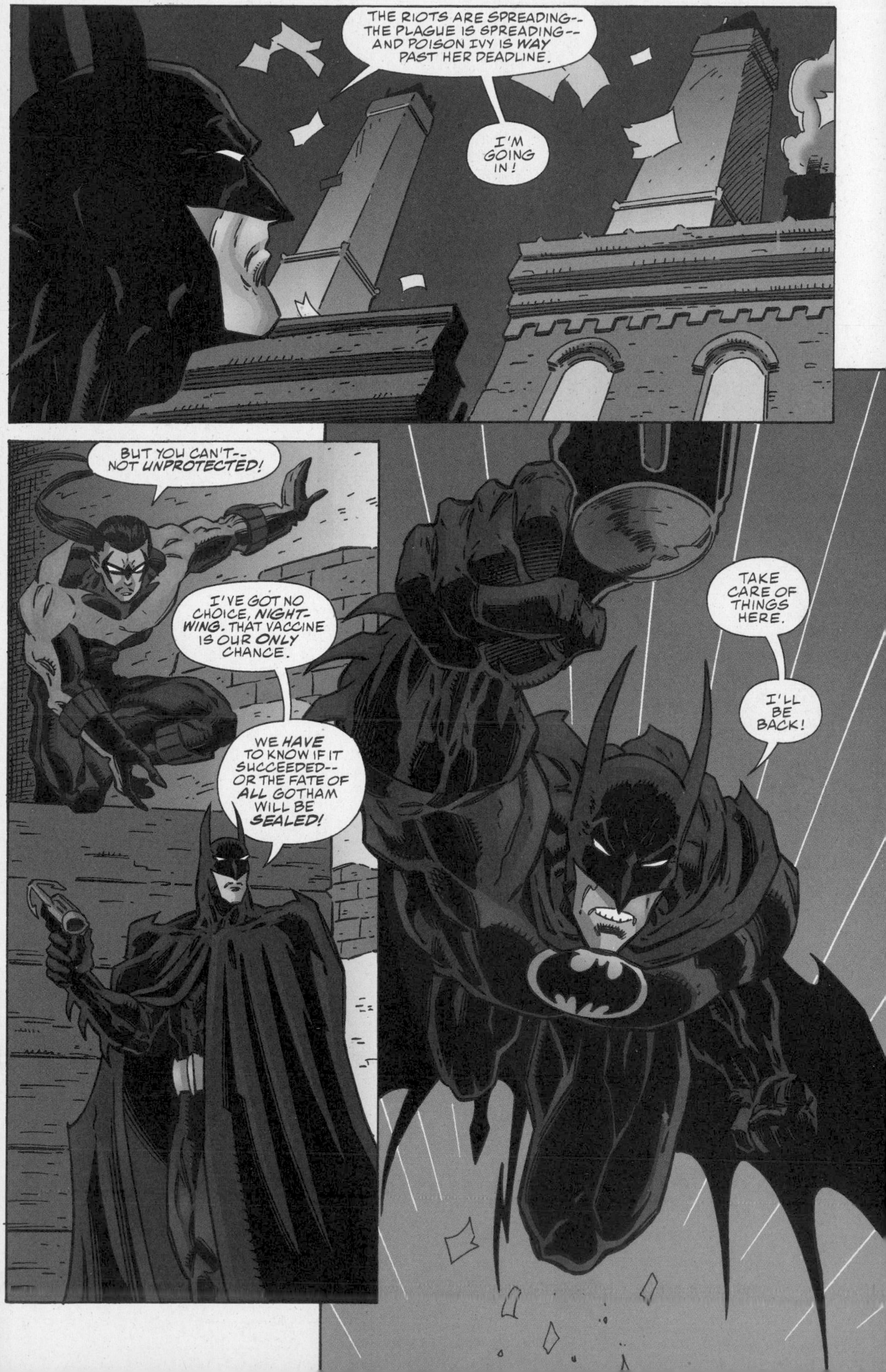
THE RIOTS ARE SPREADING-- THE PLAGUE IS SPREADING-- AND POISON IVY IS WAY PAST HER DEADLINE.
I'M GOING IN!
BUT YOU CAN'T-- NOT UNPROTECTED!
I'VE GOT NO CHOICE, NIGHTWING. THAT VACCINE IS OUR ONLY CHANCE.
WE HAVE TO KNOW IF IT SUCCEEDED-- OR THE FATE OF ALL GOTHAM WILL BE SEALED!
TAKE CARE OF THINGS HERE.
I'LL BE BACK!

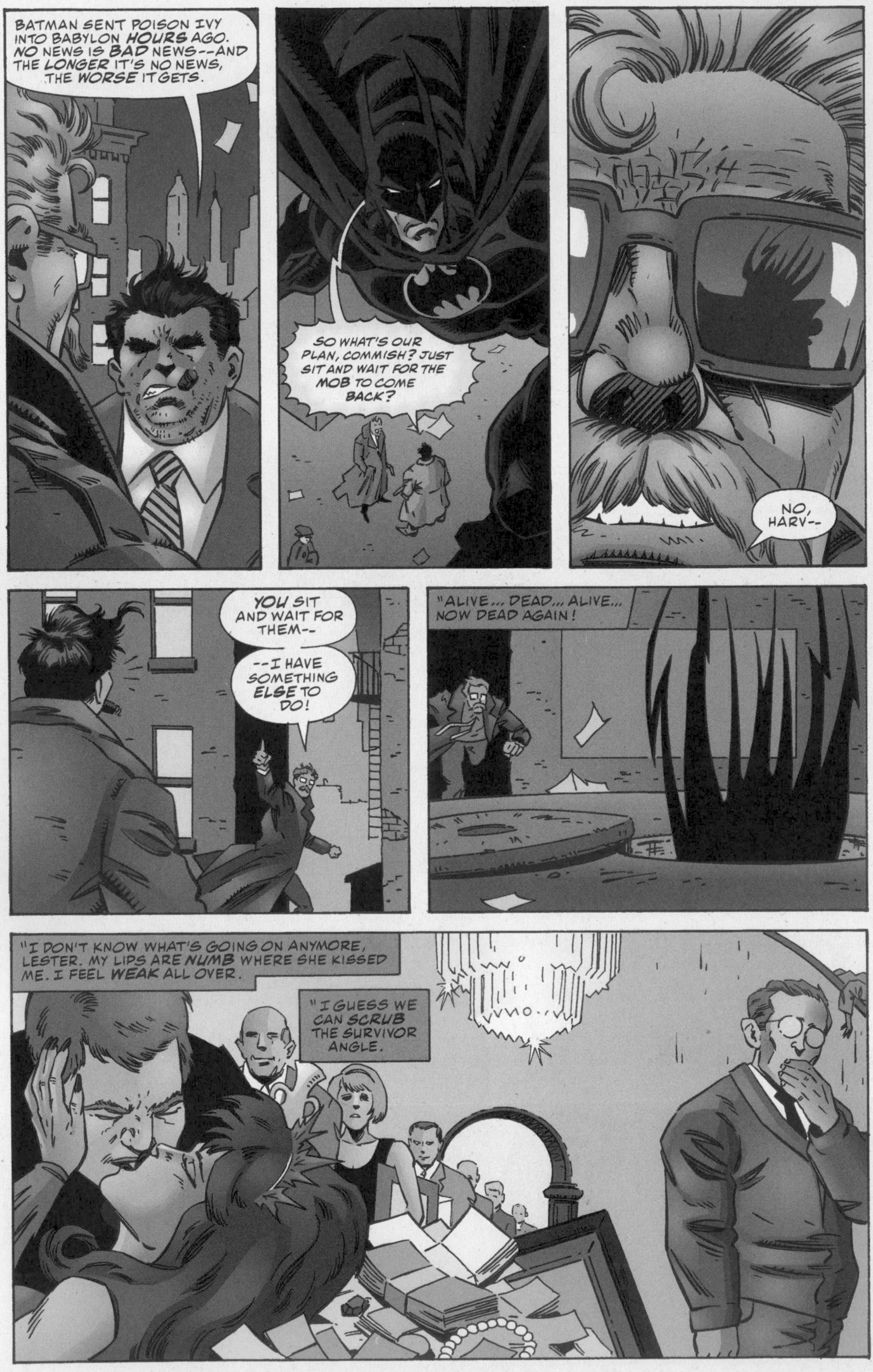

BATMAN SENT POISON IVY INTO BABYLON HOURS AGO. NO NEWS IS BAD NEWS--AND THE LONGER IT'S NO NEWS, THE WORSE IT GETS.
SO WHAT'S OUR PLAN, COMMISH? JUST SIT AND WAIT FOR THE MOB TO COME BACK?
NO, HARV--
YOU SIT AND WAIT FOR THEM--
--I HAVE SOMETHING ELSE TO DO!
"ALIVE... DEAD... ALIVE... NOW DEAD AGAIN!
"I DON'T KNOW WHAT'S GOING ON ANYMORE, LESTER. MY LIPS ARE NUMB WHERE SHE KISSED ME. I FEEL WEAK ALL OVER.
"I GUESS WE CAN SCRUB THE SURVIVOR ANGLE.

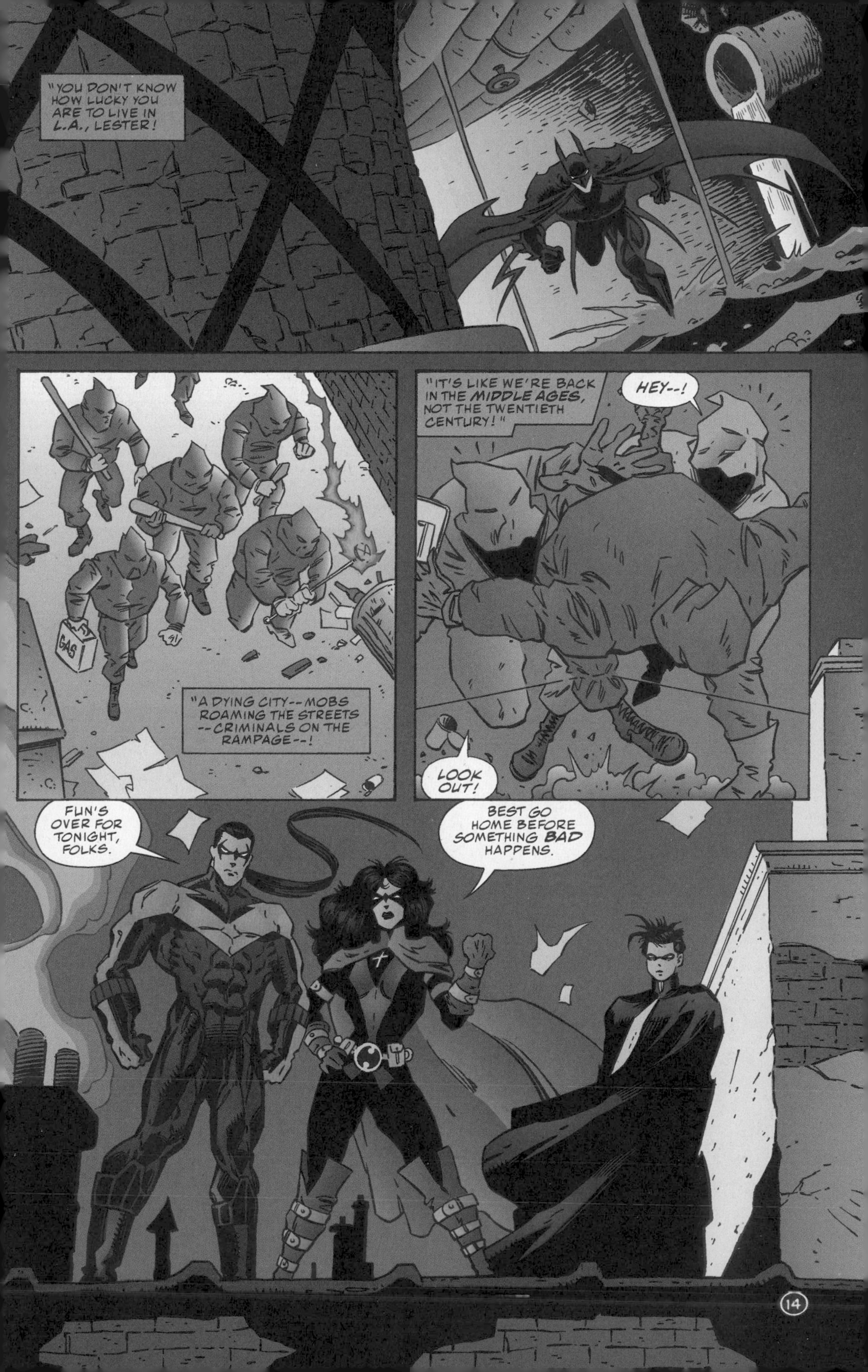
"YOU DON'T KNOW HOW LUCKY YOU ARE TO LIVE IN L.A., LESTER!
"A DYING CITY--MOBS ROAMING THE STREETS --CRIMINALS ON THE RAMPAGE--!
GAS
"IT'S LIKE WE'RE BACK IN THE MIDDLE AGES, NOT THE TWENTIETH CENTURY!"
HEY--!
LOOK OUT!
FUN'S OVER FOR TONIGHT, FOLKS.
BEST GO HOME BEFORE SOMETHING BAD HAPPENS.

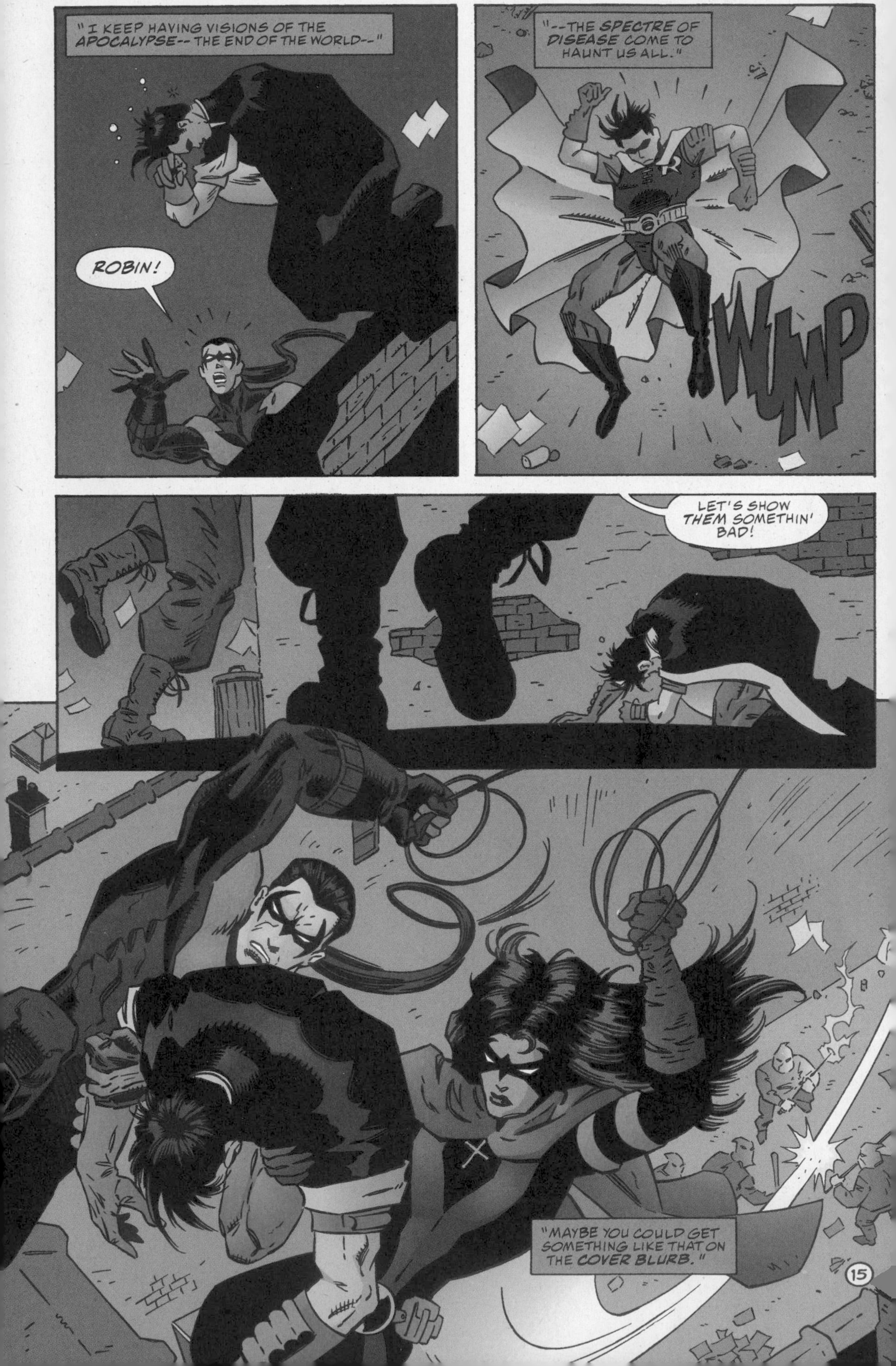
"I KEEP HAVING VISIONS OF THE APOCALYPSE-- THE END OF THE WORLD--"
ROBIN!
"--THE SPECTRE OF DISEASE COME TO HAUNT US ALL."
WUMP
LET'S SHOW THEM SOMETHIN' BAD!
"MAYBE YOU COULD GET SOMETHING LIKE THAT ON THE COVER BLURB."

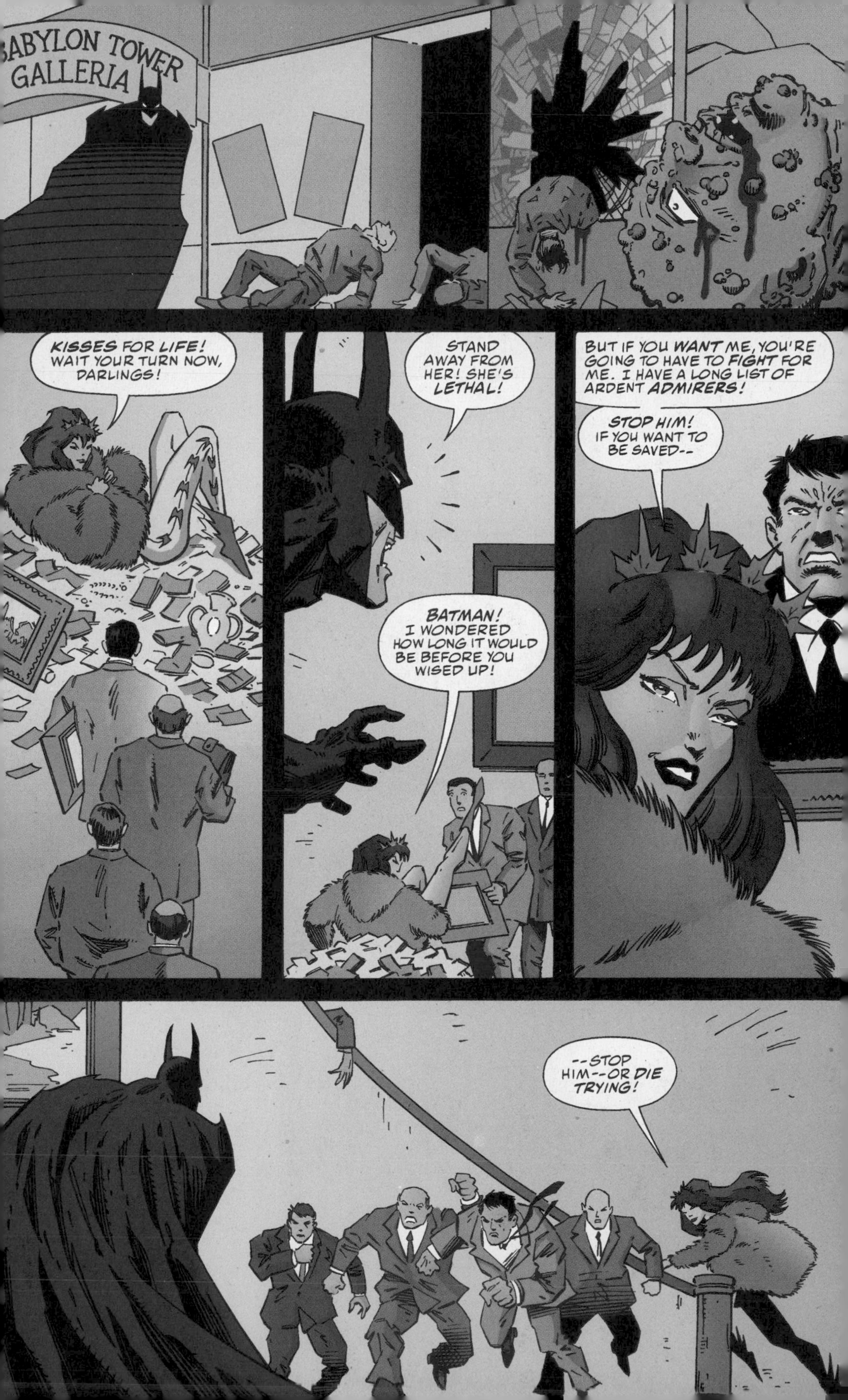
BABYLON TOWER GALLERIA
KISSES FOR LIFE! WAIT YOUR TURN NOW, DARLINGS!
STAND AWAY FROM HER! SHE'S LETHAL!
BATMAN! I WONDERED HOW LONG IT WOULD BE BEFORE YOU WISED UP!
BUT IF YOU WANT ME, YOU'RE GOING TO HAVE TO FIGHT FOR ME. I HAVE A LONG LIST OF ARDENT ADMIRERS!
STOP HIM! IF YOU WANT TO BE SAVED--
--STOP HIM--OR DIE TRYING!

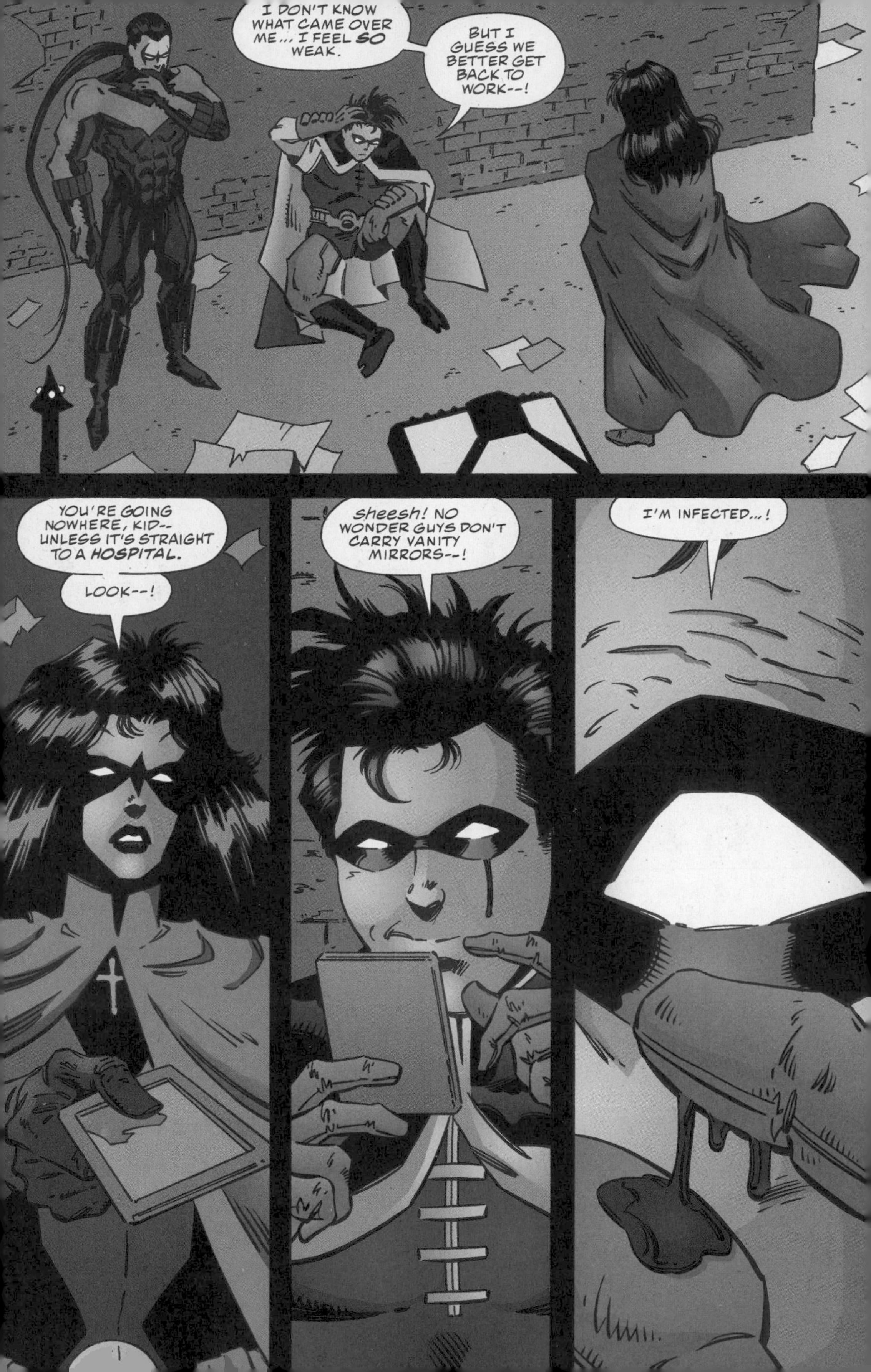
I DON'T KNOW WHAT CAME OVER ME... I FEEL SO WEAK.
BUT I GUESS WE BETTER GET BACK TO WORK--!
YOU'RE GOING NOWHERE, KID-- UNLESS IT'S STRAIGHT TO A HOSPITAL.
LOOK--!
sheesh! NO WONDER GUYS DON'T CARRY VANITY MIRRORS--!
I'M INFECTED...!

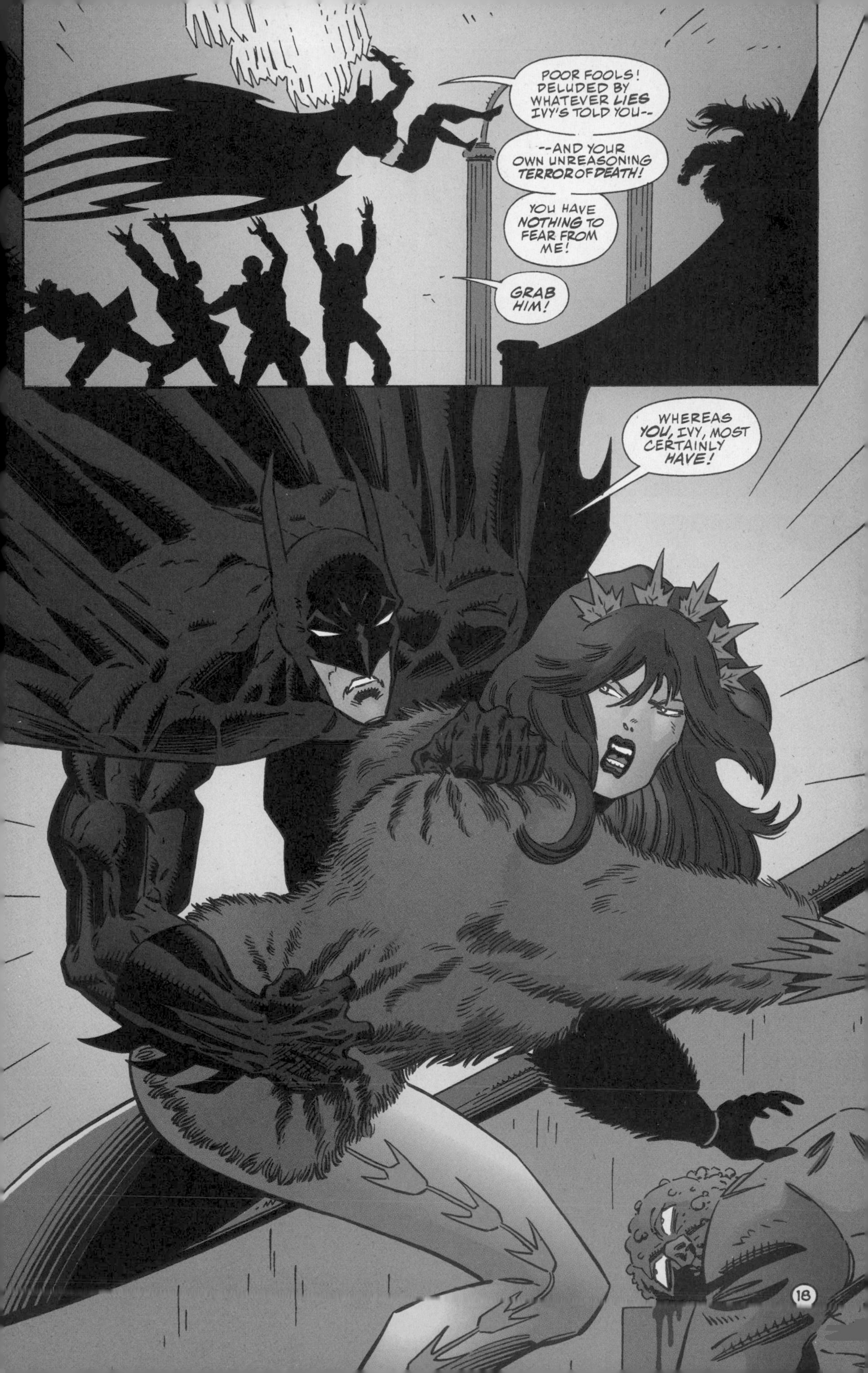
POOR FOOLS! DELUDED BY WHATEVER LIES IVY'S TOLD YOU--
--AND YOUR OWN UNREASONING TERROR OF DEATH!
YOU HAVE NOTHING TO FEAR FROM ME!
GRAB HIM!
WHEREAS YOU, IVY, MOST CERTAINLY HAVE!

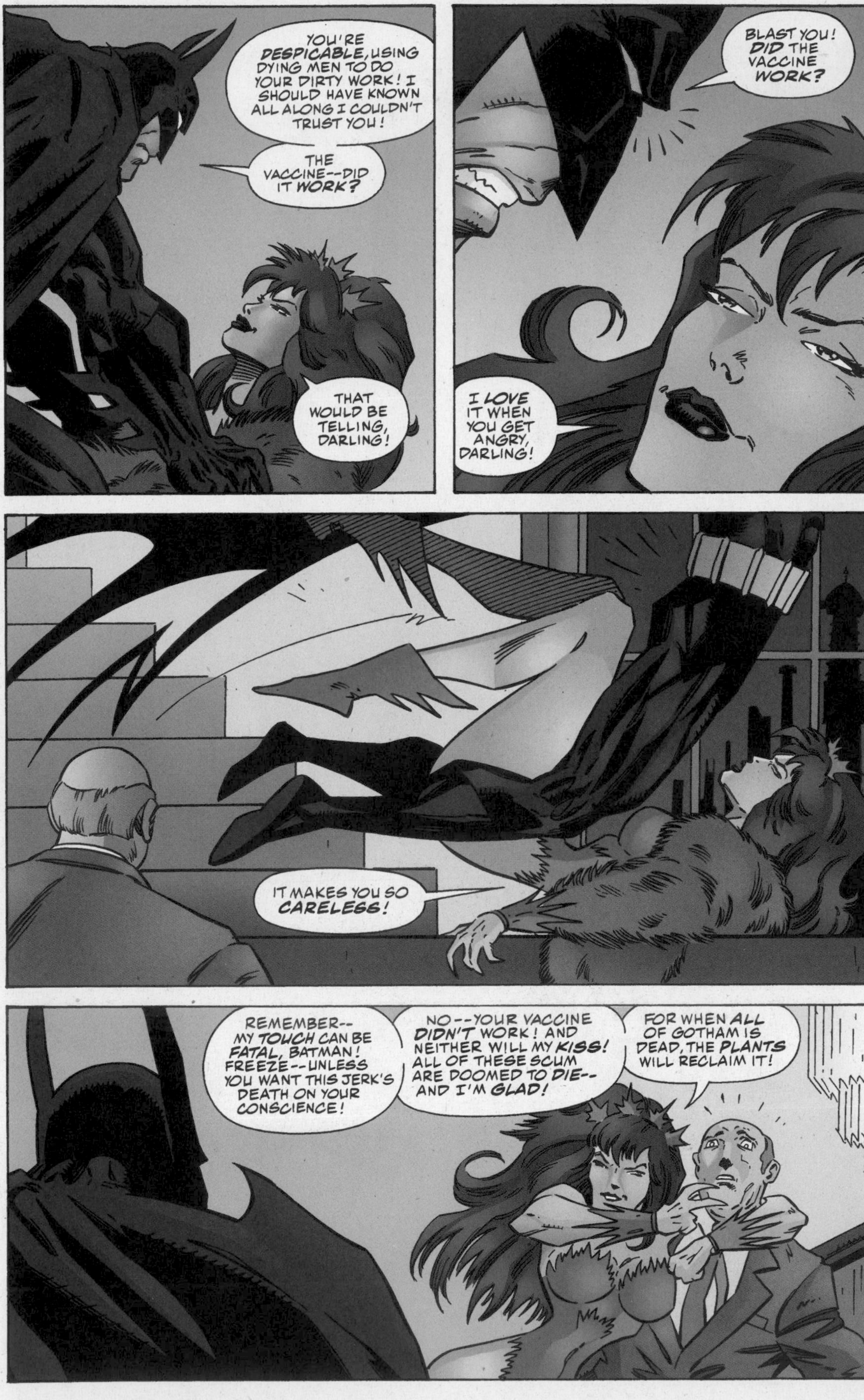
YOU'RE DESPICABLE, USING DYING MEN TO DO YOUR DIRTY WORK! I SHOULD HAVE KNOWN ALL ALONG I COULDN'T TRUST YOU!
THE VACCINE--DID IT WORK?
THAT WOULD BE TELLING, DARLING!
BLAST YOU! DID THE VACCINE WORK?
I LOVE IT WHEN YOU GET ANGRY, DARLING!
IT MAKES YOU SO CARELESS!
REMEMBER-- MY TOUCH CAN BE FATAL, BATMAN! FREEZE--UNLESS YOU WANT THIS JERK'S DEATH ON YOUR CONSCIENCE!
NO--YOUR VACCINE DIDN'T WORK! AND NEITHER WILL MY KISS! ALL OF THESE SCUM ARE DOOMED TO DIE-- AND I'M GLAD!
FOR WHEN ALL OF GOTHAM IS DEAD, THE PLANTS WILL RECLAIM IT!

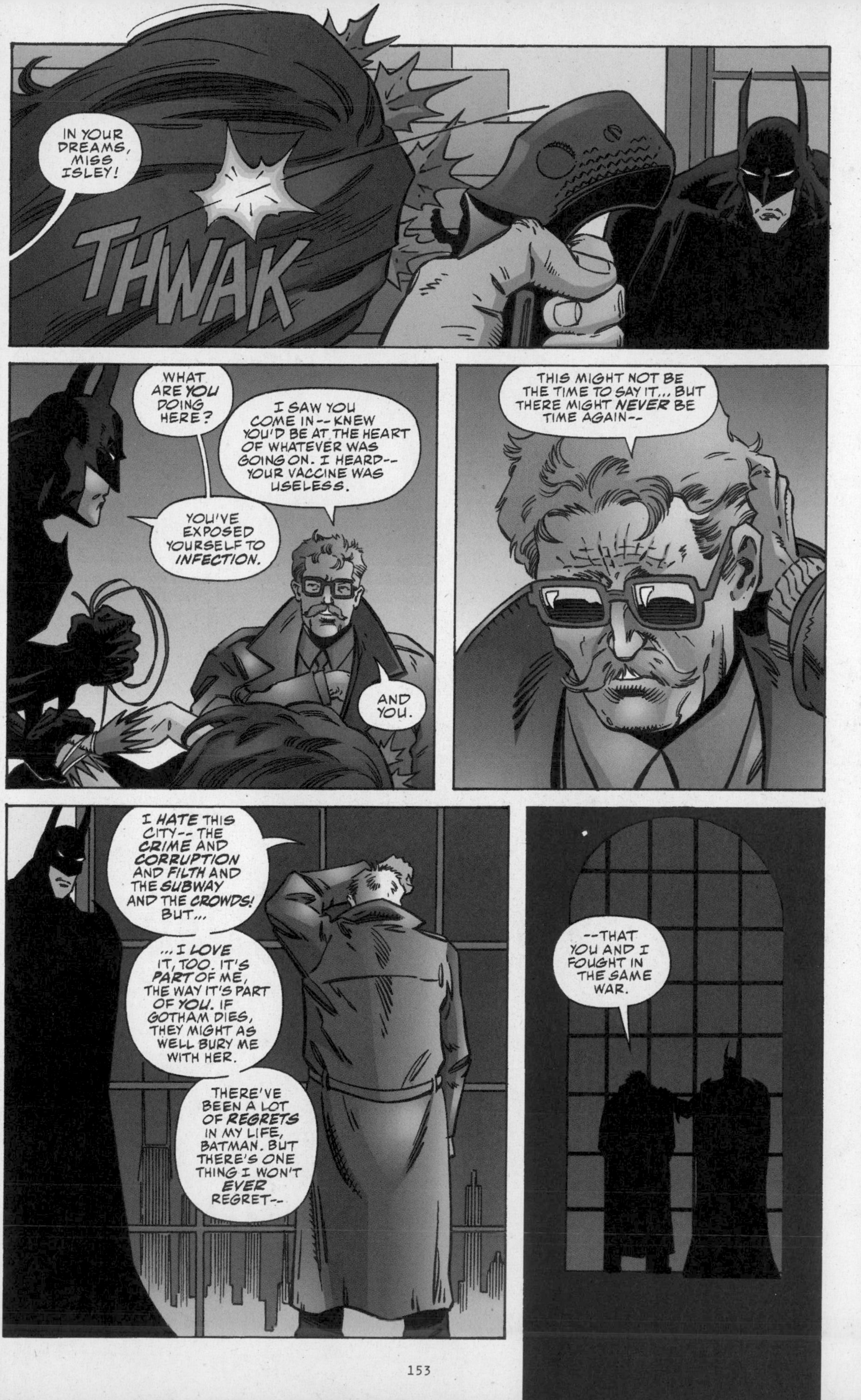
IN YOUR DREAMS, MISS ISLEY!
THWAK
WHAT ARE YOU DOING HERE?
YOU'VE EXPOSED YOURSELF TO INFECTION.
I SAW YOU COME IN-- KNEW YOU'D BE AT THE HEART OF WHATEVER WAS GOING ON. I HEARD-- YOUR VACCINE WAS USELESS.
AND YOU.
THIS MIGHT NOT BE THE TIME TO SAY IT... BUT THERE MIGHT NEVER BE TIME AGAIN--
I HATE THIS CITY-- THE CRIME AND CORRUPTION AND FILTH AND THE SUBWAY AND THE CROWDS! BUT...
...I LOVE IT, TOO. IT'S PART OF ME, THE WAY IT'S PART OF YOU. IF GOTHAM DIES, THEY MIGHT AS WELL BURY ME WITH HER.
THERE'VE BEEN A LOT OF REGRETS IN MY LIFE, BATMAN. BUT THERE'S ONE THING I WON'T EVER REGRET--
--THAT YOU AND I FOUGHT IN THE SAME WAR.

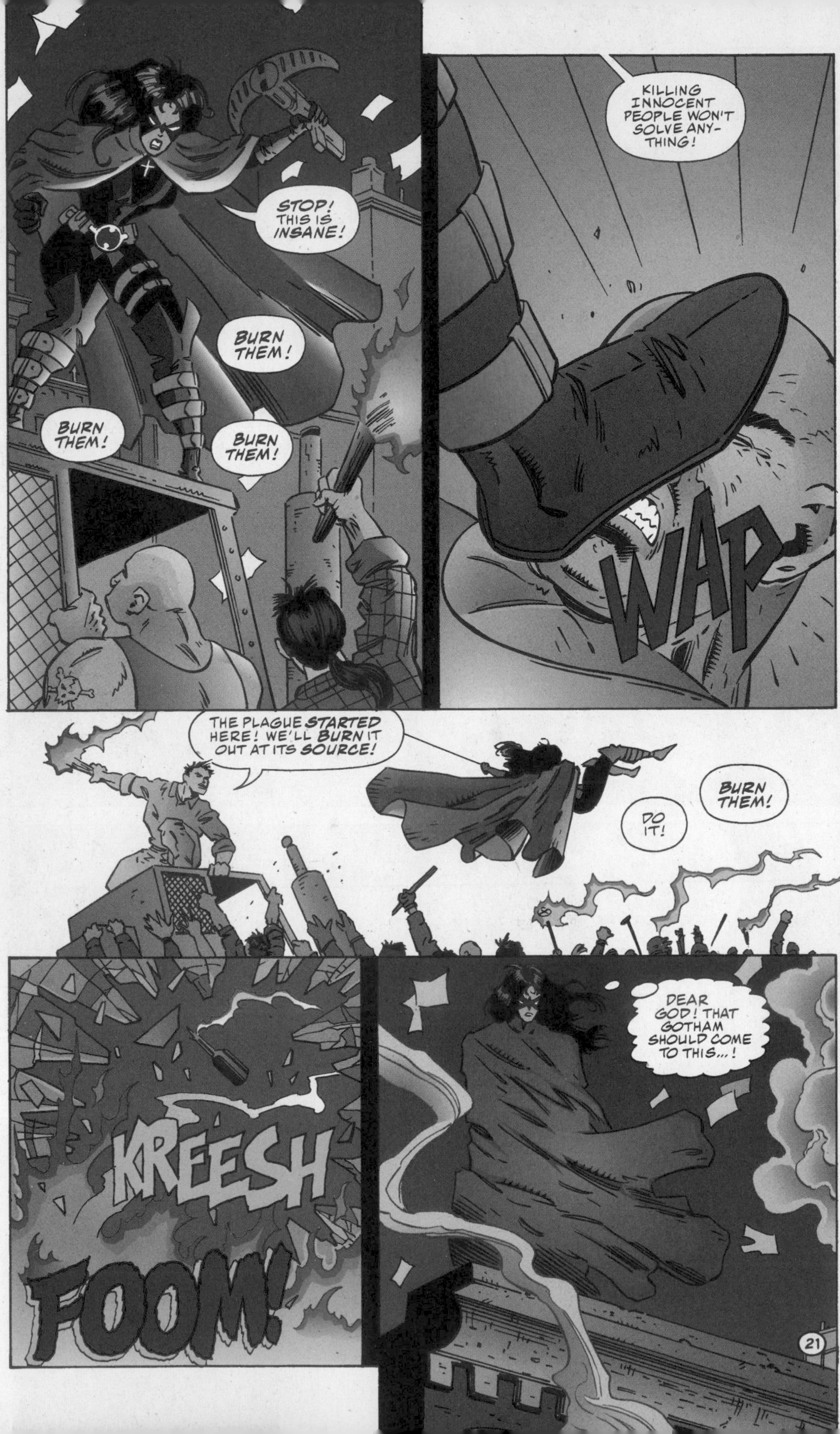
STOP! THIS IS INSANE!
BURN THEM!
BURN THEM!
BURN THEM!
KILLING INNOCENT PEOPLE WON'T SOLVE ANY-THING!
WAP
THE PLAGUE STARTED HERE! WE'LL BURN IT OUT AT ITS SOURCE!
BURN THEM!
DO IT!
KREESH
FOOM!
DEAR GOD! THAT GOTHAM SHOULD COME TO THIS...!

"THERE'S A RED GLOW OUTSIDE, LESTER. FLAMES FLICKER BELOW. THE MOB HAS TORCHED US."

DEAR GOD... PLEASE HELP ME!

"WHICH DEATH IS WORSE? THE CLENCH? FIRE? OR A DARK ANGEL'S KISS?"

I DON'T WANT TO DIE!

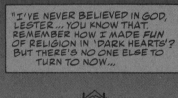

"I'VE NEVER BELIEVED IN GOD, LESTER... YOU KNOW THAT. REMEMBER HOW I MADE FUN OF RELIGION IN 'DARK HEARTS'? BUT THERE'S NO ONE ELSE TO TURN TO NOW..."

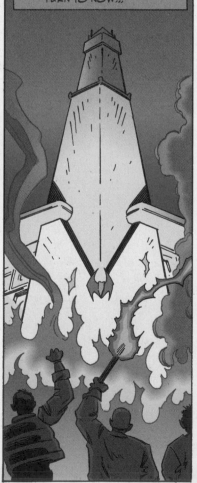

"...AND SOMEHOW, I DON'T THINK GOD CARES."

TO BE CONTINUED

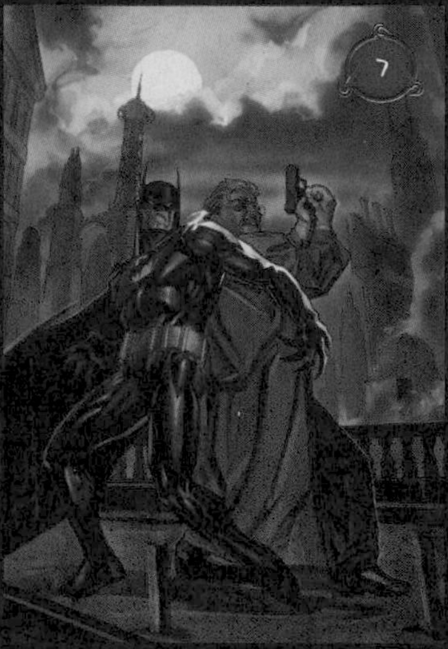
7

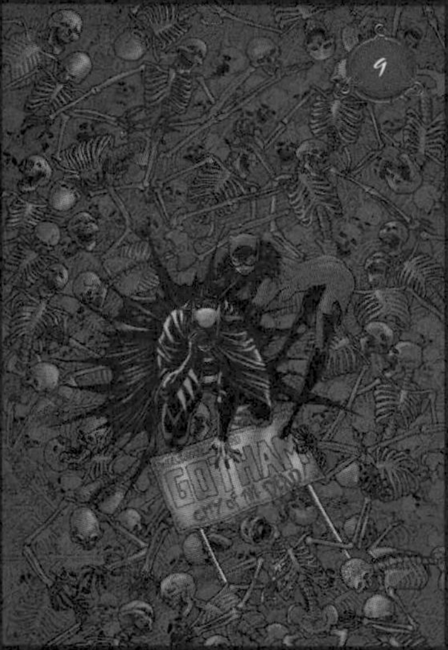
9

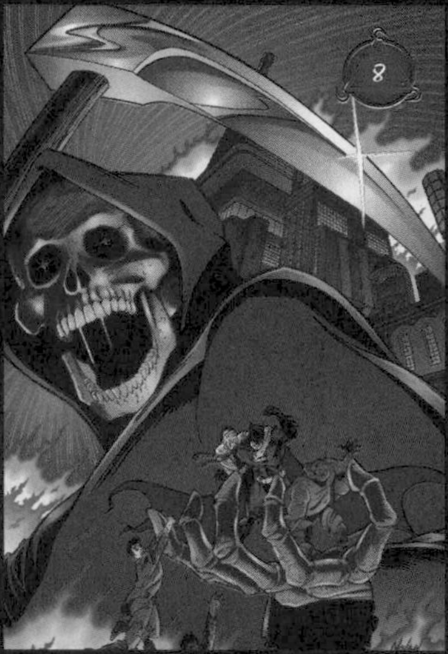
8

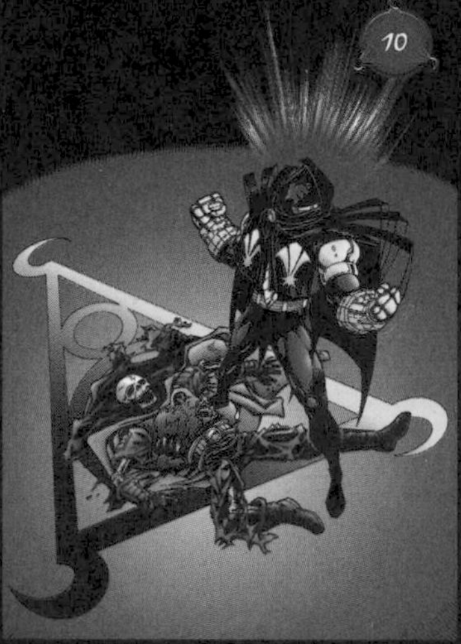
10

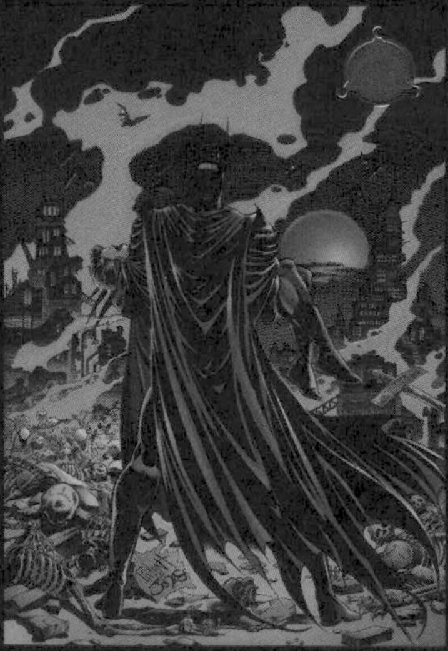

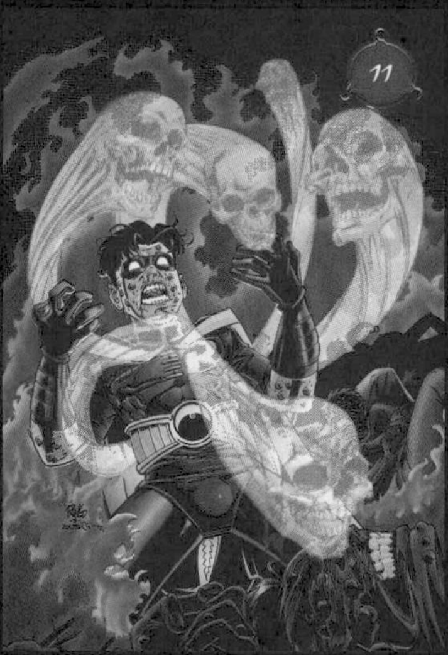
11

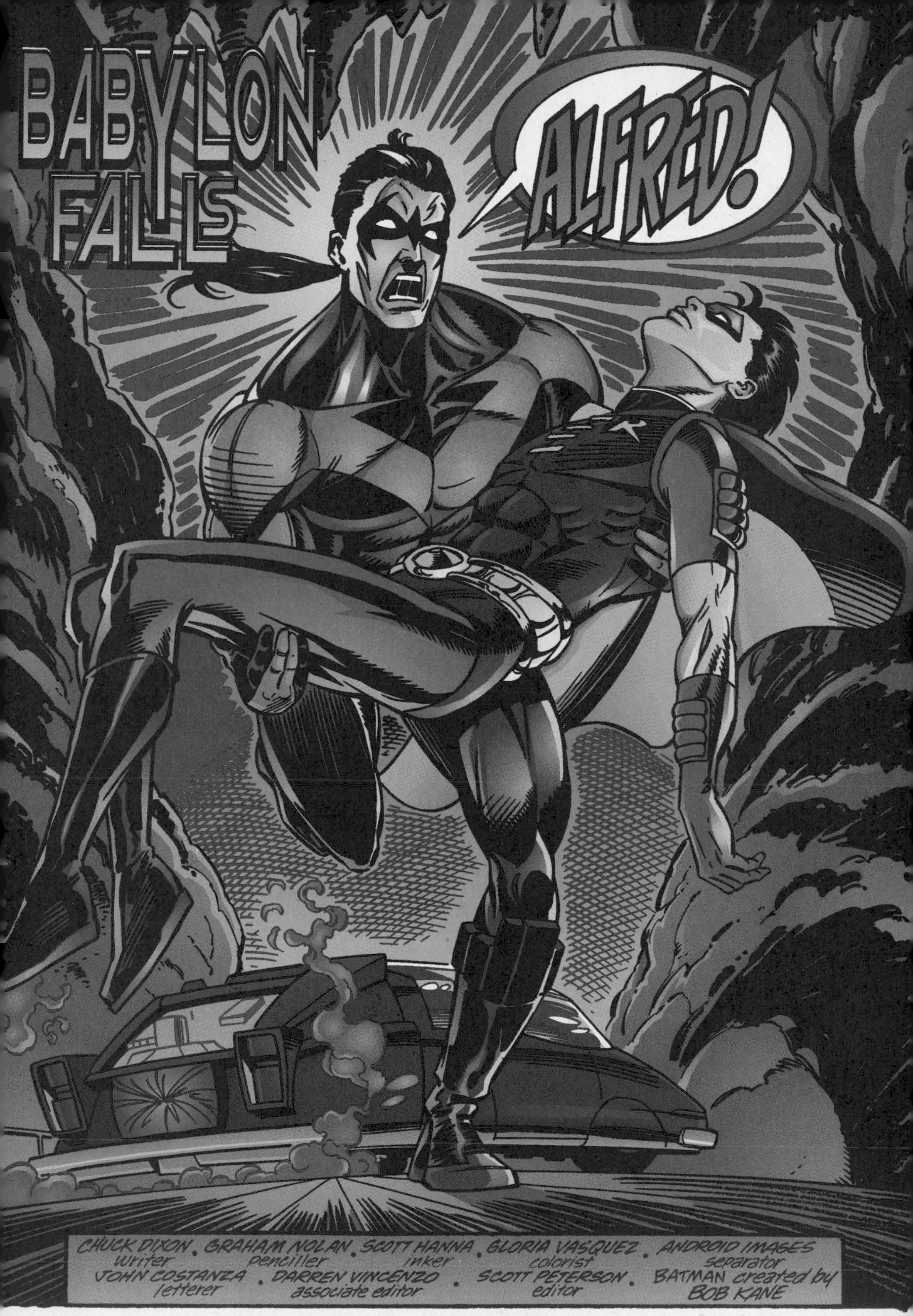
BABYLON FALLS
ALFRED!
CHUCK DIXON . GRAHAM NOLAN . SCOTT HANNA . GLORIA VASQUEZ . ANDROID IMAGES
writer penciller inker colorist separator
JOHN COSTANZA . DARREN VINCENZO . SCOTT PETERSON . BATMAN created by
letterer associate editor editor BOB KANE

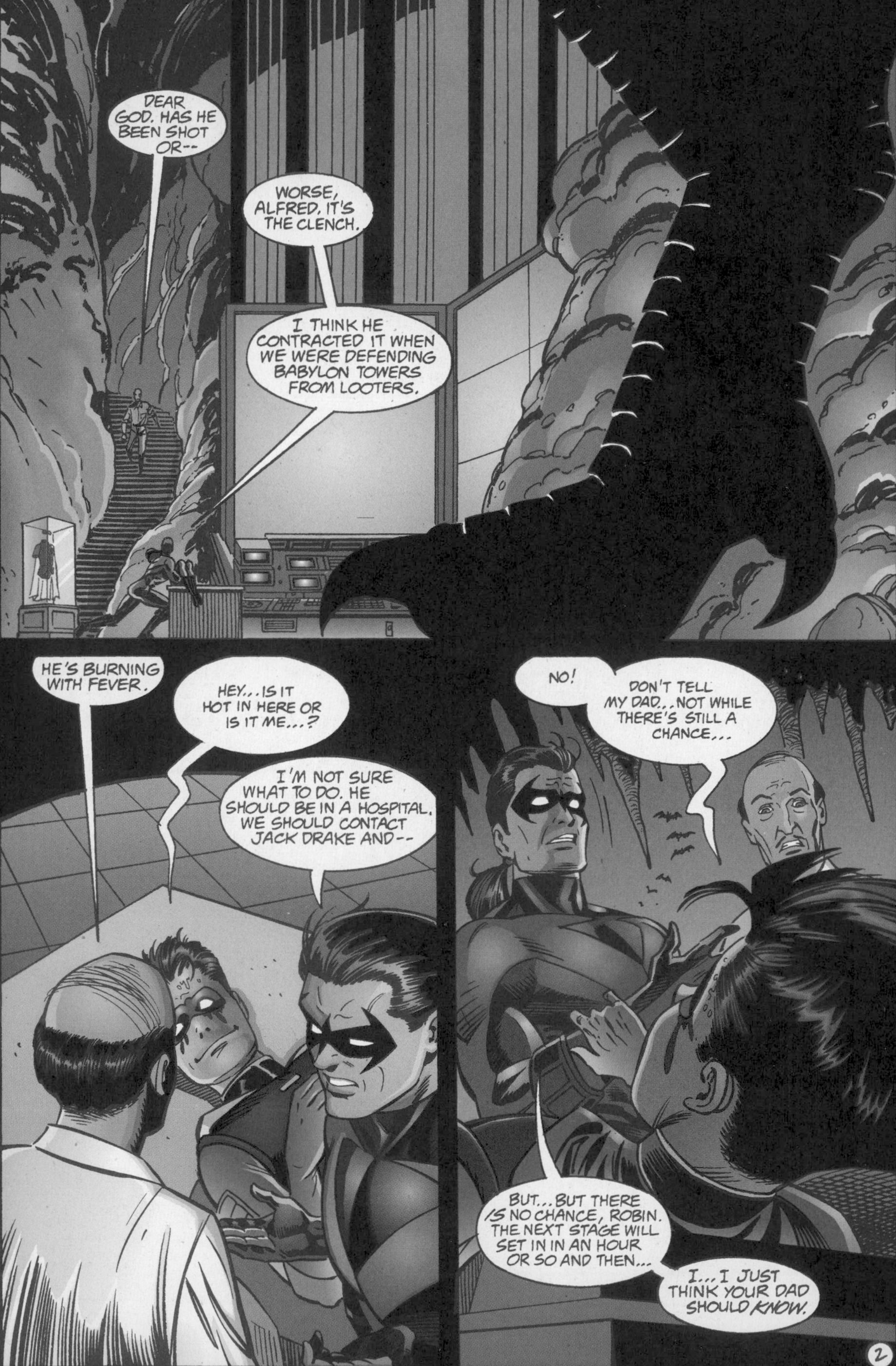
DEAR GOD. HAS HE BEEN SHOT OR--
WORSE, ALFRED. IT'S THE CLENCH.
I THINK HE CONTRACTED IT WHEN WE WERE DEFENDING BABYLON TOWERS FROM LOOTERS.
HE'S BURNING WITH FEVER.
HEY...IS IT HOT IN HERE OR IS IT ME...?
I'M NOT SURE WHAT TO DO. HE SHOULD BE IN A HOSPITAL. WE SHOULD CONTACT JACK DRAKE AND--
NO!
DON'T TELL MY DAD...NOT WHILE THERE'S STILL A CHANCE...
BUT...BUT THERE IS NO CHANCE, ROBIN. THE NEXT STAGE WILL SET IN IN AN HOUR OR SO AND THEN...
I...I JUST THINK YOUR DAD SHOULD KNOW.

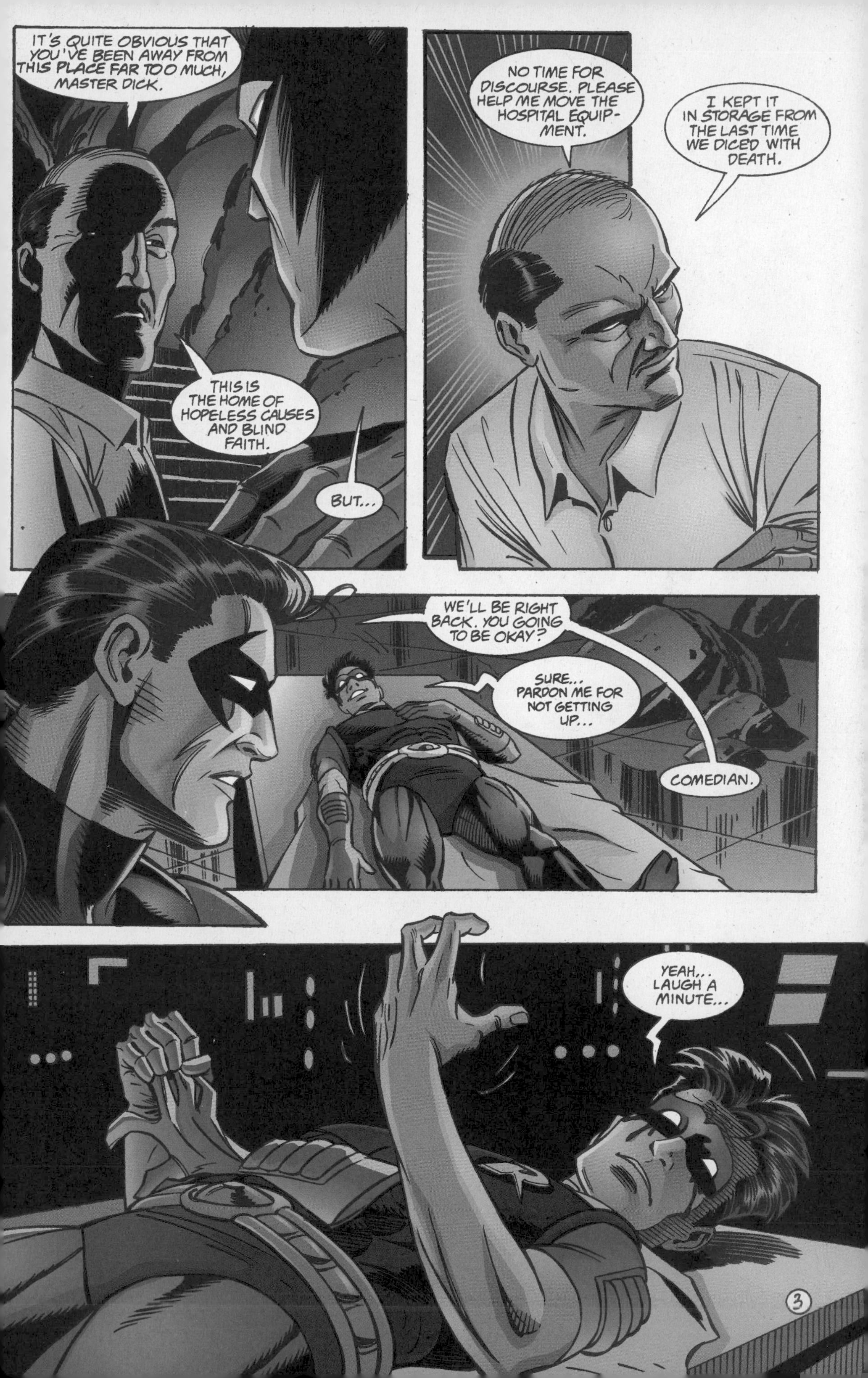
IT'S QUITE OBVIOUS THAT YOU'VE BEEN AWAY FROM THIS PLACE FAR TOO MUCH, MASTER DICK.
THIS IS THE HOME OF HOPELESS CAUSES AND BLIND FAITH.
BUT...
NO TIME FOR DISCOURSE. PLEASE HELP ME MOVE THE HOSPITAL EQUIP-MENT.
I KEPT IT IN STORAGE FROM THE LAST TIME WE DICED WITH DEATH.
WE'LL BE RIGHT BACK. YOU GOING TO BE OKAY?
SURE... PARDON ME FOR NOT GETTING UP...
COMEDIAN.
YEAH... LAUGH A MINUTE...
3

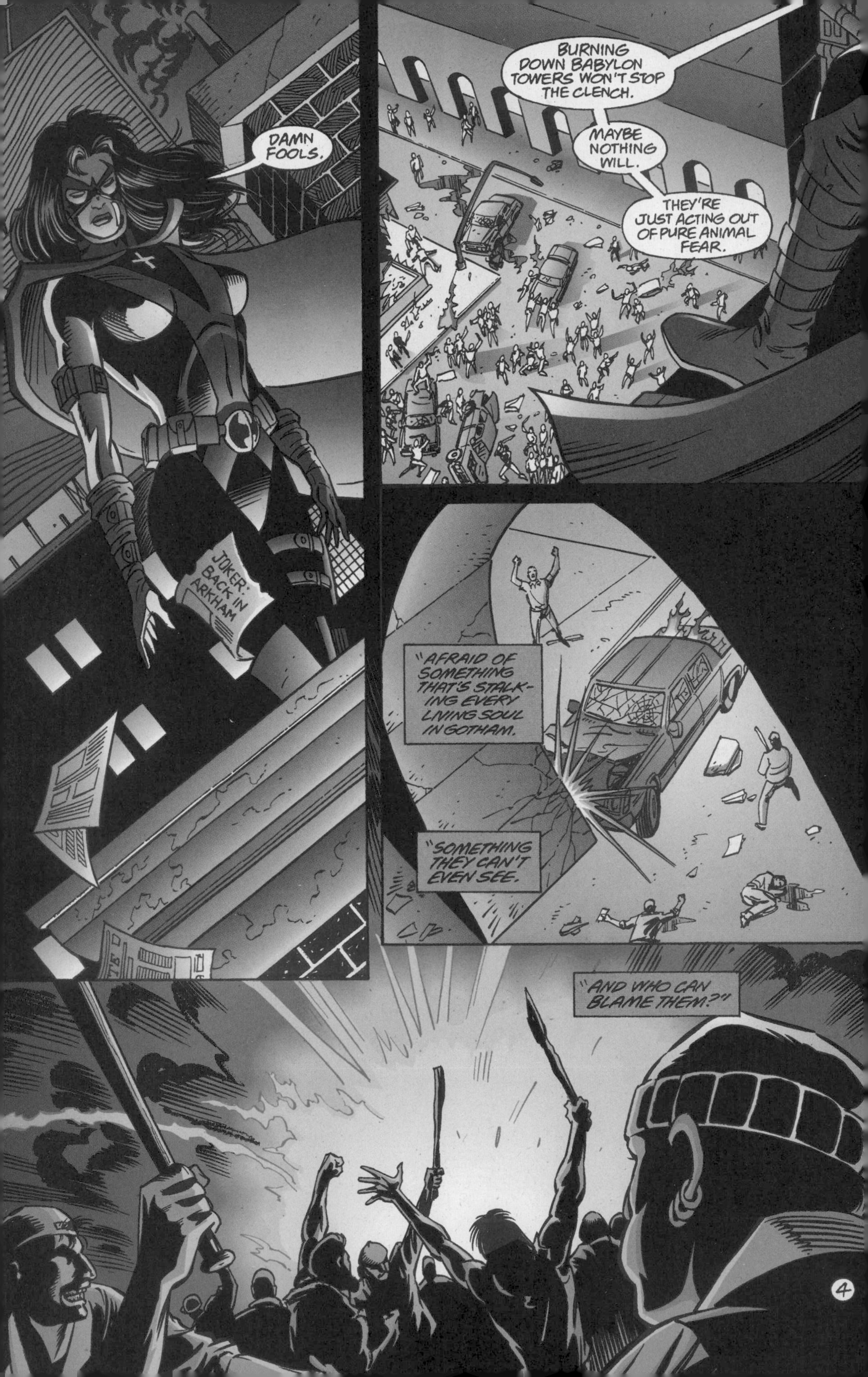
DAMN FOOLS.
BURNING DOWN BABYLON TOWERS WON'T STOP THE CLENCH.
MAYBE NOTHING WILL.
THEY'RE JUST ACTING OUT OF PURE ANIMAL FEAR.
JOKER: BACK IN ARKHAM
"AFRAID OF SOMETHING THAT'S STALKING EVERY LIVING SOUL IN GOTHAM.
"SOMETHING THEY CAN'T EVEN SEE.
"AND WHO CAN BLAME THEM?"
4

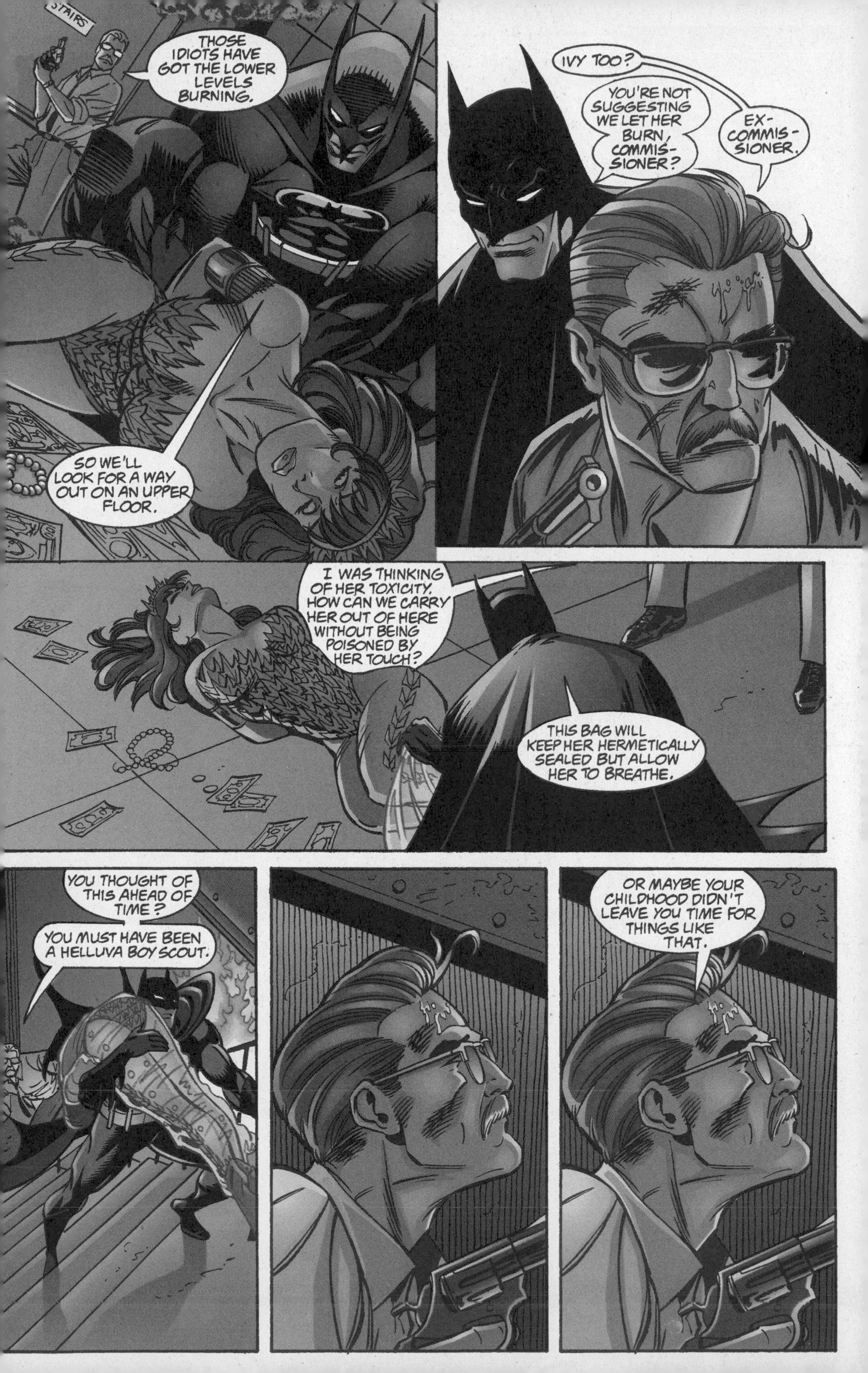
STAIRS
THOSE IDIOTS HAVE GOT THE LOWER LEVELS BURNING.
SO WE'LL LOOK FOR A WAY OUT ON AN UPPER FLOOR.
IVY TOO?
YOU'RE NOT SUGGESTING WE LET HER BURN, COMMISSIONER?
EX-COMMISSIONER.
I WAS THINKING OF HER TOXICITY. HOW CAN WE CARRY HER OUT OF HERE WITHOUT BEING POISONED BY HER TOUCH?
THIS BAG WILL KEEP HER HERMETICALLY SEALED BUT ALLOW HER TO BREATHE.
YOU THOUGHT OF THIS AHEAD OF TIME?
YOU MUST HAVE BEEN A HELLUVA BOY SCOUT.
OR MAYBE YOUR CHILDHOOD DIDN'T LEAVE YOU TIME FOR THINGS LIKE THAT.

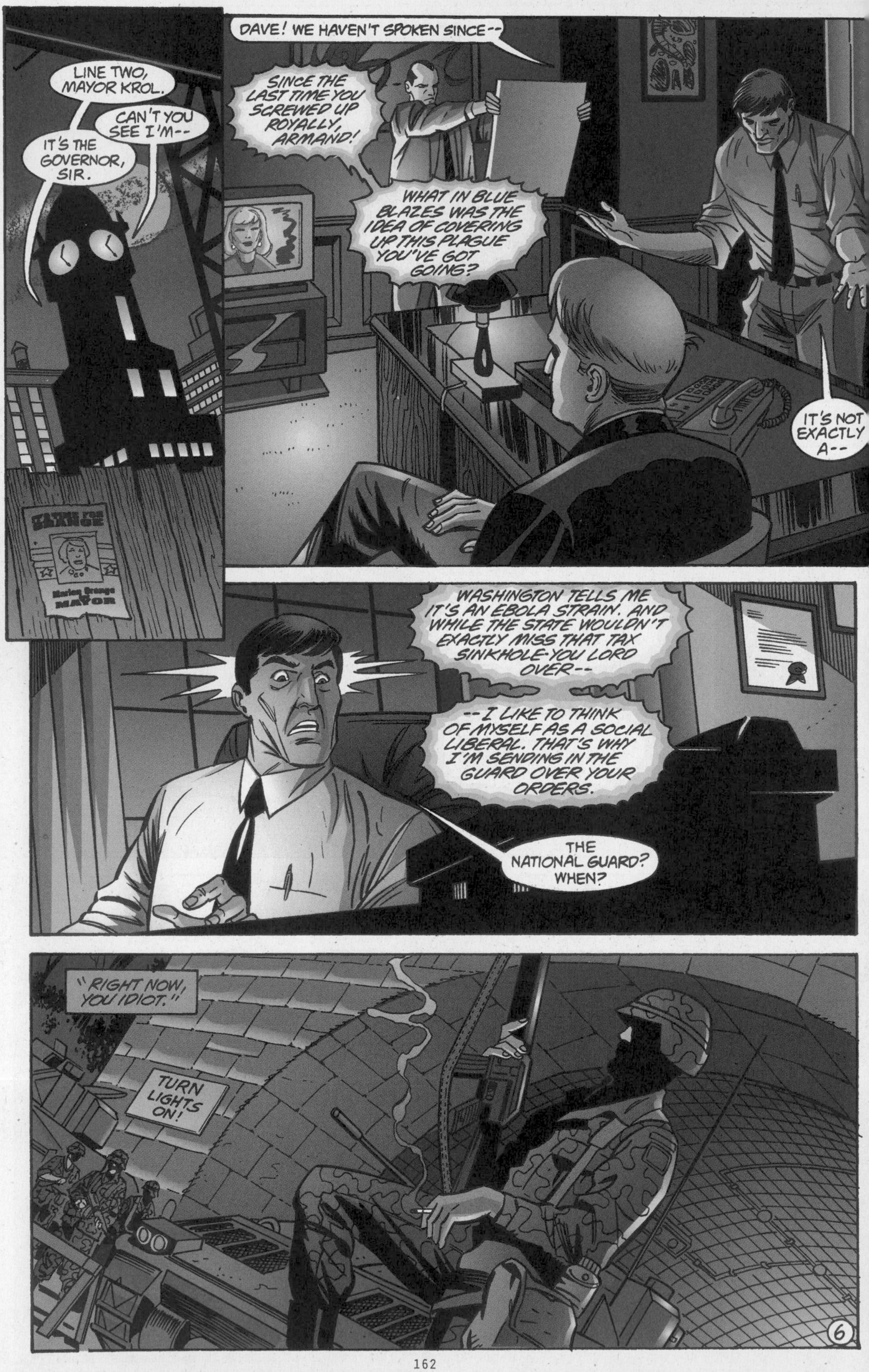
LINE TWO, MAYOR KROL.
CAN'T YOU SEE I'M--
IT'S THE GOVERNOR, SIR.
DAVE! WE HAVEN'T SPOKEN SINCE--
SINCE THE LAST TIME YOU SCREWED UP ROYALLY, ARMAND!
WHAT IN BLUE BLAZES WAS THE IDEA OF COVERING UP THIS PLAGUE YOU'VE GOT GOING?
IT'S NOT EXACTLY A--
WASHINGTON TELLS ME IT'S AN EBOLA STRAIN. AND WHILE THE STATE WOULDN'T EXACTLY MISS THAT TAX SINKHOLE YOU LORD OVER--
--I LIKE TO THINK OF MYSELF AS A SOCIAL LIBERAL. THAT'S WHY I'M SENDING IN THE GUARD OVER YOUR ORDERS.
THE NATIONAL GUARD? WHEN?
"RIGHT NOW, YOU IDIOT."
TURN LIGHTS ON!
6

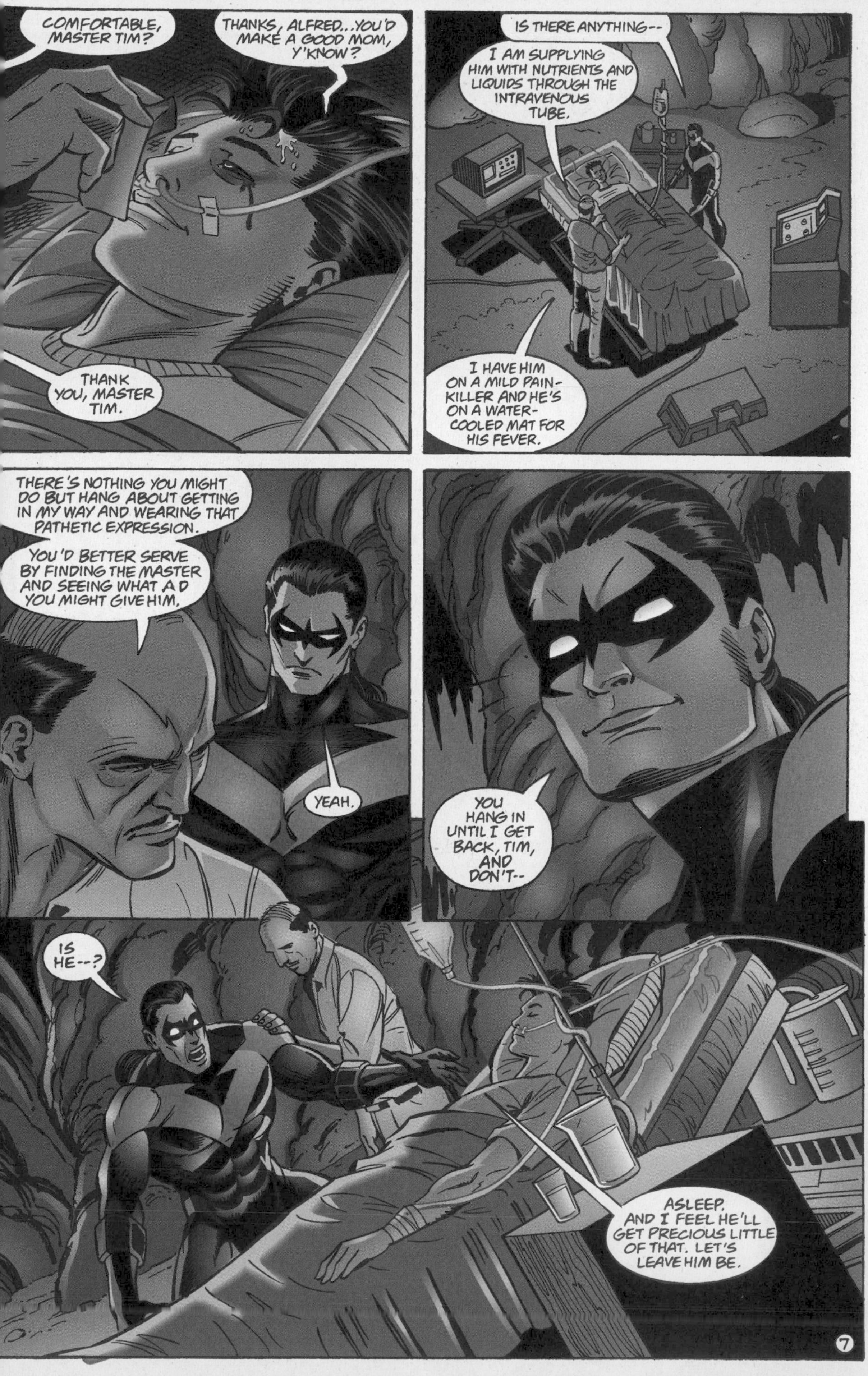
COMFORTABLE, MASTER TIM?
THANKS, ALFRED...YOU'D MAKE A GOOD MOM, Y'KNOW?
THANK YOU, MASTER TIM.
IS THERE ANYTHING--
I AM SUPPLYING HIM WITH NUTRIENTS AND LIQUIDS THROUGH THE INTRAVENOUS TUBE.
I HAVE HIM ON A MILD PAIN-KILLER AND HE'S ON A WATER-COOLED MAT FOR HIS FEVER.
THERE'S NOTHING YOU MIGHT DO BUT HANG ABOUT GETTING IN MY WAY AND WEARING THAT PATHETIC EXPRESSION.
YOU'D BETTER SERVE BY FINDING THE MASTER AND SEEING WHAT A D YOU MIGHT GIVE HIM.
YEAH.
YOU HANG IN UNTIL I GET BACK, TIM, AND DON'T--
IS HE--?
ASLEEP. AND I FEEL HE'LL GET PRECIOUS LITTLE OF THAT. LET'S LEAVE HIM BE.

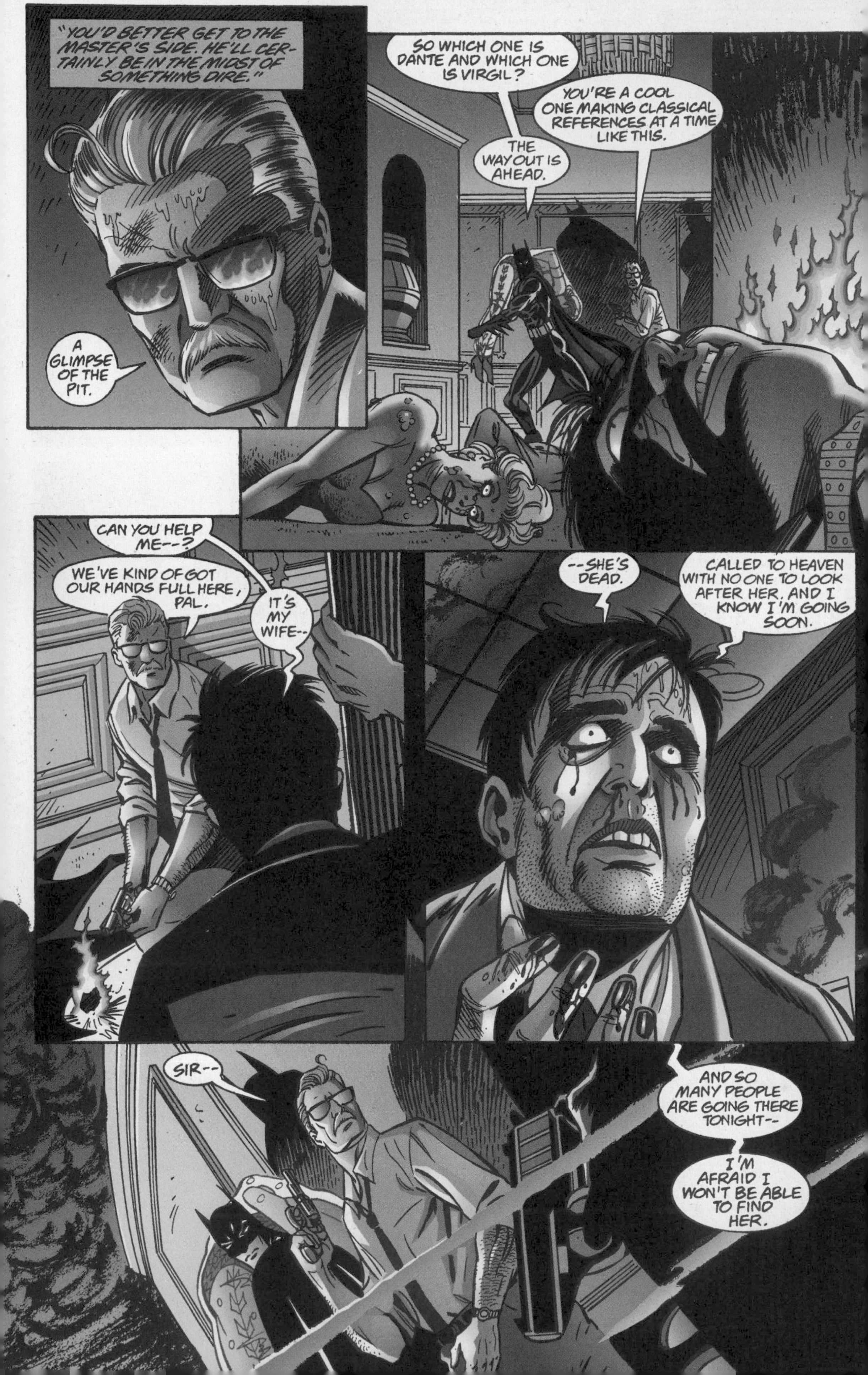
"YOU'D BETTER GET TO THE MASTER'S SIDE. HE'LL CERTAINLY BE IN THE MIDST OF SOMETHING DIRE."
A GLIMPSE OF THE PIT.
SO WHICH ONE IS DANTE AND WHICH ONE IS VIRGIL?
THE WAY OUT IS AHEAD.
YOU'RE A COOL ONE MAKING CLASSICAL REFERENCES AT A TIME LIKE THIS.
CAN YOU HELP ME--?
WE'VE KIND OF GOT OUR HANDS FULL HERE, PAL.
IT'S MY WIFE--
--SHE'S DEAD.
CALLED TO HEAVEN WITH NO ONE TO LOOK AFTER HER. AND I KNOW I'M GOING SOON.
SIR--
AND SO MANY PEOPLE ARE GOING THERE TONIGHT--
I'M AFRAID I WON'T BE ABLE TO FIND HER.

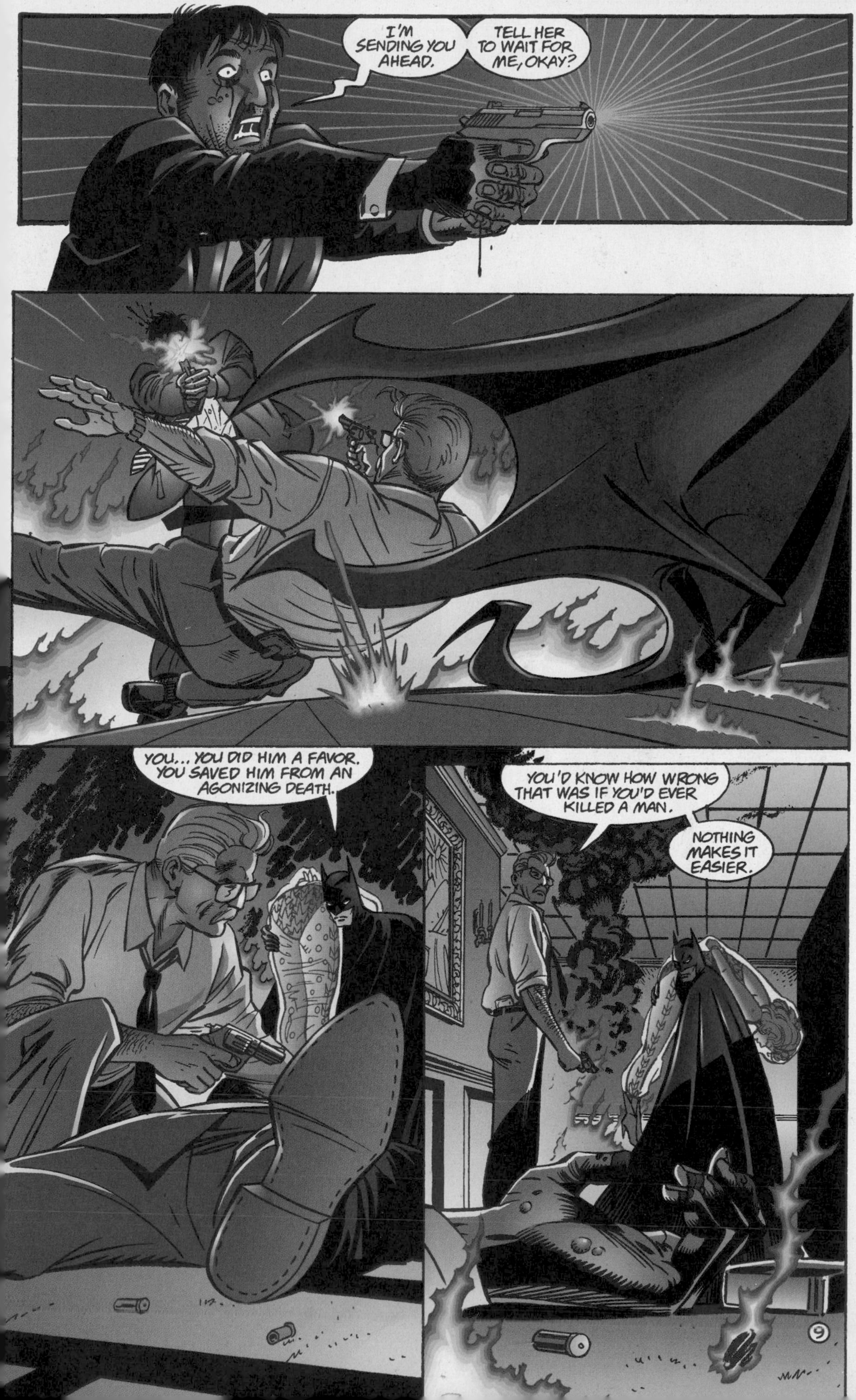
I'M SENDING YOU AHEAD.
TELL HER TO WAIT FOR ME, OKAY?
YOU... YOU DID HIM A FAVOR. YOU SAVED HIM FROM AN AGONIZING DEATH.
YOU'D KNOW HOW WRONG THAT WAS IF YOU'D EVER KILLED A MAN.
NOTHING MAKES IT EASIER.
9

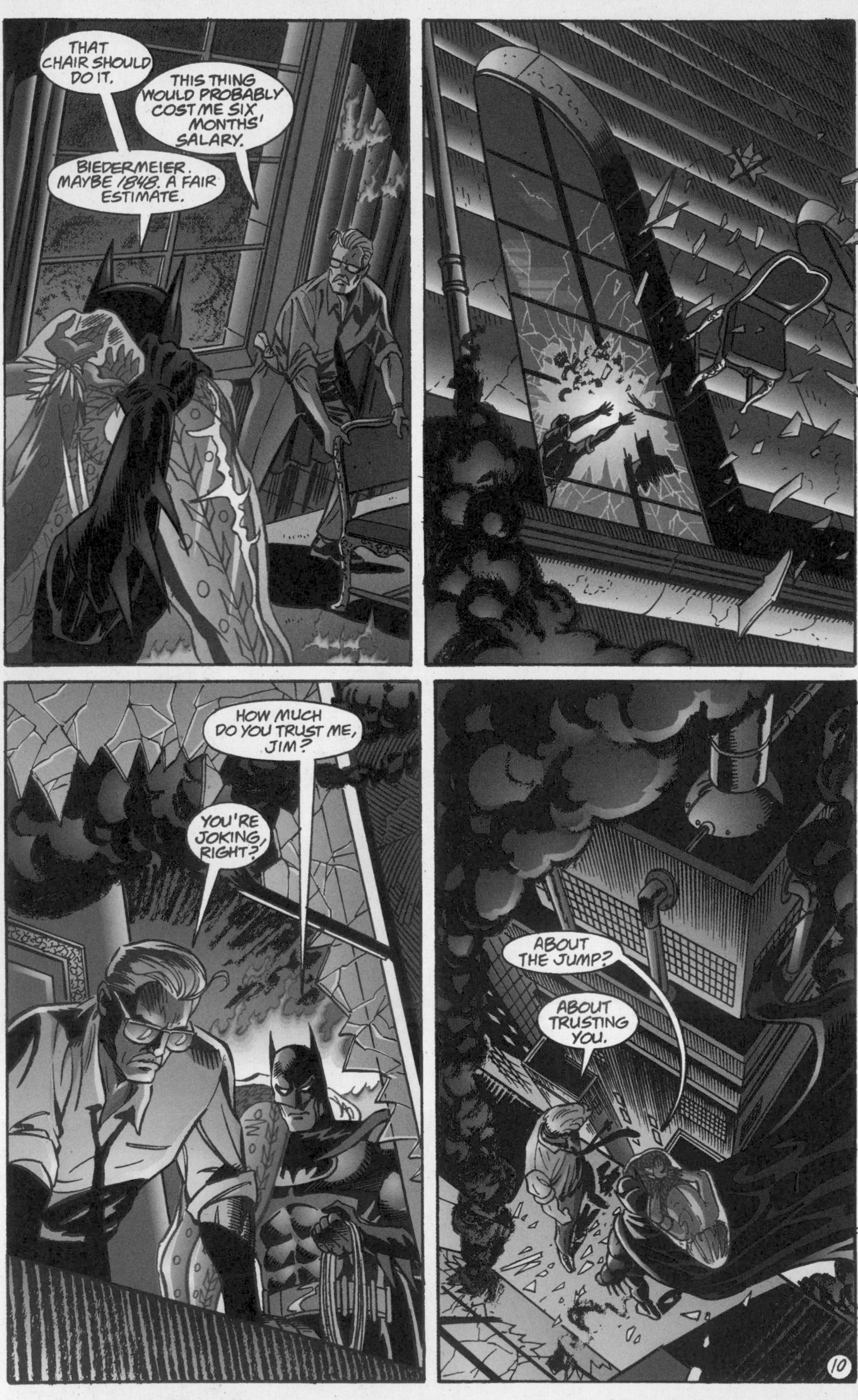
THAT CHAIR SHOULD DO IT.
THIS THING WOULD PROBABLY COST ME SIX MONTHS' SALARY.
BIEDERMEIER. MAYBE 1848. A FAIR ESTIMATE.
HOW MUCH DO YOU TRUST ME, JIM?
YOU'RE JOKING, RIGHT?
ABOUT THE JUMP?
ABOUT TRUSTING YOU.
10

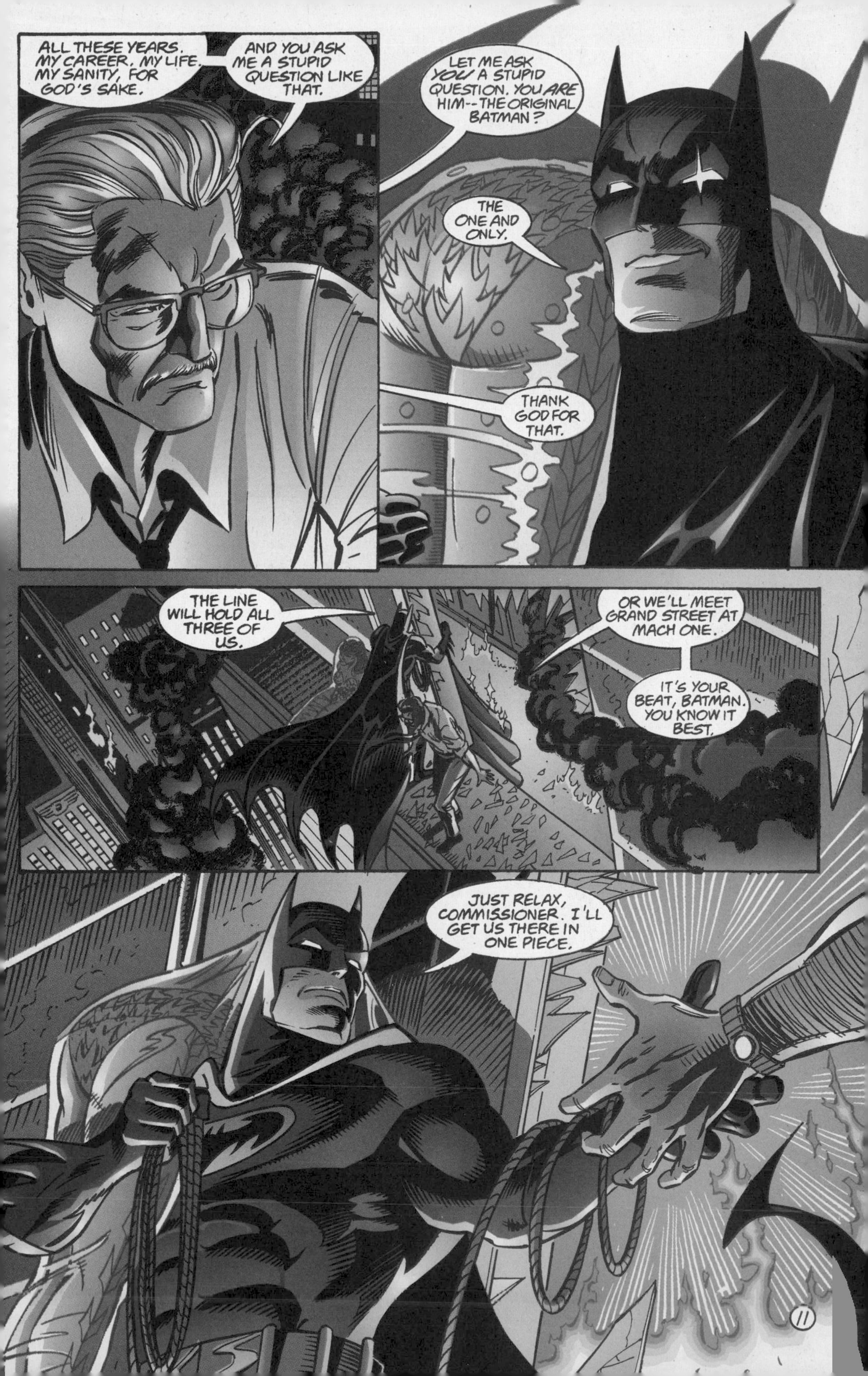
ALL THESE YEARS. MY CAREER. MY LIFE. MY SANITY, FOR GOD'S SAKE.
AND YOU ASK ME A STUPID QUESTION LIKE THAT.
LET ME ASK *YOU* A STUPID QUESTION. YOU *ARE* HIM--THE ORIGINAL BATMAN?
THE ONE AND ONLY.
THANK GOD FOR THAT.
THE LINE WILL HOLD ALL THREE OF US.
OR WE'LL MEET GRAND STREET AT MACH ONE.
IT'S YOUR BEAT, BATMAN. YOU KNOW IT BEST.
JUST RELAX, COMMISSIONER. I'LL GET US THERE IN ONE PIECE.
11

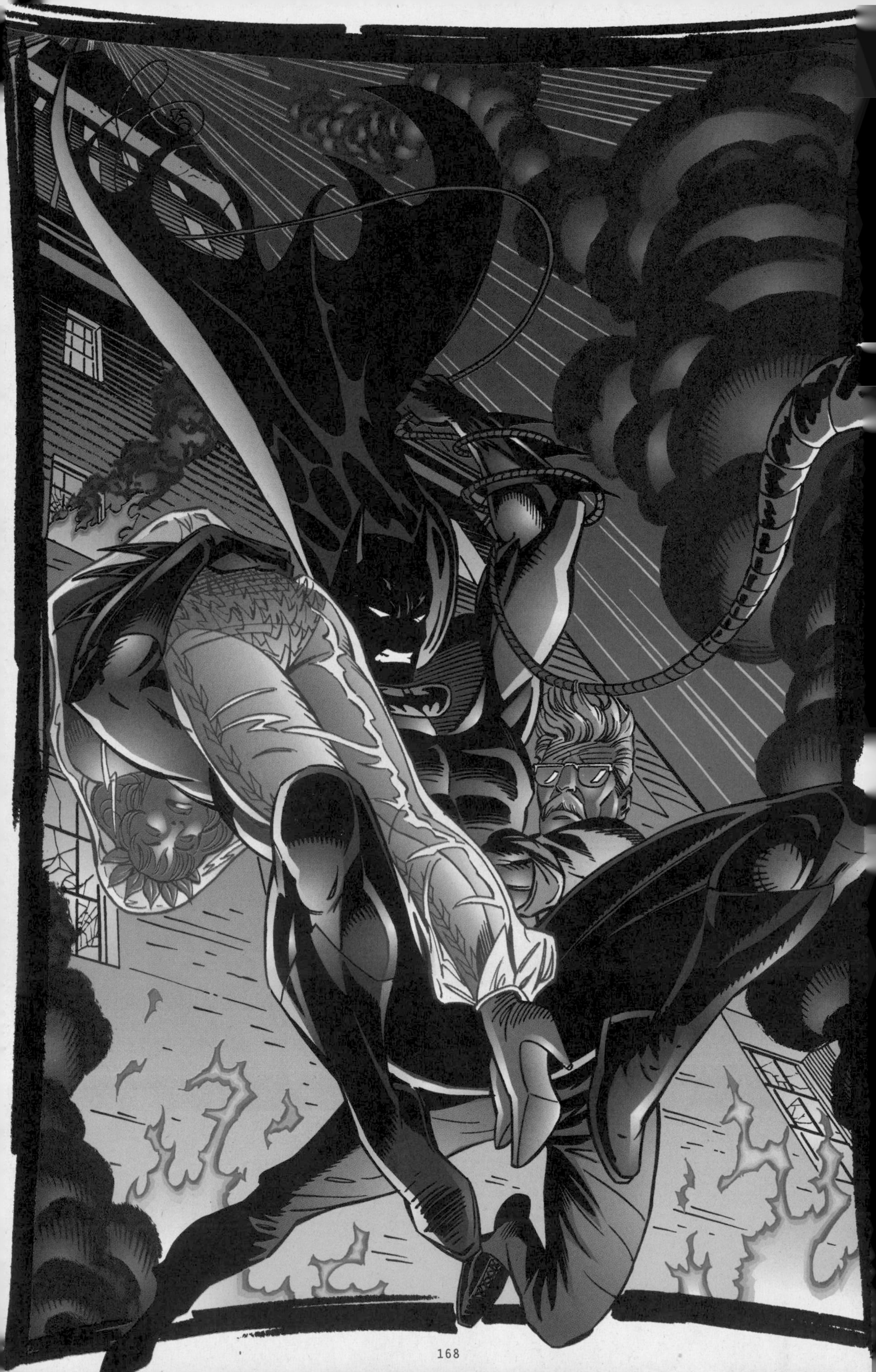

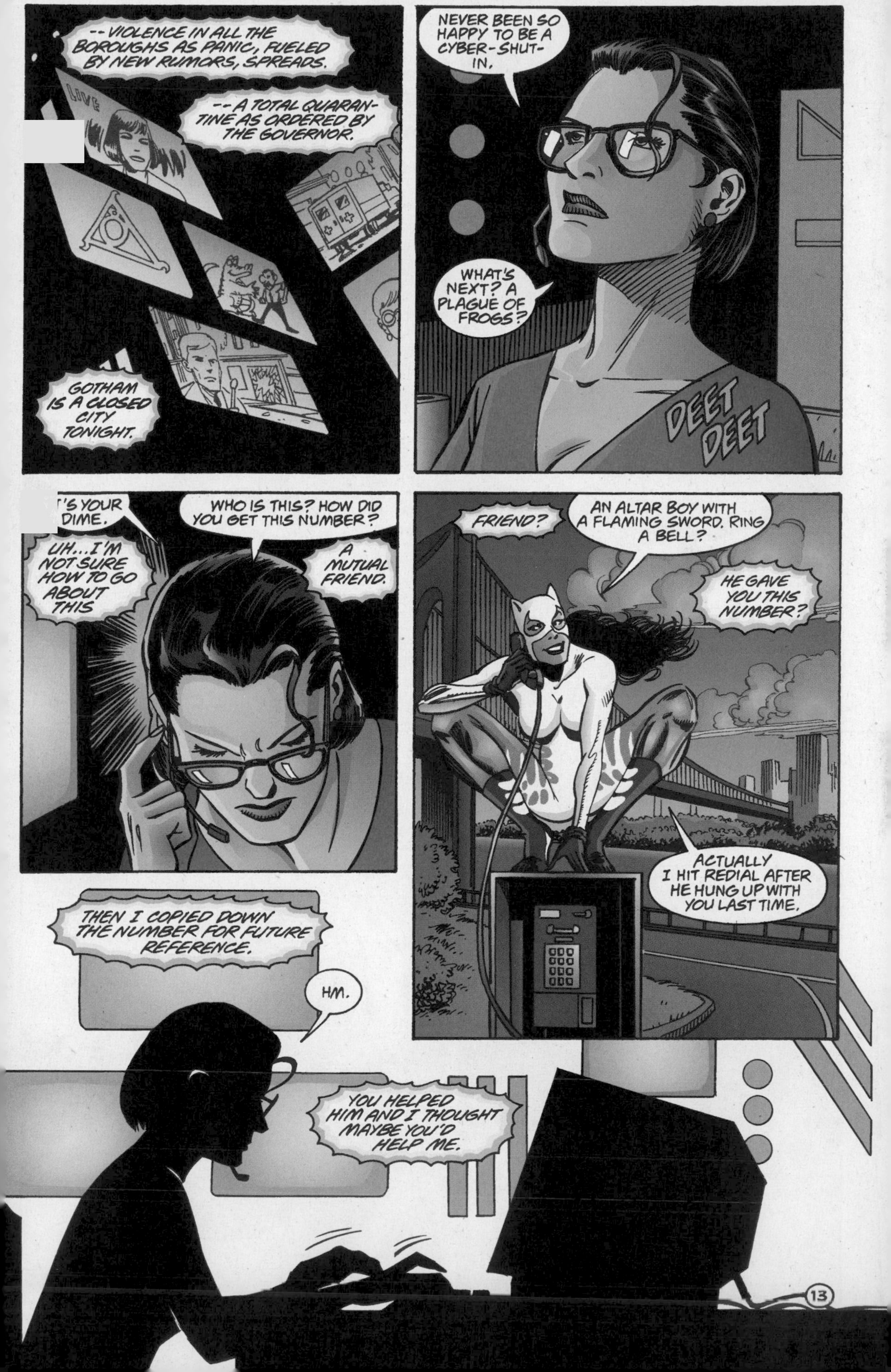
--VIOLENCE IN ALL THE BOROUGHS AS PANIC, FUELED BY NEW RUMORS, SPREADS.
--A TOTAL QUARANTINE AS ORDERED BY THE GOVERNOR.
LIVE
GOTHAM IS A CLOSED CITY TONIGHT.
NEVER BEEN SO HAPPY TO BE A CYBER-SHUT-IN.
WHAT'S NEXT? A PLAGUE OF FROGS?
DEET DEET
T'S YOUR DIME.
UH...I'M NOT SURE HOW TO GO ABOUT THIS
WHO IS THIS? HOW DID YOU GET THIS NUMBER?
A MUTUAL FRIEND.
FRIEND?
AN ALTAR BOY WITH A FLAMING SWORD. RING A BELL?
HE GAVE YOU THIS NUMBER?
ACTUALLY I HIT REDIAL AFTER HE HUNG UP WITH YOU LAST TIME.
THEN I COPIED DOWN THE NUMBER FOR FUTURE REFERENCE.
HM.
YOU HELPED HIM AND I THOUGHT MAYBE YOU'D HELP ME.

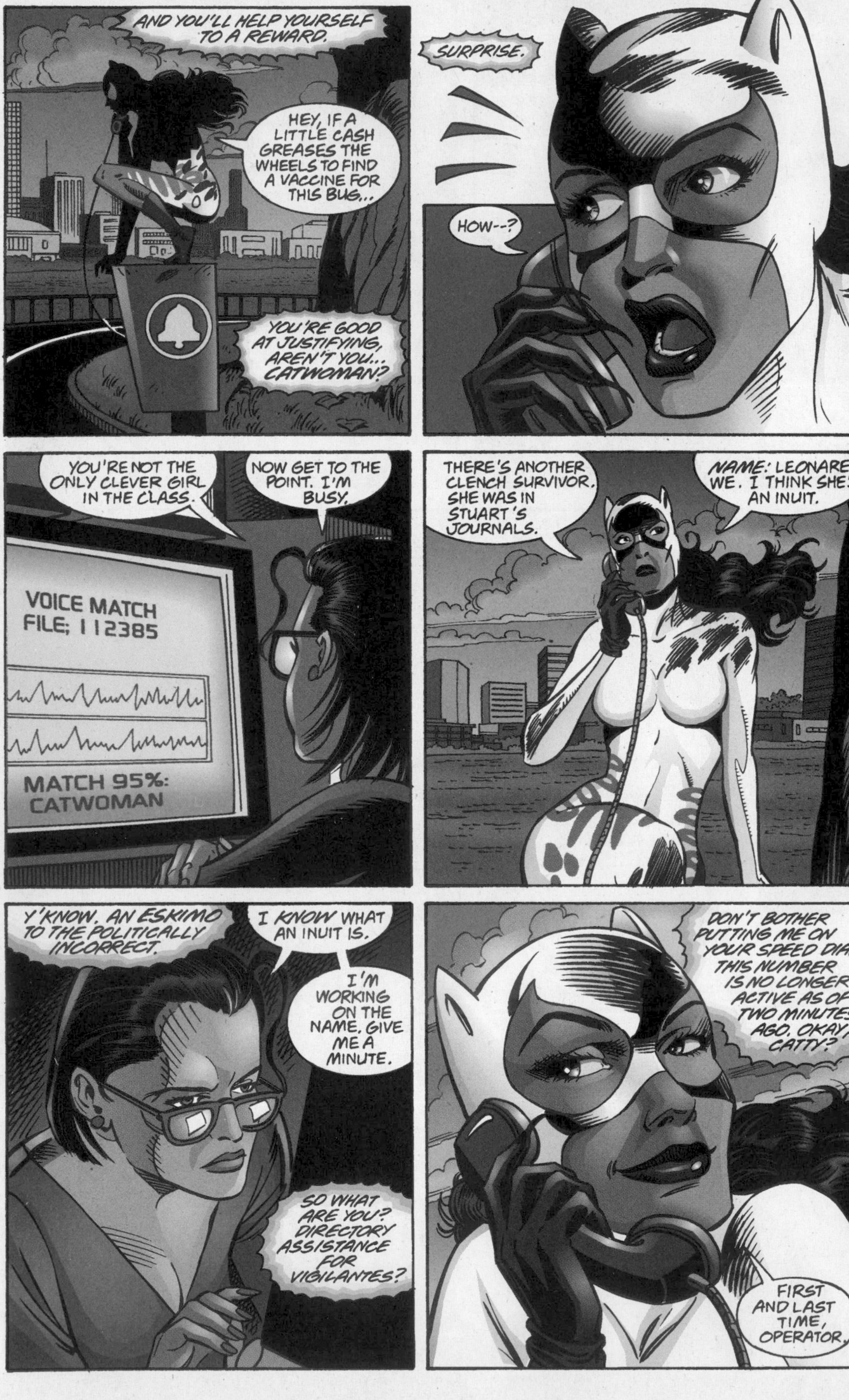
AND YOU'LL HELP YOURSELF TO A REWARD.
HEY, IF A LITTLE CASH GREASES THE WHEELS TO FIND A VACCINE FOR THIS BUG...
YOU'RE GOOD AT JUSTIFYING, AREN'T YOU... CATWOMAN?
SURPRISE.
HOW--?
YOU'RE NOT THE ONLY CLEVER GIRL IN THE CLASS.
NOW GET TO THE POINT. I'M BUSY.
VOICE MATCH
FILE; 112385
MATCH 95%: CATWOMAN
THERE'S ANOTHER CLENCH SURVIVOR. SHE WAS IN STUART'S JOURNALS.
NAME: LEONARE WE. I THINK SHE'S AN INUIT.
Y'KNOW. AN ESKIMO TO THE POLITICALLY INCORRECT.
I KNOW WHAT AN INUIT IS.
I'M WORKING ON THE NAME. GIVE ME A MINUTE.
SO WHAT ARE YOU? DIRECTORY ASSISTANCE FOR VIGILANTES?
DON'T BOTHER PUTTING ME ON YOUR SPEED DIAL. THIS NUMBER IS NO LONGER ACTIVE AS OF TWO MINUTES AGO. OKAY, CATTY?
FIRST AND LAST TIME, OPERATOR.

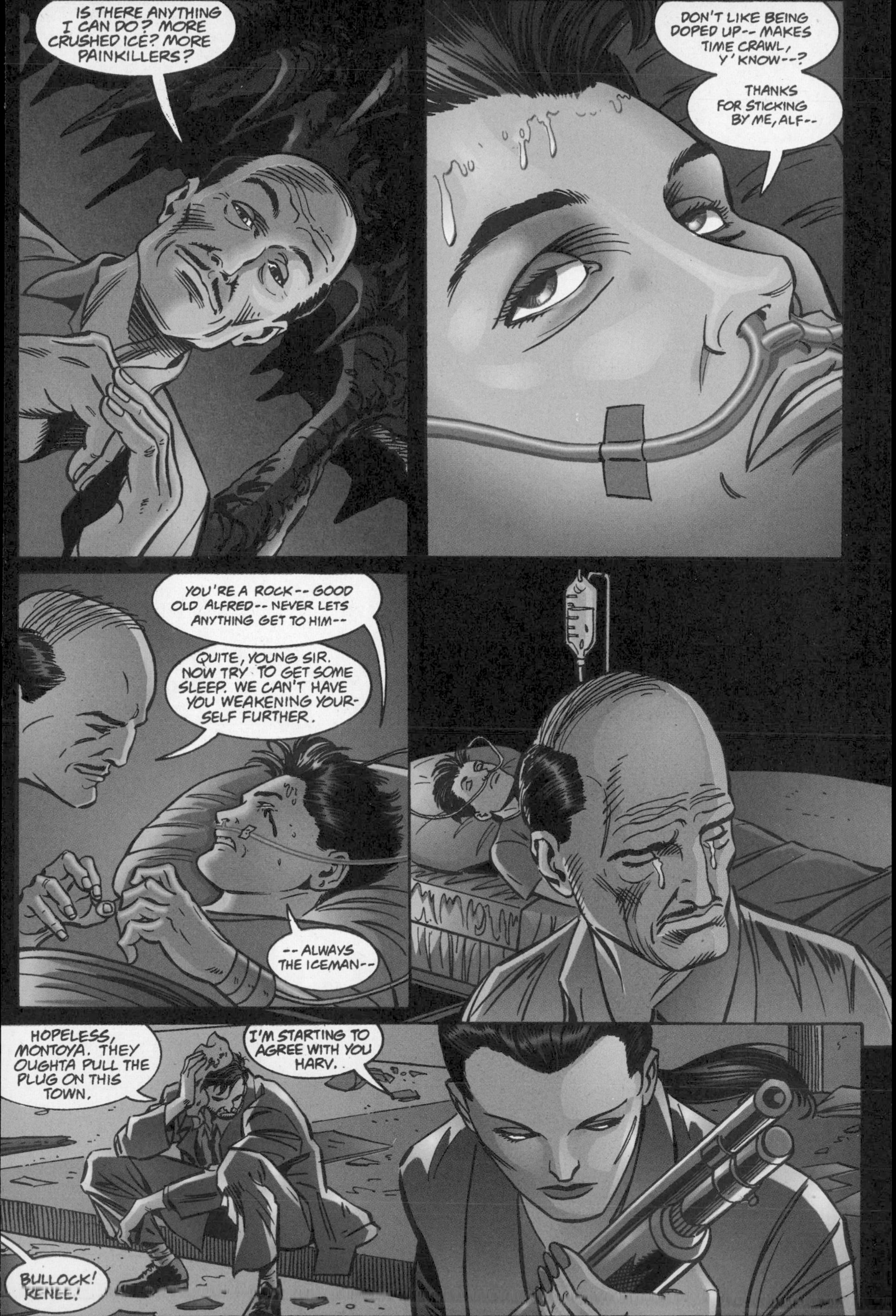
IS THERE ANYTHING I CAN DO? MORE CRUSHED ICE? MORE PAINKILLERS?
DON'T LIKE BEING DOPED UP-- MAKES TIME CRAWL, Y'KNOW--?
THANKS FOR STICKING BY ME, ALF--
YOU'RE A ROCK-- GOOD OLD ALFRED-- NEVER LETS ANYTHING GET TO HIM--
QUITE, YOUNG SIR. NOW TRY TO GET SOME SLEEP. WE CAN'T HAVE YOU WEAKENING YOURSELF FURTHER.
--ALWAYS THE ICEMAN--
HOPELESS, MONTOYA. THEY OUGHTA PULL THE PLUG ON THIS TOWN.
I'M STARTING TO AGREE WITH YOU HARV.
BULLOCK! RENEE!

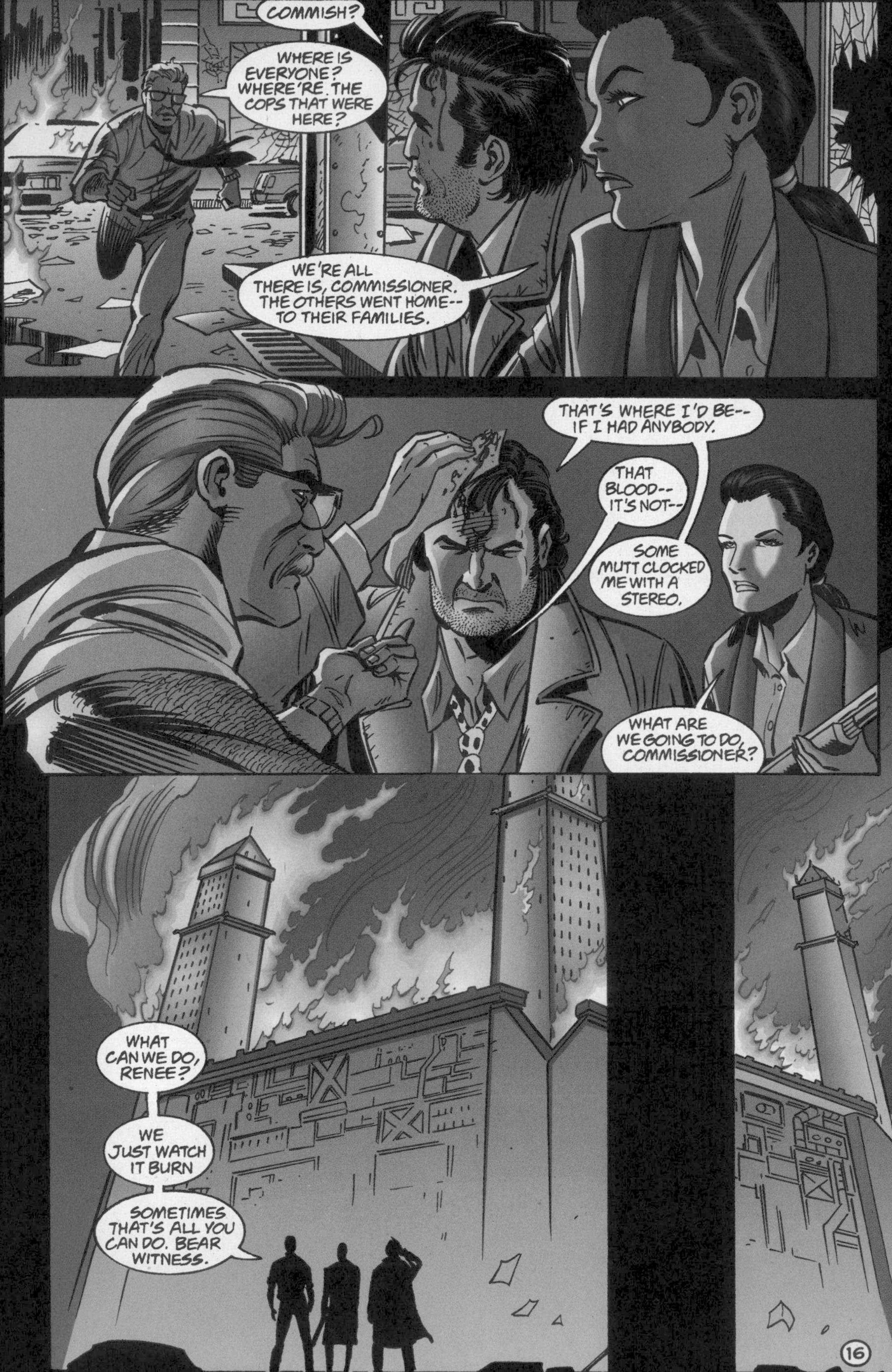
COMMISH?
WHERE IS EVERYONE? WHERE'RE THE COPS THAT WERE HERE?
WE'RE ALL THERE IS, COMMISSIONER. THE OTHERS WENT HOME-- TO THEIR FAMILIES.
THAT'S WHERE I'D BE-- IF I HAD ANYBODY.
THAT BLOOD-- IT'S NOT--
SOME MUTT CLOCKED ME WITH A STEREO.
WHAT ARE WE GOING TO DO, COMMISSIONER?
WHAT CAN WE DO, RENEE?
WE JUST WATCH IT BURN
SOMETIMES THAT'S ALL YOU CAN DO. BEAR WITNESS.

I THINK IT WAS REALLY OVER-HANDED OF THE GOVERNOR TO DO THIS TO YOU.

I MEAN... MARTIAL LAW?

IT'S SO POLITICAL. IT'S SO PARTISAN.

DO ME A FAVOR AND SHUT UP, HOWE. YOU'RE AS GUILTY AS I AM.

BUT WHO CARES, RIGHT?

IN A FEW WEEKS I WON'T BE MAYOR AND YOU WON'T BE TOP COP.

AND I CAN PUT A SPIN ON THIS. HELL, IF GARY HART CAN TRY A--

UH?

UH... UH...

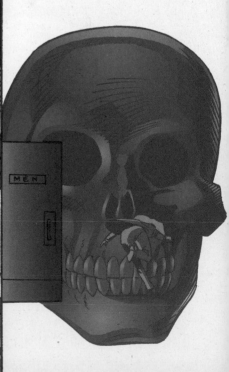

MEN

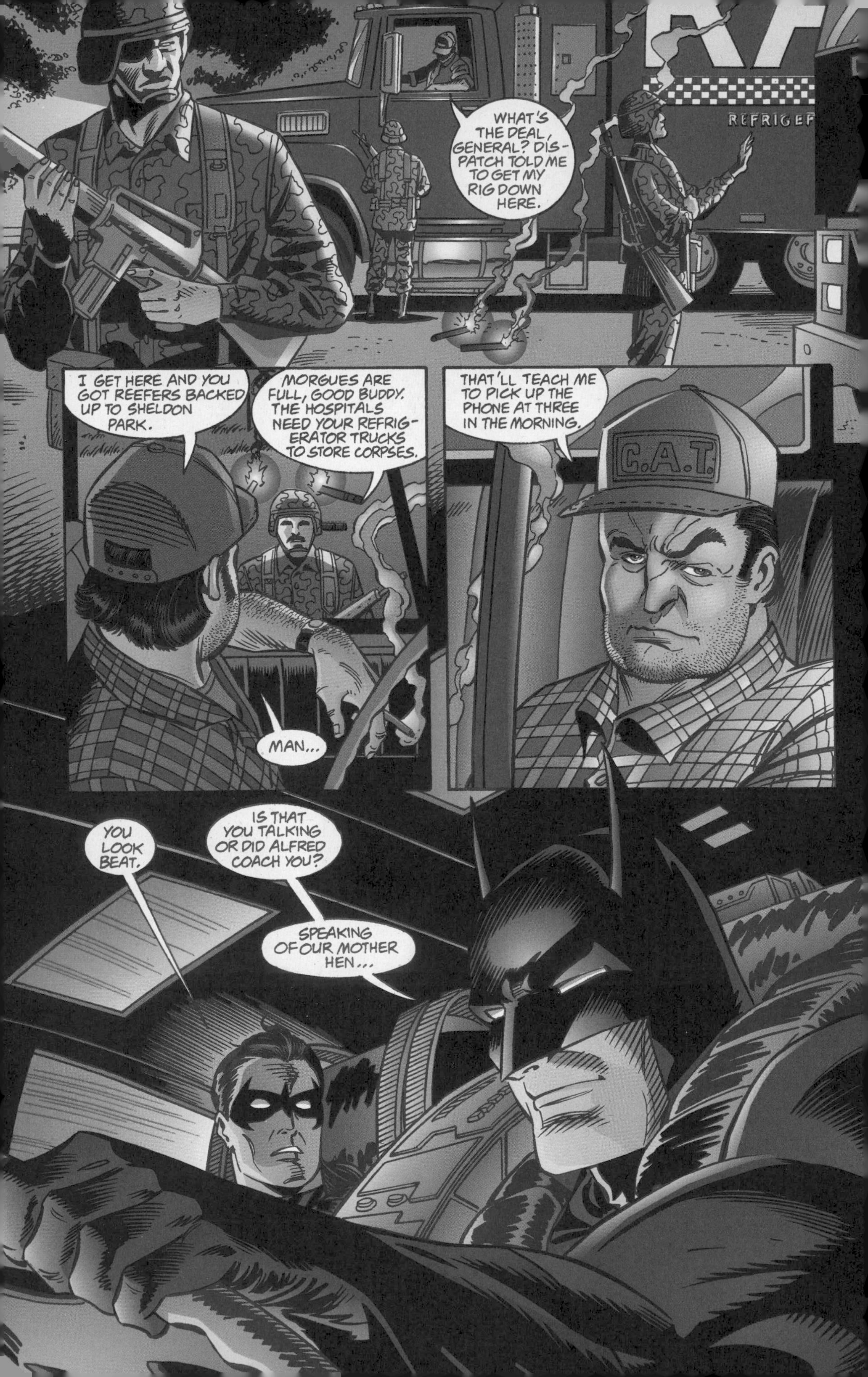
REFRIGEF
WHAT'S THE DEAL, GENERAL? DIS-PATCH TOLD ME TO GET MY RIG DOWN HERE.
I GET HERE AND YOU GOT REEFERS BACKED UP TO SHELDON PARK.
MORGUES ARE FULL, GOOD BUDDY. THE HOSPITALS NEED YOUR REFRIG-ERATOR TRUCKS TO STORE CORPSES.
MAN...
THAT'LL TEACH ME TO PICK UP THE PHONE AT THREE IN THE MORNING.
C.A.T.
YOU LOOK BEAT.
IS THAT YOU TALKING OR DID ALFRED COACH YOU?
SPEAKING OF OUR MOTHER HEN...

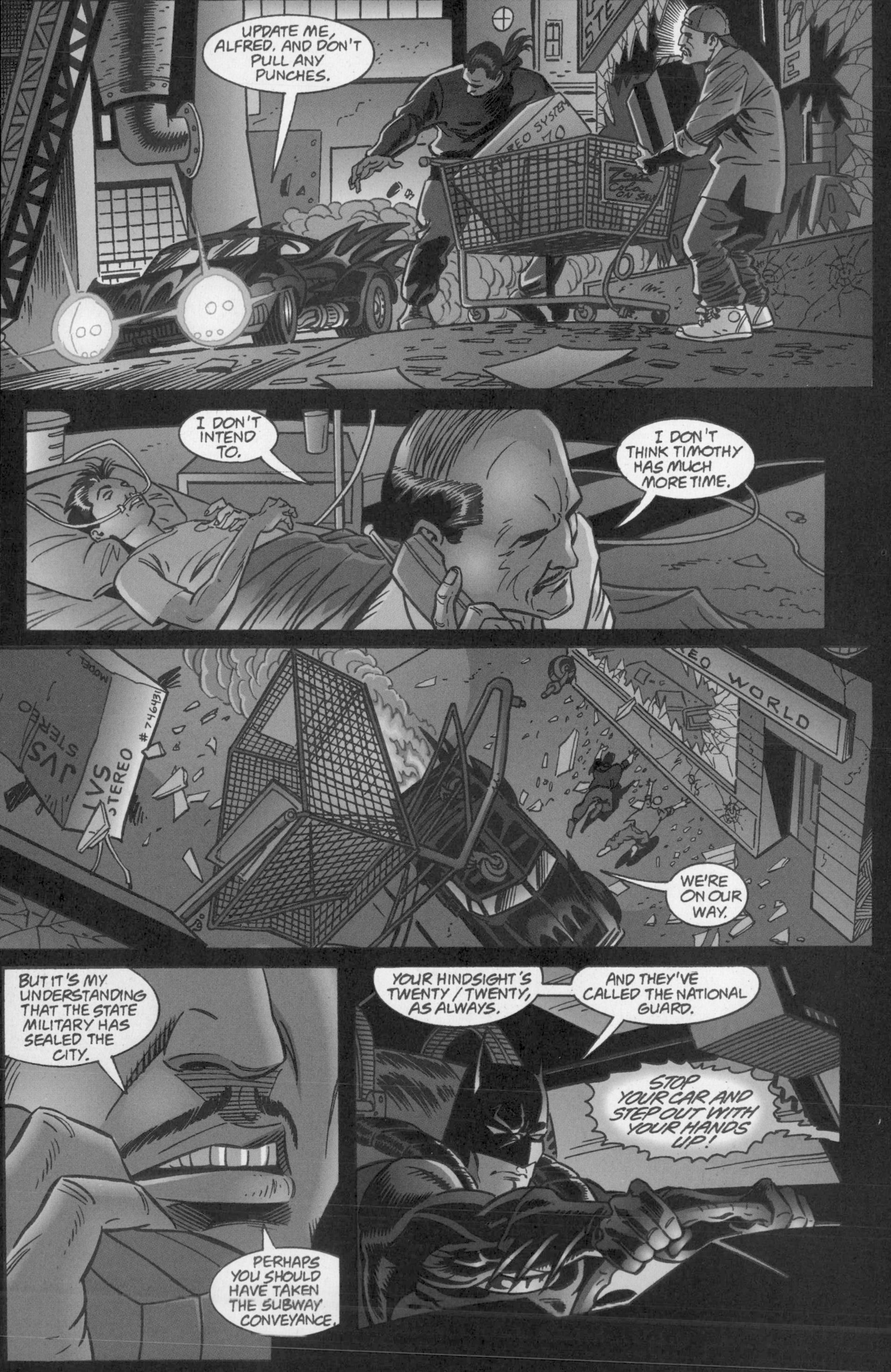
UPDATE ME, ALFRED. AND DON'T PULL ANY PUNCHES.
I DON'T INTEND TO.
I DON'T THINK TIMOTHY HAS MUCH MORE TIME.
JVS STEREO
WE'RE ON OUR WAY.
BUT IT'S MY UNDERSTANDING THAT THE STATE MILITARY HAS SEALED THE CITY.
PERHAPS YOU SHOULD HAVE TAKEN THE SUBWAY CONVEYANCE.
YOUR HINDSIGHT'S TWENTY / TWENTY, AS ALWAYS.
AND THEY'VE CALLED THE NATIONAL GUARD.
STOP YOUR CAR AND STEP OUT WITH YOUR HANDS UP!

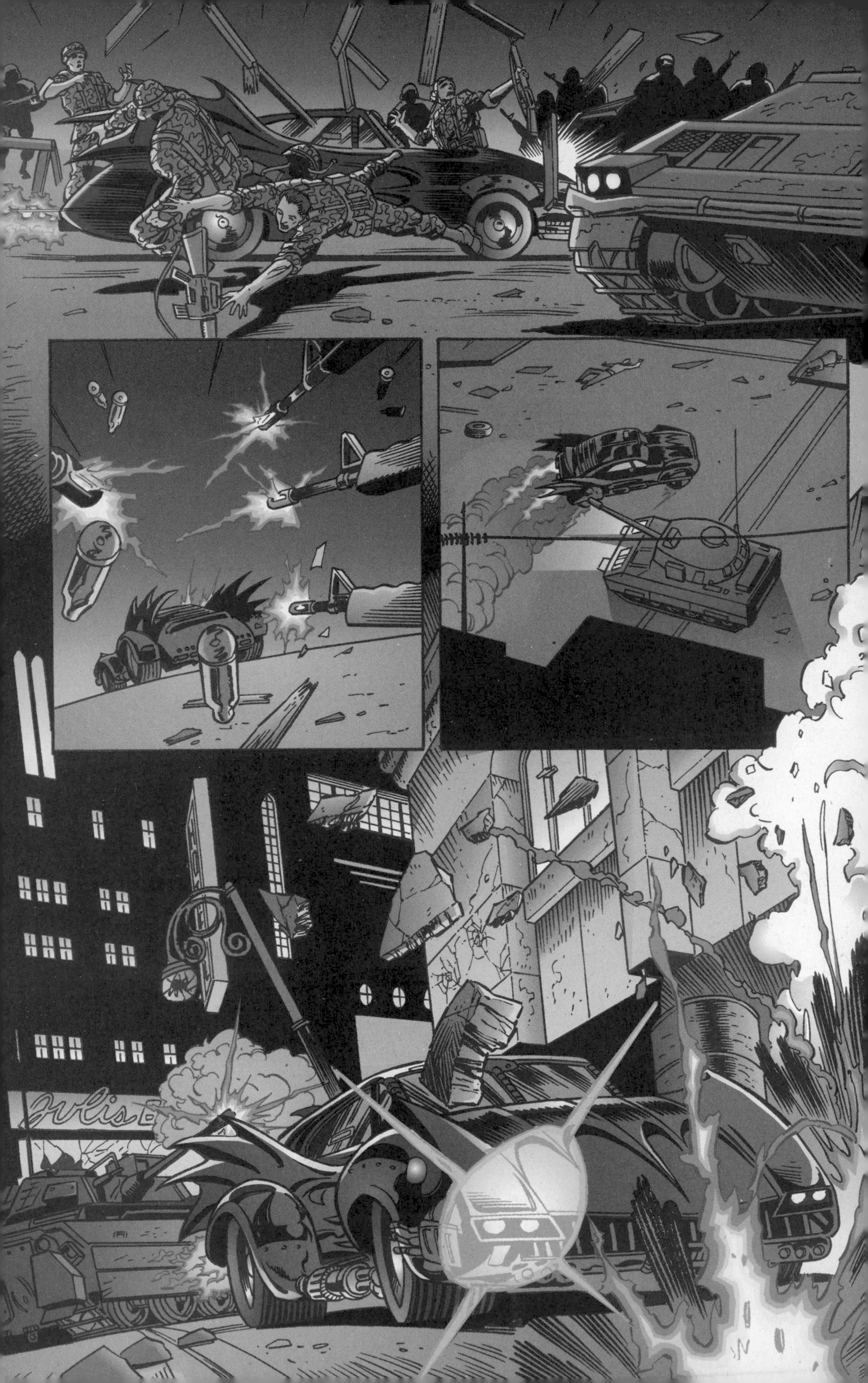

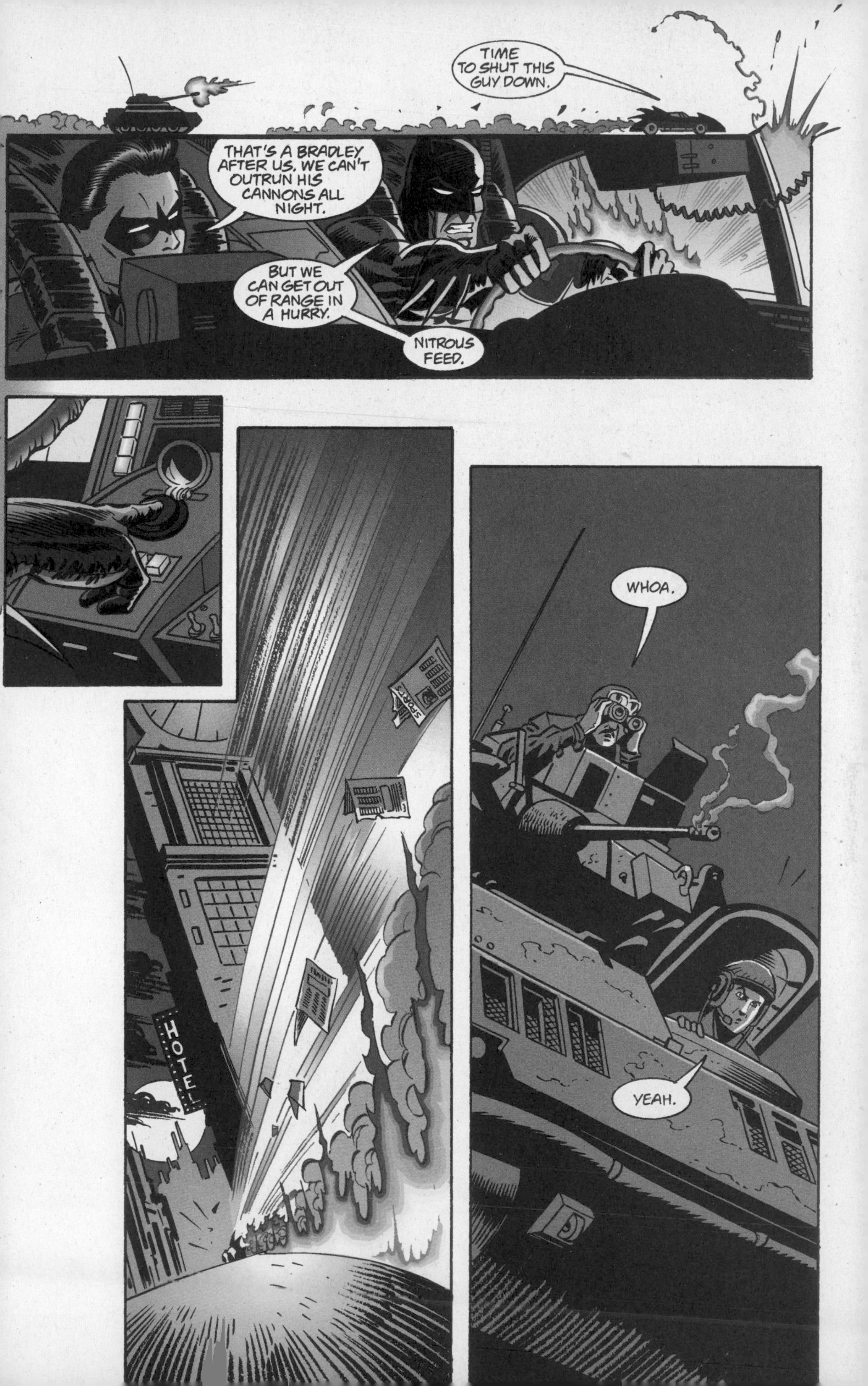
TIME TO SHUT THIS GUY DOWN.
THAT'S A BRADLEY AFTER US. WE CAN'T OUTRUN HIS CANNONS ALL NIGHT.
BUT WE CAN GET OUT OF RANGE IN A HURRY.
NITROUS FEED.
SPORTS
HOTEL
WHOA.
YEAH.

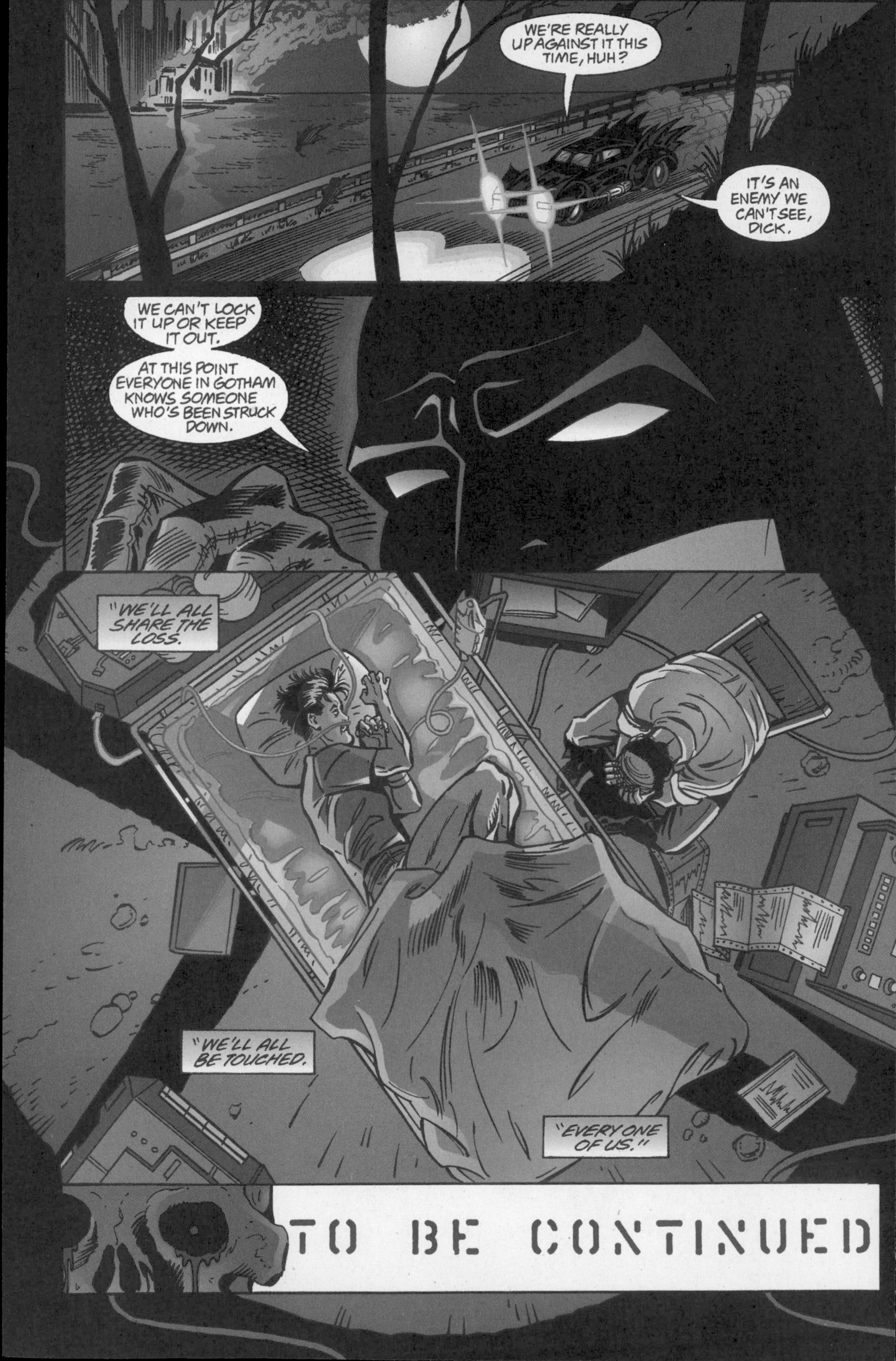
WE'RE REALLY UP AGAINST IT THIS TIME, HUH?
IT'S AN ENEMY WE CAN'T SEE, DICK.
WE CAN'T LOCK IT UP OR KEEP IT OUT.
AT THIS POINT EVERYONE IN GOTHAM KNOWS SOMEONE WHO'S BEEN STRUCK DOWN.
"WE'LL ALL SHARE THE LOSS.
"WE'LL ALL BE TOUCHED.
"EVERY ONE OF US."
TO BE CONTINUED

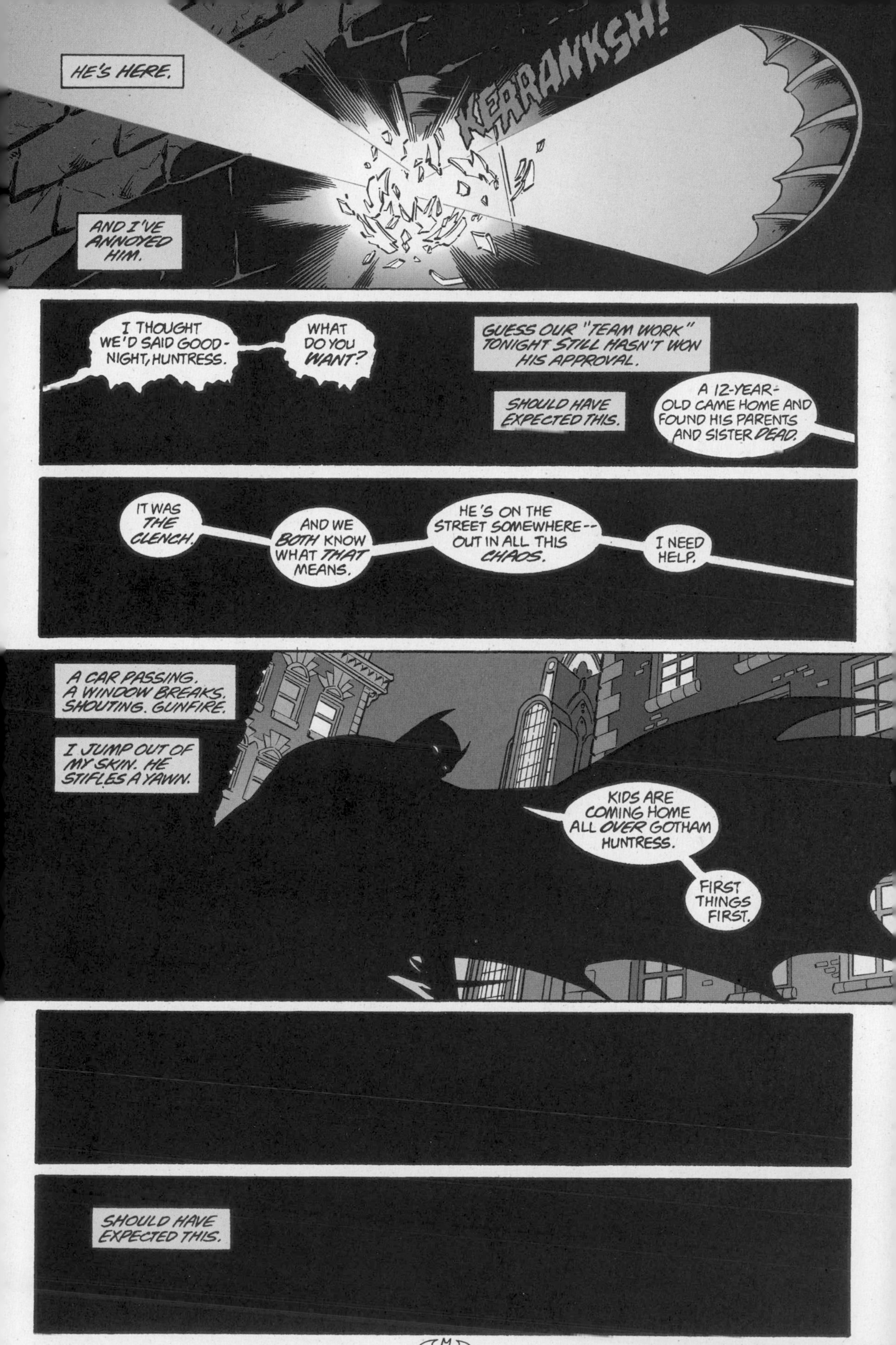
HE'S HERE.
KERRANKSH!
AND I'VE ANNOYED HIM.
I THOUGHT WE'D SAID GOOD-NIGHT, HUNTRESS.
WHAT DO YOU WANT?
GUESS OUR "TEAM WORK" TONIGHT STILL HASN'T WON HIS APPROVAL.
SHOULD HAVE EXPECTED THIS.
A 12-YEAR-OLD CAME HOME AND FOUND HIS PARENTS AND SISTER DEAD.
IT WAS THE CLENCH.
AND WE BOTH KNOW WHAT THAT MEANS.
HE'S ON THE STREET SOMEWHERE-- OUT IN ALL THIS CHAOS.
I NEED HELP.
A CAR PASSING. A WINDOW BREAKS. SHOUTING. GUNFIRE.
I JUMP OUT OF MY SKIN. HE STIFLES A YAWN.
KIDS ARE COMING HOME ALL OVER GOTHAM HUNTRESS.
FIRST THINGS FIRST.
SHOULD HAVE EXPECTED THIS.

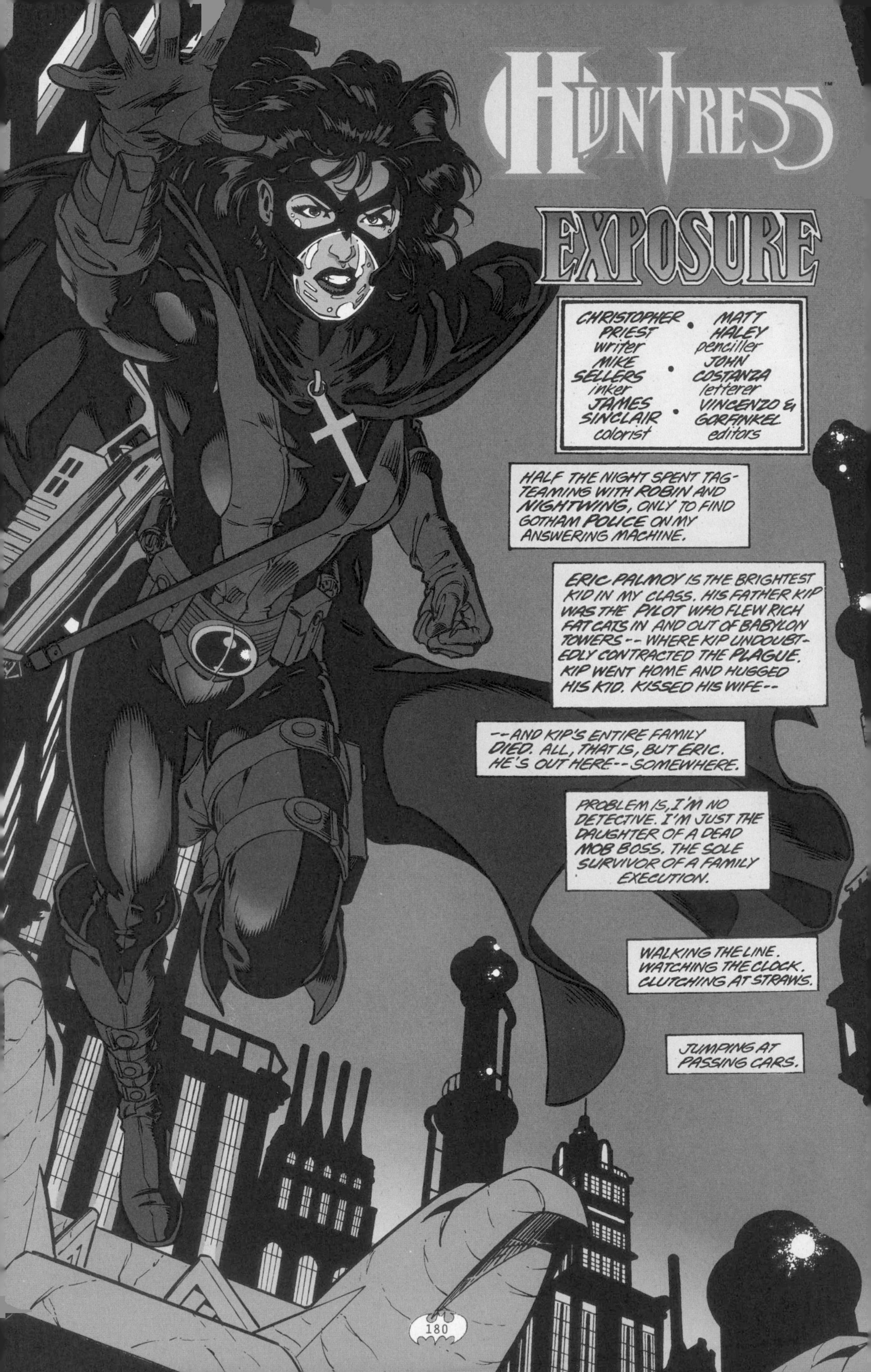

HUNTRESS™
EXPOSURE
CHRISTOPHER PRIEST writer • MATT HALEY penciller
MIKE SELLERS inker • JOHN COSTANZA letterer
JAMES SINCLAIR colorist • VINCENZO & GORFINKEL editors
HALF THE NIGHT SPENT TAG-TEAMING WITH ROBIN AND NIGHTWING, ONLY TO FIND GOTHAM POLICE ON MY ANSWERING MACHINE.
ERIC PALMOY IS THE BRIGHTEST KID IN MY CLASS. HIS FATHER KIP WAS THE PILOT WHO FLEW RICH FAT CATS IN AND OUT OF BABYLON TOWERS-- WHERE KIP UNDOUBTEDLY CONTRACTED THE PLAGUE. KIP WENT HOME AND HUGGED HIS KID. KISSED HIS WIFE--
--AND KIP'S ENTIRE FAMILY DIED. ALL, THAT IS, BUT ERIC. HE'S OUT HERE--SOMEWHERE.
PROBLEM IS, I'M NO DETECTIVE. I'M JUST THE DAUGHTER OF A DEAD MOB BOSS. THE SOLE SURVIVOR OF A FAMILY EXECUTION.
WALKING THE LINE. WATCHING THE CLOCK. CLUTCHING AT STRAWS.
JUMPING AT PASSING CARS.

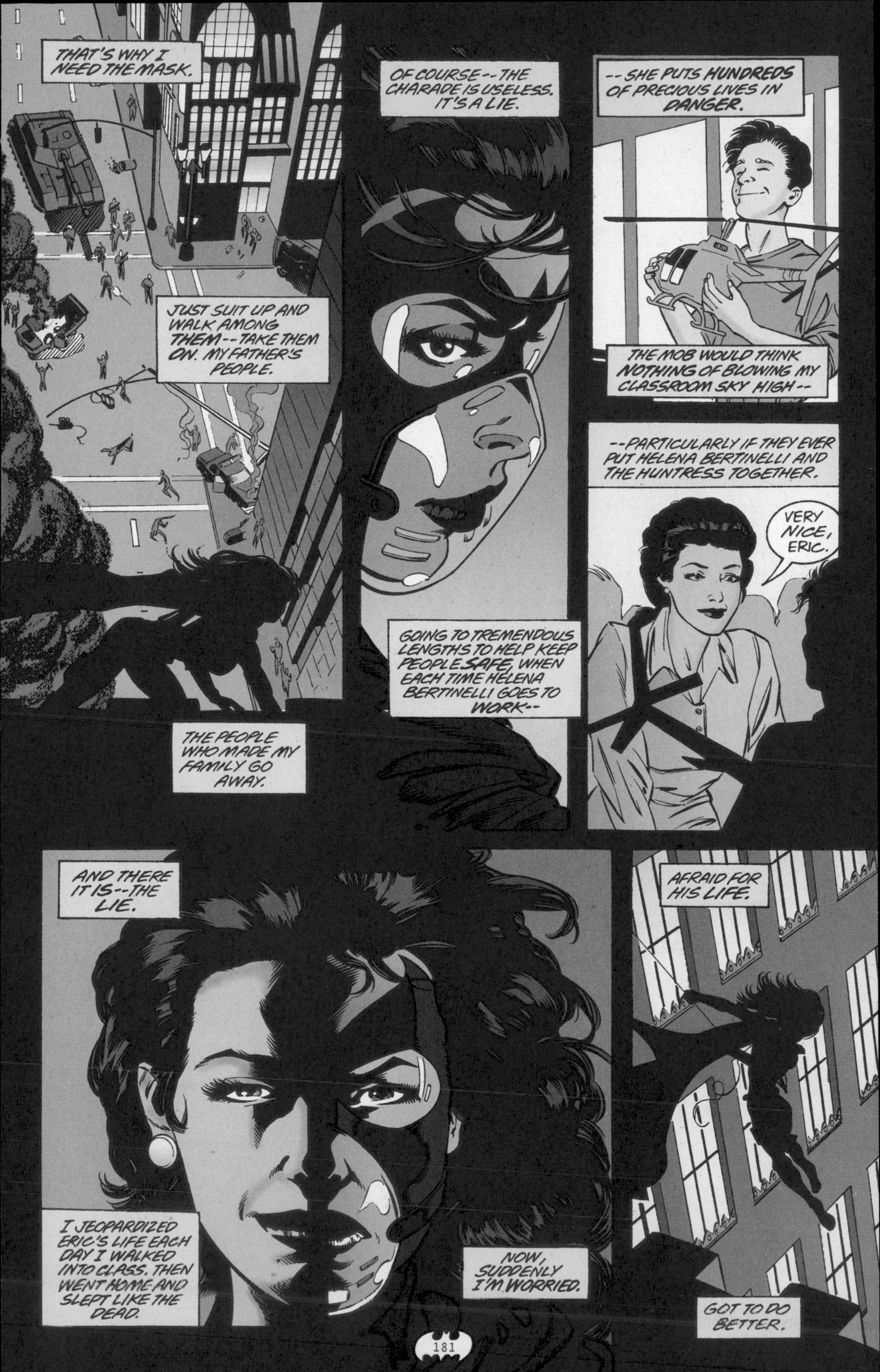
THAT'S WHY I NEED THE MASK.
JUST SUIT UP AND WALK AMONG THEM--TAKE THEM ON. MY FATHER'S PEOPLE.
THE PEOPLE WHO MADE MY FAMILY GO AWAY.
OF COURSE--THE CHARADE IS USELESS. IT'S A LIE.
GOING TO TREMENDOUS LENGTHS TO HELP KEEP PEOPLE SAFE, WHEN EACH TIME HELENA BERTINELLI GOES TO WORK--
--SHE PUTS HUNDREDS OF PRECIOUS LIVES IN DANGER.
THE MOB WOULD THINK NOTHING OF BLOWING MY CLASSROOM SKY HIGH--
--PARTICULARLY IF THEY EVER PUT HELENA BERTINELLI AND THE HUNTRESS TOGETHER.
VERY NICE, ERIC.
AND THERE IT IS--THE LIE.
I JEOPARDIZED ERIC'S LIFE EACH DAY I WALKED INTO CLASS. THEN WENT HOME AND SLEPT LIKE THE DEAD.
NOW, SUDDENLY I'M WORRIED.
AFRAID FOR HIS LIFE.
GOT TO DO BETTER.

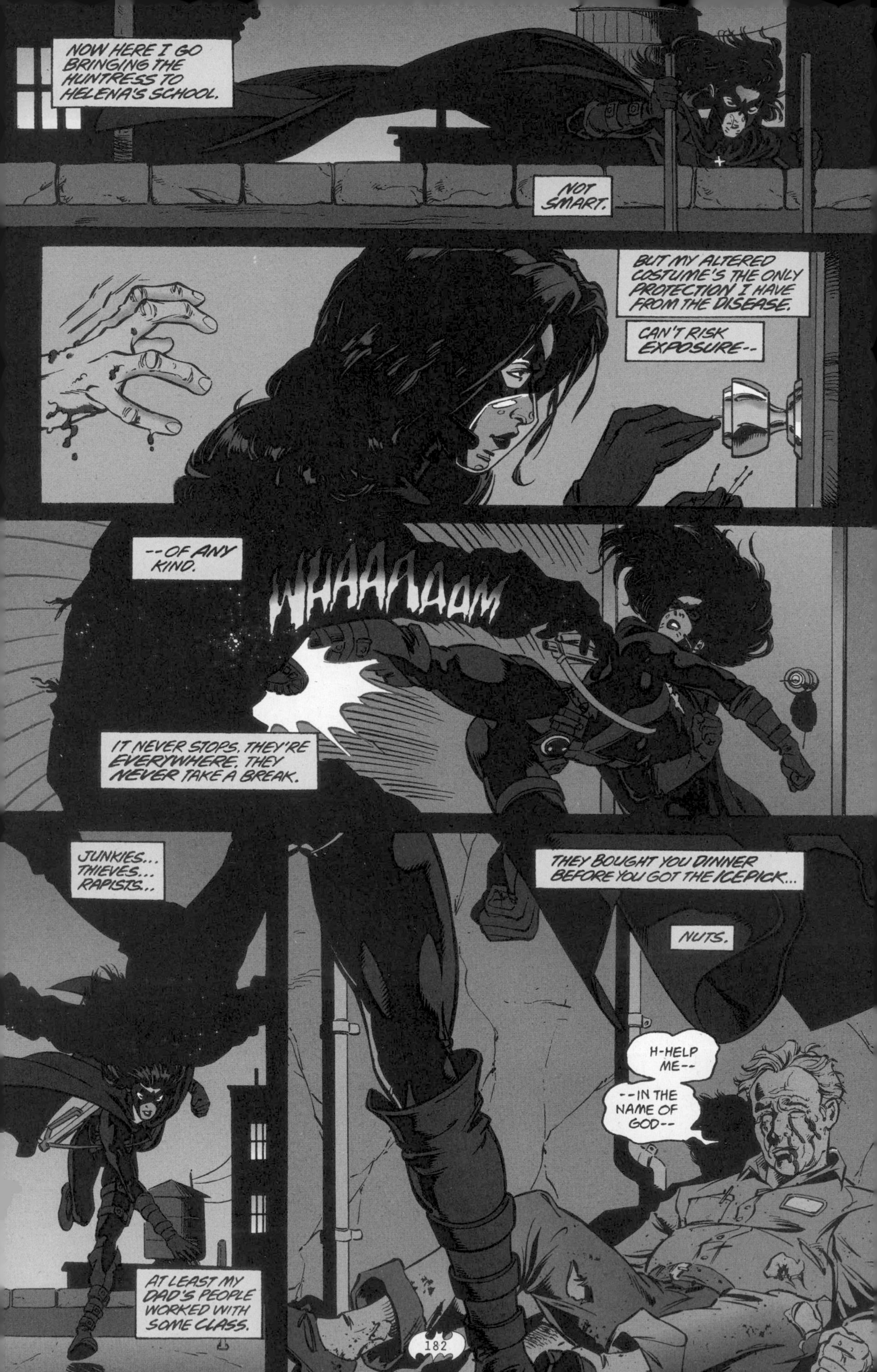
NOW HERE I GO BRINGING THE HUNTRESS TO HELENA'S SCHOOL.
NOT SMART.
BUT MY ALTERED COSTUME'S THE ONLY PROTECTION I HAVE FROM THE DISEASE.
CAN'T RISK EXPOSURE--
--OF ANY KIND.
WHAAAAAM
IT NEVER STOPS. THEY'RE EVERYWHERE. THEY NEVER TAKE A BREAK.
JUNKIES... THIEVES... RAPISTS...
AT LEAST MY DAD'S PEOPLE WORKED WITH SOME CLASS.
THEY BOUGHT YOU DINNER BEFORE YOU GOT THE ICEPICK...
NUTS.
H-HELP ME--
--IN THE NAME OF GOD--

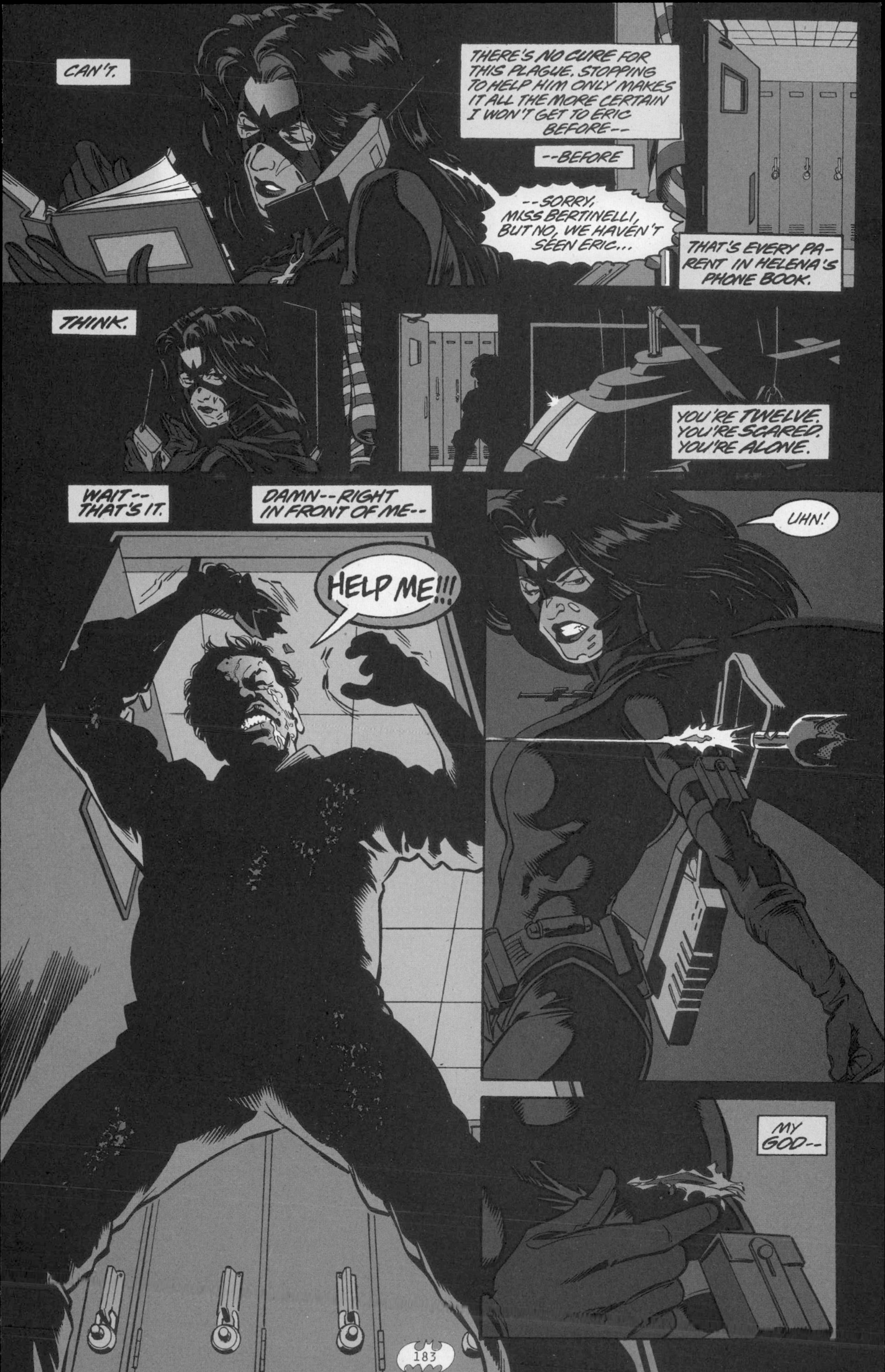
CAN'T.
THERE'S NO CURE FOR THIS PLAGUE. STOPPING TO HELP HIM ONLY MAKES IT ALL THE MORE CERTAIN I WON'T GET TO ERIC BEFORE--
--BEFORE
--SORRY, MISS BERTINELLI, BUT NO, WE HAVEN'T SEEN ERIC...
THAT'S EVERY PARENT IN HELENA'S PHONE BOOK.
THINK.
YOU'RE TWELVE. YOU'RE SCARED. YOU'RE ALONE.
WAIT-- THAT'S IT.
DAMN--RIGHT IN FRONT OF ME--
HELP ME!!!
UHN!
MY GOD--

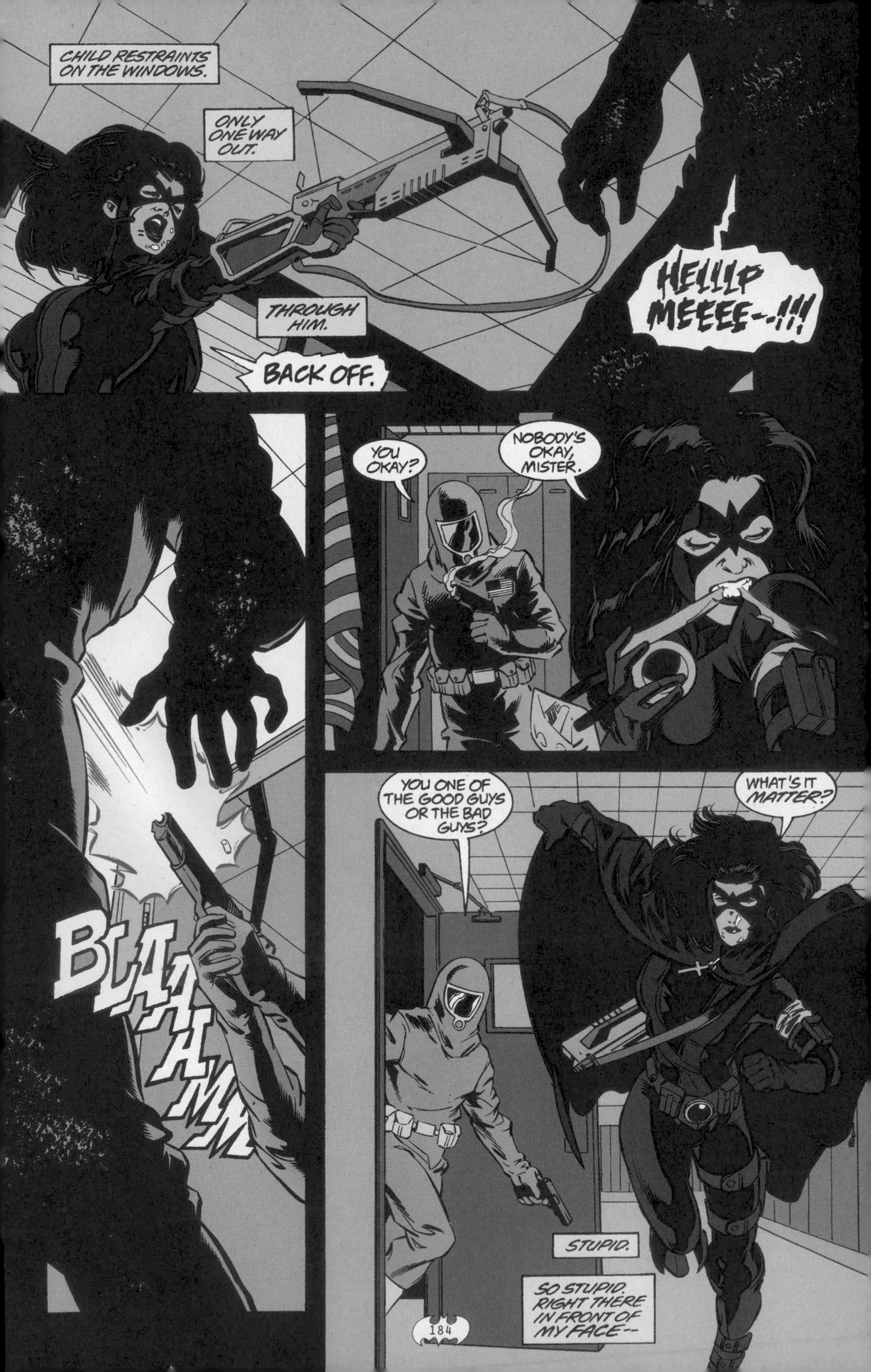

CHILD RESTRAINTS ON THE WINDOWS.
ONLY ONE WAY OUT.
THROUGH HIM.
BACK OFF.
HELLLP MEEEE--!!!
BLAAHMM
YOU OKAY?
NOBODY'S OKAY, MISTER.
YOU ONE OF THE GOOD GUYS OR THE BAD GUYS?
WHAT'S IT MATTER?
STUPID.
SO STUPID. RIGHT THERE IN FRONT OF MY FACE--

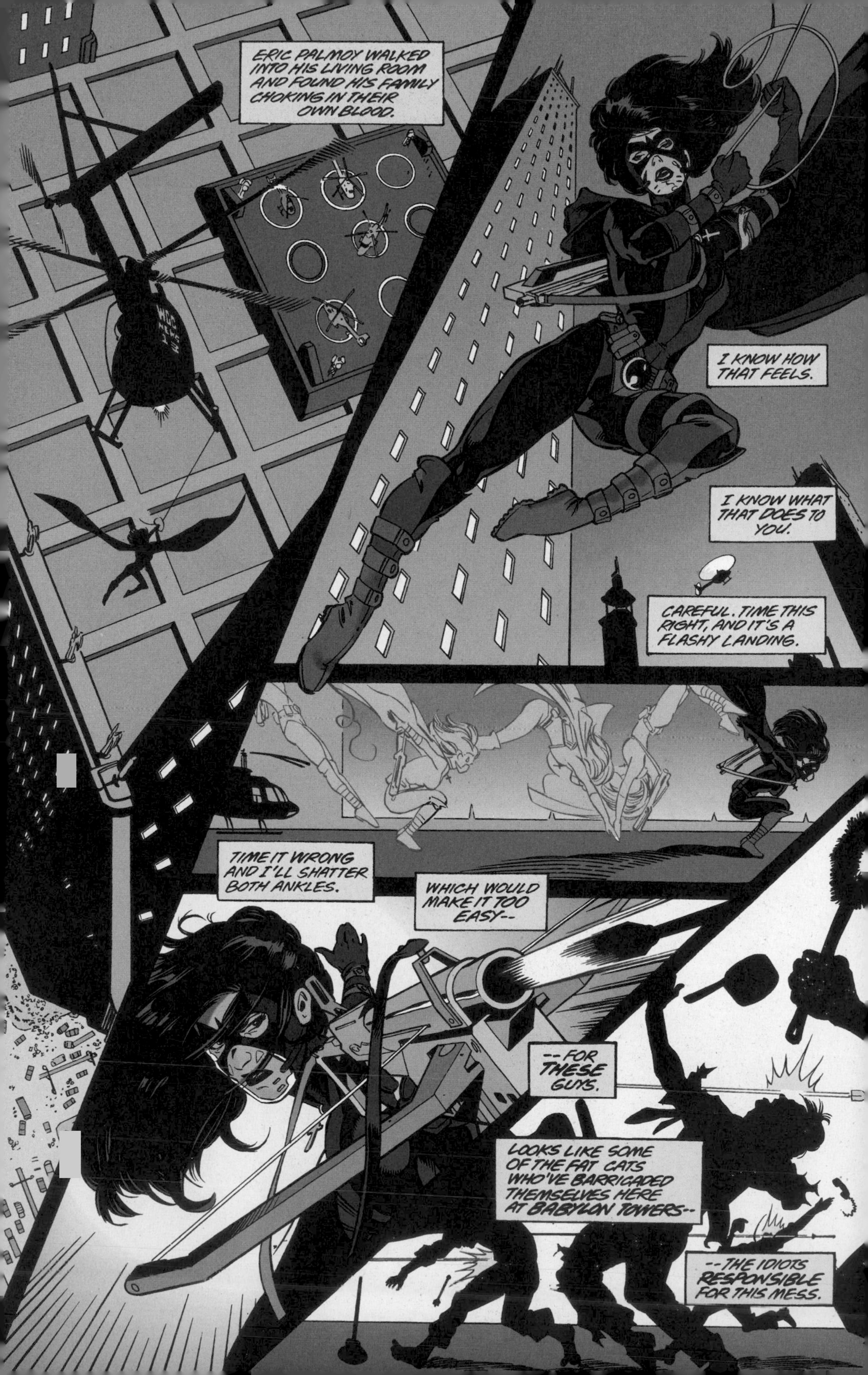
ERIC PALMOY WALKED INTO HIS LIVING ROOM AND FOUND HIS FAMILY CHOKING IN THEIR OWN BLOOD.
I KNOW HOW THAT FEELS.
I KNOW WHAT THAT DOES TO YOU.
CAREFUL. TIME THIS RIGHT, AND IT'S A FLASHY LANDING.
TIME IT WRONG AND I'LL SHATTER BOTH ANKLES.
WHICH WOULD MAKE IT TOO EASY--
--FOR THESE GUYS.
LOOKS LIKE SOME OF THE FAT CATS WHO'VE BARRICADED THEMSELVES HERE AT BABYLON TOWERS--
--THE IDIOTS RESPONSIBLE FOR THIS MESS.

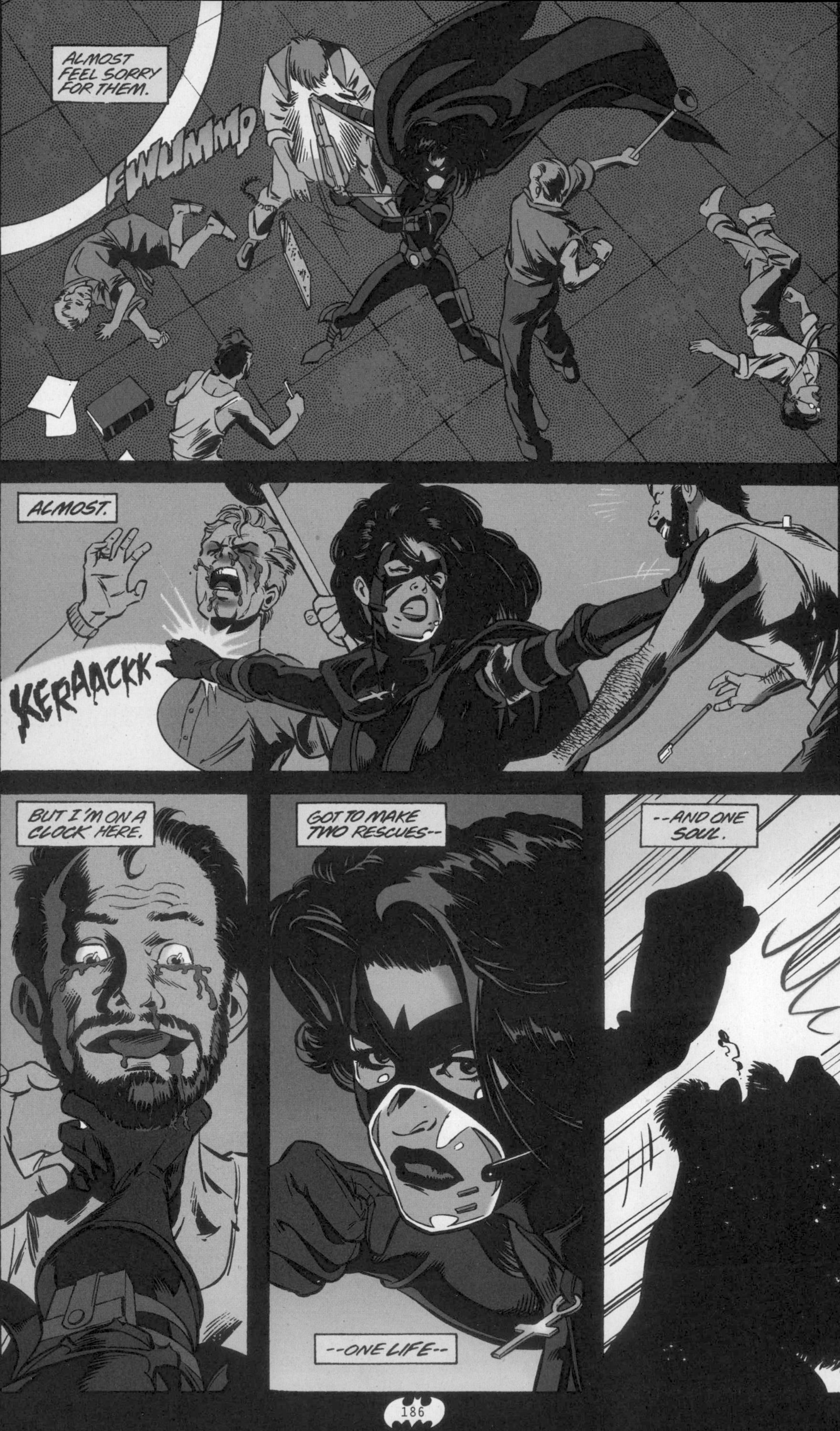

ALMOST FEEL SORRY FOR THEM.
FWUMMP
ALMOST.
KERAACKK
BUT I'M ON A CLOCK HERE.
GOT TO MAKE TWO RESCUES--
--ONE LIFE--
--AND ONE SOUL.

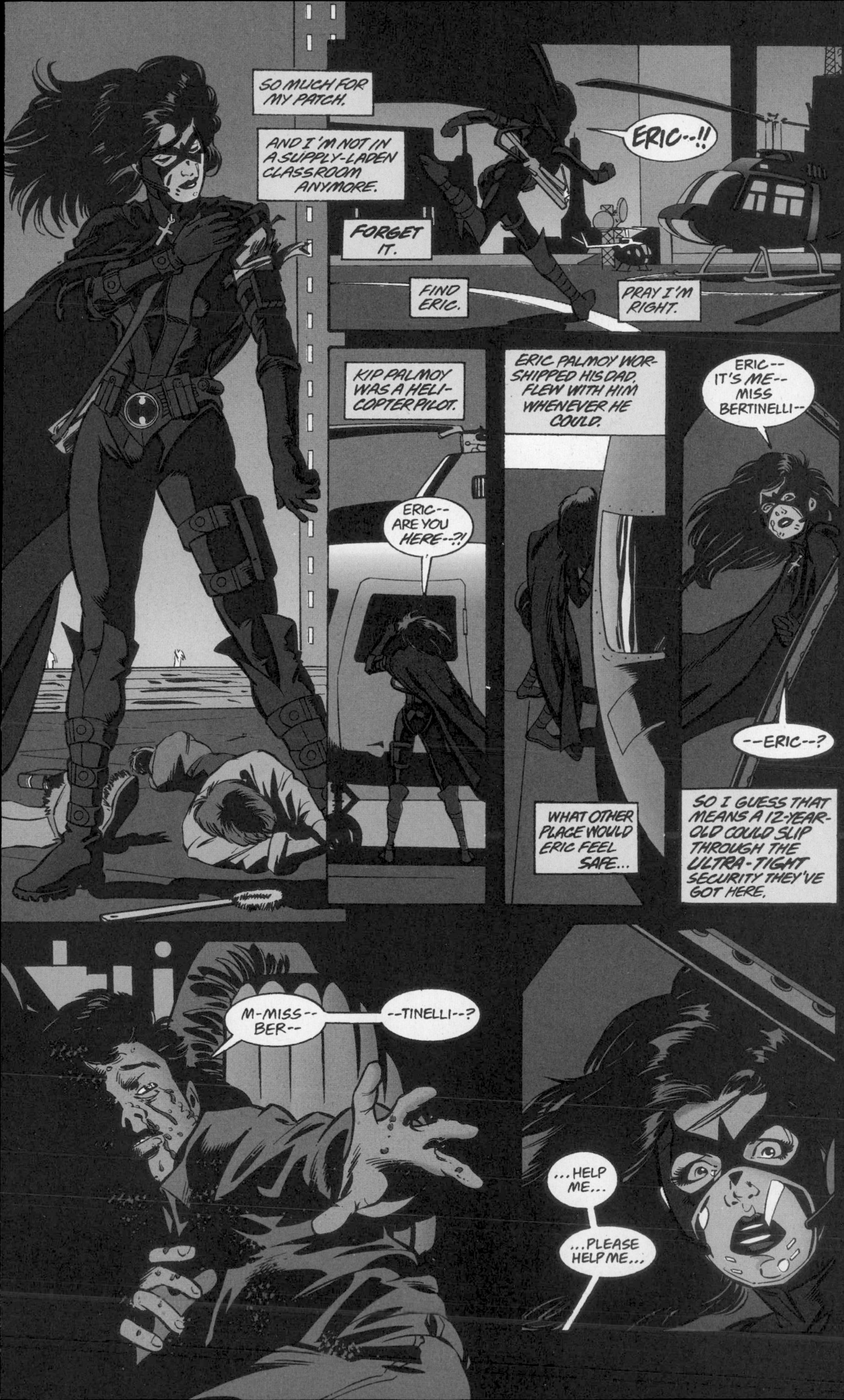
SO MUCH FOR MY PATCH.
AND I'M NOT IN A SUPPLY-LADEN CLASSROOM ANYMORE.
FORGET IT.
ERIC--!!
FIND ERIC.
PRAY I'M RIGHT.
KIP PALMOY WAS A HELI-COPTER PILOT.
ERIC-- ARE YOU HERE--?!
ERIC PALMOY WOR-SHIPPED HIS DAD. FLEW WITH HIM WHENEVER HE COULD.
WHAT OTHER PLACE WOULD ERIC FEEL SAFE...
ERIC-- IT'S ME-- MISS BERTINELLI--
--ERIC--?
SO I GUESS THAT MEANS A 12-YEAR-OLD COULD SLIP THROUGH THE ULTRA-TIGHT SECURITY THEY'VE GOT HERE.
M-MISS BER--
--TINELLI--?
...HELP ME...
...PLEASE HELP ME...

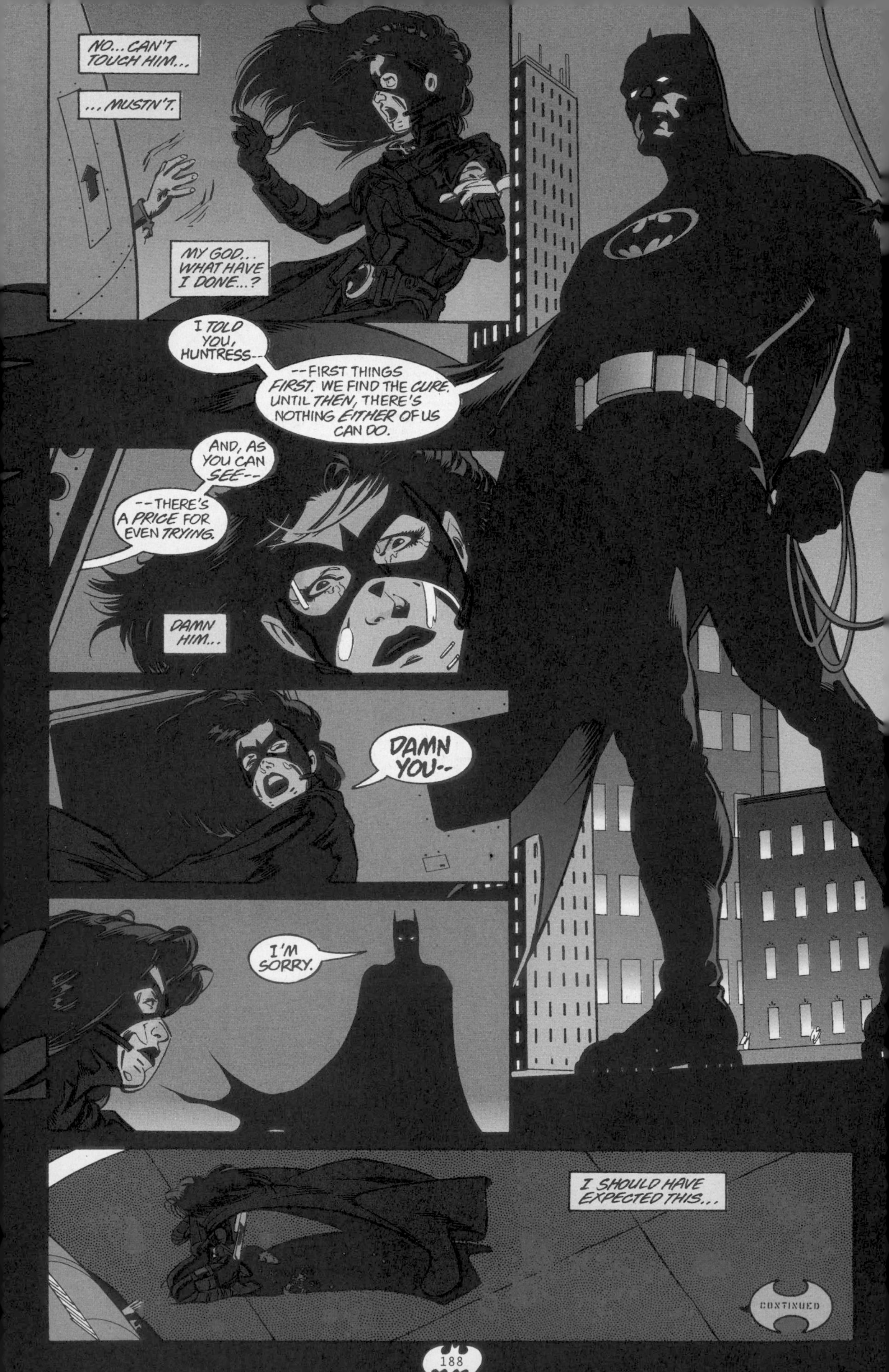
NO... CAN'T TOUCH HIM...
...MUSTN'T.
MY GOD... WHAT HAVE I DONE...?
I TOLD YOU, HUNTRESS--
--FIRST THINGS FIRST. WE FIND THE CURE. UNTIL THEN, THERE'S NOTHING EITHER OF US CAN DO.
AND, AS YOU CAN SEE--
--THERE'S A PRICE FOR EVEN TRYING.
DAMN HIM...
DAMN YOU--
I'M SORRY.
I SHOULD HAVE EXPECTED THIS...
CONTINUED

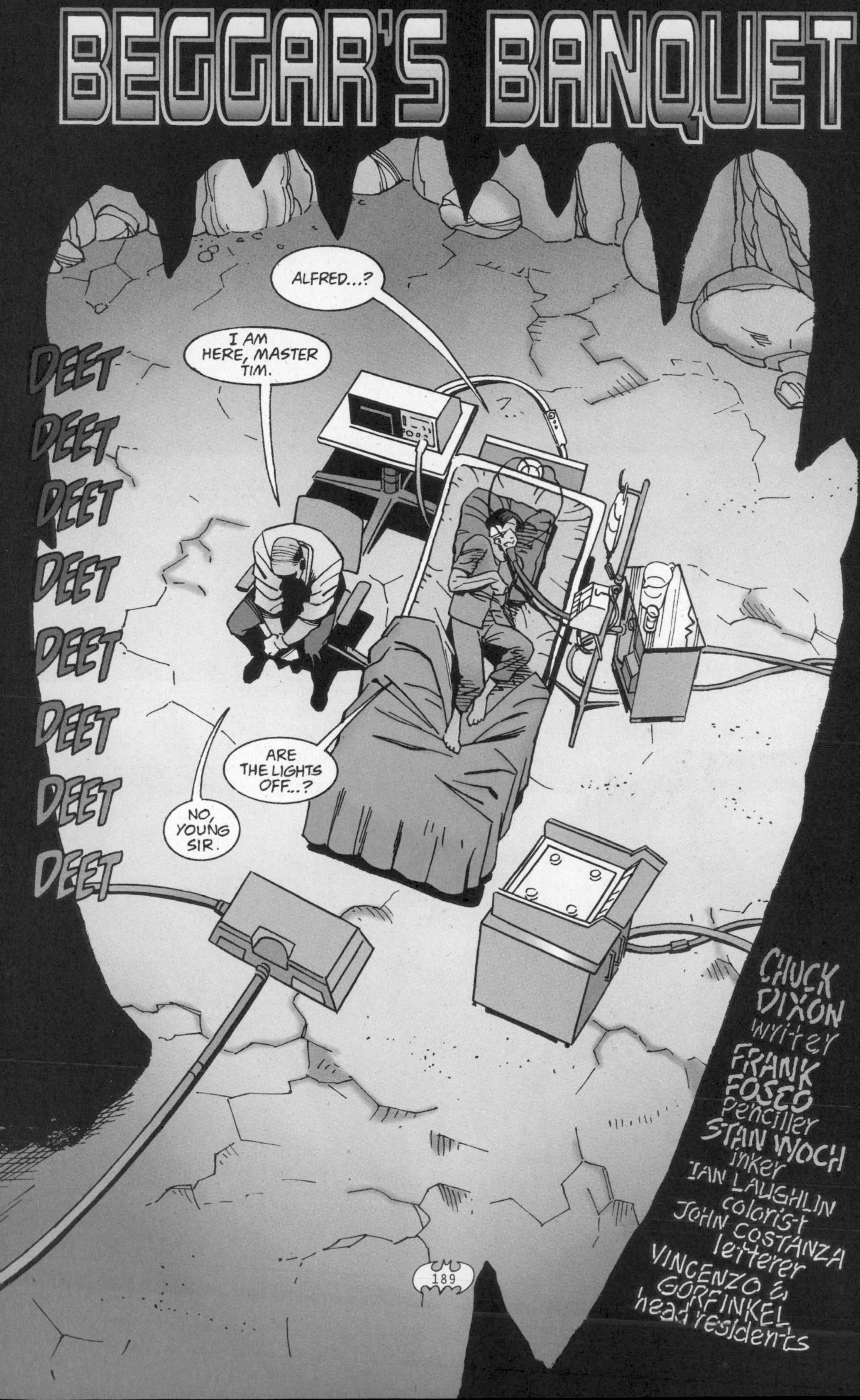
BEGGAR'S BANQUET
ALFRED...?
I AM HERE, MASTER TIM.
DEET DEET DEET DEET DEET DEET DEET DEET
ARE THE LIGHTS OFF...?
NO, YOUNG SIR.
CHUCK DIXON writer
FRANK FOSCO penciller
STAN WOCH inker
IAN LAUGHLIN colorist
JOHN COSTANZA letterer
VINCENZO & GORFINKEL head residents

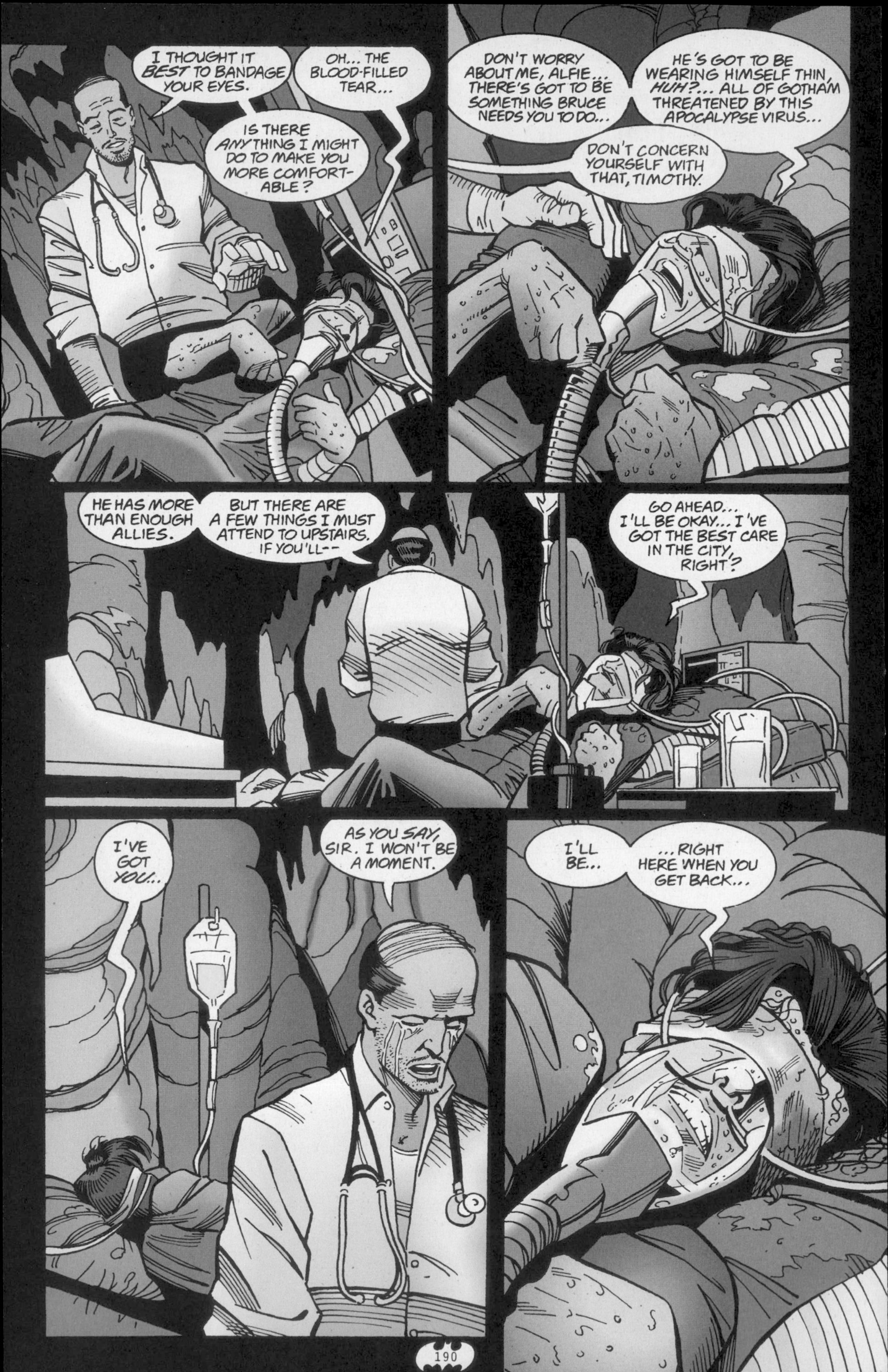
I THOUGHT IT BEST TO BANDAGE YOUR EYES.
OH... THE BLOOD-FILLED TEAR...
IS THERE ANYTHING I MIGHT DO TO MAKE YOU MORE COMFORTABLE?
DON'T WORRY ABOUT ME, ALFIE... THERE'S GOT TO BE SOMETHING BRUCE NEEDS YOU TO DO...
HE'S GOT TO BE WEARING HIMSELF THIN, HUH?... ALL OF GOTHAM THREATENED BY THIS APOCALYPSE VIRUS...
DON'T CONCERN YOURSELF WITH THAT, TIMOTHY.
HE HAS MORE THAN ENOUGH ALLIES.
BUT THERE ARE A FEW THINGS I MUST ATTEND TO UPSTAIRS. IF YOU'LL--
GO AHEAD... I'LL BE OKAY... I'VE GOT THE BEST CARE IN THE CITY, RIGHT?
I'VE GOT YOU...
AS YOU SAY, SIR. I WON'T BE A MOMENT.
I'LL BE...
...RIGHT HERE WHEN YOU GET BACK...

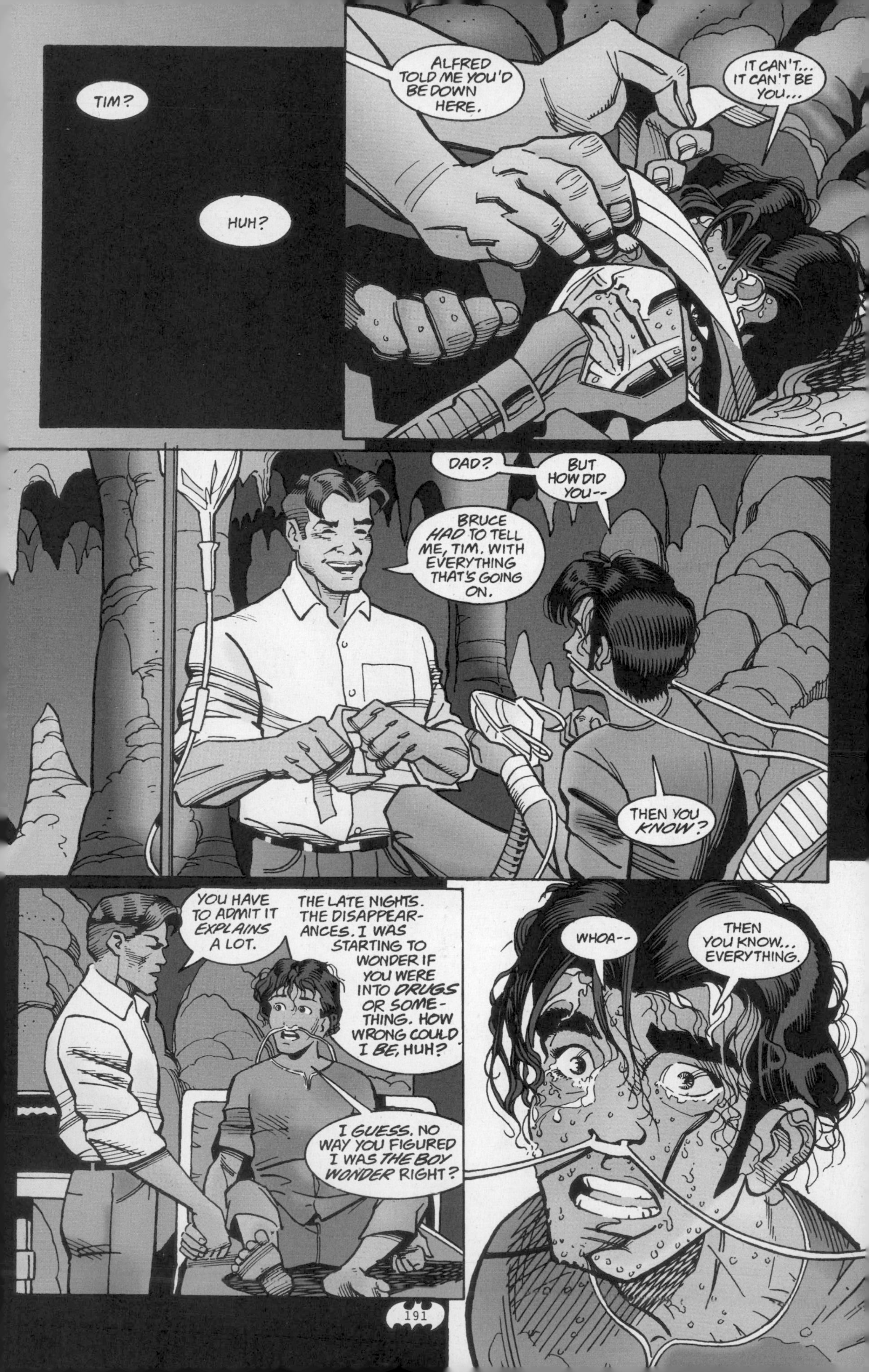
TIM?
HUH?
ALFRED TOLD ME YOU'D BE DOWN HERE.
IT CAN'T... IT CAN'T BE YOU...
DAD?
BUT HOW DID YOU--
BRUCE *HAD* TO TELL ME, TIM. WITH EVERYTHING THAT'S GOING ON.
THEN YOU *KNOW*?
YOU HAVE TO ADMIT IT *EXPLAINS* A LOT.
THE LATE NIGHTS. THE DISAPPEAR-ANCES. I WAS STARTING TO WONDER IF YOU WERE INTO *DRUGS* OR SOME-THING. HOW WRONG COULD I *BE*, HUH?
I *GUESS*. NO WAY YOU FIGURED I WAS *THE BOY WONDER* RIGHT?
WHOA--
THEN YOU KNOW... EVERYTHING.
191

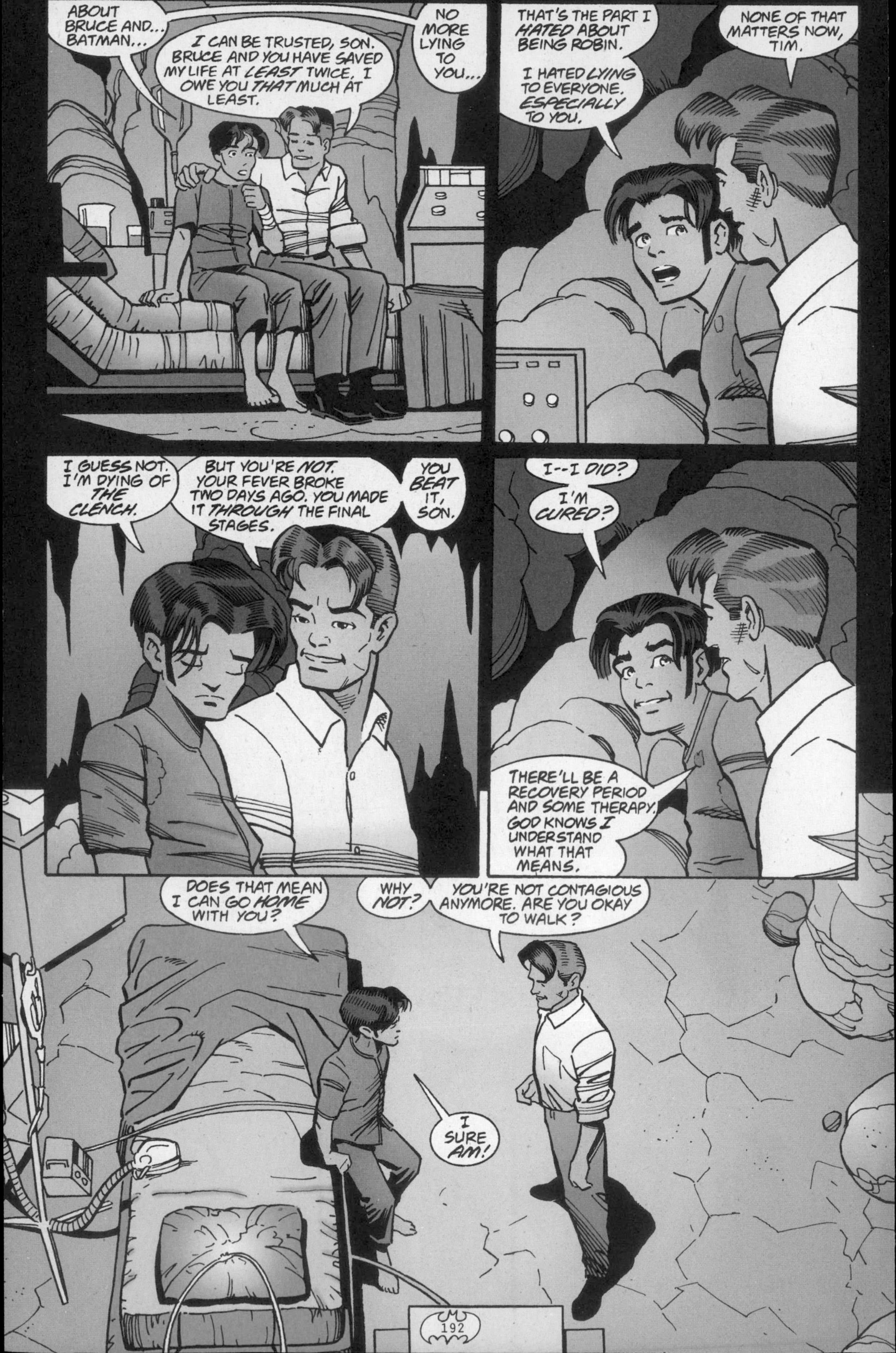
ABOUT BRUCE AND... BATMAN...
NO MORE LYING TO YOU...
I CAN BE TRUSTED, SON. BRUCE AND YOU HAVE SAVED MY LIFE AT LEAST TWICE. I OWE YOU THAT MUCH AT LEAST.
THAT'S THE PART I HATED ABOUT BEING ROBIN.
I HATED LYING TO EVERYONE. ESPECIALLY TO YOU.
NONE OF THAT MATTERS NOW, TIM.
I GUESS NOT. I'M DYING OF THE CLENCH.
BUT YOU'RE NOT. YOUR FEVER BROKE TWO DAYS AGO. YOU MADE IT THROUGH THE FINAL STAGES.
YOU BEAT IT, SON.
I--I DID?
I'M CURED?
THERE'LL BE A RECOVERY PERIOD AND SOME THERAPY. GOD KNOWS I UNDERSTAND WHAT THAT MEANS.
DOES THAT MEAN I CAN GO HOME WITH YOU?
WHY NOT?
YOU'RE NOT CONTAGIOUS ANYMORE. ARE YOU OKAY TO WALK?
I SURE AM!

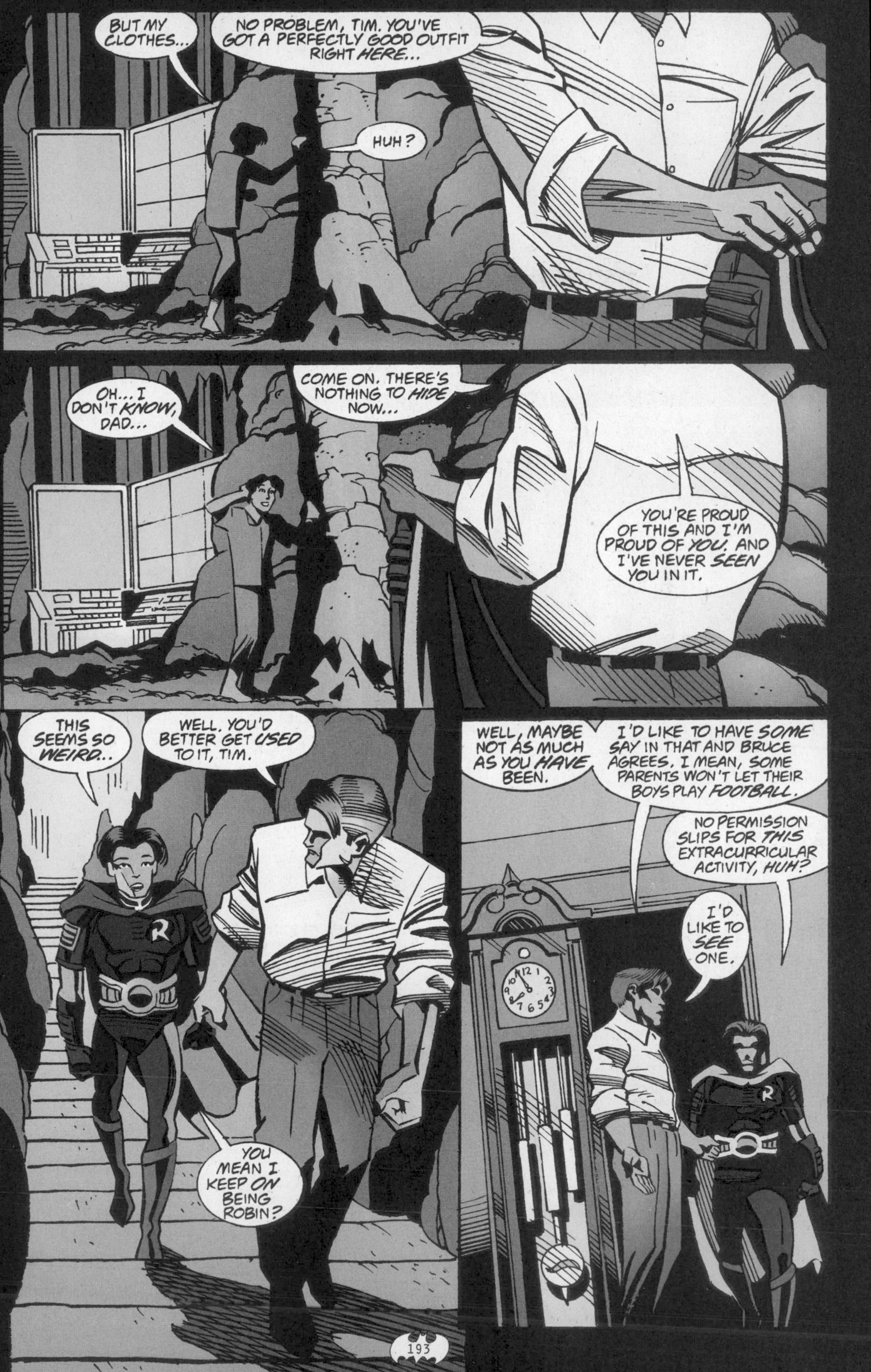
BUT MY CLOTHES...
NO PROBLEM, TIM. YOU'VE GOT A PERFECTLY GOOD OUTFIT RIGHT HERE...
HUH?
OH... I DON'T KNOW, DAD...
COME ON. THERE'S NOTHING TO HIDE NOW...
YOU'RE PROUD OF THIS AND I'M PROUD OF YOU. AND I'VE NEVER SEEN YOU IN IT.
THIS SEEMS SO WEIRD..
WELL, YOU'D BETTER GET USED TO IT, TIM.
YOU MEAN I KEEP ON BEING ROBIN?
WELL, MAYBE NOT AS MUCH AS YOU HAVE BEEN.
I'D LIKE TO HAVE SOME SAY IN THAT AND BRUCE AGREES. I MEAN, SOME PARENTS WON'T LET THEIR BOYS PLAY FOOTBALL.
NO PERMISSION SLIPS FOR THIS EXTRACURRICULAR ACTIVITY, HUH?
I'D LIKE TO SEE ONE.

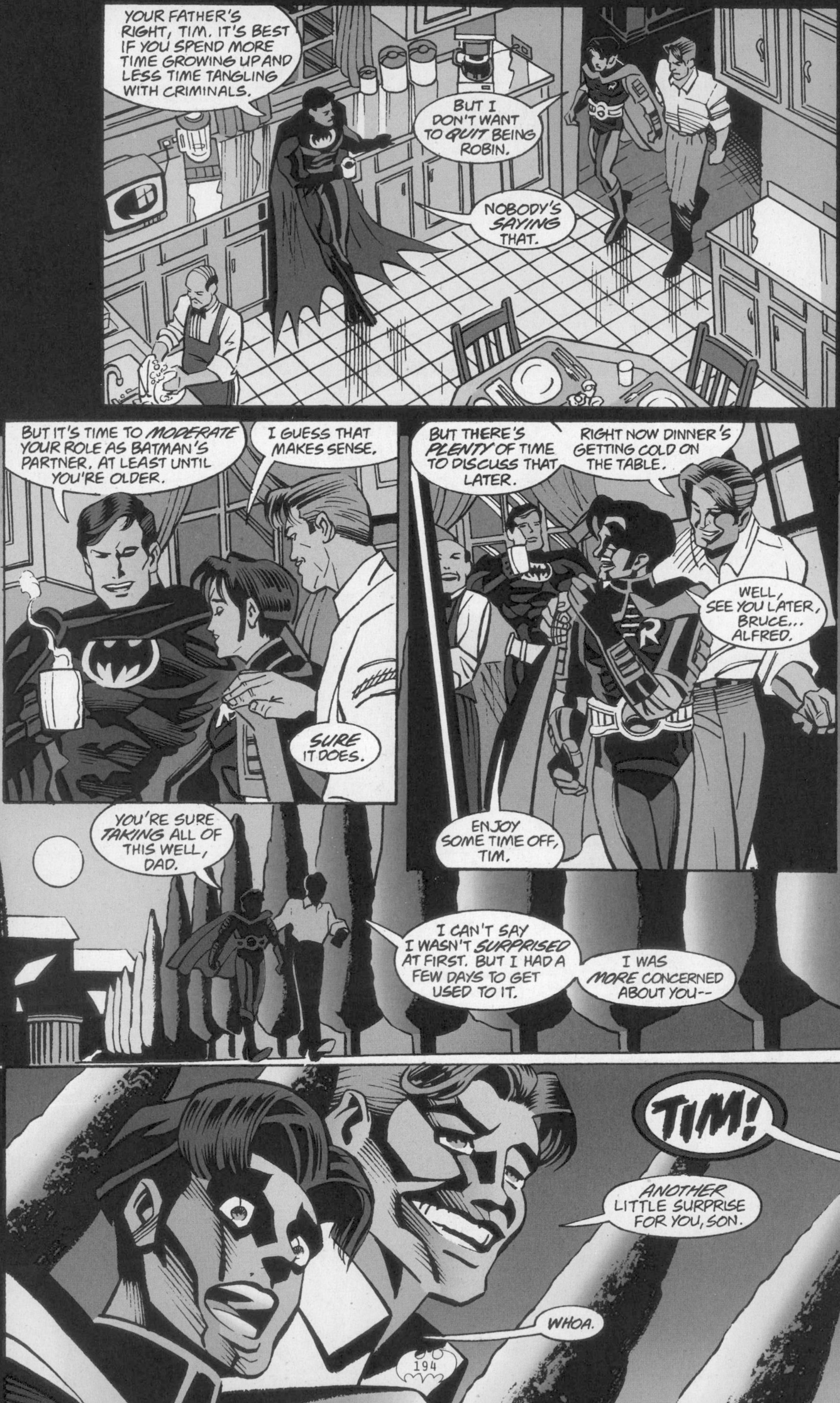
YOUR FATHER'S RIGHT, TIM. IT'S BEST IF YOU SPEND MORE TIME GROWING UP AND LESS TIME TANGLING WITH CRIMINALS.
BUT I DON'T WANT TO QUIT BEING ROBIN.
NOBODY'S SAYING THAT.
BUT IT'S TIME TO MODERATE YOUR ROLE AS BATMAN'S PARTNER. AT LEAST UNTIL YOU'RE OLDER.
I GUESS THAT MAKES SENSE.
SURE IT DOES.
BUT THERE'S PLENTY OF TIME TO DISCUSS THAT LATER.
RIGHT NOW DINNER'S GETTING COLD ON THE TABLE.
WELL, SEE YOU LATER, BRUCE... ALFRED.
ENJOY SOME TIME OFF, TIM.
YOU'RE SURE TAKING ALL OF THIS WELL, DAD.
I CAN'T SAY I WASN'T SURPRISED AT FIRST. BUT I HAD A FEW DAYS TO GET USED TO IT.
I WAS MORE CONCERNED ABOUT YOU--
TIM!
ANOTHER LITTLE SURPRISE FOR YOU, SON.
WHOA.

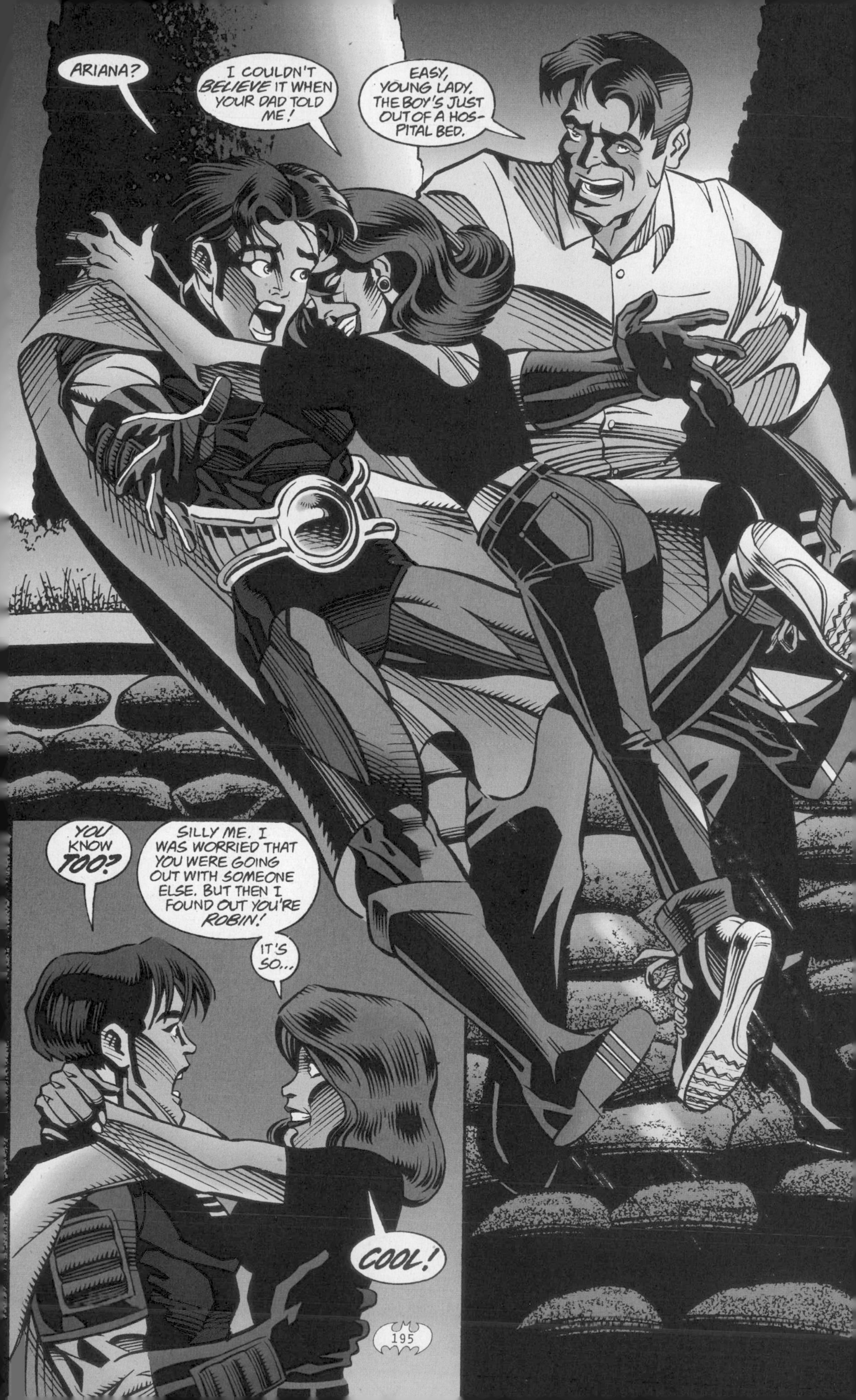
ARIANA?
I COULDN'T BELIEVE IT WHEN YOUR DAD TOLD ME!
EASY, YOUNG LADY. THE BOY'S JUST OUT OF A HOS-PITAL BED.
YOU KNOW TOO?
SILLY ME. I WAS WORRIED THAT YOU WERE GOING OUT WITH SOMEONE ELSE. BUT THEN I FOUND OUT YOU'RE ROBIN!
IT'S SO...
COOL!

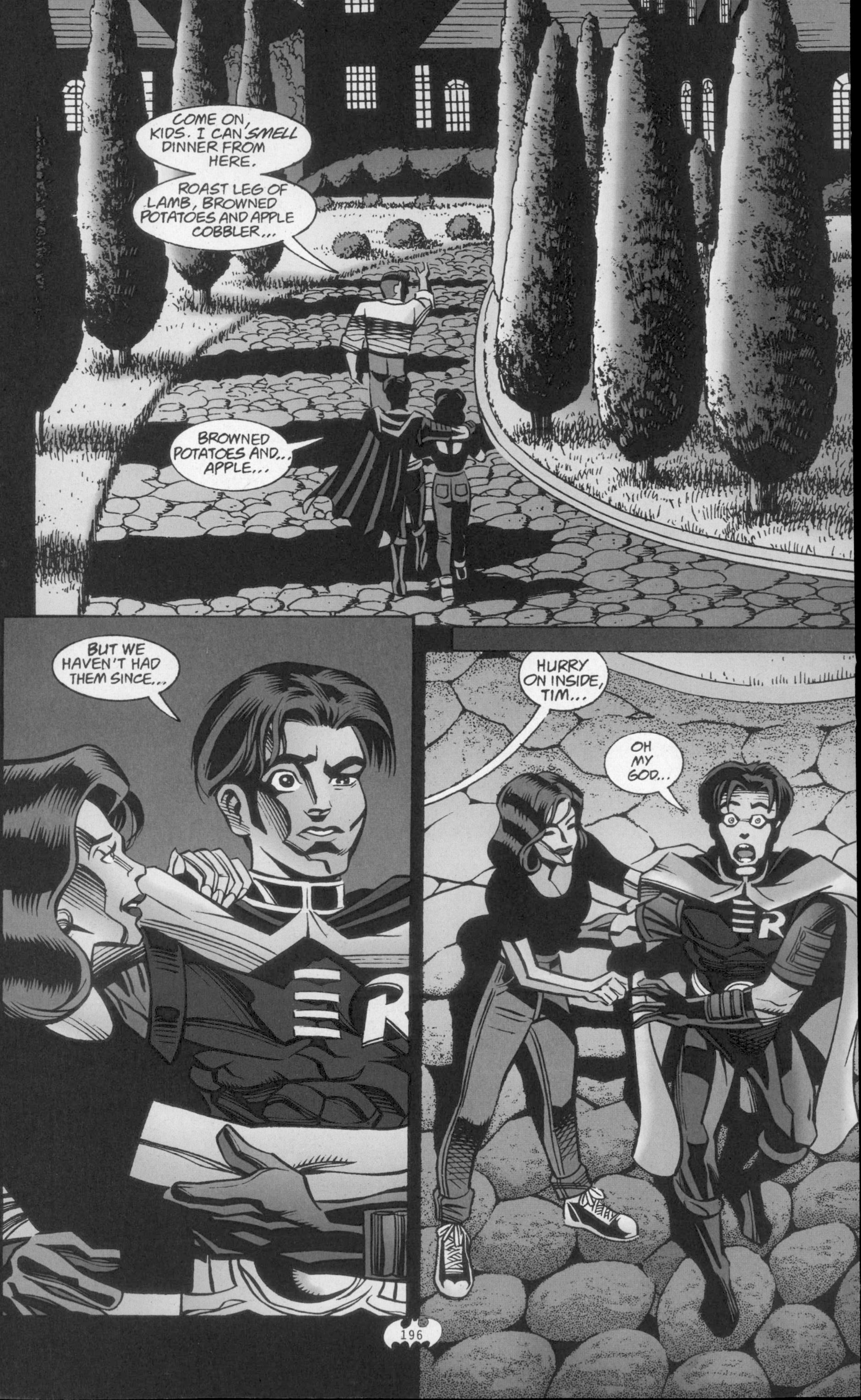
COME ON, KIDS. I CAN'T SMELL DINNER FROM HERE.
ROAST LEG OF LAMB, BROWNED POTATOES AND APPLE COBBLER...
BROWNED POTATOES AND... APPLE...
BUT WE HAVEN'T HAD THEM SINCE...
HURRY ON INSIDE, TIM...
OH MY GOD...

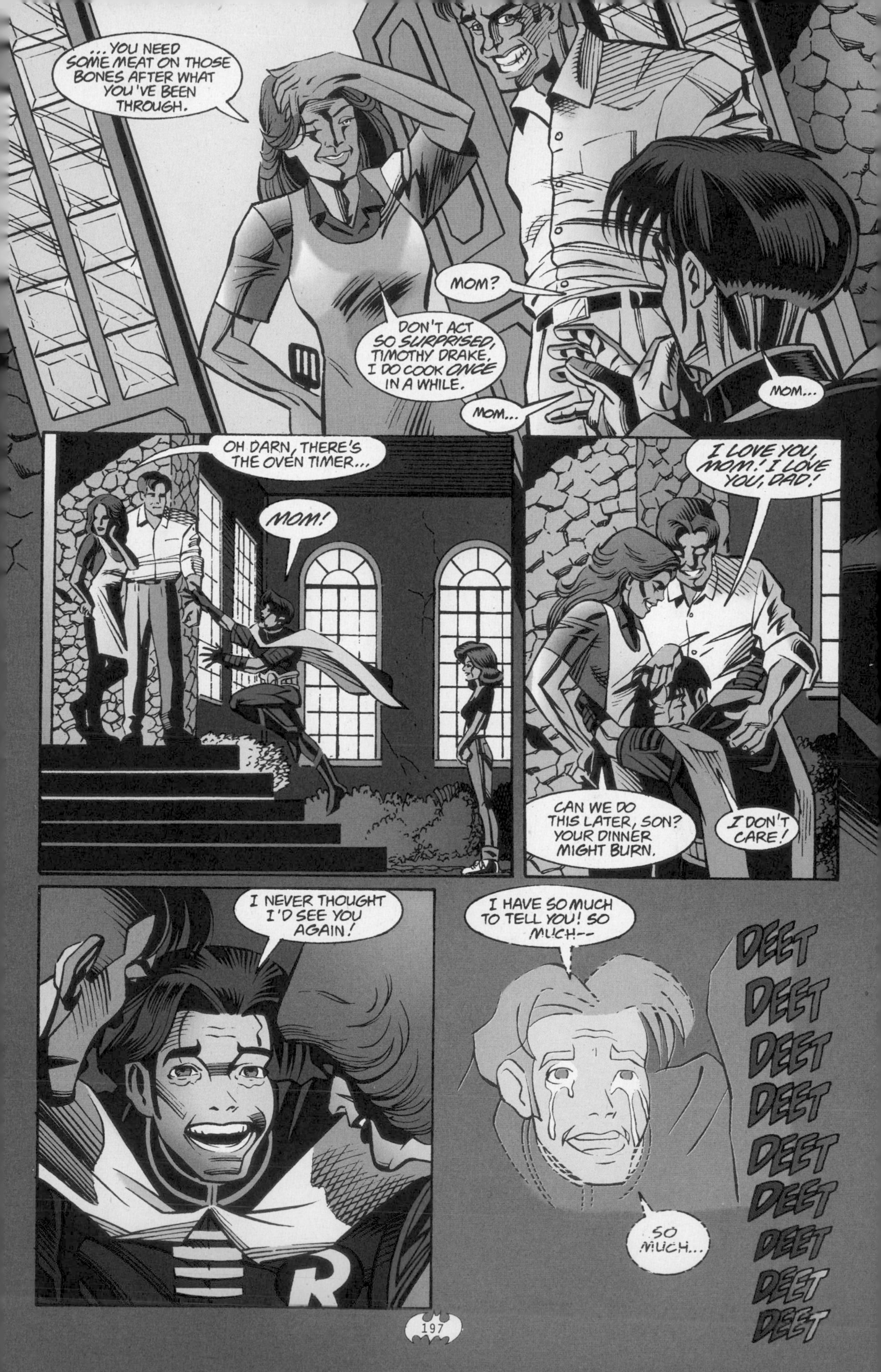

...YOU NEED SOME MEAT ON THOSE BONES AFTER WHAT YOU'VE BEEN THROUGH.
MOM?
DON'T ACT SO SURPRISED, TIMOTHY DRAKE. I DO COOK ONCE IN A WHILE.
MOM...
MOM...
OH DARN, THERE'S THE OVEN TIMER...
MOM!
I LOVE YOU, MOM! I LOVE YOU, DAD!
CAN WE DO THIS LATER, SON? YOUR DINNER MIGHT BURN.
I DON'T CARE!
I NEVER THOUGHT I'D SEE YOU AGAIN!
I HAVE SO MUCH TO TELL YOU! SO MUCH--
SO MUCH...
DEET DEET DEET DEET DEET DEET DEET DEET DEET

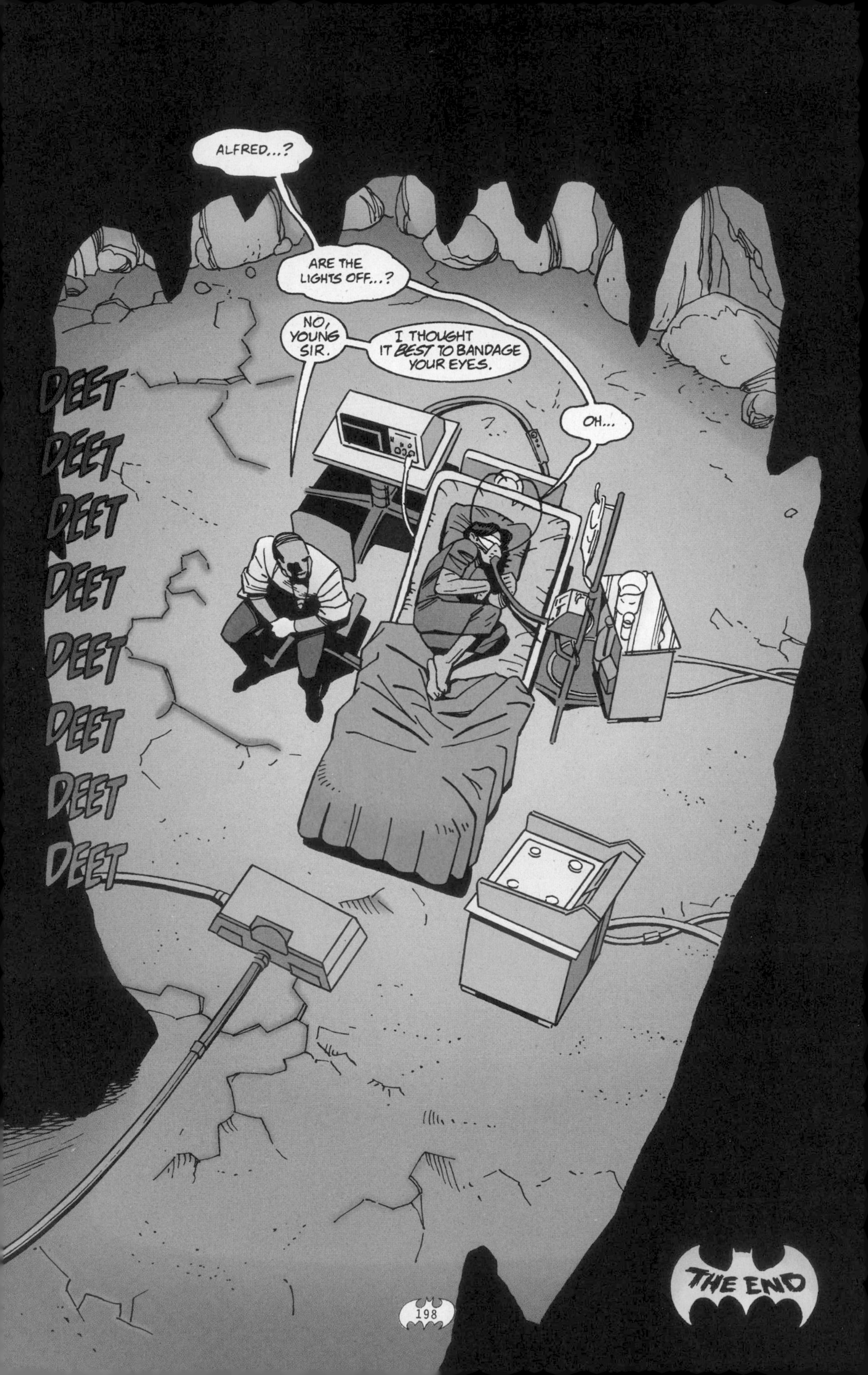
ALFRED...?
ARE THE LIGHTS OFF...?
NO, YOUNG SIR.
I THOUGHT IT BEST TO BANDAGE YOUR EYES.
OH...
DEET
DEET
DEET
DEET
DEET
DEET
DEET
DEET
THE END

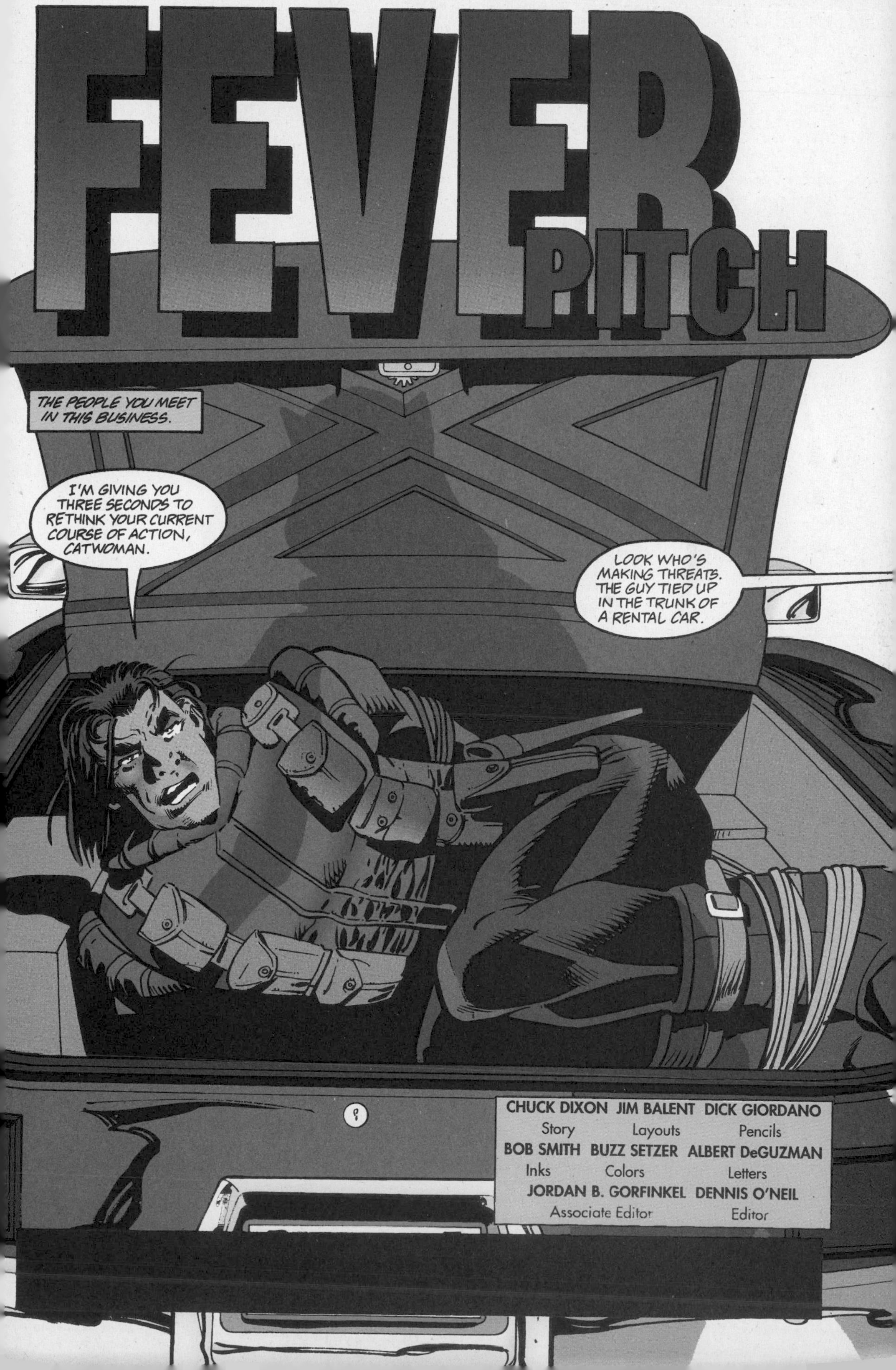
FEVER PITCH
THE PEOPLE YOU MEET IN THIS BUSINESS.
I'M GIVING YOU THREE SECONDS TO RETHINK YOUR CURRENT COURSE OF ACTION, CATWOMAN.
LOOK WHO'S MAKING THREATS. THE GUY TIED UP IN THE TRUNK OF A RENTAL CAR.
CHUCK DIXON Story JIM BALENT Layouts DICK GIORDANO Pencils
BOB SMITH Inks BUZZ SETZER Colors ALBERT DeGUZMAN Letters
JORDAN B. GORFINKEL Associate Editor DENNIS O'NEIL Editor

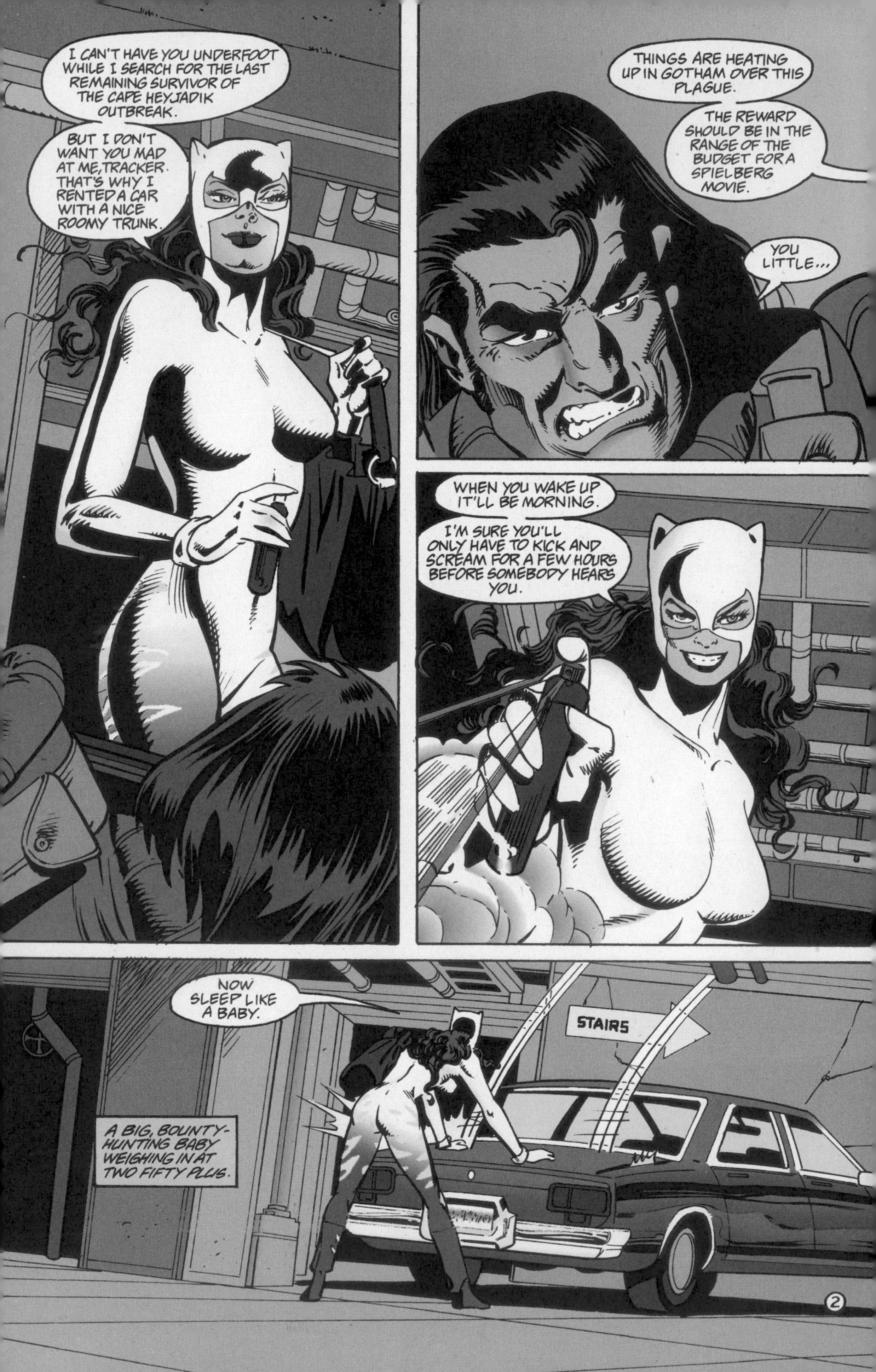
I CAN'T HAVE YOU UNDERFOOT WHILE I SEARCH FOR THE LAST REMAINING SURVIVOR OF THE CAPE HEYJADIK OUTBREAK.
BUT I DON'T WANT YOU MAD AT ME, TRACKER. THAT'S WHY I RENTED A CAR WITH A NICE ROOMY TRUNK.
THINGS ARE HEATING UP IN GOTHAM OVER THIS PLAGUE.
THE REWARD SHOULD BE IN THE RANGE OF THE BUDGET FOR A SPIELBERG MOVIE.
YOU LITTLE...
WHEN YOU WAKE UP IT'LL BE MORNING.
I'M SURE YOU'LL ONLY HAVE TO KICK AND SCREAM FOR A FEW HOURS BEFORE SOMEBODY HEARS YOU.
NOW SLEEP LIKE A BABY.
STAIRS
A BIG, BOUNTY-HUNTING BABY WEIGHING IN AT TWO FIFTY PLUS.

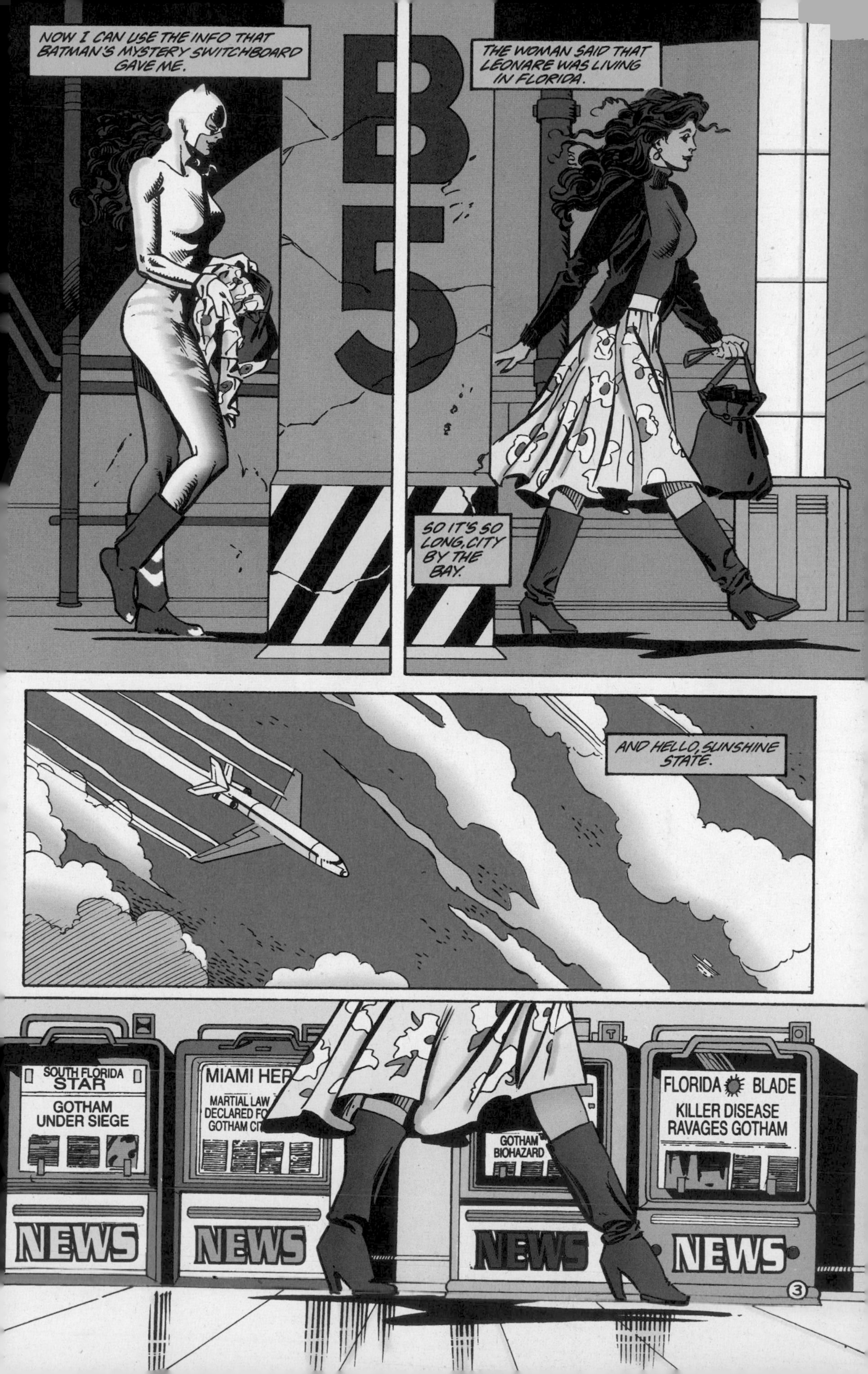
NOW I CAN USE THE INFO THAT BATMAN'S MYSTERY SWITCHBOARD GAVE ME.
THE WOMAN SAID THAT LEONARE WAS LIVING IN FLORIDA.
SO IT'S SO LONG, CITY BY THE BAY.
AND HELLO, SUNSHINE STATE.
SOUTH FLORIDA STAR
GOTHAM UNDER SIEGE
MIAMI HER
MARTIAL LAW DECLARED FO GOTHAM CI
GOTHAM BIOHAZARD
FLORIDA BLADE
KILLER DISEASE RAVAGES GOTHAM
NEWS
NEWS
NEWS
NEWS
3

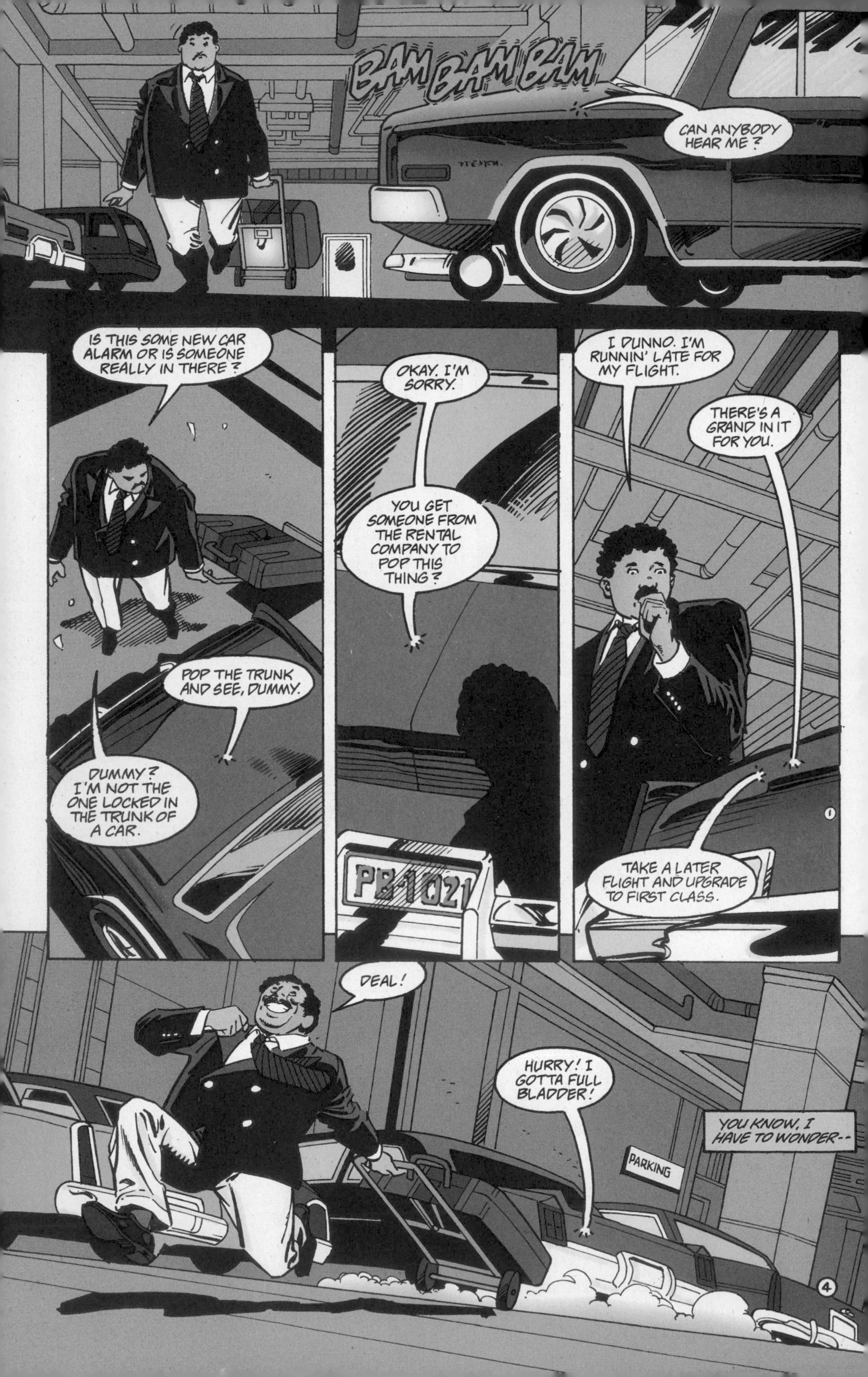
BAM BAM BAM
CAN ANYBODY HEAR ME?
IS THIS SOME NEW CAR ALARM OR IS SOMEONE REALLY IN THERE?
POP THE TRUNK AND SEE, DUMMY.
DUMMY? I'M NOT THE ONE LOCKED IN THE TRUNK OF A CAR.
OKAY. I'M SORRY.
YOU GET SOMEONE FROM THE RENTAL COMPANY TO POP THIS THING?
PB-1021
I DUNNO. I'M RUNNIN' LATE FOR MY FLIGHT.
THERE'S A GRAND IN IT FOR YOU.
TAKE A LATER FLIGHT AND UPGRADE TO FIRST CLASS.
DEAL!
HURRY! I GOTTA FULL BLADDER!
PARKING
YOU KNOW, I HAVE TO WONDER--
4

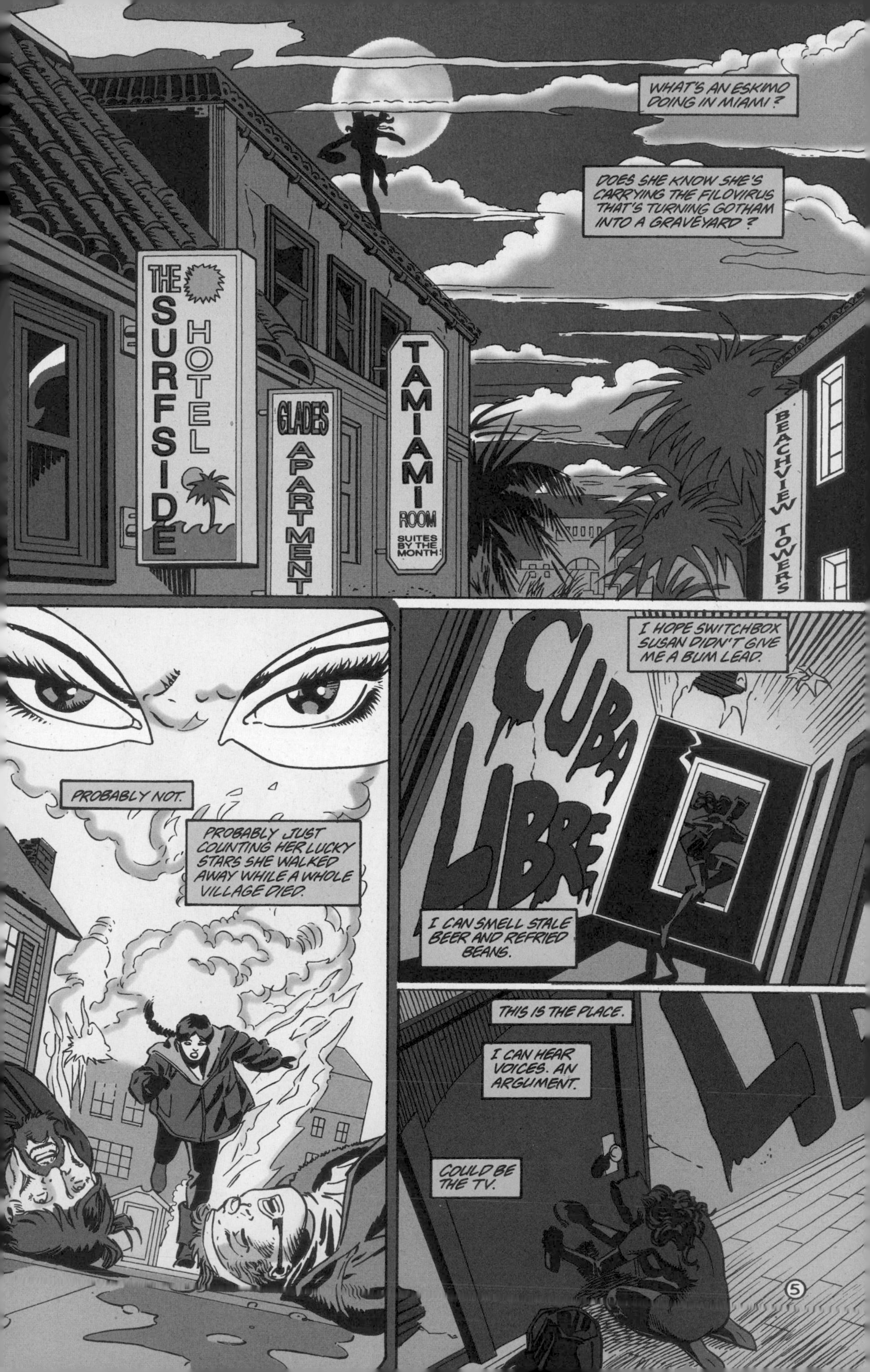
WHAT'S AN ESKIMO DOING IN MIAMI?
DOES SHE KNOW SHE'S CARRYING THE FILOVIRUS THAT'S TURNING GOTHAM INTO A GRAVEYARD?
THE SURFSIDE HOTEL
GLADES APARTMENT
TAMIAMI ROOM SUITES BY THE MONTH
BEACHVIEW TOWERS
PROBABLY NOT.
PROBABLY JUST COUNTING HER LUCKY STARS SHE WALKED AWAY WHILE A WHOLE VILLAGE DIED.
I HOPE SWITCHBOX SUSAN DIDN'T GIVE ME A BUM LEAD.
CUBA LIBRE
I CAN SMELL STALE BEER AND REFRIED BEANS.
THIS IS THE PLACE.
I CAN HEAR VOICES. AN ARGUMENT.
COULD BE THE TV.

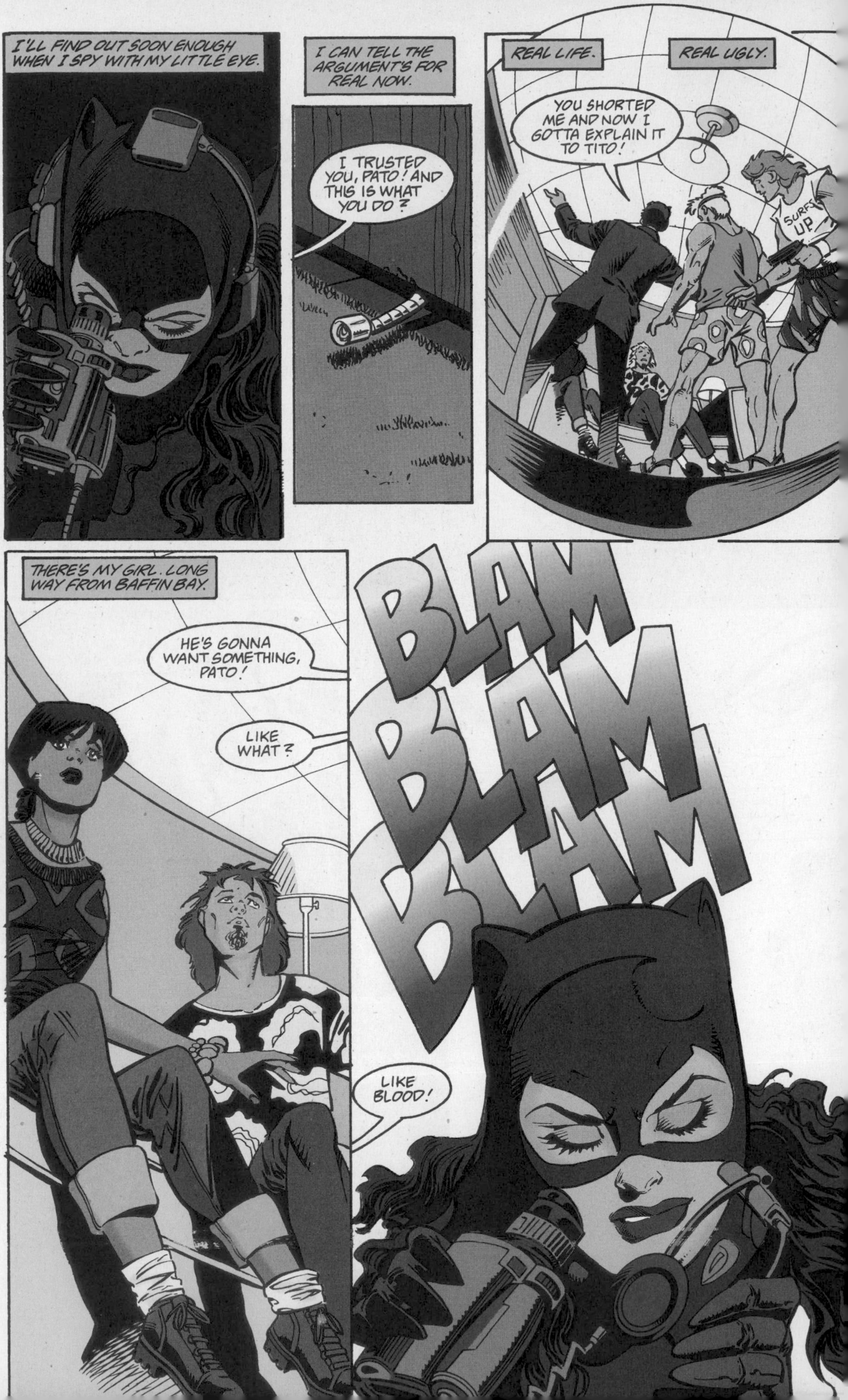
I'LL FIND OUT SOON ENOUGH WHEN I SPY WITH MY LITTLE EYE.
I CAN TELL THE ARGUMENT'S FOR REAL NOW.
I TRUSTED YOU, PATO! AND THIS IS WHAT YOU DO?
REAL LIFE.
REAL UGLY.
YOU SHORTED ME AND NOW I GOTTA EXPLAIN IT TO TITO!
SURF'S UP
THERE'S MY GIRL. LONG WAY FROM BAFFIN BAY.
HE'S GONNA WANT SOMETHING, PATO!
LIKE WHAT?
BLAM BLAM BLAM
LIKE BLOOD!

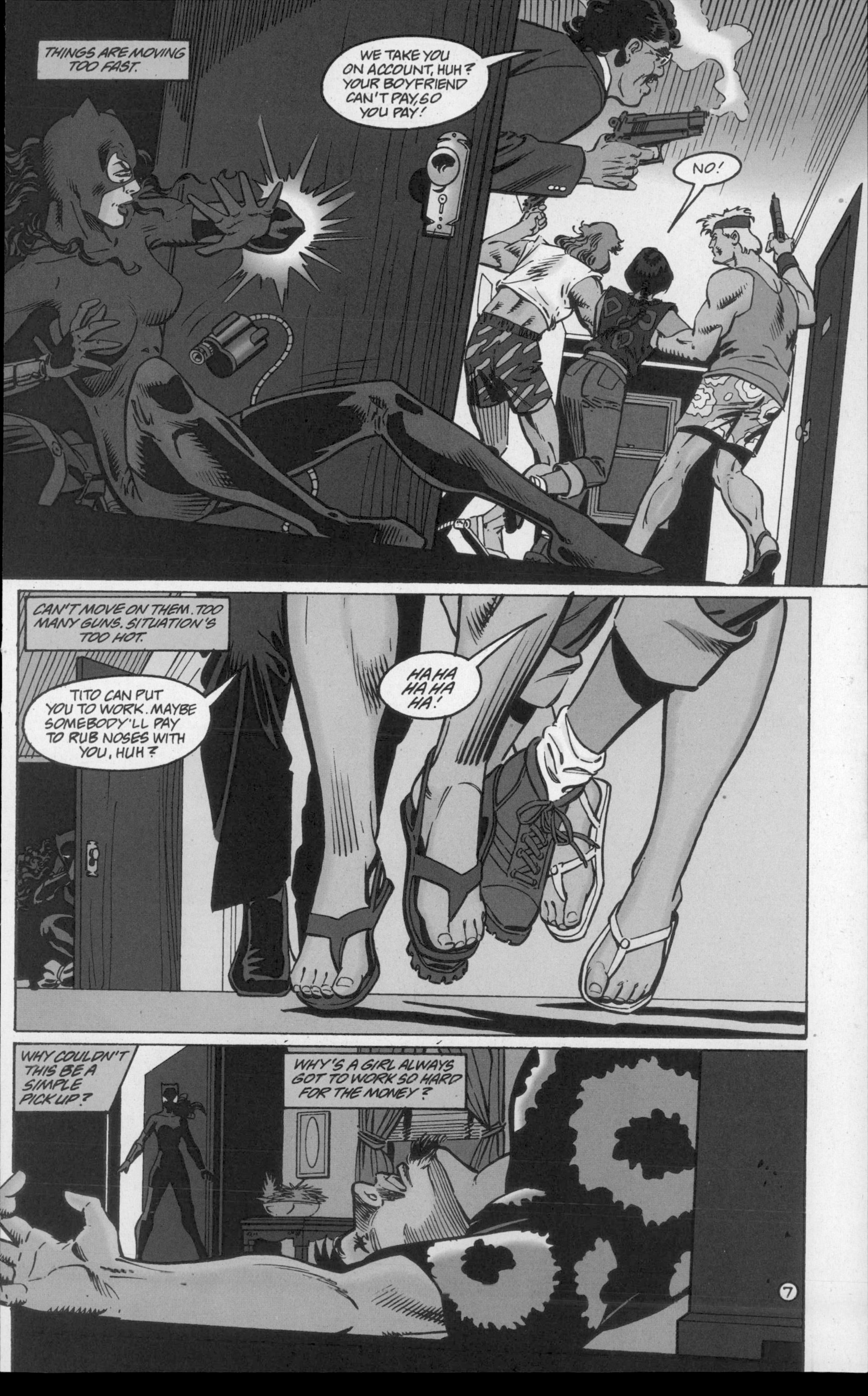

THINGS ARE MOVING TOO FAST.
WE TAKE YOU ON ACCOUNT, HUH? YOUR BOYFRIEND CAN'T PAY, SO YOU PAY!
NO!
CAN'T MOVE ON THEM. TOO MANY GUNS. SITUATION'S TOO HOT.
TITO CAN PUT YOU TO WORK. MAYBE SOMEBODY'LL PAY TO RUB NOSES WITH YOU, HUH?
HA HA HA HA HA!
WHY COULDN'T THIS BE A SIMPLE PICK UP?
WHY'S A GIRL ALWAYS GOT TO WORK SO HARD FOR THE MONEY?
7

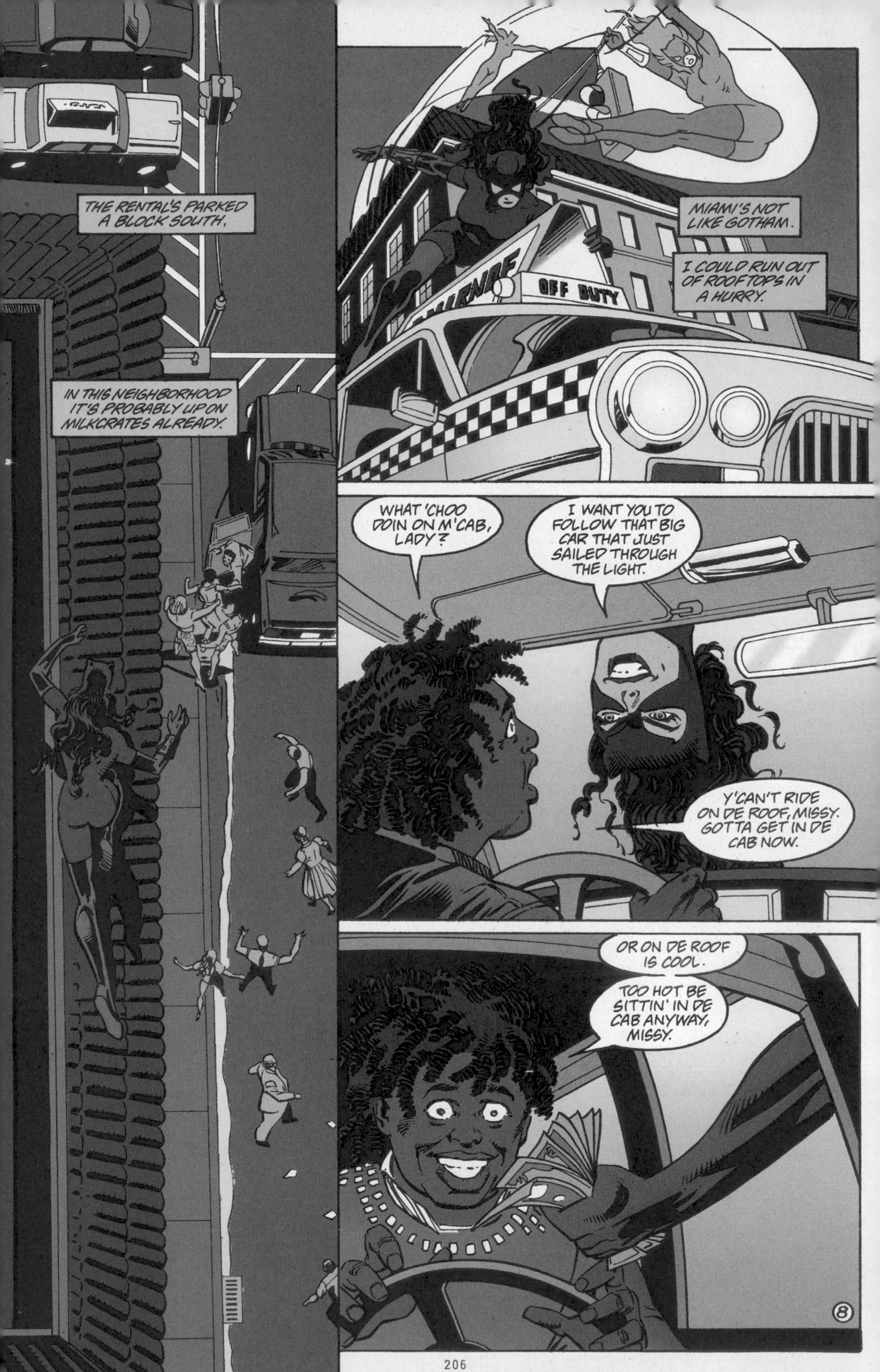
THE RENTAL'S PARKED A BLOCK SOUTH.
IN THIS NEIGHBORHOOD IT'S PROBABLY UP ON MILKCRATES ALREADY.
MIAMI'S NOT LIKE GOTHAM.
I COULD RUN OUT OF ROOFTOPS IN A HURRY.
OFF DUTY
WHAT 'CHOO DOIN ON M'CAB, LADY?
I WANT YOU TO FOLLOW THAT BIG CAR THAT JUST SAILED THROUGH THE LIGHT.
Y'CAN'T RIDE ON DE ROOF, MISSY. GOTTA GET IN DE CAB NOW.
OR ON DE ROOF IS COOL.
TOO HOT BE SITTIN' IN DE CAB ANYWAY, MISSY.
8

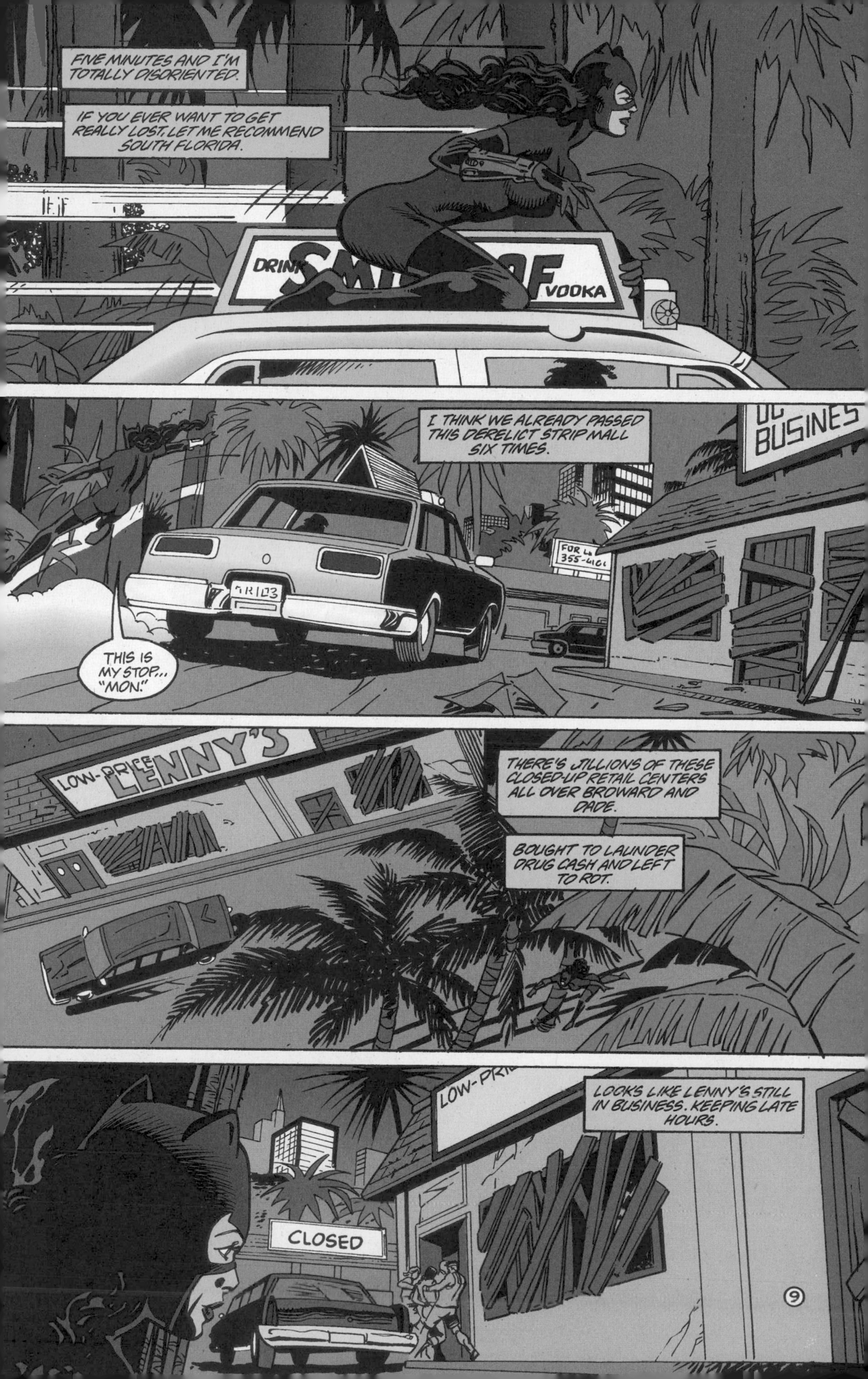
FIVE MINUTES AND I'M TOTALLY DISORIENTED.
IF YOU EVER WANT TO GET REALLY LOST, LET ME RECOMMEND SOUTH FLORIDA.
DRINK SMIRNOFF VODKA
I THINK WE ALREADY PASSED THIS DERELICT STRIP MALL SIX TIMES.
BUSINES
THIS IS MY STOP... "MON."
LOW-PRICE LENNY'S
THERE'S JILLIONS OF THESE CLOSED-UP RETAIL CENTERS ALL OVER BROWARD AND DADE.
BOUGHT TO LAUNDER DRUG CASH AND LEFT TO ROT.
LOW-PRI
LOOKS LIKE LENNY'S STILL IN BUSINESS. KEEPING LATE HOURS.
CLOSED
9

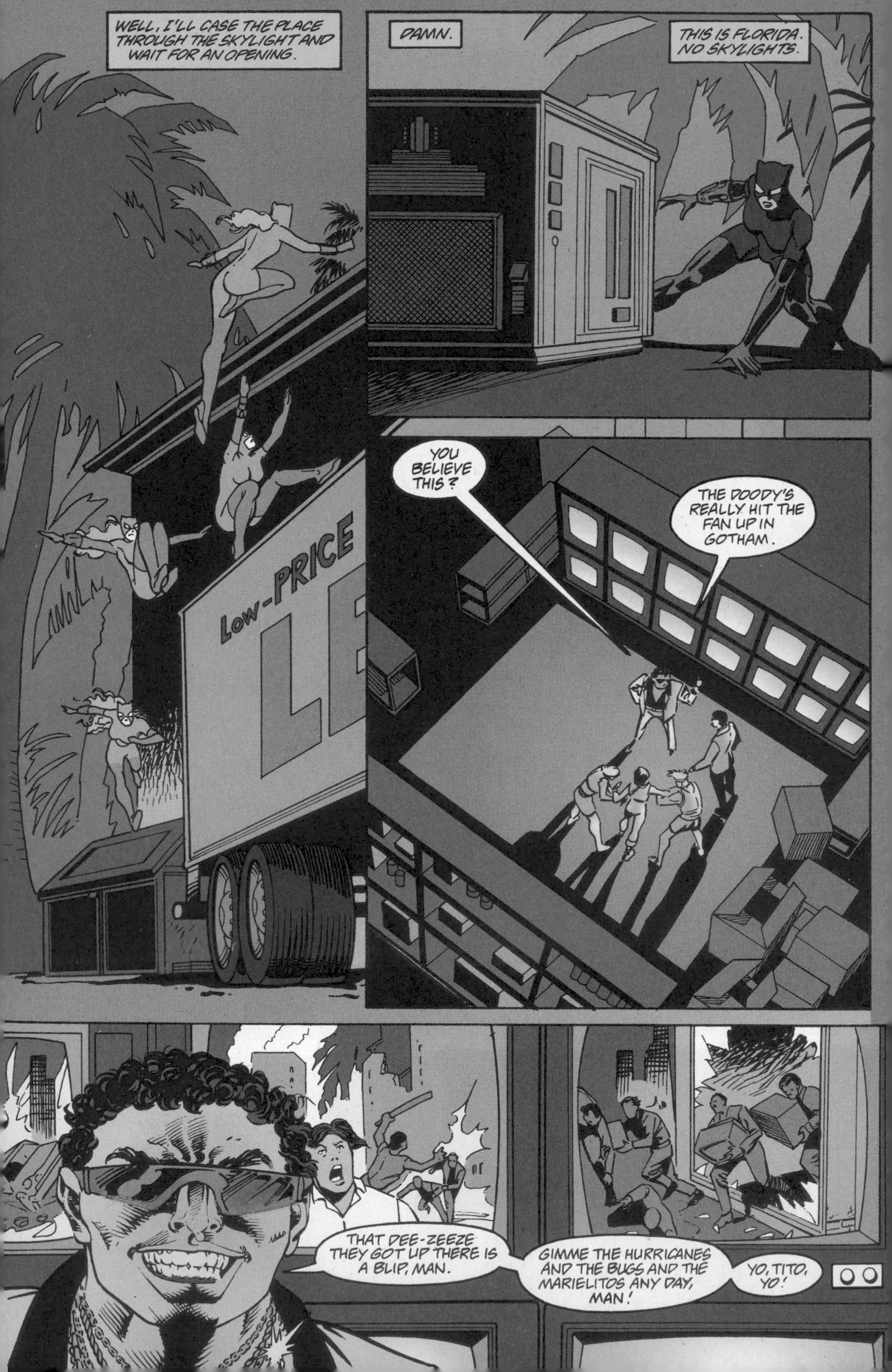
WELL, I'LL CASE THE PLACE THROUGH THE SKYLIGHT AND WAIT FOR AN OPENING.
DAMN.
THIS IS FLORIDA. NO SKYLIGHTS.
Low-PRICE LE
YOU BELIEVE THIS?
THE DOODY'S REALLY HIT THE FAN UP IN GOTHAM.
THAT DEE-ZEEZE THEY GOT UP THERE IS A BLIP, MAN.
GIMME THE HURRICANES AND THE BUGS AND THE MARIELITOS ANY DAY, MAN!
YO, TITO, YO!

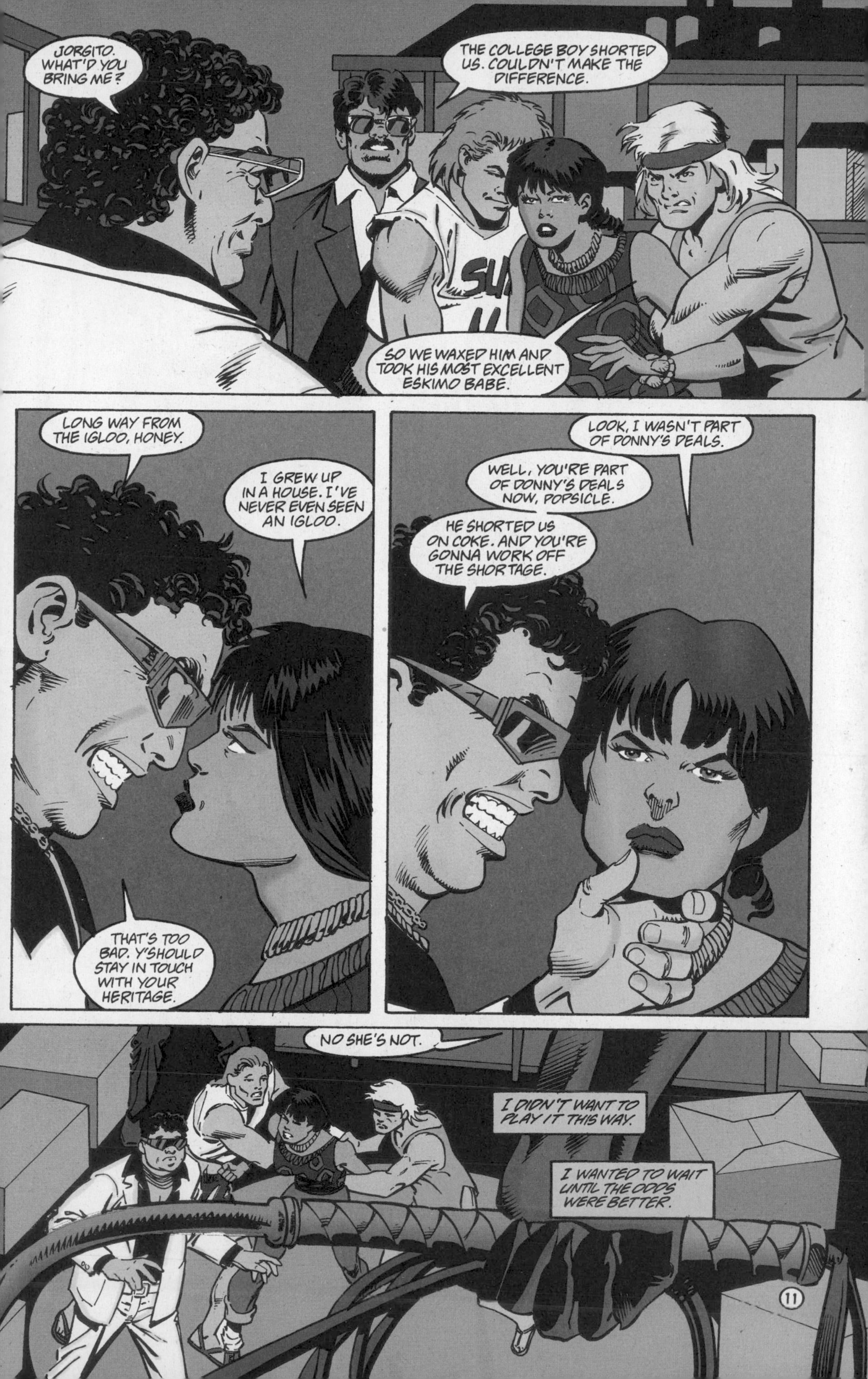
JORGITO. WHAT'D YOU BRING ME?
THE COLLEGE BOY SHORTED US. COULDN'T MAKE THE DIFFERENCE.
SO WE WAXED HIM AND TOOK HIS MOST EXCELLENT ESKIMO BABE.
LONG WAY FROM THE IGLOO, HONEY.
I GREW UP IN A HOUSE. I'VE NEVER EVEN SEEN AN IGLOO.
THAT'S TOO BAD. Y'SHOULD STAY IN TOUCH WITH YOUR HERITAGE.
LOOK, I WASN'T PART OF DONNY'S DEALS.
WELL, YOU'RE PART OF DONNY'S DEALS NOW, POPSICLE.
HE SHORTED US ON COKE. AND YOU'RE GONNA WORK OFF THE SHORTAGE.
NO SHE'S NOT.
I DIDN'T WANT TO PLAY IT THIS WAY.
I WANTED TO WAIT UNTIL THE ODDS WERE BETTER.

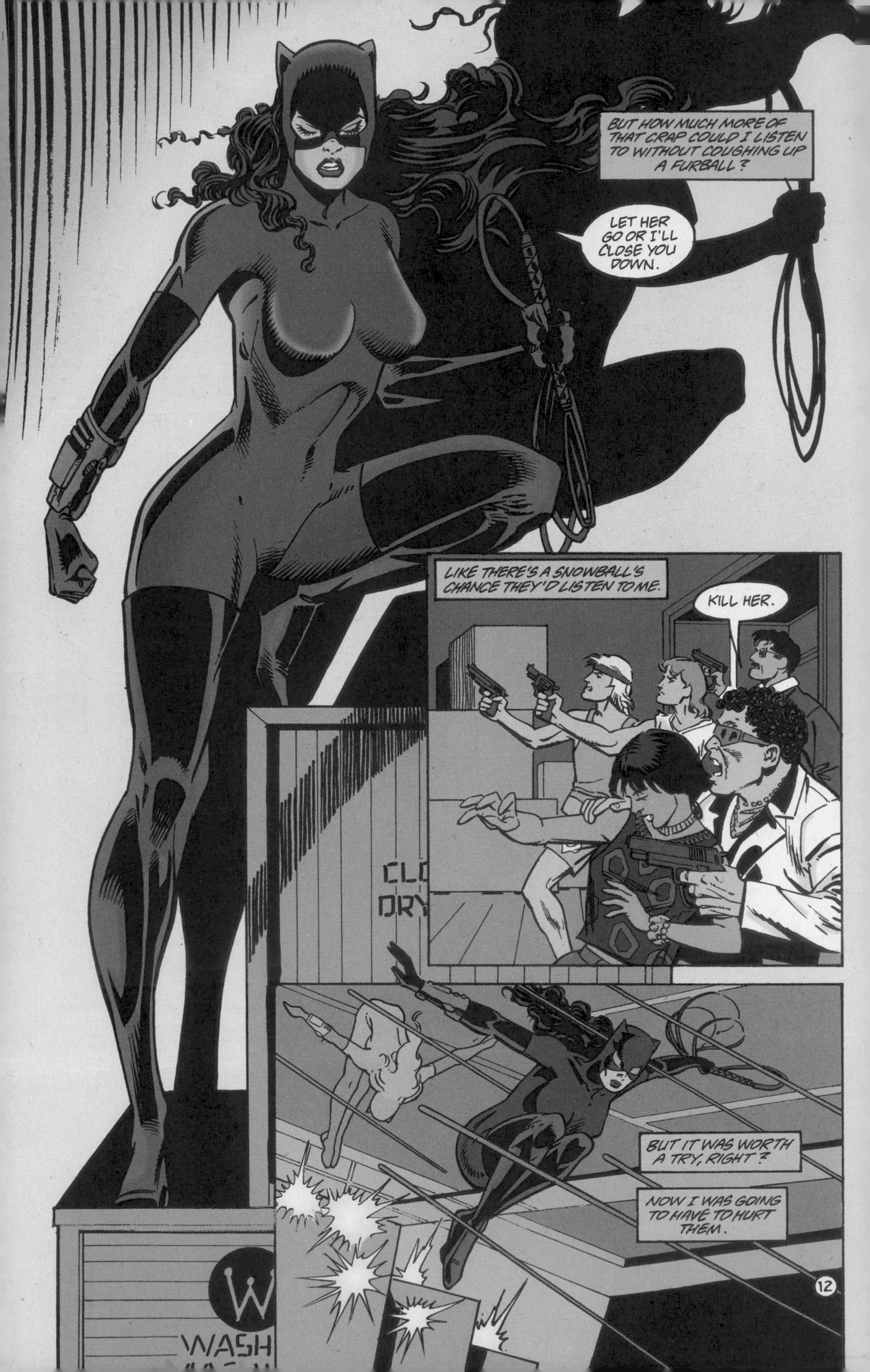

BUT HOW MUCH MORE OF THAT CRAP COULD I LISTEN TO WITHOUT COUGHING UP A FURBALL?
LET HER GO OR I'LL CLOSE YOU DOWN.
LIKE THERE'S A SNOWBALL'S CHANCE THEY'D LISTEN TO ME.
KILL HER.
BUT IT WAS WORTH A TRY, RIGHT?
NOW I WAS GOING TO HAVE TO HURT THEM.

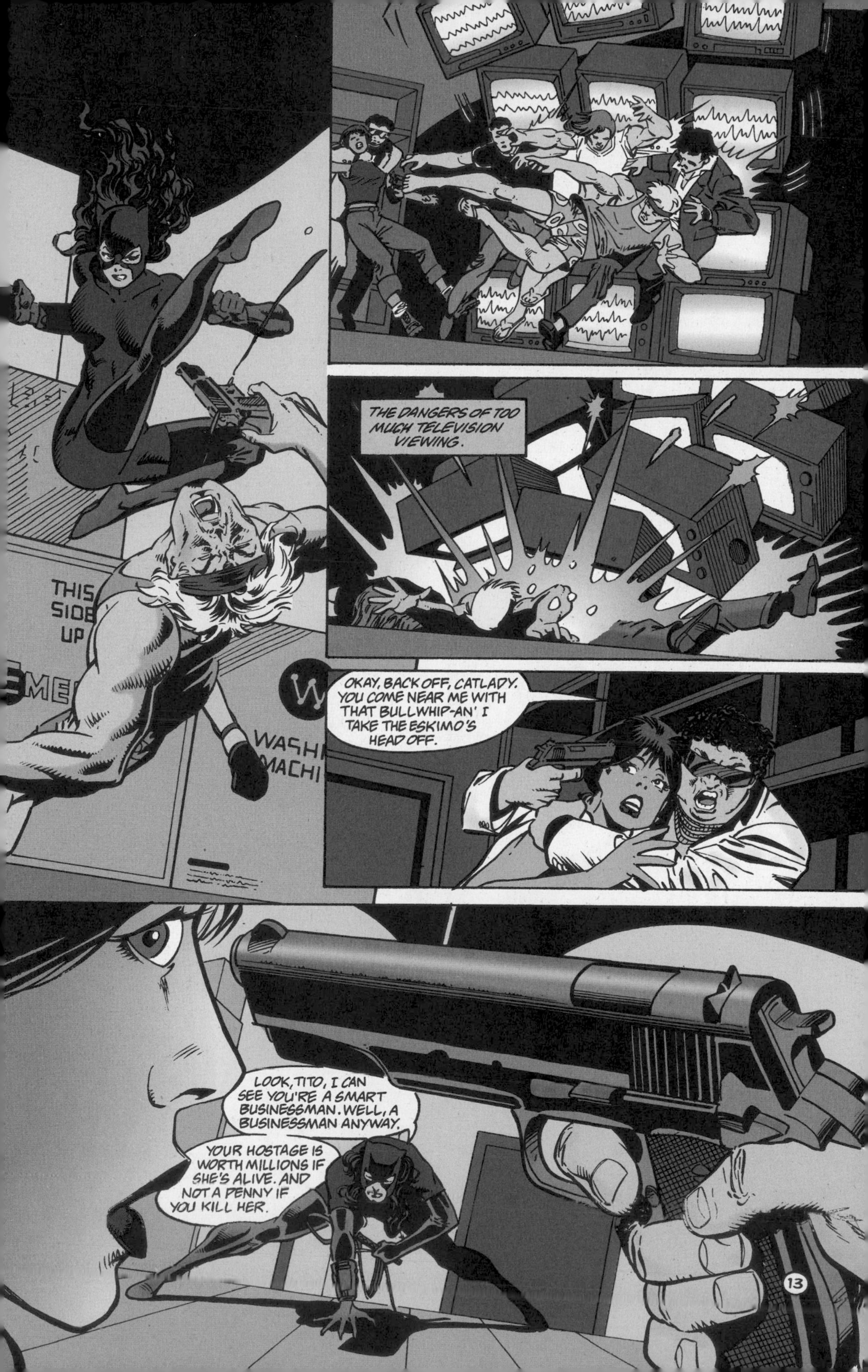

THIS SIDE UP
WASHI MACHI
THE DANGERS OF TOO MUCH TELEVISION VIEWING.
OKAY, BACK OFF, CATLADY. YOU COME NEAR ME WITH THAT BULLWHIP-AN' I TAKE THE ESKIMO'S HEAD OFF.
LOOK, TITO, I CAN SEE YOU'RE A SMART BUSINESSMAN. WELL, A BUSINESSMAN ANYWAY.
YOUR HOSTAGE IS WORTH MILLIONS IF SHE'S ALIVE. AND NOT A PENNY IF YOU KILL HER.

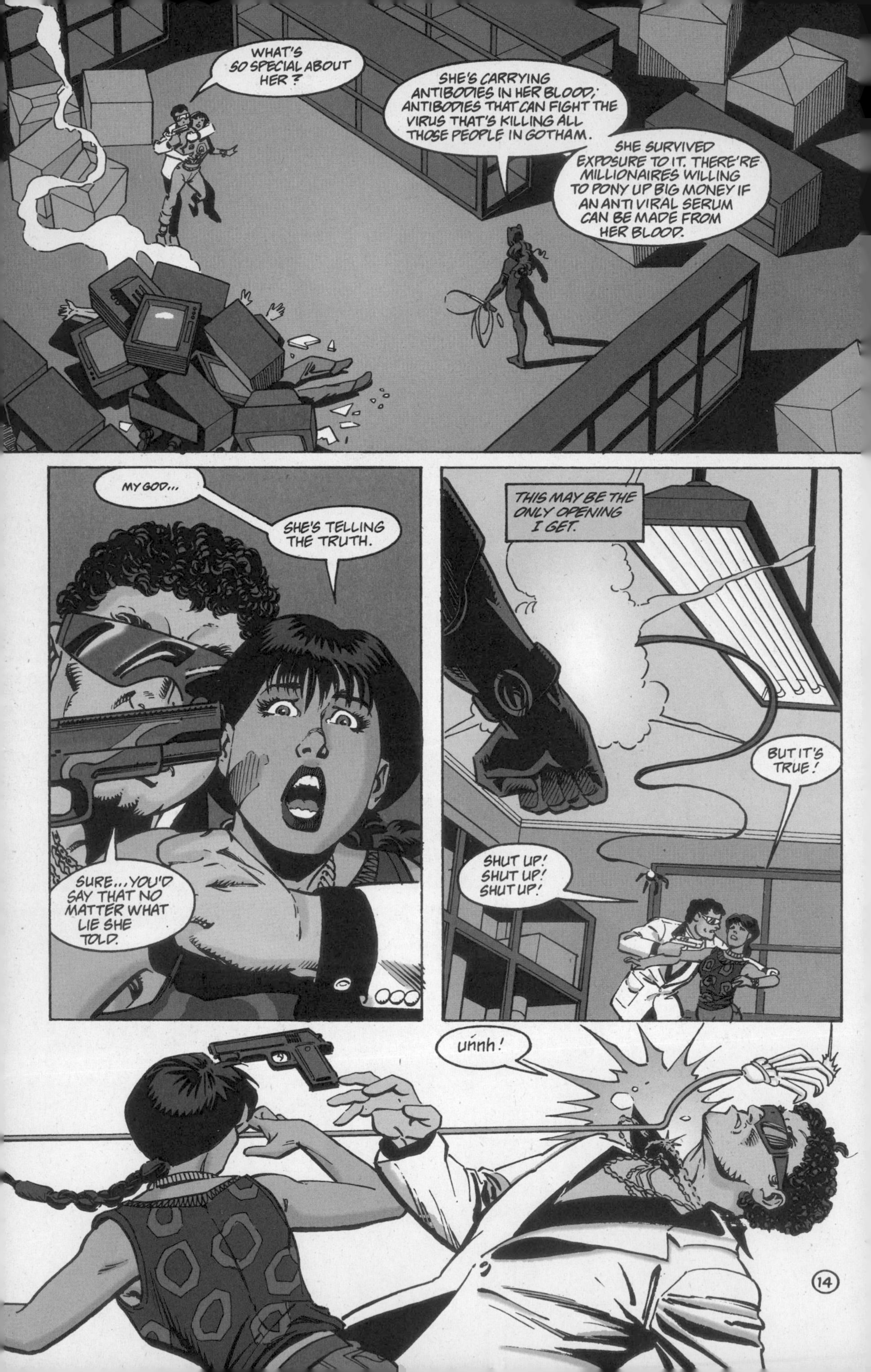

WHAT'S SO SPECIAL ABOUT HER?
SHE'S CARRYING ANTIBODIES IN HER BLOOD; ANTIBODIES THAT CAN FIGHT THE VIRUS THAT'S KILLING ALL THOSE PEOPLE IN GOTHAM.
SHE SURVIVED EXPOSURE TO IT. THERE'RE MILLIONAIRES WILLING TO PONY UP BIG MONEY IF AN ANTI VIRAL SERUM CAN BE MADE FROM HER BLOOD.
MY GOD...
SHE'S TELLING THE TRUTH.
SURE... YOU'D SAY THAT NO MATTER WHAT LIE SHE TOLD.
THIS MAY BE THE ONLY OPENING I GET.
BUT IT'S TRUE!
SHUT UP! SHUT UP! SHUT UP!
uńnh!

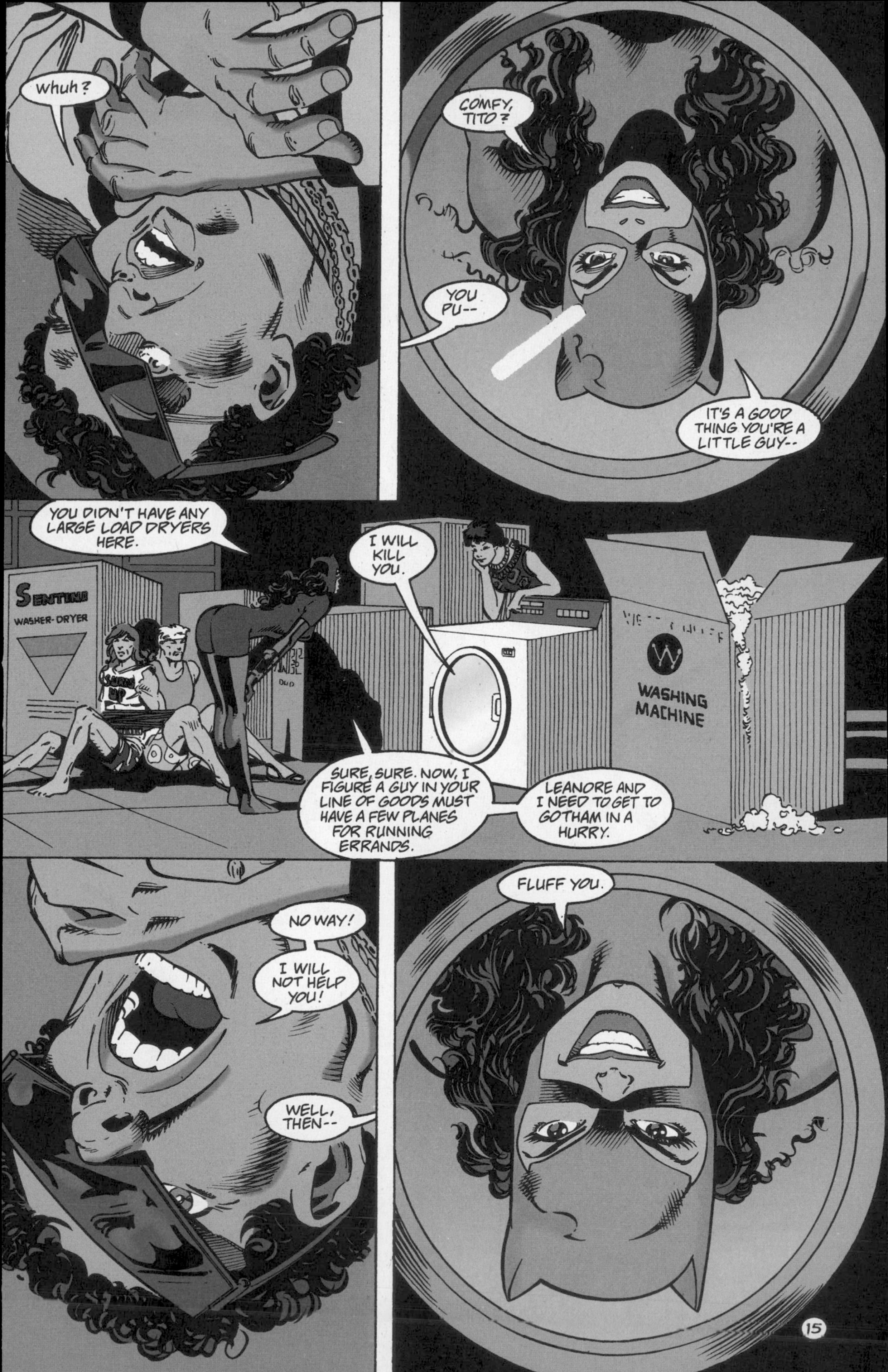

Whuh?
COMFY, TITO?
YOU PU--
IT'S A GOOD THING YOU'RE A LITTLE GUY--
YOU DIDN'T HAVE ANY LARGE LOAD DRYERS HERE.
I WILL KILL YOU.
WASHER-DRYER
WASHING MACHINE
SURE, SURE. NOW, I FIGURE A GUY IN YOUR LINE OF GOODS MUST HAVE A FEW PLANES FOR RUNNING ERRANDS.
LEANORE AND I NEED TO GET TO GOTHAM IN A HURRY.
NO WAY!
I WILL NOT HELP YOU!
WELL, THEN--
FLUFF YOU.

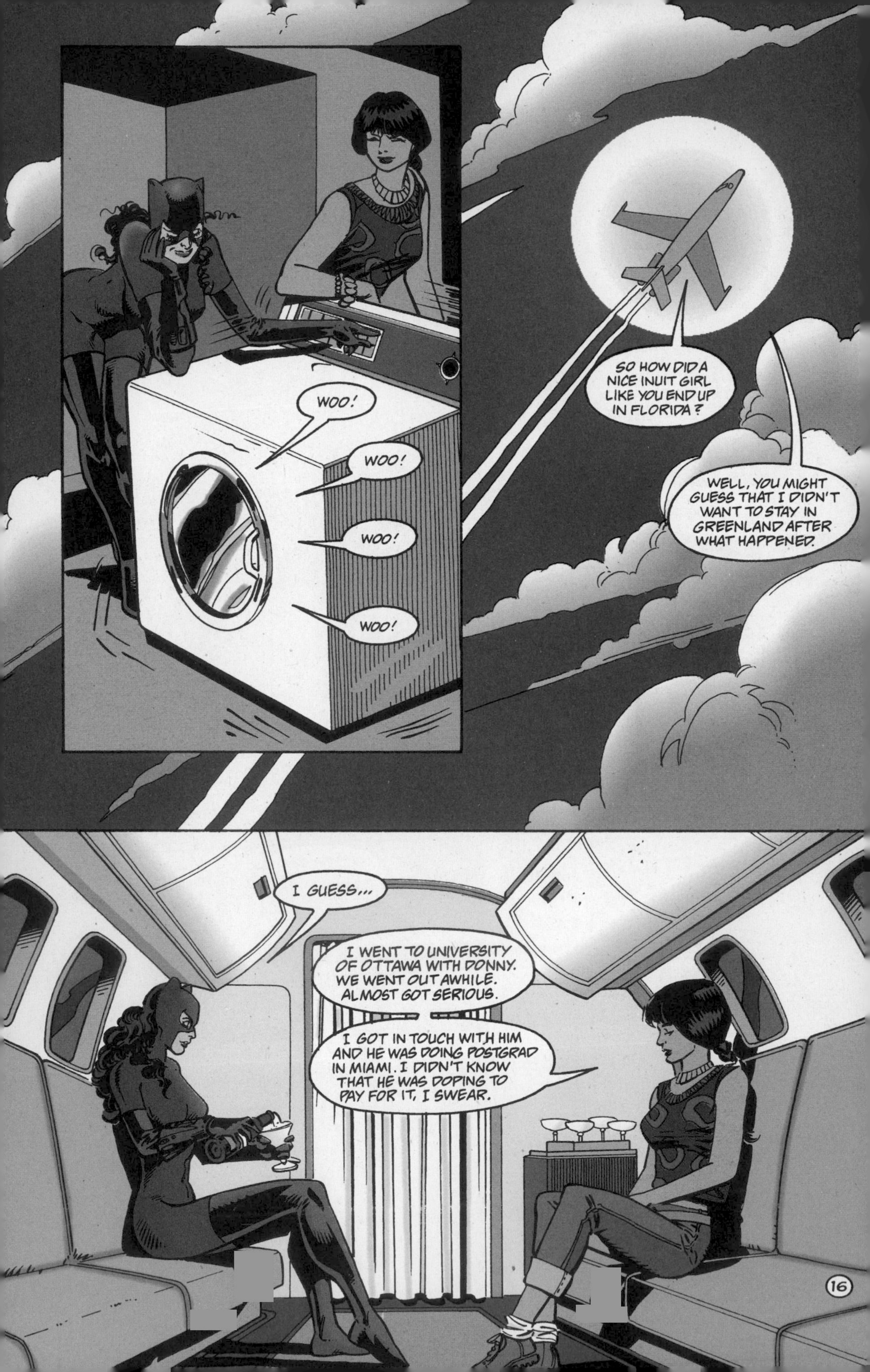
WOO!
WOO!
WOO!
WOO!
SO HOW DID A NICE INUIT GIRL LIKE YOU END UP IN FLORIDA?
WELL, YOU MIGHT GUESS THAT I DIDN'T WANT TO STAY IN GREENLAND AFTER WHAT HAPPENED.
I GUESS...
I WENT TO UNIVERSITY OF OTTAWA WITH DONNY. WE WENT OUT AWHILE. ALMOST GOT SERIOUS.
I GOT IN TOUCH WITH HIM AND HE WAS DOING POSTGRAD IN MIAMI. I DIDN'T KNOW THAT HE WAS DOPING TO PAY FOR IT, I SWEAR.

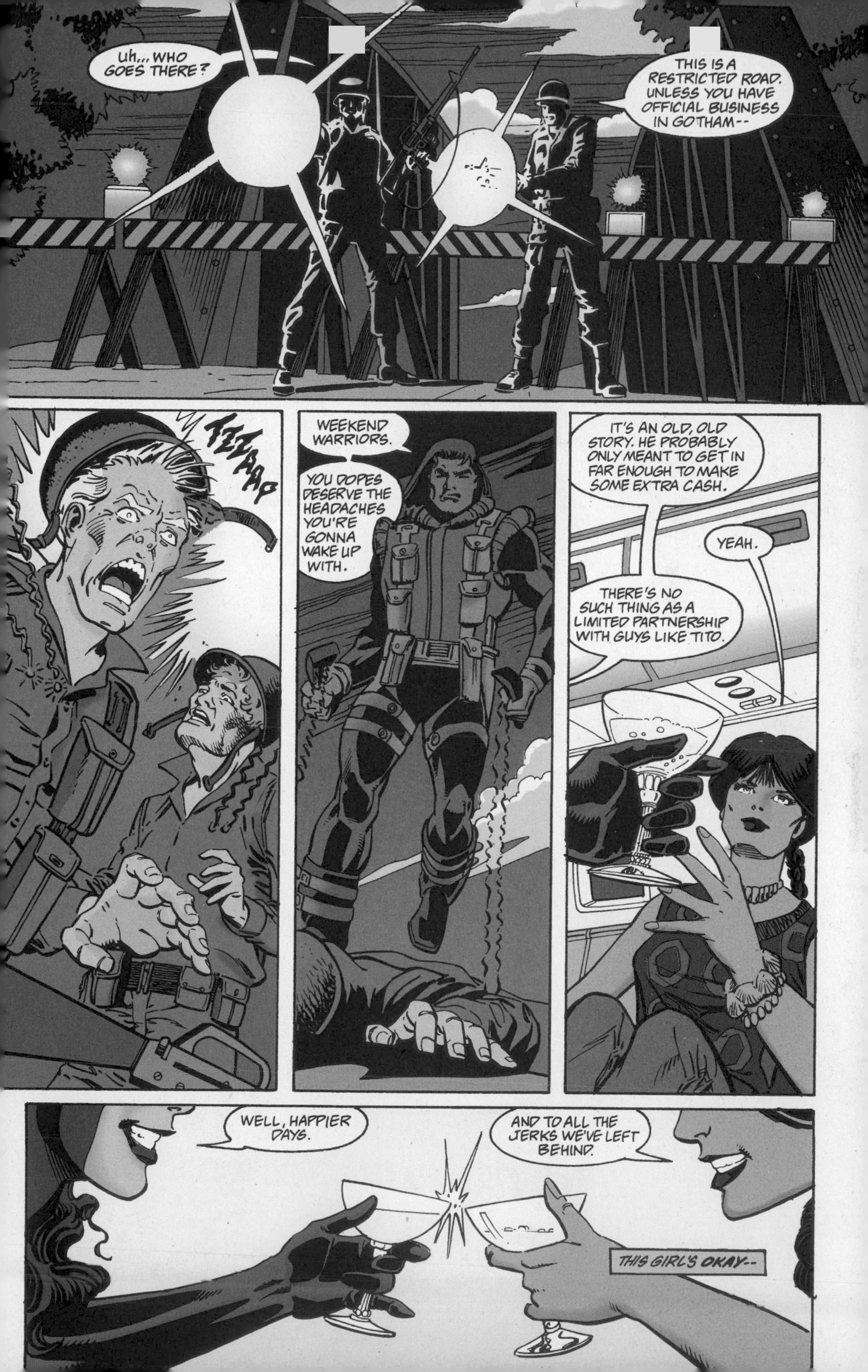

UH... WHO GOES THERE?
THIS IS A RESTRICTED ROAD. UNLESS YOU HAVE OFFICIAL BUSINESS IN GOTHAM--
WEEKEND WARRIORS.
YOU DOPES DESERVE THE HEADACHES YOU'RE GONNA WAKE UP WITH.
IT'S AN OLD, OLD STORY. HE PROBABLY ONLY MEANT TO GET IN FAR ENOUGH TO MAKE SOME EXTRA CASH.
YEAH.
THERE'S NO SUCH THING AS A LIMITED PARTNERSHIP WITH GUYS LIKE TITO.
WELL, HAPPIER DAYS.
AND TO ALL THE JERKS WE'VE LEFT BEHIND.
THIS GIRL'S OKAY--

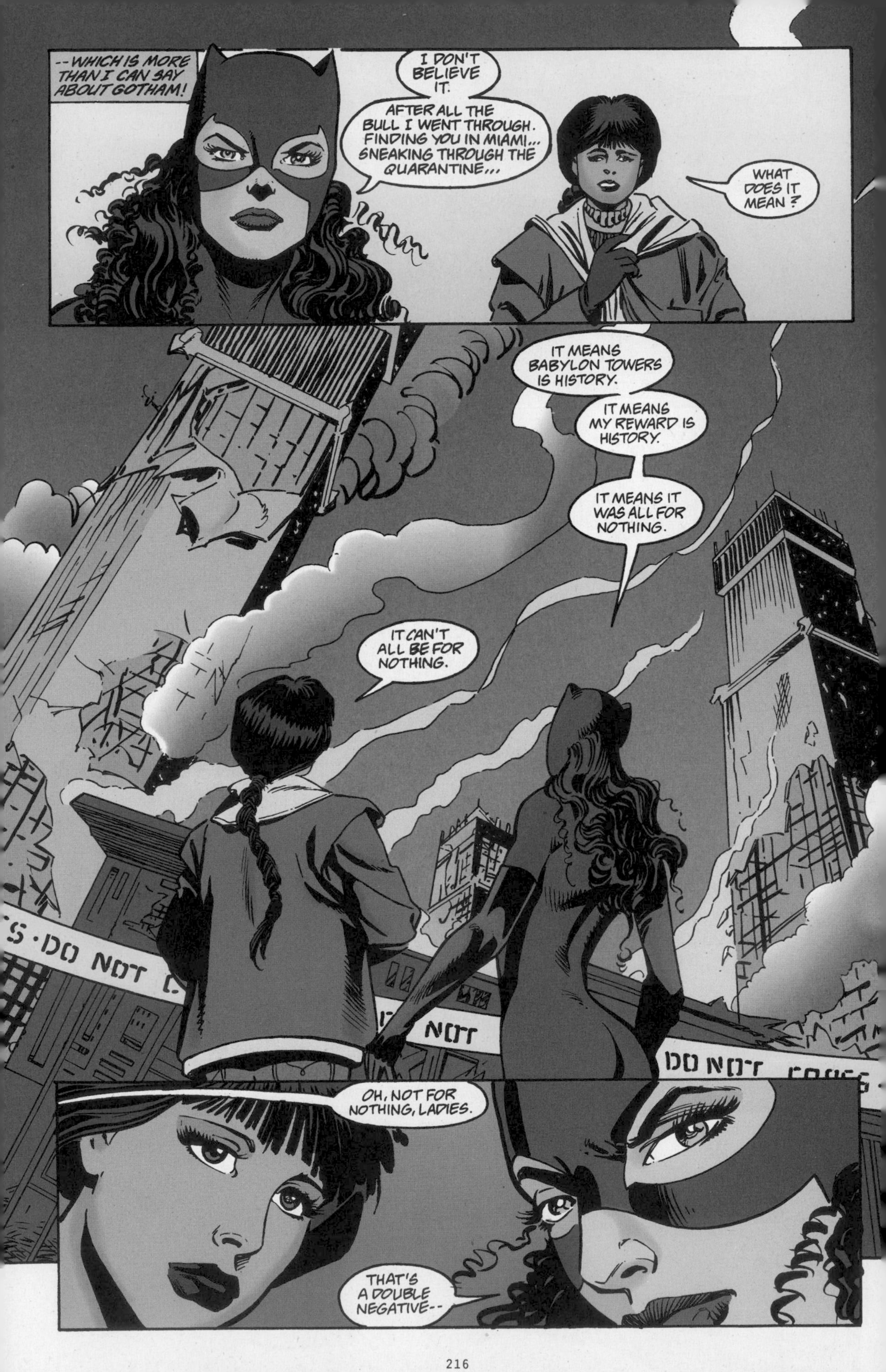
--WHICH IS MORE THAN I CAN SAY ABOUT GOTHAM!
I DON'T BELIEVE IT.
AFTER ALL THE BULL I WENT THROUGH. FINDING YOU IN MIAMI... SNEAKING THROUGH THE QUARANTINE...
WHAT DOES IT MEAN ?
IT MEANS BABYLON TOWERS IS HISTORY.
IT MEANS MY REWARD IS HISTORY.
IT MEANS IT WAS ALL FOR NOTHING.
IT CAN'T ALL BE FOR NOTHING.
S·DO NOT C
NOT
DO NOT CROSS
OH, NOT FOR NOTHING, LADIES.
THAT'S A DOUBLE NEGATIVE--

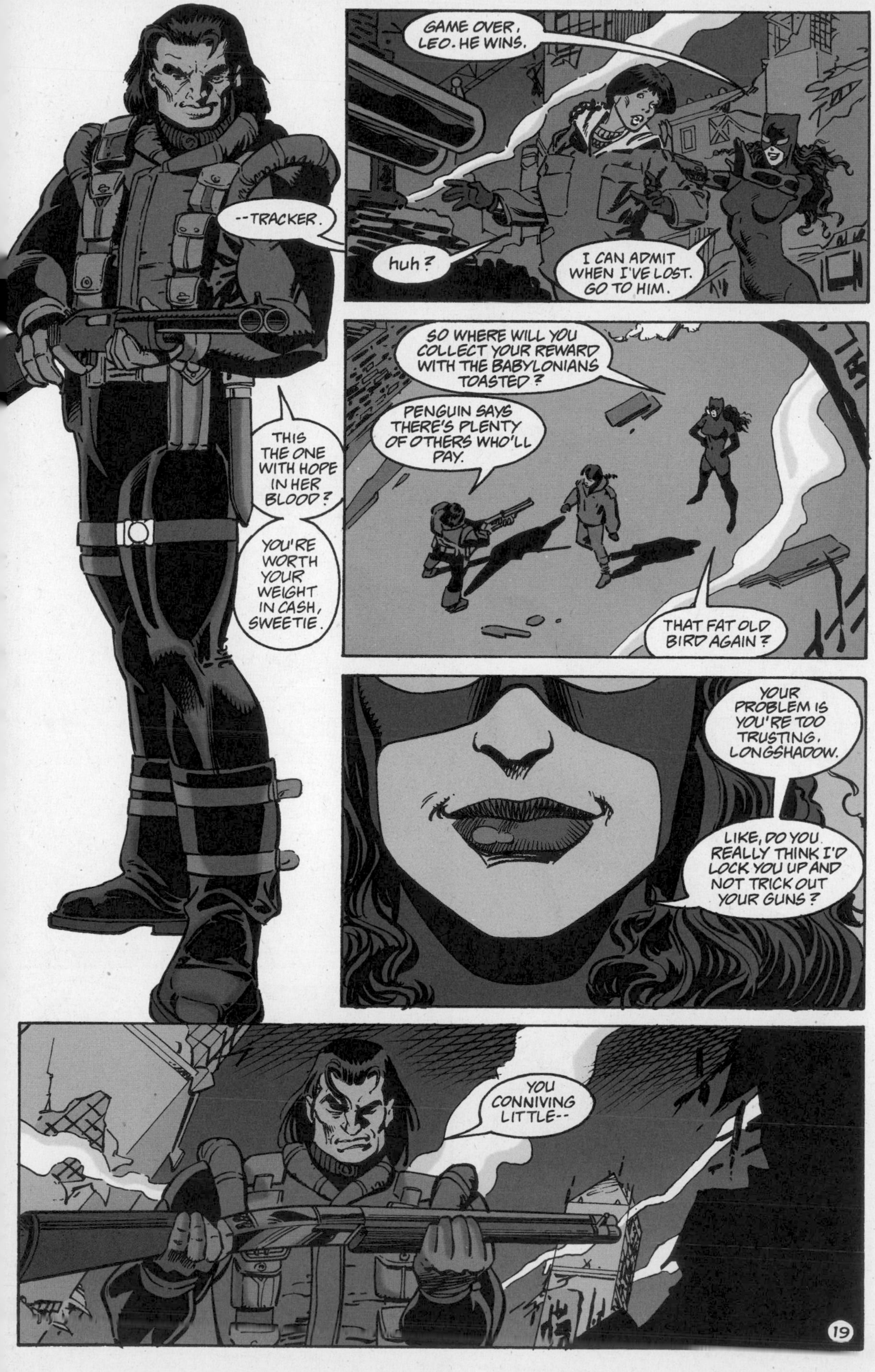
GAME OVER, LEO. HE WINS.
--TRACKER.
huh?
I CAN ADMIT WHEN I'VE LOST. GO TO HIM.
THIS THE ONE WITH HOPE IN HER BLOOD?
YOU'RE WORTH YOUR WEIGHT IN CASH, SWEETIE.
SO WHERE WILL YOU COLLECT YOUR REWARD WITH THE BABYLONIANS TOASTED?
PENGUIN SAYS THERE'S PLENTY OF OTHERS WHO'LL PAY.
THAT FAT OLD BIRD AGAIN?
YOUR PROBLEM IS YOU'RE TOO TRUSTING, LONGSHADOW.
LIKE, DO YOU REALLY THINK I'D LOCK YOU UP AND NOT TRICK OUT YOUR GUNS?
YOU CONNIVING LITTLE--
19

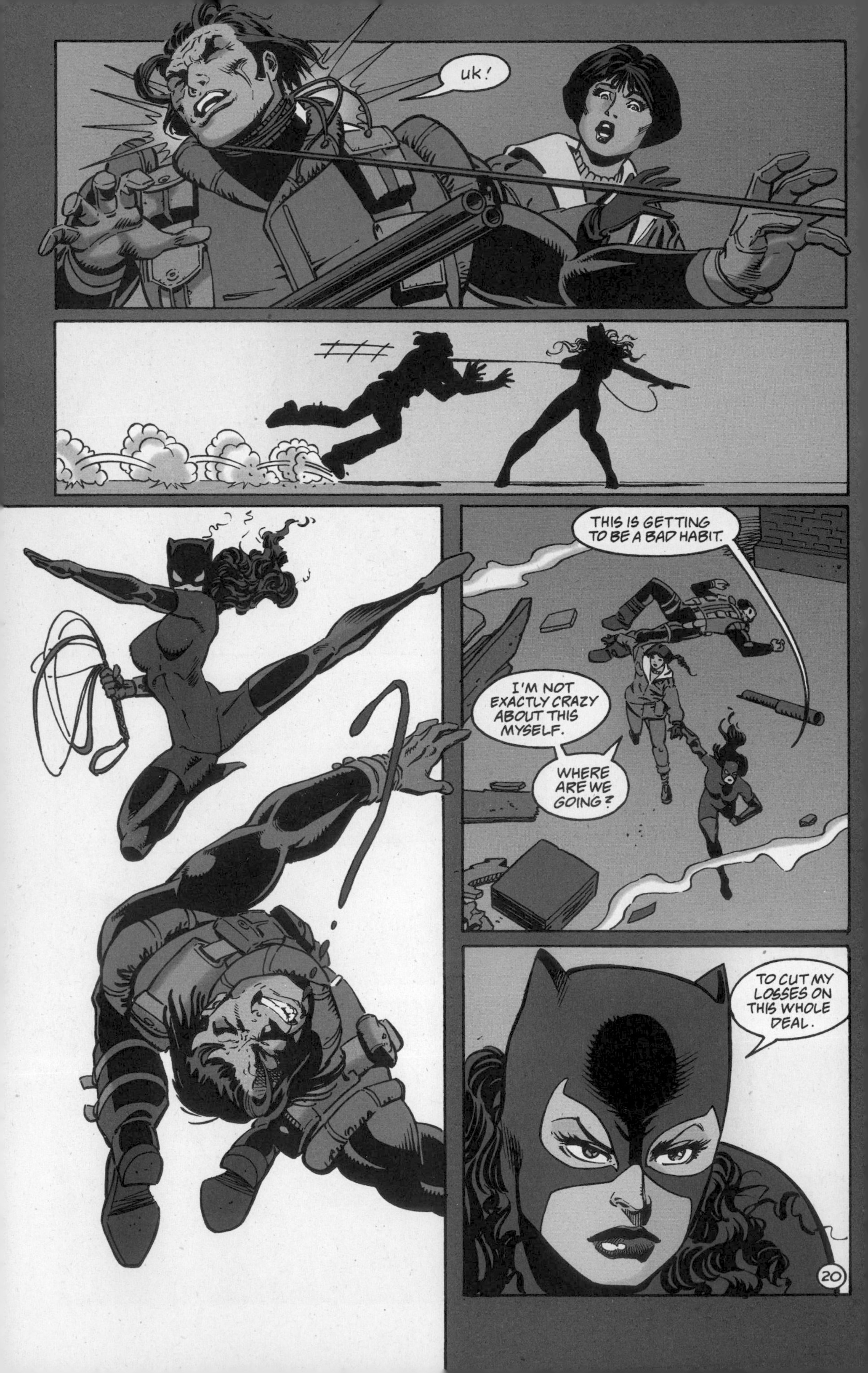
uk!
THIS IS GETTING TO BE A BAD HABIT.
I'M NOT EXACTLY CRAZY ABOUT THIS MYSELF.
WHERE ARE WE GOING?
TO CUT MY LOSSES ON THIS WHOLE DEAL.
20

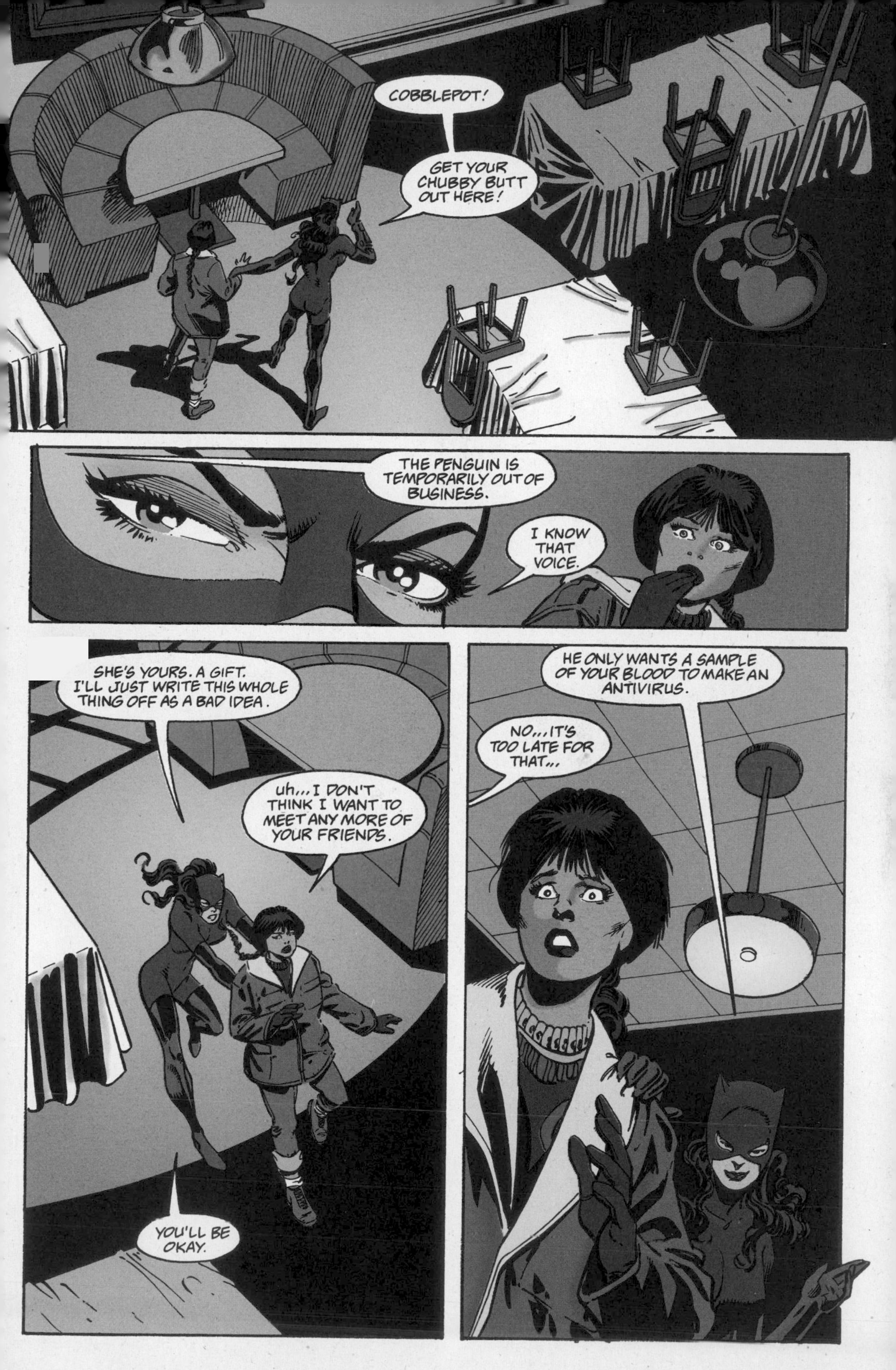
COBBLEPOT!
GET YOUR CHUBBY BUTT OUT HERE!
THE PENGUIN IS TEMPORARILY OUT OF BUSINESS.
I KNOW THAT VOICE.
SHE'S YOURS. A GIFT. I'LL JUST WRITE THIS WHOLE THING OFF AS A BAD IDEA.
uh... I DON'T THINK I WANT TO MEET ANY MORE OF YOUR FRIENDS.
YOU'LL BE OKAY.
HE ONLY WANTS A SAMPLE OF YOUR BLOOD TO MAKE AN ANTIVIRUS.
NO... IT'S TOO LATE FOR THAT...

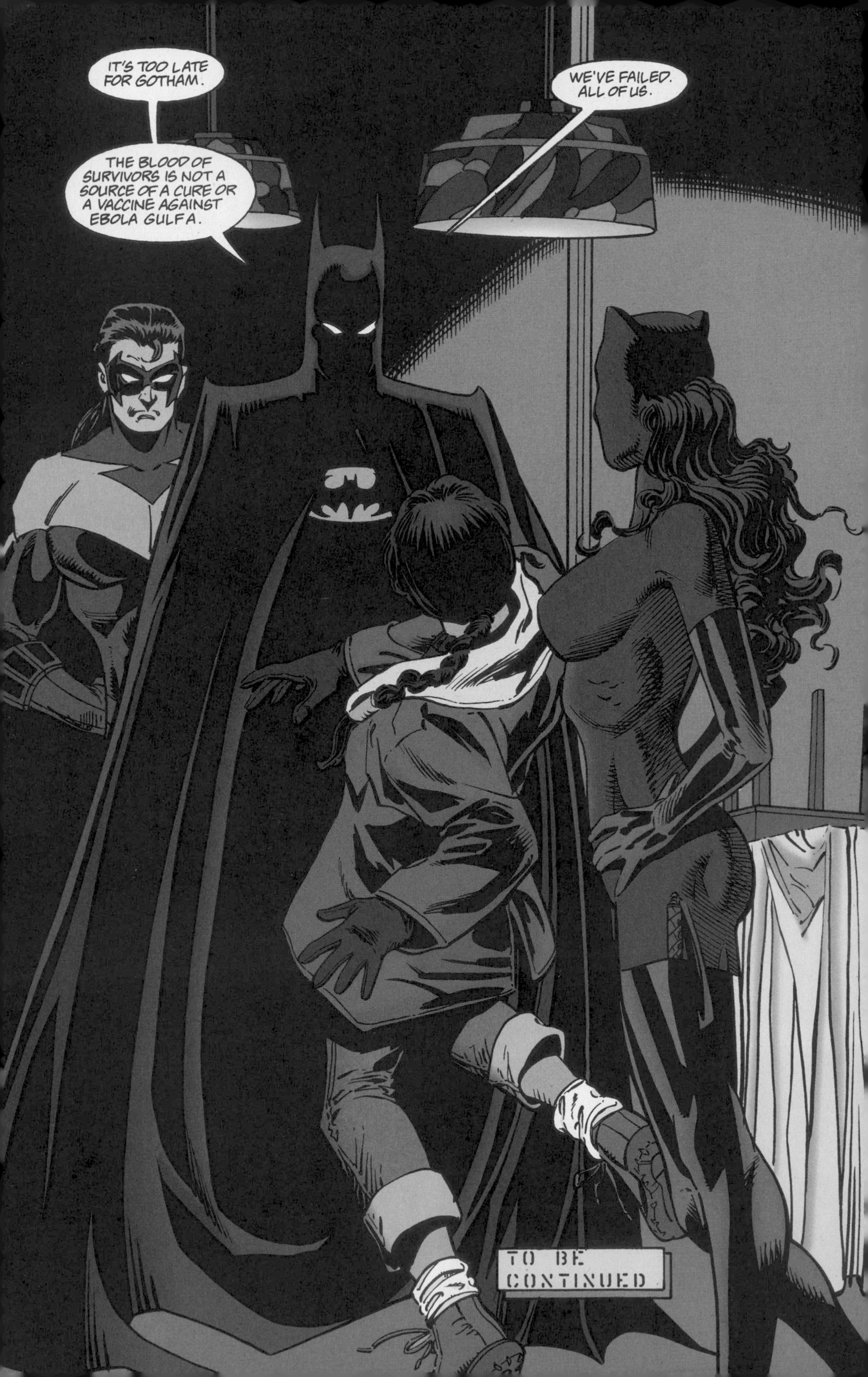
IT'S TOO LATE FOR GOTHAM.
THE BLOOD OF SURVIVORS IS NOT A SOURCE OF A CURE OR A VACCINE AGAINST EBOLA GULFA.
WE'VE FAILED. ALL OF US.
TO BE CONTINUED

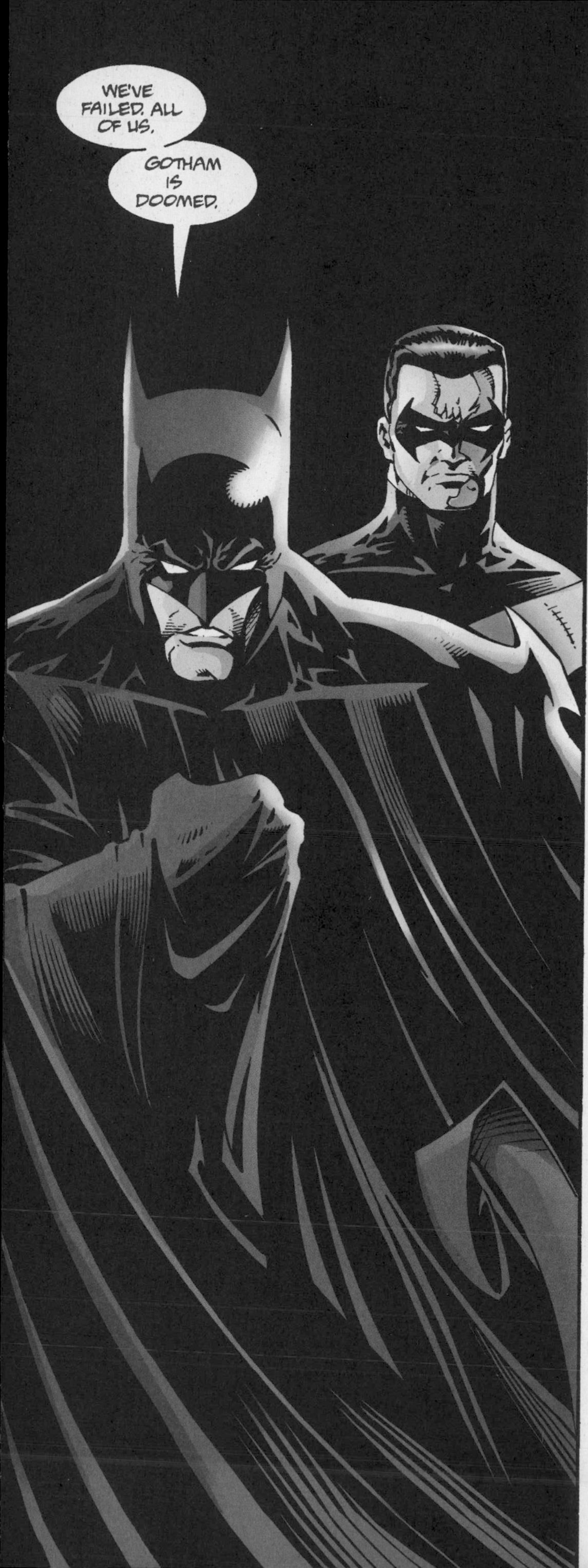
WE'VE FAILED. ALL OF US.
GOTHAM IS DOOMED.

AZRAEL

PART 10: CONTAGION

WRITER
DENNIS O'NEIL
PENCILS
BARRY KITSON
INKS
JAMES PASCOE
COLORIST
DEMETRIUS BASSOUKOS
SEPARATIONS
DIGITAL HELLFIRE
LETTERER
KEN BRUZENAK
ASSISTANT EDITOR
CHUCK KIM
EDITOR
ARCHIE GOODWIN

AZRAEL CREATED BY DENNIS O'NEIL AND JOE QUESADA

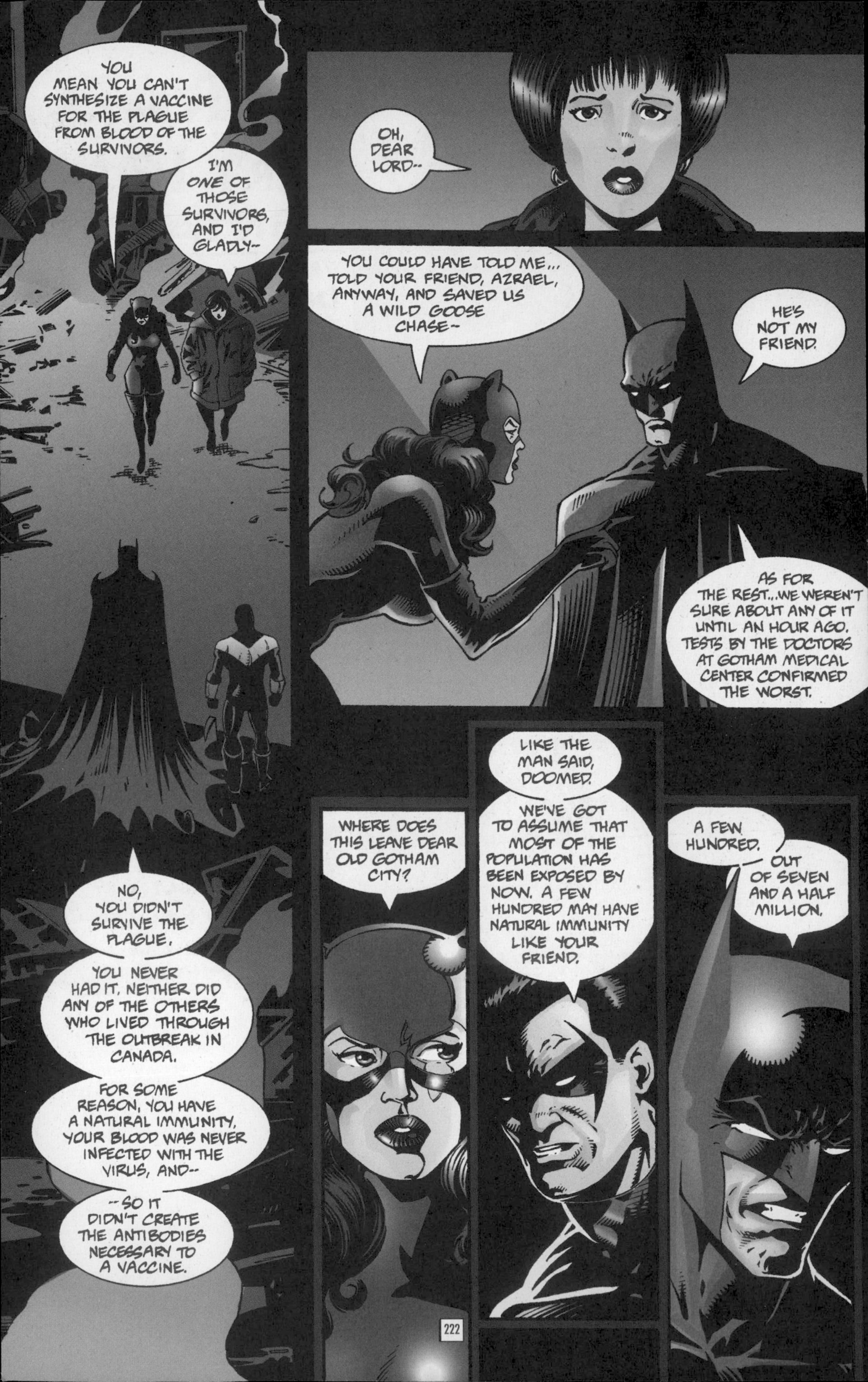
YOU MEAN YOU CAN'T SYNTHESIZE A VACCINE FOR THE PLAGUE FROM BLOOD OF THE SURVIVORS.
I'M ONE OF THOSE SURVIVORS, AND I'D GLADLY--
OH, DEAR LORD--
YOU COULD HAVE TOLD ME... TOLD YOUR FRIEND, AZRAEL, ANYWAY, AND SAVED US A WILD GOOSE CHASE--
HE'S NOT MY FRIEND.
AS FOR THE REST...WE WEREN'T SURE ABOUT ANY OF IT UNTIL AN HOUR AGO. TESTS BY THE DOCTORS AT GOTHAM MEDICAL CENTER CONFIRMED THE WORST.
NO, YOU DIDN'T SURVIVE THE PLAGUE.
YOU NEVER HAD IT, NEITHER DID ANY OF THE OTHERS WHO LIVED THROUGH THE OUTBREAK IN CANADA.
FOR SOME REASON, YOU HAVE A NATURAL IMMUNITY, YOUR BLOOD WAS NEVER INFECTED WITH THE VIRUS, AND--
--SO IT DIDN'T CREATE THE ANTIBODIES NECESSARY TO A VACCINE.
WHERE DOES THIS LEAVE DEAR OLD GOTHAM CITY?
LIKE THE MAN SAID, DOOMED.
WE'VE GOT TO ASSUME THAT MOST OF THE POPULATION HAS BEEN EXPOSED BY NOW. A FEW HUNDRED MAY HAVE NATURAL IMMUNITY LIKE YOUR FRIEND.
A FEW HUNDRED.
OUT OF SEVEN AND A HALF MILLION.

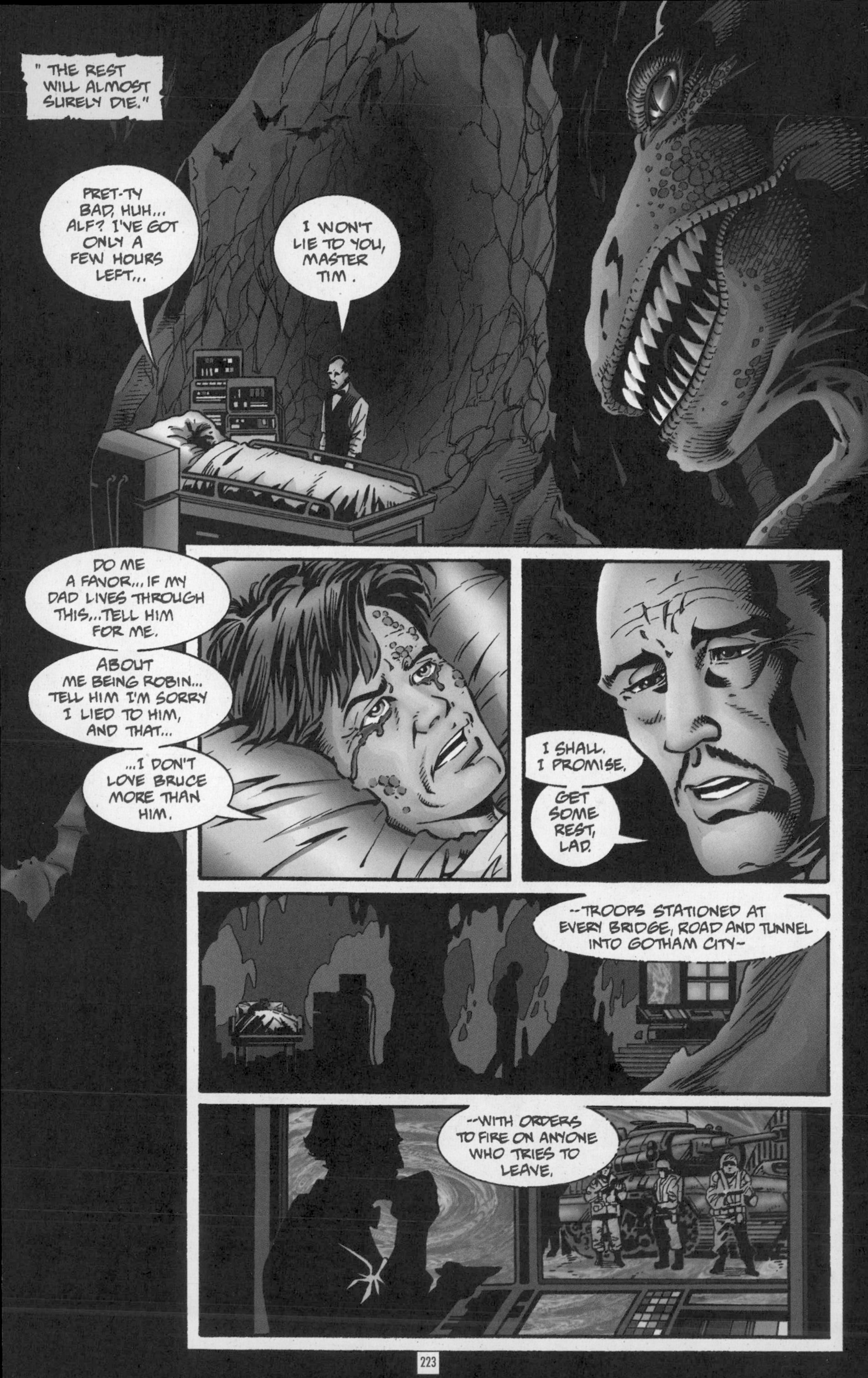
"THE REST WILL ALMOST SURELY DIE."
PRET-TY BAD, HUH... ALF? I'VE GOT ONLY A FEW HOURS LEFT...
I WON'T LIE TO YOU, MASTER TIM.
DO ME A FAVOR... IF MY DAD LIVES THROUGH THIS...TELL HIM FOR ME.
ABOUT ME BEING ROBIN... TELL HIM I'M SORRY I LIED TO HIM, AND THAT...
...I DON'T LOVE BRUCE MORE THAN HIM.
I SHALL. I PROMISE.
GET SOME REST, LAD.
--TROOPS STATIONED AT EVERY BRIDGE, ROAD AND TUNNEL INTO GOTHAM CITY--
--WITH ORDERS TO FIRE ON ANYONE WHO TRIES TO LEAVE.

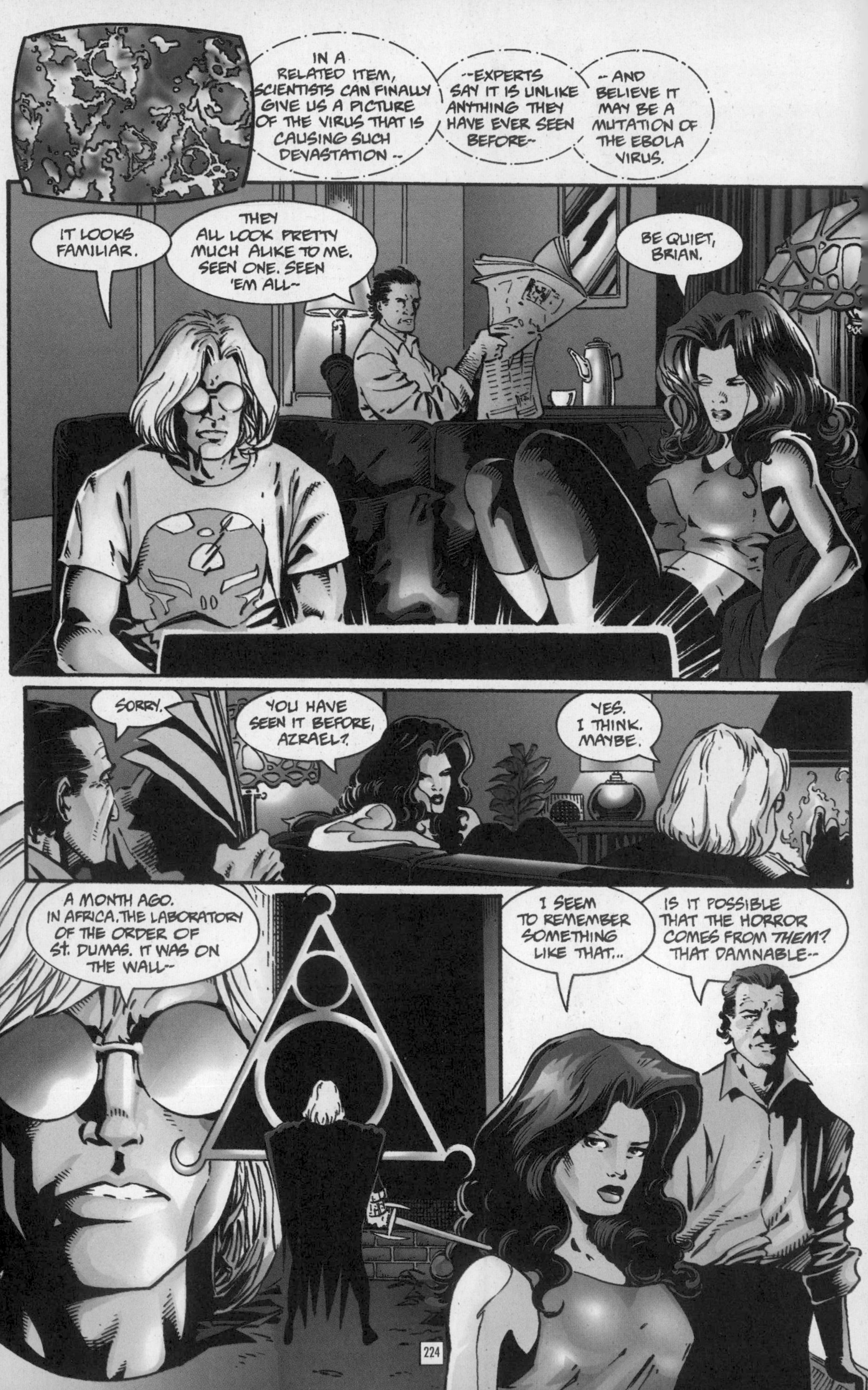
IN A RELATED ITEM, SCIENTISTS CAN FINALLY GIVE US A PICTURE OF THE VIRUS THAT IS CAUSING SUCH DEVASTATION --
--EXPERTS SAY IT IS UNLIKE ANYTHING THEY HAVE EVER SEEN BEFORE--
-- AND BELIEVE IT MAY BE A MUTATION OF THE EBOLA VIRUS.
IT LOOKS FAMILIAR.
THEY ALL LOOK PRETTY MUCH ALIKE TO ME. SEEN ONE. SEEN 'EM ALL--
BE QUIET, BRIAN.
SORRY.
YOU HAVE SEEN IT BEFORE, AZRAEL?
YES. I THINK. MAYBE.
A MONTH AGO. IN AFRICA. THE LABORATORY OF THE ORDER OF St. DUMAS. IT WAS ON THE WALL--
I SEEM TO REMEMBER SOMETHING LIKE THAT...
IS IT POSSIBLE THAT THE HORROR COMES FROM *THEM*? THAT DAMNABLE--

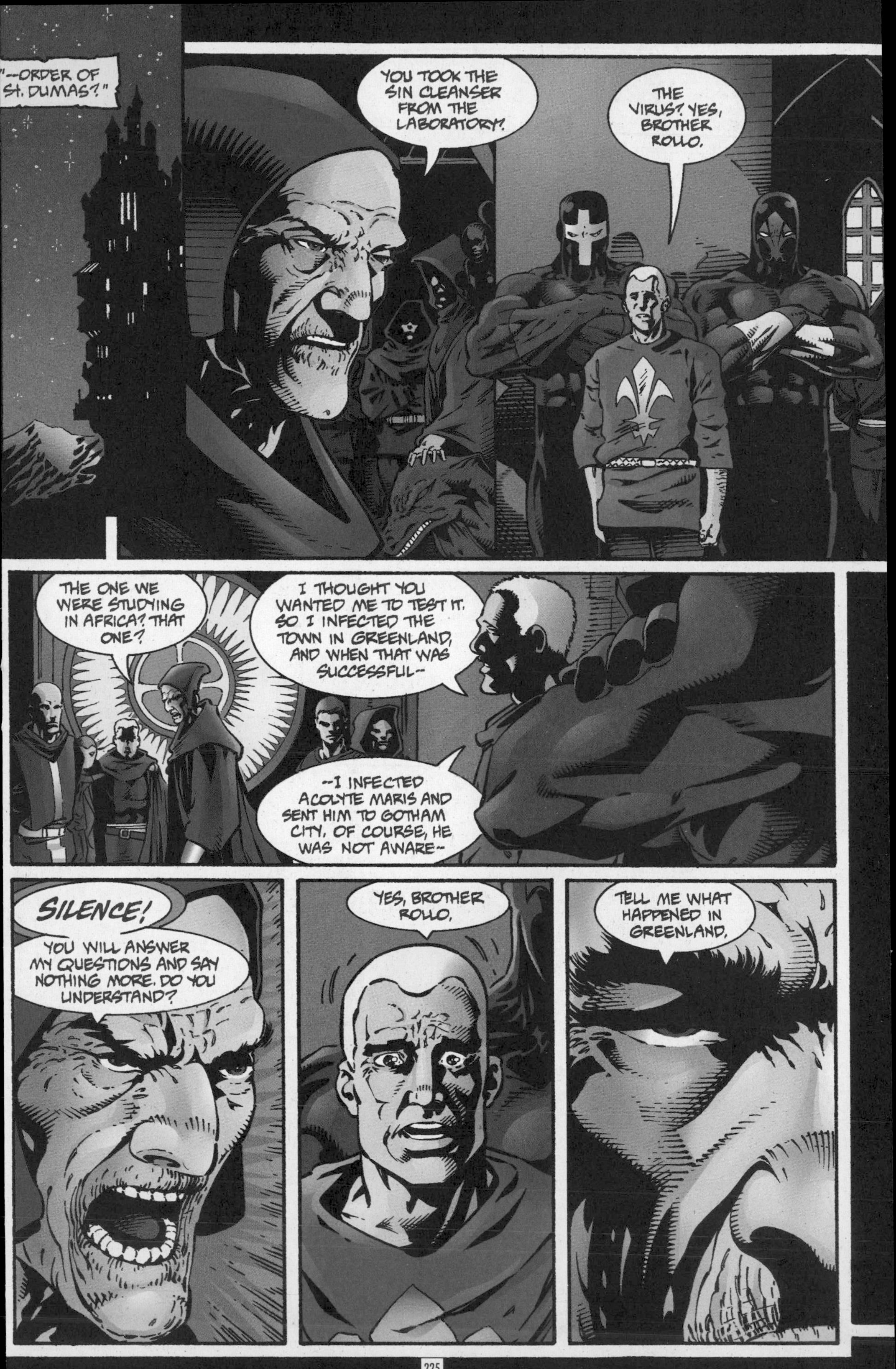
"--ORDER OF ST. DUMAS?"
YOU TOOK THE SIN CLEANSER FROM THE LABORATORY?
THE VIRUS? YES, BROTHER ROLLO.
THE ONE WE WERE STUDYING IN AFRICA? THAT ONE?
I THOUGHT YOU WANTED ME TO TEST IT. SO I INFECTED THE TOWN IN GREENLAND, AND WHEN THAT WAS SUCCESSFUL--
--I INFECTED ACOLYTE MARIS AND SENT HIM TO GOTHAM CITY. OF COURSE, HE WAS NOT AWARE--
SILENCE!
YOU WILL ANSWER MY QUESTIONS AND SAY NOTHING MORE. DO YOU UNDERSTAND?
YES, BROTHER ROLLO.
TELL ME WHAT HAPPENED IN GREENLAND.

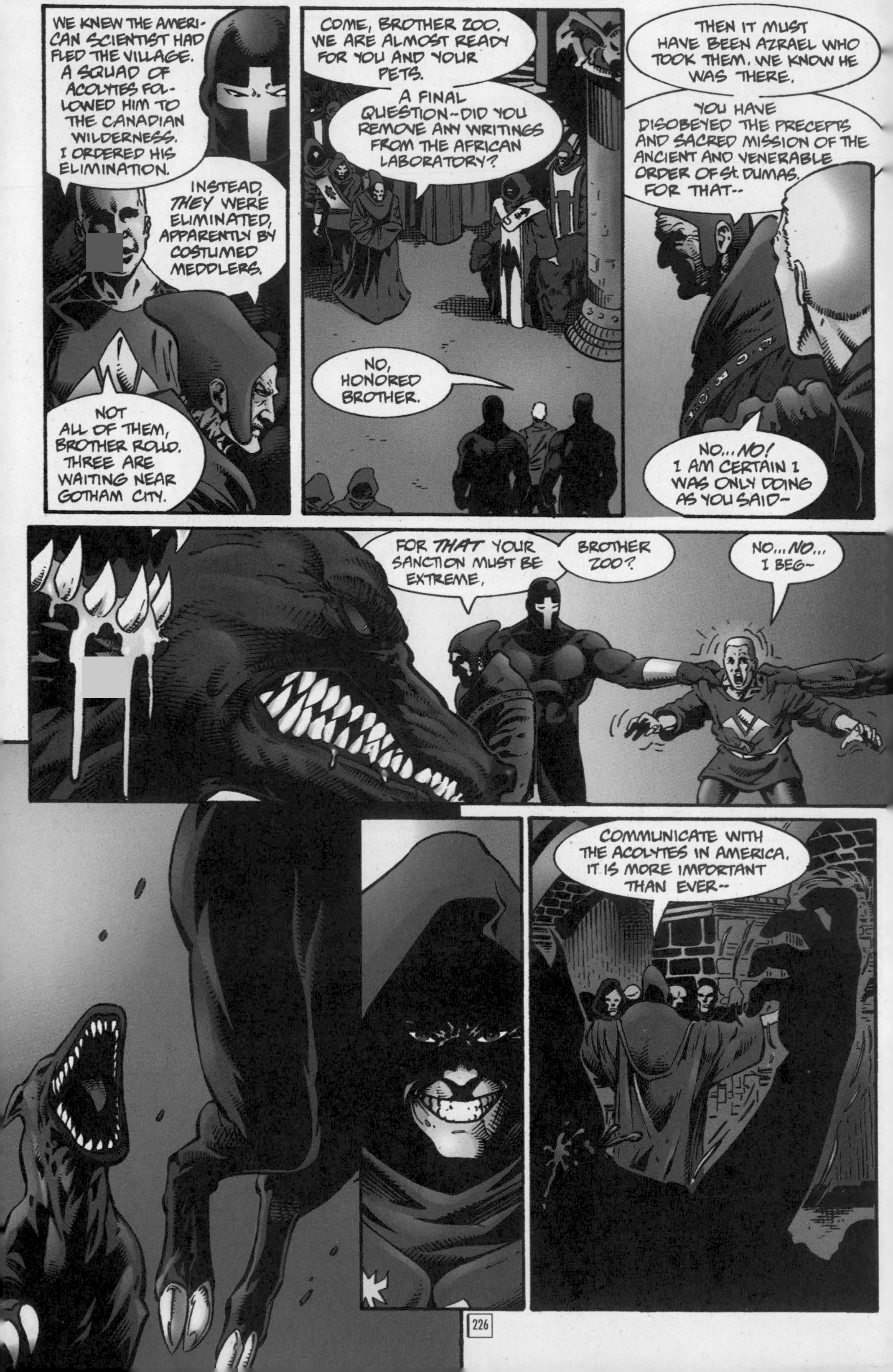
WE KNEW THE AMERICAN SCIENTIST HAD FLED THE VILLAGE. A SQUAD OF ACOLYTES FOLLOWED HIM TO THE CANADIAN WILDERNESS. I ORDERED HIS ELIMINATION.
INSTEAD, *THEY* WERE ELIMINATED, APPARENTLY BY COSTUMED MEDDLERS.
NOT ALL OF THEM, BROTHER ROLLO. THREE ARE WAITING NEAR GOTHAM CITY.
COME, BROTHER ZOO. WE ARE ALMOST READY FOR YOU AND YOUR PETS.
A FINAL QUESTION--DID YOU REMOVE ANY WRITINGS FROM THE AFRICAN LABORATORY?
NO, HONORED BROTHER.
THEN IT MUST HAVE BEEN AZRAEL WHO TOOK THEM. WE KNOW HE WAS THERE.
YOU HAVE DISOBEYED THE PRECEPTS AND SACRED MISSION OF THE ANCIENT AND VENERABLE ORDER OF St. DUMAS. FOR THAT--
NO...*NO!* I AM CERTAIN I WAS ONLY DOING AS YOU SAID--
FOR *THAT* YOUR SANCTION MUST BE EXTREME,
BROTHER ZOO?
NO...*NO*... I BEG--
COMMUNICATE WITH THE ACOLYTES IN AMERICA. IT IS MORE IMPORTANT THAN EVER--

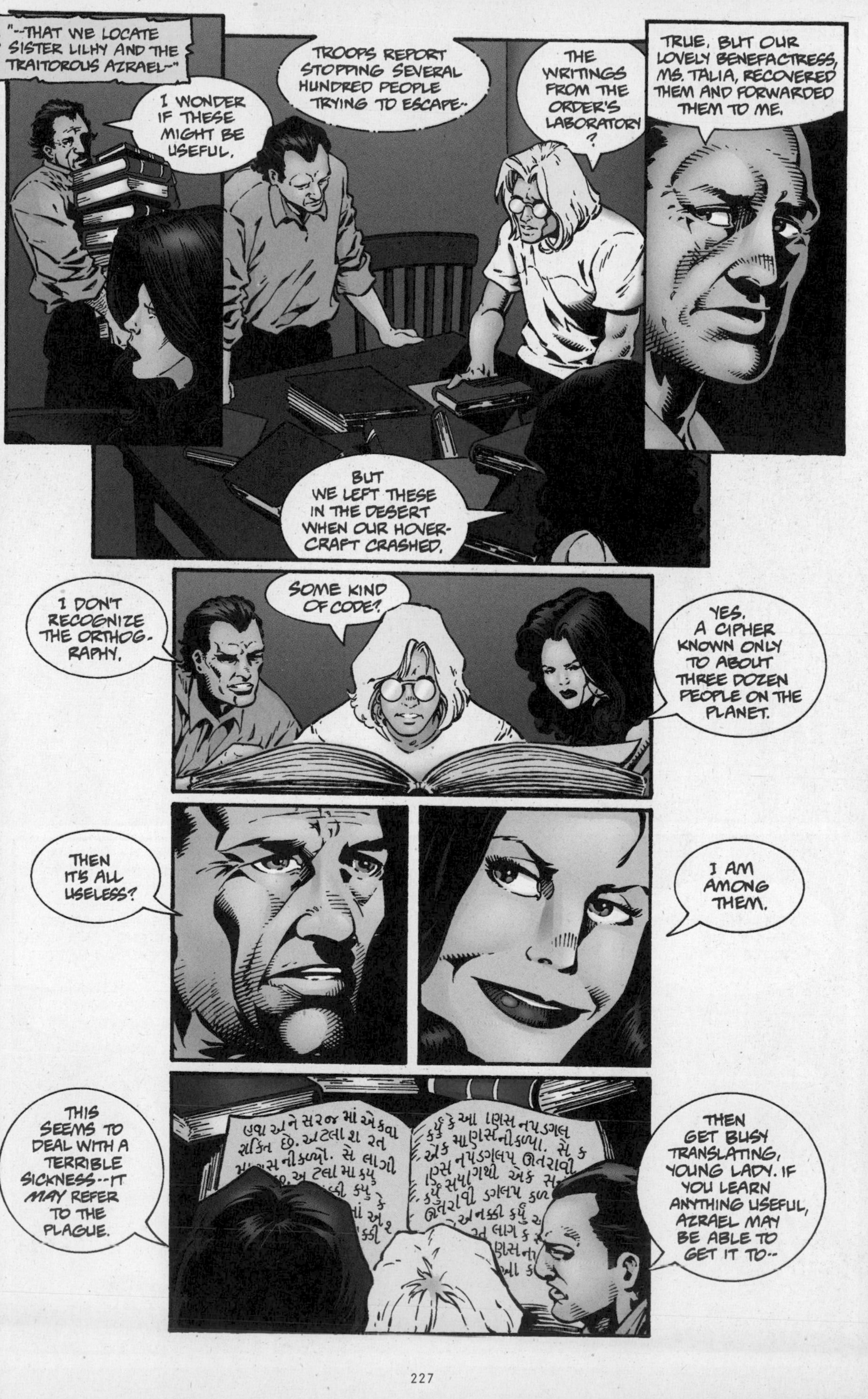
"--THAT WE LOCATE SISTER LILHY AND THE TRAITOROUS AZRAEL--"
TROOPS REPORT STOPPING SEVERAL HUNDRED PEOPLE TRYING TO ESCAPE--
THE WRITINGS FROM THE ORDER'S LABORATORY?
TRUE, BUT OUR LOVELY BENEFACTRESS, MS. TALIA, RECOVERED THEM AND FORWARDED THEM TO ME.
I WONDER IF THESE MIGHT BE USEFUL.
BUT WE LEFT THESE IN THE DESERT WHEN OUR HOVER-CRAFT CRASHED.
I DON'T RECOGNIZE THE ORTHOG-RAPHY.
SOME KIND OF CODE?
YES. A CIPHER KNOWN ONLY TO ABOUT THREE DOZEN PEOPLE ON THE PLANET.
THEN IT'S ALL USELESS?
I AM AMONG THEM.
THIS SEEMS TO DEAL WITH A TERRIBLE SICKNESS--IT MAY REFER TO THE PLAGUE.
THEN GET BUSY TRANSLATING, YOUNG LADY. IF YOU LEARN ANYTHING USEFUL, AZRAEL MAY BE ABLE TO GET IT TO--

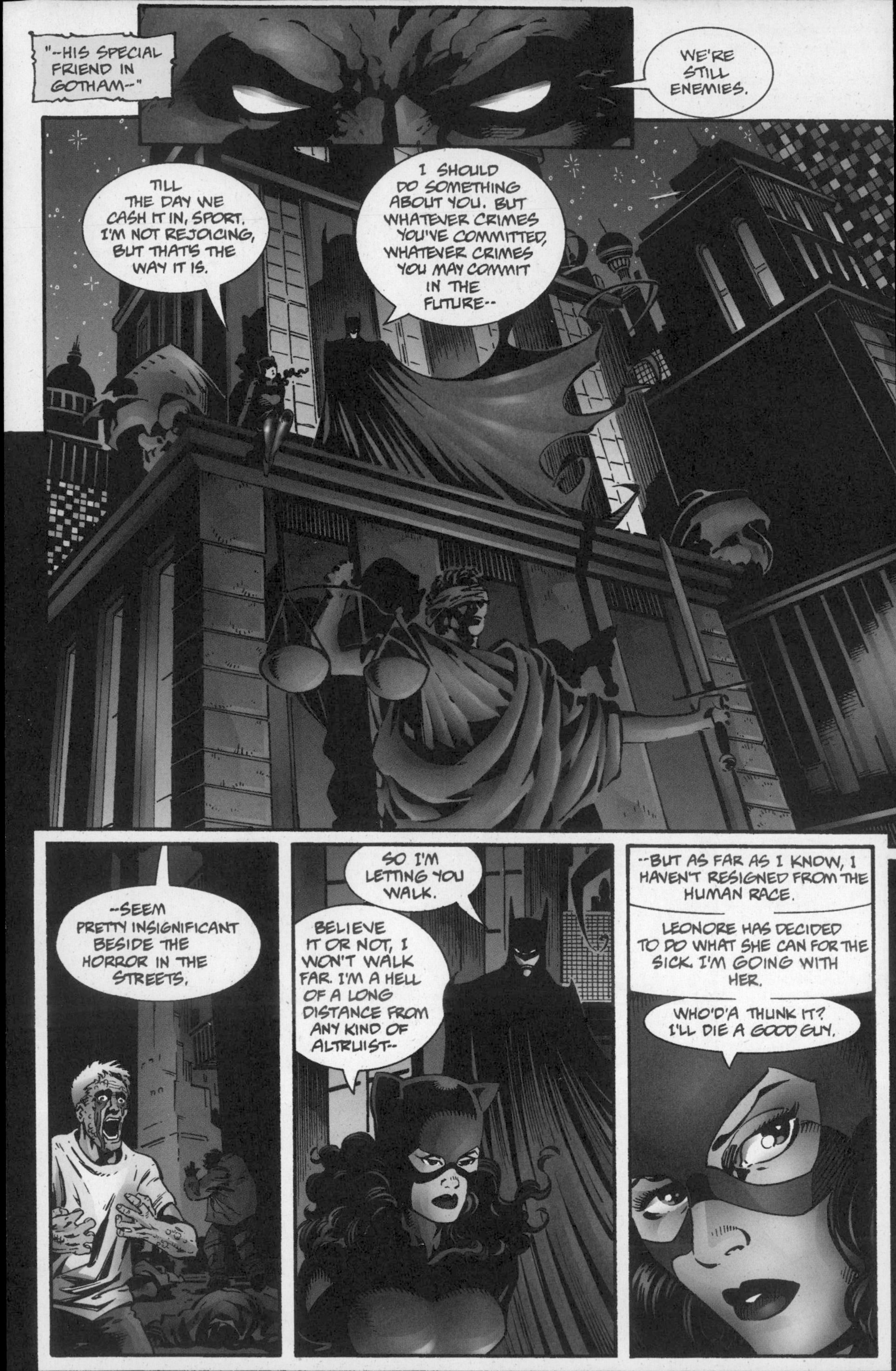
"--HIS SPECIAL FRIEND IN GOTHAM--"
WE'RE STILL ENEMIES.
TILL THE DAY WE CASH IT IN, SPORT. I'M NOT REJOICING, BUT THAT'S THE WAY IT IS.
I SHOULD DO SOMETHING ABOUT YOU. BUT WHATEVER CRIMES YOU'VE COMMITTED, WHATEVER CRIMES YOU MAY COMMIT IN THE FUTURE--
--SEEM PRETTY INSIGNIFICANT BESIDE THE HORROR IN THE STREETS.
SO I'M LETTING YOU WALK.
BELIEVE IT OR NOT, I WON'T WALK FAR. I'M A HELL OF A LONG DISTANCE FROM ANY KIND OF ALTRUIST--
--BUT AS FAR AS I KNOW, I HAVEN'T RESIGNED FROM THE HUMAN RACE.
LEONORE HAS DECIDED TO DO WHAT SHE CAN FOR THE SICK. I'M GOING WITH HER.
WHO'D'A THUNK IT? I'LL DIE A GOOD GUY.

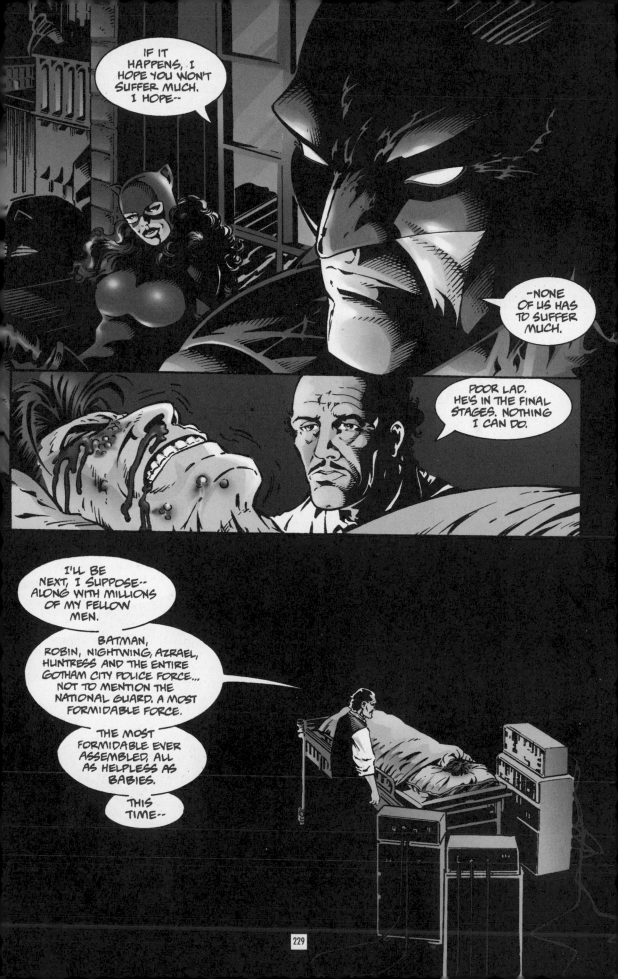

IF IT HAPPENS, I HOPE YOU WON'T SUFFER MUCH. I HOPE--

--NONE OF US HAS TO SUFFER MUCH.

POOR LAD. HE'S IN THE FINAL STAGES. NOTHING I CAN DO.

I'LL BE NEXT, I SUPPOSE-- ALONG WITH MILLIONS OF MY FELLOW MEN.

BATMAN, ROBIN, NIGHTWING, AZRAEL, HUNTRESS AND THE ENTIRE GOTHAM CITY POLICE FORCE... NOT TO MENTION THE NATIONAL GUARD. A MOST FORMIDABLE FORCE.

THE MOST FORMIDABLE EVER ASSEMBLED, ALL AS HELPLESS AS BABIES.

THIS TIME--

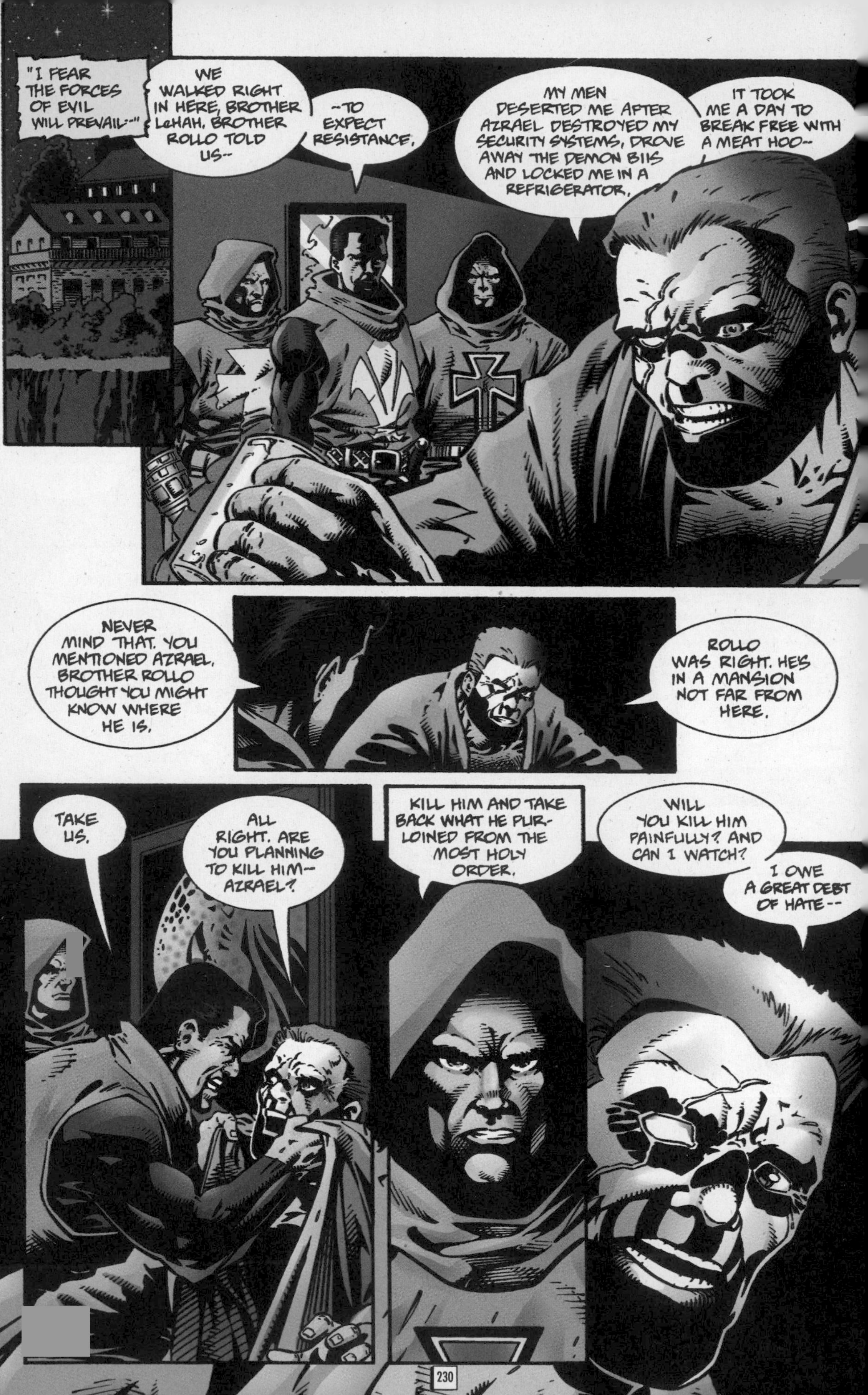
"I FEAR THE FORCES OF EVIL WILL PREVAIL--"
WE WALKED RIGHT IN HERE, BROTHER LeHAH. BROTHER ROLLO TOLD US--
--TO EXPECT RESISTANCE.
MY MEN DESERTED ME AFTER AZRAEL DESTROYED MY SECURITY SYSTEMS, DROVE AWAY THE DEMON BIIS AND LOCKED ME IN A REFRIGERATOR.
IT TOOK ME A DAY TO BREAK FREE WITH A MEAT HOO--
NEVER MIND THAT. YOU MENTIONED AZRAEL. BROTHER ROLLO THOUGHT YOU MIGHT KNOW WHERE HE IS.
ROLLO WAS RIGHT. HE'S IN A MANSION NOT FAR FROM HERE.
TAKE US.
ALL RIGHT. ARE YOU PLANNING TO KILL HIM--AZRAEL?
KILL HIM AND TAKE BACK WHAT HE PURLOINED FROM THE MOST HOLY ORDER.
WILL YOU KILL HIM PAINFULLY? AND CAN I WATCH?
I OWE A GREAT DEBT OF HATE--

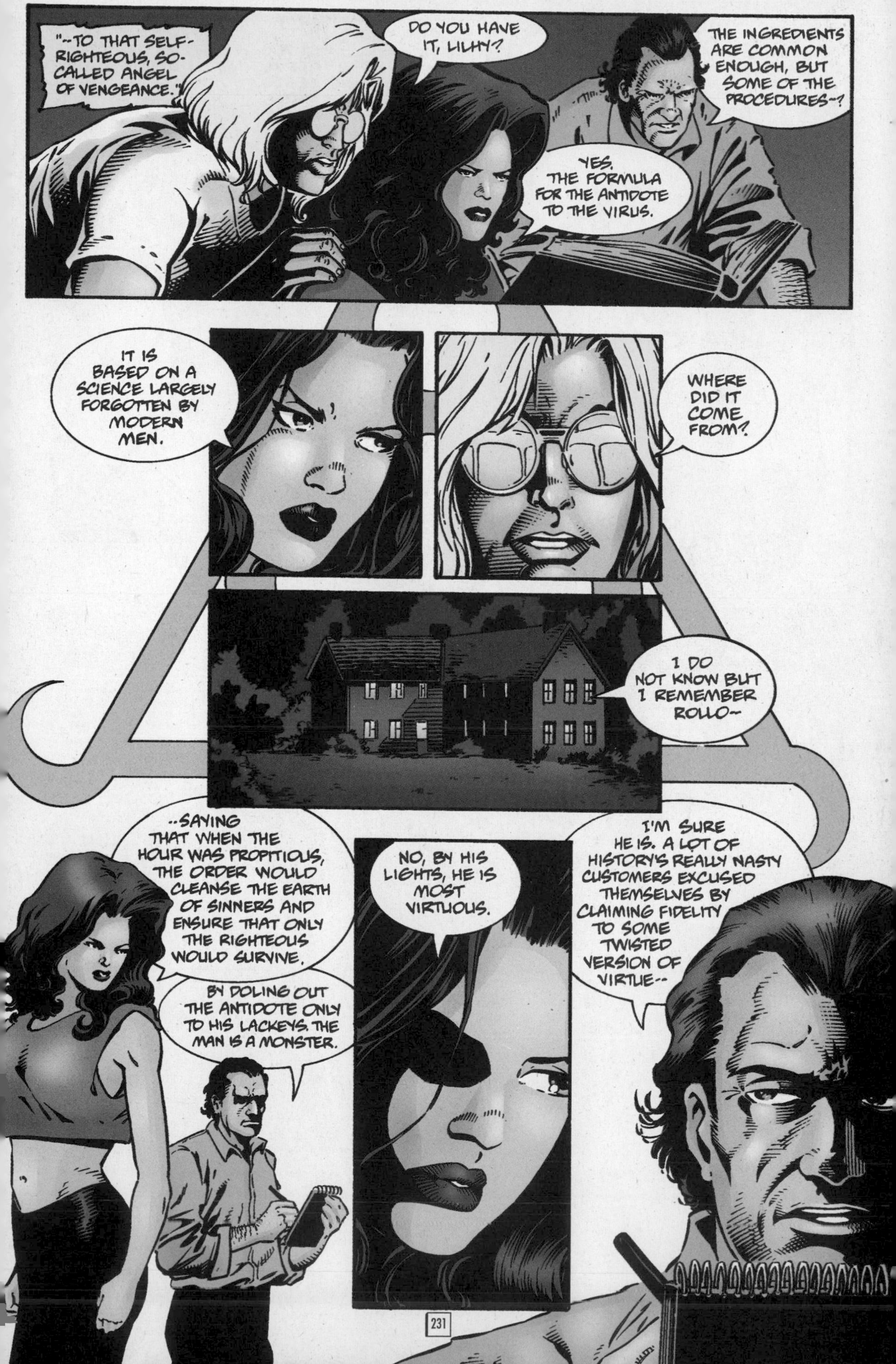
"--TO THAT SELF-RIGHTEOUS, SO-CALLED ANGEL OF VENGEANCE."
DO YOU HAVE IT, LILHY?
THE INGREDIENTS ARE COMMON ENOUGH, BUT SOME OF THE PROCEDURES--?
YES. THE FORMULA FOR THE ANTIDOTE TO THE VIRUS.
IT IS BASED ON A SCIENCE LARGELY FORGOTTEN BY MODERN MEN.
WHERE DID IT COME FROM?
I DO NOT KNOW BUT I REMEMBER ROLLO--
..SAYING THAT WHEN THE HOUR WAS PROPITIOUS, THE ORDER WOULD CLEANSE THE EARTH OF SINNERS AND ENSURE THAT ONLY THE RIGHTEOUS WOULD SURVIVE.
BY DOLING OUT THE ANTIDOTE ONLY TO HIS LACKEYS. THE MAN IS A MONSTER.
NO, BY HIS LIGHTS, HE IS MOST VIRTUOUS.
I'M SURE HE IS. A LOT OF HISTORY'S REALLY NASTY CUSTOMERS EXCUSED THEMSELVES BY CLAIMING FIDELITY TO SOME TWISTED VERSION OF VIRTUE--

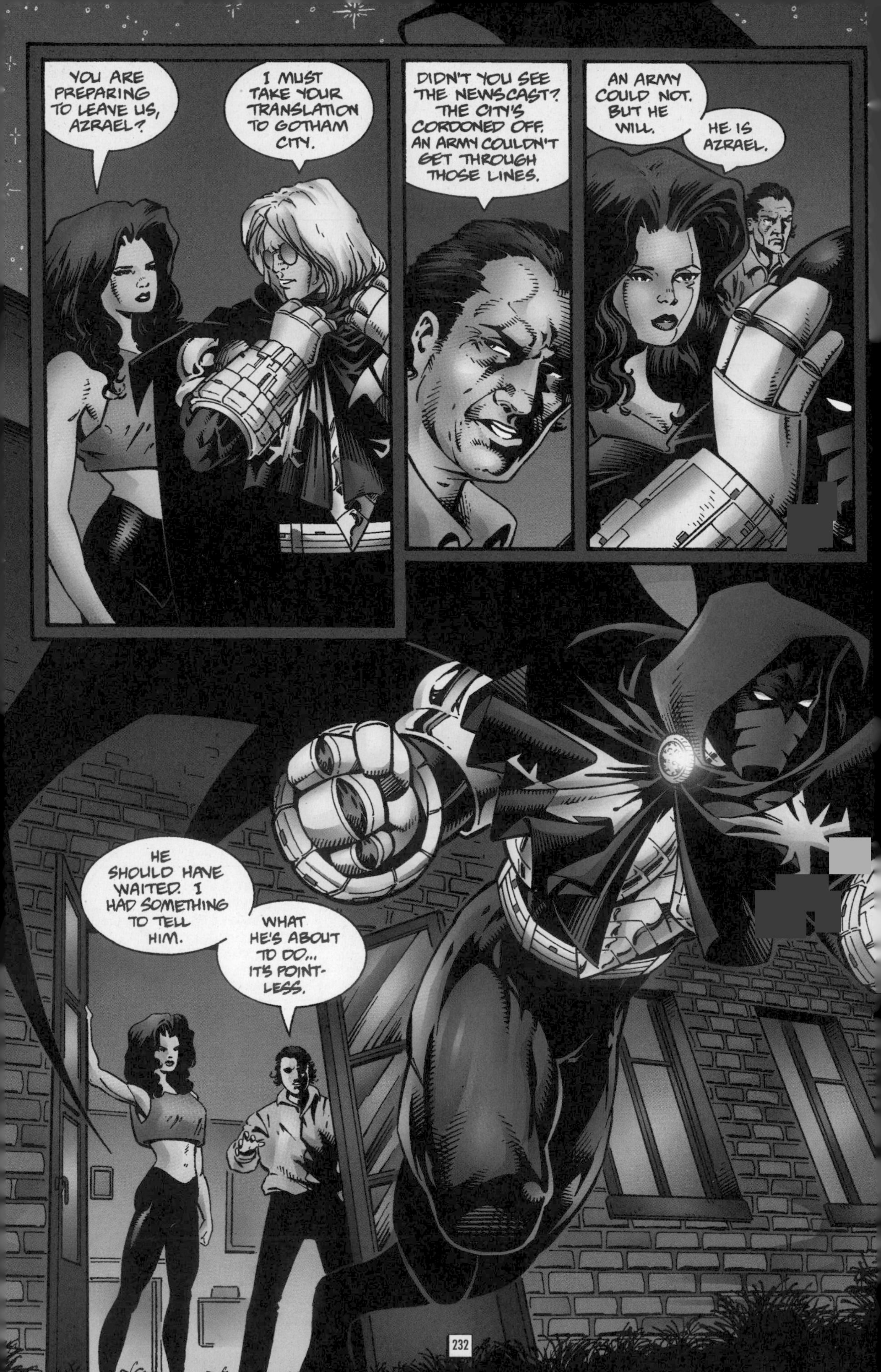
YOU ARE PREPARING TO LEAVE US, AZRAEL?
I MUST TAKE YOUR TRANSLATION TO GOTHAM CITY.
DIDN'T YOU SEE THE NEWSCAST? THE CITY'S CORDONED OFF. AN ARMY COULDN'T GET THROUGH THOSE LINES.
AN ARMY COULD NOT. BUT HE WILL.
HE IS AZRAEL.
HE SHOULD HAVE WAITED. I HAD SOMETHING TO TELL HIM.
WHAT HE'S ABOUT TO DO... IT'S POINTLESS.

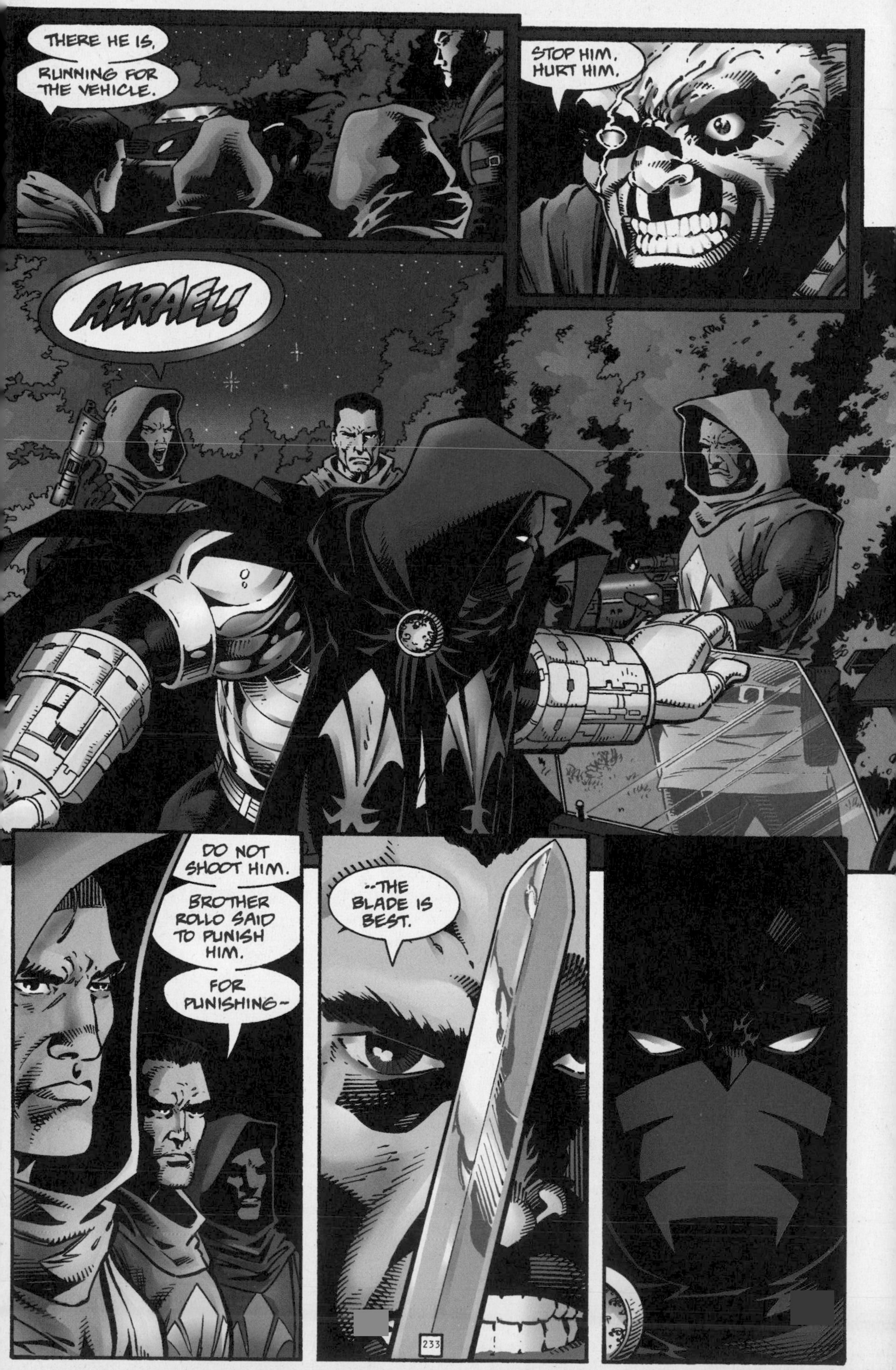

THERE HE IS, RUNNING FOR THE VEHICLE.
STOP HIM. HURT HIM.
AZRAEL!
DO NOT SHOOT HIM.
BROTHER ROLLO SAID TO PUNISH HIM.
FOR PUNISHING–
--THE BLADE IS BEST.

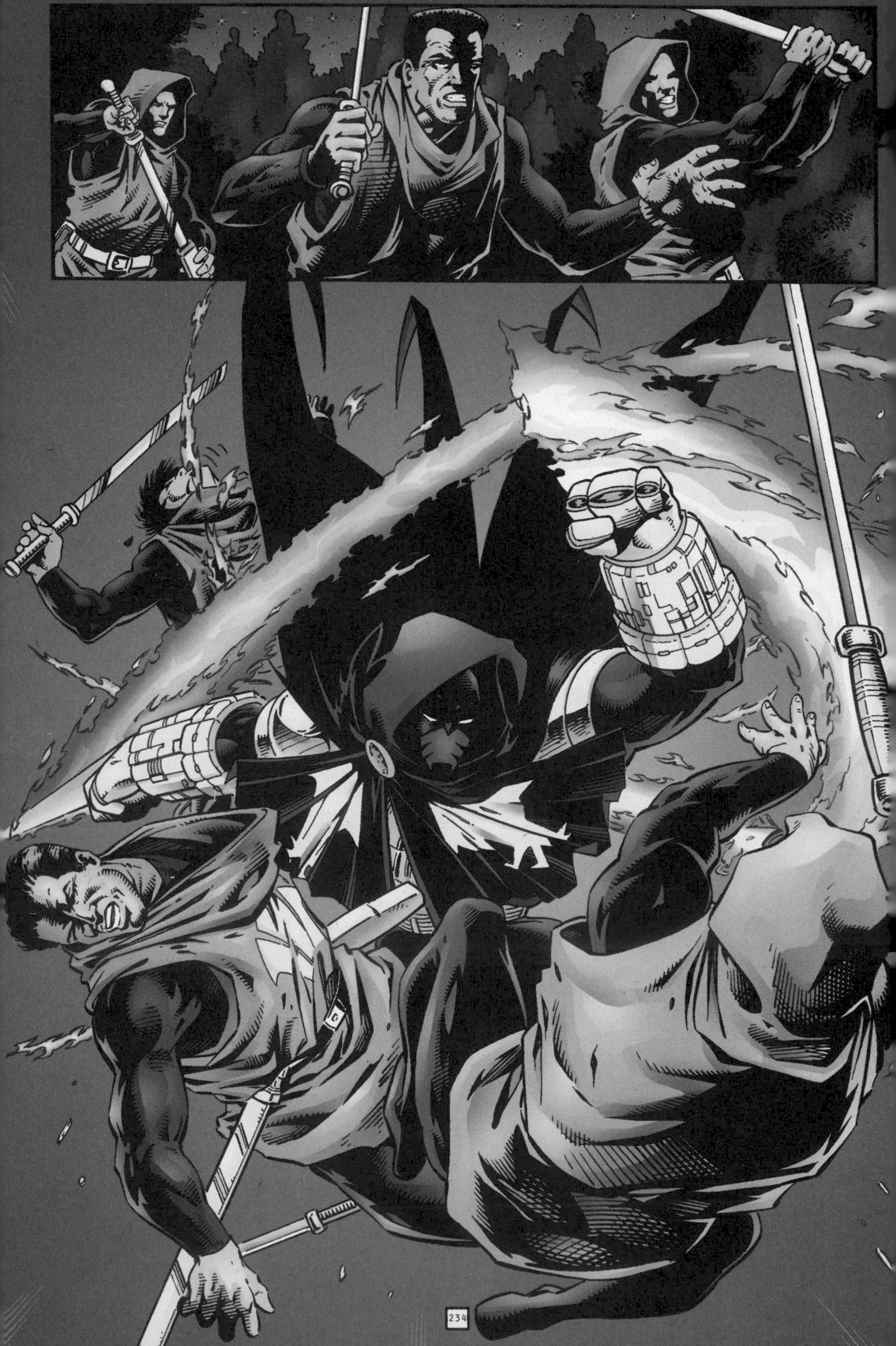

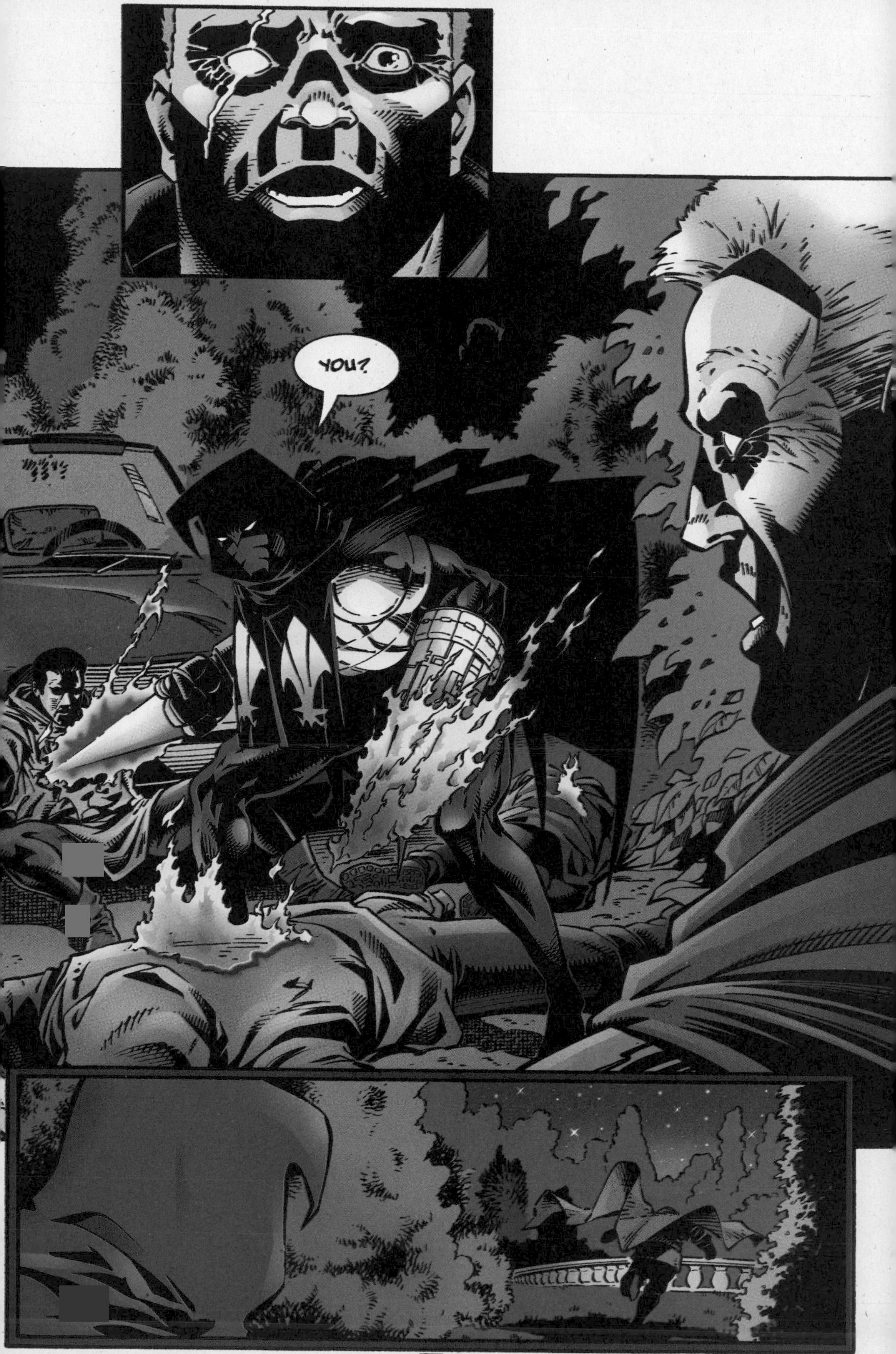
YOU?

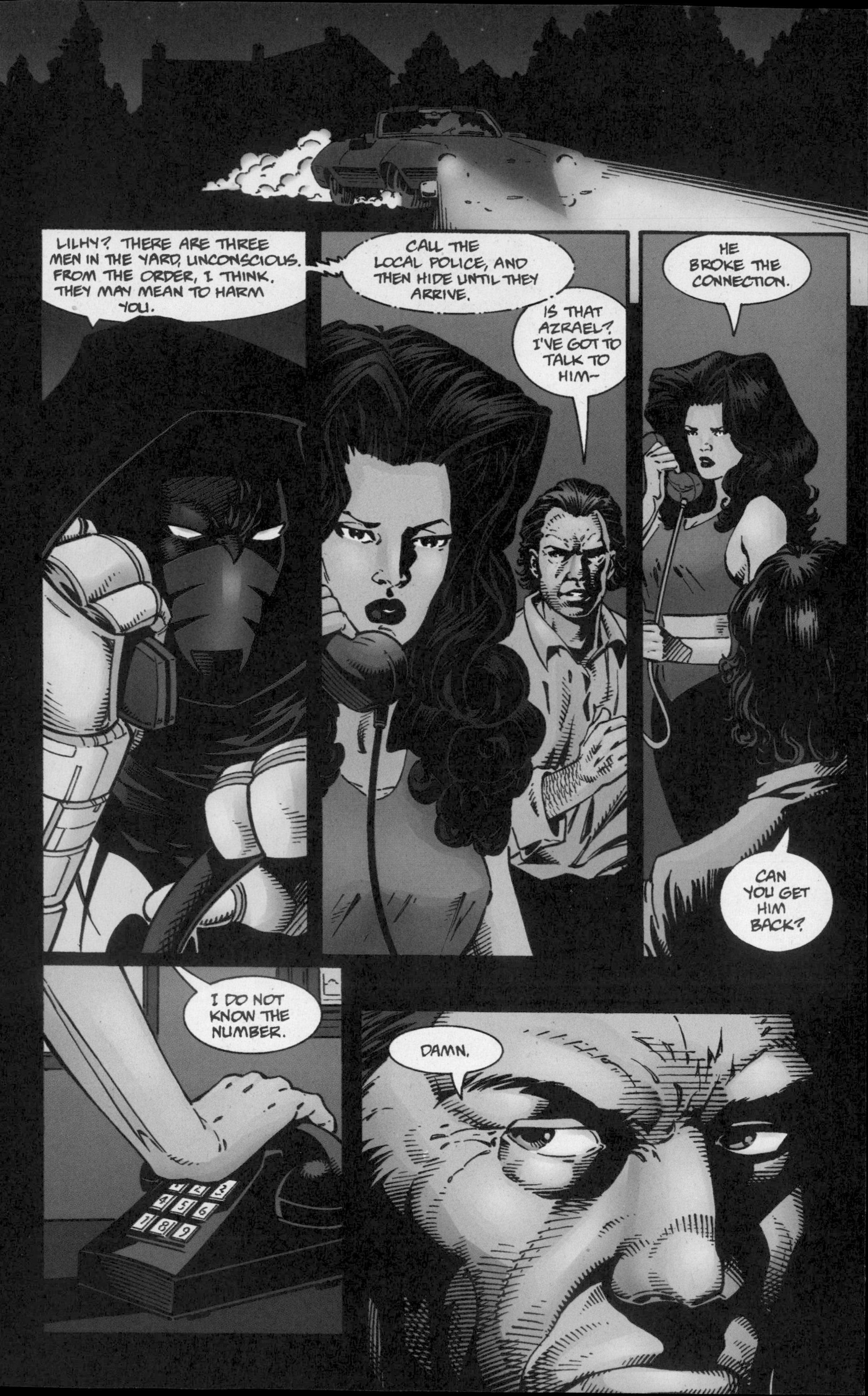
LILHY? THERE ARE THREE MEN IN THE YARD, UNCONSCIOUS. FROM THE ORDER, I THINK. THEY MAY MEAN TO HARM YOU.
CALL THE LOCAL POLICE, AND THEN HIDE UNTIL THEY ARRIVE.
IS THAT AZRAEL? I'VE GOT TO TALK TO HIM–
HE BROKE THE CONNECTION.
CAN YOU GET HIM BACK?
I DO NOT KNOW THE NUMBER.
DAMN.

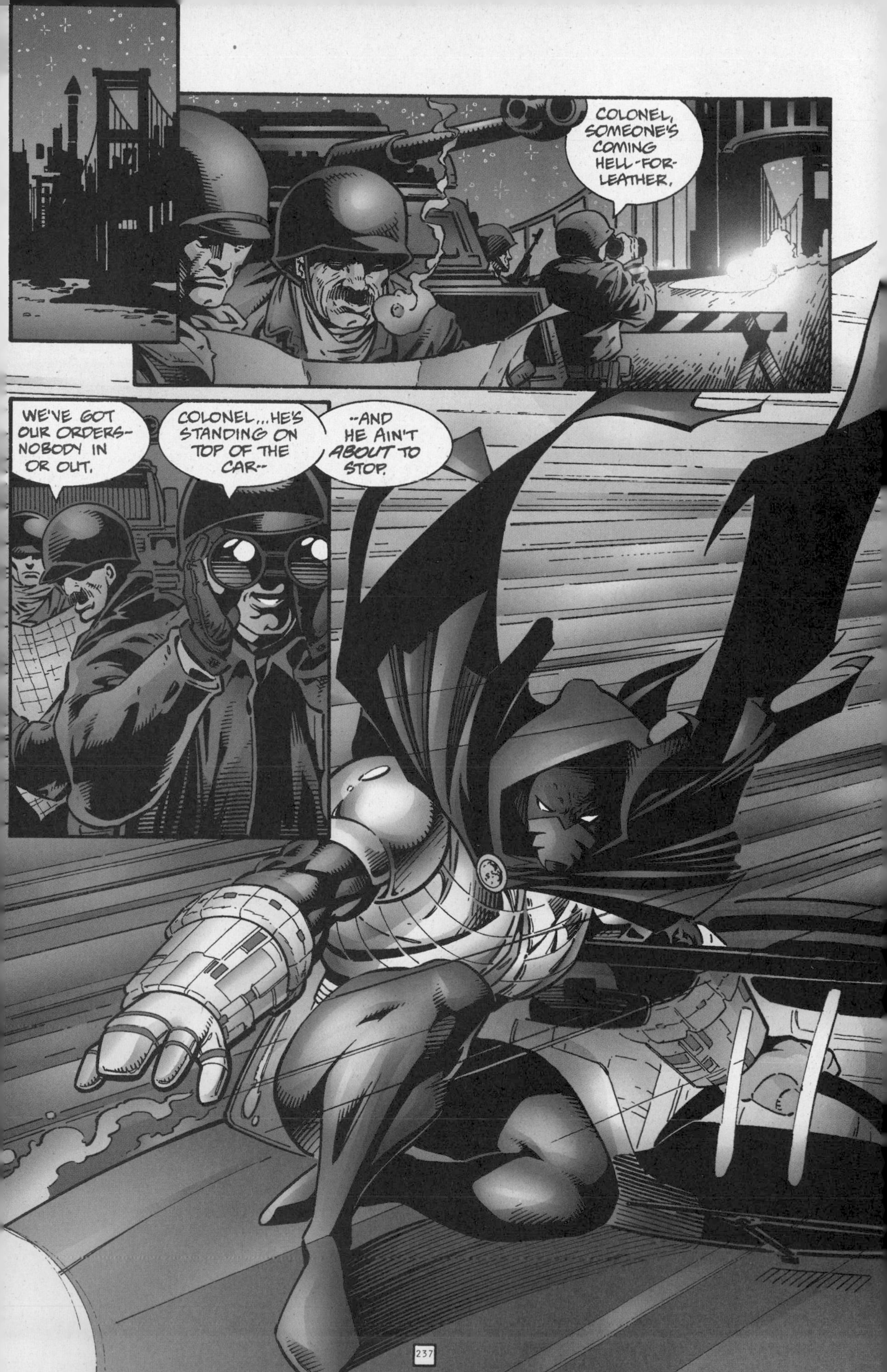
COLONEL, SOMEONE'S COMING HELL-FOR-LEATHER.
WE'VE GOT OUR ORDERS-- NOBODY IN OR OUT.
COLONEL...HE'S STANDING ON TOP OF THE CAR--
--AND HE AIN'T ABOUT TO STOP.

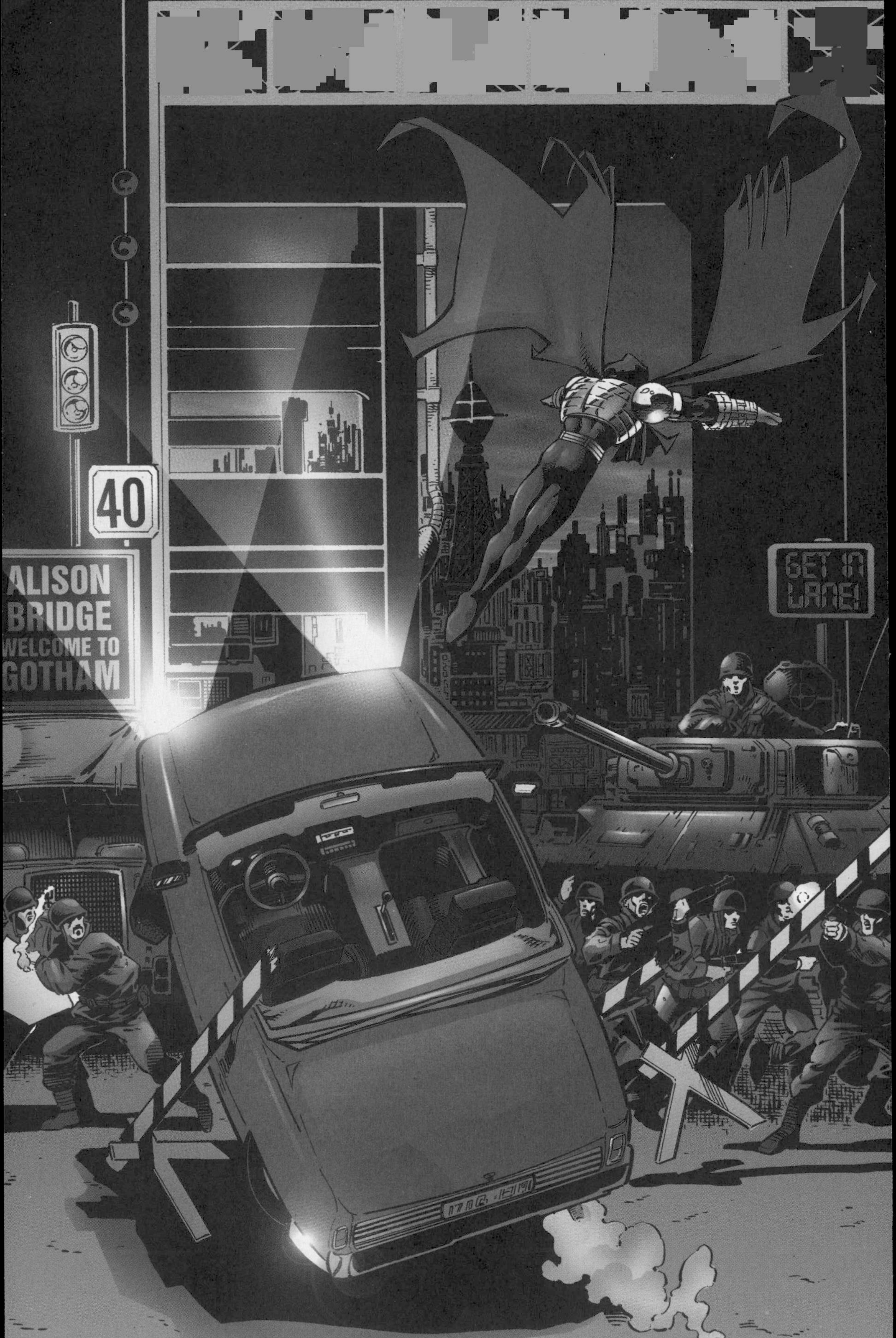
ALISON
BRIDGE
WELCOME TO
GOTHAM
40
GET IN
LANE!

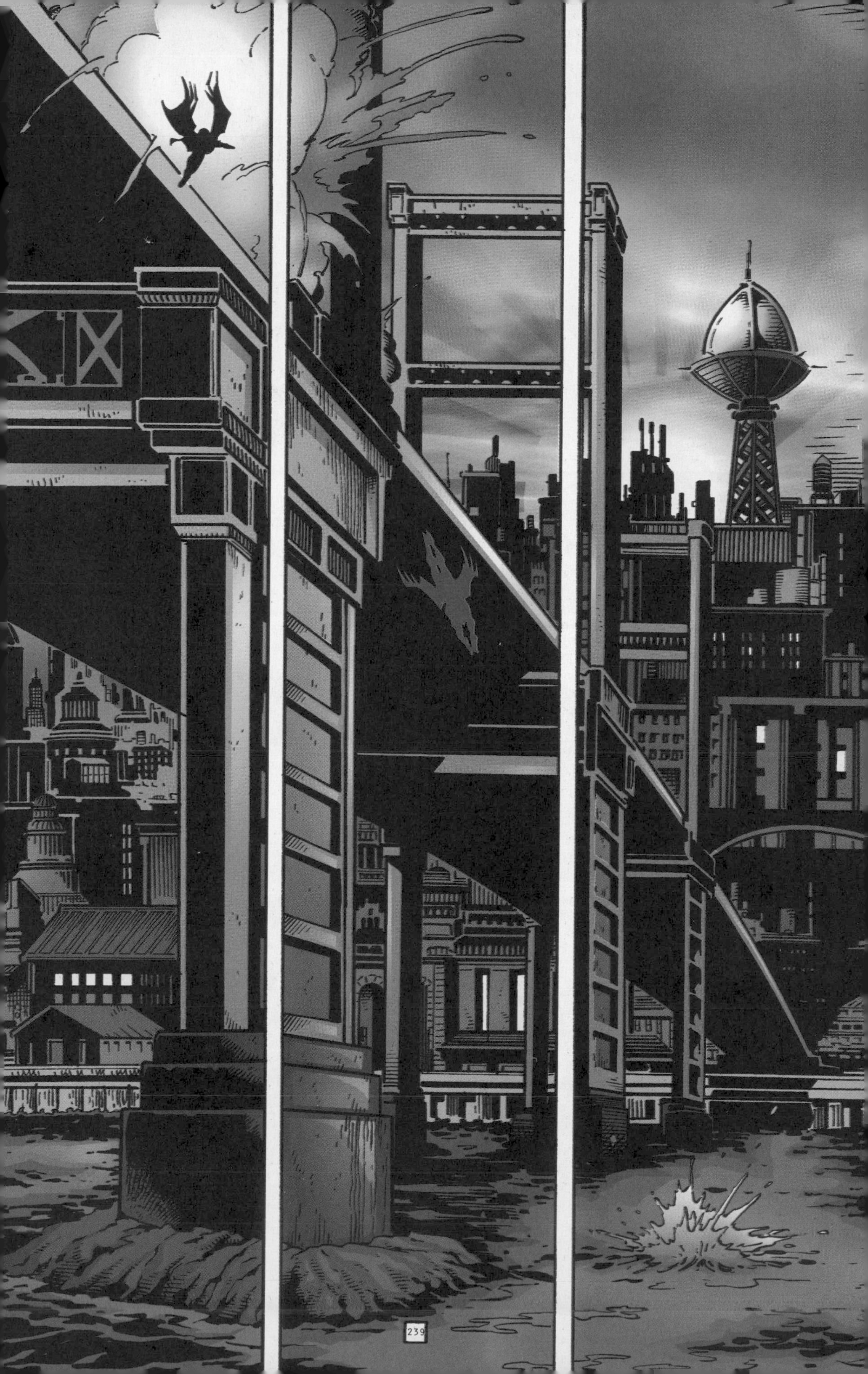

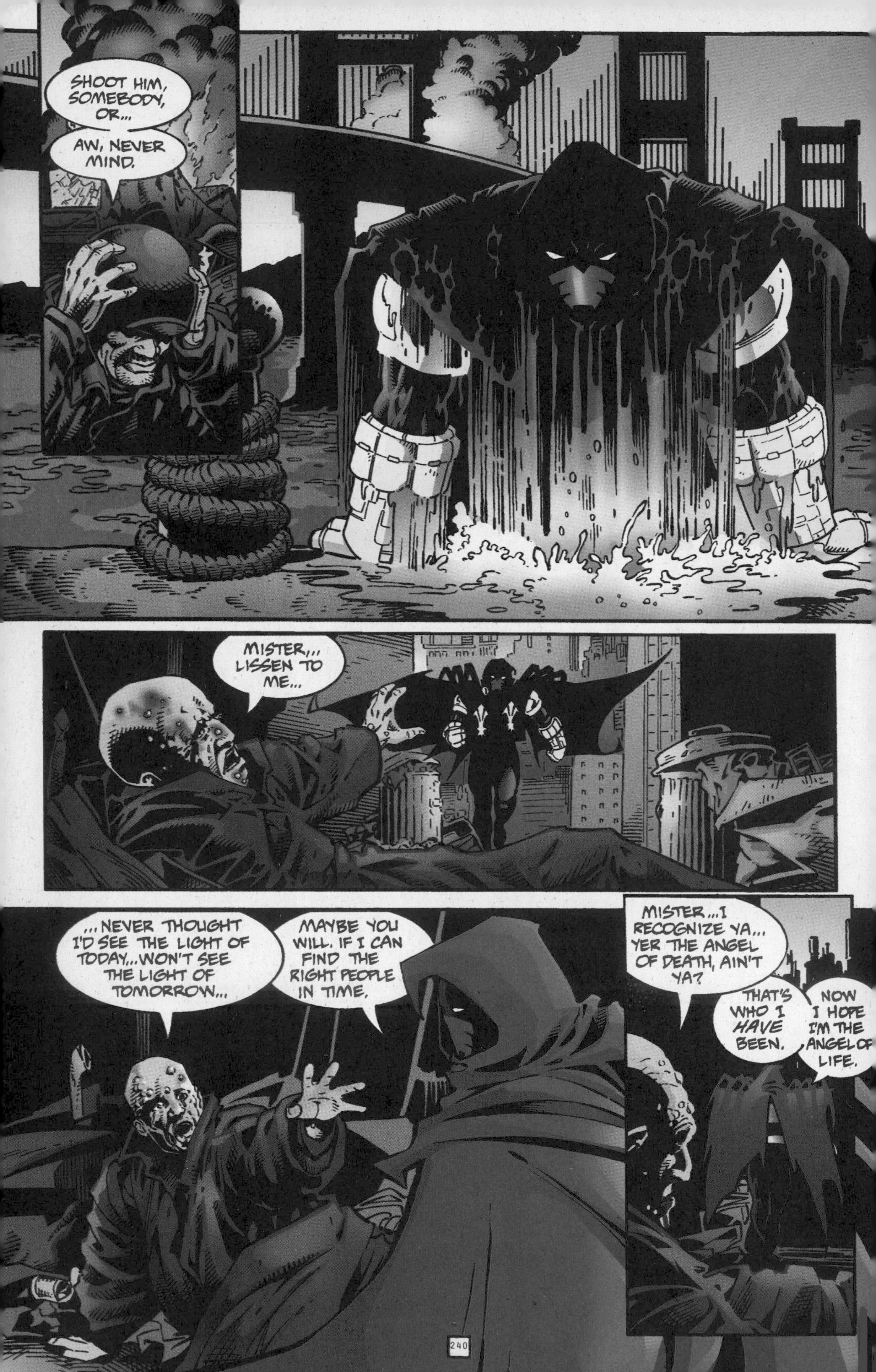
SHOOT HIM, SOMEBODY, OR...
AW, NEVER MIND.
MISTER,,, LISSEN TO ME...
...NEVER THOUGHT I'D SEE THE LIGHT OF TODAY,...WON'T SEE THE LIGHT OF TOMORROW...
MAYBE YOU WILL. IF I CAN FIND THE RIGHT PEOPLE IN TIME.
MISTER...I RECOGNIZE YA... YER THE ANGEL OF DEATH, AIN'T YA?
THAT'S WHO I *HAVE* BEEN.
NOW I HOPE I'M THE ANGEL OF LIFE.

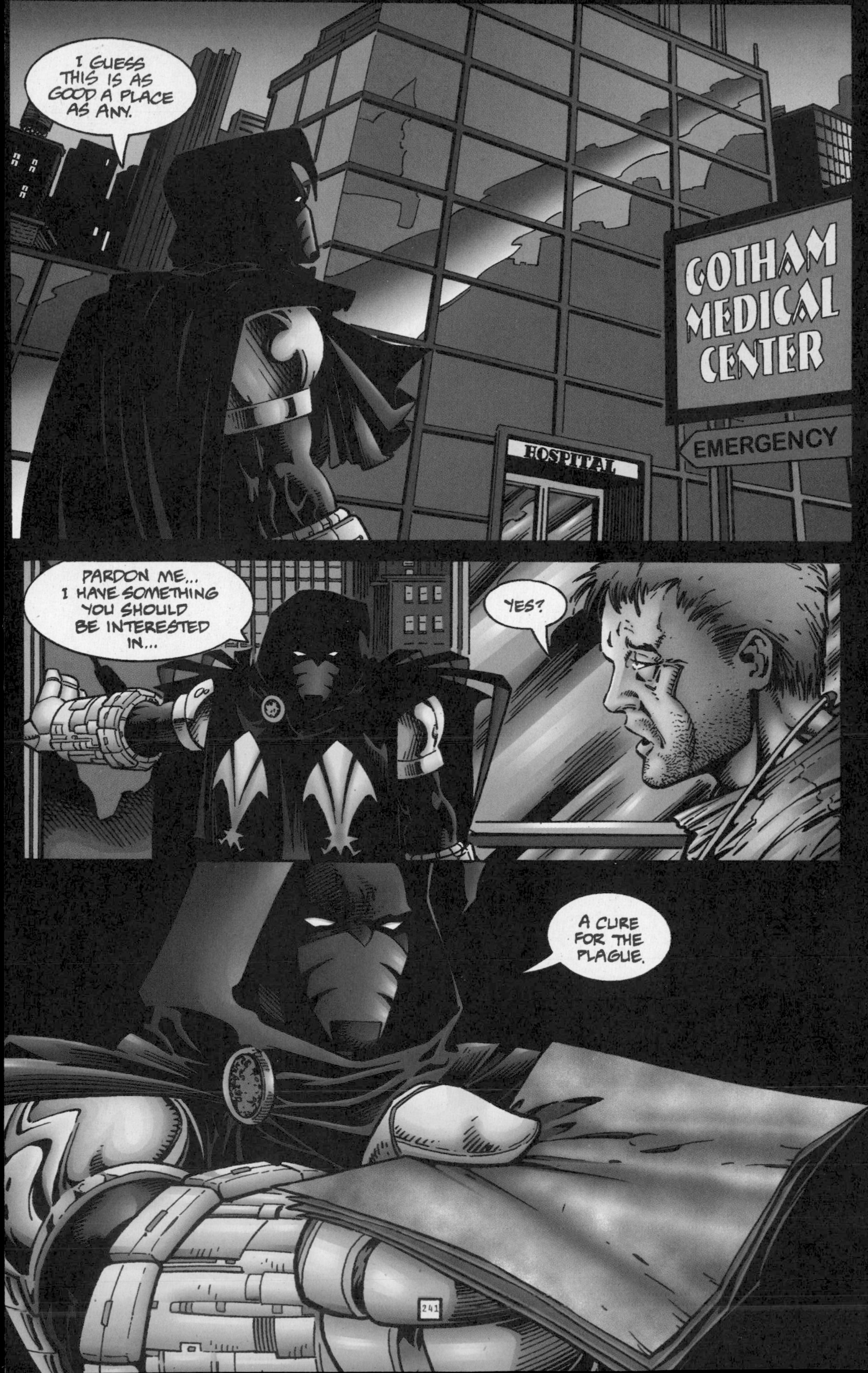
I GUESS THIS IS AS GOOD A PLACE AS ANY.
GOTHAM MEDICAL CENTER
EMERGENCY
HOSPITAL
PARDON ME... I HAVE SOMETHING YOU SHOULD BE INTERESTED IN...
YES?
A CURE FOR THE PLAGUE.

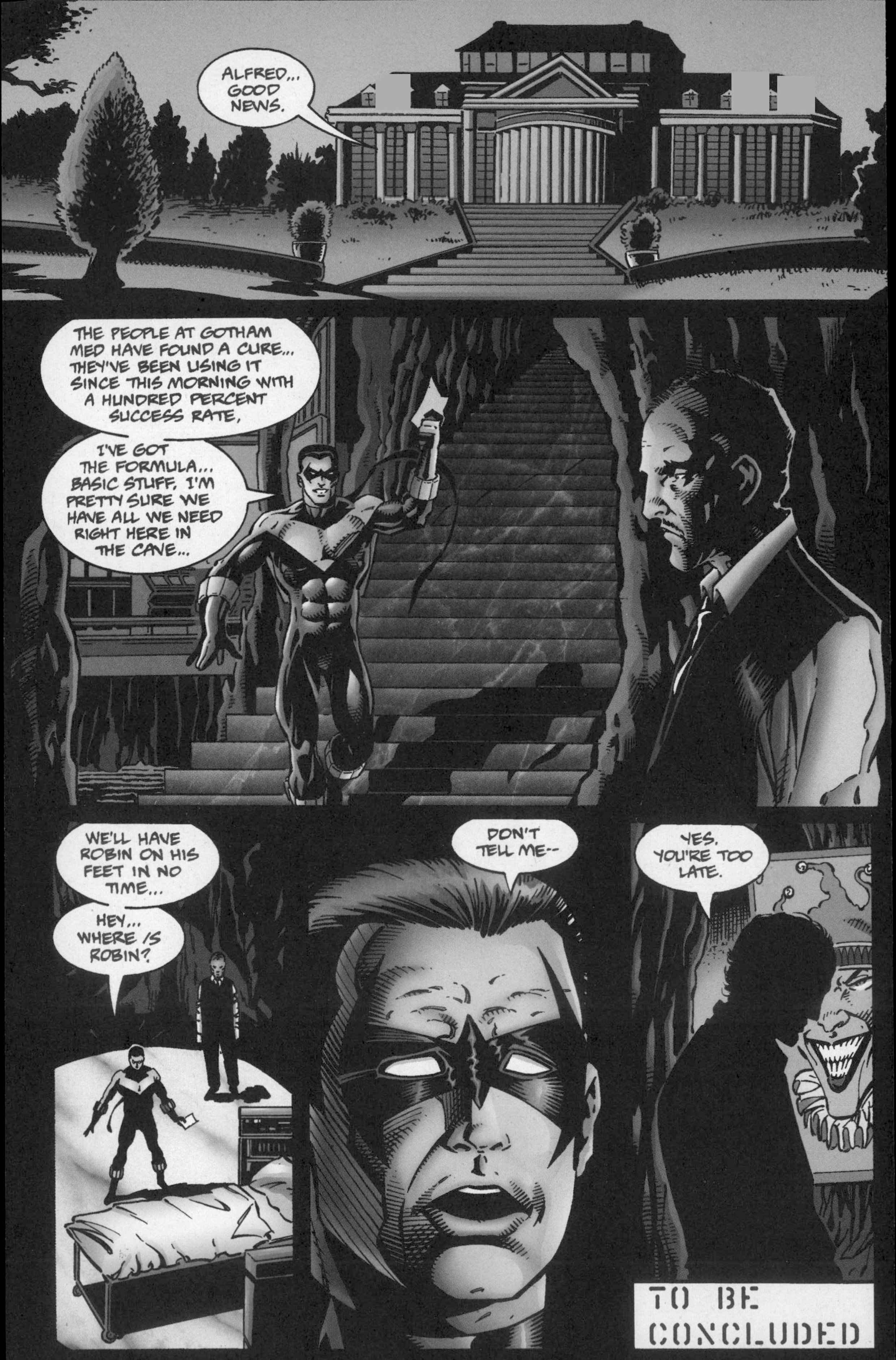
ALFRED... GOOD NEWS.
THE PEOPLE AT GOTHAM MED HAVE FOUND A CURE... THEY'VE BEEN USING IT SINCE THIS MORNING WITH A HUNDRED PERCENT SUCCESS RATE.
I'VE GOT THE FORMULA... BASIC STUFF. I'M PRETTY SURE WE HAVE ALL WE NEED RIGHT HERE IN THE CAVE...
WE'LL HAVE ROBIN ON HIS FEET IN NO TIME...
HEY... WHERE IS ROBIN?
DON'T TELL ME--
YES. YOU'RE TOO LATE.
TO BE CONCLUDED

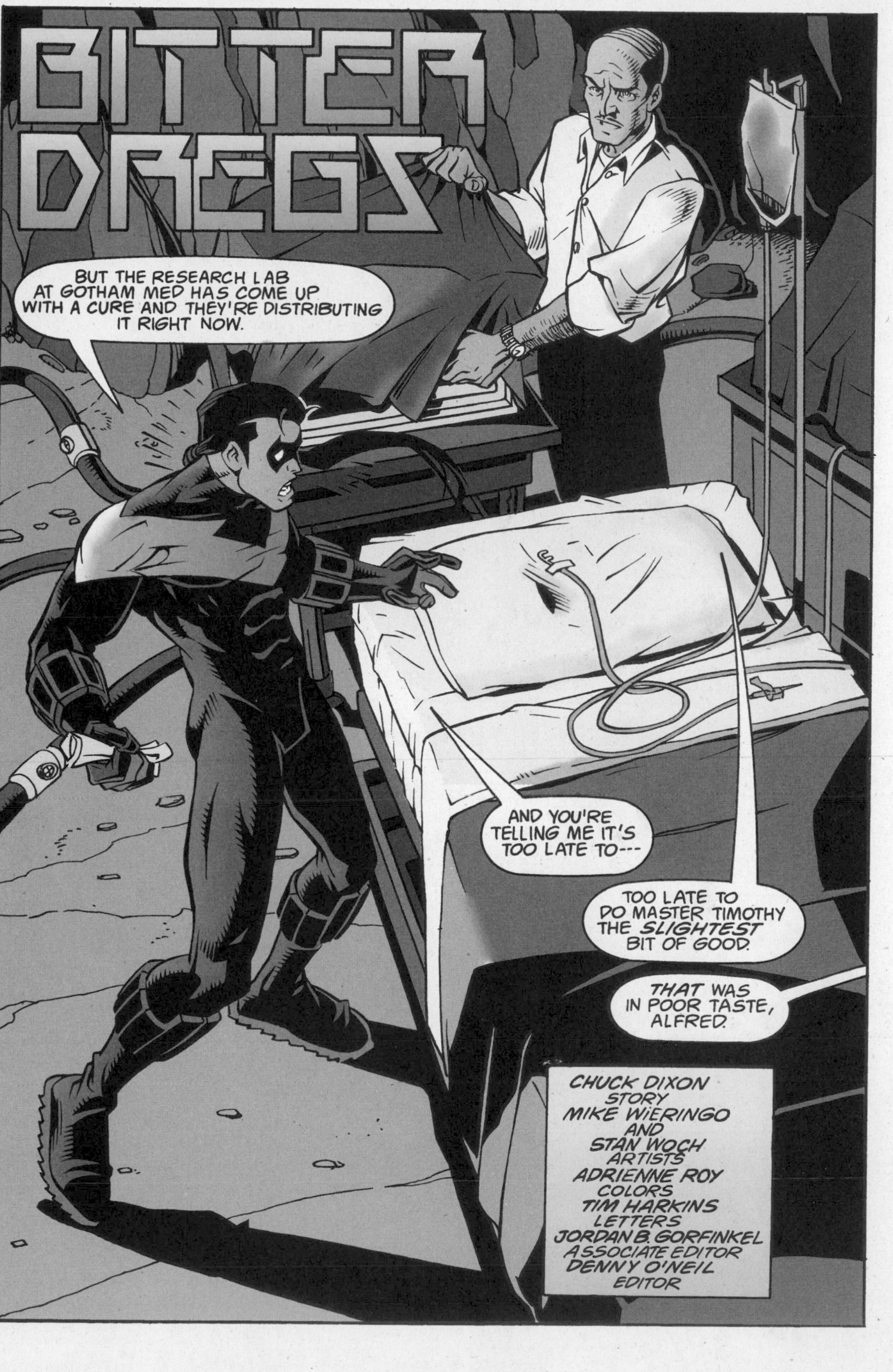
BITTER DREGS
BUT THE RESEARCH LAB AT GOTHAM MED HAS COME UP WITH A CURE AND THEY'RE DISTRIBUTING IT RIGHT NOW.
AND YOU'RE TELLING ME IT'S TOO LATE TO---
TOO LATE TO DO MASTER TIMOTHY THE *SLIGHTEST* BIT OF GOOD.
THAT WAS IN POOR TASTE, ALFRED.
CHUCK DIXON STORY
MIKE WIERINGO AND STAN WOCH ARTISTS
ADRIENNE ROY COLORS
TIM HARKINS LETTERS
JORDAN B. GORFINKEL ASSOCIATE EDITOR
DENNY O'NEIL EDITOR

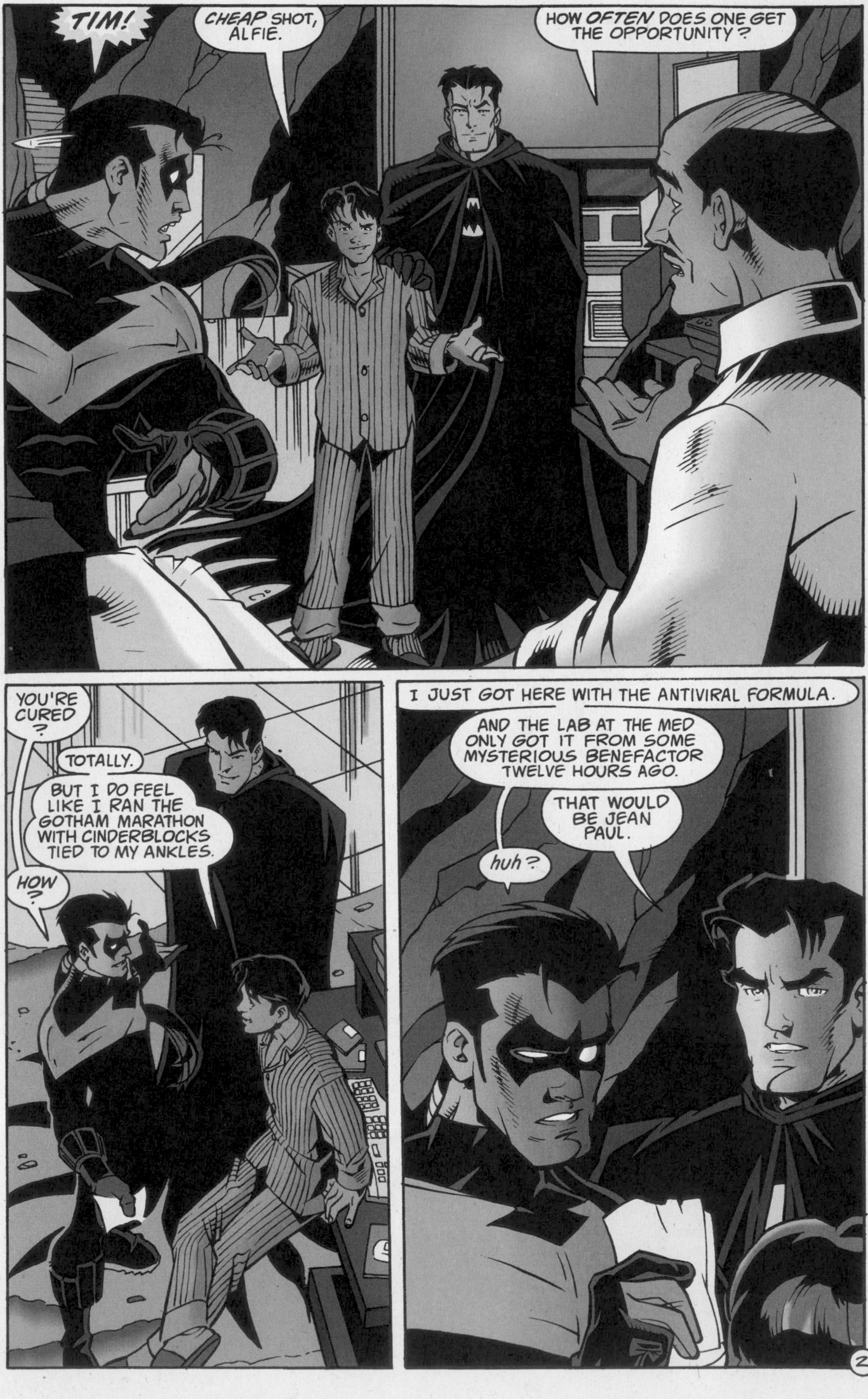
TIM!
CHEAP SHOT, ALFIE.
HOW OFTEN DOES ONE GET THE OPPORTUNITY?
YOU'RE CURED?
TOTALLY.
BUT I DO FEEL LIKE I RAN THE GOTHAM MARATHON WITH CINDERBLOCKS TIED TO MY ANKLES.
HOW?
I JUST GOT HERE WITH THE ANTIVIRAL FORMULA.
AND THE LAB AT THE MED ONLY GOT IT FROM SOME MYSTERIOUS BENEFACTOR TWELVE HOURS AGO.
THAT WOULD BE JEAN PAUL.
huh?
2

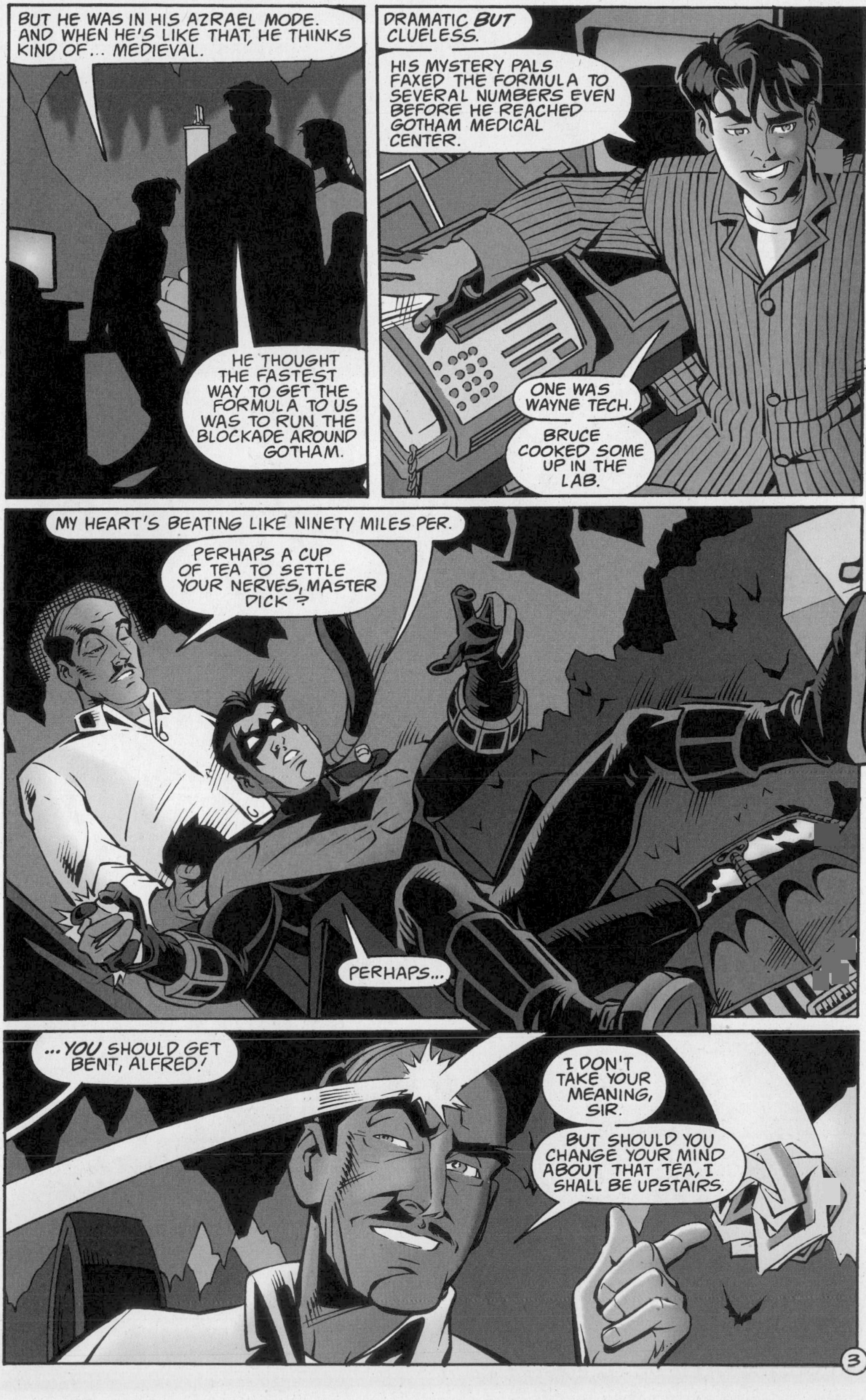
BUT HE WAS IN HIS AZRAEL MODE. AND WHEN HE'S LIKE THAT, HE THINKS KIND OF... MEDIEVAL.
HE THOUGHT THE FASTEST WAY TO GET THE FORMULA TO US WAS TO RUN THE BLOCKADE AROUND GOTHAM.
DRAMATIC *BUT* CLUELESS.
HIS MYSTERY PALS FAXED THE FORMULA TO SEVERAL NUMBERS EVEN BEFORE HE REACHED GOTHAM MEDICAL CENTER.
ONE WAS WAYNE TECH.
BRUCE COOKED SOME UP IN THE LAB.
MY HEART'S BEATING LIKE NINETY MILES PER.
PERHAPS A CUP OF TEA TO SETTLE YOUR NERVES, MASTER DICK?
PERHAPS...
...*YOU* SHOULD GET BENT, ALFRED!
I DON'T TAKE YOUR MEANING, SIR.
BUT SHOULD YOU CHANGE YOUR MIND ABOUT THAT TEA, I SHALL BE UPSTAIRS.
3

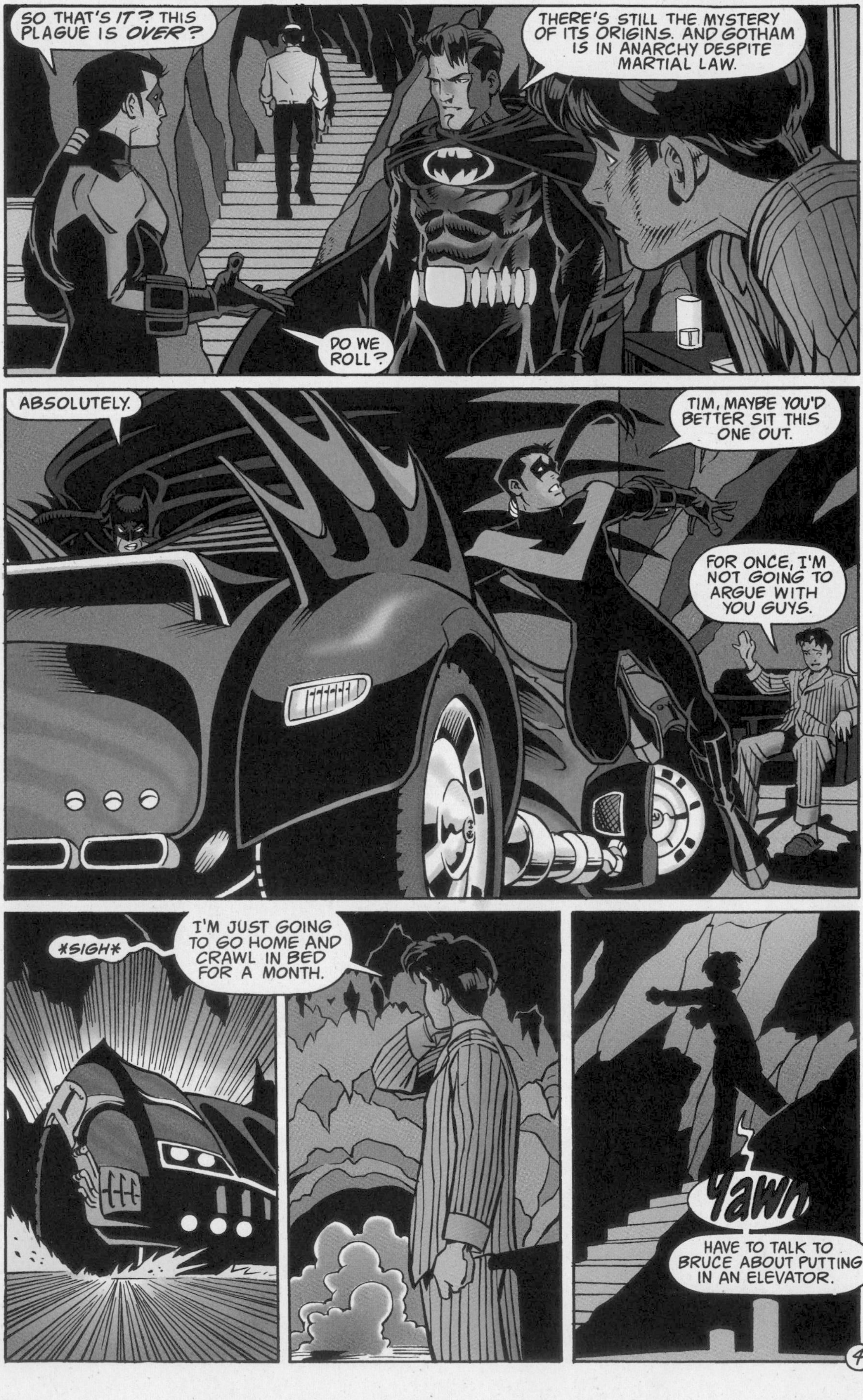
SO THAT'S IT? THIS PLAGUE IS OVER?
THERE'S STILL THE MYSTERY OF ITS ORIGINS. AND GOTHAM IS IN ANARCHY DESPITE MARTIAL LAW.
DO WE ROLL?
ABSOLUTELY.
TIM, MAYBE YOU'D BETTER SIT THIS ONE OUT.
FOR ONCE, I'M NOT GOING TO ARGUE WITH YOU GUYS.
SIGH
I'M JUST GOING TO GO HOME AND CRAWL IN BED FOR A MONTH.
YAWN
HAVE TO TALK TO BRUCE ABOUT PUTTING IN AN ELEVATOR.
4

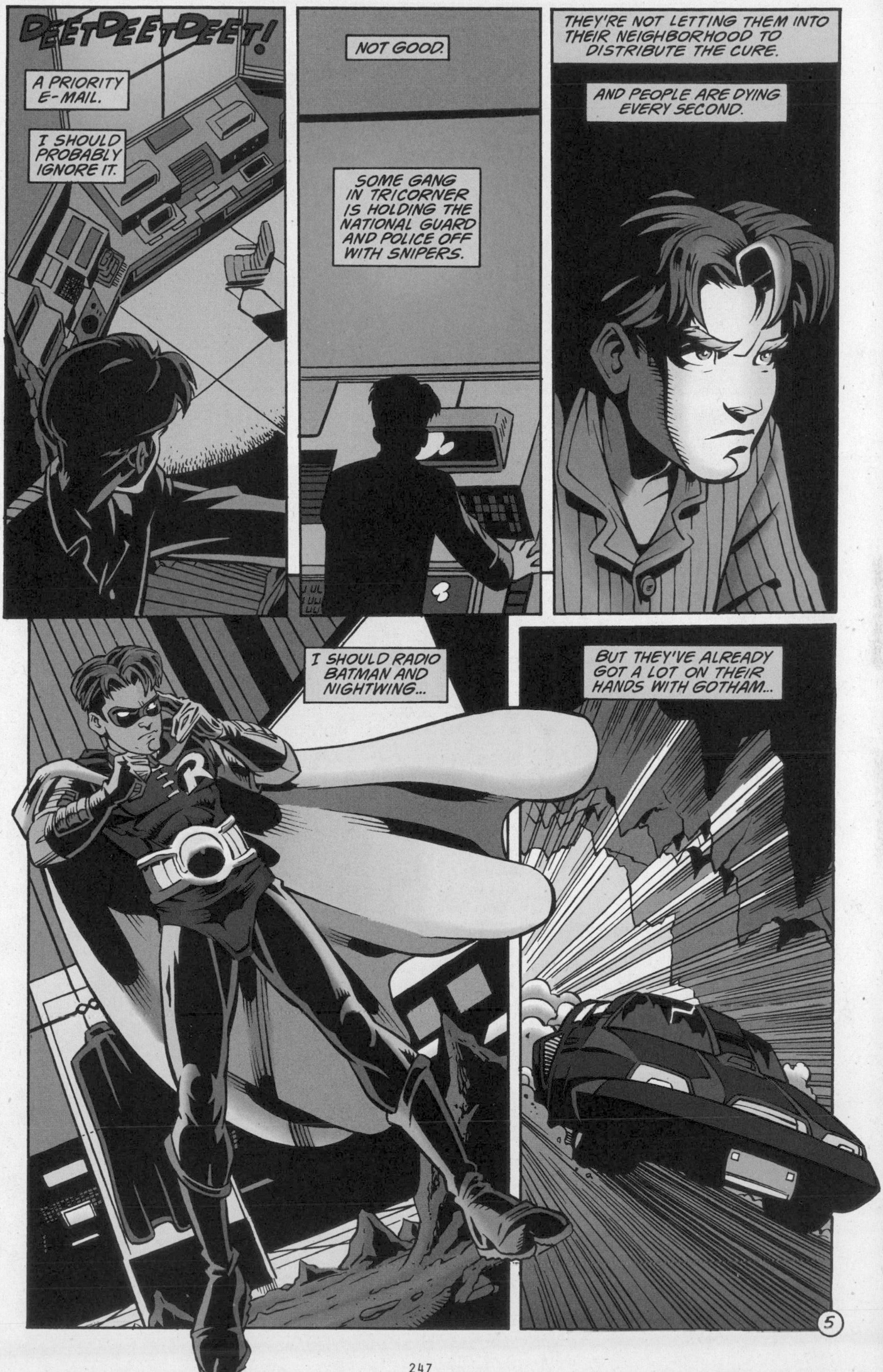
DEETDEETDEET!
A PRIORITY E-MAIL.
I SHOULD PROBABLY IGNORE IT.
NOT GOOD.
SOME GANG IN TRICORNER IS HOLDING THE NATIONAL GUARD AND POLICE OFF WITH SNIPERS.
THEY'RE NOT LETTING THEM INTO THEIR NEIGHBORHOOD TO DISTRIBUTE THE CURE.
AND PEOPLE ARE DYING EVERY SECOND.
I SHOULD RADIO BATMAN AND NIGHTWING...
BUT THEY'VE ALREADY GOT A LOT ON THEIR HANDS WITH GOTHAM...
5

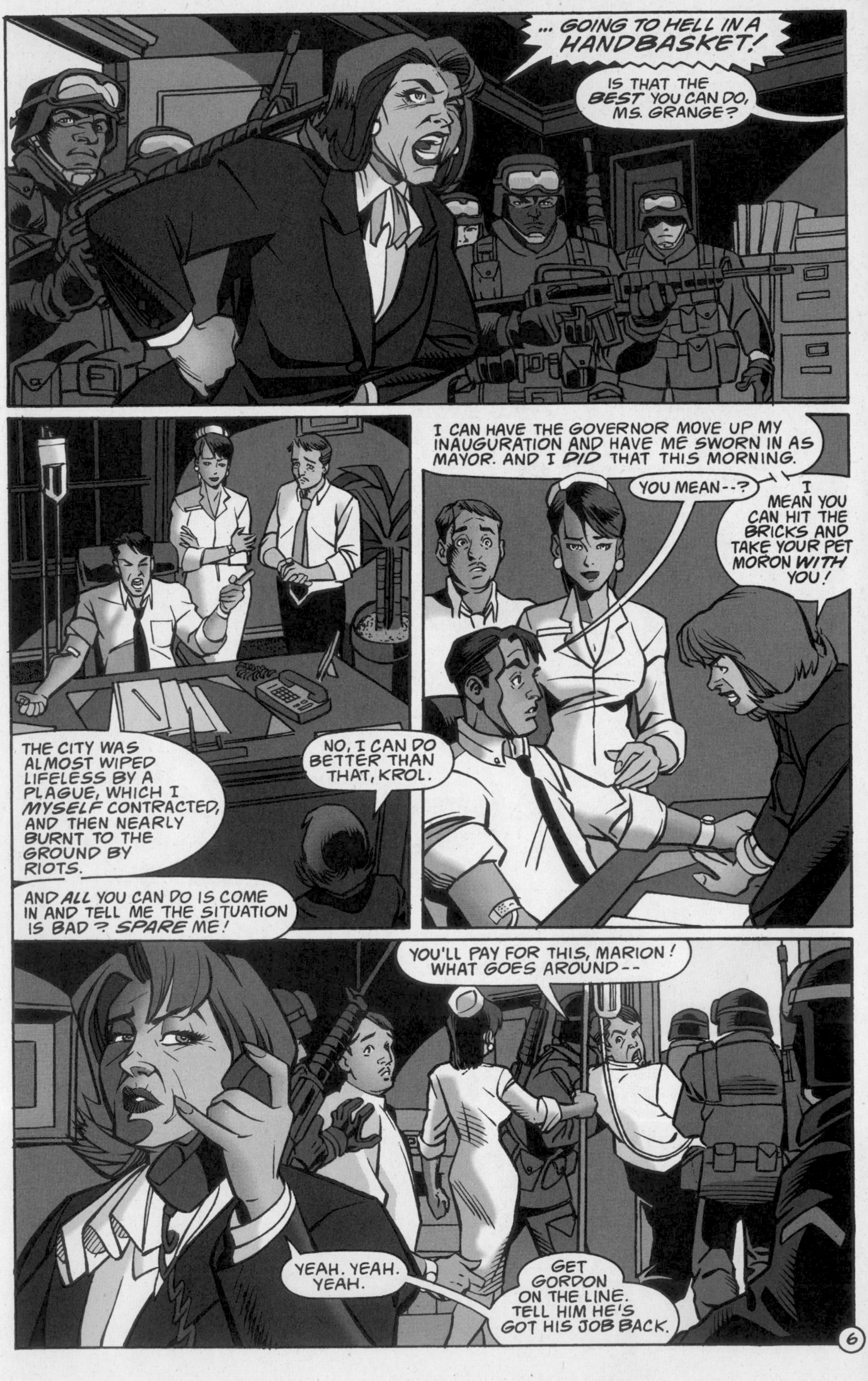
... GOING TO HELL IN A HANDBASKET!
IS THAT THE BEST YOU CAN DO, MS. GRANGE?
THE CITY WAS ALMOST WIPED LIFELESS BY A PLAGUE, WHICH I MYSELF CONTRACTED, AND THEN NEARLY BURNT TO THE GROUND BY RIOTS.
AND ALL YOU CAN DO IS COME IN AND TELL ME THE SITUATION IS BAD? SPARE ME!
NO, I CAN DO BETTER THAN THAT, KROL.
I CAN HAVE THE GOVERNOR MOVE UP MY INAUGURATION AND HAVE ME SWORN IN AS MAYOR. AND I DID THAT THIS MORNING.
YOU MEAN--?
I MEAN YOU CAN HIT THE BRICKS AND TAKE YOUR PET MORON WITH YOU!
YOU'LL PAY FOR THIS, MARION! WHAT GOES AROUND--
YEAH. YEAH. YEAH.
GET GORDON ON THE LINE. TELL HIM HE'S GOT HIS JOB BACK.
6

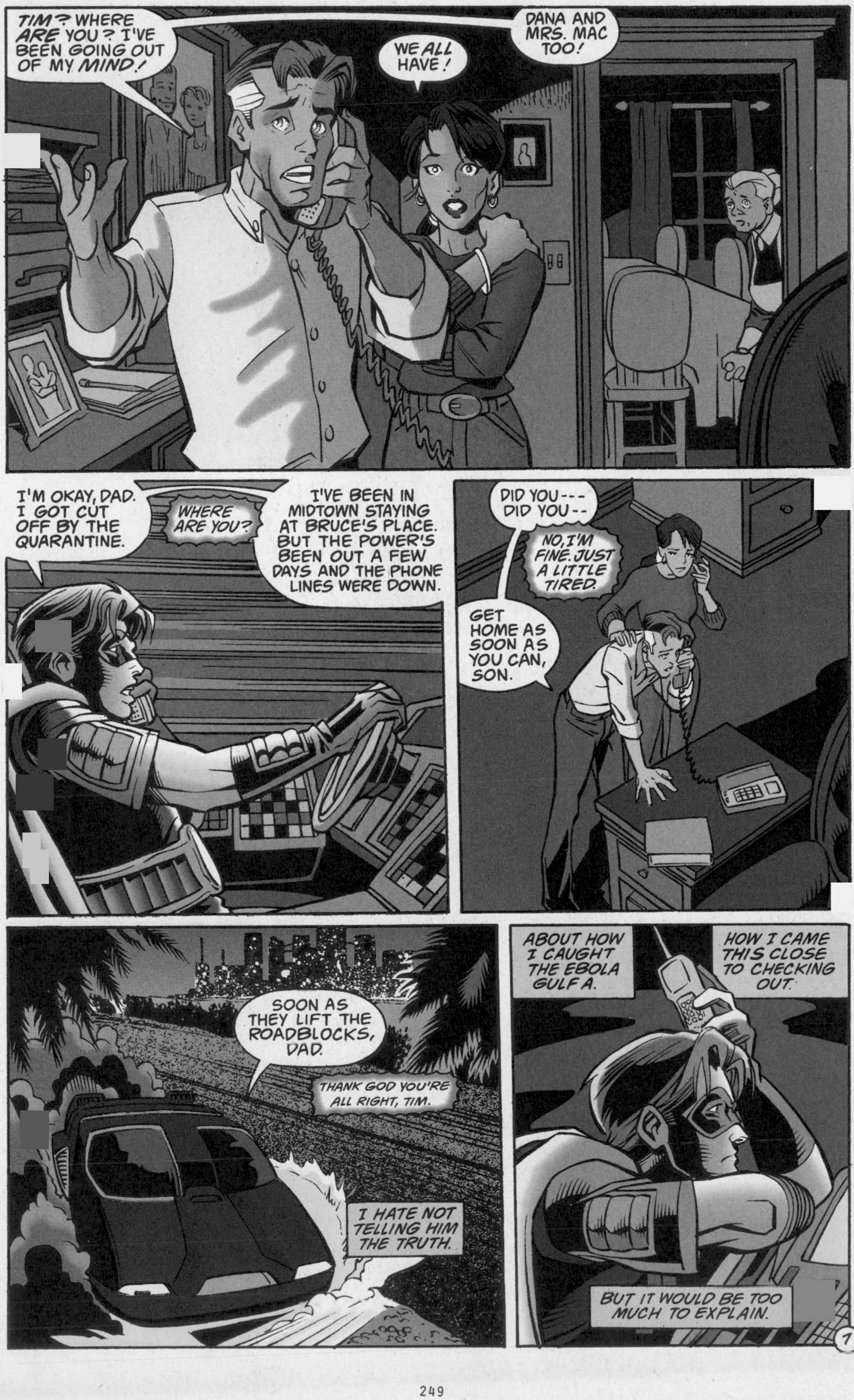
TIM? WHERE ARE YOU? I'VE BEEN GOING OUT OF MY MIND!
WE ALL HAVE!
DANA AND MRS. MAC TOO!
I'M OKAY, DAD. I GOT CUT OFF BY THE QUARANTINE.
WHERE ARE YOU?
I'VE BEEN IN MIDTOWN STAYING AT BRUCE'S PLACE. BUT THE POWER'S BEEN OUT A FEW DAYS AND THE PHONE LINES WERE DOWN.
DID YOU--- DID YOU--
NO, I'M FINE. JUST A LITTLE TIRED.
GET HOME AS SOON AS YOU CAN, SON.
SOON AS THEY LIFT THE ROADBLOCKS, DAD.
THANK GOD YOU'RE ALL RIGHT, TIM.
I HATE NOT TELLING HIM THE TRUTH.
ABOUT HOW I CAUGHT THE EBOLA GULF A.
HOW I CAME THIS CLOSE TO CHECKING OUT.
BUT IT WOULD BE TOO MUCH TO EXPLAIN.
7

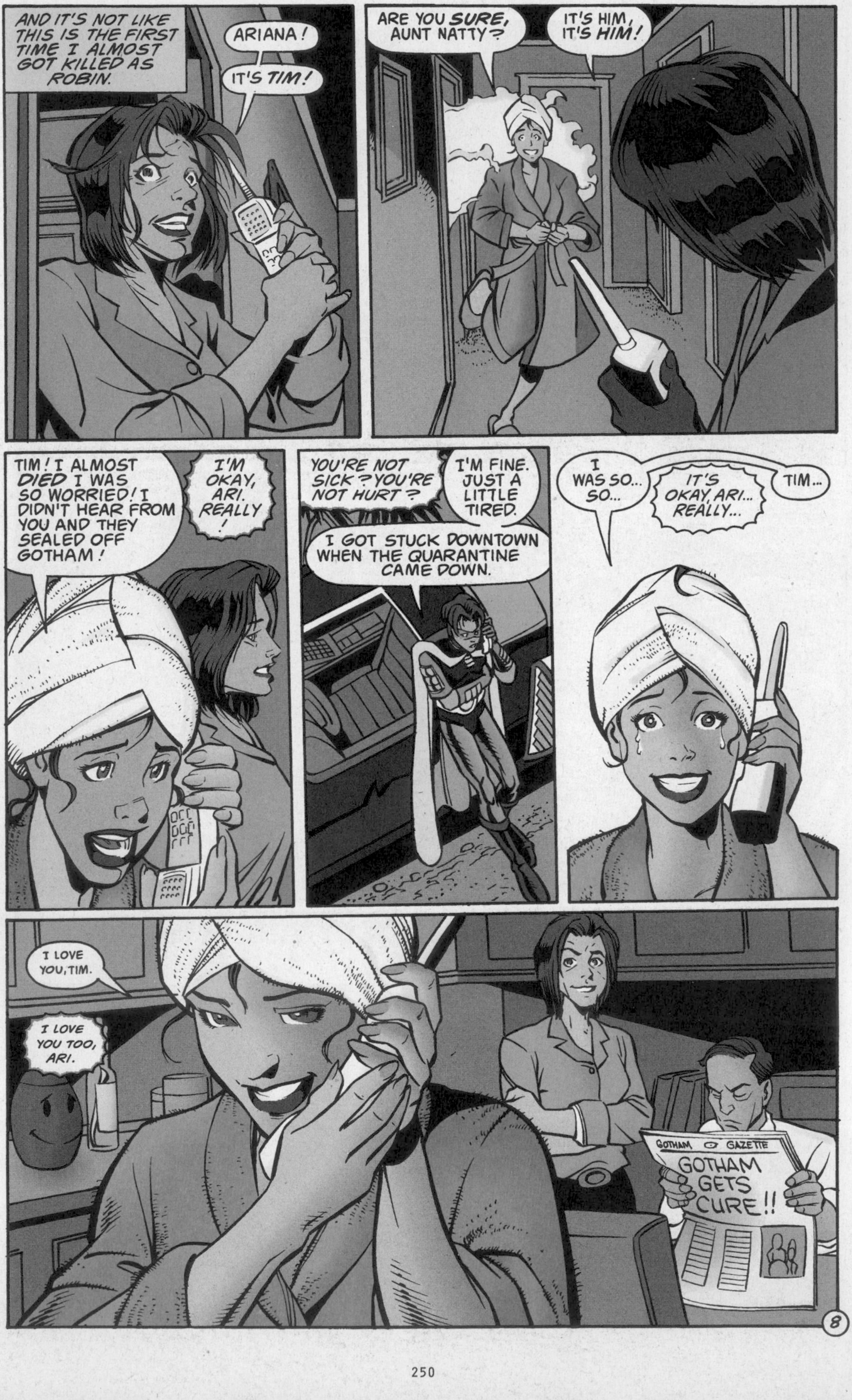
AND IT'S NOT LIKE THIS IS THE FIRST TIME I ALMOST GOT KILLED AS ROBIN.
ARIANA!
IT'S TIM!
ARE YOU SURE, AUNT NATTY?
IT'S HIM, IT'S HIM!
TIM! I ALMOST DIED I WAS SO WORRIED! I DIDN'T HEAR FROM YOU AND THEY SEALED OFF GOTHAM!
I'M OKAY, ARI. REALLY!
YOU'RE NOT SICK? YOU'RE NOT HURT?
I'M FINE. JUST A LITTLE TIRED.
I GOT STUCK DOWNTOWN WHEN THE QUARANTINE CAME DOWN.
I WAS SO... SO...
IT'S OKAY, ARI... REALLY...
TIM...
I LOVE YOU, TIM.
I LOVE YOU TOO, ARI.
GOTHAM GAZETTE
GOTHAM GETS CURE!!
8

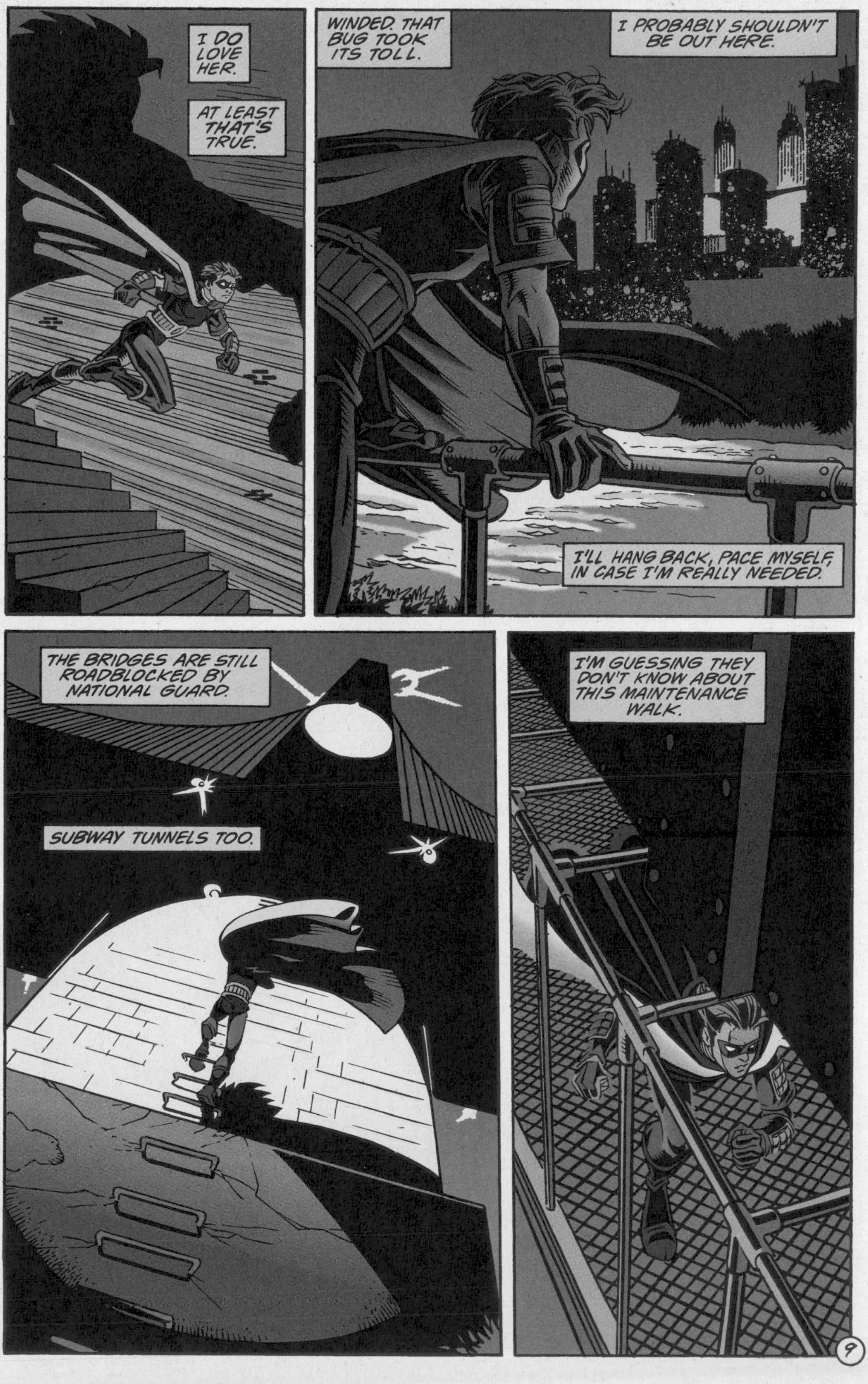

I DO LOVE HER.
AT LEAST THAT'S TRUE.
WINDED. THAT BUG TOOK ITS TOLL.
I PROBABLY SHOULDN'T BE OUT HERE.
I'LL HANG BACK, PACE MYSELF, IN CASE I'M REALLY NEEDED.
THE BRIDGES ARE STILL ROADBLOCKED BY NATIONAL GUARD.
SUBWAY TUNNELS TOO.
I'M GUESSING THEY DON'T KNOW ABOUT THIS MAINTENANCE WALK.
9

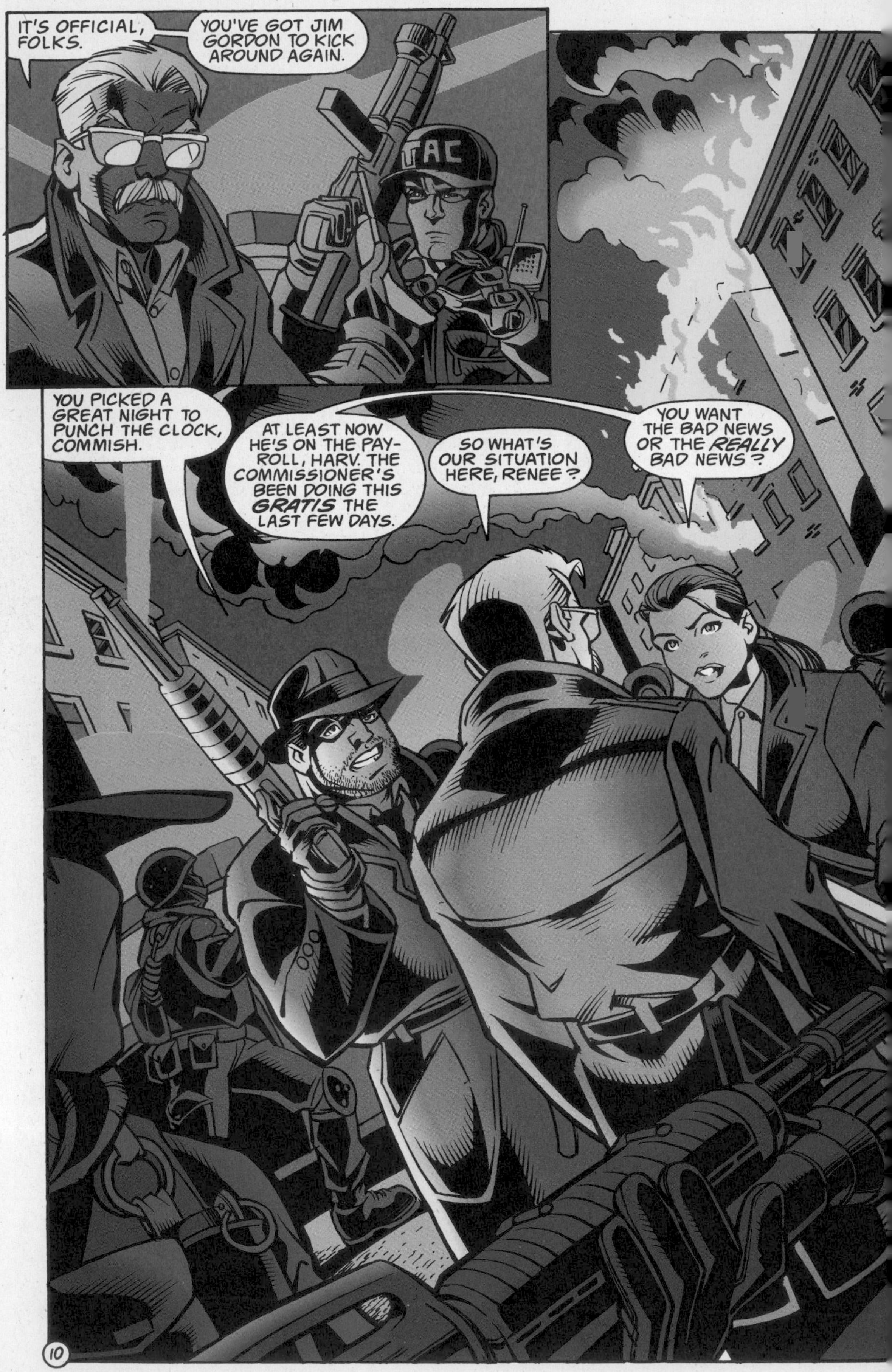
IT'S OFFICIAL, FOLKS.
YOU'VE GOT JIM GORDON TO KICK AROUND AGAIN.
TAC
YOU PICKED A GREAT NIGHT TO PUNCH THE CLOCK, COMMISH.
AT LEAST NOW HE'S ON THE PAYROLL, HARV. THE COMMISSIONER'S BEEN DOING THIS *GRATIS* THE LAST FEW DAYS.
SO WHAT'S OUR SITUATION HERE, RENEE?
YOU WANT THE BAD NEWS OR THE *REALLY* BAD NEWS?
10

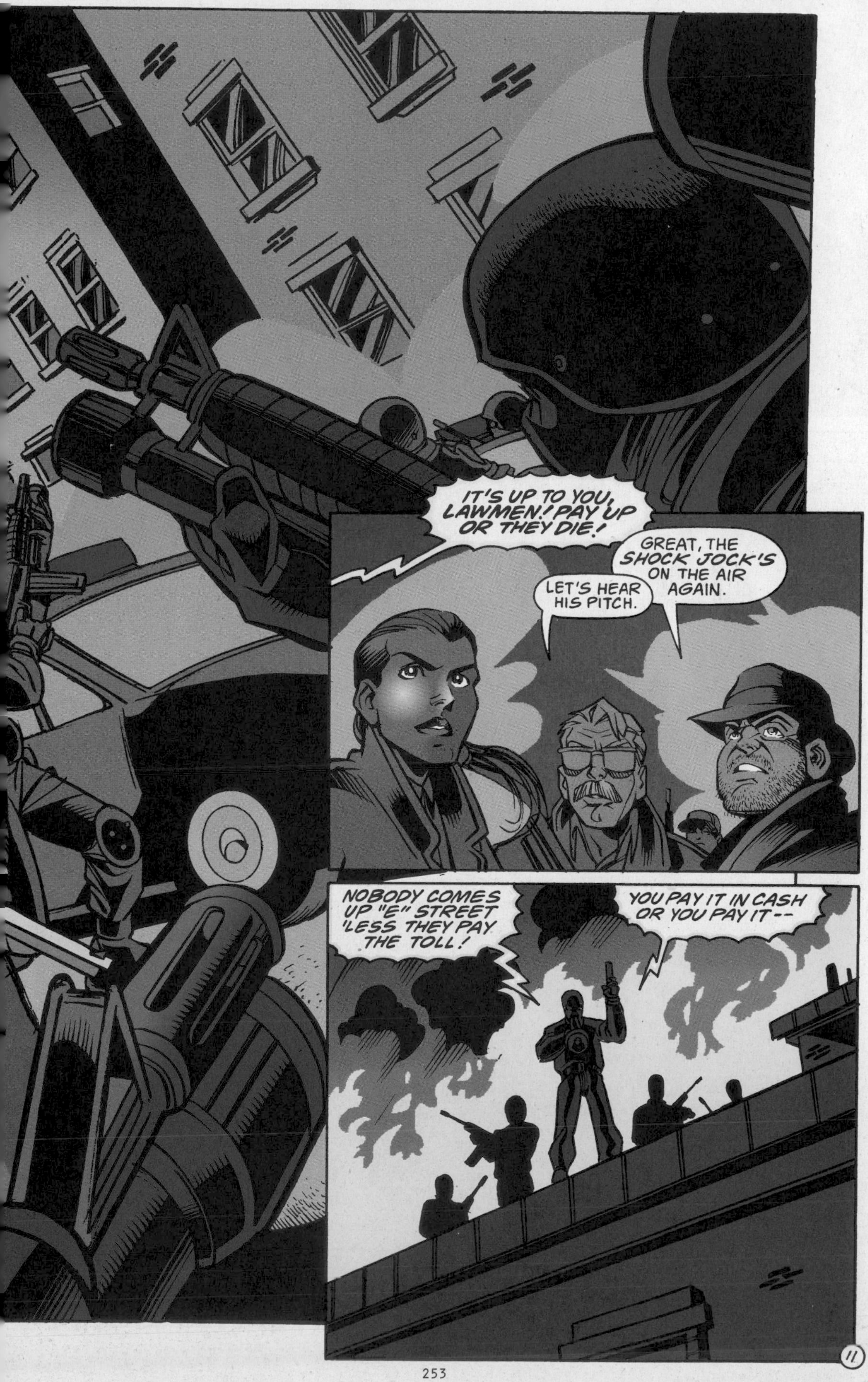
IT'S UP TO YOU, LAWMEN! PAY UP OR THEY DIE!
GREAT, THE SHOCK JOCK'S ON THE AIR AGAIN.
LET'S HEAR HIS PITCH.
NOBODY COMES UP "E" STREET 'LESS THEY PAY THE TOLL!
YOU PAY IT IN CASH OR YOU PAY IT--
11

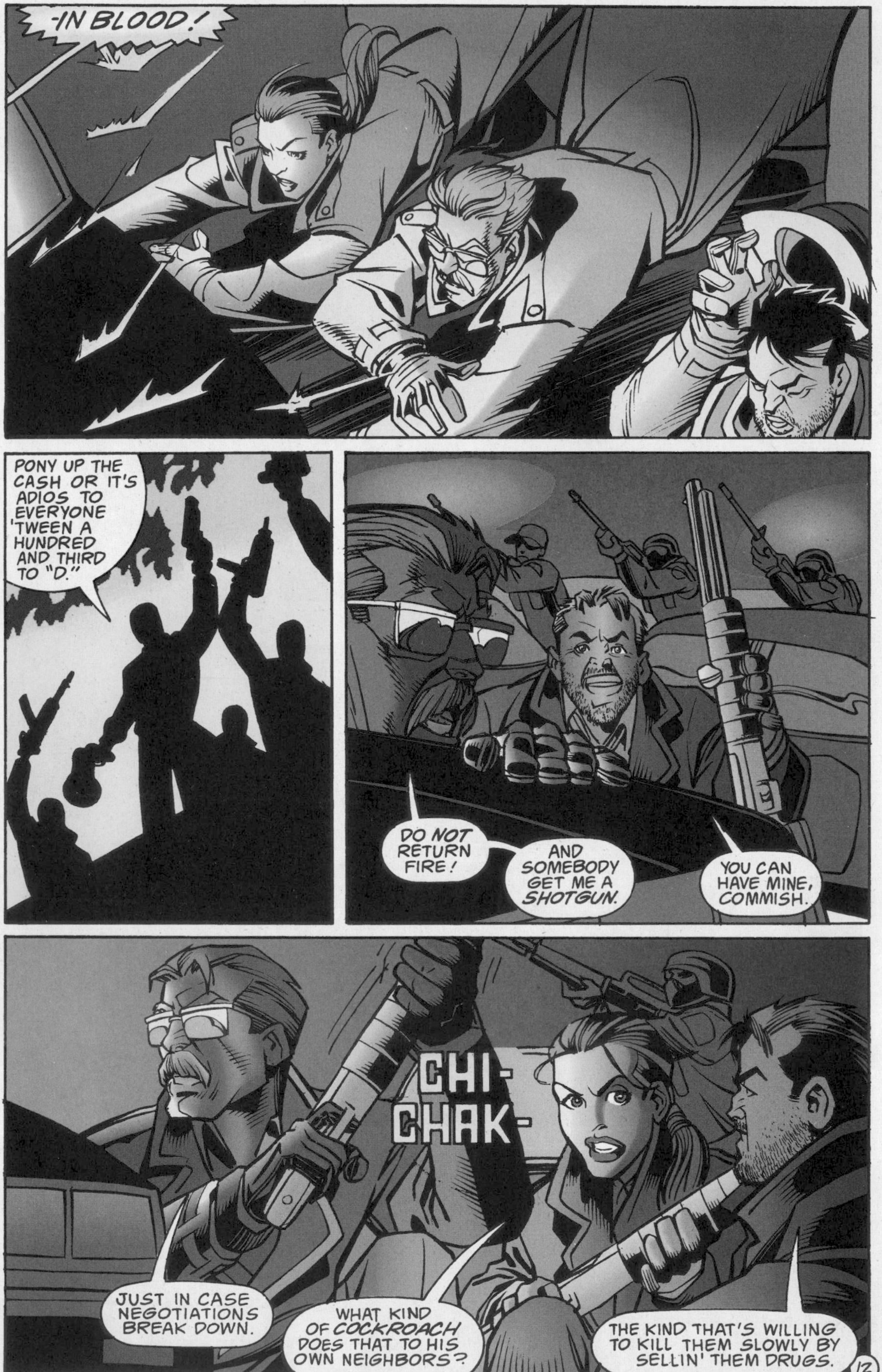
-IN BLOOD!
PONY UP THE CASH OR IT'S ADIOS TO EVERYONE 'TWEEN A HUNDRED AND THIRD TO "D."
DO NOT RETURN FIRE!
AND SOMEBODY GET ME A SHOTGUN.
YOU CAN HAVE MINE, COMMISH.
CHI-CHAK-
JUST IN CASE NEGOTIATIONS BREAK DOWN.
WHAT KIND OF COCKROACH DOES THAT TO HIS OWN NEIGHBORS?
THE KIND THAT'S WILLING TO KILL THEM SLOWLY BY SELLIN' THEM DRUGS.
12

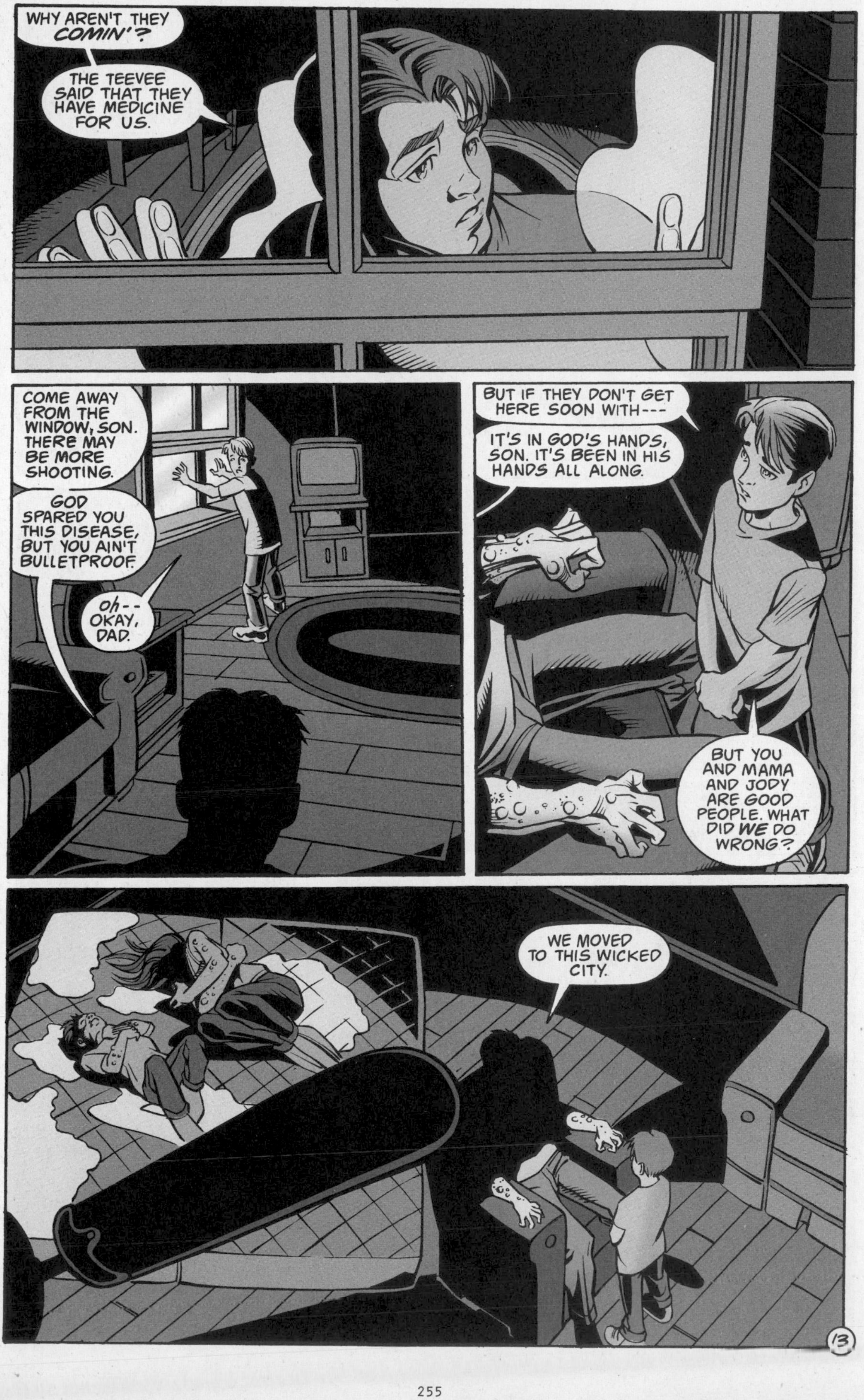
WHY AREN'T THEY COMIN'?
THE TEEVEE SAID THAT THEY HAVE MEDICINE FOR US.
COME AWAY FROM THE WINDOW, SON. THERE MAY BE MORE SHOOTING.
GOD SPARED YOU THIS DISEASE, BUT YOU AIN'T BULLETPROOF.
OH-- OKAY, DAD.
BUT IF THEY DON'T GET HERE SOON WITH---
IT'S IN GOD'S HANDS, SON. IT'S BEEN IN HIS HANDS ALL ALONG.
BUT YOU AND MAMA AND JODY ARE GOOD PEOPLE. WHAT DID WE DO WRONG?
WE MOVED TO THIS WICKED CITY.
13

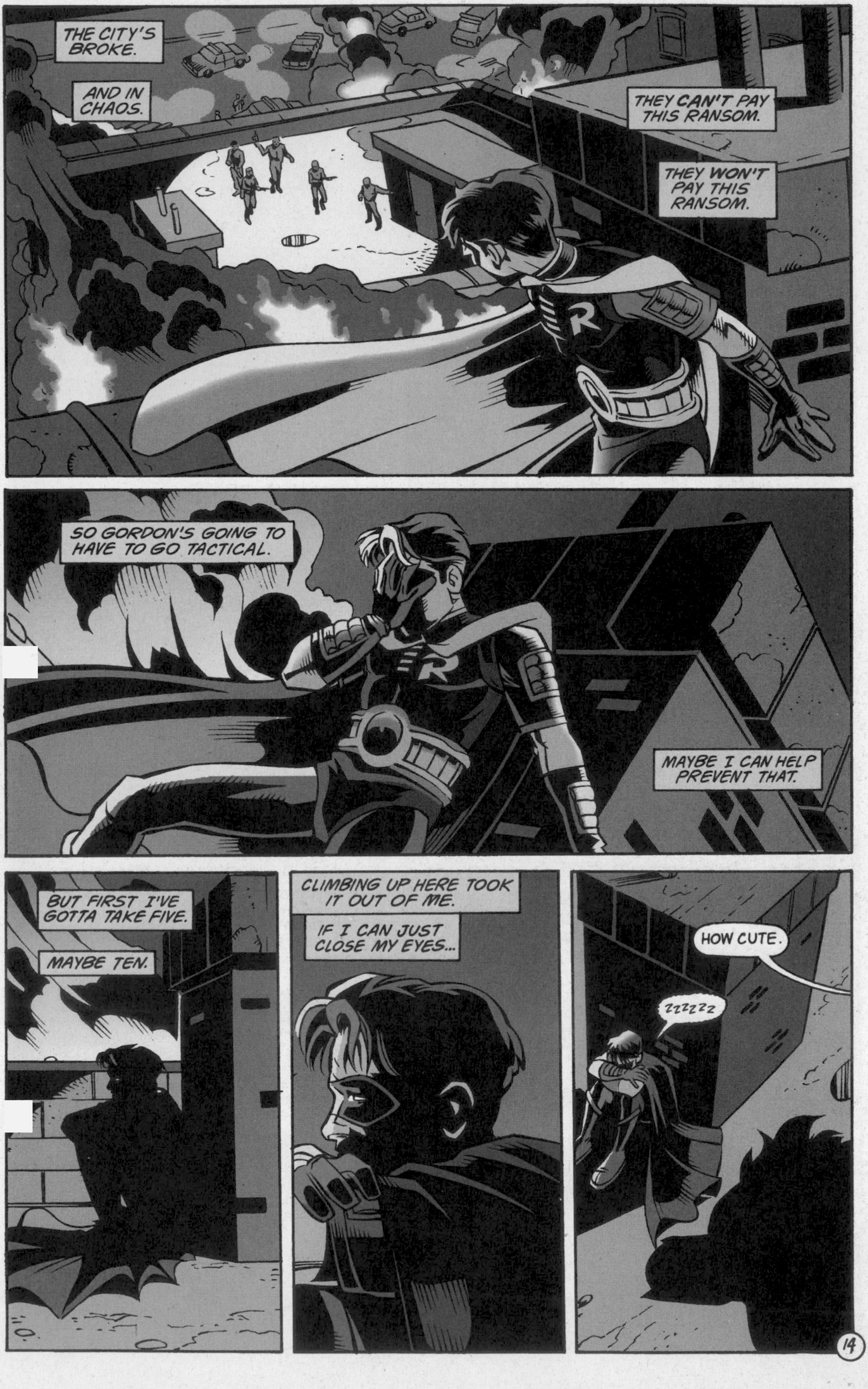
THE CITY'S BROKE.
AND IN CHAOS.
THEY CAN'T PAY THIS RANSOM.
THEY WON'T PAY THIS RANSOM.
SO GORDON'S GOING TO HAVE TO GO TACTICAL.
MAYBE I CAN HELP PREVENT THAT.
BUT FIRST I'VE GOTTA TAKE FIVE.
MAYBE TEN.
CLIMBING UP HERE TOOK IT OUT OF ME.
IF I CAN JUST CLOSE MY EYES...
HOW CUTE.
ZZZZZZ
14

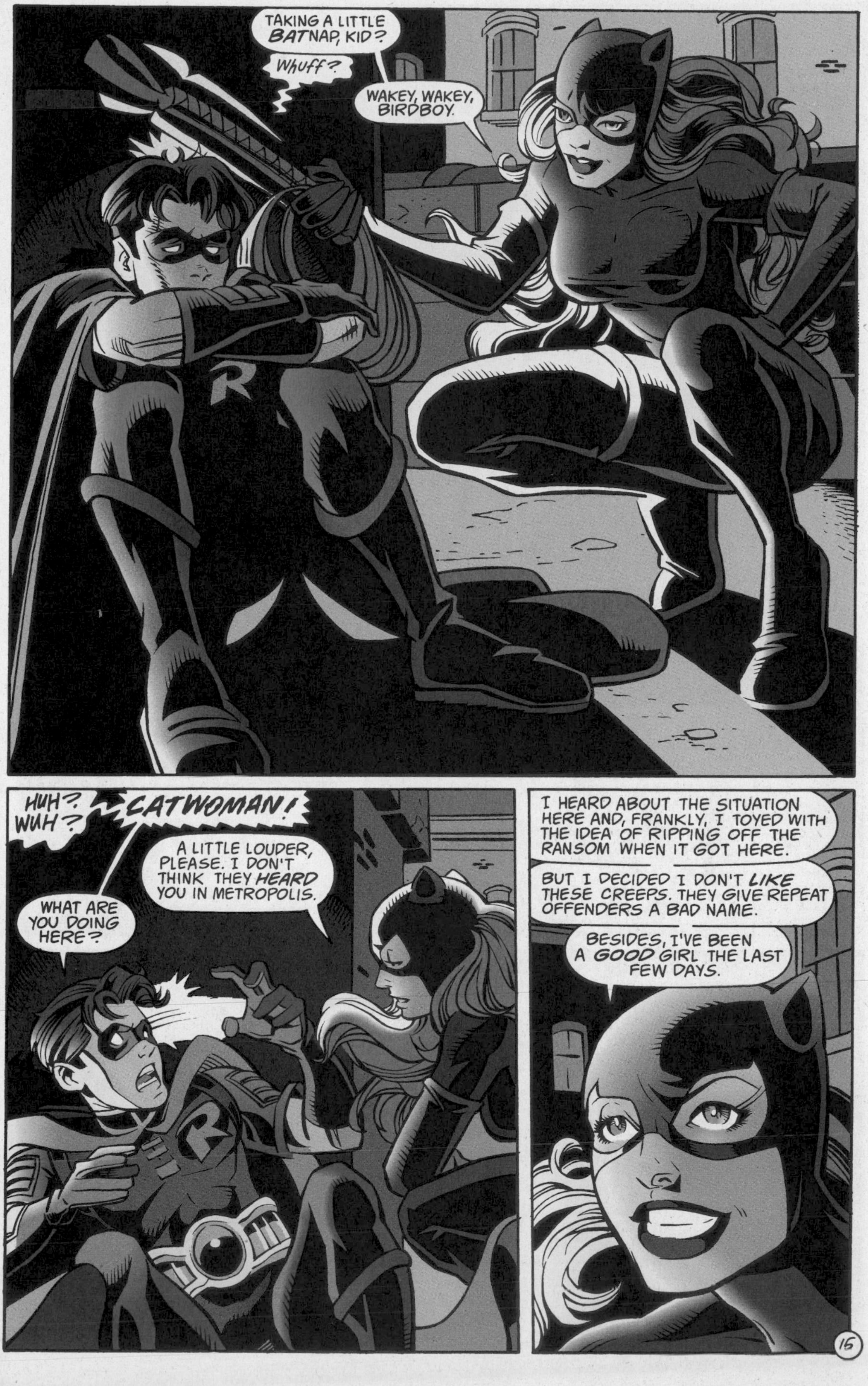
TAKING A LITTLE BATNAP, KID?
Whuff?
WAKEY, WAKEY, BIRDBOY.
HUH? WUH?
CATWOMAN!
WHAT ARE YOU DOING HERE?
A LITTLE LOUDER, PLEASE. I DON'T THINK THEY HEARD YOU IN METROPOLIS.
I HEARD ABOUT THE SITUATION HERE AND, FRANKLY, I TOYED WITH THE IDEA OF RIPPING OFF THE RANSOM WHEN IT GOT HERE.
BUT I DECIDED I DON'T LIKE THESE CREEPS. THEY GIVE REPEAT OFFENDERS A BAD NAME.
BESIDES, I'VE BEEN A GOOD GIRL THE LAST FEW DAYS.
15

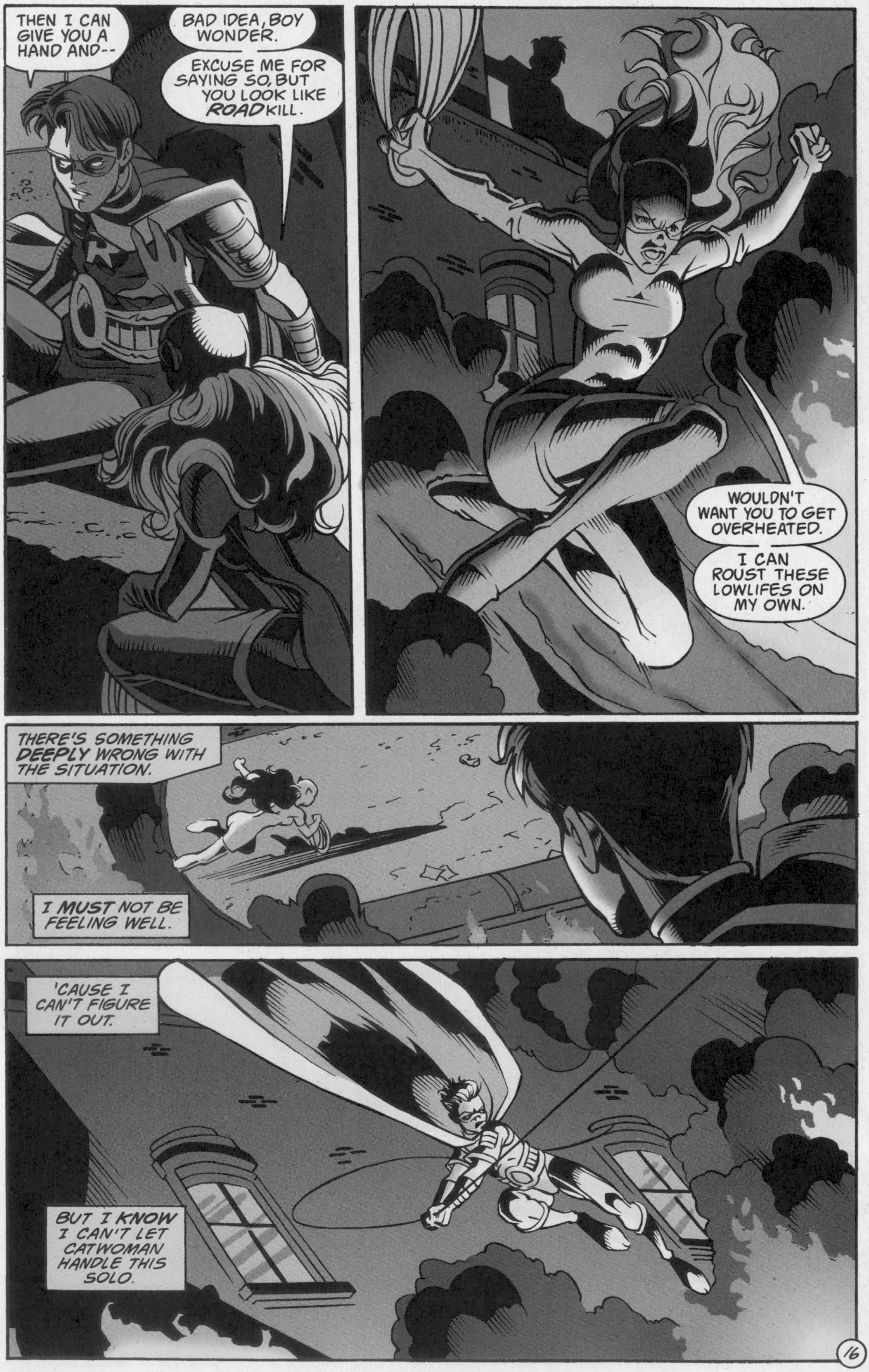
THEN I CAN GIVE YOU A HAND AND--
BAD IDEA, BOY WONDER.
EXCUSE ME FOR SAYING SO, BUT YOU LOOK LIKE ROADKILL.
WOULDN'T WANT YOU TO GET OVERHEATED.
I CAN ROUST THESE LOWLIFES ON MY OWN.
THERE'S SOMETHING DEEPLY WRONG WITH THE SITUATION.
I MUST NOT BE FEELING WELL.
'CAUSE I CAN'T FIGURE IT OUT.
BUT I KNOW I CAN'T LET CATWOMAN HANDLE THIS SOLO.
16

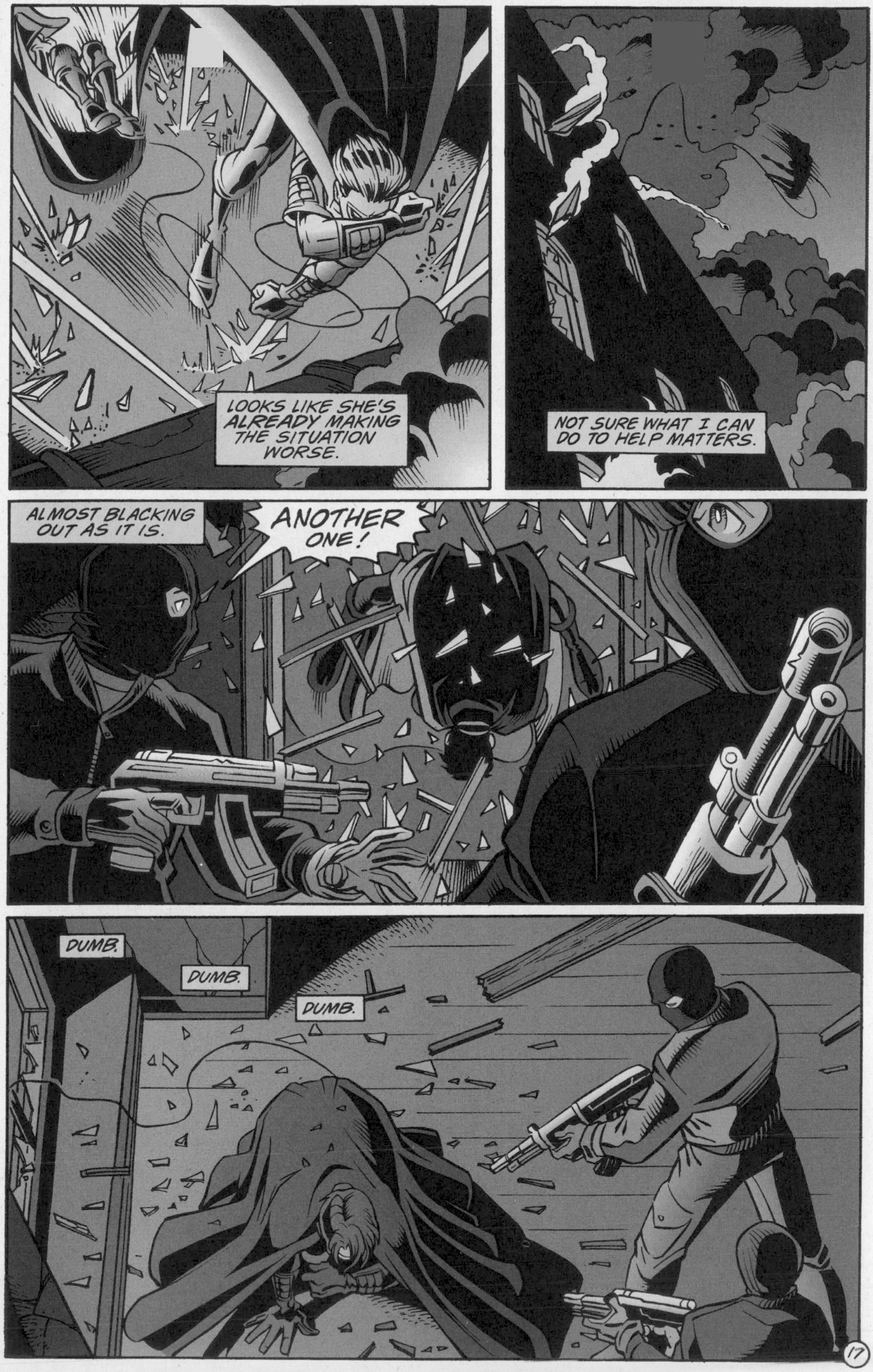
LOOKS LIKE SHE'S ALREADY MAKING THE SITUATION WORSE.
NOT SURE WHAT I CAN DO TO HELP MATTERS.
ALMOST BLACKING OUT AS IT IS.
ANOTHER ONE!
DUMB.
DUMB.
DUMB.
17

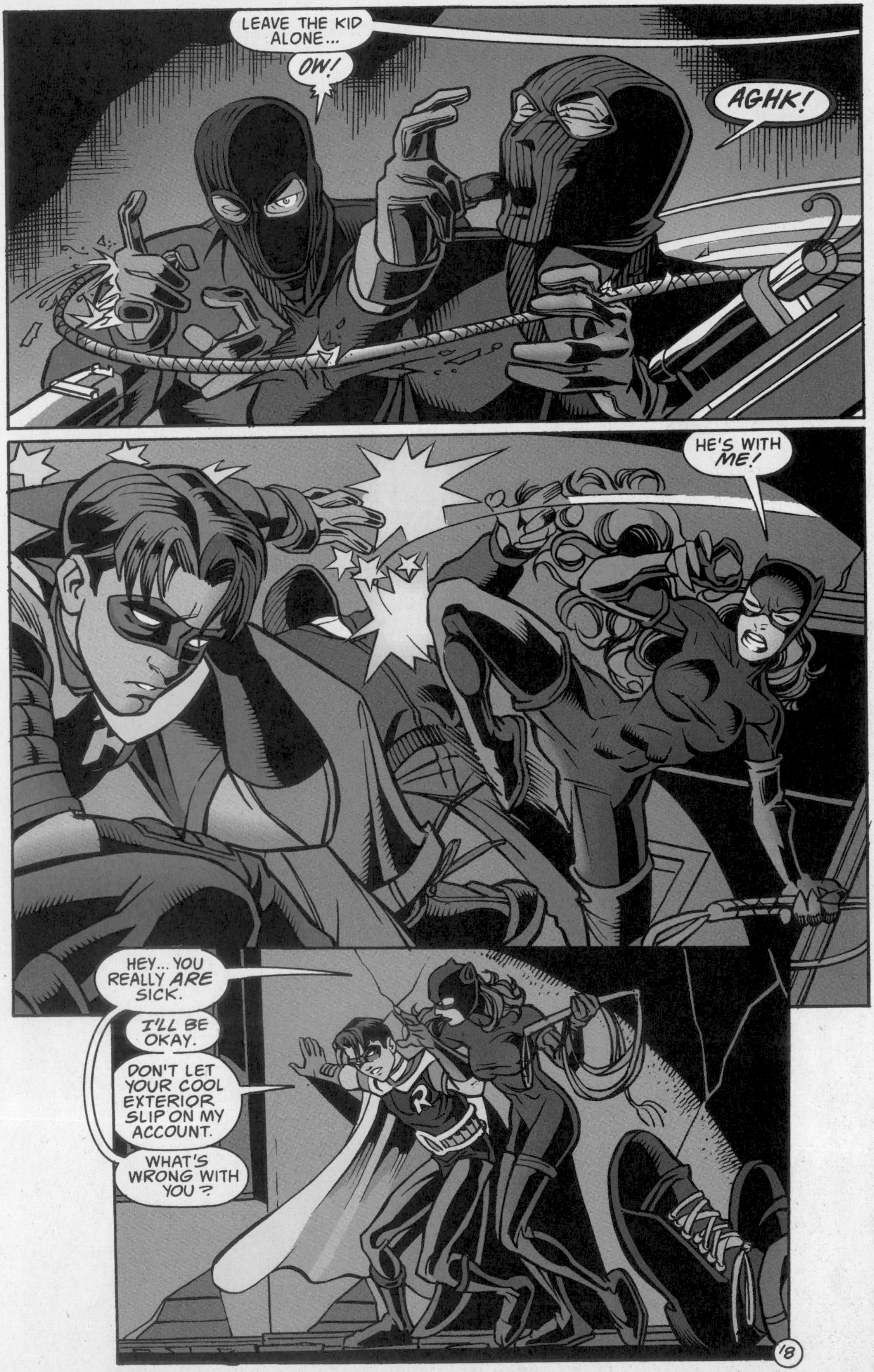
LEAVE THE KID ALONE...
OW!
AGHK!
HE'S WITH ME!
HEY... YOU REALLY ARE SICK.
I'LL BE OKAY.
DON'T LET YOUR COOL EXTERIOR SLIP ON MY ACCOUNT.
WHAT'S WRONG WITH YOU?
18

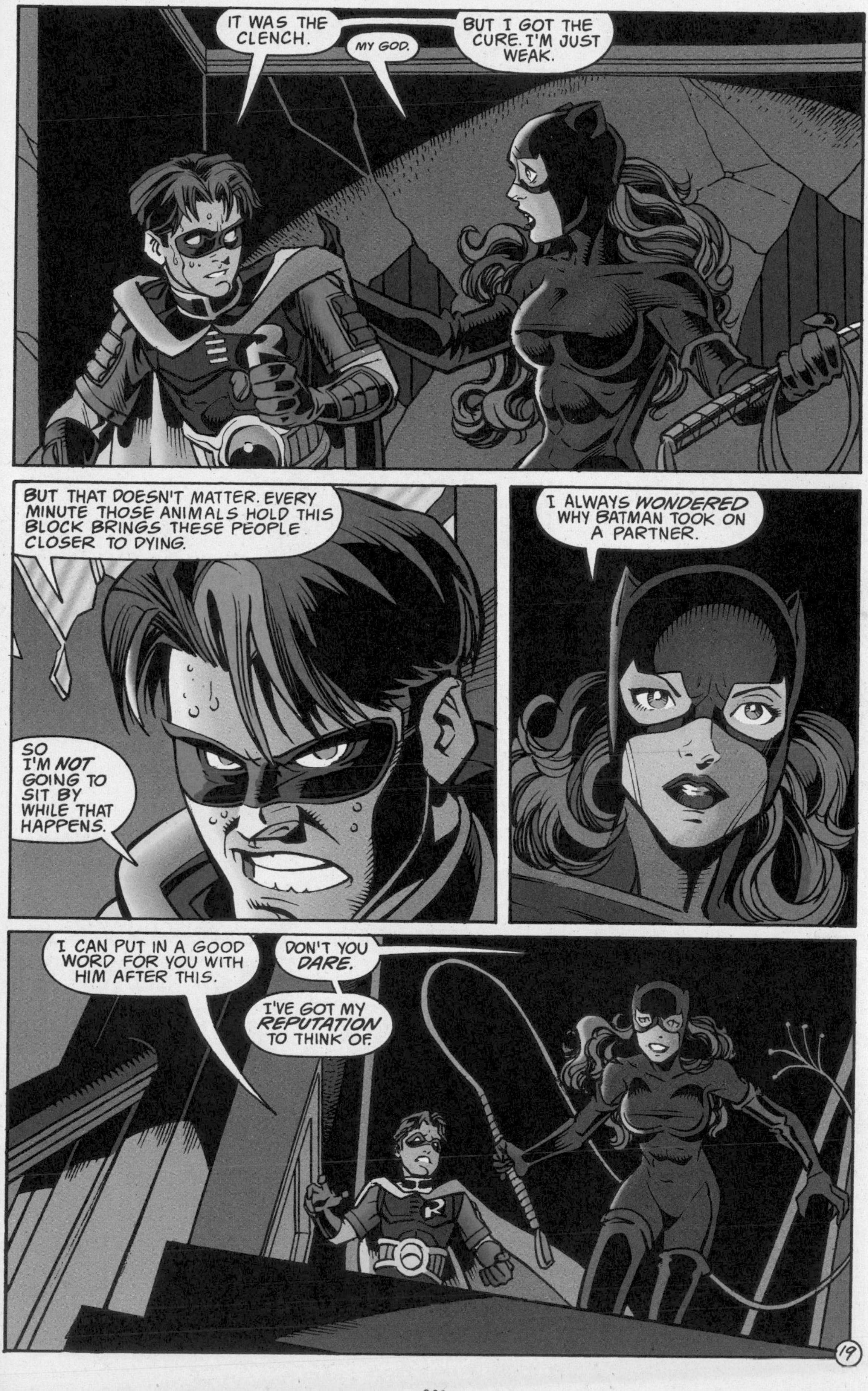
IT WAS THE CLENCH.
MY GOD.
BUT I GOT THE CURE. I'M JUST WEAK.
BUT THAT DOESN'T MATTER. EVERY MINUTE THOSE ANIMALS HOLD THIS BLOCK BRINGS THESE PEOPLE CLOSER TO DYING.
SO I'M *NOT* GOING TO SIT BY WHILE THAT HAPPENS.
I ALWAYS *WONDERED* WHY BATMAN TOOK ON A PARTNER.
I CAN PUT IN A GOOD WORD FOR YOU WITH HIM AFTER THIS.
DON'T YOU *DARE.*
I'VE GOT MY *REPUTATION* TO THINK OF.
19

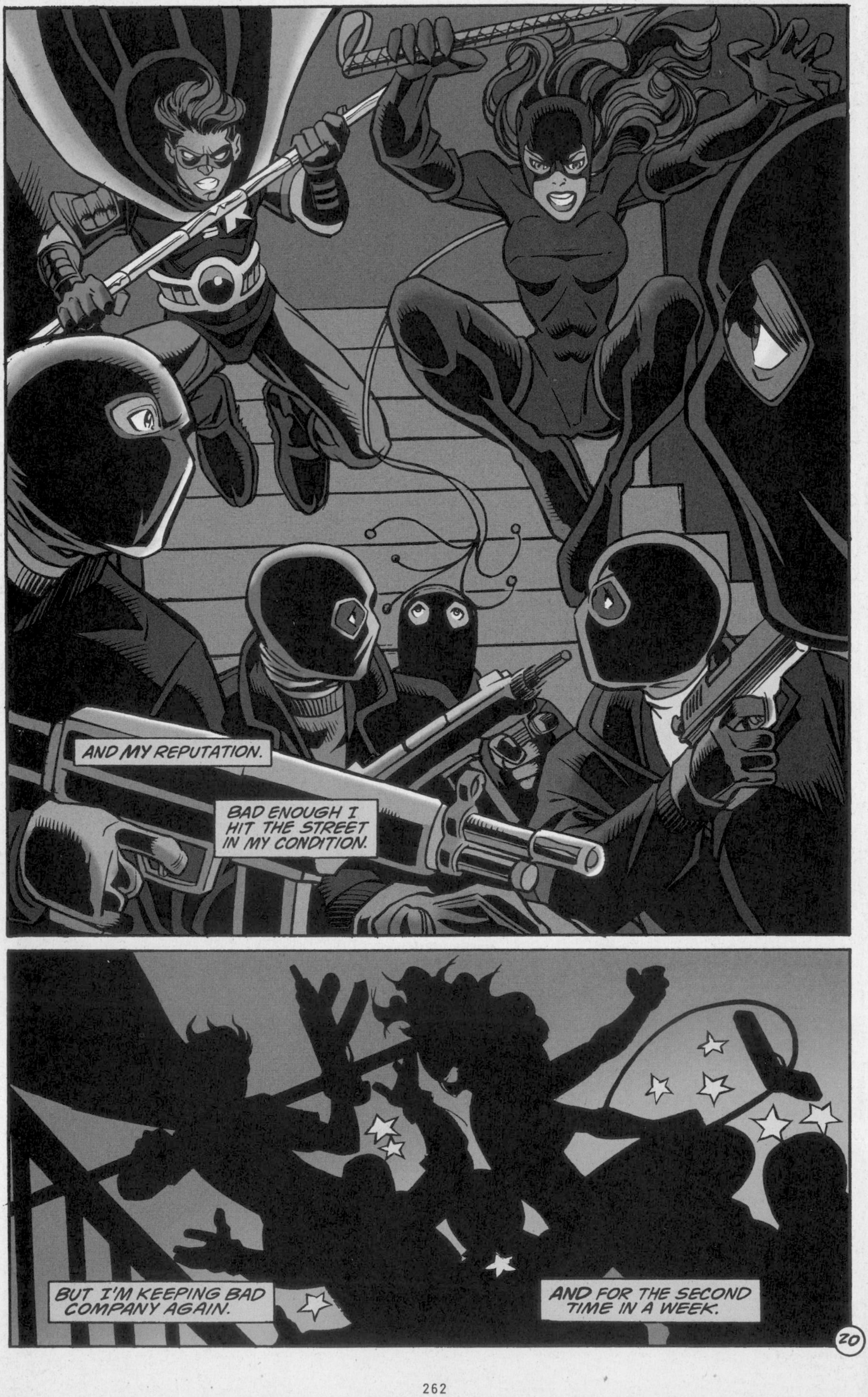
AND MY REPUTATION.
BAD ENOUGH I HIT THE STREET IN MY CONDITION.
BUT I'M KEEPING BAD COMPANY AGAIN.
AND FOR THE SECOND TIME IN A WEEK.
20

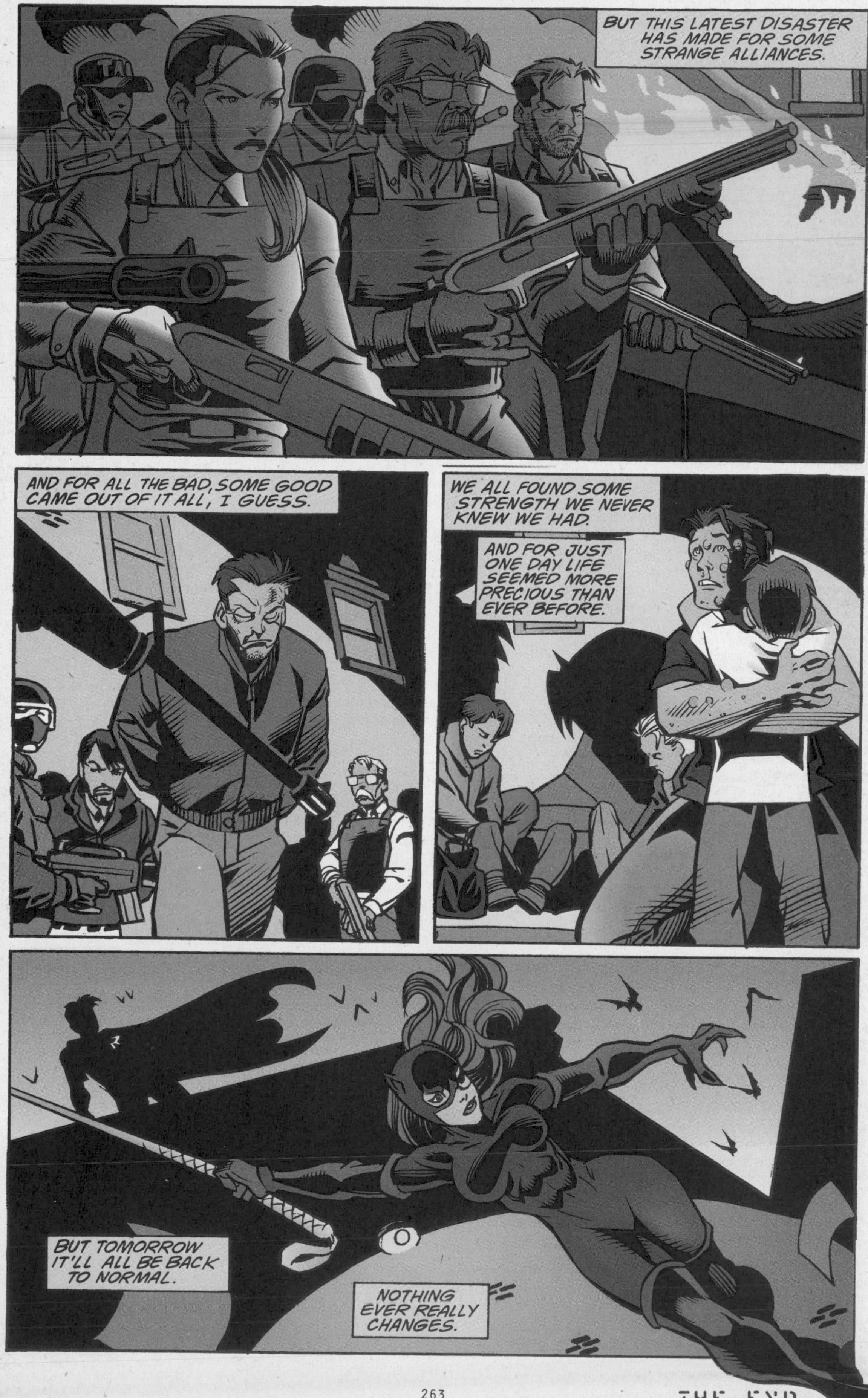
BUT THIS LATEST DISASTER HAS MADE FOR SOME STRANGE ALLIANCES.
AND FOR ALL THE BAD, SOME GOOD CAME OUT OF IT ALL, I GUESS.
WE ALL FOUND SOME STRENGTH WE NEVER KNEW WE HAD.
AND FOR JUST ONE DAY LIFE SEEMED MORE PRECIOUS THAN EVER BEFORE.
BUT TOMORROW IT'LL ALL BE BACK TO NORMAL.
NOTHING EVER REALLY CHANGES.

THE END

BATMAN
THE QUEST FOR JUSTICE CONTINUES IN THESE BOOKS FROM DC:

FOR READERS OF ALL AGES

**THE BATMAN ADVENTURES:
THE LOST YEARS**
Hilary Bader/Bo Hampton/
Terry Beatty

THE BATMAN ADVENTURES
K. Puckett/T. Templeton/
R. Burchett/various

**BATMAN & SUPERMAN
ADVENTURES: World's Finest**
Paul Dini/Joe Staton/
Terry Beatty

BATMAN BEYOND
Hilary Bader/Rick Burchett/
various

**BATMAN: THE DARK KNIGHT
ADVENTURES**
Kelley Puckett/Mike Parobeck/
Rick Burchett

BATMAN: WAR ON CRIME
Paul Dini/Alex Ross

GRAPHIC NOVELS

BATMAN: ARKHAM ASYLUM
Suggested for mature readers
Grant Morrison/Dave McKean

BATMAN: FORTUNATE SON
Gerard Jones/Gene Ha

BATMAN: THE KILLING JOKE
Suggested for mature readers
Alan Moore/Brian Bolland/
John Higgins

**THE BATMAN ADVENTURES:
MAD LOVE**
Paul Dini/Bruce Timm

BATMAN: NIGHT CRIES
Archie Goodwin/Scott Hampton

BATMAN: BLOODSTORM
Doug Moench/Kelley Jones/
John Beatty

BATMAN: CRIMSON MIST
Doug Moench/Kelley Jones/
John Beatty

BATMAN: THE CHALICE
Chuck Dixon/John Van Fleet

**BATMAN/DEADMAN:
DEATH AND GLORY**
James Robinson/John Estes

BATMAN/DRACULA: RED RAIN
Doug Moench/Kelley Jones/
Malcolm Jones III

BATMAN: SON OF THE DEMON
Mike Barr/Jerry Bingham

COLLECTIONS

**THE KNIGHTFALL Trilogy
BATMAN: KNIGHTFALL Part 1:
Broken Bat
BATMAN: KNIGHTFALL Part 2:
Who Rules the Night
BATMAN: KNIGHTFALL Part 3:
KnightsEnd**
Various writers and artists

BATMAN: ANARKY
Alan Grant/Norm Breyfogle/
various

**BATMAN: A DEATH IN
THE FAMILY**
Jim Starlin/Jim Aparo/
Mike DeCarlo

**BATMAN: A LONELY PLACE
OF DYING**
Marv Wolfman/George Pérez/
various

BATMAN BLACK AND WHITE
Various writers and artists

BATMAN: CATACLYSM
Various writers and artists

**BATMAN: COLLECTED LEGENDS
OF THE DARK KNIGHT**
J. Robinson/J.F. Moore/
A. Grant/T. Sale/C. Russell/
K. O'Neill

**BATMAN: THE DARK KNIGHT
RETURNS
10TH ANNIVERSARY EDITION**
Frank Miller/Klaus Janson/
Lynn Varley

**BATMAN: DARK KNIGHT
DYNASTY**
M. Barr/S. Hampton/G. Frank/
S. McDaniels/various

BATMAN: DARK LEGENDS
Various writers and artists

BATMAN: FACES
Matt Wagner

**BATMAN: FEATURING
TWO-FACE AND THE RIDDLER**
Various writers and artists

BATMAN: FOUR OF A KIND
Various writers and artists

BATMAN: GOTHIC
Grant Morrison/Klaus Janson

BATMAN: HAUNTED KNIGHT
Jeph Loeb/Tim Sale

BATMAN IN THE SIXTIES
Various writers and artists

BATMAN IN THE SEVENTIES
Various writers and artists

BATMAN: THE LONG HALLOWEEN
Jeph Loeb/Tim Sale

BATMAN: MANBAT
Jamie Delano/John Bolton

**BATMAN: NO MAN'S LAND
VOL. 1**
B. Gale/D. Grayson/
A. Maleev/D. Eaglesham/
W. Faucher

**BATMAN: NO MAN'S LAND
VOL. 2**
Various writers and artists

BATMAN: OTHER REALMS
Mark Kneece/Bo Hampton/
Scott Hampton

BATMAN: PRODIGAL
Various writers and artists

BATMAN: SHAMAN
Dennis O'Neil/Ed Hannigan/
John Beatty

**BATMAN: STRANGE
APPARITIONS**
S. Englehart/M. Rogers/
T. Austin/various

BATMAN: SWORD OF AZRAEL
Dennis O'Neil/Joe Quesada/
Kevin Nowlan

BATMAN: TALES OF THE DEMON
Dennis O'Neil/Neal Adams/
various

BATMAN: THE MOVIES
Dennis O'Neil/various

BATMAN: THRILLKILLER
Howard Chaykin/Dan Brereton

BATMAN: VENOM
Dennis O'Neil/Trevor Von Eeden/
various

**BATMAN VS. PREDATOR:
THE COLLECTED EDITION**
Dave Gibbons/Andy Kubert/
Adam Kubert

**BATMAN VS. PREDATOR II:
BLOODMATCH**
Doug Moench/Paul Gulacy/
Terry Austin

**BATMAN VS. PREDATOR III:
BLOOD TIES**
Chuck Dixon/Rodolfo Damaggio/
Robert Campanella

BATMAN: YEAR ONE
Frank Miller/David Mazzucchelli

**THE GREATEST BATMAN
STORIES EVER TOLD Vol. 1**
Various writers and artists

**THE GREATEST JOKER
STORIES EVER TOLD**
Various writers and artists

CATWOMAN: THE CATFILE
Chuck Dixon/Jim Balent/
Bob Smith

NIGHTWING: ROUGH JUSTICE
Chuck Dixon/Scott McDaniels/
Karl Story

NIGHTWING: TIES THAT BIND
Dennis O'Neil/Alan Grant/
various

**NIGHTWING: A KNIGHT
IN BLÜDHAVEN**
Chuck Dixon/Scott McDaniel/
Karl Story

ROBIN: A HERO REBORN
Chuck Dixon/Tom Lyle/
Bob Smith

ARCHIVE EDITIONS

BATMAN ARCHIVES Vol. 1
(DETECTIVE COMICS 27-50)
BATMAN ARCHIVES Vol. 2
(DETECTIVE COMICS 51-70)
BATMAN ARCHIVES Vol. 3
(DETECTIVE COMICS 71-86)
BATMAN ARCHIVES Vol. 4
(DETECTIVE COMICS 87-102)
All by B. Kane/B. Finger/D. Sprang/
various

**BATMAN: THE DARK KNIGHT
ARCHIVES Vol. 1**
(BATMAN 1-4)
**BATMAN: THE DARK KNIGHT
ARCHIVES Vol. 2**
(BATMAN 5-8)
All by Bob Kane/Bill Finger/various

**WORLD'S FINEST COMICS
ARCHIVES Vol. 1**
(SUPERMAN 76,
WORLD'S FINEST 71-85)
B. Finger/E. Hamilton/C. Swan/
various

TO FIND MORE COLLECTED EDITIONS AND MONTHLY COMIC BOOKS FROM DC COMICS,
CALL 1-888-COMIC BOOK FOR THE NEAREST COMICS SHOP OR GO TO YOUR LOCAL BOOK STORE.

Visit us at www.dccomics.com